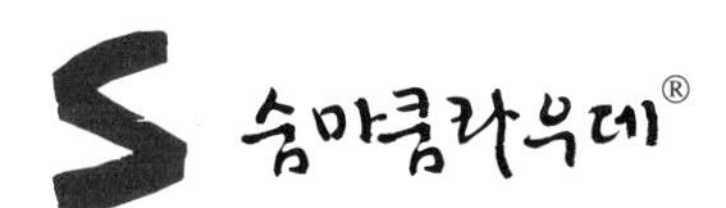

독해

ENGLISH READING COMPREHENSION

MANUAL

SUMMA CUM LAUDE-ENGLISH

COPYRIGHT

숨마쿰라우데® [독해 매뉴얼]

지은이 소개

김대성 보성고등학교 교사
고려대학교 영어교육과 (졸)
서울시 교육청 전국연합학력평가 출제위원

육상태 현대고등학교 교사
한국교원대학교 영어교육학과 (졸)
서울시 교육청 전국연합학력평가 출제위원

윤진호 동덕여자고등학교 교사
서울대학교 영어교육과 (졸)
서울시 교육청 전국연합 학력평가 출제위원

김재남 동덕여자고등학교 교사
한국외국어대학교 영어통번역학 (졸)

성정혜 EBS 영어 영역 강사
강남구청 인터넷 수능 방송 강사

1판 7쇄 발행일 : 2023년 3월 27일
지은이 : 김대성, 육상태, 윤진호, 김재남, 성정혜
펴낸이 : 이동준, 정재현
기획 및 편집 : 박희라, 안혜원
디자인 : 굿윌디자인

펴낸곳 : (주)이룸이앤비
출판신고번호 : 제2009 – 000168호
주소 : 경기도 성남시 수정구 위례광장로 21-9 KCC웰츠타워 2층 2018호
대표전화 : 02 – 424 – 2410
팩스 : 070 – 4275 – 5512
홈페이지 : www.erumenb.com
ISBN : 978 – 89 – 5990 – 366 – 5

THINK MORE ABOUT YOUR FUTURE

INTRODUCTION

[이 책을 펴내면서]

수년 전, 모 일간지에서 고등학교 입학을 앞두고 있는 학생들에게 고등학교에서의 영어 학습법에 관해 조언의 글을 써 달라는 요청을 받았습니다. 당시 '영어를 입에 붙이라고' 조언을 해 주었습니다. 머릿속으로 생각하는 영어가 아닌, 입 밖으로 내뱉는 영어를 하라는 취지였습니다. 귀로 들으면서 입으로 읊조리고, 눈으로 보면서 입으로 읊조리라는 의미였습니다. 그러한 조언의 글을 쓰면서 필자는 언젠가 기회가 되면, 고등학교 1학년생이 읊조릴 수 있는 좋은 글들로부터 시작하여 수능 영어 수준의 맛을 고루 느껴볼 수 있는 글을 담은 책을 만들어야겠다고 생각했습니다. 그리고 지금, 그런 취지의 책이 나왔습니다.

본 책은 수능에 출제되는 문제 유형을 기본 틀로 하되 고등학교 1학년 학생들이 읊조릴 수 있는 수준의 지문부터 난이도를 점차 높여서 수능 수준의 지문까지 다루고 있습니다. 아울러, 수능 및 평가원 기출 문제 중 우수한 지문을 선정하여 대표 예제로 제시하였고, 대표 예제에 대한 지문의 구조도 분석하여 글의 흐름 및 구조를 보다 잘 이해할 수 있도록 하였습니다. 또한, 기출 문제와 새로 출제한 문제가 적절히 섞여 있는 Exercise를 제공하며, 각 단원에 내신 서술형 문제를 추가하여 내신도 대비할 수 있도록 하였습니다.

이 책은 유형편과 소재편, 그리고 Mini Test로 구성됩니다. 유형편은 단원별로 쉬운 문항부터 시작하여 점차 난이도가 높아지도록 문항을 구성하였으며 마지막 문항은 내신 서술형 문항이 포함된 고난도 문항을 배치하였습니다. 소재편은 수능에서 출제되는 소재를 분석하고 이를 바탕으로 구성하였습니다. 통상, 이 책에서 다루어지는 소재가 수능에서 나온다고 보면 됩니다. 따라서, 어떤 소재가 주로 다루어지고, 어떤 소재가 어떤 유형으로 나오는지에 대한 감을 익혀나가시기 바랍니다.

수능의 문제 유형과 소재가 총망라되고, 수준별로 구성이 되어 있어서 자신의 수준에 맞게 공부할 수 있는, 학년별로 최적화된 집필진에 의해 체계적으로 구성된 본 책을 통해 영어의 아름다움을 체감할 수 있기를 기원합니다.

저자 일동

SUMMA CUM LAUDE-ENGLISH

STRUCTURE

[이 책의 구성과 특징]

PART Ⅰ 유형편

수능에 나오는 독해의 모든 유형을 다루며, 각 유형별로 문제를 해결하기 위한 전략 및 해법을 제시하였습니다. 대표 예제로 유형을 익힌 후 **Exercise 문제**로 각 유형을 충분히 연습해 볼 수 있습니다.

한눈에 보는 구조

대표 예제의 글의 구조를 분석하여 지문에 대한 이해도를 높입니다.

유형 해결 전략

각 유형별 대표 예제를 토대로 유형별 해결 전략이 어떻게 적용되는지를 보여줍니다.

Bonus Tip

유형별로 문제 풀이에 도움이 되는 유용한 정보를 추가적으로 제공합니다.

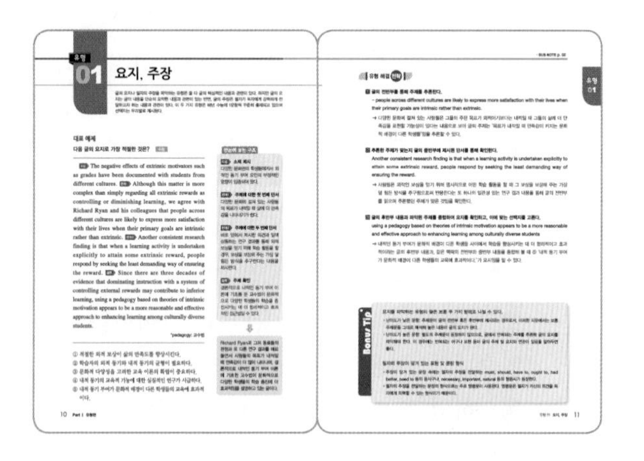
01 요지, 주장

PART Ⅱ 소재편

수능에 주로 출제되는 소재들을 선별하여 해당 소재와 관련된 지문을 집중적으로 학습할 수 있도록 하였습니다. 대표 예제로 소재에 따른 지문을 익힌 후 **Exercise 문제**로 소재별 지문을 충분히 연습해 볼 수 있습니다.

한눈에 보는 구조

대표 예제의 글의 구조를 분석하여 지문에 대한 이해도를 높입니다.

각 소재별로 최근 5개년 기출 지문들을 분석하여 자주 출제되었던 주요 어휘들을 정리하였습니다.

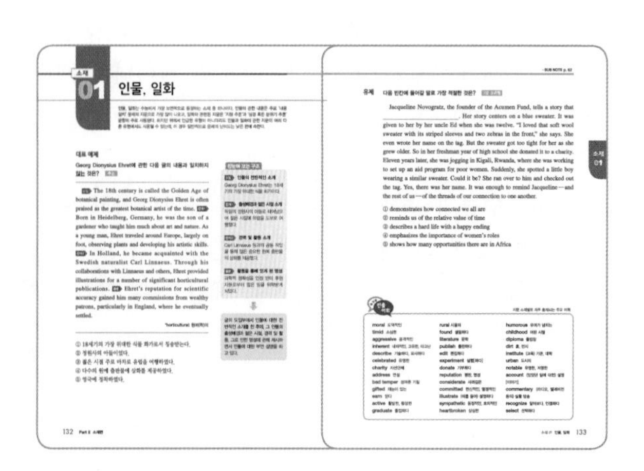
01 인물, 일화

THINK MORE ABOUT YOUR FUTURE

STRUCTURE

PART Ⅲ Mini Test

이제까지 학습한 내용을 최종적으로 점검하고 확인해 볼 수 있도록 **Mini Test 8회분**을 제공합니다.

각 회별로 3개의 고난도 문항을 제공하며, 제한 시간을 설정하여 실전에 대비할 수 있도록 하였습니다.

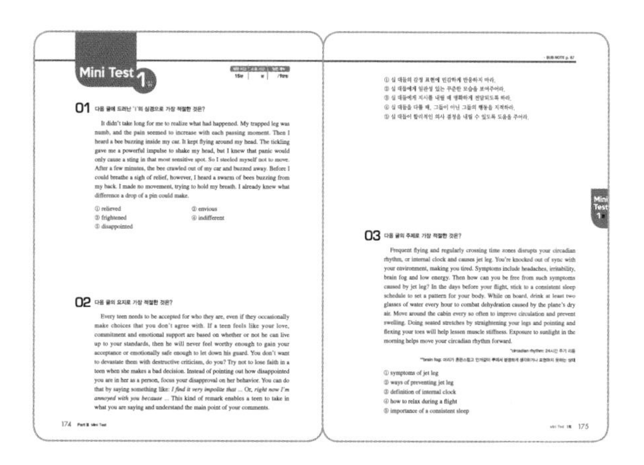

SUB NOTE (정답 및 해설)

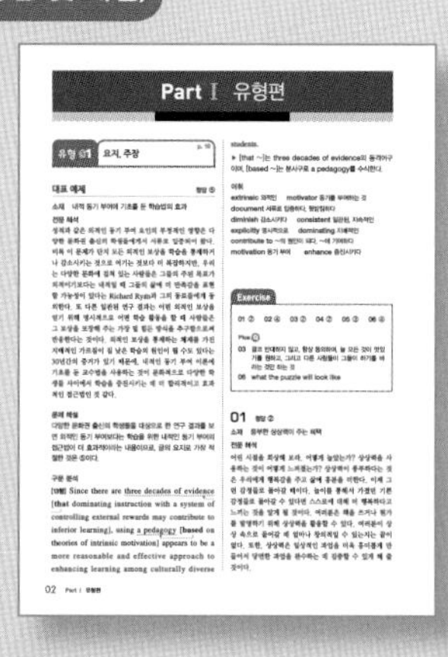

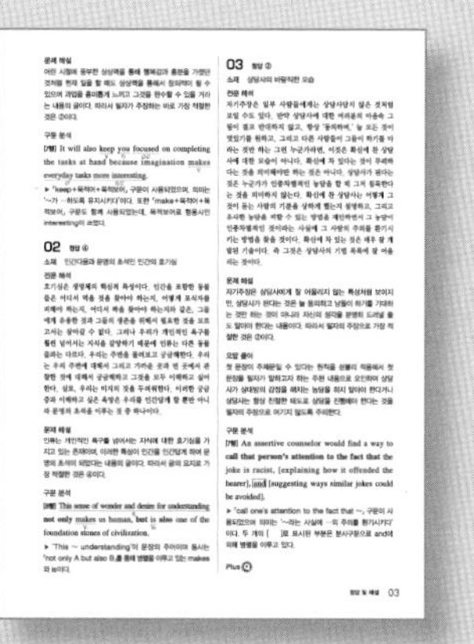

각 문항별로 소재, 정확한 전문 해석, 자세한 문제 해설 및 구문 분석, 어휘를 수록하여 혼자서 공부하는 데에도 어려움이 없도록 구성하였습니다. 오답의 선택지를 고를 가능성이 있는 문항에 대해서는 해설에서 오답 풀이를 제공합니다.

SUMMA CUM LAUDE-ENGLISH

CONTENTS

[이 책의 차례]

PART I 유형편

THINK MORE ABOUT YOUR FUTURE

CONTENTS

PART Ⅱ 소재편

PART Ⅲ Mini Test

SUMMA CUM LAUDE-ENGLISH

SCHEDULE

[36일 완성 **Study Plan**] PART I 유형편은 18일, PART II 소재편은 10일, PART III Mini Test는 8일을 목표로 하여 총 '36일'에 완성하는 학습 계획표입니다.

PART I 유형편			
Day	Chapter	page	Check
Day 01	유형 01 요지, 주장	p. 10	☐ ____월 ____일
Day 02	유형 02 주제, 제목	p. 16	☐ ____월 ____일
Day 03	유형 03 글의 목적	p. 22	☐ ____월 ____일
Day 04	유형 04 심경, 분위기	p. 28	☐ ____월 ____일
Day 05	유형 05 내용 일치	p. 34	☐ ____월 ____일
Day 06	유형 06 실용문의 이해	p. 40	☐ ____월 ____일
Day 07	유형 07 도표의 이해	p. 46	☐ ____월 ____일
Day 08	유형 08 어휘 추론	p. 52	☐ ____월 ____일
Day 09	유형 09 어법성 판단	p. 58	☐ ____월 ____일
Day 10	유형 10 지칭 추론	p. 64	☐ ____월 ____일
Day 11	유형 11 빈칸 추론	p. 70	☐ ____월 ____일
Day 12	유형 12 연결어 추론	p. 78	☐ ____월 ____일
Day 13	유형 13 무관한 문장 찾기	p. 84	☐ ____월 ____일
Day 14	유형 14 글의 순서 배열	p. 90	☐ ____월 ____일
Day 15	유형 15 문장 삽입	p. 96	☐ ____월 ____일
Day 16	유형 16 요약문 완성	p. 102	☐ ____월 ____일
Day 17	유형 17 장문 독해(1) 일반 장문	p. 108	☐ ____월 ____일
Day 18	유형 18 장문 독해(2) 순서 장문	p. 118	☐ ____월 ____일
PART II 소재편			
Day 19	소재 01 인물, 일화	p. 132	☐ ____월 ____일
Day 20	소재 02 교육, 학교	p. 136	☐ ____월 ____일
Day 21	소재 03 철학, 종교, 심리	p. 140	☐ ____월 ____일
Day 22	소재 04 문학, 언어, 예술, 문화	p. 144	☐ ____월 ____일
Day 23	소재 05 역사, 지리	p. 148	☐ ____월 ____일
Day 24	소재 06 정치, 경제, 사회, 법	p. 152	☐ ____월 ____일
Day 25	소재 07 환경, 자원, 생태계	p. 156	☐ ____월 ____일
Day 26	소재 08 의학, 건강, 식품, 영양	p. 160	☐ ____월 ____일
Day 27	소재 09 스포츠, 취미, 여행, 여가	p. 164	☐ ____월 ____일
Day 28	소재 10 컴퓨터, 정보, 미디어, 교통	p. 168	☐ ____월 ____일
PART III Mini Test			
Day 29	Mini Test 1회	p. 174	☐ ____월 ____일
Day 30	Mini Test 2회	p. 180	☐ ____월 ____일
Day 31	Mini Test 3회	p. 186	☐ ____월 ____일
Day 32	Mini Test 4회	p. 192	☐ ____월 ____일
Day 33	Mini Test 5회	p. 198	☐ ____월 ____일
Day 34	Mini Test 6회	p. 204	☐ ____월 ____일
Day 35	Mini Test 7회	p. 210	☐ ____월 ____일
Day 36	Mini Test 8회	p. 216	☐ ____월 ____일

PART I

유형편

숨마쿰라우데®

[독해 매뉴얼]

유형 **01~18**

유형 01 요지, 주장

글의 요지나 필자의 주장을 파악하는 유형은 둘 다 글의 핵심적인 내용과 관련이 있다. 하지만 글의 요지는 글의 내용을 단순히 요약한 내용과 관련이 있는 반면, 글의 주장은 필자가 독자에게 강력하게 전달하고자 하는 내용과 관련이 있다. 이 두 가지 유형은 매년 수능에 1문항씩 꾸준히 출제되고 있으며 선택지는 우리말로 제시된다.

대표 예제

다음 글의 요지로 가장 적절한 것은? 수능

도입》 The negative effects of extrinsic motivators such as grades have been documented with students from different cultures. 전개1》 Although this matter is more complex than simply regarding all extrinsic rewards as controlling or diminishing learning, we agree with Richard Ryan and his colleagues that people across different cultures are likely to express more satisfaction with their lives when their primary goals are intrinsic rather than extrinsic. 전개2》 Another consistent research finding is that when a learning activity is undertaken explicitly to attain some extrinsic reward, people respond by seeking the least demanding way of ensuring the reward. 결론》 Since there are three decades of evidence that dominating instruction with a system of controlling external rewards may contribute to inferior learning, using a pedagogy based on theories of intrinsic motivation appears to be a more reasonable and effective approach to enhancing learning among culturally diverse students.

*pedagogy: 교수법

① 적절한 외적 보상이 삶의 만족도를 향상시킨다.
② 학습자의 외적 동기와 내적 동기의 균형이 필요하다.
③ 문화적 다양성을 고려한 교육 이론의 확립이 중요하다.
④ 내적 동기의 교육적 기능에 대한 실질적인 연구가 시급하다.
⑤ 내적 동기 부여가 문화적 배경이 다른 학생들의 교육에 효과적이다.

한눈에 보는 구조

도입》 **소재 제시**
다양한 문화권의 학생들에게서 외적인 동기 부여 요인의 부정적인 영향이 입증되어 왔다.

전개1》 **주제에 대한 첫 번째 단서**
다양한 문화에 걸쳐 있는 사람들의 목표가 내적일 때 삶에 더 만족감을 나타내기가 쉽다.

전개2》 **주제에 대한 두 번째 단서**
바로 앞에서 제시한 의견과 일맥상통하는 연구 결과를 통해 외적 보상을 얻기 위해 학습 활동을 할 경우, 보상을 보장해 주는 가장 덜 힘든 방식을 추구한다는 내용을 제시한다.

결론》 **주제 확인**
결론적으로 내적인 동기 부여 이론에 기초를 둔 교수법이 문화적으로 다양한 학생들의 학습을 증진시키는 데 더 합리적이고 효과적인 접근법일 수 있다.

Richard Ryan과 그의 동료들의 관점과 또 다른 연구 결과를 예로 들면서 사람들의 목표가 내적일 때 만족감이 더 많이 나타나며, 결론적으로 내적인 동기 부여 이론에 기초한 교수법이 문화적으로 다양한 학생들의 학습 증진에 더 효과적임을 설명하고 있는 글이다.

유형 해결 전략

1 글의 전반부를 통해 주제를 추론한다.

~ people across different cultures are likely to express more satisfaction with their lives when their primary goals are intrinsic rather than extrinsic.

→ 다양한 문화에 걸쳐 있는 사람들은 그들의 주된 목표가 외적이기보다는 내적일 때 그들의 삶에 더 만족감을 표현할 가능성이 있다는 내용으로 보아 글의 주제는 '목표가 내적일 때 만족감이 커지는 문화적 배경이 다른 학생들'임을 추론할 수 있다.

2 추론한 주제가 맞는지 글의 중반부에 제시된 단서를 통해 확인한다.

Another consistent research finding is that when a learning activity is undertaken explicitly to attain some extrinsic reward, people respond by seeking the least demanding way of ensuring the reward.

→ 사람들은 외적인 보상을 얻기 위해 명시적으로 어떤 학습 활동을 할 때 그 보상을 보장해 주는 가장 덜 힘든 방식을 추구함으로써 반응한다는 또 하나의 일관성 있는 연구 결과 내용을 통해 글의 전반부를 읽으며 추론했던 주제가 맞은 것임을 확인한다.

3 글의 후반부 내용과 파악된 주제를 종합하여 요지를 확인하고, 이에 맞는 선택지를 고른다.

using a pedagogy based on theories of intrinsic motivation appears to be a more reasonable and effective approach to enhancing learning among culturally diverse students

→ 내적인 동기 부여가 문화적 배경이 다른 학생들 사이에서 학습을 향상시키는 데 더 합리적이고 효과적이라는 글의 후반부 내용과, 같은 맥락의 전반부와 중반부 내용을 종합해 볼 때 ⑤ '내적 동기 부여가 문화적 배경이 다른 학생들의 교육에 효과적이다.'가 요지임을 알 수 있다.

Bonus Tip

요지를 파악하는 유형의 글은 보통 두 가지 형태로 나뉠 수 있다.

- 난이도가 낮은 문항: 주제문이 글의 전반부 혹은 후반부에 제시되는 경우로서, 이러한 지문에서는 보통 주제문을 그대로 해석해 놓은 내용이 글의 요지가 된다.
- 난이도가 높은 문항: 별도의 주제문이 등장하지 않으므로, 글에서 반복되는 주제를 추론해 글의 요지를 파악해야 한다. 이 경우에는 반복되는 어구나 표현 등이 글의 주제 및 요지와 연관이 있음을 알아두면 좋다.

필자의 주장이 담겨 있는 표현 및 문장 형식

- 주장이 담겨 있는 문장 속에는 필자의 주장을 전달하는 must, should, have to, ought to, had better, need to 등의 동사구나, necessary, important, natural 등의 형용사가 등장한다.
- 필자의 주장을 전달하는 문장의 형식으로는 주로 명령문이 사용된다. 명령문은 필자가 자신의 의견을 독자에게 피력할 수 있는 형식이기 때문이다.

Exercise

01 다음 글에서 필자가 주장하는 바로 가장 적절한 것은? 고2 교육청

Think back to when you were a kid. How did you play? How did using your imagination make you feel? Being imaginative gives us feelings of happiness and adds excitement to our lives. It's time to get back to those emotions. If you can return to the joyful feelings that you had through play, you'll find that you feel happier about yourself. You can use your imagination to write books or invent something. There is no end to how creative you can be when you move into your imagination. It will also keep you focused on completing the tasks at hand because imagination makes everyday tasks more interesting.

① 다양한 취미 활동을 통해 경험의 폭을 넓혀라.
② 어린 시절처럼 생활 속에서 상상력을 발휘하라.
③ 생활 속에서 즐거움을 찾는 방법을 이웃과 나눠라.
④ 아이들의 눈높이에 맞추어 아이들의 행동을 이해하라.
⑤ 아이들이 상상력을 통해 스스로 문제를 해결하게 하라.

02 다음 글의 요지로 가장 적절한 것은? 고2 교육청

Curiosity is the essence of life. Animals including humans cannot live without knowing what is useful to them and what is needed for their survival: where to find food, how to avoid predators, where to find mates, etc. However, the human species differs from other animals because we thirst for knowledge that reaches far beyond our personal needs. We look around us and we wonder. We wonder about our surroundings and about what we observe both near and far and we want to understand it all. Indeed, we fear the unknown. This sense of wonder and desire for understanding not only makes us human, but is also one of the foundation stones of civilization.

① 인간과 동물의 호기심은 본질적으로 같다.
② 인간의 호기심은 오랜 진화 과정의 산물이다.
③ 사물과 현상에 대한 이해는 사람마다 다를 수 있다.
④ 호기심과 앎에 대한 욕구가 인간다움과 문명의 바탕이다.
⑤ 미지의 것에 대한 두려움은 비합리적인 사고로 이어진다.

03 다음 글에서 필자가 주장하는 바로 가장 적절한 것은? 수능

Assertiveness may seem to some people to be uncharacteristic of counselors. If your picture of a counselor is someone who never disagrees, always "goes along," wants everything to be nice all the time, and only does what other people want him or her to do, **this** is not a picture of an assertive counselor. Being assertive does not have to mean being disagreeable. Being a counselor does not mean that you should simply be silent when someone tells a racist joke. An assertive counselor would find a way to call that person's attention to the fact that the joke is racist, explaining how it offended the hearer, and suggesting ways similar jokes could be avoided. Being assertive is a highly developed skill—it should fit nicely in the counselor's repertoire of techniques.

① 상담사는 상대방의 감정을 해치는 농담을 하지 말아야 한다.
② 상담사는 자기 생각을 분명하게 드러낼 줄도 알아야 한다.
③ 상담사는 항상 친절한 태도로 상담을 진행해야 한다.
④ 상담사는 정기적으로 상담 기술 교육을 받아야 한다.
⑤ 상담사는 상담 기록을 철저히 관리해야 한다.

Plus Q

밑줄 친 **this**가 가리키는 바를 우리말로 쓰시오.

01 **imagination** 상상력, 상상 **imaginative** 상상력이 풍부한, 창의적인 **emotion** 감정 **joyful** 기쁜 **invent** 발명하다 **creative** 창의적인 **complete** 완수하다, 완성하다 **task** 과업, 일, 과제 **at hand** 당면한, 가까이 있는

02 **curiosity** 호기심 **essence** 핵심적 특성, 본질 **predator** 포식자 **human species** 인류 **differ from** ~와 다르다 **thirst for** ~을 갈망하다 **surroundings** 주변, 환경 **observe** 관찰하다 **unknown** 미지의 **foundation stone** 초석 **civilization** 문명

03 **assertiveness** 자기주장, 단호함 **uncharacteristic of** ~답지 않은 **assertive** 확신에 찬, 적극적인 **disagreeable** 무례한 **racist** 인종차별적인 **call one's attention to** ~에 …의 주의를 환기시키다 **repertoire** 목록

04 다음 글의 요지로 가장 적절한 것은?

A man I knew was always racing impatiently into the future. If we met for a drink after work, the first thing he did was talk about where we'd go for dinner, not about ordering drinks like most people typically do. At dinner, he rushed through dessert to get to a movie. At the movie, he was on his feet before the last frame faded. He was making plans for the next day, next week, and next year. Never did he live in the here and now. As a result, he couldn't enjoy life fully. Life has its own timetable. It takes nine months to make a baby, 21 years to make an adult. Stick to the present and put all of your energy into it. That's the way life is supposed to be.

① 노후 대책 수립은 빠를수록 좋다.
② 현재의 삶에 충실히 하는 것이 좋다.
③ 삶의 여유는 경제적 풍요에서 나온다.
④ 시간이 지나면 모든 문제가 해결된다.
⑤ 미래를 준비하는 삶의 자세가 필요하다.

05 다음 글에서 필자가 주장하는 바로 가장 적절한 것은?

One day a bright and likeable student once told me that he was very troubled over a creative writing assignment. The prospect of getting anything less than an A had him feeling deeply depressed. Eventually, he discovered the distortion: "In my culture, if you don't reach your goals, you don't deserve to live," he told me. I asked him, "Where is it written that someone who isn't perfect is worthless?" He thought for a while and said, "That's the first time someone has told me that I don't have to be perfect in order to be worthwhile." You might question your worth should you fail to earn a certain salary, lose an argument, or make a mistake. That is what you should avoid at any cost. If you must judge yourself, you should try judging your performance only, not the core self.

① 잘하는 분야에 집중함으로써 자신의 가치를 높이려고 하라.
② 상대와의 충분한 의사소통을 통해 문제를 해결하도록 하라.
③ 부족한 한 부분이 당신의 가치 자체를 대변하지 않도록 하라.
④ 자존감을 높이기 위해서는 자신이 하는 일에 정통하려고 하라.
⑤ 문제에 대한 관점의 차이는 문화의 차이에 의한 것임을 인식하라.

06 다음 글의 요지로 가장 적절한 것은?

In any organization, people have different pieces of the organizational puzzle. Members may have detailed descriptions of their roles and responsibilities, but very often they lack information about the "big picture"—about the overall vision of the organization. While people may be able to work on the puzzle anyway, randomly sticking their pieces here and there in an attempt to make them fit, they lack the essential information that will enable them to contribute to the whole. It's possible that after many random tries, the persistent few will eventually assemble the puzzle. What's more likely is that many other participants will become frustrated, lose interest, and quit. The leader's job is to paint the big picture, to convey the vision, and to give people a clear sense of **[like / what / will / the / look / puzzle]** when everyone has put the pieces in place.

① 조직의 전체 목표는 조직원들의 이득에 위배되지 않아야 한다.
② 조직의 발전에 필수적인 정보는 조직 내에서 충분히 공유되어야 한다.
③ 지도자는 조직원들이 각자의 비전을 성취하도록 최대한 지원해야 한다.
④ 조직원들이 체계적으로 일하도록 지도자는 전체적인 비전을 제시해야 한다.
⑤ 지도자는 생산성을 높이기 위해 조직원들의 임무를 상세하게 규정해야 한다.

Plus Q

윗글의 괄호 안에 있는 단어들을 어법과 문맥에 맞게 배열하시오.

➡

04 **impatiently** 성급하게 **typically** 대개, 전형적으로 **rush through dessert** 디저트를 서둘러 먹다 **on one's feet** 일어서서 **frame** 영화의 한 화면 **fade** 사라지다 **here and now** 현재 **timetable** 시간표 **stick to** 고수하다, 붙잡고 늘어지다
05 **bright** 총명한 **likeable** 호감이 가는 **assignment** 과제 **distortion** 왜곡 **deserve** ~할 가치가 있다 **question** 의구심을 품다 **argument** 논쟁 **at any cost** 기필코, 꼭 **performance** 실적, 성과 **core** 핵심
06 **organizational** 조직의 **detailed** 세부적인 **description** 묘사, 설명 **overall** 전체의 **randomly** 되는대로, 임의로 **in an attempt to** ~하려는 시도로 **essential** 필수적인 **contribute** 기여하다 **persistent** 끈질긴, 고집하는 **convey** 전달하다 **put ~ in place** ~을 제자리에 놓다

유형 02

주제, 제목

주제, 제목 추론은 글의 지엽적인 부분에 치우치지 않고 전체적인 개념을 이해하여 핵심 내용을 찾는 유형이다. 제목은 압축된 주제이므로, 주제보다 더 구체적으로 표현하거나 비유적인 어구로 나타내는 경향이 있다. 제목, 주제 추론은 각각 1문항씩 출제되고 있으며, 선택지는 제목은 영어로, 주제는 영어와 한글로 제시되었으나 최근에는 영어로 제시되는 경향이 있다.

대표 예제

다음 글의 제목으로 가장 적절한 것은? 수능

도입 When we remark with surprise that someone "looks young" for his or her chronological age, we are observing that we all age biologically at different rates. 전개1 Scientists have good evidence that this apparent difference is real. It is likely that age changes begin in different parts of the body at different times and that the rate of annual change varies among various cells, tissues, and organs, as well as from person to person. 전개2 Unlike the passage of time, biological aging resists easy measurement. What we would like to have is one or a few measurable biological changes that mirror all other biological age changes without reference to the passage of time, so that we could say, for example, that someone who is chronologically eighty years old is biologically sixty years old. 전개3 This kind of measurement would help explain why one eighty-year-old has so many more youthful qualities than does another eighty-year-old, who may be biologically eighty or even ninety years old.

① In Search of a Mirror Reflecting Biological Aging
② Reasons for Slow Aging in the Modern Era
③ A Few Tips to Guess Chronological Age
④ Secrets of Biological Aging Disclosed
⑤ Looking for the Fountain of Youth

한눈에 보는 구조

도입 **소재 제시**
생활 연령에 비해 '젊어 보인다'고 말할 때, 생물학적으로는 서로 다른 속도로 나이가 든다는 것을 말하는 것이다.

전개1 **과학자 인용**
겉으로 보이는 차이가 진짜라는 타당한 근거를 가지고 있다.

전개2 **주제 제시**
생물학적 연령은 측정이 쉽지 않으므로, 시간의 경과와 관계없이 생물학적 나이 변화를 반영하는 하나 또는 몇 개의 측정 가능한 생물학적 변화가 필요하다.

전개3 **주제에 대한 부연 설명**
생물학적 연령 측정은 80세인 어떤 사람이 동갑보다 더 많은 젊음의 특징을 가지는 이유를 설명해 준다.

생활 연령과 생물학적 연령을 대조하여 글을 전개하였으며, 글의 중반 이후에 글쓴이가 강조하고자 하는 내용(주제)이 나오고 있다.

유형 해결 전략

1 처음 한두 문장에 주제나 제목에 관한 단서가 있다.

글의 도입부에 제시된 looks young, chronological age, age biologically 등을 통해 이 글의 소재가 '생활 연령과 생물학적 연령'임을 알 수 있으며, 이것은 제목의 단서가 된다.

2 반복적으로 사용된 어휘나 어구는 반드시 주제와 관련이 있으며, 내용이 전환되는 부분에 특히 주의를 기울인다.

글의 중반에 Unlike라는 전치사가 나오고 있으므로 그 뒤를 주목해서 읽을 필요가 있으며, biological aging resists easy measurement, one or a few measurable biological changes, mirror all other biological age changes, This kind of measurement would help라는 핵심 어구가 반복적으로 제시되고 있다. 즉 이를 통해 글에서 생물학적 연령 측정이 어려움에도 불구하고 측정하려고 애쓰는 이유를 말하려는 것으로 이해할 수 있으며, 이 내용을 압축한 표현이 글의 제목이 된다.

→ 주제문: What we would like to have is one or a few measurable biological changes that mirror all other biological age changes without reference to the passage of time, ~
(우리가 갖고 싶은 것은 ~ 시간의 경과와는 관계없이 모든 다른 생물학적 나이 변화를 반영하는 하나 또는 몇 개의 측정 가능한 생물학적 변화이다.)

3 너무 포괄적이거나 지엽적이지 않으면서, 글의 전체 내용을 담고 있는 선택지를 고른다.

chronological age, youth와 같은 어구들은 본문에서 언급되기는 하였으나 글의 일부분만을 포함하고 있으며, slow aging, tips, secrets와 같은 어구들은 본문의 내용과 직접적인 연관성이 없다. 따라서 모든 것을 종합해 볼 때 ① '생물학적 노화를 반영하는 거울을 찾아서'가 글의 제목으로 가장 적절하다.

② 현대 시대에서 느린 노화의 이유들 → 지문에서 다루지 않은 내용의 선택지
③ 생활 연령을 짐작할 수 있는 몇 가지 비결 → 지문에서 다루지 않은 내용의 선택지
④ 밝혀진 생물학적 노화의 비밀들 → 지문의 내용과 정반대인 선택지
⑤ 청춘의 샘 찾기 → 지문에 나온 어휘를 활용했지만 내용상 관계 없는 선택지

Bonus Tip

주제문의 단서와 위치

- 글의 흐름 전환을 나타내는 역접의 연결어(but, however, yet, still, nevertheless 등) 이후에 주제문이 나올 가능성이 많으므로, 주목할 필요가 있다.
- 예시의 연결어(for example, for instance 등)는 주제문을 보다 구체적으로 설명하기 위한 장치이므로, 예를 드는 연결어 앞문장이 주제문일 가능성이 높다.
- 결론이나 요약을 이끌어내는 연결어(therefore, thus, consequently, as a result, in short 등) 다음에는 글의 전체적인 내용을 다시 한 번 요약 정리하여 표현한 문장이 나오므로, 그 문장이 주제문일 가능성이 높다.

Exercise

01 다음 글의 주제로 가장 적절한 것은? 고2 교육청

Emotions usually get a bad reputation. They are often seen as something to be regulated or managed. People even think emotions are harmful if they get out of control. However, all emotions have a point. They played an important part in our evolutionary history and helped us survive. For example, by seeing disgust on someone's face when presented with moldy food, we were able to avoid eating something dangerous. By communicating happiness, we were able to develop beneficial social interactions. Even anger was an important emotion to our ancestors, motivating us to seek food when we were hungry, to fight off predators and to compete for scarce resources.

*moldy: 곰팡이가 낀

① reasons we need to hide our emotions
② difficulties of reading others' emotions
③ contributions of emotions to human survival
④ ways of expressing emotions in different cultures
⑤ differences between emotional and physical responses

02 다음 글의 제목으로 가장 적절한 것은? 고1 교육청

Give children options and allow them to make their own decisions — on how much they would like to eat, whether they want to eat or not, and what they would like to have. For example, include them in the decision-making process of what you are thinking of making for dinner — "Lisa, would you like to have pasta and meatballs, or chicken and a baked potato?" When discussing how much they should eat during dinner, serve them a reasonable amount; if they claim they are still "hungry" after they are through, ask them to wait five to ten minutes, and if they continue to feel hunger, then they can have a second plate of food. These are fantastic behaviors that, when taught properly, teach brilliant self-confidence and self-control.

① Be a Role Model to Your Children
② Hunger: The Best Sauce for Children
③ Table Manners: Are They Important?
④ Good Nutrition: Children's Brain Power
⑤ Teach Children Food Independence

03 다음 글의 주제로 가장 적절한 것은? 고3 교육청

Work was once seen as human penance for evil beginnings in the Garden of Eden. Over the years, as socioeconomic classes arose in society in the Middle Ages, work began to be seen as the curse of the poor. The wealthy in society did all they could to avoid labor, perhaps except for war, which was seen as noble. Eventually enlightened philosophers such as St. Thomas Aquinas and his contemporaries taught that work was important, especially if we used our surplus to help others. Their teachings influenced reformers such as Martin Luther, who explained that work was virtuous if we had integrity and were honest in our dealings with our fellow men. Later, as America and Canada expanded into new territories, work in contemporary society was described as a privilege of the free. Then, as we entered the 1900s, Henry Ford and other industrialists convinced us that work led to progress for our society and our families.

*penance: 속죄

① various ways to improve working conditions
② changes in the perception of work over time
③ efforts to raise awareness about workers' rights
④ influences of the working class on modern society
⑤ relationships between working hours and productivity

Plus Q

노동(work)을 바라보는 세 가지 시각을 윗글에서 찾아 쓰시오.

➡

01 **reputation** 평판 **regulate** 조절하다 **have a point** 나름의 의미[이유]가 있다 **evolutionary** 진화의 **disgust** 혐오, 역겨움 **beneficial** 유익한 **interaction** 상호작용 **ancestor** 조상 **motivate** 자극하다 **predator** 포식자 **scarce** 부족한

02 **option** 선택권, 선택의 자유 **serve** (음식을) 차려내다 **reasonable** 적당한, 알맞은 **amount** 양, 총액 **be through** 끝내다, 마치다 **plate** 접시, 1인분(의 요리) **fantastic** 멋진, 환상적인 **properly** 제대로, 올바르게 **brilliant** 훌륭한, 찬란히 빛나는 **self-confidence** 자신감 **self-control** 자기통제 **role model** 역할 모델 **independence** 독립심, 자립정신

03 **curse** 저주 **eventually** 마침내 **enlightened** 계몽된 **contemporary** 동시대 사람 **surplus** 잉여 **virtuous** 덕이 높은 **integrity** 진실성 **territory** 영역 **privilege** 특권

04 다음 글의 제목으로 가장 적절한 것은?

Public ownership of companies is intended to spread the bounty of capitalism widely. But the relationship of stock owners to the companies in which they invest tends to be impersonal. They seldom care about what a firm makes — whether it is cheap weapons, poisonous pesticides, or ridiculous entertainment. They pay little attention to how it markets its products, or how it treats its customers, or how it affects the community where it operates. As long as it makes profits, they endorse its management. But let the CEO's performance slip one quarter, and they hasten to take their nest egg elsewhere. Not surprisingly, managers learn quickly that the quarterly report is almighty, and they live in terror of its recurring shadow ever after.

*bounty: 관대함 **nest egg: 자금의 밑천

① The Investment Is the Adventure Itself
② Profits: Judging Standards of Stock Owners
③ The More We Get, the Less Satisfied We Get
④ Investors: More Intelligent Than Anyone Else
⑤ Company: An Organism Operated by the Capital

05 다음 글의 주제로 가장 적절한 것은?

You probably have felt it: those early hours of the afternoon, after lunch has settled, when your eyes begin to droop and your mind goes fuzzy with drowsiness. It's much better to take a nap, and wake up refreshed and ready to work again. And if your boss catches you sleeping at work, tell him or her that it's all in the name of productivity. Thirty people in a Harvard University study were tested four times a day on how quickly they could process information. They were shown flashing images of lines on a screen and asked to identify which direction they were slanted. The performance of the ten people who stayed awake the entire day declined by 50 percent on their last test, while the people who napped for an hour in the early afternoon did as well on their last test as on their first. Even those who napped for half an hour did better than the ones who did not sleep.

① how to improve productivity
② effects of naps on productivity
③ how to select useful information
④ appropriate amount of time for naps
⑤ importance of getting along at the workplace

06 다음 글의 제목으로 가장 적절한 것은?

Each sound in a musical work evokes some response, if **it** is noticed. A changed rhythm, a note in a chord, or the instrument playing a melody affects a listener's response. A sensitivity to what is heard in music is as important as remembering it. Listening to music with no feeling must be something like watching a soccer game in which the goals have been removed. Likewise, listening to music with no feeling has little point. The psychological involvement is missing, and only a sterile, intellectual experience remains. How can you become more responsive to musical sounds? It seems simple, but just trying to be more sensitive to what you hear is a good first step. Open yourself up to the qualities of music. You can play a short section of a work, say, five seconds. Then ask yourself, what response did I have to that portion of the music?

① Respond to Music Emotionally
② Musical Sounds: Healing Us or Not?
③ Are Women More Sensitive than Men?
④ Psychology Leads to Intellectual Curiosity
⑤ What Is Common Between Music and Soccer?

Plus Q

밑줄 친 **it**이 가리키는 것을 본문에서 찾아 쓰시오.

➡

04 **ownership** 소유권 **intend** 의도하다 **capitalism** 자본주의 **stock** 주식 **invest** 투자하다 **impersonal** 비인간적인 **firm** 회사; 확고한 **poisonous** 독성이 있는 **pesticide** 살충제 **ridiculous** 우스꽝스러운 **entertainment** 오락(물) **affect** 영향을 주다 **operate** 영업하다, 가동시키다 **endorse** 지지하다, 승인하다 **quarterly** 분기의 **almighty** 절대적인 힘을 가지고 있는 **terror** 두려움, 공포 **recurring** 되풀이하여 발생하는

05 **droop** (특히 지치거나 약해져서) 아래로 처지다[늘어지다] **go fuzzy** 오락가락하다 **drowsiness** 졸음 **take a nap** 낮잠을 자다 **in the name of** ~의 이름으로, ~라는 명목으로 **identify** 확인하다 **direction** 방향 **slant** 기울다, 경사지다 **decline** 줄어들다

06 **evoke** 불러일으키다 **note** 음표 **chord** 화음 **sensitivity** 자극 감응, 민감성, 감성 **involvement** 관여, 개입 **sterile** 빈약한, 메마른, 단조로운 **section** 구간 **portion** 부분

유형

03 글의 목적

필자가 쓴 글의 의도를 파악하는 유형으로 일상적으로 접할 수 있는 소재가 많이 다뤄지며, 안내문, 편지글, 광고문, 이메일 등의 실용문의 형태로 주로 출제된다. 이 유형은 세부 내용에 초점을 맞추기보다 글을 종합적으로 이해하여 요지를 파악하는 것이 중요하다. 해마다 1문항씩 출제되며, 선택지는 한글로 제시된다.

대표 예제

다음 글의 목적으로 가장 적절한 것은? 수능

머리말 Dear Coach Johnson,

My name is Christina Markle, Bradley Markle's mother. 서론 Bradley and I were thrilled to learn that you're holding your Gymnastics Summer Camp again this year. So I didn't hesitate to sign up and pay the non-refundable deposit for the second week program, which is from July 13 to 17. 본론 But today I remembered that our family is going to get back from a trip on July 13, and I'm afraid Bradley won't be able to make it on the very first day of the program. 결론 Rather than make him skip the day, I'd like to check to see if he could switch to the third week program. Please let us know if that's possible. Thank you.

Sincerely,
Christina Markle

① 캠프 참가를 위해 여행 일정을 조정하려고
② 캠프 참가 시기를 변경할 수 있는지 문의하려고
③ 캠프 등록 시 지불한 예치금 환불을 요구하려고
④ 캠프 일정이 분명하지 않은 것에 대해 항의하려고
⑤ 예약한 캠프 프로그램의 변경된 내용을 확인하려고

한눈에 보는 구조

머리말 **관계 명시**
한 아이의 어머니가 코치에게 쓴 글이다.

서론 **소재 제시**
올해 개최되는 하계 체조 캠프의 2주차 프로그램(7월 13~17일)에 등록을 했고 환불이 되지 않는 보증금을 지불했다.

본론 **필자가 처한 문제 상황 설명**
가족 여행에서 돌아오는 날짜가 신청한 프로그램이 시작하는 날과 겹쳐 첫날부터 참가할 수 없게 되었다.

결론 **목적 제시**
참가 시기를 3주차 프로그램으로 변경할 수 있는지 묻고 있다.

캠프 프로그램 참가 일정 변경이 가능한지 문의하는 편지글로, 본론에서 기존에 신청한 프로그램 기간과 가족 여행 일정이 겹친다는 상황을 설명하고 있으며, 결론에서 글의 목적(글쓴이의 의도)이 드러나 있다.

유형 해결 전략

1 글의 초반에 드러나는 소재어와 대상을 통해 대략적인 상황, 예상 독자를 파악한다.

글의 전반부에 제시된 Dear Coach Johnson, Gymnastics Summer Camp를 보면 이 글의 소재가 '하계 체조 캠프'이며 이 캠프의 코치에게 쓰는 글임을 쉽게 알 수 있다.

2 주로 글의 중반부에 제시되는 연결어에 유의하며 상황 전환의 흐름을 정확히 읽어간다.

글의 중반부에 But today I remembered that ~, and I'm afraid Bradley won't be able to make it ~. 이라는 문장이 제시되고 있다. 이를 통해 이미 신청한 프로그램 기간과 관련한 문제가 발생했다는 것을 알 수 있다.

3 목적을 나타내는 주요 어휘 및 표현이 포함된 핵심 문장을 찾는다.

글의 후반부에 제시된 Rather than make him skip the day, I'd like to check ~. 라는 문장에서 이 글을 쓴 의도를 정확히 밝히고 있다.

→ 핵심 문장: I'd like to check to see if he could switch to the third week program.
(세 번째 주 프로그램으로 바꿀 수 있는지 알기 위해 확인을 하고 싶습니다.)

4 필자의 진정한 의도와 자연스럽게 연결되는 선택지를 고른다.

'캠프, 일정(시기), 변경'과 같이 지문에서 사용된 핵심 어휘가 포함된 선택지로 가능성을 줄이고 나서, 뒤에 이어지는 '조정, 문의, 요구, 항의, 확인'이라는 의도와 가장 밀접하게 연결되는 것을 고른다. 예치금 환불 요구나 일정에 대한 항의는 지문의 내용과는 거리가 멀다.

① 캠프 참가를 위해 여행 일정을 조정하려고 → 핵심 어휘는 포함하나 조정 대상이 잘못된 매력적인 오답
③ 캠프 등록 시 지불한 예치금 환불을 요구하려고 → 지문의 어휘를 활용했지만 내용상 관계 없는 선택지
④ 캠프 일정이 분명하지 않은 것에 대해 항의하려고 → 지문에서 다루지 않은 내용의 선택지
⑤ 예약한 캠프 프로그램의 변경된 내용을 확인하려고 → 확인한다는 의도를 제외한 나머지 내용이 불일치

Bonus Tip

목적을 찾는 단서

- 상황의 전환을 나타내는 연결어(but, however, yet 등) 이후에 주로 문제점이 제기된다.
- 문장의 시작 혹은 중간에 위치하는 부사(luckily, unfortunately, also, rarely 등)도 중요한 단서가 되므로 놓치지 않고 글의 분위기(긍정, 부정, 혹은 중립) 및 흐름 파악에 활용한다.
- 의도를 나타내는 어구가 포함되어 있는 문장이 핵심 문장일 가능성이 높다.

핵심 문장에 자주 사용되는 표현

- You need to ~
- I would like to ~
- Please ~ / Could you ~
- We aim/hope/want to ~
- You must/should/have to ~
- You'd better ~
- It would be ~ if ~
- We note that ~
- I suggest that ~
- I think it's important that ~
- Thank you for ~
- I'd appreciate it if ~
- It seems that ~
- Avoid ~ / Do not ~
- I look forward to ~

Exercise

01 다음 글의 목적으로 가장 적절한 것은? 고2 교육청

To the Student Council,

We are the members of the 11th grade band. Currently, since we have no practice room of our own, we have to practice twice a week in the multipurpose room. For the past two weeks, band practice has been canceled because other groups needed to use the room. Since the band tournament is only one month away, we are asking to be the only group to use the multipurpose room after school for this entire month. Principal Cooper has said that the entire student council must vote on our proposal. We hope that you will understand our situation and vote in our favor.

Sincerely,
The 11th Grade Band

① 다목적실 사용 규정에 대해 문의하려고
② 밴드 경연 대회 참가 승인을 요청하려고
③ 밴드부 연습실 장비의 추가 구입을 건의하려고
④ 밴드 연습 시간 연장에 대한 반대 의사를 밝히려고
⑤ 다목적실 단독 사용에 대한 학생회의 협조를 구하려고

02 다음 글의 목적으로 가장 적절한 것은? 고2 교육청

At Jayden Corporation, we are committed to safeguarding the privacy of all employees, former and current. If you receive a telephone, e-mail, or written request for any information regarding a former employee, do not provide any details of employment. Please pass along the inquiry to Human Resources. Human Resources will determine whether any such inquiry is for legitimate reasons. In certain situations, the HR Department may contact a former employee to request permission to provide information to an outside agency, business, or individual. If there are any questions about this policy, please contact Human Resources.

① 직원 대상 법률 상담 서비스를 소개하려고
② 다른 부서와의 긴밀한 정보 교류를 독려하려고
③ 회사 기밀 유출에 대한 처벌 기준을 공지하려고

④ 개인 정보 수집에 대한 전체 직원의 동의를 요청하려고
⑤ 이전 직원 관련 정보 요청에 대한 대응 방법을 안내하려고

03 다음 글의 목적으로 가장 적절한 것은? 고3 교육청

Dear C&G Waste Services,

Westwood High School is currently establishing a paper recycling program. With the help of students and staff, we aim to significantly reduce the amount of paper that goes into the trash by recycling paper. We currently have a dumpster that will hold the paper recycling, but we need containers for individual classrooms to meet our goal. We would like to request 20 containers. We also need 2,000 clear trash bags in order to allow students and staff to get the paper to the recycle dumpster. So, we are asking your company if it will donate **these items** so that we may succeed in conserving our natural resources. Please contact me if you have any questions. We look forward to establishing a partnership with C&G Waste Services. We know that these types of partnerships help us give back to the community and enhance actions our students can take towards helping the environment.

Sincerely,
Anna Wilson

① 빈번한 쓰레기 미수거에 대해 항의하려고
② 구입한 물품의 배송 지연에 대해 문의하려고
③ 재활용 쓰레기 수거 일정의 변경을 요청하려고
④ 지역 환경 보호 운동을 선도한 것에 대해 감사하려고
⑤ 종이 재활용 프로그램 운영에 필요한 물품 기부를 부탁하려고

Plus Q

밑줄 친 these items가 가리키는 것을 본문에서 찾아 영어로 쓰시오.

➡

01 **student council** 학생회, 학생자치위원회 **currently** 현재, 지금 **multipurpose** 다목적의, 용도가 많은 **cancel** 취소하다 **tournament** 경연 대회 **proposal** 제안, 신청 **in one's favor** ~을 지지하여
02 **be committed to** ~에 전념하다 **safeguard** 보호하다 **regarding** ~에 관한 **employee** 직원 **inquiry** 문의 **Human Resources(HR)** 인사부 **determine** 결정하다 **legitimate** 합당한
03 **establish** 구축하다 **significantly** 크게, 상당히 **dumpster** 대형 쓰레기 수거함 **conserve** 보존하다 **natural resources** 천연자원 **look forward to** ~를 기대하다 **partnership** 협력 관계 **enhance** 강화하다

04 다음 글의 목적으로 가장 적절한 것은?

I came to know the fact that you will be leaving our firm shortly. We are very sorry to lose you since your work has always been most satisfactory and we were hoping that you would remain with J&E for many years. I understand that you are leaving for personal reasons that have nothing to do with this organization. I will be happy to provide you with a letter of recommendation, if you so request. You may find this helpful in securing a position with another firm in your new locale. Please advise my secretary of your intent in this matter, so that we can have it prepared for you before your departure. I know that I speak for everyone here at J&E in wishing you the very best of luck in the future.

① 회사에 사직 의사를 밝히려고
② 다른 지역의 회사에 지원하려고
③ 비서에게 이직에 관해 충고하려고
④ 추천서 제공이 가능함을 안내하려고
⑤ 문제를 일으킨 직원에게 해고를 통보하려고

05 다음 글의 목적으로 가장 적절한 것은?

We are sorry that your recent shipment of supplies was defective. We understand your disappointment and apologize for any inconvenience that this may have caused your organization. In an effort to improve the overall quality of our products and the way that they are being shipped, we have switched to a new delivery company and new packaging. This effort should prevent damage to our products and will expedite orders. We will replace your entire order and have it shipped by the end of this week. There is no cost to you since this was an error on our part. We look forward to continuing serving your business and hope that you will continue ordering products from us. If there is anything else that we can do to reduce your inconvenience, please feel free to contact us.

① 제품의 품질 개선을 건의하려고
② 배송 회사의 교체를 요구하려고
③ 추가적인 비용 청구에 항의하려고
④ 배송 관련 문제에 대해 사과하려고
⑤ 지속적인 서비스 이용에 감사하려고

06 다음 글의 목적으로 가장 적절한 것은?

In order to better serve you and improve our business processes, we are implementing a significant upgrade to our Enterprise Resource Planning systems. In planning the upcoming changes, we have made every effort to minimize the disruption for our business partners. There are, however, a few things we want you to know about: brief interruption for orders and shipping, changes to reference numbers for open transactions, and modifications in formatting of transactional documents. We want you to be aware of this information so you could anticipate these changes and ensure that you have sufficient inventory on-hand during the interruption of shipping to avoid any damage to your work. **Express** our appreciation to you for your support of BD Biosciences products, we will continue to communicate with you about this important transition. If you have any questions, you can contact Customer Service toll-free at 855-236-2772.

① 거래 내역에 대해 문의하려고
② 단골 고객들에게 감사를 표현하려고
③ 시스템 개선에 따른 변경 사항을 알리려고
④ 배송 지연에 대한 피해 보상을 요구하려고
⑤ 거래 절차 변경에 대한 지원을 요청하려고

Plus Q

밑줄 친 부분을 어법에 맞게 고쳐 쓰시오.

➡

04 **come to** ~하게 되다 **shortly** 곧 **satisfactory** 만족스러운 **have nothing to do with** ~와는 관계가 없다 **organization** 조직 **letter of recommendation** 추천서 **secure** 얻다, 확보하다 **locale** 지역, 장소 **secretary** 비서 **intent** 의도 **speak for** ~대신 말하다, ~를 대변하다
05 **shipment** 배송 **defective** 결함이 있는 **inconvenience** 불편 **in an effort to** ~하려는 노력으로 **switch** 전환하다, 바꾸다 **damage** 피해 **expedite** 더 신속히 처리하다 **reduce** 줄이다
06 **improve** 개선하다 **implement** 시행하다 **significant** 중요한 **upcoming** 다가오는, 곧 있을 **disruption** 혼란 **interruption** 중단 **modification** 수정, 변경 **transactional** 거래의 **anticipate** 예상하다 **ensure** 보장하다 **sufficient** 충분한 **on-hand** 보유(량) **appreciation** 감사 **transition** (다른 상황으로의) 이행, 과도; 변화

유형

04 심경, 분위기

심경을 파악하는 문항은 필자나 등장인물의 심리 상태를 추론하는 유형이며, 분위기를 파악하는 문항은 글의 등장인물이 처한 상황을 추론하는 유형이다. 모두 구체적인 단서를 근거로 정답을 찾아야 하는데, 심경이나 분위기를 묘사하는 어휘 혹은 표현이 그러한 근거로서 역할을 한다. 최근에는 분위기를 묻는 문항은 출제되지 않고 있으며, 심경을 묻는 문항만이 수능에 1문항씩 매년 출제되고 있다.

대표 예제

다음 글에 드러난 'I'의 심경으로 가장 적절한 것은? 수능

도입》 I'm leaving early tomorrow morning, finally! I've always wanted to explore the Amazon, the unknown and mysterious world. At this hour, the great Emerald Amazon Explorer should be at the port waiting for me to get on board. 전개》 Freshwater dolphins will escort me on the playful river, and 500 species of birds, half a dozen species of monkeys, and numerous colorful butterflies will welcome me into their kingdom. I wish I could camp in the wild and enjoy the company of mosquitos, snakes, and spiders. I'd love to make the world's largest rainforest home. 결말》 My heart swells as much as my chubby bags; yet, I'd better get some sleep since a long, tough journey is ahead of me.

① excited
② exhausted
③ frustrated
④ indifferent
⑤ relieved

한눈에 보는 구조

도입》 **상황 제시**
나는 내일 미지의 신비스러운 세계인 아마존을 탐험하러 떠날 예정이고, Emerald Amazon Explorer 호가 항구에서 나를 기다리고 있을 것이다.

전개》 **아마존에 대한 기대와 예상**
많은 야생 생물들이 나를 환영해서 그들의 왕국으로 데려갈 것이며, 아마존의 야생에서 야영을 하면서 야생 생물들과 함께 즐기고 싶다.

결말》 **현재 기분에 대한 요약**
내 가슴은 불룩한 가방만큼 부풀어 올라 있다.

아마존을 탐험할 예정인 글쓴이는 아마존에서 야생 생물들이 자신을 반길 것이고, 그들과 그곳에서 즐기기를 바라고 있다는 것을 기술하며, 마지막으로 자신의 마음이 부풀어 있다고 설명함으로써 자신의 '흥분된' 심경을 나타내고 있다.

유형 해결 전략

1 필자가 처한 상황이나 경험하고 있는 사건을 파악한다.

- I'm leaving early tomorrow morning, finally!
  (나는 드디어 내일 아침 일찍 떠날 예정이다!)
- I've always wanted to explore the Amazon, the unknown and mysterious world.
  (나는 항상 미지의 신비스러운 세계인 아마존을 탐험하고 싶었다.)

→ 필자가 처한 상황은 항상 탐험하고 싶어 했던 아마존으로 내일 떠난다는 것이다.

2 필자의 심경을 추측할 수 있는 어휘 및 표현을 찾는다.

- 500 species of birds, half a dozen species of monkeys, and numerous colorful butterflies will welcome me into their kingdom
  (500종의 새들, 6종의 원숭이들, 그리고 수많은 화려한 나비들이 나를 맞이해 그들의 왕국으로 데려갈 것이다.)
- I wish I could camp in the wild and enjoy the company of mosquitos, snakes, and spiders.
  (야생에서 야영을 하면서 모기, 뱀, 그리고 거미들과 함께 즐길 수 있다면 좋겠다.)
- My heart swells as much as my chubby bags
  (내 가슴은 나의 불룩한 가방만큼 많이 부풀어 오른다.)

→ welcome, I wish I could camp, enjoy, My heart swells 등을 통해 필자는 아마존 탐험을 기대하고 있음을 알 수 있다.

3 필자가 처한 상황과 심경을 추측할 수 있는 어휘 및 표현을 총체적으로 고려해서 필자의 심경을 파악한다.

→ 필자는 내일 아마존 탐험을 떠날 예정이며, 아마존에서 벌어질 일을 예상하면서 기대에 부풀어 있음을 알 수 있다. 따라서 필자의 심경으로 가장 적절한 것은 ① '흥분된'이다.

Bonus Tip

심경 · 분위기를 나타내는 어휘 및 표현

go smoothly(순조롭게 진행되다), cheer(환호하다), sing a song of celebration(축하의 노래를 하다), solitude(외로움, 외톨이임), a narrow stiff road(좁고 가파른 길), terrified(무서워하는), catch one's breath(헐떡이다), feel at ease(편안함을 느끼다), speechless(말이 나오지 않은, 형언할 수 없는), fulfill one's lifelong dream(평생의 꿈을 이루다), heart begins to beat(심장이 뛰기 시작하다), comforting words(위로의 말), the heart starts to pound(심장이 뛰기 시작하다), anxious(근심하는, 갈망하는), tears of delight(기쁨의 눈물), butterflies in the stomach(가슴이 두근거림), My mind was completely blank.(내 마음은 완전히 멍한 상태였다.), the heart swells(마음이 부푼다)

심경 문항 선택지로 주로 나오는 단어

anticipating(기대하는), ashamed(부끄러워하는), tense(긴장한), scared(두려워하는), relieved(안도해하는), depressed(우울해하는), irritated(짜증이 난), frightened(두려워하는), grateful(감사해하는), sympathetic(공감하는), perplexed(당혹해하는), envious(질투하는), indifferent(무관심한)

Exercise

01 다음 글의 상황에 나타난 분위기로 가장 적절한 것은? 평가원

On my first day in the Emergency Center, I was about to drink my coffee when the first call came. I quickly picked up the line, "9-1-1." My voice was trembling and my heart was racing. A woman cried, "My husband's not breathing!" I instructed her to begin CPR. I was trying to be as steady as I could, but I was shaking. The situation was absolutely critical. While she was performing CPR, I immediately notified the nearby hospital. After a few tense moments, she came back on the line and shouted, "Where's the ambulance?" I replied, "It's getting there as quickly as it can."

① festive ② urgent
③ romantic ④ mysterious
⑤ monotonous

02 다음 글에 드러난 'I'의 심경으로 가장 적절한 것은? 고2 교육청

One afternoon, as I wandered around the shops near my hotel, I saw a poor gypsy woman sitting on the sidewalk outside the subway station. She looked tired and lonely, and her eyes were fixed firmly on the ground. A young toddler played at her feet merrily, not knowing her mother's sadness. Then, a young woman who worked at a nearby tourist shop came out of the shop, holding some food. She went over to the gypsy woman, smiled at the child and handed over the food. While the shop assistant was happily responding to the toddler's playful touches, I saw a smile flashing across the gypsy woman's face. It was a heartwarming moment. That day I learned a lesson in human kindness.

① moved ② bored
③ nervous ④ indifferent
⑤ depressed

03 다음 글에 드러난 Gabby의 심경 변화로 가장 적절한 것은? 평가원

Stepping up to the microphone, Gabby could feel the sweat starting to run down her face and neck. She tried to take a deep breath, but couldn't. As her name was called, Gabby became more afraid of speaking before a large audience. Then, she suddenly remembered the words of a woman who had gradually overcome the same fear: "Fear, rapid heartbeat, quick breathing, and sweating are simply the body's declaration that we are ready to fight." **Recalling this**, Gabby calmed down and remembered clearly what she had to say. Assured, Gabby smiled and started to deliver her speech. The words flowed out like water, and her beating heart gave her more and more mental strength. The performance was successful. She had overcome her fear.

① hopeful → scared
② indifferent → refreshed
③ jealous → delighted
④ anxious → confused
⑤ worried → confident

Plus Q

윗글의 밑줄 친 **Recalling this**를 접속사가 들어간 형태로 다시 쓰시오.

➡

01 **emergency center** 응급 센터 **tremble** 떨다, 떨리다 **race** (심장이) 아주 빨리 고동치다 **instruct** 지시하다 **CPR(=cardiopulmonary resuscitation)** 심폐소생술 **steady** 차분한, 침착한 **critical** 위기의, 위급한 **notify** 통지하다, 알리다 **tense** 긴장된

02 **wander** 돌아다니다 **sidewalk** 보도 **fix** 고정시키다 **firmly** 단단히 **toddler** 아장아장 걷는 아기 **hand over** ~을 건네주다 **flash** 휙 지나가다 **heartwarming** 마음이 따뜻한 **lesson** 교훈

03 **overcome** 극복하다 **heartbeat** 심장 박동 **sweat** 땀을 흘리다 **declaration** 선언 **recall** 상기하다 **assured** 자신 있는, 확신이 있는 **deliver** (연설을) 하다

04 다음 글에 드러난 'I'의 심경으로 가장 적절한 것은?

On my final day of classes, the principal greeted me as I entered the school building. "Will you come with me, please?" he said sternly. "There is a problem with your room." He looked straight ahead as he led me down the hall. What now? I wondered. When I arrived at my room, I couldn't believe what I saw. It was amazing! There were sprays of flowers in each corner, bouquets on the students' desks and filing cabinets, and a huge blanket of flowers lying on my desk. I wondered how they could have done this. Most of them came from families so poor that they relied on the school assistance program for clothing and meals. I started to cry and they joined me. That was not the only tribute they paid me, though. Two years later, all fourteen students graduated, and six earned college scholarships.

① envious ② regretful
③ delighted ④ sympathetic
⑤ disappointed

05 다음 글의 상황에 나타난 분위기로 가장 적절한 것은?

Chris Jenkins decided to catch up on some yard work at his trout-fishing farm in Australia. Ziggy, his dog, kept him company, while Stella, his friend, napped about 60 yards away. When Chris stood up to stretch, he banged his head on the railing around the fishing area, lost his balance, and slipped into the icy water. Unfortunately, Chris did not know how to swim. What is worse, his heavy clothes weighed him down. Perhaps Ziggy knew that she was too light to pull him out, barking frantically to wake up Stella. Within seconds, Stella hurtled into the lake, and Chris tried to grab her leg and hold on.

① solemn and serious
② funny and pleasant
③ desolate and gloomy
④ desperate and urgent
⑤ relaxed and peaceful

06 다음 글에 드러난 Hana의 심경 변화로 가장 적절한 것은?

The early morning mist had become a light rain, and on the pier black umbrellas were seen here and there, making recognizing Mr. Johnson even harder. Hana searched desperately for a face that resembled the photo she had studied so long and hard. What if he hadn't come? How could I get to his place by myself? Hana took a deep breath and lifted her head. At that moment, she saw a man in a black coat, carrying an umbrella, come quickly to her side. He was of slight build, not much taller than she, and his face was pale. He bowed stiffly and murmured, "You have had a long trip, Miss Omiya." Hana caught her breath. "You are Mr. Johnson? Oh, my! I was anxious about what I'm supposed to do if you don't show up."

① lonely → pleased
② worried → relieved
③ excited → embarrassed
④ frightened → surprised
⑤ sympathetic → indifferent

Plus Q

다음 빈칸에 들어갈 단어를 본문에서 찾아 쓰시오.

If something is ____________, it is very light in color or almost white.

➡

04 **principal** 교장 **sternly** 준엄하게, 엄격하게 **look straight ahead** 곧장 앞을 응시하다 **amazing** 놀라운 **spray** 다발 **rely on A for B** B를 A에 의존하다 **assistance** 지원 **tribute** 경의, 찬사, 존경
05 **catch up on** (밀린 일을) 하다 **trout** 송어 **company** 동반, 동석 **nap** 낮잠을 자다 **bang** 쾅하고 부딪치다 **railing** 난간 **weigh down** ~의 무게로 가라앉다 **bark** 짖다 **frantically** 미친 듯이 **hurtle** 돌진하다 **grab** 잡다 **hold on** 버티다
06 **mist** 안개 **pier** 부두 **desperately** 필사적으로 **slight** 홀쭉한 **build** 체격 **pale** 창백한 **stiffly** 뻣뻣하게 **murmur** 중얼거리다 **be anxious about** ~에 대해 걱정하다 (*cf.* **be anxious to** ~하고 싶어 하다) **show up** 나타나다

유형

05 내용 일치

글의 내용과 선택지를 비교하여 일치 여부를 판단하는 유형으로, 선택지에서 제시되는 정보를 중심으로 정확한 내용 파악이 필요하다. 각 선택지는 대개 하나의 정보를 확인하는 형태로 출제되는데, 한 선택지 안에 두 가지 정보가 제시되는 경우도 있으며, 대개 그 선택지가 답이 되는 경향이 있으므로 두 정보가 모두 지문의 내용과 일치하는지 꼼꼼하게 살펴야 한다. 수능에서는 매년 1문항씩 출제되고 있다.

대표 예제

Protogenes에 관한 다음 글의 내용과 일치하지 않는 것은?

수능

도입 Known for his devotion to each of his paintings, Protogenes was an ancient Greek painter and a rival of Apelles. He was born in Caunus, on the coast of Caria, but lived most of his life in Rhodes. Little else is known of him. 전개1 But there are some accounts of his paintings. The *Ialysus* and the *Satyr* were the most well-known among his works. Protogenes spent approximately seven years painting the *Ialysus*, a depiction of a local hero of a town in Rhodes. After remaining in Rhodes for at least 200 years, it was carried off to Rome. There later it was destroyed by fire. 전개2 Protogenes worked on the *Satyr* during Demetrius Poliorcetes' attack on Rhodes from 305 to 304 B.C. Interestingly, the garden in which he painted the *Satyr* was in the middle of the enemy's camp. Protogenes is said to have been about seventy years of age when the *Satyr* was completed.

① 고대 그리스 화가였다.
② 일생의 대부분을 Rhodes에서 지냈다.
③ *Ialysus*를 그리는 데 대략 7년을 보냈다.
④ 적진과 멀리 떨어진 곳에서 *Satyr*를 그렸다.
⑤ *Satyr*를 완성했을 때는 약 70세였다고 전해진다.

한눈에 보는 구조

도입 **설명 대상 소개**
_ 고대 그리스의 화가
_ 출생지와 거주지
_ 그 외 인물에 대해 알려진 것은 거의 없음.

전개1 **작품에 대한 기술 1**
그의 그림에 대해서는 몇 가지 알 수 있음.
_ Ialysus: Rhodes의 한 마을의 지역 영웅을 묘사 / 그리는 데 7년이 걸림.

전개2 **작품에 대한 기술 2**
_ Satyr: 기원전 305년에서 304년에 적진 한가운데서 그렸으며 70세에 완성함.

Protogenes라는 고대 그리스 화가의 유명한 작품 두 개를 열거의 방식으로 설명하고 있는 글이다.

유형 해결 전략

1 지시문과 글의 도입부를 통해 소재를 확인한다.

Known for his devotion to each of his paintings, Protogenes was an ancient Greek painter ~.

→ 고대 그리스 화가인 Protogenes에 관한 글임을 알 수 있다.

2 지문에 제시되는 관련 정보와 선택지의 내용을 일일이 대조하면서 확인한다.

선택지의 순서는 지문에 제시되는 정보의 순서와 일치하므로, 하나하나 차분하게 대조하며 확인한다.

① 고대 그리스 화가였다. → Protogenes was an ancient Greek painter (일치)

② 일생의 대부분을 Rhodes에서 지냈다. → ~, but lived most of his life in Rhodes (일치)

③ *Ialysus*를 그리는 데 대략 7년을 보냈다. → Protogenes spent approximately seven years painting the *Ialysus* (일치)

④ 적진과 멀리 떨어진 곳에서 *Satyr*를 그렸다. → the garden in which he painted the *Satyr* was in the middle of the enemy's camp (불일치)

⑤ *Satyr*를 완성했을 때는 약 70세였다고 전해진다. → Protogenes is said to have been about seventy years of age when the *Satyr* was completed. (일치)

3 선택지에 두 개의 정보가 제시되는 경우, 어느 한 정보가 다른 정보에 영향을 끼치지 않도록 꼼꼼하게 읽는다.

선택지에 제시된 두 개의 정보 중 하나가 일치할 경우, 섣불리 맞는다고 생각하고 다른 정보를 가볍게 보며 실수하는 경우가 종종 있다. 두 정보를 개별적으로 생각하며 꼼꼼하게 일치 여부를 따진다.

④ 적진과 멀리 떨어진 곳에서 *Satyr*를 그렸다. → *Satyr*를 그리긴 했지만, 지문의 in the middle of the enemy's camp와 상반되는 내용이므로 정답으로 선택하면 된다.

4 글의 후반부에 제시된 정보에 더욱 유의한다.

일치 여부가 드러나면 바로 답을 낼 수 있는 유형이라는 특징을 고려해 볼 때, ①, ②번보다는 ③, ④, ⑤번 중의 하나에 답이 있을 확률이 높으므로 후반부 내용을 특히 유의해서 살펴본다.

Bonus Tip

내용 일치 문항 선택지 구성 원리

- 선택지는 글의 전개 순서에 따라 제시되므로, 지문의 내용과 선택지를 순서대로 대조한다.
- 선택지는 지문의 내용을 직역하여 제시하는 것이 원칙이다.
- 선택지는 주로 하나의 정보를 담고 있으나, 때로는 두 개의 정보가 들어 있기도 하며 이 경우 답과 상당한 밀접성을 가질 확률이 높다는 점을 기억한다.
- 글에 언급된 정보의 일부만을 바꾸어 오답으로 제시하는 경우가 많으므로, 이에 유의한다.

Exercise

01 addax에 관한 다음 글의 내용과 일치하지 않는 것은? 고1 교육청

The addax is a kind of antelope found in some areas in the Sahara Desert. It has twisted horns and short, thick legs. It is an endangered mammal and there are only about 500 left in the wild. The head and body length of the addax measures 150 – 170 centimeters. Males are slightly taller than females. The coat of the addax changes in color depending on the season. In winter, the addax is grayish-brown with white legs. During summer, their coat gets lighter, and is almost completely white. The addax prefers sandy desert areas and stony deserts. The addax is mostly active at night due to the heat of the desert.

*antelope: (동물) 영양 **coat: (동물의) 털

① 다리가 짧고 두껍다.
② 멸종 위기에 처해 있다.
③ 수컷이 암컷보다 약간 더 크다.
④ 계절에 따라 털 색깔이 변한다.
⑤ 주로 낮에 활동적이다.

02 tarsier에 관한 다음 글의 내용과 일치하지 않는 것은? 고2 교육청

Tarsiers are little primates not much bigger than rats. Their resemblance to the rat is exaggerated by their thin tail, which is much longer than their overall body length. All tarsiers are completely nocturnal and have a number of remarkable physical adaptations for this lifestyle. They have an excellent sense of hearing. Tarsiers also have enormous eyes in comparison with their body size; their eyes make up nearly one-fourth the size of their faces. The habitat of the tarsier is generally tropical rain forest and they are found in dense bamboo thickets. During the day, they lie in holes in tree trunks and in dark, thickly tangled vegetation. At night, they hunt for insects, spiders, and small lizards. Tarsiers can rotate their heads at least 180 degrees, which gives them a wide field of vision for spotting prey.

① 몸통보다 긴 꼬리를 지니고 있다.
② 뛰어난 청력을 가지고 있다.
③ 눈이 얼굴 크기의 약 4분의 1을 차지한다.
④ 열대우림 지역에 주로 서식한다.
⑤ 채식 위주의 먹잇감을 찾아다닌다.

03 North Yungas Road에 관한 다음 글의 내용과 일치하지 않는 것은? 고3 교육청

North Yungas Road, known as 'Death Road,' connects the Yungas region of northern Bolivia to the capital, La Paz. The road was built in the 1930s during the Chaco War by Paraguayan prisoners of war. Starting from La Paz, this road first climbs to 4,650 meters, and then gradually descends to 1,200 meters at the town of Coroico. This drop is one of the longest stretches of continuous downhill road in the world. It's mostly a single-lane road with no guard rails, and it has cliffs of up to 600 meters. The hazards include landslides and tumbling rocks, constant fog, tropical downpours and limited visibility. Unlike the rest of Bolivia, one of the local road rules specifies that vehicles are required to drive on the left side of the road to give the driver a better view of the vehicle's outside wheel and make passing safer.

① 전쟁 포로들에 의해 만들어졌다.
② 세계에서 가장 긴 내리막길 중 하나가 있다.
③ 대부분이 가드레일이 없는 일차선 도로이다.
④ 지속적인 안개와 열대성 폭우 같은 위험이 있다.
⑤ 차량을 도로의 오른편에서 운행해야 한다.

Plus 

차량을 도로의 왼편에서 운행하도록 명시한 이유 두 가지를 우리말로 쓰시오.

➡

01 **the Sahara Desert** 사하라 사막 **twisted** 나선형의, 비틀어진 **horn** 뿔 **endangered** 멸종 위기에 처한 **mammal** 포유동물 **measure** (치수 · 길이 · 양 등이) ~이다 **slightly** 약간 **depending on** ~에 따라서 **grayish-brown** 회갈색의 **active** 활동적인 **due to** ~ 때문에
02 **primates** 영장류 **rat** 쥐 **resemblance** 유사함, 닮음 **nocturnal** 야행성의 **remarkable** 뛰어난, 주목할 만한 **enormous** 거대한 **habitat** 서식지 **tangle** 얽히다 **vegetation** 초목
03 **region** 지역 **capital** 수도 **descend** 내려가다 **downhill** 내리막의 **hazard** 위험 **landslide** 산사태 **downpour** 폭우 **specify** 명시하다 **vehicle** 차량

04 Dorothy Hodgkin에 관한 다음 글의 내용과 일치하지 않는 것은?

Dorothy Hodgkin was born in Cairo, Egypt, in 1910 and her father, John Crowfoot, was a British archaeologist. During World War I, Dorothy and her sisters were sent to England for safety reasons. She received her schooling at the Sir John Leman School. After she graduated from the school, Dorothy joined Somerville College of Women at Oxford University. Fortunately, she was financially supported by one of her relatives, who paid her tuition fees. She received her Bachelor's degree from Oxford University in 1932. She then assisted John Desmond Bernal, a famous crystallographer, at Cambridge University. In 1934, Hodgkin returned to Oxford to complete her doctorate program as well as to teach. After World War II, Hodgkin became the first scientist in Britain to use a computer to analyze the molecular structure of complex chemicals and this enabled her to produce three-dimensional models.

*crystallographer: 결정학자

① 아버지가 영국의 고고학자였다.
② 1차 세계 대전 때 영국으로 가게 되었다.
③ 친척 중 한 명으로부터 등록금 후원을 받았다.
④ 캠브리지 대학에서 학사 학위를 받았다.
⑤ 컴퓨터를 이용해 화학물질의 분자 구조를 분석했다.

05 Wilma Rudolph에 관한 다음 글의 내용과 일치하지 않는 것은?

Wilma Rudolph was the twentieth of twenty-two children. She was born prematurely and doctors didn't expect her to survive. She did, but at the age of four she contracted double pneumonia and scarlet fever, which left her left leg paralyzed. At age nine, she removed the metal leg brace she had depended on for the past five years and began walking without it. By thirteen, she had developed a rhythmic walk, which doctors said was a miracle. That same year, she decided she wanted to begin running. She entered her first race and came in last. For the next three years, she entered every race she could. She kept on running until the day came that she won a race. Eventually, the little girl who was not supposed to live and then who was not supposed to be able to walk again would go on to win three Olympic gold medals.

① 20번째 자식이며 조산으로 태어났다.
② 5년간 금속 의족을 사용했다.
③ 첫 번째 달리기 대회에서 중도에 포기했다.
④ 첫 경주 후 3년 동안 참가할 수 있는 모든 대회에 나갔다.
⑤ 올림픽에서 금메달을 세 개 땄다.

06 Ellen West에 관한 다음 글의 내용과 일치하지 않는 것은?

Ellen West was a troubled patient who suffered from anorexia nervosa and possibly other mental illness. Ellen had fluctuations with her weight and had an extreme fear of gaining weight. It eventually led to the development of depression. In order to stay thin, she started to take some medicine. She was given permission to marry her cousin at the age of 28. She became obsessed with wanting a child; however, she would not adjust her eating habits, which resulted in a miscarriage. She decided to discontinue her use of medicine in order to get pregnant, but her fears of weight gain overpowered her and she began using it again. When Ellen turned 30, she decided to become a vegetarian in hopes of maintaining her thin figure. It wasn't until after three years of marriage that she informed her husband of her severe eating disorder and depression.

① 체중 증가에 대한 두려움 때문에 우울증에 걸렸다.
② 날씬함을 유지하기 위해서 약을 복용하기 시작했다.
③ 체중 걱정으로 인해 아이를 낳고 싶어 하지 않았다.
④ 30살 때 채식주의자가 되기로 결심했다.
⑤ 결혼 생활 3년 후에 남편에게 자신의 심각한 문제를 알렸다.

Plus Q

Ellen West가 유산하게 된 이유를 본문에서 찾아 10자 내외의 우리말로 쓰시오.

➡

04 **archaeologist** 고고학자 **financially** 재정적으로 **relative** 친척 **tuition fee** 등록금 **bachelor's degree** 학사 학위 **assist** ~의 조수 노릇을 하다, 돕다 **complete** 마치다, 완성하다 **analyze** 분석하다 **molecular** 분자의

05 **prematurely** 조산으로 **contract** (병에) 걸리다 **double pneumonia** 양측 폐렴 **scarlet fever** 성홍열 **paralyzed** 마비된 **metal leg brace** 금속으로 된 다리 지지대 **eventually** 결국

06 **fluctuation** 오르내림 **development** 발병 **depression** 우울증 **obsessed with** ~에 집착하는 **adjust** 조정[조절]하다 **result in** 결국 ~이 되다 **miscarriage** 유산 **discontinue** 그만두다 **overpower** 압도하다, 제압하다 **vegetarian** 채식주의자

유형

06 실용문의 이해

제시된 실용문 속의 정보와 일치하거나 일치하지 않는 선택지를 판단하는 유형으로, '단편 영화제 관람, 방과 후 학교 등록, 미술 전시회 초대' 등 행사 혹은 활동 참여에 관한 주제가 주로 제시되고 있다. 날짜 혹은 기간, 장소, 참가 대상, 세부 일정, 예약, 참가비용과 같은 정보가 선택지로 보통 주어진다. 다른 유형과 비교하여 난이도는 쉬운 편에 속하며, 해마다 2문항씩 출제되고 있다.

대표 예제

2015 Annual Teen Programmers Conference에 관한 다음 안내문의 내용과 일치하는 것은? 수능

도입 **2015 Annual Teen Programmers Conference**
November 21 & 22, 10:00 a.m. – 5:00 p.m.

Hosted by the Teen Programmers Association

Is the computer screen your universe? Then join our conference held at West State University's Brilliance Hall, and challenge yourself! Here you'll meet the leaders in modern computer science.

전개1 **The conference includes:**

- Lectures by renowned industry figures, including Warwick Meade
- 10 separate seminars on hardware / software, programming, and new applications
- Exhibitions of their latest products by 12 major firms

전개2 **Ticket Prices:**

- Total Pass: $25 (includes buffet lunch)
- Lectures & Seminars Only: $15
- Exhibitions Only: $10

Booking is essential. Reserve your tickets at www.tiinprogrammers.org.

---

① 3일간 진행된다.
② 시청의 대강당에서 개최된다.
③ 12개의 개별 세미나가 열린다.
④ Total Pass에 점심 뷔페가 포함된다.
⑤ 예약하지 않아도 참가할 수 있다.

한눈에 보는 구조

도입 **개략적인 회의 소개**
2015년도 십 대 프로그래머 연례 회의가 십 대 프로그래머 협회 주최로 11월 21일~22일 간 West 주립대학의 Brilliance Hall에서 개최된다.

전개1 **회의 세부 내용 소개**
유명한 업계 인물들의 강연, 10개의 개별 세미나, 12개 주요 회사들의 최신 제품 전시회가 회의에 포함된다.

전개2 **입장권 가격 안내**
전체 행사 입장권은 25달러, 강연과 세미나만 이용하면 15달러, 전시회만 관람할 경우 10달러이다.

회의 기간, 장소, 세부 내용, 입장권 가격이 순서대로 제시되며, 이 중 입장권 가격 항목에서 정답을 쉽게 찾을 수 있다.

유형 해결 전략

1 지시문과 도입부 내용을 통해 소재를 확인한다.

글의 지시문과 도입부를 통해 '십 대가 참여하는 프로그래머 연례 회의'가 글의 소재임을 알 수 있다. 또한 도입부에서 회의 기간 및 시간, 주최 기관, 장소에 관한 정보를 파악할 수 있다.

2 선택지를 먼저 빠르게 읽고 지문에서 확인할 사항을 미리 파악한다.

선택지를 보면 지문에서 확인할 정보는 기간, 장소, 세부 내용, 입장권 가격, 예약 필요 여부이다. 세세한 숫자나 고유 명사들은 지문과 대조할 때 살펴본다.

3 선택지와 지문을 대조하며 일치 여부를 신속하고 정확하게 확인한다.

① 3일간 진행된다. → November 21 & 22

② 시청의 대강당에서 개최된다.
→ join our conference held at West State University's Brilliance Hall

③ 12개의 개별 세미나가 열린다.
→ 10 separate seminars on hardware / software, programming, and new applications

④ Total Pass에 점심 뷔페가 포함된다. → Total Pass: $25 (includes buffet lunch)

⑤ 예약하지 않아도 참가할 수 있다. → Booking is essential.

→ 회의는 11월 21일~22일의 2일 간, 주립대학의 한 건물에서 열리고, 10개의 개별 세미나가 진행될 예정으로 예약이 필수임을 알 수 있다. 따라서 안내문의 내용과 일치하는 것은 전체 입장권 가격에 점심 뷔페가 포함되어 있다는 내용의 ④이다.

Bonus Tip

실용문의 항목별 주요 표현

항목	주요 표현
날짜 혹은 기간	• from Monday to Friday • It is a 4-week program beginning on ~
참가 가능 대상 제한 대상	• Children aged 8-10 • Entries are limited[restricted] to ~ • Participants must be at least 16 years of age.
등록 [참가] 비용	• Free admission for ~ • All tickets are non-refundable. • Admission is free, but donations are welcome.
예약	• Reservations are required. • All seats are reservation only.
문의 방법	• For more[further] details, contact us at ~ • For additional information[inquiries], please visit our website at ~

Exercise

01 Zookeeper Experience at Dudley Zoo에 관한 다음 안내문의 내용과 일치하지 않는 것은? 고2 교육청

Zookeeper Experience at Dudley Zoo

During Zookeeper Experience, you will learn what it takes to work in an animal care career, participating in the following activities:

- Preparing animal diets
- Helping to weigh and care for animals
- Taking part in animal training

WHO: Animal lovers aged 9 – 18

TIME: 9:30 a.m. – 11:30 a.m.

– We schedule one Zookeeper Experience per day.

COST: $50

– Zoo admission is included.

WHAT TO BRING: A water bottle and your camera

– Photo opportunities are provided.

Please visit our website at www.dudleyzoo.com to make a reservation.

① 동물의 먹이를 준비하는 활동을 포함한다.
② 9세부터 18세까지의 동물 애호가를 대상으로 한다.
③ 하루에 한 번 운영된다.
④ 동물원 입장료는 참가비와 별도이다.
⑤ 사진 촬영 기회가 제공된다.

2015 National Essay Contest에 관한 다음 안내문의 내용과 일치하는 것은? 평가원

고 난도

2015 NATIONAL ESSAY CONTEST

The Evergreen Foundation is excited to call for submissions for the 2015 National Essay Contest! This contest is designed to encourage high school students **become** more aware of the importance of our environment.

Contest Theme

- How can we preserve our forests?

Requirements & Submission Guidelines

- High school students only
- Only one essay per student
- Essays must be between 1,500 and 2,000 words.
- Due by July 15, 2015

We will announce the winners of this year's contest on August 15, 2015.

Only essays submitted by email will be accepted.
(email: 2015essay@evergreeners.org)

For more information, visit www.evergreeners.org.

① 주제가 정해져 있지 않다.
② 대학생을 대상으로 한다.
③ 1인당 1편의 에세이만 제출할 수 있다.
④ 수상자는 2015년 7월 15일에 발표된다.
⑤ 에세이는 직접 방문하여 제출해야 한다.

Plus Q

밑줄 친 부분을 어법에 맞게 고쳐 쓰시오.

➡

01 **zookeeper** 동물원 사육사 **participate in** ~에 참여하다 **diet** 음식, 먹이 **take part in** ~에 참가하다 **admission** 입장 **opportunity** 기회 **make a reservation** 예약하다

02 **foundation** 재단 **call for** 요구하다 **submission** 제출 **encourage** 권장하다 **become aware of** ~을 알게 되다 **preserve** 보존하다 **due** ~하기로 되어 있는[예정된] **accept** 받아 주다[수락하다]

03 Summer Camp Youth Volunteer Program에 관한 다음 안내문의 내용과 일치하는 것은?

Summer Camp Youth Volunteer Program

Applications are now closed for Summer 2016. If you have applied for Summer 2016, here are the next steps:

- April 8: all volunteers are chosen and schedules are assigned
- June 4, 5, or 15: all volunteers need to attend one orientation

Youth volunteers work with our Summer Camps, supporting the informal science education. They help the Educator and Assistant with classroom preparation and management, and work with the kids on experiments and activities. Volunteers help provide a fun and safe environment while assisting campers in their exploration of science during the Camps that run June 13 – August 26 at the Museum in Durham. Volunteers must work 8:30 am – 3:30 pm.

Requirements

- Have experience working with young children and in positions of responsibility
- Volunteers must be able to work two weeks of camp. The weeks do not need to be consecutive.

Contact our Volunteer Coordinator with any questions via email at emman@ncmls.org.

① 두 번의 예비교육에 참석해야 한다.
② 봉사자들을 위한 과학 교육이 제공된다.
③ 하계 캠프는 3개월 동안 진행된다.
④ 책임지는 자리에서 근무한 경험이 필요하다.
⑤ 자원봉사자들은 2주간 연속하여 활동해야 한다.

Breitenbush Hot Springs에 관한 다음 안내문의 내용과 일치하지 않는 것은?

Breitenbush Hot Springs

Join us for a workshop, personal retreat or just the day!
(Reservations are required for all visits.)

Reservation Hours: Monday through Saturday 9 am – 4 pm
We are now taking reservations through September, 2016.

Lodging Rates Include:
- Three bountiful, organic, vegetarian meals daily
- Round-the-clock access to the hot springs

Important Information
Reservations for weekend nights are for a two-night minimum.
Single-night reservations for Friday or Saturday must be made one week in advance.

Discounts
Guests who stay 7 days or more receive a 10% lodging discount. We do not combine discounts.

For further information, please contact us at office@breitenbush.com.

① 모든 방문에 예약이 필수이다.
② 일요일에는 예약을 받지 않는다.
③ 정해진 시간에 온천 이용이 가능하다.
④ 주말 예약은 2박 이상이어야 한다.
⑤ 중복 할인을 제공하지 않는다.

Plus Q

금요일이나 토요일의 1박 예약을 위해 필요한 조건을 우리말로 쓰시오.

➡

03 **application** 신청 **assign** 배정하다 **informal** 격식에 얽매이지 않는 **management** 관리 **environment** 환경 **assist** 돕다 **exploration** 탐험, 탐구 **responsibility** 책임 **consecutive** 연속적인 **coordinator** 진행자 **via** 통하여

04 **retreat** 조용한 곳 **lodging** 임시 숙소 **rate** 요금 **bountiful** 풍부한, 많은 **vegetarian** 채식의 **round-the-clock** 24시간 계속되는 **access** 입장, 이용 **in advance** 미리, 사전에 **combine** 결합하다

도표의 이해

도표에 제시된 수치 정보와 지문에 제시된 정보가 일치하는지의 여부를 판단하는 유형으로, 도표에서의 수치나 변화 추이에 주목하여 도표를 정확하게 파악한 뒤, 도표와 지문에 제시된 내용이 일치하는지를 순서대로 대조하면 된다. 수능에서 매년 1문항씩 출제되고 있으며, 도표의 내용과 일치하지 않는 것을 묻는다.

대표 예제

다음 도표의 내용과 일치하지 않는 것은? 수능

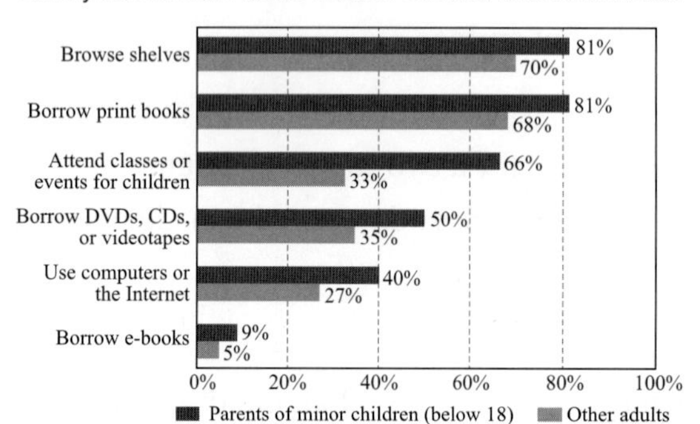

도입 The above graph shows the results of a survey conducted in 2012. It compares the percentage of parents of minor children (hereafter, parents) and that of other adults in terms of their involvement in six library activities. 전개 ①Most notably, the percentage of parents is higher than that of other adults in all activity types. ②The percentage of parents who browsed shelves is the same as that of parents who borrowed print books. ③The percentage gap between parents and other adults is largest in the activity of attending classes or events for children and is smallest in the activity of using computers or the Internet. ④The percentage of other adults who browsed shelves is twice as high as that of other adults who borrowed DVDs, CDs, or videotapes. ⑤Finally, the percentage of parents who borrowed e-books is less than 10% but is higher than that of other adults who did the same activity.

한눈에 보는 구조

도입 도표의 대략적인 소개
_ 2012년 조사
_ 미성년 자녀의 부모와 다른 성인의 6개의 도서관 활동 참여 비교

전개 도표의 세부 설명
서가 둘러보기, 인쇄된 책 빌리기, 수업이나 행사 참여, DVD와 CD 또는 비디오테이프 빌리기, 컴퓨터나 인터넷 사용하기, 전자 도서 빌리기의 6개 항목에서 부모와 다른 성인을 비교하고 있다.

6개 항목의 도서관 활동에 있어서 미성년 자녀의 부모와 다른 성인의 참여 비율을 나타낸 도표를 분석하는 글로 도입에서는 도표의 개략적인 소개를 하고 있으며, 나머지 부분에서는 도표에 대한 세부적인 설명을 하고 있다.

유형 해결 전략

1 도표의 제목 및 내용을 먼저 파악한다.

도표의 제목: Library Activities of Parents of Minor Children and Other Adults

→ 미성년 자녀의 부모와 다른 성인의 도서관 활동과 관련된 도표임을 알 수 있다.

도표의 내용: 서가 둘러보기, 인쇄된 책 빌리기, 수업이나 행사 참여, DVD와 CD 또는 비디오테이프 빌리기, 컴퓨터나 인터넷 사용하기, 전자 도서 빌리기의 6개 항목에서 부모와 다른 성인을 비교하고 있다. / 모든 활동 유형에서 부모의 비율이 그 외 성인의 비율보다 더 높다.

2 선택지로 제시된 지문 내용을 수치화하고 도표와의 일치 여부를 확인한다.

① 모든 활동에서 부모의 비율 > 다른 성인의 비율 → 도표와 일치

② 서가를 둘러본 부모의 비율(81%) = 인쇄된 책을 빌린 부모의 비율(81%) → 도표와 일치

③ 부모 참여율 − 다른 성인 참여율

(大) 수업이나 행사 참가 (33% point) → 도표와 일치

(小) 컴퓨터나 인터넷 사용 (13% point) → 도표와 불일치

전자 도서 대여(4% point)로 수정되어야 올바른 문장이다.

④ 서가를 둘러본 성인의 비율(70%) = 2×DVD, CD, 비디오테이프를 빌린 성인(35%) → 도표와 일치

⑤ 전자 도서를 빌린 부모의 비율(9%) > 전자 도서를 빌린 성인의 비율(5%) → 도표와 일치

Bonus Tip

증감 표현

- 증가: increase, grow, go up, multiply, rise, be on the rise[increase], soar 등
- 감소: decrease, drop, go down, decline, fall, be on the fall[decrease], reduce 등
- 전치사 by와 to+수치
  - _ by+수치: 정도(수치만큼의 증감)을 나타냄.
  - _ to+수치: 증감하여 최종 결과가 됨.

배수, 분수 표현

- They sold **three times as many cars** in 2010 **as** in 2016.
  = They sold **three times more cars** in 2010 **than** in 2016.
- 1/2: a[one] half, a[one] second
  1/4: a[one] quarter, a[one] fourth
  3/4: three quarters, three fourths

기타 표현

- 꾸준하게: continually, continuously, gradually, steadily
- 급격하게: drastically, radically, rapidly, sharply, steeply
- 일정하게: constantly

Exercise

01 다음 도표의 내용과 일치하지 않는 것은? 고2 교육청

Who 11-Year-Old Australians Consulted If They Had Problems

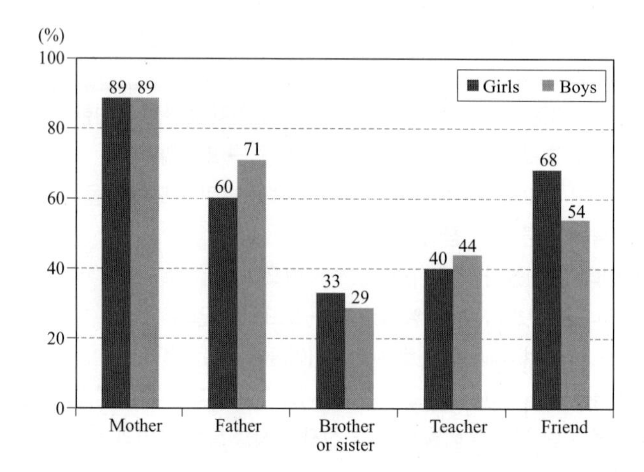

The above graph shows who Australian girls and boys aged eleven consulted if they had problems. ① Mothers were the most consulted source if girls and boys had problems. ② For boys, fathers were the second most consulted source, followed by friends. ③ The percentage of girls who consulted teachers was 20 percentage points higher than that of girls who consulted fathers. ④ The percentage of boys who consulted teachers was higher than that of girls who consulted teachers by 4 percentage points. ⑤ More girls went to their friends than to their brothers or sisters if they had problems.

02 다음 도표의 내용과 일치하지 않는 것은? 고3 교육청

A Shift in U.S. Immigrant Sources

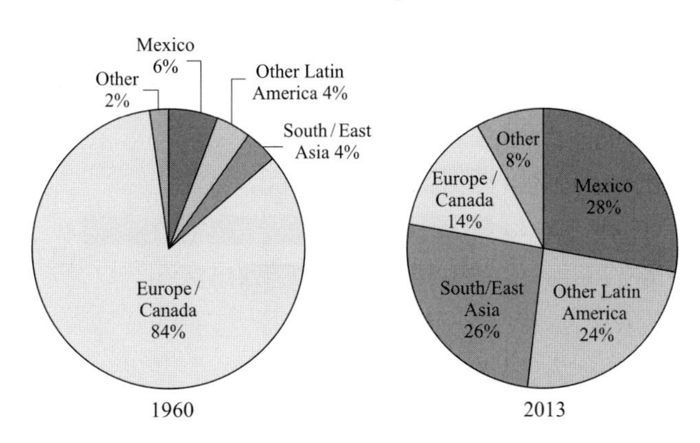

The two pie charts above show the change in percentage of five U.S. immigrant sources between 1960 and 2013. ① In 1960, Europe/Canada was the largest source of U.S. immigrants, but it dropped _______ fourth place in 2013. ② The largest source for the nation's immigrants in 2013 was Mexico. ③ The percentage of Mexico and Other Latin America together only accounted for 10% in 1960, but it increased _______ more than 50% in 2013. ④ The percentage of immigrant population born in South/East Asia increased to 26% in 2013, which was more than seven times that of 1960. ⑤ Though Europe/Canada was a dominant source making up more than 80% of U.S. immigrants in 1960, no single source contributed more than 30% in 2013.

Plus Q

윗글의 밑줄 친 빈칸 두 곳에 공통으로 들어갈 전치사를 쓰시오.

➡

01 **consult** 조언을 구하다 **source** 원천, 근원 **follow** 뒤를 잇다 **percentage** 비율
percentage point 퍼센트 포인트(백분율로 나타낸 수치가 이전 수치에 비해 증가하거나 감소한 양)
02 **immigrant** 이민자, 이주민 **drop** 떨어지다 **account for** ~을 차지하다 **population** 인구, (모든) 주민
dominant 지배적인 **make up** 구성하다, 이루다 **contribute** 기여하다, 이바지하다

03 다음 도표의 내용과 일치하지 않는 것은?

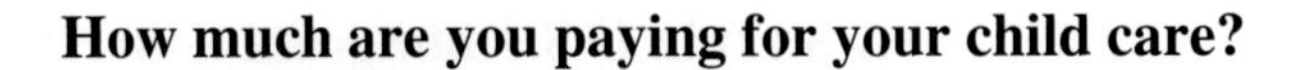

How much are you paying for your child care?

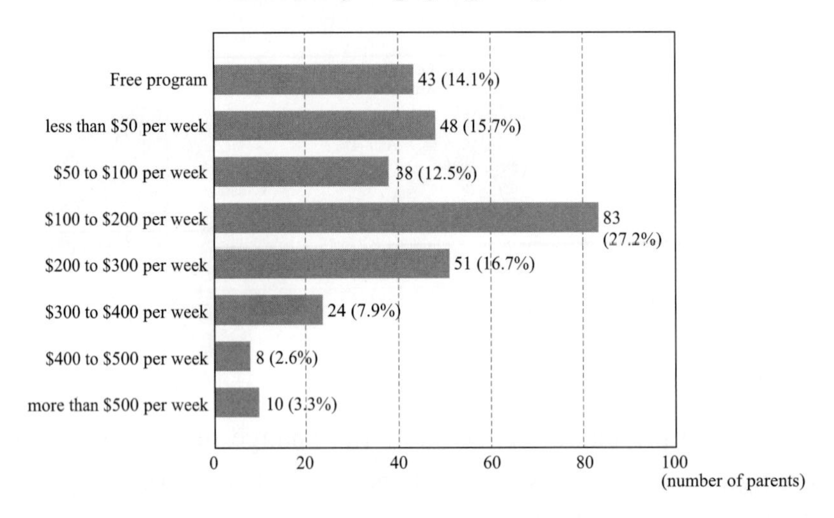

The graph above shows how much parents in Tompkins County in America pay for their child care per week. Three hundred and five parents answered this survey. ① The largest number of parents answered that they pay from 100 to 200 dollars per week for child care, which accounts for 27.2 percent. ② The second largest number of parents, which is 16.7 percent, said they pay from 200 to 300 dollars per week for child care. ③ The number of parents who use a free child care program accounts for 14.1 percent, which ranks third. ④ The number of parents who pay 200 to 300 dollars per week for child care is more than twice as many as that of parents who pay 300 to 400 dollars per week. ⑤ The smallest number of parents responded they pay 400 to 500 dollars per week for child care, which occupies 2.6 percent among the whole.

04 다음 도표의 내용과 일치하지 않는 것은?

Urban Female Population Composition 1991 and 2011, Age Group 20-49 years

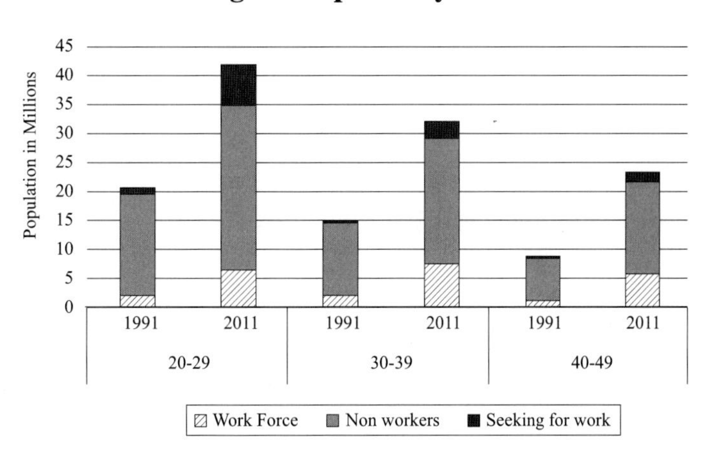

The above graph shows urban female population composition both in 1991 and 2011 by three age groups: 20-29, 30-39, and 40-49. ① In 2011, the size of urban female population of each age group was more than double **that** of 1991. ② In 2011, the urban female population of the 20-29 group in workforce was almost the same as that of the same group seeking work, while the urban female population of the 30-39 group in workforce was smaller than that of the same group seeking work. ③ In both years, the urban female population of the 40-49 group in workforce was smaller than that of the other two age groups in workforce. ④ In both years, non workers of the 20-29 group were more than those of the other two groups. ⑤ The size of the urban female population of all age groups seeking work in 2011 was larger than that of those in 1991.

Plus Q

밑줄 친 that이 가리키는 것을 본문에서 찾아 쓰시오.

➡

03 **pay** 지불하다 **child care** 보육 **rank** 순위가 ~이다 **respond** 응답하다 **occupy** 차지하다, 점유하다 **whole** 전체(의)
04 **urban** 도시의 **composition** 구성 **size** 규모 **workforce** 노동 인구 **seek** 추구하다, 찾다

유형

08 어휘 추론

어휘 추론 문항은 주어진 세 개의 네모에서 맞는 표현을 고르거나, 다섯 개의 밑줄 친 부분에서 틀린 표현을 고르는 형태로 출제된다. 네모나 밑줄 친 부분에 대한 단서는 주변에 주어지기 때문에, 논리적 흐름을 잘 파악해서 해당 부분의 옳고 그름을 판단해야 한다. 비교적 난이도가 높은 유형으로 수능에서 매년 1문항씩 출제되고 있다.

대표 예제

(A), (B), (C)의 각 네모 안에서 문맥에 맞는 낱말로 가장 적절한 것은? 수능

도입 The Atitlán Giant Grebe was a large, flightless bird that had evolved from the much more widespread and smaller Pied-billed Grebe. By 1965 there were only around 80 birds left on Lake Atitlán. 전개1 One immediate reason was easy enough to spot: the local human population was cutting down the reed beds at a furious rate. This (A) [accommodation / destruction] was driven by the needs of a fast growing mat-making industry. 전개2 But there were other problems. An American airline was intent on developing the lake as a tourist destination for fishermen. However, there was a major problem with this idea: the lake (B) [lacked / supported] any suitable sporting fish! To compensate for this rather obvious defect, a specially selected species of fish called the Large-mouthed Bass was introduced. The introduced individuals immediately turned their attentions to the crabs and small fish that lived in the lake, thus (C) [competing / cooperating] with the few remaining grebes for food. 전개3 There is also little doubt that they sometimes gobbled up the zebra-striped Atitlán Giant Grebe's chicks.

*reed: 갈대

**gobble up: 게걸스럽게 먹다

한눈에 보는 구조

도입 소재 제시
1965년 무렵에 Atitlán Giant Grebe가 Atitlán 호수에 약 80마리만이 남아 있었다.

전개1 Atitlán Giant Grebe의 수가 적어지게 된 이유 1
매트 제조 산업의 필요에 의해 갈대밭이 파괴되었기 때문이다.

전개2 Atitlán Giant Grebe의 수가 적어지게 된 이유 2
호수가 낚시꾼들을 위한 관광지로 개발되면서, 스포츠용 물고기가 없어서 큰입농어가 도입되었는데, 이 물고기들이 호수에 사는 게와 작은 물고기를 놓고 논병아리와 경쟁하였기 때문이다.

전개3 Atitlán Giant Grebe의 수가 적어지게 된 이유 3
큰입농어들이 Atitlán Giant Grebe 새끼들을 먹어치웠기 때문이다.

도입에서 소재 제시와 이것이 처한 상황에 대해 언급하고 있으며 전개에서 이에 대한 원인에 대해 설명하고 있는 글이다. 원인과 결과, 열거의 전개 방식으로 글이 전개되고 있다.

	(A)		(B)		(C)
①	accommodation	……	lacked	……	competing
②	accommodation	……	supported	……	cooperating
③	destruction	……	lacked	……	competing
④	destruction	……	supported	……	cooperating
⑤	destruction	……	lacked	……	cooperating

유형 해결 전략

1 글의 도입부를 통해 제시된 사건(소재)이 무엇인지를 파악한다.

By 1965 there were only around 80 birds left on Lake Atitlán.
사건의 내용 → Atitlán 호수에 Atitlán Giant Grebe가 약 80마리만이 남아 있게 되었다.

2 (A), (B), (C)의 각 네모에 맞는 표현을 찾기 위해 네모 주변의 단서를 찾는다.

(A) the local human population was cutting down the reed beds at a furious rate
→ 현지의 인간들이 맹렬한 속도로 갈대밭을 베어 넘어뜨렸기 때문이다. 이러한 내용과 일맥상통하는 단어가 무엇일지 생각해본다.

(B) To compensate for this rather obvious defect, a specially selected species of fish called the Large-mouthed Bass was introduced.
→ 물고기와 관련된 문제점을 해결하기 위해 큰입농어라 불리는 특별히 선택된 물고기 종이 도입되었다. 도입된 이유는 물고기가 적었기 때문이었을 것이다.

(C) The introduced individuals immediately turned their attentions to the crabs and small fish / they sometimes gobbled up the zebra-striped Atitlan Giant Grebe's chicks
→ 큰입농어들은 호수에 서식하는 게와 작은 물고기에게로 관심을 돌렸으며, Atitlán Giánt Grebe의 새끼들도 먹어치웠다. 이들이 이러한 행동을 보인 이유는 무엇일지를 생각해본다.

3 (A), (B), (C)의 단서를 통해 문맥상 적절한 어휘를 선택한다.

(A) 현지의 인간들이 갈대밭을 베어 버린 것은 파괴 행위이므로 destruction이 적절하다.
(B) 스포츠용 물고기가 적었기 때문에 새로운 물고기를 도입한 것이므로 lacked가 적절하다.
(C) 호수에 사는 게와 작은 물고기, 그리고 Atitlán Giant Grebe의 새끼들을 먹어치운 큰입농어들은 논병아리와 먹이를 놓고 경쟁을 했기 때문이라고 추론할 수 있으므로 competing이 적절하다.

Bonus Tip

네모 유형에서 쌍으로 출제된 기출 어휘

inferior 열등한 superior 우등한	insufficient 불충분한 sufficient 충분한	hostile 적대적인 favorable 호의적인
abundant 풍부한 scarce 부족한	damaged 손상된 recovered 회복된	uncomplicated 복잡하지 않은 intricate 복잡한
vulnerable 취약한 immune 면역력이 있는	benefit 이득 loss 손실	valid 타당한 biased 편견을 가진

Exercise

01 다음 글의 밑줄 친 부분 중, 문맥상 낱말의 쓰임이 적절하지 않은 것은? 고2 교육청

Historical evidence points to workers being exploited by employers in the ① absence of appropriate laws. This means that workers are not always compensated for their ② contributions, for their increased productivity, as economic theory would suggest. Employers will be able to exploit workers if they are not legally ③ controlled. Thus, the minimum wage laws may be the only way to prevent many employees from working at wages that are ④ above the poverty line. This point of view means that minimum wage laws are a source of correcting for existing market failure, ⑤ enhancing the power of markets to create efficient results.

02 (A), (B), (C)의 각 네모 안에서 문맥에 맞는 낱말로 가장 적절한 것은? 고2 교육청

Do you know one of the best remedies for coping with family tension? Two words: "I'm sorry." It's amazing how hard some people find them to say. They think it implies weakness or defeat. Nothing of the kind. In fact, it is exactly the (A) [same / opposite]. Another good way of relieving tension is a row! The sea is ever so much calmer after a storm. A row has another (B) [advantage / disadvantage]. When tempers are raised, unspoken truths usually come out. They may hurt a bit, especially at the time. Yet, at the end, you know each other a bit better. Lastly, most of the tensions and quarrels between children are (C) [natural / risky]. Even when they seem to be constant, wise parents don't worry too much.

*row: 말다툼

	(A)		(B)		(C)
①	same	……	advantage	……	natural
②	opposite	……	advantage	……	natural
③	opposite	……	advantage	……	risky
④	opposite	……	disadvantage	……	risky
⑤	same	……	disadvantage	……	risky

03 다음 글의 밑줄 친 부분 중, 문맥상 낱말의 쓰임이 적절하지 않은 것은? 평가원

An Egyptian executive, after entertaining his Canadian guest, offered him joint partnership in a new business venture. The Canadian, delighted with the offer, suggested that they meet again the next morning with their ① respective lawyers to finalize the details. The Egyptian never showed up. The surprised and disappointed Canadian tried to understand what **go** wrong: Did Egyptians ② lack punctuality? Was the Egyptian expecting a counter-offer? Were lawyers unavailable in Cairo? None of these explanations proved to be correct; rather, the problem was ③ caused by the different meaning Canadians and Egyptians attach to inviting lawyers. The Canadian regarded the lawyers' ④ absence as facilitating the successful completion of the negotiation; the Egyptian interpreted it as signaling the Canadian's mistrust of his verbal commitment. Canadians often use the impersonal formality of a lawyer's services to finalize ⑤ agreements. Egyptians, by contrast, more frequently depend on the personal relationship between bargaining partners to accomplish the same purpose.

*punctuality: 시간 엄수

Plus Q

윗글의 밑줄 친 부분을 어법에 맞게 고쳐 쓰시오.

➡ ....

01 exploit 착취하다　appropriate 적절한　compensate for 보상하다　contribution 기여
productivity 생산성　minimum wage 최저 임금　poverty line 빈곤선(생계유지에 필요한 최저 소득 기준)
enhance 강화하다

02 remedy 처방　cope with ~에 대처하다　tension 갈등, 긴장 상태　amazing 놀라운
imply 의미하다, 암시하다　weakness 약함　defeat 패배　relieve (고통 · 부담 따위를) 덜다　calm 잔잔한
temper 화, 짜증　unspoken 입 밖에 내지 않은　quarrel 싸움, 말다툼　constant 지속적인, 계속되는

03 executive 중역　joint partnership 합작 제휴　venture 벤처 (사업)　finalize 마무리하다
detail 세부 사항　counter-offer 수정 제안　correct 정확한　facilitate 용이하게 하다
completion 완성, 마무리　negotiation 협상　interpret 해석하다　mistrust 불신　verbal 구두의
commitment 약속, 위임　impersonal 사사롭지 않은　formality 형식상의 절차
accomplish 완수하다, 성취하다

04 (A), (B), (C)의 각 네모 안에서 문맥에 맞는 낱말로 가장 적절한 것은?

It's almost instinctive. You see a lovely baby, and you start to smile or make a face to draw some kind of response. But even if you get a (A) [blank / meaningful] stare back, don't think that the baby is doing nothing. In fact, the baby is processing every change in the shape and rhythm of your mouth and face. At birth, babies are (B) [blind / receptive] to any language and facial expressions. With time, they learn to focus on the sounds, muscle movements and facial rhythms of the language to which they are exposed. It's all part of the way babies learn. It seems that even language depends on (C) [visual / audible] triggers. So go ahead and smile at the next infant you encounter. Just be expressive about it.

	(A)		(B)		(C)
①	blank	……	blind	……	visual
②	blank	……	receptive	……	visual
③	blank	……	receptive	……	audible
④	meaningful	……	blind	……	audible
⑤	meaningful	……	receptive	……	visual

05 다음 글의 밑줄 친 부분 중, 문맥상 낱말의 쓰임이 적절하지 않은 것은?

After a year or so of intense dependence, infants begin to feel the need to ①assert their autonomy. At some level they sense that unless they begin to take charge of their actions they will never grow up into fully functioning persons. Consequently, they ②insist on doing things their own way, and if they are prevented from doing so, they are ready to throw tantrums — it is the classic age of the "terrible twos." As they grow to realize the vastness of the world outside their homes, most children eventually become intimidated by their own ③insignificance. At that point, they become ④concerned with fitting in with their peers and with being accepted and recognized by a community larger than the family. This is the stage of ⑤disobedience, and for a great many people it is the beginning of the road to personal development.

06 (A), (B), (C)의 각 네모 안에서 문맥에 맞는 낱말로 가장 적절한 것은?

While a fertile imagination is the source of inspiration in seeking new knowledge, it can also be dangerous if not balanced by strong (A) [criticism / support]. This is, of course, quite different from saying it should be repressed or crushed. This imagination merely enables us to wander into the darkness of the unknown where, by the dim light of the knowledge that we carry, we may (B) [glimpse / overlook] something that seems interesting. But when we bring it out and examine it more closely it could prove to be only trash whose glitter had caught our attention. Things not clearly seen often take on grotesque forms. Imagination can be the source of frustration. To forget **this** is to court despair. In fact, many hypotheses from imagination prove to be (C) [wrong / right] whatever their origin may be.

	(A)		(B)		(C)
①	criticism	……	glimpse	……	wrong
②	criticism	……	glimpse	……	right
③	criticism	……	overlook	……	wrong
④	support	……	overlook	……	right
⑤	support	……	overlook	……	wrong

Plus Q

밑줄 친 **this**가 가리키는 바를 우리말로 쓰시오.

➡

04 **instinctive** 본능적인 **draw response** 반응을 이끌어내다 **stare** 응시, 빤히 쳐다보기 **process** 처리하다 **facial expression** 얼굴 표정 **expose** 노출시키다 **depend on** ~에 달려 있다 **trigger** 자극, 유인 **infant** 유아, 아기 **encounter** 마주치다

05 **intense** 열심인, 강렬한 **assert** 주장하다 **autonomy** 자율성 **insist** 주장하다, 우기다 **tantrum** 화, 성냄 **classic** 전형적인, 고전적인 **vastness** 광대함 **intimidated** 위협적인 **insignificance** 하찮음 **peer** 또래, 동료 **community** 공동체 **disobedience** 반항, 불순종

06 **fertile** 풍부한, 비옥한 **source** 원천 **inspiration** 영감 **repress** 억압하다 **crush** 짓밟다 **wander** 방황하다 **dim** 희미한 **trash** 쓰레기 **glitter** 반짝임, 빛남 **take on** 띠다, 떠맡다 **grotesque** 기괴한 **frustration** 좌절 **court** 자초하다, 불러들이다 **despair** 절망

어법성 판단

문법 사항의 이해를 묻는 유형으로, 어법에 맞는 표현을 고르거나 어법상 틀린 것을 고르는 2가지 형태 중 하나로 출제된다. 어법에 맞는 표현을 고르는 문제는 (A), (B), (C)가 들어 있는 문장과 그 앞뒤의 관계를 파악하여 풀이하도록 하며, 밑줄 친 다섯 개의 부분 중 어법상 틀린 것을 고르는 문제는 밑줄 친 부분에 필요한 어법 요소가 무엇인지를 파악하는 것이 중요하다. 어법 문제는 해마다 1문항씩 출제되고 있다.

대표 예제

다음 글의 밑줄 친 부분 중, 어법상 틀린 것은? 수능

도입》 Oxygen is what it is all about. Ironically, the stuff that gives us life eventually kills it. The ultimate life force lies in tiny cellular factories of energy, called mitochondria, ① that burn nearly all the oxygen we breathe in. But breathing has a price. The combustion of oxygen that keeps us alive and active ② sending out by-products called oxygen free radicals. They have Dr. Jekyll and Mr. Hyde characteristics. 전개1》 On the one hand, they help guarantee our survival. For example, when the body mobilizes ③ to fight off infectious agents, it generates a burst of free radicals to destroy the invaders very efficiently. 전개2》 On the other hand, free radicals move ④ uncontrollably through the body, attacking cells, rusting their proteins, piercing their membranes and corrupting their genetic code until the cells become dysfunctional and sometimes give up and die. 결론》 These fierce radicals, ⑤ built into life as both protectors and avengers, are potent agents of aging.

*oxygen free radical: 활성 산소

**membrane: (해부학) 얇은 막

한눈에 보는 구조

도입》 **주제 제시**
산소 연소는 활성 산소라고 불리는 부산물을 내보내며, 활성 산소는 이중적인 특징을 갖고 있다.

전개1》 **주제에 대한 부연 설명 1**
활성 산소는 신체 감염원을 파괴하기 위해 생산되어 인간의 생존 보장을 돕는다.

전개2》 **주제에 대한 부연 설명 2 (전개 1의 대조되는 역할 설명)**
활성 산소는 세포를 공격하여 제대로 기능을 못하게 하고 죽게 만든다.

결론》 **주제의 재진술**
활성 산소는 생명체의 일부로서 보호자이자 동시에 보복자의 역할을 한다.

글의 처음과 마지막 부분에 글의 주제를 반복하여 드러내고 있다. 중반에 예시와 대조의 방법을 이용하여 주제를 부연 설명하고 있다.

유형 해결 전략

1 글의 초반에 제시된 주제를 파악하고 글의 흐름을 예측한다.

글의 초반의 ~by-products called oxygen free radicals. They have Dr. Jekyll and Mr. Hyde characteristics. 부분에서 '~활성 산소라고 불리는 부산물들은 이중적인 특징을 가진다'는 주제를 제시하므로 활성 산소의 긍정적인 역할과 부정적인 역할이 다뤄질 것임을 예측할 수 있다.

2 밑줄 친 부분이 속한 문장 구조를 분석하고, 그 부분의 역할이 무엇인지 판단한다.

주어, 동사, 목적어, 수식어구 등으로 이루어지는 문장의 기본적인 구조를 이해하며 밑줄 친 부분이 해당 문장에서 필수 요소가 맞는지, 그리고 어떤 역할을 하고 있는지를 분석한다. 각각의 밑줄 친 부분은 주격 관계대명사, 동사, 부사적 용법의 to부정사, 동사를 수식하는 부사, 과거분사의 역할이 필요한 자리이다.

3 문법 지식과 함께 정확한 해석을 통해 정답을 찾는다.

① that: 그 뒤에 주어가 없는 불완전한 문장이 이어지므로 접속사가 아니라 tiny cellular factories of energy를 선행사로 수식하는 주격 관계대명사로 쓰였음을 알 수 있다. '우리가 들이쉬는 거의 모든 산소를 태우는 아주 작은 에너지 세포 공장'이라고 자연스럽게 해석되므로 어법상 오류가 없다.

② sending: 동사원형+-ing의 형태로 동명사, 현재분사, 동사의 진행형 중 하나로 판단해 볼 수 있다. 그러나 해석을 해보면 주어인 '우리를 살아있게 하고 활동적이게 유지하는 산소의 연소'에 이어질 동사가 없어 문장이 완전하지 않으므로 비문임을 알 수 있다.

③ to fight: 목적을 나타내는 to부정사의 부사적 용법으로, '싸워 물리치기 위해'라고 자연스럽게 해석된다.

④ uncontrollably: 동사 move를 수식하는 부사로서 '통제할 수 없을 정도로 돌아다니면서'라고 해석된다.

⑤ built: These fierce radicals를 대상으로 부연 설명하는 과거분사로 쓰여 '보호자인 동시에 보복자로 생명체의 일부가 되어 있는 이런 사나운 활성 산소'라고 무리 없이 해석된다.

Bonus Tip

시험에 주로 출제되는 문법 및 유의사항

- 분사구문(현재분사, 과거분사), 관계사(관계대명사, 관계부사, 전치사+관계대명사), 수 일치(단수, 복수), 태(능동, 수동)의 문법 요소가 주로 제시된다.
- 주어와 동사 사이에 수식어구가 포함되어 거리가 멀어질 경우 정확한 해석을 이끌어내는 것이 쉽지 않다. 밑줄 친 부분이 포함된 문장에서 주어와 동사를 확인한 뒤에 밑줄 친 부분이 수식하거나 설명하는 대상이 무엇인지 판단하도록 한다.
- 형태가 비슷한 자동사와 타동사, 접속사나 관계대명사로 쓰이는 that, 부정사가 아닌 전치사로 사용되는 to 등 혼동하기 쉬운 문법을 정확히 구별할 수 있어야 한다.

형태가 비슷한 자동사와 타동사

- rise-rose-risen (자: 오르다)
- raise-raised-raised (타: 올리다)
- lie-lay-lain (자: 놓여 있다)
- lie-lied-lied (자: 거짓말하다)
- lay-laid-laid (타: 놓다)

전치사 to로 사용하는 숙어

- be used to 명사(구)/동명사 (~에 익숙하다)
  cf. be used to 동사 (~하는 데 사용되다)
- look forward to (~을 기대하다)
- respond to (~에 반응하다)
- object to (~에 반대하다)

Exercise

01 다음 글의 밑줄 친 부분 중, 어법상 틀린 것은? 고2 교육청

Language is one of the primary features that distinguishes humans from other animals. Many animals, including dolphins, whales, and birds, ① do indeed communicate with one another through patterned systems of sounds, scents, and other chemicals, or movements. Furthermore, some nonhuman primates ② have been taught to use sign language to communicate with humans. However, the complexity of human language, its ability to convey nuanced emotions and ideas, and its importance for our existence as social animals ③ setting it apart from the communication systems used by other animals. In many ways, language is the essence of culture. It provides the single most common variable ④ by which different cultural groups are identified. Language not only facilitates the cultural diffusion of innovations, it also helps to shape the way we think about, perceive, and ⑤ name our environment.

02 (A), (B), (C)의 각 네모 안에서 어법에 맞는 표현으로 가장 적절한 것은? 고2 교육청

If we create a routine, we don't have to expend precious energy every day prioritizing everything. We must simply expend a small amount of initial energy to create the routine, and then all that is left to do is follow it. There is a huge body of scientific research to explain the mechanism (A) [which / by which] routine enables difficult things to become easy. One simplified explanation is that as we repeatedly do a certain task the neurons, or nerve cells, (B) [make / making] new connections through communication gateways called 'synapses.' With repetition, the connections strengthen and it becomes easier for the brain to activate them. For example, when you learn a new word it takes several repetitions at various intervals for the word to be mastered. To recall the word later you will need to activate the same synapses until eventually you know the word without consciously thinking about (C) [it / them].

(A)		(B)		(C)
① which	……	make	……	them
② which	……	making	……	them
③ by which	……	make	……	them
④ by which	……	making	……	it
⑤ by which	……	make	……	it

03 다음 글의 밑줄 친 부분 중, 어법상 <u>틀린</u> 것은? 고3 교육청

The Internet and communication technologies play an ever-increasing role in the social lives of young people in developed societies. Adolescents have been quick to immerse themselves in technology with most ① <u>using</u> the Internet to communicate. Young people treat the mobile phone as an essential necessity of life and often prefer to use text messages to communicate with their friends. Young people also ② <u>increasingly</u> access social networking websites. As technology and the Internet are a familiar resource for young people, it is logical ③ <u>what</u> they would seek assistance from this source. This [**been / by / has / in / the increase / shown / websites**] that provide therapeutic information for young people. A number of 'youth friendly' mental health websites ④ <u>have</u> been developed. The information ⑤ <u>presented</u> often takes the form of Frequently Asked Questions, fact sheets and suggested links. It would seem, therefore, logical to provide online counselling for young people.

Plus Q

윗글의 괄호 안에 있는 어구들을 어법과 문맥에 맞게 배열하시오.

➡

01 **primary** 주요한 **scent** 향기, 냄새 **complexity** 복잡성 **existence** 존재, 실존 **set apart from** ~에서 구별하다 **variable** 변수 **identify** 확인하다 **facilitate** 가능하게 하다 **diffusion** 발산, 보급 **perceive** 인지하다
02 **routine** 정해진 절차 **expend** 쓴다[들이다] **prioritize** 우선순위를 정하다 **initial** 처음의 **gateway** 관문 **repetition** 반복 **strengthen** 강화되다 **activate** 활성화시키다 **interval** 간격 **eventually** 결국 **consciously** 의식적으로
03 **ever-increasing** 계속 증가하는 **adolescent** 청소년 **immerse oneself in** ~에 몰두하다, ~에 빠져들다 **necessity** 필수품 **logical** 논리적인 **assistance** 원조, 지원 **therapeutic** 치료(법)의 **fact sheet** 자료표

04 다음 글의 밑줄 친 부분 중, 어법상 틀린 것은?

Man's ability over all other creatures on this Earth is the ability to think. All successful people use it to improve their lives and control their own destiny. Only you can take the initial step toward the unleashing of the power within your own mind. The power is awesome and at times can be ① frightening. However, man has power of the mind ② that many people cannot or would not believe. Anthony Robbins has recently written a book ③ entitled *Unlimited Power*, which explains the theories of Neuro Linguistic Programming, the power of the mind and how to gain control and use it. NLP was originally developed by John Grinder as a communication system ④ used the central nervous system. Through this system, Mr. Robbins has put forth a complete outline on how to achieve goals that you probably felt ⑤ were impossible.

05 (A), (B), (C)의 각 네모 안에서 어법에 맞는 표현으로 가장 적절한 것은?

We're so used to (A) [have / having] exotic fruits and vegetables out of season that at first it's difficult to accept that we can get organic fruits and vegetables that are in season. Of course, a lot of organic food is produced abroad and flown to our supermarkets and this makes it more (B) [available / availably], but vitamins and mineral content is lost if food has been on a long journey. It's therefore much better to buy locally produced products. Many supermarkets recognize the fact that organic means big business. But remember that just because it says it's organic on the packet, it doesn't mean that it's better for you, especially if it (C) [has processed / has been processed]. Once organic products have been turned into a cake or biscuit, for example, you'll have the same concerns attached to the conventional versions of these foods: high sugar and fat.

	(A)		(B)		(C)
①	have	……	available	……	has processed
②	have	……	availably	……	has been processed
③	having	……	available	……	has processed
④	having	……	availably	……	has processed
⑤	having	……	available	……	has been processed

06 다음 글의 밑줄 친 부분 중, 어법상 틀린 것은?

The population of the United States is increasingly heterogeneous, ① moving toward a plurality of ethnic, religious, and regional groups. Each of these groups ② has traditional food habits that differ—slightly or significantly—from the so-called typical American majority diet. Effective nutrition counseling, education, and food service require that these variations ③ are acknowledged and understood within the context of culture. It is our goal to provide dietitians, nutritionists, and food service professionals ________ the broad overview ④ needed to avoid ethnocentric assumptions and the nutrition specifics helpful in working with each group discussed. We have attempted ⑤ to combine the conceptual ________ the technical in a way that is useful to other health professionals as well.

Plus Q

윗글의 밑줄 친 빈칸 두 곳에 공통으로 들어갈 전치사를 쓰시오.

➡

04 improve 개선하다 initial 처음의 unleash 불러일으키다, 촉발시키다 awesome 경탄할 만한 entitle 제목을 붙이다 linguistic 언어의 nervous system 신경계 put forth 제시하다 outline 틀, 개요
05 exotic 외국의 organic 유기농의 available 이용할 수 있는 content 함유량 recognize 인식하다 packet 통 process 가공하다 turn into ~으로 바꿔 놓다 concern 우려 conventional 전통적인
06 heterogeneous 여러 종류의 plurality 많은 수 significantly 상당히 so-called 이른바 typical 전형적인 nutrition 영양 variation 변화, 차이 acknowledge 인정하다 dietitian 영양사 nutritionist 영양학자 avoid 피하다 ethnocentric 자기 민족 중심적인 assumption 추정 conceptual 개념의

유형

10 지칭 추론

글의 등장인물(대상)들 사이의 관계를 파악하여 가리키는 대상이 나머지 넷과 다른 하나를 고르는 유형으로, 지문을 정확하게 읽고 글의 흐름을 파악하는 능력이 필요로 된다. 선택지 ①번은 처음 한두 문장에 나온 명사를 대명사로 받는 것이며, 다른 대명사가 나오기 위해서는 그 앞에 다른 명사가 언급되어야 하므로, 정답은 그 이전 선택지와의 간격이 먼 경향이 있다. 수능에서 매년 1문항씩 출제되고 있다.

대표 예제

밑줄 친 he[his]가 가리키는 대상이 나머지 넷과 다른 것은?

수능

발단 The dancers stood on a two-step elevated stage, so that there was a natural gap between those who came to dance and those who came to watch. The host randomly pulled the name of a well-known dancer, Linx, out of a hat. People cheered. 전개 According to the format, Linx had to "call out" another dancer to battle him on stage. Instead of deliberately choosing someone, however, ① he decided to select his opponent randomly by making himself into a human spin-wheel. He propelled himself into a backspin, covered ② his eyes, and extended his arm above his head. 위기 When his body finally stopped spinning, ③ his arm pointed away from the dancers on stage and directly at Dan Tres, standing among the spectators. The crowd erupted in "Ohhhhs!" because ④ he was an older family man who had not danced hip-hop in many years, while the much younger Linx was a nimble b-boy. 결말 Linx looked embarrassed, but nonetheless ⑤ he called out the respected elder to battle.

*nimble: 동작이 날렵한

한눈에 보는 구조

발단 주요 인물 등장
댄서들이 무대 위에 있고, Linx라는 유명한 댄서가 무작위로 뽑혔다.

전개 구체적인 상황 묘사
대회 진행 방식에 따라, Linx는 무대에서 대결할 상대 선수를 호명해야 했는데, 자신을 인간 회전판으로 만들어 무작위로 대결 상대를 선택하기로 하였다.

위기 문제 상황 발생
그의 팔이 가리킨 사람은 여러 해 동안 힙합을 추지 않은 나이 든 남자였다.

결말 문제 해결 및 갈등 해소
Linx는 당황한 것처럼 보였지만, 그 연장자를 호명하였다.

댄스 경연장에서 무작위로 호명된 댄서가 대회 진행 방식에 따라 상대 선수를 지명하는 과정을 시간 순서에 따라 서술한 글이다.

유형 해결 전략

1 첫 번째 대명사가 나올 때까지 꼼꼼히 읽으면서 그 대명사가 지칭하는 대상을 정확히 파악한다.

①번 대명사가 he이므로 the host나 Linx 중 한 사람인데, 무대에서 대결할 상대 선수를 호명하는 것은 Linx가 해야 할 일이므로 ①은 Linx를 지칭한다.

2 이후에는 밑줄 친 대명사가 포함된 부분만 골라 빠르게 읽는다.

대명사 대신 Linx를 대입해서 읽는다. ④에 Linx를 대입하면, 'Linx는 힙합을 여러 해 동안 추지 않은 나이 든 남자였지만, 반면 Linx는 날렵한 비보이였다'라는 어색한 문장이 되므로 정답은 ④이다.

3 밑줄과 밑줄의 간격이 유난히 먼 경우, 그 중간 문장을 주의 깊게 읽는다.

이 문제에서는 ③과 ④의 간격이 그다지 멀지 않지만, ④앞에 Dan Tres라는 다른 인물이 등장하기 때문에 ④는 Dan Tres를 지칭하는 것임을 확인할 수 있다.

Bonus Tip

글의 중반에 새로운 인물이 등장하면, 그 이후의 선택지에 주의를 기울인다.

On a spring day in New York's Central Park, **a balloon salesman** was busy trying to sell ① his balloons. In order to gain the attention of those walking in the park, from time to time ② he would release a brightly colored balloon and let it rise into the sky. In the sunny afternoon, **a little African-American boy** approached ③ him. The boy was shy and had a poor self-image. ④ He had been watching the man and had a question for him.

→ 글 초반에는 a balloon salesman만 등장하며, 중반 이후에 새로운 인물 a little African-American boy가 등장하고 있다. 새로운 인물 등장 이후에 정답 선택지가 제시될 가능성이 높으므로(여기서는 ④), 그 이후의 선택지에 주의를 기울인다.

대명사 it의 경우 가주어나 가목적어를 활용하는 경우도 있으므로 속지 않도록 주의한다.

- I like paragliding so much that I always do **it** every weekend. **It** seems as if I were flying at that very moment.
  → 앞의 it은 paragliding을 받는 대명사, 뒤의 It은 가주어이다.

they의 경우 능동, 수동에 유의해 사람인지 사물인지만 알아도 정답을 찾을 수 있다.

- People in ancient times created many kinds of tools due to material scarcity. Thus, **they** had abundant knowledge of the materials around them. In many cases, **they** are made into practical uses.
  → 앞의 they는 people, 뒤의 they는 materials를 가리킨다. 사람이 실용적인 용도로 만들어질 수 없기 때문에 수동으로 되어 있는 것만 봐도 구별해 낼 수 있다.

Exercise

01 밑줄 친 부분이 가리키는 대상이 나머지 넷과 다른 것은? 고1 교육청

When Gandhi was fifteen, he stole a piece of gold from his brother's bracelet. Gandhi was so troubled by his guilt that one day ① he decided to tell his father what he had done. He wrote a letter asking his father to punish ② him. Then, Gandhi handed the letter to his father who was lying ill in bed. His father quietly sat up and read the letter and soaked it with ③ his tears. A little later, his father tore up the letter. Through his father's action of tearing up the letter, Gandhi knew ④ he was forgiven. From that day on, ⑤ he always kept his father's tears and love in his heart and went on to be a great leader.

*soak: (흠뻑) 적시다

**tear: 눈물; 찢다

02 밑줄 친 부분이 가리키는 대상이 나머지 넷과 다른 것은? 고2 교육청

Jake's own flying dream began at a village festival. He was four years old. His uncle, a tall silent pilot, had bought ① him a red party balloon from a charity stall, and tied it to the top button of Jake's shirt. The balloon seemed to have a mind of its own. It was filled with helium, a gas four times lighter than air, though Jake did not understand this at the time. It pulled mysteriously at ② his button. "Maybe you will fly," Jake's uncle remarked. He led ③ his nephew up a grassy bank so they could look over the whole festival. Below Jake stretched the little tents and the stalls. Above ④ him bobbed the big red balloon, shiny and beautiful. It kept pulling him towards the sky, and ⑤ he began to feel unsteady on his feet. Then his uncle let go of his hand, and Jake's dream began.

*stall: 가판대

**bob: 까닥까닥 움직이다

• SUB NOTE p. 30

03 밑줄 친 부분이 가리키는 대상이 나머지 넷과 다른 것은? 고3 교육청

Carlos Sanchez's long-time friend, Frank Sandoval, had fallen on hard times and was about to lose ① his home. Frank's wife was sick and their two small children were temporarily staying with his mother. Carlos hadn't talked to Frank for several months and decided one day to call him and see how ② he was. When Frank confided in Carlos about his situation, Carlos immediately went to Frank's home. When he walked in, ③ he was shocked to see his friend so thin and frail. He sat down with Frank and asked him how much money ④ he needed. Frank told him it was hopeless, that it was too much to pay back. Carlos pulled out his checkbook and wrote ⑤ him a check for fifty thousand dollars. He told Frank that things would get better—and they **did**. Three years later, Frank paid Carlos back with interest.

Plus Q

밑줄 친 **did**가 가리키는 것을 본문에서 찾아 어법에 맞게 쓰시오.

➡ ....

01 steal(-stole-stolen) 훔치다 bracelet 팔찌 be troubled by ~로 괴로워하다 guilt 죄책감 punish 벌하다 hand 건네다 lie ill in bed 병석에 누워 있다 quietly 조용히 forgive 용서하다 go on 계속 나아가다

02 village 마을 silent 과묵한, 조용한 charity 자선 stall (특히 시장의) 가판대 button 단추 helium 헬륨 mysteriously 신기하게 remark 말하다 nephew 조카 grassy 풀이 무성한 bank 강둑 stretch 펼쳐지다 shiny 반짝이는 let go of ~을 놓다

03 fall on hard times 재정적으로 힘든 시기를 겪다 be about to 막 ~하려는 참이다 temporarily 일시적으로 confide (비밀을) 털어놓다 immediately 곧장 frail 허약한 hopeless 절망적인 pay ~ back ~에게 돈을 갚다 interest 이자

04 밑줄 친 he[him]이 가리키는 대상이 나머지 넷과 다른 것은?

There was a farmer who sold a pound of butter to a baker. One day the baker decided to weigh the butter to see if ① he was getting a pound, and he found that he was not. This angered ② him and he took the farmer to court. The judge asked the farmer if ③ he was using any measure. The farmer replied, "Your Honor, I am primitive. I don't have a proper measure, but I do have a scale." The judge asked, "Then how do you weigh the butter?" The farmer replied, "Your Honor, long before the baker started buying butter from me, I have been buying a pound loaf of bread from ④ him. Every day when the baker brings the bread, I put it on the scale and give ⑤ him the same weight in butter. If anyone is to be blamed, it is the baker."

05 밑줄 친 부분이 가리키는 대상이 나머지 넷과 다른 것은?

Louis Stone was an inventive newspaper reporter in the 1890s. ① He worked for the *Evening Citizen* of Winstead, Connecticut. Turning away from producing the typical boring newspaper story, ② he wrote whoppers instead. But readers liked his stories even when they found out they weren't true. The self-righteous editor of *Evening Citizen* didn't fire ③ him. Instead, he was elated by the sudden increase in its circulation. By allowing him to keep writing his whoppers, ④ he helped Stone to become famous as the Winstead Liar. With the full support of the editor, ⑤ he also wrote accounts of a cat that could whistle "Yankee Doodle," a tree that grew baked apples, a hen that laid red, white, and blue eggs on the Fourth of July, and a man who painted a spider web on his bald head to keep flies away.

*whopper: 터무니없는 허풍

06 밑줄 친 he[his]가 가리키는 대상이 나머지 넷과 다른 것은?

A boy was born to a couple after eleven years of married life. They were a loving couple and the boy was **the apple of their eye**. One morning, when the boy was around two years old, the husband saw a medicine bottle open on ① his way out. He was late for work, so ② he asked his wife to cap the bottle and put it back in the cupboard. The wife, busy with work in the kitchen, totally forgot what ③ he had asked her to do. The boy went to the medicine bottle and drank it all. It happened to be a poisonous medicine meant for adults to be consumed in small doses. When ④ he started vomiting, the wife took him to the hospital, where he died. The wife was stunned. The distracted husband came to the hospital and saw the dead child. And then ⑤ he looked at his wife and uttered just four words. "I love you, darling."

Plus Q

밑줄 친 the apple of their eye의 뜻을 문맥을 통해 유추하여 10자 이내의 우리말로 쓰시오.

➡

04 **weigh** ~의 무게를 재다 **anger** 화나게 하다 **measure** 도량 단위, 치수 **primitive** 미개한, 원시의 **proper** 적절한 **scale** 저울 **loaf** 덩어리 **blame** 비난하다

05 **inventive** 창의력이 풍부한 **story** 뉴스 기사 **self-righteous** 독선적인 **fire** 해고하다 **be elated by** ~으로 의기양양하다, 우쭐하다 **circulation** 발행 부수 **account** 이야기 **baked** 잎이 없는

06 **medicine bottle** 약병 **cap** 마개를 하다 **cupboard** 찬장 **poisonous** 독이 있는 **consume** 먹다, 마시다 **in small doses** 소량으로 **vomit** 구토하다 **stun** 망연자실하게 만들다

유형

11 빈칸 추론

지문의 주제나 핵심 어구를 빈칸으로 두는 경우가 많기 때문에 주제나 요지 추론 유형의 연장선으로 볼 수 있다. 단어, 구, 절이 빈칸으로 제시되고, 장문 독해에 속한 빈칸 추론을 포함해 매년 5문항 정도가 출제된다. 빈칸 추론은 빈칸이 지문의 처음이나 마지막에 있는지, 아니면 중간에 있는지의 '빈칸의 위치'에 따라 문제를 푸는 접근 방식이 달라진다.

대표 예제

다음 빈칸에 들어갈 말로 가장 적절한 것은? 수능

도입 When two cultures come into contact, they do not exchange every cultural item. If that were the case, there would be no cultural differences in the world today. Instead, only a small number of cultural elements ever spread from one culture to another. 전개1 Which cultural item is accepted depends largely on the item's use and compatibility with already existing cultural traits. 전개2 For example, it is not likely that men's hair dyes designed to "get out the gray" will spread into parts of rural Africa where a person's status is elevated with advancing years. 전개3 Even when a(n) ______________ is consistent with a society's needs, there is still no guarantee that it will be accepted. 전개4 For example, most people in the United States using US customary units (e.g., inch, foot, yard, mile, etc.) have resisted adopting the metric system even though making such a change would enable US citizens to interface with the rest of the world more efficiently.

*metric system: 미터법

① categorization　② innovation
③ investigation　④ observation
⑤ specification

한눈에 보는 구조

도입 **주제 제시**
두 문화가 접촉할 때, 적은 수의 문화적 요소만 확산된다.

전개1 **주제에 대한 이유 1**
문화 항목의 수용 여부는 용도와 기존의 문화적 특성과의 양립 가능성 여부에 달려 있다.

전개2 **이유 1에 대한 예시**
나이가 듦에 따라 지위가 올라가는 아프리카 시골 지역에서는 염색약이 받아들여 질 것 같지 않다.

전개3 **주제에 대한 이유 2**
사회의 필요와 일치해도 수용하지 않을 수 있다.

전개4 **이유 2에 대한 예시**
미국인은 관습적 단위를 사용하면서 미터법 채택에 저항한다.

글의 초반에 주제가 명료하게 드러나고, 주제에 대한 두 가지 이유가 각각의 예시를 통해 구체화되고 있다.

유형 해결 전략

1 빈칸이 지문 중간에 있는 경우이므로, 빈칸이 있는 문장부터 읽는다.

Even when a(n) ________ is consistent with a society's needs, there is still no guarantee that it will be accepted.
(________이 한 사회의 필요와 일치할 때조차도, 여전히 그것이 받아들여질 것이라는 보장은 없다.)

2 빈칸 다음 문장을 꼼꼼하게 읽으면서 최대한 많은 정보를 추론해내야 정답을 빨리 찾을 수 있다.

빈칸 다음 문장에서 For example의 예시의 연결어가 사용되고 있다. 예시는 앞의 내용을 구체화시키는 역할을 하므로, 빈칸이 속한 문장이 예시 문장에서 어떻게 다른 방식으로 표현되었는지 비교해보면 답을 찾기 쉽다.

→ 'Even when a(n) ________ is consistent with a society's needs'가 'even though making such a change would enable US citizens to interface with the rest of the world more efficiently'와 서로 대구를 이룬다. 빈칸에는 making such a change에 상응하는 표현인 ②innovation이 와야 한다.

3 빈칸을 유추할 수 없는 경우에는 빈칸의 앞 문장을 꼼꼼하게 읽는다.

이 문제에서는 빈칸 앞 문장이 이유 1에 대한 예시이므로 정답을 찾는 데 직접적으로 도움이 되지는 않는다. 그러나 이유 1이 예시를 통해 구체화되고 있다는 구조적인 힌트를 얻어, 이유 2와 예시의 구조와의 유사성을 발견하여 답을 찾는 데 도움을 준다.

Bonus Tip

빈칸이 지문의 처음이나 마지막에 있을 경우 대부분 주제문에 해당한다.

지문에 전환 관계의 접속사가 있는지를 확인해야 하며 지문의 결론 부분에서 주제를 한 번 더 강조할 확률이 높다는 점을 명심해야 한다.

주제나 요지가 드러나는 부분의 핵심 단어에 빈칸이 들어가는 경우가 대부분이다.

지문에서 자주 반복되는 단어와 비슷한 의미를 가진 단어가 선택지에 제시될 수 있으며 그것이 답으로 처리되는 경우가 많다.

예시가 여러 개 제시될 경우 예시를 충분히 활용해야 한다.

주제문을 분명하게 드러내지 않고 예시를 두세 개 제시하고 그 예시들을 통해서 빈칸의 내용을 추론하게 할 수 있으므로, 예시들이 공통으로 시사하는 바를 파악하도록 한다.

지문 속 근거가 아닌 상식에 입각하여 답을 고르지 않도록 한다.

글을 정확하게 파악하지 못할 경우, 빈칸이 속한 문장의 내용과 상식적으로 가장 부합하는 선택지를 고르는 경향이 있는데, 상식적으로 가장 적합한 선택지는 매력적인 오답으로 활용될 확률이 높다는 점을 명심해야 한다.

Exercise

01 다음 빈칸에 들어갈 말로 가장 적절한 것은? 고1 교육청

When you're eager to get your slice of the pie, why would you be interested in giving a hand to other people so that they can get their piece? If Ernest Hamwi had taken that attitude when he was selling zalabia, a very thin Persian waffle, at the 1904 World's Fair, he might have ended his days as a street vendor. Hamwi noticed that a nearby ice-cream vendor ran out of bowls to serve to his customers. Most people would have sniffed, "Not my problem," perhaps even hoping the ice-cream vendor's misfortune would mean more customers for them. Instead, Hamwi rolled up a waffle and put a scoop of ice cream on top, creating one of the world's first ice-cream cones. He ____________________ and, in the process, made a fortune.

*vendor: 상인 **sniff: 콧방귀를 뀌며 말하다

① opened a new shop
② helped his neighbor
③ joined the big event
④ kept his recipe secret
⑤ learned from his failure

02 다음 빈칸에 들어갈 말로 가장 적절한 것은? 고2 교육청

Patients should be aware that ____________________ about who should be treated for various conditions. For example, expert committees in Europe and the United States set different guidelines about when to treat high blood pressure. The group of American experts believed that for mild elevation of blood pressure the benefits exceeded the risks from treatment. They wrote guidelines suggesting that patients with mild blood pressure elevation take medicine. But in Europe, an expert committee with access to the same scientific data set different guidelines that don't advise treatment for mild elevation of blood pressure. In Europe, people with the same symptoms would not be encouraged to take medicine. Different groups of experts can disagree significantly about what is "best practice."

*elevation: 상승

① there is a universal guideline
② there can be moral considerations
③ their family is responsible for the decision
④ there can be differing views among specialists
⑤ they benefit from following their doctors' advice

03 다음 빈칸에 들어갈 말로 가장 적절한 것은? 고3 교육청

While there is no denying that exceptional players like Emmitt Smith can put points on the board and enhance team success, new research suggests there is a limit to the benefit top talents bring to a team. Researchers compared the amount of individual talent on teams with the teams' success, and they found striking examples of ________________. The researchers looked at three sports: basketball, soccer, and baseball. In each sport, they calculated both the percentage of top talent on each team and the teams' success over several years. For both basketball and soccer, they found that top talent did in fact predict team success, but only up to a point. ____(A)____, there was not simply a point of diminishing returns with respect to top talent; there was in fact a cost. Basketball and soccer teams with the greatest proportion of elite athletes performed worse than those with more moderate proportions of top level players.

*diminishing returns: 수확 체감

① more talent hurting the team
② practice leading to perfection
③ top players being more cooperative
④ coaches being the key to team management
⑤ supporters interrupting the flow of the game

Plus Q

윗글의 빈칸 (A)에 들어갈 적절한 연결어를 쓰시오.

➡

01 **be eager to** 간절히 ~하고 싶어 하다 **give a hand** 도움을 주다 **attitude** 마음가짐, 태도 **fair** 박람회 **run out of** ~이 동나다, ~을 다 써버리다 **bowl** 그릇, 사발 **serve** (고객의) 시중을 들다 **customer** 고객 **misfortune** 불행, 불운 **roll up** ~을 말아 올리다 **scoop** 한 숟가락[국자](의 양) **make a fortune** 많은 돈을 벌다, 재산을 모으다 **recipe** 조리법

02 **patient** 환자 **condition** 질환, 병 **committee** 위원회 **guideline** 지침 **blood pressure** 혈압 **mild** 가벼운, 온화한 **benefit** 이득; 이득을 얻다 **exceed** 넘다, 능가하다 **treatment** 치료, 처리, 대우 **take medicine** 약을 복용하다 **access** 접근 **symptom** 증상 **encourage** 권하다, 장려하다 **disagree** 의견이 다르다(일치하지 않다) **significantly** 상당히, 뚜렷이 **moral** 도덕적 **specialist** 전문의, 전문가

03 **exceptional** 매우 뛰어난 **enhance** 높이다, 더하다 **compare** 비교하다 **striking** 주목할 만한, 두드러진 **calculate** 계산하다, 추산하다 **predict** 예견하다, 예측하다 **with respect to** ~와 관련하여 **cost** 손실, 대가 **proportion** 비율 **moderate** 많지 않은, 보통의

04 다음 빈칸에 들어갈 말로 가장 적절한 것은?

Nobody is flawless. You will always be able to find a point of criticism on anyone, if you would look for it. However, remember that you are not flawless, either. It is much better to accept people as they are, and learn to make the best of any relationship, than to continuously criticize them and beat them down. Even the greatest leaders on earth had their share of flaws, but they learned from their mistakes and used these lessons for their advancement. Gandhi, Mandela and Mother Teresa all experienced rejection at some time, and all made errors in their days. Yet, they became immortal in their own ways. It may be good to consider this when thinking of __________ others.

① assisting ② educating ③ protecting
④ condemning ⑤ encouraging

05 다음 빈칸에 들어갈 말로 가장 적절한 것은?

Although we are always with ourselves, it is amazing that many of us don't really know a lot about ourselves. Why? Because we fail to take the time to connect with the source within. Through our upbringing and education, we often lose contact with our core being. And it is only through deep contemplation, self-evaluation, and genuine efforts, combined with an investment of time, that we can restore this contact. However, because we, human beings, are dynamic creatures, we also change all the time. This means that getting to know ourselves is ________________. And that makes it a painstaking effort. But it is worth our while, because we can do so much more if only we get to know ourselves better: We could learn more about our likes and dislikes, our preferred goals, and the ways to keep ourselves happy and contented.

① a never-ending process
② a very confusing situation
③ something that rarely happens
④ a major requirement for socialization
⑤ different from understanding the world

06 다음 빈칸에 들어갈 말로 가장 적절한 것은?

The pleasure principle controls us when we choose the easy solution first and then pay for it with feelings of discomfort, e.g., if we eat ice cream we feel good for a while, but later pay for it with an increase in weight. When we go into a store and see something we don't have money for, we use our credit cards: Why can't I have it now? It is hard to see the value of postponing certain purchases. All one can see is an evening of elegant dining, a new mobile phone or the beautiful clothes that can be purchased with credit cards. There is no pain and no sacrifice—until the bills become due. Some people become shackled to credit card debts. Try to be aware of those moments when we choose and regularly ____________________—exercise instead of looking at the TV; buy an apple instead of a bar of chocolate, etc.

*shackle: 족쇄를 채우다

① do good and selfless acts
② get in touch with the latest findings
③ make time to do the things you enjoy
④ take the more difficult short-term way out
⑤ have a project going that is for the community

04 **flawless** 결점 없는, 완벽한 **criticism** 비판 **continuously** 계속적으로
have one's share of 많은 ~을 지니다 **advancement** 발달 **rejection** 거부, 거절
in one's days 한창 젊었을 때에 **immortal** 불멸의
05 **upbringing** 양육, 교육 **core** 속, 핵심 **contemplation** 심사숙고 **self-evaluation** 자기 평가
genuine 진심에서 우러난 **investment** 투자 **restore** 회복하다 **dynamic** 역동적인
painstaking 수고를 아끼지 않는, 공들인
06 **pleasure principle** 쾌락 욕구 원칙(고통은 피하고 쾌락을 추구하려는 본능) **pay for** ~에 대한 대가를 치르다
postpone 연기하다 **sacrifice** 희생 **due** 지급 기일이 된 **way out** 출구

07 다음 빈칸에 들어갈 말로 가장 적절한 것은?

Often, we don't have a good notion of what our talents are, because we ______________________. For instance, John Gardner was a modest college teacher until he was drafted into the army during World War II. In the service he was forced to take on managerial responsibilities, which he discovered fit his talents even better than teaching did. When he returned to civilian life, he was given increasingly more demanding administrative jobs, until he was named chairman of the Carnegie Foundation, and then was asked by President Lyndon B. Johnson to serve as the first secretary of health, education, and welfare. This sort of experience convinced Gardner that most of us use only a small part of our natural abilities and may never find out what we are really capable of doing.

① have had our talents exaggerated
② have been evaluated by unfair standards
③ have never had a chance to try them out
④ haven't overcome obstacles we met in the past
⑤ haven't figured out the duty and the responsibility

08 다음 빈칸에 들어갈 말로 가장 적절한 것은?

What happens when fate brings someone special into your life? In no time, your heart pounds as strongly as it can, your tongue feels like sandpaper, and your palms turn into a waterfall. Suddenly "Hello" becomes the hardest word in the English language. Why does this particular person blow you away like a tornado through a trailer camp? That's because you have the ability to ________________, buried deeply in your brain. This skill has strong evolutionary roots, dating from when an instantaneous "fight or flight" decision was a matter of life or death. You have developed an incredible subconscious capability to sense whether someone will be fun to be with and fulfill your needs.

① tell right from wrong
② size someone up instantly
③ learn from past experiences
④ adjust to new environment easily
⑤ sense biological signs immediately

09 다음 빈칸에 들어갈 말로 가장 적절한 것은?

The value of mindless action depends on ____________. Our actions may lead us to something that we will think about and explore further, or they may lead nowhere. A good example is the way babies learn language. Many sounds that a baby hears or produces lead nowhere with regard to language. A baby bangs, a car drives by, a spoon falls on the floor, or the baby bumps the crib. These are all sounds that have no meaning in language. But other sounds can have great meaning simply by being accidentally picked up by someone else. For example, a baby accidentally says something close to "mama," which makes the mother who happens to hear it happy. Then those language sounds are repeated over and over, and they begin to have meaning. So-called statistical learning begins.

① curiosity ② chance ③ acceptance
④ willingness ⑤ contribution

Plus Q

by chance의 의미를 갖는 단어를 본문에서 찾아 쓰시오.

➡

07 **notion** 생각, 개념 **modest** 보통의, 겸손한 **be drafted** 징집되다 **service** 복무, 봉사 **take on** 떠맡다 **managerial** 관리의 **fit** ~에 맞다 **civilian** 민간의 **demanding** 까다로운 **administrative** 행정의 **name** 임명하다 **foundation** 재단, 협회 **secretary** 장관, 비서 **convince** 확신시키다 **natural** 타고난

08 **sandpaper** 사포 **waterfall** 분수 **trailer camp** 이동 주택 캠프장 **evolutionary** 진화적인 **instantaneous** 순간의, 즉시의 **incredible** 놀라운 **subconscious** 잠재적인 **capability** 능력 **fulfill** 실현시키다, 완수하다 **size up** 평가하다, 판단하다

09 **mindless** 생각 없는 **lead nowhere** 아무것도 아니다, 아무 도움도 안 되다 **with regard to** ~에 관해서 **bang** 큰 소리를 내다 **crib** 유아용 침대 **close to** ~와 유사한 **over and over** 반복해서 **statistical** 통계적인

유형

12 연결어 추론

두 개의 빈칸에 글의 논리적 흐름에 맞는 연결어를 추론해 넣는 유형이다. 빈칸 앞뒤의 글의 흐름을 통해 앞뒤가 인과 관계인지, 주제와 예시의 관계인지, 역접의 관계인지 등을 파악해서 적절한 연결어를 추론해야 한다. 선택지로 제시되는 연결어의 의미를 정확하게 파악해 놓을 필요가 있다. 수능에서 거의 매년 1문항씩 출제되고 있다.

대표 예제

다음 글의 빈칸 (A), (B)에 들어갈 말로 가장 적절한 것은?

평가원

도입 Feedback is usually most effective when you offer it at the earliest opportunity, particularly if your objective is to teach someone a skill. 전개1 ______(A)______, if you are teaching your friend how to make your famous egg rolls, you provide a step-by-step commentary as you watch your pupil. If he makes a mistake, you don't wait until the egg rolls are finished to tell him that he left out the cabbage. He needs immediate feedback to finish the rest of the sequence successfully. 전개2 Sometimes, ______(B)______, if a person is already sensitive and upset about something, delaying feedback can be wise. 결론 Use your critical thinking skills to analyze when feedback will do the most good. Rather than automatically offering immediate correction, use the just-in-time approach and provide feedback just before the person might make another mistake.

	(A)		(B)
①	For example	……	however
②	For example	……	as a result
③	In addition	……	in fact
④	Similarly	……	moreover
⑤	Similarly	……	therefore

한눈에 보는 구조

도입 **소재 제시**
기술을 가르치는 경우 빠른 피드백은 일반적으로 효과적이다.

전개1 **예시 제시**
에그롤을 만드는 법을 가르치는 경우, 배우는 사람이 실수를 할 때마다 즉각적으로 피드백을 주는데, 이것은 필요한 과정이다.

전개2 **글의 흐름 전환**
_ 피드백의 시기와 관련된 또 다른 관점을 제시한다.
_ 어떤 사람이 예민하고 당황해하고 있다면 피드백을 미루는 것이 현명할 수 있다.

결론 **주제 제시**
_ 피드백을 주는 시기에 대해 조언한다.
_ 피드백을 주는 시기를 분석하는 데 비판적 사고 기능을 활용하되, 즉각적인 피드백을 제공하기보다는 다른 실수를 하기 전, 적기에 피드백을 제공하라.

피드백을 주는 적절한 시기에 관한 글로, 글의 마지막 부분에서 주제가 드러나 있다.

• SUB NOTE p. 37

유형 해결 전략

1 도입부를 통해 글의 소재 및 방향을 파악해 둔다.

Feedback is usually most effective when you offer it at the earliest opportunity

→ 피드백을 가급적 빨리 주는 것이 대개는 효과적이라는 내용을 통해 '피드백을 주는 시기'에 관한 글임을 추론할 수 있다.

2 (A), (B) 빈칸 앞뒤의 논리적 흐름을 파악한다.

(A)의 앞: particularly if your objective is to teach someone a skill
→ 누군가에게 기술을 가르치는 경우를 설명하고 있다.
(A)의 뒤: if you are teaching your friend how to make your famous egg rolls
→ 친구에게 에그롤을 만드는 법을 가르치면서 그가 실수를 하면 끝날 때까지 기다리지 않고 바로 잘못된 점을 말한다는 구체적인 예가 제시되어 있다.

(B)의 앞: He needs immediate feedback to finish the rest of the sequence successfully.
→ 에그롤의 연속 과정을 성공적으로 마치기 위해서는 즉각적인 피드백이 필요하다.
(B)의 뒤: if a person is already sensitive and upset about something, delaying feedback can be wise
→ 어떤 사람이 어떤 일에 관해 이미 예민하고 당황해하고 있으면 피드백을 미루는 것이 현명할 수 있다.
(B)의 앞뒤에서 immediate와 delaying이 대비를 이룬다.

3 파악된 (A), (B) 빈칸 앞뒤의 논리적 흐름에 맞는 연결어를 선택한다.

(A) 앞에는 기술을 가르치는 경우에 즉각적인 피드백이 효과적이라는 내용이 나와 있고, 뒤에는 그에 대한 자세한 예가 나오므로 For example이 적절하다.
(B) 앞에는 에그롤을 가르치면서는 즉각적인 피드백이 필요하다는 내용이 나와 있으며, 뒤에는 사람에 따라 피드백을 미루는 것이 현명할 수 있다는 역접의 내용이 나오므로 however가 적절하다.

Bonus Tip

시험에 자주 출제되는 연결어

1. 예시: for example, for instance (예를 들어)
2. 첨가: in addition, besides, moreover, furthermore (게다가, 더욱이)
3. 비교: similarly, likewise (마찬가지로)
4. 대조, 역접: by contrast(대조적으로), on the other hand(반면에), on the contrary(그와는 반대로), conversely (반대로, 거꾸로 말해서), however (그러나), nevertheless (그럼에도 불구하고), nonetheless(그렇기는 하지만, 그럼에도 불구하고)
5. 결론, 요약: therefore (그러므로), thus (따라서), hence (그런 이유로, 따라서), as a result (결과적으로), in conclusion (결론적으로), in short (간단히 말해서)
6. 환언: in other words, that is (즉, 다시 말해서)
7. 강조, 부연: in fact (사실, 그러나 실은), indeed (사실은), in effect (사실상, 실제적으로)
8. 조건: otherwise (그렇지 않으면)

Exercise

01 다음 글의 빈칸 (A), (B)에 들어갈 말로 가장 적절한 것은? 고2 교육청

If you ask someone to name three sports, most likely he or she will be able to answer with ease. After all, nearly everyone has an idea about what types of activities are regarded as sports and which are not. Most of us think we know what sports are. ___(A)___, the line drawn between examples of sports, leisure, and play is not always clear. In fact, devising a definition that establishes clear and clean parameters around what types of activities should be included and excluded is relatively difficult to do. Activities that are regarded as play today may gain the status of sport in the future. ___(B)___, many people once played badminton in their backyards but this activity was hardly considered a sport. Since 1992, however, badminton has been an Olympic sport!

*parameter: 규정 요소

	(A)		(B)
①	However	……	For example
②	However	……	In conclusion
③	Moreover	……	In conclusion
④	Similarly	……	For example
⑤	Similarly	……	In other words

02 다음 글의 빈칸 (A), (B)에 들어갈 말로 가장 적절한 것은? 고2 교육청

Fishing is the most obvious ocean-based economic activity. People in many coastal areas make their living by fishing, and fish and shellfish make up a major part of their diet. ___(A)___, about one billion people worldwide rely on fish as their main source of animal protein. In terms of fishing as an economic activity, the largest segment of world fisheries is commercial fishing. Fish caught by commercial fishermen include salmon, tuna, shellfish and other edible species such as squid. Consumers are used to buying these seafoods in grocery stores, restaurants, and village markets around the world. ___(B)___, the supply is not infinite. As the world's population swells, the demand for fishing products puts intense pressure on fish populations. The worldwide catch of ocean fish swelled from 81 million tons in 2003 to 148 million tons in 2010.

(A)		(B)
① Instead	……	Likewise
② Instead	……	However
③ In fact	……	Likewise
④ In fact	……	However
⑤ For example	……	Moreover

03 다음 글의 빈칸 (A), (B)에 들어갈 말로 가장 적절한 것은? 평가원

Problems can be distinguished according to whether they are reasonable or unreasonable. Reasonable problems are of the kind that can be solved in a step-by-step manner. A crossword puzzle is of this nature. Given a sufficient vocabulary, the empty spaces can be filled in one by one. Unreasonable problems, ___(A)___, cannot be treated this way because the task contains some 'trick' or 'catch' that must be understood before someone can arrive at a solution. This feature frustrates any step-by-step process that proceeds without the realization that "things aren't what they seem." ___(B)___, successful problem solving in these cases requires that the person **acquires** an insight into the nature of the trick. Riddles provide commonplace instances of such insight problems, such as the classic riddle that the Sphinx posed to Oedipus.

(A)		(B)
① in contrast	……	Hence
② in contrast	……	Nevertheless
③ for example	……	Hence
④ for example	……	Besides
⑤ in addition	……	Nevertheless

Plus Q

윗글의 밑줄 친 **acquires**를 어법에 맞게 고쳐 쓰시오.

➡

01 **draw** 긋다 **devise** 궁리하다, 고안하다 **establish** 규명하다, 확립하다 **exclude** 제외하다 **status** 지위 **backyard** 뒤뜰
02 **obvious** 분명한 **rely on** ~에 의존하다 **segment** 부분 **fisheries** 어업 **commercial** 상업적인 **edible** 먹을 수 있는 **squid** 오징어 **intense** 강한 **swell** 부풀다
03 **distinguish** 구분하다 **sufficient** 충분한 **treat** 다루다 **catch** 함정 **feature** 특성 **proceed** 진행되다 **insight** 통찰 **riddle** 수수께끼 **commonplace** 흔한 **pose** (문제 등을) 제기하다

04 다음 글의 빈칸 (A), (B)에 들어갈 말로 가장 적절한 것은?

When we experience pain or discomfort, the natural inclination is to try to avoid the pain or do something to get rid of the source of the pain. In the case of outer discomfort caused by a neighbor's loud radio, ____(A)____, we might take a drive to get away from the noise or ask the neighbor to turn down the volume. However, for inner pain this kind of approach is usually counterproductive. For example, one who fears a panic attack tenses up and tries to fight it. This makes the panic attack more intense and longer lasting. A better approach would be to relax, and let the attack come and then pass. ____(B)____, people who have experienced traumatic events may try fruitlessly to get rid of the memories. It would be better to accept and process the memory. If someone experiences chronic pain, one of the worst things to do is to tense up and fight it.

	(A)		(B)
①	as a result	……	Similarly
②	as a result	……	Besides
③	in fact	……	Besides
④	for example	……	Therefore
⑤	for example	……	Similarly

05 다음 글의 빈칸 (A), (B)에 들어갈 말로 가장 적절한 것은?

The growth of electronic channels is creating a fundamental change in the nature of marketing. The customers are moving from face-to-face contacts with the suppliers who were earlier located in fixed locations that operate during fixed hours, to remote contacts that operate "anywhere, anytime." More and more services now fall into the category of arm's length relationships rather than the face-to-face interactions. ____(A)____, the customers would still find it difficult to get rid of the marketplace, for it is the physical environment that attracts them, as in destination resorts. Furthermore, the physical environment is progressing. The shopping malls, which earlier had retail stores alone are now being redesigned to create a "total experience." ____(B)____, the redesigned malls seek to provide food services, health clubs, entertainment, exhibitions, and above all a chance to socialize.

*destination resort: 사람들이 특별히 찾는 리조트

(A)		(B)
① However	……	Nevertheless
② However	……	In other words
③ Likewise	……	Nevertheless
④ Likewise	……	In other words
⑤ Besides	……	Consequently

06 다음 글의 빈칸 (A), (B)에 들어갈 말로 가장 적절한 것은?

For years I have tried to help people control their minds. One of the most important things that I have found is that if you want to change how you feel and behave, then change the way you use your physiology. ______(A)______, if you are feeling depressed, but you stand up straight, put your chest out, and put a smile on your face, you won't feel depressed any longer. Scientists have verified this. They have found that people have beaten lie detectors by putting themselves in a physiological state, posture, and breathing pattern similar to ____________ of when they are telling the truth. ______(B)______, you can reprogram yourself by changing how you use your body and your thought processes.

*physiology: 생리(생물체의 생물학적 기능과 작용)

(A)		(B)
① For example	……	In addition
② For example	……	Therefore
③ Likewise	……	In addition
④ However	……	Therefore
⑤ However	……	In other words

Plus Q

윗글의 빈칸에 들어갈 대명사를 어법에 맞게 쓰시오.

➡

04 **discomfort** 불편함 **inclination** 성향, 경향 **get away** 탈출하다 **counterproductive** 역효과를 낳는 **panic** 극심한 공포 **tense** 긴장되다 **intense** 강렬한 **chronic** 만성적인
05 **electronic** 전자의 **channel** (*pl.*) 유통 체계 **supplier** 공급자 **operate** 영업하다, 운용하다 **remote** 원거리의, 먼 **fall** 속하다 **category** 범주 **retail** 소매의
06 **control** 통제하다 **depressed** 우울한 **straight** 똑바로 **chest** 가슴 **verify** 확인하다 **beat** 이기다 **lie detector** 거짓말 탐지기 **state** 상태 **posture** 자세

유형

13 무관한 문장 찾기

글의 주제나 흐름에서 벗어나는 문장을 고르는 유형으로, 대부분 첫 문장부터 주제와 핵심 어구가 주어지므로 내용의 일관성을 중점적으로 판단하여 풀이한다. 그러나 주제가 명확하지 않고 단계적으로 전개되는 경우 각 문장의 전후 관계를 파악하여 연결이 매끄럽지 않은 문장을 찾아야 한다. 수능에서 해마다 1문항씩 출제되고 있다.

대표 예제

다음 글에서 전체 흐름과 관계 없는 문장은? 수능

도입 Food intake is essential for the survival of every living organism. The failure to detect spoiled or toxic food can have deadly consequences. Therefore, it is not surprising that humans use all their five senses to analyze food quality. 전개1 ① A first judgment about the value of a food source is made on its appearance and smell. ② Food that looks and smells attractive is taken into the mouth. ③ The value of a particular food is an estimation of how good it is, based on its level of vitamins, minerals, or calories. 전개2 ④ Here, based on a complex sensory analysis that is not only restricted to the sense of taste but also includes smell, touch, and hearing, the final decision whether to swallow or reject food is made. 결론 ⑤ Frequently, this complex interaction between different senses is inappropriately referred to as 'taste' although it should be better called flavor perception, because it uses multiple senses.

한눈에 보는 구조

도입 **주제 제시**
음식 섭취는 모든 생물의 생존에 필수적이며, 인간은 음식의 질을 분석하기 위해 오감을 모두 사용한다.

전개1 **주제에 대한 부연 설명** 1
외관과 냄새로 음식 재료의 가치를 최초로 판단하고, 보기에 매력적이고 냄새가 매혹적인 음식을 섭취한다.

전개2 **주제에 대한 부연 설명** 2
후각, 촉각, 청각을 포함한 복합적인 감각 분석을 통해 음식을 섭취할지 혹은 거부할지에 대한 최종 결정을 내린다.

결론
감각 간의 복잡한 상호작용은 여러 가지 감각을 사용하므로 향미 지각으로 불리는 편이 더 낫다.

글의 주제를 먼저 제시한 뒤, 음식 섭취의 과정을 설명하면서 주제를 부연하고 있다. 특정 음식의 가치에 대한 평가를 다루고 있는 ③번 문장은 이러한 흐름에서 벗어난다는 것을 알 수 있다.

유형 해결 전략

1 글의 도입부에 제시되는 주제를 파악하고, 글의 흐름을 예상한다.

Therefore, it is not surprising that humans use all their five senses to analyze food quality.

→ '음식 섭취와 관련한 인간의 오감 활용'이라는 주제로 이야기가 전개될 것임을 예상할 수 있다.

2 주제와의 연관성 및 앞뒤의 흐름을 선택지의 내용을 고려하여 따져본다.

음식 섭취와 관련한 오감의 활용 → ① 음식의 가치(질)에 대한 첫 판단은 시각과 후각을 통해 이루어짐. → ② 시각과 후각을 통한 평가가 매혹적인 경우 음식을 입속으로 넣게 됨. → ③ 특정 음식의 가치는 비타민, 미네랄, 칼로리의 수준에 근거함. → ④ 입속으로 들어간 음식의 섭취나 거부에 대한 최종 결정은 미각뿐 아니라 후각, 촉각, 청각을 통해 이루어짐. → ⑤ 감각 간의 복합적 상호작용을 향미지각으로 부르는 것이 더 나음.

→ 음식 섭취와 관련한 오감의 활용을 음식 섭취의 과정에 따라 전개하고 있다. 따라서 특정 음식의 가치 결정 기준에 관해 언급하고 있는 ③은 글의 전체 흐름과 관계가 없다.

3 문장에 사용되는 지시어를 오답 소거의 중요한 단서로 활용한다.

⑤번 문장의 경우, this complex interaction이 ④번 문장의 a complex sensory analysis와 연관되어 있으므로, ④, ⑤번 문장이 하나의 흐름에 맞게 제시되어 있다고 판단할 수 있다.

Bonus Tip

무관한 문장을 찾는 단서

- 선택지의 내용을 볼 때는 특히 주어를 유심히 살펴본다. 앞 문장에서 글의 일관성과 통일성에 큰 역할을 하지 않는 요소를 가져와 주어로 다루며 부연하는 문장이 정답일 가능성이 높다.
- 지시어, 대명사가 쓰인 경우, 반드시 지시 대상을 찾아서 논리적 일관성이 있는지를 확인한다.
- 연결어가 쓰인 경우, 정확히 앞뒤 문장을 이어서 해석하며 흐름이 자연스러운지 판단한다.
- 글이 전개되는 여러 방식을 알아두면 맥락을 빠르게 이해하는 데 도움이 된다.

다양한 글의 전개 방식

예시	초반에 주제나 상황을 제시하고 그에 대한 뒷받침 사실을 구체적으로 하나씩 나열하는 방식
비교와 대조	여러 대상 간의 유사점을 다룬 뒤 차이점을 제시하는 방식
원인과 결과	특정 사건을 제시하며 그에 대한 인과 관계를 언급하는 방식
통념과 비판	일반적 견해(통념)를 초반에 언급한 뒤 그것에 대한 반대되는 필자의 주장과 의견을 덧붙이는 방식
문제점과 해결책	주로 시사적인 문제점을 초반에 제기하고 그에 대한 필자의 해결 방안을 기술하는 방식

Exercise

01 다음 글에서 전체 흐름과 관계 없는 문장은? 고2 교육청

Both mammals and birds are noisy creatures. They commonly make their presence felt, and communicate, by sound, but birds are far better at it. ① Many mammals produce different sounds for different objects, but few can match the range of meaningful sounds that birds may give voice to. ② Apart from human beings, mammals on the whole are not melodious and there is little evidence that they intend to be. ③ Some mammals bellow, but few sing, apart from human beings and perhaps whales. ④ Some mammals are different in where they live, how they move around and what they eat. ⑤ Yet many birds are famed for their songs and some of the most glorious songsters are the ones we encounter most often.

*bellow: 큰 소리로 울부짖다

02 다음 글에서 전체 흐름과 관계 없는 문장은? 고2 교육청

Black ice refers to a thin coating of glazed ice on a surface. While not truly black, it is virtually transparent, allowing black asphalt roadways or the surface below to be seen through it—hence the term "black ice". ① Black ice is often practically invisible to drivers or persons stepping on it. ② There is, thus, a risk of sudden sliding and subsequent accidents. ③ To ensure safe driving, it is best to examine your car before starting. ④ On December 1, 2013, heavy post-Thanksgiving weekend traffic encountered black ice on the westbound I-290 expressway in Worcester, Massachusetts. ⑤ A chain reaction series of crashes resulted, involving three tractor-trailers and over 60 other vehicles.

• SUB NOTE p. 42

03 다음 글에서 전체 흐름과 관계 없는 문장은? 고3 교육청

Not until the rise of ecology at the beginning of the twentieth century did people begin to think seriously of land as a natural system with interconnecting parts. ①A century earlier, Thomas Jefferson had vigorously promoted an orderly division of the American land, beginning with the Northwest Territory. ②Surveyors were sent forth to draw rectangular grids on the land, dividing the wilds into counties, townships, and ultimately homesteads, with little concern for terrain or other natural features. ③They adopted the environmentally friendly system even though they did not see a profit in it. ④That system had its virtues, but in time ecology made the lines appear artificial. ⑤As some observers would come to see it, **the rectangular grid system caused as much harm as it did good**.

*homestead: 정부 공여 농지

Plus Q

밑줄 친 부분을 우리말로 해석하시오.

➡

01 mammal 포유류, 포유동물 presence 존재 object 물체 match ~에 필적하다 range 범위 melodious 노래하는, 가락이 아름다운 evidence 증거 be famed for ~로 유명하다 glorious 멋진, 눈부시게 아름다운 songster 명금(고운 소리로 우는 새), 가수 encounter 마주치다

02 refer to 지칭하다 coating 막, 코팅 glazed 광을 낸 virtually 사실상 transparent 투명한 practically 사실상 invisible 보이지 않는 subsequent 뒤따르는 tractor-trailer 견인 트레일러

03 ecology 생태(계); 생태학 interconnecting 서로 연결된 vigorously 활발히 surveyor 측량사 send ~ forth ~를 (다른 곳으로) 보내다[파견하다] rectangular 직사각형의 grid 격자무늬 concern 고려 terrain 지형 adopt 택하다 virtue 장점 artificial 인위적인 observer 관찰자

04 다음 글에서 전체 흐름과 관계 없는 문장은?

Refugees are people who cross international borders in order to flee human rights abuses and conflict. However, refugees are more than simply a human rights issue. Refugee movements are also an inherent part of international politics. ① The causes, consequences, and responses to refugees are all closely associated with world politics. ② The causes of refugee movements, for instance, are grounded on conflict, state failure, and the inequalities of international political economy. ③ The world's economy is influenced not only by changes in political circumstances but also by assumptions on which people base their decisions. ④ The consequences of these movements have been connected with security, the spread of conflict, terrorism, and transnationalism. ⑤ Therefore, responding to refugees represents a challenge to world order and justice and to the facilitation of international cooperation.

05 다음 글에서 전체 흐름과 관계 없는 문장은?

In the information age, we have arrived at a point where information is no longer scarce; instead, it's overwhelming. The amount of it makes some people nervous and tense, leading to information overload. ① This occurs when the volume of the information supply exceeds the limited human information processing capacity. ② Those people experience a strong loss of concentration, a high level of stress, and feelings of guilt because they still have so much to read and digest. ③ However, it is not what information does to people that counts, but what people do with information. ④ As a result, they feel overwhelmed and unable to cope with the information flow. ⑤ The vastly increased information flow over the last 20 years does not present any problems to technology, but our brains have not quite found the right answer to it.

06 다음 글에서 전체 흐름과 관계 없는 문장은?

One of the major issues plaguing human potential in the corporate world today is "work-life balance." The work-life balance conversation that has recently dominated the corporate landscape implies that work and life are separate. ① In this way, we set work and life against each other, and the thought that follows is that you are either working too much and living too little or vice versa. ② The term work-life balance itself is fatally flawed for it diminishes our ability to prove that work can be a richly rewarding part of a person's life and should in many ways be personal. ③ You cannot separate the personal and professional aspects of an individual's life. ④ You can consider them separately to gain insight, but the practical separation of **the two** is impossible. ⑤ Therefore, work-life balance can be acquired only when you understand that they have little to do with each other.

*vice versa: 거꾸로, 반대로

Plus Q

문맥상 밑줄 친 **the two**가 가리키는 것을 본문에서 찾아 영어로 쓰시오.

➡

04 **refugee** 난민 **border** 국경 **flee** 달아나다 **abuse** 남용 **conflict** 분쟁 **inherent** 내재한 **politics** 정치 **consequence** 결과 **associate** 연관 짓다 **ground** 바탕을 두다 **inequality** 불평등 **circumstance** 환경 **assumption** 추정 **transnationalism** 다국적주의 **facilitation** 활성화 **cooperation** 협력

05 **scarce** 희소한 **overwhelming** 압도적인 **overload** 과부하 **occur** 발생하다 **exceed** 초과하다 **capacity** 용량 **concentration** 집중력 **guilt** 죄책감 **digest** (내용을) 완전히 이해하다, 소화하다 **cope with** 대처하다 **vastly** 엄청나게

06 **plague** 괴롭히다 **potential** 잠재력 **dominate** 지배하다 **imply** 넌지시 나타내다 **fatally** 치명적으로 **flawed** 결함이 있는 **diminish** 깎아내리다 **rewarding** 보람 있는 **separation** 분리 **have little to do with** ~와 연관이 거의 없다

유형

14 글의 순서 배열

글의 순서 배열은 주어진 글을 읽고 다음에 이어지는 글의 순서를 찾는 유형으로, 글의 내용에 따라 시간의 흐름 및 사건의 전개 순서일 경우도 있고, 글의 논리적 순서를 파악해야 하는 경우도 있다. 매년 수능에 1문항씩 출제되어 오다가 최근에는 2문항씩 출제되고 있으며 3점 문항으로 출제된 적도 있다.

대표 예제

주어진 글 다음에 이어질 글의 순서로 가장 적절한 것은? 수능

도입≫ Some people make few intentional changes in life. Sure, over time they may get fatter, gather lines, and go gray.

(A) They train for marathons, quit smoking, switch fields, write plays, take up the guitar, or learn to tango even if they never danced before in their lives. 결론≫ What is the difference between these two groups of people?

(B) 전개≫ But they wear their hair the same way, buy the same brand of shoes, eat the same breakfast, and stick to routines for no reason other than the ease of a comfortable, predictable life. Yet as both research and real life show, many others do make important changes.

(C) It's their perspective. People who change do not question whether change is possible or look for reasons they cannot change. They simply decide on a change they want and do what is necessary to accomplish it. Changing, which always stems from a firm decision, becomes job number one.

① (A)−(C)−(B)　② (B)−(A)−(C)
③ (B)−(C)−(A)　④ (C)−(A)−(B)
⑤ (C)−(B)−(A)

한눈에 보는 구조

도입≫ **소재 제시**
시간이 흐르면서 자연스럽게 변화가 일어나는 것을 제외하고, 살면서 의도적인 변화를 거의 하지 않는 사람들이 있다.

전개≫ **비교와 대조를 통한 전개**
의도적인 변화를 하지 않는 사람들은 판에 박힌 일상을 고수하는데, 이와는 반대로 실제로 살면서 중요한 변화를 하는 많은 다른 사람들이 있다.

결론≫ **주제 제시**
변화를 하는 사람들과 의도적인 변화를 하지 않는 두 집단 간의 차이는 의도적인 변화에 대한 그들의 시각이다.

글의 도입에서 살면서 의도적인 변화를 거의 하지 않는 사람들에 대해 소개한 후, 대조의 방식으로 실제로 살면서 중요한 변화를 하는 사람들과 비교를 하고 있다. 그 다음, 이 두 집단 간의 차이가 무엇인지 질문을 던져 놓고 마지막 부분에서 그에 대한 대답을 제시하고 있다. 따라서 글의 순서는 (B)−(A)−(C)가 된다.

유형 해결 전략

1 주어진 글을 통해 무엇에 관한 내용인지 소재를 파악한다.

주어진 글 → 살면서 의도적인 변화를 거의 하지 않는 사람들이 있고 그들은 그저 시간이 흐르는 대로 노화에 따른 변화가 일어난다.

2 대명사가 가리키는 것이 무엇인지 파악하고, 각 단락의 마지막 부분과 다음 단락의 처음 부분과 연결되는 내용을 찾아본다.

(B) → they는 주어진 글에 제시된 살면서 의도적인 변화를 하지 않는 사람들을 가리키고 그들의 태도를 구체적으로 보여준다. 그들은 똑같은 방식의 머리를 하고, 똑같은 상표의 신발을 사고, 똑같은 아침을 먹으며 판에 박힌 일상을 고수한다. Yet 다음에는 중요한 변화를 하는 사람들이 있다는 언급을 한다.

(A) → They는 변화를 하는 사람들을 가리키고 그들이 하는 다양한 활동을 보여준다. 그들은 마라톤을 위해 훈련을 하고, 담배를 끊고, 분야를 바꾸고, 희곡을 쓰고, 기타를 배우고, 또는 살면서 전에 한 번도 춤을 춰 본 적이 없다고 해도 탱고를 배운다. 마지막에 '그 두 집단의 차이는 무엇인가'라는 질문을 한다.

3 마지막 부분을 연결하여 글의 전체적인 흐름이 자연스러운지 확인한다.

(C) → '그것은 그들의 시각이다.'라고 시작하는 문장은 (A)에서 던진 질문에 대한 대답이고 변화를 하는 사람들이 가진 변화에 대한 태도를 설명하는 내용으로 글이 마무리된다.

글 전체 흐름 → 변화를 하지 않는 사람들의 모습에 대한 언급이 먼저 나오고, (B)에 있는 Yet 다음에 변화를 하는 사람들이 하는 다양한 활동을 보여주는 것이 (A)에 제시되며 (A)의 마지막에 질문을 던지고 그 질문에 대한 답을 (C)에서 하고 있다.

Bonus Tip

글의 순서를 찾는 단서

- 고유명사나 일반 명사가 먼저 제시되고 그것을 대신하는 대명사가 그 다음에 제시되므로 대명사가 무엇을 가리키는지 파악하는 것이 글의 순서를 찾는 데 큰 힌트가 된다.
- 부정관사(a/an)가 있는 명사가 순서상 먼저 나오고 그 다음에 그것에 대해 정관사(the)를 붙여서 가리키므로 그런 표현적인 부분도 순서의 단서가 될 수 있다.
- 글이 논리적인 순서를 찾아야 하는 경우에는 연결어가 순서를 찾는 단서가 될 수 있다.

_ 일반 명제 다음에 그에 대한 사례를 제시하는 연결어: For example, For instance 등

_ 글의 흐름이 전환되거나 역접이 되는 연결어: However, Instead, Nevertheless, By contrast 등

_ 유사한 내용이 이어지는 연결어: Similarly, Likewise 등

_ 앞 문장과의 인과관계를 보여주는 연결어: Therefore, Thus, As a result, Consequently 등

- 글이 사건의 전개 순서나 시간의 흐름에 따라 전개되고 있는지 아니면 논리적으로 연결되는 내용인지 파악한다.

_ 사건의 전개나 시간의 흐름에 따른 순서일 경우: 진행되는 사건의 내용에 따라 순서를 정하면 되므로 상대적으로 난이도는 쉽게 여겨질 수 있다.

_ 글의 논리적 연결을 고려하여 순서를 정하는 경우: 상대적으로 난이도가 어렵게 여겨질 수 있고 내용에 따른 문장 간의 연결고리를 파악해서 순서를 찾아야 한다.

Exercise

01 주어진 글 다음에 이어질 글의 순서로 가장 적절한 것은? 고2 교육청

For some people, there is an irony to success. Many people who achieve great success don't always feel it.

(A) Achievement is something you reach or attain, like a goal. It is something tangible, clearly defined and measurable. It comes when you pursue and obtain what you want.

(B) Success, in contrast, is a feeling or a state of being. "She feels successful. She *is* successful," we say, using the verb *to be* to suggest this state of *being*.

(C) For example, some who achieve fame talk about the loneliness that often goes with it. That's because success and achievement are not the same thing, yet too often we mistake one for the other.

*tangible: 실체가 있는

① (A)−(C)−(B) ② (B)−(A)−(C) ③ (B)−(C)−(A)
④ (C)−(A)−(B) ⑤ (C)−(B)−(A)

02 주어진 글 다음에 이어질 글의 순서로 가장 적절한 것은? 고2 교육청

Every day in each of my classes I randomly select two students who are given the title of "official questioners." These students are assigned the responsibility to ask at least one question during that class.

(A) In a serious tone, she answered that she'd been extremely nervous when I appointed her at the beginning of class. But then, during that class, she felt differently from how she'd felt during other lectures.

(B) After being the day's official questioner, one of my students, Carrie, visited me in my office. Just to break the ice, I asked in a lighthearted way, "Did you feel honored to be named one of the first 'official questioners' of the semester?"

(C) It was a lecture just like the others, but this time, she said, she was forced to have a higher level of consciousness; she was more aware of the content of the lecture and discussion. She also admitted that as a result she got more out of that class.

① (A)−(C)−(B) ② (B)−(A)−(C) ③ (B)−(C)−(A)
④ (C)−(A)−(B) ⑤ (C)−(B)−(A)

03 주어진 글 다음에 이어질 글의 순서로 가장 적절한 것은? 수능

Sometimes, after punishment has been administered a few times, it needn't be continued, because the mere threat of punishment is enough to induce the desired behavior.

(A) Avoidance training, however, doesn't always work in our favor. For instance, a child who has been repeatedly criticized for poor performance on math may learn to dodge difficult math problems in order to avoid further punishment.

(B) Unfortunately, because of this avoidance, the child fails to develop his math skills and therefore improve the capabilities he has, and so a vicious cycle has set in. The avoidance must be unlearned through some positive experiences with math in order for this cycle to be broken.

(C) Psychologists call this avoidance training because the person is learning to avoid the possibility of a punishing consequence. Avoidance training is responsible for many everyday behaviors. It has taught you to carry an umbrella when it looks like rain to avoid the punishment of getting wet, and to keep your hand away from a hot iron to avoid the punishment of a burn.

① (A)−(C)−(B) ② (B)−(A)−(C) ③ (B)−(C)−(A)
④ (C)−(A)−(B) ⑤ (C)−(B)−(A)

Plus Q

다음 빈칸에 들어갈 표현을 본문에서 찾아 쓰시오.

The more pesticides are used, the more resistant the insects become, and so even the more pesticides have to be used. It's a ____________.

➡

01 **achievement** 성취, 업적 **attain** 달성하다 **measurable** 측정할 수 있는 **obtain** 얻다 **state** 상태 **fame** 명성, 명예 **loneliness** 고독, 외로움 **mistake ~ for ...** ~을 …로 오인하다[혼동하다]
02 **randomly** 무작위로 **assign** (임무를) 부여하다 **appoint** 지명하다 **lighthearted** 쾌활한, 명랑한 **honored** 영광인, 명예로운 **consciousness** 의식 **be aware of** ~을 알다
03 **administer** 가하다, 주다 **induce** 끌어내다 **avoidance** 회피 **dodge** 요리조리 피하다 **capability** 능력 **vicious cycle** 악순환 **set in** 시작되다 **unlearn** 배우지 않았던 상태로 되돌리다

04 주어진 글 다음에 이어질 글의 순서로 가장 적절한 것은?

> A top financial analyst used the World Wide Web to dig up some fresh news on Waste Management Incorporated (WMI), a company he was tracking.

(A) Some customers were getting multiple bills, others weren't getting any. Too often, the garbage wasn't getting picked up on time. The analyst used the chat room postings as a springboard. He developed e-mail contacts with many of the employees and added to his collection of information.

(B) By visiting various investment chat rooms, the analyst learned that Waste Management employees were venting about one snafu after another; many were attributable to incompatible computer systems at different units of the company.

(C) Armed with clear evidence suggesting inadequate firmwide systems, as well as other problems, the analyst advised his clients that something smelled rotten at WMl. Investors who stayed away from it, breathed a sigh of relief a few months later when WMI's share price collapsed.

*snafu: 대혼란

① (A)−(C)−(B) ② (B)−(A)−(C) ③ (B)−(C)−(A)
④ (C)−(A)−(B) ⑤ (C)−(B)−(A)

05 주어진 글 다음에 이어질 글의 순서로 가장 적절한 것은?

> The word *totem* is taken from the Ojibwa, an Algonquin people of Canada.

(A) Frequently the relationship is a ritual one, the animal is considered sacred, and there are specific taboos associated with it, and the members of the group may even believe themselves to be descended from the totemic species.

(B) The expression *ototeman*, from which the word *totem* comes, means roughly, "He is a relative of mine," and expresses membership in the exogamic group. Ojibwa clans were named after animal species, so that people might say *makwa nth-totem*: "My clan is a bear."

(C) Subsequent researchers applied the term *totemism* liberally to similar phenomena elsewhere, and it came to be used as a general concept, referring to any situation in which a special relationship was thought to exist between a social group and one or more classes of material objects, specifically animals and plants.

*exogamic: 종족 외의

① (A)－(C)－(B) ② (B)－(A)－(C) ③ (B)－(C)－(A)
④ (C)－(A)－(B) ⑤ (C)－(B)－(A)

06 주어진 글 다음에 이어질 글의 순서로 가장 적절한 것은?

Rice stalks lower their heads when they are mature and corn kernels remain on the shoots even when they are ripe.

(A) These mutant seeds have been spread intentionally, which means that the plants have become artificial species not found in nature, having been bred to keep their seeds intact. By nurturing these cultivars, the most preferred seeds are produced.

(B) However, rice and corn are mutants, and they have been modified to keep their seeds attached for the purpose of convenient and efficient harvesting. Humans have continuously selected and bred such mutants, through breeding technology, in order for these phenomena to occur.

(C) **This** may not seem strange, but, in reality, these types of rice and corn should not survive in nature. Normally, when they mature, seeds should fall down to the ground in order to germinate.

*cultivar: 재배 변종 식물

① (A)－(C)－(B) ② (B)－(A)－(C) ③ (B)－(C)－(A)
④ (C)－(A)－(B) ⑤ (C)－(B)－(A)

Plus Q
밑줄 친 **This**가 가리키는 것을 본문에서 찾아 쓰시오.

➡

04 **dig up** ~에 대해 알아내다[들추다] **track** 추적하다 **springboard** 출발점, 도약판 **vent** (감정 등을) 드러내다 **attributable to** ~의 탓인 **incompatible** 호환되지 않는 **rotten** 썩은 **collapse** (가격이) 폭락하다
05 **ritual** 의식(儀式)적인 **sacred** 신성한 **descended from** ~에서 유래한 **clan** 부족, 씨족 **subsequent** 그 후의 **phenomena** (자연) 현상 **concept** 개념
06 **stalk** 줄기 **mature** 다 익은, 성숙한 **kernel** 낟알 **shoot** 햇가지 **ripe** (과일 · 곡물이) 익은 **mutant** 돌연변이의 **intact** 원래 상태 그대로의, 손대지 않은 **modify** 수정[변경]하다 **germinate** 발아하다

유형

15 문장 삽입

글의 흐름이 단절된 곳이나 글의 흐름에 논리적 비약이 있는 곳을 찾아 주어진 문장을 넣는 유형이다. 글의 전체적 통일성과 유기적 연결성을 파악하는 능력을 측정하고자 하는 유형으로서 난이도가 가장 높은 유형 중 하나이다. 위치를 찾을 때 전체적인 글의 흐름도 중요하지만 연결어, 대명사 등이 주요 단서 역할을 할 때도 있다. 매년 수능에 1문항씩 출제되어 오다가 최근에는 2문항씩 출제되고 있다.

대표 예제

글의 흐름으로 보아, 주어진 문장이 들어가기에 가장 적절한 곳은? 수능

Surprised by the vision of an unfamiliar silhouette pushing into the house, these dogs were using their eyes instead of their noses.

도입 Remember when you were little and you imagined that adults had infinite power? Surely someone who could drive the car, open the juice container, and reach the sink could make it stop raining. (①) I think that's the same expectation that we have with respect to our dogs and their ability to smell. (②) Because they are so good at using their noses, we assume that they can smell anything, anytime. (③) 전개1 But dogs use other senses, too, and the brains of both humans and dogs tend to intensify one sense at a time. (④) 전개2 Many owners have been snapped at by their dogs when they returned home with a new hairdo or a new coat. (⑤) 결론 Their noses may be remarkable, but they're not always switched on.

한눈에 보는 구조

도입 소재 제시
어렸을 때 어른들이 무한한 힘을 가졌다고 상상했었던 것처럼, 우리는 개의 냄새를 맡는 능력에 관해서도 비슷한 기대를 갖고 있으며, 그들은 언제 어떤 것이든지 냄새를 맡을 수 있다고 추정한다.

전개1 글의 흐름 전환
개들은 다른 감각도 사용하며, 한 번에 한 가지 감각을 증강하는 경향이 있다.

전개2 전환에 대한 부연 설명
많은 주인이 머리 모양을 새로 하거나 새 코트를 입고 집에 돌아왔을 때, 개가 달려든 적이 있다.

결론 요지 진술
결론적으로 개의 코는 뛰어나기는 하지만 항상 작동되어 있는 상태로 유지되는 것은 아니다.

우리는 개의 냄새를 맡는 능력에 대해 기대하면서 개들은 언제 어떤 것이든지 냄새를 맡을 수 있을 것이라고 추정하지만 개들은 한 번에 한 가지 감각을 증강하기 때문에 항상 냄새를 맡을 준비가 되어 있지 않다는 내용의 글이다. 글의 마지막 부분에 요지가 분명히 드러나 있다.

• SUB NOTE p. 48

유형 해결 전략

1 글의 전반적인 주제 혹은 요지를 파악한다.

글의 요지: 개도 한 번에 한 가지 감각을 증강하기 때문에 개는 냄새를 언제든지 잘 맡을 수 없다.

2 주어진 문장을 읽고, 그 내용을 정확히 파악해 둔다.

Surprised by the vision of an unfamiliar silhouette pushing into the house, these dogs were using their eyes instead of their noses. (낯선 검은 윤곽이 집으로 밀고 들어오는 것을 보고 깜짝 놀라, 이 개들은 코 대신 눈을 사용하고 있었다.)

→ 주어진 문장은 이 문장의 앞에 언급된 내용에 대해 설명하는 내용임을 추정할 수 있다.

3 글을 읽어가면서 흐름이 단절된 곳이나 논리적 비약이 있는 곳을 찾는다.

③ 뒤의 문장에서 글의 흐름 전환이 이루어지고 있으며, 개들이 한 번에 한 가지 감각을 증강한다는 내용으로 이에 대한 예가 ④ 뒤의 문장(Many owners have been snapped at by their dogs when they returned home with a new hairdo or a new coat.)에서 제시되고 있으므로, 두 문장은 유기적으로 연결되어 있다.

→ 많은 주인들이 머리 모양을 새로 하고 왔을 때 개가 달려드는 경험을 왜 하게 되는지에 대한 설명이 ④의 뒤의 문장 다음에 제시되어야 하는데, 주어진 문장은 ④의 뒤의 문장의 원인에 대한 설명이 되므로, 주어진 문장이 들어갈 가장 적절한 곳은 ⑤이다.

Bonus Tip

문제 풀이에 도움이 되는 주어진 문장의 특성

1. 연결사로 시작하는 경우

- for example이 있는 경우, 주어진 문장의 앞에는 좀 더 일반적이면서 주어진 문장과 같은 맥락의 문장이 올 것이다.
- however, in contrast 혹은 on the other hand가 있는 경우에는 주어진 문장부터 주제에 대한 다른 관점이 제시된다는 것에 유의한다.
- in other words가 있는 경우에는 주어진 문장과 같은 내용이지만 약간 다르게 표현된 문장이 앞에 나올 수 있다는 것에 유의한다.
- in addition, also, furthermore 등이 있는 경우에는 주어진 문장은 같은 맥락의 바로 뒷 문장에 온다는 것에 유의한다.
- similarly, likewise가 있는 경우, 주어진 문장부터는 앞에서 제시된 예와 다른 예가 제시되지만 근본적인 맥락은 같다는 것에 유의한다.

이외에도 다양한 연결사로 시작되는 경우에 그 연결사의 기능을 잘 파악해서 연결사를 문제 풀이의 단서로 사용할 수 있다.

2. 주어진 문장 속에 대명사가 있는 경우

주어진 문장 속에 대명사, 즉 it, they, them, he, she, him, her 등이 있는 경우가 있다. 이 경우 일반적으로 주어진 문장의 앞 문장 속에 각각의 대명사가 가리키는 명사가 존재하므로, 주어진 문장의 대명사와 수가 일치하는가 등을 따져보면 문제 풀이에 도움이 될 수 있다.

Exercise

01 글의 흐름으로 보아, 주어진 문장이 들어가기에 가장 적절한 곳은? 고2 교육청

> I once worked with a group of students in the final year of senior school, who listened out for the slang used in their school.

Slang is actually quite difficult for linguists to find out about. You will have your local slang that you use in your school or in your town, and there's no way I would ever know about it unless you told me what it was. (①) Indeed, in your area you'll probably have several different kinds of slang. (②) The slang that kids use in primary school is likely to be different from what is used in secondary school. (③) If your town has several schools, there are often differences in the kind of slang heard in each school. (④) And there may even be words that are used differently within a single school. (⑤) They found that the slang used by first-year students was very different from their own.

*slang: 은어, 속어

02 글의 흐름으로 보아, 주어진 문장이 들어가기에 가장 적절한 곳은? 고2 교육청

> Dyeing hair blond, for instance, was a common practice among ancient Roman men, as it was believed that blond hair provided a more youthful appearance.

There has been a huge rise in popularity of male grooming products. (①) Men all over the world are spending billions of dollars on everything from cosmetics to plastic surgery. (②) As to the reason for men's grooming, experts say that men consider their appearance as an important factor for social success. (③) Experts further searched the history of men's grooming for such cases in various countries. (④) Similarly, ancient Egyptian men regularly shaved their body hair and applied various cosmetics to their skin. (⑤) We could say appearance was important to men in the past and it certainly is to men in the present.

*grooming: 몸단장

• SUB NOTE p. 48

03 글의 흐름으로 보아, 주어진 문장이 들어가기에 가장 적절한 곳은? 평가원

Still, many believe we will eventually reach a point at which conflict with the finite nature of resources is inevitable.

Can we sustain our standard of living in the same ecological space while consuming the resources of that space? This question is particularly relevant since we are living in an era of skyrocketing fuel costs and humans' ever-growing carbon footprints. (①) Some argue that we are already at a breaking point because we have nearly exhausted the Earth's finite carrying capacity. (②) However, it's possible that innovations and cultural changes can expand Earth's capacity. (③) We are already seeing this as the world economies are increasingly looking at "green," renewable industries like solar and hydrogen energy. (④) That means survival could ultimately depend on getting the human population below its carrying capacity. (⑤) Otherwise, without population control, the demand for resources will eventually exceed an ecosystem's ability to provide it.

Plus Q

다음 두 문장의 빈칸에 공통으로 들어갈 단어를 윗글에서 찾아 쓰시오.

•Even a short walk ____________ her.
•Within three years they had ____________ their resources.

➡

01 senior school (영국의) 고등학교 linguist 언어학자 local 지역의, 현지의 unless ~하지 않으면 primary school 초등학교 secondary school 중등학교(11세에서 16세 또는 18세까지의 학생들이 다니는 학교)
02 dye 염색하다 ancient 고대의 blond 금발의 provide 주다, 공급하다 youthful 젊은 appearance 외모 huge 큰, 거대한 popularity 인기 male 남성의 product 상품 cosmetics 화장품 plastic surgery 성형 수술 as to ~에 관해 factor 요소 shave (털을) 깎다, 면도하다 apply 바르다
03 eventually 결국 conflict 갈등 finite 유한한 inevitable 불가피한 sustain 유지하다, 지속하다 ecological 생태의 relevant 적절한, 타당한 era 시대 skyrocketing 치솟는 carrying capacity 환경 수용력 innovation 혁신 renewable 재생 가능한 hydrogen 수소 ultimately 궁극적으로 exceed 초과하다

04 글의 흐름으로 보아, 주어진 문장이 들어가기에 가장 적절한 곳은?

> You wouldn't want that, so instead of writing you decide a private discussion would suit you just as well.

Let's assume an otherwise competent associate has ruined an important potential deal. (①) Your first inclination might be to fire off an angry, disappointed, and frustrated-sounding memo or e-mail. (②) On second thought you worry if the senior vice president somehow sees a copy, your coworker's job performance may be called into serious question, or worse. (③) The poor soul will still be able to perceive your feelings from your tone of voice and facial expressions. (④) Moreover, the strong disappointment you feel will be expressed, but so too will your understanding that occasionally things go wrong. (⑤) Nothing personal, you might say, only a friendly little chat that allows you to convey your point but allows the listener to know you don't hate him or her.

05 글의 흐름으로 보아, 주어진 문장이 들어가기에 가장 적절한 곳은?

> Eventually it was substituted with character by the bourgeoisie.

In the Medieval Age, when personal attention was focused more on securing a place in the next world, virtue was what every good Christian aspired to. (①) To lead a virtuous life and to be of good virtue assured eternal salvation. (②) In the Modern Age, virtue began drifting to the margins as society became increasingly production oriented. (③) By the nineteenth century, *character* had become one of the most important descriptive words in the English vocabulary. (④) The term *character* became associated with hard work, industriousness, frugality, and integrity, etc. (⑤) To be of good character was the highest compliment one could extend to a bourgeois man or woman.

*bourgeoisie: 유산계급

06 글의 흐름으로 보아, 주어진 문장이 들어가기에 가장 적절한 곳은?

> The goal of plantations is to produce wood products, with little or no regard to the many other services, resources, and habitat that real forests provide.

Rates of forest loss are especially high in Africa, Latin America, the Caribbean, and much of Asia. (①) According to reports, the exceptions are China and India, where large investments in forest plantations distort the data to hide the ongoing rates of loss of natural forests. (②) However, industrial timber plantations are very different from real forests. (③) To this end, they are generally intensely managed, evenly spaced, monoculture fields of imported species with the highest wood yields. (④) Such plantations are not helpful for biological diversity, resistance to disease, or provision of the many other nontimber forest products that people and animals depend on for survival. (⑤) Tree plantations can generally only sustain 10 percent of the species that lived in the forests and are best described as "green deserts!"

Plus Q

윗글의 내용과 일치하도록 빈칸에 적절한 단어를 본문에서 찾아 쓰시오. (단, 필요하면 어형을 바꿀 것)

> Plantations that produce industrial timbers do not provide enough resources that are necessary for the species in the forests to ____________.

➡

04 **suit** 적합하다 **otherwise** 다른 경우라면 **competent** 유능한 **associate** 동료 **potential** 잠재적인 **inclination** 경향, 성향 **fire off** (흔히 화가 나서 말 · 글을) 급히 하다[쓰다] **on second thought** 다시 생각해보고서 **call ~ into question** ~에 의문을 제기하다 **perceive** 인지하다 **tone of voice** 어조 **convey** 전달하다

05 **substitute** 대체하다 **character** 품성, 인격 **Medieval** 중세의 **attention** 관심 **secure** 확보하다 **aspire** 열망하다 **virtuous** 덕이 높은 **assure** 보장하다 **eternal** 영원한 **salvation** 구원 **drift** 표류하다 **margin** 가장자리 **oriented** ~지향인 **industriousness** 부지런함, 꾸준함 **frugality** 절약, 검소 **integrity** 진실성, 청렴

06 **plantation** 조림지 **regard** 고려, 배려 **resource** 자원 **habitat** 서식지 **rate** 속도, 비율 **loss** 손실 **exception** 예외 **investment** 투자 **distort** 왜곡하다 **ongoing** 현재 진행 중인 **timber** 목재 **intensely** 열심히, 굉장하게 **evenly** 고르게, 균등하게 **spaced** 공간이 띄어진 **monoculture** 단일 (작물) 재배 **biological** 생물적인 **diversity** 다양성 **resistance** 저항 **sustain** 부양하다, 지탱하다

유형

16 요약문 완성

글의 내용을 한 문장으로 요약한 문장의 빈칸 (A)와 (B)에 들어갈 적절한 어휘나 어구를 채워 넣는 유형으로 요지를 추론하는 유형의 변형이라고 볼 수 있다. 따라서 글을 읽으면서 요지를 파악하고 자신이 파악한 요지와 제시된 요약문을 비교하면서 빈칸에 어울리는 어구를 선택지에서 고르면 된다. 중급 정도의 난이도에 속하는 유형으로, 수능에서는 매년 1문항씩 출제되고 있다.

대표 예제

다음 글의 내용을 한 문장으로 요약하고자 한다. 빈칸 (A)와 (B)에 들어갈 말로 가장 적절한 것은? 수능

도입 Performance must be judged in terms of what is under the control of the individuals being evaluated rather than those influences on performance that are beyond their control. 전개1 There can be broad, influential factors, sometimes of an economic nature, that hold down the performance of everyone being judged. 전개2 One example is in sales. If there is a general downturn in the economy and products or services are not being purchased with the same frequency as in the previous year, sales could be down, for example, by an average of 15%. This 15% (actually −15%) figure would then represent "average" performance. Perhaps the best salesperson in the year had only a 3% drop in sales over the previous year. 결론 Thus, "good" performance in this situation is a smaller loss compared to some average or norm group.

In performance evaluation, we should consider ____(A)____ factors affecting the individual's performance rather than ____(B)____ figures only.

한눈에 보는 구조

도입 **주제 제시**
실적은 평가를 받는 개인의 통제 하에 있는 것의 측면에서 판단되어야 한다.

전개1 **주제에 대한 부연 설명**
판단을 받고 있는 모든 사람에게 영향을 미치는 광범위한 실적 억제 요인이 있을 수 있다.

전개2 **주제에 대한 예시**
매출액이 15%만큼 감소되었을 때 이 수치가 '평균' 실적을 나타낼 것이다. 하지만 그 해의 가장 우수한 사원은 3%만 감소했을 것이다.

결론 **주제의 구체화**
제시된 상황에서 '훌륭한' 실적은 기준 집단과 비교했을 때 더 적은 양의 감소를 말한다. 즉, 실적 평가에서 단순한 수치만을 보기보다 상황적인 요인을 고려해야 한다.

실적 평가는 평가를 받는 개인의 통제 하에 있는 것의 측면에서 판단되어야 한다는 내용의 글로, 도입부에 주제가 분명히 드러나며 매출액의 예를 통해 주제를 구체화하고 있다.

	(A)		(B)
①	contextual	……	put aside
②	contextual	……	rely on
③	controllable	……	put aside
④	positive	……	ignore
⑤	positive	……	rely on

유형 해결 전략

1 글의 도입부를 통해 주제를 파악한다.

Performance must be judged in terms of what is under the control of the individuals being evaluated rather than those influences on performance that are beyond their control.

→ 글의 주제는 '개인이 통제할 수 있는 것에 의해서 이루어져야 하는 개인의 실적에 대한 평가'이다.

2 글의 중반부를 읽으면서 주제를 구체화하기 위해 제시된 단서들을 확보한다.

주제를 구체화하기 위해 제시된 예: 매출액 변동에 대한 분석
_ 전반적인 경기 침체로 이전 해보다 평균 15%의 매출액 감소
_ 하지만 그 해의 가장 우수한 사원은 단지 3%만 감소함

→ 우수한 사원의 감소량과 평균 매출 감소량을 비교했을 때 우수한 사원은 '훌륭한' 실적을 냈다고 평가할 수 있다.

3 수집된 단서를 기반으로 요약문을 읽고, 빈칸에 들어갈 가장 적절한 선택지를 고른다.

(A) 평균 매출 감소량과 우수한 사원의 감소량을 비교해서 우수성을 평가해야 한다는 의미는 상황적인 요소를 고려해야 한다는 것을 의미한다. → contextual(상황적인)이 적절하다.
(B) 실적 평가를 할 때 단순한 수치, 즉 평균 매출 감소량에만 의존해서 그것을 모두에게 적용하는 것은 지양해야 한다는 맥락이다. → rely on(의존하다)이 적절하다.

Bonus Tip

요약문 완성의 지문 소재에 따른 문항 풀이 방법

(1) 실험에 대한 과정과 결과를 설명한 지문
이 경우 요약문에 반영이 되는 것은 실험의 결과가 기술되는 지문의 후반부 내용이다. 그러므로 실험의 과정이 설명된 지문이 요약문 지문으로 사용되었을 경우에는, 실험의 결과가 기술된 부분이나 주제문의 역할을 하는 문장을 찾아 주의 깊게 볼 필요가 있다.
(2) 인문학의 여러 분야와 관련된 내용이 설명되어 있는 지문
심리학, 인류학, 경영학 등에 관한 내용으로 각각의 학문에서 사용되는 특정한 개념, 사건, 혹은 상황에 대한 내용이 등장한다. 이러한 소재가 사용된 지문에는 지문을 대표하는 주제문이 없는 것이 일반적이다. 따라서 독해를 하면서 필자가 말하고자 하는 글의 요지가 무엇인지를 추론해야 한다.

Exercise

01 다음 글의 내용을 한 문장으로 요약하고자 한다. 빈칸 (A)와 (B)에 들어갈 말로 가장 적절한 것은? 고2 교육청

When I was in eighth grade, we were studying longitude and latitude in geography class. Every day for a week, we had a quiz, and I kept getting longitude and latitude confused. I went home and almost cried because I was so frustrated and embarrassed that I couldn't keep them straight in my mind. I stared and stared at those words until suddenly I figured out what to do. I told myself, when you see that *n* in longitude it will remind you of the word *north*. Therefore, it will be easy to remember that longitude lines go from north to south. It worked; I got them all right on the next quiz, and the next, and on the test.

*longitude: 경도 **latitude: 위도

→ The above story suggests that ___(A)___ what you are learning with what you already know helps you ___(B)___ the learning material.

	(A)		(B)
①	associating	……	memorize
②	associating	……	publish
③	presenting	……	publish
④	replacing	……	evaluate
⑤	replacing	……	memorize

02 다음 글의 내용을 한 문장으로 요약하고자 한다. 빈칸 (A)와 (B)에 들어갈 말로 가장 적절한 것은? 평가원

Certain species are more crucial to the maintenance of their ecosystem than others. Such species, called keystone species, are vital in determining the nature and structure of the entire ecosystem. The fact that other species depend on or are greatly affected by the keystone species is revealed when the keystone species is removed. It is in this sense that we should draw attention to fig trees. Different species of fig trees may be keystone species in tropical rain forests. Although figs collectively produce a continuous crop of fruits, fruit-eating monkeys, birds, bats, and other vertebrates of the forest do not normally consume large quantities of figs in their diets. During the time of year when other fruits are less plentiful, however, fig trees become important in sustaining fruit-eating vertebrates. **Should the fig trees disappear**, most of the fruit-eating vertebrates would be eliminated. Protecting fig trees in such tropical rainforest ecosystems is an important conservation goal because it increases the likelihood that monkeys, birds, bats, and other vertebrates will survive.

*fig: 무화과 **vertebrate: 척추동물

→ As a keystone species in tropical rain forests, fig trees support fruit-eating animals' survival when other fruits are ____(A)____, and thus ____(B)____ their ecosystem.

	(A)		(B)
①	insufficient	……	preserve
②	insufficient	……	create
③	poisonous	……	purify
④	poisonous	……	reshape
⑤	abundant	……	clean

Plus Q

윗글의 밑줄 친 **Should the fig trees disappear를 If**로 시작되는 어구로 다시 쓰시오.

➡

01 **geography** 지리 **confused** 혼동하는 **frustrated** 좌절한 **embarrassed** 창피한, 난처해 하는 **stare** 바라보다 **figure out** 알아차리다 **associate** 관련지어 생각하다, 연상

02 **crucial** 결정적인, 중대한 **maintenance** 유지 **ecosystem** 생태계 **keystone species** 핵심종 **vital** 매우 중요한 **determine** 결정하다 **structure** 구조 **reveal** 드러내다 **crop** 수확; 곡물 **sustain** 먹여 살리다, 부양하다 **eliminate** 제거하다, 없애다 **conservation** 보존 **likelihood** 가능성 **poisonous** 독이 있는 **purify** 정화하다 **reshape** 모양을 새로 만들다 **abundant** 풍부한

03 다음 글의 내용을 한 문장으로 요약하고자 한다. 빈칸 (A)와 (B)에 들어갈 말로 가장 적절한 것은?

Mention the word manliness these days and you'll probably be greeted with giggles. Many people today associate manliness with cartoonish images of men sitting on their sofas, drinking beer and watching the big game. Or, just as likely, they don't think much about manliness at all. Whatever image they have in mind when you mention "manliness," it is just a laughing matter, and it probably has nothing to do with virtue. But if you search the annals of Western thought, you'll probably discover that this shallow conception of manliness is relatively new. For two thousand years, many of the world's great thinkers explored the subject of manliness, imagining it not as something silly. Instead, they considered it as the culmination of the virtues as expressed in the life of a man. Manliness was considered a virtue in and of itself, the attainment of which had to be actively sought.

→ Manliness, although generally described as ___(A)___ these days, had been regarded as something worth ___(B)___.

	(A)		(B)
①	negative	……	escaping
②	negative	……	pursuing
③	acceptable	……	pursuing
④	acceptable	……	reporting
⑤	comparative	……	escaping

04 다음 글의 내용을 한 문장으로 요약하고자 한다. 빈칸 (A)와 (B)에 들어갈 말로 가장 적절한 것은?

Even though science is about material things and physical relationships, and is represented in technologies and artifacts, it is shared through words and formulae. Almost all of what any biologist knows about evolutionary theory, for example, will not have come from observing material evidence but from communicating, through language, with other biologists. Ask chemists to explain the Periodic Table and they will use names for the elements which were given to them by other chemists. Astronomers and physicists know about 'supernovas'; however, what they know is not just the result of looking through their telescopes but of reading and hearing how their colleagues have tried to explain the data at **their** disposal.

*Periodic Table: 주기율표 **supernova: 초신성

> → Most scientific knowledge is acquired not by the scientist's ____(A)____ scientific experiences, but by ____(B)____ what he or she knows through language.

	(A)		(B)
①	individual	……	sharing
②	individual	……	asserting
③	essential	……	sharing
④	unexpected	……	asserting
⑤	unexpected	……	specifying

Plus Q

밑줄 친 **their**가 가리키는 것을 본문에서 찾아 쓰시오.

➡

03 manliness 남성다움 giggle 킥킥 웃음 associate 연관시키다, 관련시키다 cartoonish 만화 같은 have nothing to do with ~와 관련이 없다 virtue 덕행 annals 기록 shallow 천박한, 피상적인 conception 개념 culmination 정점 attainment 달성 pursue 추구하다

04 material 물질적인 physical 물리적인 represent 대표하다 artifact 인공물 formula 공식 (*pl.* formulae) evolutionary 진화의 observe 관찰하다 evidence 증거 chemist 화학자 element 원소, 요소 astronomer 천문학자 physicist 물리학자 telescope 망원경 colleague 동료 at one's disposal 자신의 마음대로

유형

17 장문 독해(1) 일반 장문

230단어 정도의 긴 글을 읽고 제목 추론과 빈칸 추론의 두 개의 물음에 답해야 하는 유형으로, 글의 전체적인 내용을 토대로 제목 문항을 풀고, 빈칸 앞뒤 문장의 흐름과 글의 주제를 고려하여 빈칸 문항을 풀도록 한다. 내용 일치 파악이나 지칭 추론을 묻는 질문이 출제된 경우도 있으며 연결사나 심경을 묻는 문항 등으로 다양하게 출제될 소지가 있다.

대표 예제

다음 글을 읽고, 물음에 답하시오. 수능

도입 We might describe science that has no known practical value as basic science or basic research. Our exploration of worlds such as Jupiter would be called basic science, and it is easy to argue that basic science is not worth the effort and expense because it has no known practical use. Of course, the problem is that we have no way of knowing what knowledge will be of use until we acquire that knowledge. 전개 In the middle of the 19th century, Queen Victoria is supposed to have asked physicist Michael Faraday what good his experiments with electricity and magnetism were. He answered, "Madam, what good is a baby?" Of course, Faraday's experiments were the beginning of the electronic age. 결론1 Many of the practical uses of scientific knowledge that fill our world — transistors, vaccines, plastics — began as basic research. Basic scientific research provides the raw materials that technology and engineering use to solve problems. 결론2 Basic scientific research has yet one more important use that is so valuable it seems an insult to refer to it as merely functional. Science is the study of nature, and as we learn more about how nature works, we learn more about what our existence in this universe means for us. The seemingly ____________ knowledge we gain from space probes to other worlds tells us about our planet and our own role in the scheme of nature. Science tells us where we are and what we are, and that knowledge is beyond value.

*space probe: 우주탐사기(機)

한눈에 보는 구조

도입 **통념 제시**
목성 탐사와 같은 기초과학은 실용적 가치를 지니지 않아서, 노력과 비용을 들일만한 가치가 없다고 주장하기 쉽다.

전개 **사례를 통한 통념 비판**
Victoria 여왕의 질문에 대한 Faraday의 대답을 예로 들어 기초과학이 무가치하다는 통념을 비판한다.

결론1 **주제 제시** 1
과학의 많은 실용적 용도가 처음에는 기초과학으로 시작되었다.

결론2 **주제 제시** 2
자연의 섭리에 대해 연구하는 기초과학은 가치를 따질 수 없다.

기초과학은 실용적이지 않다는 통념에 대해 Faraday의 사례를 통해 반박하고 있으며 자연의 섭리에 대해 연구하는 기초과학은 실용성의 여부를 떠나 그 가치를 따질 수가 없는 것이라고 말하는 내용의 글이다.

01 윗글의 제목으로 가장 적절한 것은?

① What Does Basic Science Bring to Us?
② The Crisis of Researchers in Basic Science
③ Common Goals of Science and Technology
④ Technology: The Ultimate Aim of Basic Science
⑤ Michael Faraday, Frontiersman of the Electronic Age!

02 윗글의 빈칸에 들어갈 말로 가장 적절한 것은?

① applicable ② impractical ③ inaccurate
④ priceless ⑤ resourceful

유형 해결 전략

1 주어진 글이 무엇에 관한 내용인지 파악한다.

첫 번째 문단은 기초과학이 실용적인 가치가 없는 것처럼 보일지라도 그 판단은 섣불리 내릴 수 없으며 실제 많은 과학적 지식의 실용적 사용은 기초연구로부터 시작되었다는 내용이다.
두 번째 문단은 기초과학 연구가 자연에 대한 연구로서 우리가 누구인지, 우리가 어디에 있는지, 우리의 역할은 무엇인지를 알려주는 학문으로 실용성의 여부를 떠나 그 가치를 따질 수 없을 만큼 중요하다는 내용이다.

2 글 전체를 포괄하는 제목으로 알맞은 표현을 찾는다.

첫 번째 문단과 두 번째 문단 모두 기초과학을 통해 얻을 수 있는 가치에 대해 말하고 있으므로, 글의 제목으로는 ① '기초과학이 우리에게 무엇을 가져다 주는가?'가 가장 적절하다.

3 빈칸에 들어갈 말을 찾기 위해 빈칸 앞뒤 문맥을 정확하게 파악한다.

빈칸 앞에서 과학은 우주 안에서의 인간 존재의 의미에 대해 알 수 있게 해주며, 그것은 단순히 기능적인 실용성의 여부로 판단할 수 없다고 했다. 따라서 빈칸이 있는 문장은 우주 탐사와 같은 겉보기에는 '비실용적'으로 보이는 지식으로부터 우리가 사는 행성과 그속에서의 우리의 역할에 대해 파악할 수 있다는 내용이 되는 것이 문맥상 자연스러우므로, 빈칸에는 ② '비실용적인'이 들어가는 것이 가장 적절하다.

Exercise

[01~02] 다음 글을 읽고, 물음에 답하시오. 고2 교육청

Today's consumers are not just looking for a good product at a fair price. They are looking beyond the product or service to the ethics of the company that supplies it. The shift in focus by consumers is evident in their concerns about the companies they purchase from. For example, there is growing interest in labor practices, environmental policies, and social responsibilities. Also, there is a pressure to get companies to present not just financial results, but also social and environmental results and impact. Companies need to respond to the pressure because customers are voicing their concerns in every way, from boycotting stores to suing companies. Some multinational companies have experienced the ____________ of ethical consumers in recent years, and have been forced to respond quickly to protect their reputations and their existence as companies.

This growing emphasis on ethical consumption is a trend that cannot be ignored. It is not going to go away. There are some important changes in the world indicating that ethical consumers will continue to be a growing force in the next few decades. Companies would do well to understand **this trend** and make efforts to deal with it.

*sue: 고소하다, 소송을 제기하다

01 윗글의 제목으로 가장 적절한 것은?

① Growing Concerns on Unemployment Rates
② Importance of Diverse Marketing Strategies
③ Multinational Companies: Burden on Nations
④ Fair Trade vs. Free Trade: Rivaling Concepts
⑤ Ever Increasing Trend of Ethical Consumerism

02 윗글의 빈칸에 들어갈 말로 가장 적절한 것은?

① anger
② decrease
③ dishonesty
④ inefficiency
⑤ helplessness

Plus Q

밑줄 친 this trend가 가리키는 것을 본문에서 찾아 쓰시오.

➡ ....

[03~04] 다음 글을 읽고, 물음에 답하시오. 고3 교육청

Ta-Nahesi Coates, a senior editor at *The Atlantic Monthly*, ran a personal blog for years. Coates posts daily on a wide array of subjects: movies, politics, economic inequalities, the Civil War, TV shows, favorite poems, or whether pro football is too dangerous to play. Coates, who is African American, is also well known as an eloquent writer on race, and he posts about that frequently. Yet his blog is amazingly abuse-free: comments spill into the hundreds without going off the rails. "This is the most hot-button issue in America, and folks have managed to keep a fairly level head," he says.

The secret is the work Coates puts into his discussion board. Before he was a blogger himself, he'd noticed the terrible comments at his favorite political blogs. Coates realized that negative comments create a loop: they poison the atmosphere, chasing off productive posters. So when he started his own personal blog, he decided to break that loop. The instant he saw something abusive, he'd delete it, banning repeat offenders. Meanwhile, he went out of his way to encourage the smart folks, responding to them personally and publicly, so they'd be encouraged to stay and talk. And Coates was unfailingly polite and courteous himself, to help set community standards. Soon several dozen regular commenters emerged, and they got to know each other, talking as much to each other as to Coates. Their cohesion helped cement the culture of ____________ even more; anyone today who looks at the blog can quickly tell this community isn't going to tolerate nastiness.

03 윗글의 제목으로 가장 적절한 것은?

① A Successful Blogger Knows How to Manage Comments
② Blogging Is a Good Way to Promote Your Business
③ Blog: A Window to See Another Foreign Culture
④ Share Hobbies with People Through Your Blog
⑤ Personal Information Slips Out of Your Blog

04 윗글의 빈칸에 들어갈 말로 가장 적절한 것은?

① civility
② competition
③ independence
④ disbelief
⑤ privacy

01~02 **consumer** 소비자 **fair** 타당한, 온당한 **ethics** 윤리 **evident** 분명한 **concern** 관심, 걱정 **labor practices** 노동 관행 **policy** 정책 **responsibility** 책임 **financial** 금전적인 **voice** 목소리를 내다 **boycott** 불매 동맹하다 **multinational** 다국적인 **reputation** 평판, 명성 **emphasis** 중요성, 강조 **trend** 추세 **ignore** 무시하다 **indicate** 알려 주다, 가리키다 **do well to** ~하는 것이 현명하다 **make efforts** 노력하다 **unemployment** 실업 **diverse** 다양한 **burden** 부담, 짐 **consumerism** 소비주의

03~04 **senior editor** 선임 편집자 **subject** 주제 **eloquent** 설득력 있는 **abuse-free** 욕설이 없는 **go off the rails** 정도를 벗어나다 **hot-button** 뜨거운, 큰 반향을 불러일으키는 **keep a level head** 분별이 있다 **loop** 고리 **poison** 나쁜 영향을 주다 **chase off** 쫓아내다 **productive** 생산적인, 건설적인 **abusive** 모욕적인 **delete** 삭제하다 **ban** 막다, 금하다 **offender** 남의 감정을 해치는 사람 **respond to** ~에 반응하다 **unfailingly** 변함없이 **courteous** 공손한 **emerge** 나타나다 **cohesion** 결속, 응집성 **cement** 견고하게 하다, 다지다 **tolerate** 용인하다 **nastiness** 불쾌함, 비열함 **civility** 예의바름, 공손함

[05~06] 다음 글을 읽고, 물음에 답하시오.

The World Wide Web offers advantages and benefits that were previously available only to professional investors. Foremost is the convenience of being able to access vast amounts of stock market data and information at any time. Anxious investors no longer have to wait until regular office hours to retrieve critical information from their stockbrokers. This information can now be accessed from their homes, offices, or any locations that allow them access to the Internet.

Internet users are no longer limited to outdated news through periodic sources such as newspapers or end-of-day television or radio broadcasts. As soon as news is released or hits the wire, Web users can access that information in real time. Such rapid spreading of information benefits individual investors. ____________ data allow them to make better informed decisions. In addition, many investors who use online brokerage services find that their trades are executed much more efficiently and rapidly than when they made buy / sell phone calls to their stockbrokers. The Internet also provides serious investors with a wide variety of analysis tools. These tools range from simple graphs and charts of historical data to a complex technical analysis that predicts the movement of stock prices. All these tools help investors by providing better information that affects their investment decisions.

05 윗글의 제목으로 가장 적절한 것은?

① How To Become a Successful Stockbroker
② The Lack of Investment in the Internet Marketing
③ The Impact of the Internet on Individual Investors
④ Be Careful, Avoid False Information on the Internet
⑤ Addicted to Trading: Online Investors Become Gamblers

06 윗글의 빈칸에 들어갈 말로 가장 적절한 것은?

① Raw
② Timely
③ Personal
④ Historical
⑤ Quantitative

Plus Q

다음 문장의 빈칸에 들어갈 단어를 본문에서 찾아 쓰시오.

________ events or situations happen occasionally, at fairly regular intervals.

➡

[07~08] 다음 글을 읽고, 물음에 답하시오.

It is hard to understand why Koreans love spicy chili peppers more than any other country. Their chili pepper consumption rose 40% from 5.2 g per person a day in 1998 to 7.2 g in 2005. The annual consumption per person is 2.6 kg, a world record. Why do they love hot chili pepper even though it is so spicy? In 1997, Professor David Julius's team at the University of California, San Francisco, solved this secret. TRPV1, one of several heat sensors in our bodies, detects high temperatures over 43°C in order to prevent burns. When we eat hot chili, capsaicin in the chili pepper binds with TRPV1 and sends heat and pain signals to the cerebrum. TRPV1 also senses the pungent chemical of wasabi and horseradish, that is, allyl isothiocyanates. There is no actual temperature increase from these chemicals, TRPV1 just sends the heat signals. The brain, thinking that we are exposed to a high temperature, reacts to lower the heat and makes the body sweat. From the brain's perspective, it is completely ____________, but we do feel heat after eating chili peppers and we use the descriptive word hot as a synonym for spicy. Endorphin is released after this heat and pain perception. This is a chemical substance released naturally from the brain when our body feels pain, which has a pain-relieving effect 100 times stronger than narcotics. This is why people are addicted to spicy foods. The more capsaicin is consumed, the more stimulation to TRPV1 occurs and the brain releases more endorphin, and overall the level of pleasure to the spiciness increases.

07 윗글의 제목으로 가장 적절한 것은?

① Use of Spices as Medicines
② Different Regions, Different Spices
③ Healthy Recipes Featuring Chili Peppers
④ Nutritional Values Contained in the Spices
⑤ Science Explains Why We Like Spicy Food

08 윗글의 빈칸에 들어갈 말로 가장 적절한 것은?

① fooled
② changed
③ damaged
④ examined
⑤ protected

05~06 **previously** 예전에 **foremost** 주요한, 가장 중요한 **convenience** 편리함 **access** 접속하다 **stock market** 주식 시장 **retrieve** (정보를) 검색하다, 알아내다 **stockbroker** 주식 중개인 **outdated** 구식의, 진부한 **periodic** 간헐적인, 정기적인 **release** 발표하다 **spreading** 확산 **brokerage** (주식) 중개 **execute** 실행하다 **analysis** 분석 **predict** 예측하다

07~08 **spicy** 매운 **chili pepper** 고추 **consumption** 소비, 섭취 **detect** 감지하다 **capsaicin** 캅사이신(고추의 매운 성분) **cerebrum** 대뇌 **pungent** 매운, 자극이 강한 **horseradish** 서양고추냉이 **expose** 노출시키다 **descriptive** 기술(記述)적인 **synonym** 유의어 **release** 배출[분비]시키다 **perception** 인식, 인지 **substance** 물질 **pain-relieving effect** 진통 효과 **narcotic** 마약 **addicted** 중독된 **stimulation** 자극

유형

18 장문 독해(2) 순서 장문

주어진 글 (A)에 이어질 (B), (C), (D)의 순서 배열, 밑줄 친 대상이 다른 하나를 고르는 지칭 추론, 지문의 내용과 같은 것 또는 다른 것을 고르는 내용 일치 문제가 하나의 긴 지문에 묶여있는 유형이다. 지문만 길게 출제될 뿐 내용은 오히려 쉬운 경우가 많으므로, 지문 길이에 신경 쓰지 말고 침착하게 문제를 풀면 된다.

대표 예제

다음 글을 읽고, 물음에 답하시오. 수능

(A)

발단 The midday sun was glorious. The high school grounds were filled with well-dressed people, posing in fancy dresses and suits for cheerful photographers. Congratulations, hugs, and laughter were contagious. Hannah looked at all the familiar faces that had been part of (a) her life for the last few years. Soon her mother would be joining them. She recalled the first day of school when she had stood in that same place, in the middle of many anxious freshmen, some of whom had become her closest friends.

(B)

결말 "Hannah, you look so serious. What are you thinking about?" "Oh, Mom, just, you know." Her mother smiled. "You'll miss this place, won't you?" Hannah nodded. "Quick," her mother said, "stand over there... and smile, Hannah. You have such a pretty smile." (b) She hurried out her cell phone, zoomed in on her daughter, and realized suddenly that she was looking at a young lady. "You're all grown-up," she whispered. Hannah took more photos with her teachers in the school garden. She wished all the memories would remain in her mind forever.

한눈에 보는 구조

발단 졸업식에 참석한 Hannah는 어머니를 기다리면서 학교에서의 첫날을 기억해냈다.

전개 그날(고등학교에서의 첫날) Hannah는 긴장했다. 고등학교 생활은 도전적이라는 것이 곧 드러났다.

절정 많은 수업 시간, 끝없는 과제, 시험과 씨름했지만, 운동회, 축제 같은 신나는 행사도 있었다. Hannah의 생각이 떠도는 사이에 어머니가 오셨다.

결말 어머니는 휴대전화 렌즈로 Hannah를 바라보며 그녀가 다 컸다는 것을 갑자기 깨달았다. Hannah는 모든 추억이 영원히 기억되기를 바랐다.

졸업식 날에 고등학교 생활의 추억을 회상하며, 그 추억이 영원히 기억되기를 현재→과거→현재의 순으로 서술하고 있다.

(C)

절정 Hannah struggled with the many class hours, the endless assignments, and the exams. However, there were exciting events like sports days and school festivals. How could (c) she ever forget her second year! She had sung and danced with her friends in the festival, part of a sensational performance. After that, she had become more confident and active. Her thoughts wandering, Hannah vaguely heard her mother's voice. "Here you are!" Her mother hurried over, and gave (d) her a bundle of lilies and roses and a big hug.

(D)

전개 That day was unusually foggy as if something mysterious were ahead. Hannah was nervous and trembling. The principal was energetically addressing them, talking of the challenges and thrills of high school life, but she could not concentrate. Later, a tall, strict-looking man introduced himself as (e) her homeroom teacher. The classroom was old, but neat and inviting. Hannah was seated in the fifth row, hallway side, even though she had wanted a window seat. High school life soon proved as challenging as the principal had predicted.

---

01 주어진 글 (A)에 이어질 내용을 순서에 맞게 배열한 것으로 가장 적절한 것은?

① (B) – (D) – (C)　② (C) – (B) – (D)
③ (C) – (D) – (B)　④ (D) – (B) – (C)
⑤ (D) – (C) – (B)

02 밑줄 친 (a)~(e) 중에서 가리키는 대상이 나머지 넷과 다른 것은?

① (a)　② (b)　③ (c)　④ (d)　⑤ (e)

03 윗글의 Hannah에 관한 내용과 일치하지 않는 것은?

① 다른 신입생들과 함께 운동장에 서 있었다.
② 학교 정원에서 선생님들과 사진을 찍었다.
③ 축제에서 노래를 부르고 춤을 추었다.
④ 교장 선생님의 말씀에 집중할 수가 없었다.
⑤ 교실에서 다섯 번째 줄 창가 자리에 앉았다.

유형 해결 전략

1 문제를 먼저 확인한 후 주어진 문단 (A)를 읽는다.

(A)의 내용 → 졸업식에 참석한 Hannah는 어머니를 기다리면서 학교에서의 첫날을 기억해냈다.

2 주어진 문단 (A)에 이어질 단락의 순서부터 정한다.

각 단락의 마지막 문장과 이어질 단락의 첫 문장에서 연결 고리를 찾아 순서를 배열하면 된다. 대명사, 정관사, 고유명사, 연결사 등이 연결 고리를 찾는 데 단서가 된다.

(B) 단락
첫 문장: "Hannah, you look so serious. What are you thinking about?" "Oh, Mom, just, you know."
마지막 문장: She wished all the memories would remain in her mind forever.

(C) 단락
첫 문장: Hannah struggled with the many class hours, the endless assignments, and the exams.
마지막 문장: Her mother hurried over, and gave (d) her a bundle of lilies and roses and a big hug.

(D) 단락
첫 문장: That day was unusually foggy as if something mysterious were ahead.
마지막 문장: High school life soon proved as challenging as the principal had predicted.

→ (A)의 마지막 문장 the first day of school과 (D)의 첫 문장 That day, (D)의 마지막 문장 challenging과 (C)의 첫 문장 struggled, (C)의 마지막 문장 Her mother와 (B)의 첫 문장 Mom이 연결 고리를 형성한다. 따라서 주어진 글 (A)에 이어질 적절한 글의 순서는 (D)–(C)–(B)이다.

3 순서가 정해지면, 밑줄 친 대명사가 포함된 문장을 중심으로 읽으며 지칭하는 바를 파악한다.

(a)가 Hannah를 가리키므로 (b)~(e)까지 Hannah를 대입해서 읽는다. (b)에 Hannah를 대입하면, 'Hannah는 자신의 휴대전화를 서둘러 꺼내, 줌 렌즈로 자신의 딸을 서서히 확대했다.'는 어색한 문장이 되므로 가리키는 대상이 다른 것은 (b)이다. (b)는 Hannah의 어머니를 가리킨다.

4 내용 일치 문제의 선택지는 지문에 제시된 순서대로 구성되고, 각 문단에서 최소 하나씩은 제시되므로 문단을 읽고 선택지의 내용을 살피며 일치 여부를 파악한다.

① (A) 단락: She recalled the first day of school when she had stood in that same place, in the middle of many anxious freshmen, ~.

→ 많은 신입생들의 한가운데에서 자신이 똑같은 곳(운동장)에 서 있었던 학교에서의 첫날을 기억해냈다고 했으므로 글의 내용과 일치한다.

② (B) 단락: Hannah took more photos with her teachers in the school garden.

→ 학교 정원에서 선생님들과 사진을 더 찍었다고 했으므로 글의 내용과 일치한다.

③ (C) 단락: She had sung and danced with her friends in the festival, part of a sensational performance.

→ 축제에서 친구들과 함께 노래를 부르고, 춤을 추었다고 했으므로 글의 내용과 일치한다.

④ (D) 단락: The principal was energetically addressing them, talking of the challenges and thrills of high school life, but she could not concentrate.

→ 교장 선생님이 고등학교 생활에 대해 이야기하고 계셨지만 집중할 수가 없었다고 했으므로 글의 내용과 일치한다.

⑤ (D) 단락: Hannah was seated in the fifth row, hallway side, even though she had wanted a window seat.

→ Hannah는 다섯 번째 줄 복도 쪽 자리에 앉았다고 했으므로 글의 내용과 일치하지 않는다.

Bonus Tip

장문 독해는 지문을 읽기 전에 문제부터 파악한다.

지문을 읽기 전에, 문제를 먼저 보고 각각의 유형을 파악해 둔다. 각 유형별로 풀이 방법이 다르므로, 유형 확인 후 각각에 맞는 유형 풀이 방법을 적용해야 한다. 문제의 유형을 확인하는 것에 그치지 않고 각 문제의 선택지도 미리 확인해 두면 문제 풀이에 도움이 된다. 문제의 선택지를 먼저 읽고 지문을 읽게 되면 대략적인 소재 및 주제, 그리고 글의 흐름을 파악하는 데 걸리는 시간이 많이 단축되기 때문이다.

모든 문장을 자세하고 분석적으로 읽기보다는 내용 파악 위주로 빠르게 읽는다.

장문 독해는 짧은 시간 안에 긴 글을 모두 읽고 판단할 수 있어야 하므로, 지나치게 모든 문장을 자세하게 읽을 필요는 없다. 일반 장문의 경우는, 글 전체에서 강조되고 있는 키워드를 중심으로 이해하도록 하며, 순서 장문의 경우는 소재가 어렵지 않게 출제되므로 각 단락의 첫 부분과 마지막 부분에 주의하며 글의 흐름 위주로 글을 읽어 나가면 어렵지 않게 풀 수 있다.

Exercise

[01~03] 다음 글을 읽고, 물음에 답하시오. 고2 교육청

(A)

William Miller stayed up after the family had gone to bed, then read until the morning. Candles were expensive, but there were plenty of pine knots, and all (a) he had to do was gather them from the woods. So William formed the habit of burning pine knots in the fireplace for his nightly reading light.

*pine knot: 관솔(송진이 엉긴 소나무의 옹이)

(B)

William's "secret life" continued for some time, though. Night after night he read as long as he could, then made (b) his way back upstairs, and slept until it was time to do the morning chores. But one night something happened that he hadn't expected. His father awoke and saw a glow downstairs. Thinking the house was on fire, (c) he came rushing down the stairs to save his home and family from going up in flames.

(C)

Instead of a house fire, however, he saw his son William lying peacefully before the fireplace reading a book he'd borrowed from a neighbor. His father grabbed a broomstick and chased his son around the room, yelling, "Young man, if you don't get to bed right now, I'll kick you out of the house!" William went up to bed, at least for this night. (d) He was only trying to get an education that he couldn't get from the teachers in the community.

(D)

But his father didn't like the habit and tried to stop it. His father felt that his son's late-night reading would cut into (e) his energy for the next day's work. And the farm required every ounce of work he could get from his son. He insisted that William retire for the night when the rest of the family did. And his father thought the growing boy should sleep soundly through the night.

• SUB NOTE p. 58

01 주어진 글 (A)에 이어질 내용을 순서에 맞게 배열한 것으로 가장 적절한 것은?

① (B) – (D) – (C)
② (C) – (B) – (D)
③ (C) – (D) – (B)
④ (D) – (B) – (C)
⑤ (D) – (C) – (B)

02 밑줄 친 (a)~(e) 중에서 가리키는 대상이 나머지 넷과 다른 것은?

① (a) ② (b) ③ (c) ④ (d) ⑤ (e)

03 윗글의 내용과 일치하지 않는 것은?

① William은 관솔을 태워 그 빛으로 책을 읽었다.
② 아버지는 밤에 일어나서 아래층의 불빛을 보았다.
③ William은 벽난로 앞에서 자다가 아버지에게 발각되었다.
④ 아버지는 빗자루를 들고 William을 쫓아다녔다.
⑤ 아버지는 William이 밤 늦게 책 읽는 것을 싫어했다.

Plus Q

밑줄 친 **William's "secret life"**가 가리키는 것을 **(D)**단락에서 찾아 두 단어로 쓰시오.

➡

[04~06] 다음 글을 읽고, 물음에 답하시오. 고3 교육청

(A)

The last Saturday of each month was always a highlight in Adrian's life. He and his dad had a regular fishing date. Adrian learned a lot about fishing and about life on these expeditions. (a) His father pointed out that there are some rocks that are too dangerous to go onto, even when the sea looks calm. It might look like a perfect spot for fishing, but rocks that are too close to the water's edge can be deceptively dangerous.

(B)

When he did so, he started catching really big fish — and his mom was delighted with the fresh fish she could cook for supper. Adrian gradually realized that it pays to listen to people with experience and knowledge of dangerous places. He also realized how stupid it was not to listen to his dad who gave (b) him precious advice free of charge!

(C)

On top of that, (c) he soon knew exactly how to make fishermen's knots and how to untie tricky knots in his fishing lines. But Adrian wasn't always keen to take his dad's advice. When his dad showed him how to bait his hook, (d) he said that a little piece of the hook should always stick out, but Adrian thought otherwise. He thought it logical for the bait to hide the hook, so he ignored his dad — but after quite a few days of catching nothing, decided to follow his dad's advice.

(D)

Many careless fishermen had lost their lives on these rocks. Concrete crosses marked the spots where these people had been swept into the sea. Adrian had had a few narrow escapes when he had ventured too close to the edge. (e) He quickly learned to respect the mighty waters of the ocean. Adrian's dad also taught him which kinds of bait were suitable for catching various kinds of fish, and he also learned which sinkers were right for the different fishing areas.

*sinker: (낚싯줄의) 추, 봉돌

유형 18

04 주어진 글 (A)에 이어질 내용을 순서에 맞게 배열한 것으로 가장 적절한 것은?

① (B) – (D) – (C)
② (C) – (B) – (D)
③ (C) – (D) – (B)
④ (D) – (B) – (C)
⑤ (D) – (C) – (B)

05 밑줄 친 (a)~(e) 중에서 가리키는 대상이 나머지 넷과 다른 것은?

① (a) ② (b) ③ (c) ④ (d) ⑤ (e)

06 윗글의 Adrian에 관한 내용과 일치하지 않는 것은?

① 아버지와 함께 정기적으로 낚시를 갔다.
② 올라가면 너무 위험한 바위가 몇 군데 있다는 말을 들었다.
③ 큰 물고기를 잡아 어머니께 드려 어머니를 기쁘게 했다.
④ 아버지의 조언에 따랐지만 며칠간 아무것도 잡지 못했다.
⑤ 물고기의 종류에 따라 어떤 미끼가 적합한지 배웠다.

01~03 **gather** 모으다 **habit** 습관 **fireplace** 벽난로 **nightly** 밤의, 밤에 활동하는 **as long as** ~하는 한 **chore** 집안일, 허드렛일 **glow** 불빛 **flame** 불길, 화염 **grab** 움켜잡다 **broomstick** 빗자루 **chase** 쫓아다니다, 뒤쫓다 **yell** 소리 지르다 **education** 교육 **community** 마을, 공동체, 지역 사회 **cut into** ~을 줄이다 **require** 필요로 하다, 요구하다 **insist** 강하게 주장하다 **retire for the night** 잠자리에 들다 **sleep soundly** 푹 자다

04~06 **highlight** 가장 빛나는 순간 **expedition** 여행, 탐험 **spot** 곳, 장소 **deceptively** 보기와는 달리, 언뜻 보기에 **precious** 귀중한, 소중한 **free of charge** 공짜로, 무료로 **on top of** ~뿐만 아니라 **fisherman's knot** 피셔맨스 노트(두 줄의 양끝을 잇는 매듭의 일종) **untie** (매듭 등을) 풀다 **fishing line** 낚싯줄 **keen** 열정적인, 열렬한 **bait** 미끼를 달다; 미끼 **hook** 낚싯바늘 **stick out** 튀어나오다 **careless** 조심성 없는 **concrete** 콘크리트로 만든 **narrow escape** 가까스로 벗어나기 **venture** 위험을 무릅쓰다 **mighty** 강력한, 힘센 **suitable** 적당한

[07~09] 다음 글을 읽고, 물음에 답하시오.

(A)

When Mr. Palmer moved into his new house, he and his new neighbor got along just fine. They would smile broadly and wave when they saw each other in the driveway. There was no fence between their yards, and it appeared they would never need one.

(B)

In Palmer's mind, the conflict reached its **low point** when another issue surfaced. One day (a) he received a note from his hostile neighbor suggesting that the dead elm tree that stood squarely on the lot line between them should be cut down. Palmer didn't like the idea of splitting the costs involved and ignored the letter.

(C)

The problems began when Palmer's children began stepping in dog droppings in their yard. The neighbor had two poodles, and (b) he was sure they were the culprits, so one day he brought up the delicate subject to the neighbor. But (c) he denied that the poodles were the problem, and before long the two neighbors descended into a messy spiral of antagonism.

(D)

A few months later (d) he suddenly heard the sound of a chain saw outside. He looked out the window and watched the dead elm tree on the lot line as it was sawn vertically down the middle, leaving half standing on his property. (e) He left it standing a few years as a conversation piece, then finally cut it down. What a price paid for hostility!

07 주어진 글 (A)에 이어질 내용을 순서에 맞게 배열한 것으로 가장 적절한 것은?

① (B) – (D) – (C)
② (C) – (B) – (D)
③ (C) – (D) – (B)
④ (D) – (B) – (C)
⑤ (D) – (C) – (B)

08 밑줄 친 (a)~(e) 중에서 가리키는 대상이 나머지 넷과 다른 것은?

① (a) ② (b) ③ (c) ④ (d) ⑤ (e)

09 윗글의 Palmer에 관한 내용과 일치하지 않는 것은?

① 새 집으로 이사 온 후 이웃과 한동안 잘 지냈다.
② 죽은 느릅나무를 베고자 하는 이웃의 쪽지를 받았다.
③ 이웃에게 받은 편지 내용을 무시했다.
④ 아이들이 밟은 똥이 이웃집 개의 똥이라고 확신했다.
⑤ 남겨진 나무의 반을 즉시 베어버렸다.

Plus Q

밑줄 친 low point의 뜻을 문맥을 통해 유추하여 5자 내외의 우리말로 쓰시오.

➡

[10~12] 다음 글을 읽고, 물음에 답하시오.

(A)

September 1942, Viktor Frankl, a prominent Jewish psychiatrist and neurologist in Vienna, was arrested and transported to a Nazi concentration camp with his wife and parents. Three years later, when his camp was liberated, most of his family, including his pregnant wife, had perished — but (a) he, prisoner number 119104, had lived. In his bestselling book, *Man's Search for Meaning*, which was written in 1946, he wrote about his experiences in the camps.

(B)

Although there was no specific response from him, it served as a good opportunity for Frankl to reflect on the meaning of life. As (b) he saw in the camps, those who found meaning even in the most terrible circumstances were less likely to suffer than those who did not. "Everything can be taken from a man but one thing," Frankl wrote in *Man's Search for Meaning*, "the last of the human freedoms — to choose one's attitude in any given set of circumstances, to choose one's own way."

(C)

Working as a therapist in the camps, Frankl gave such an example in his book; the suicidal inmate (c) he encountered there. Like many others in the camps, he was hopeless and thought that there was nothing more to expect from life, nothing to live for. "In his case," Frankl writes, "it was a question of getting him to realize that life was still expecting something from him; something in the future was expected of him." For the man, it was his young child, who was then living in a foreign country. And (d) he survived.

(D)

In the book, Frankl concluded that the difference between those who had lived and those who had died came down to one thing: Meaning, an insight (e) he came to early in life. When he was a high school student, one of his science teachers declared to the class, "Life is nothing more than a combustion process, a process of oxidation. Frankl jumped out of his chair and responded, "Sir, if this is so, then what can be the meaning of life?"

10 주어진 글 (A)에 이어질 내용을 순서에 맞게 배열한 것으로 가장 적절한 것은?

① (B) – (D) – (C)
② (C) – (B) – (D)
③ (C) – (D) – (B)
④ (D) – (B) – (C)
⑤ (D) – (C) – (B)

11 밑줄 친 (a)~(e) 중에서 가리키는 대상이 나머지 넷과 다른 것은?

① (a) ② (b) ③ (c) ④ (d) ⑤ (e)

12 윗글의 Frankl에 관한 내용과 일치하지 않는 것은?

① 아내가 나치 수용소에서 죽었다.
② 1946년에 수용소 경험에 대해 책을 썼다.
③ 사람에게서 태도를 선택할 자유를 앗아갈 수 없다고 책에 적었다.
④ 아이를 잃고 자살한 수감자에 관한 내용을 책에 담았다.
⑤ 삶과 죽음을 결정하는 것은 삶의 의의라고 결론지었다.

07~09 **driveway** 차도, 진입로 **conflict** 갈등 **surface** 표면화되다 **hostile** 적개심에 불타는 **squarely** 굳건히, 공평하게 **split** 나누다 **dropping** 똥 **culprit** 범인 **bring up** 제기하다 **delicate** 민감한 **descend into** (나쁜 상황 속으로) 서서히 빠져들다 **spiral** 나선형의 것 **antagonism** 적대감 **chain saw** 동력 사슬톱 **vertically** 수직으로 **property** 소유물, 땅 **hostility** 적개심, 적의

10~12 **prominent** 저명한 **psychiatrist** 정신과 의사 **neurologist** 신경과 전문의 **arrest** 체포하다 **concentration camp** 수용소 **liberate** 해방하다 **perish** (끔찍하게) 죽다 **therapist** 치료사 **inmate** 수감자 **encounter** 만나다 **come down to** 결국 ~이 되다, ~에 이르다 **insight** 통찰력, 식견 **combustion** 연소 **oxidation** 산화

There is only one thing that
makes a dream impossible to achieve:
the fear of failure.

- Paulo Coelho

PART Ⅱ

소재편

소재 **01~10**

숨마쿰라우데®

[독해 매뉴얼]

소재

01 인물, 일화

인물, 일화는 수능에서 가장 보편적으로 등장하는 소재 중 하나이다. 인물에 관한 내용은 주로 '내용 일치' 문제의 지문으로 가장 많이 나오고, 일화와 관련된 지문은 '지칭 추론'과 '심경 혹은 분위기 추론' 문항에 주로 사용된다. 하지만 위에서 언급한 유형이 아니더라도 인물과 일화에 관한 지문이 여러 다른 유형에서도 사용될 수 있는데, 이 경우 일반적으로 문제의 난이도는 낮은 편에 속한다.

대표 예제

Georg Dionysius Ehret에 관한 다음 글의 내용과 일치하지 않는 것은? 수능

도입〉 The 18th century is called the Golden Age of botanical painting, and Georg Dionysius Ehret is often praised as the greatest botanical artist of the time. 전개1〉 Born in Heidelberg, Germany, he was the son of a gardener who taught him much about art and nature. As a young man, Ehret traveled around Europe, largely on foot, observing plants and developing his artistic skills. 전개2〉 In Holland, he became acquainted with the Swedish naturalist Carl Linnaeus. Through his collaborations with Linnaeus and others, Ehret provided illustrations for a number of significant horticultural publications. 결론〉 Ehret's reputation for scientific accuracy gained him many commissions from wealthy patrons, particularly in England, where he eventually settled.

*horticultural: 원예(학)의

① 18세기의 가장 위대한 식물 화가로서 칭송받는다.
② 정원사의 아들이었다.
③ 젊은 시절 주로 마차로 유럽을 여행하였다.
④ 다수의 원예 출판물에 삽화를 제공하였다.
⑤ 영국에 정착하였다.

한눈에 보는 구조

도입〉 인물의 전반적인 소개
Georg Dionysius Ehret는 18세기의 가장 위대한 식물 화가이다.

전개1〉 출생배경과 젊은 시절 소개
독일의 정원사의 아들로 태어났으며 젊은 시절에 유럽을 도보로 여행했다.

전개2〉 경력 및 활동 소개
Carl Linnaeus 등과의 공동 작업을 통해 많은 중요한 원예 출판물의 삽화를 제공했다.

결론〉 활동을 통해 얻게 된 명성
과학적 정확성을 인정 받아 후원자들로부터 많은 일을 위탁받게 되었다.

글의 도입부에서 인물에 대한 전반적인 소개를 한 후에, 그 인물의 출생배경과 젊은 시절, 경력 및 활동, 그로 인한 명성에 관해 제시하면서 인물에 대한 부연 설명을 하고 있다.

유제 다음 빈칸에 들어갈 말로 가장 적절한 것은? 고2 교육청

Jacqueline Novogratz, the founder of the Acumen Fund, tells a story that ______________________. Her story centers on a blue sweater. It was given to her by her uncle Ed when she was twelve. "I loved that soft wool sweater with its striped sleeves and two zebras in the front," she says. She even wrote her name on the tag. But the sweater got too tight for her as she grew older. So in her freshman year of high school she donated it to a charity. Eleven years later, she was jogging in Kigali, Rwanda, where she was working to set up an aid program for poor women. Suddenly, she spotted a little boy wearing a similar sweater. Could it be? She ran over to him and checked out the tag. Yes, there was her name. It was enough to remind Jacqueline — and the rest of us — of the threads of our connection to one another.

① demonstrates how connected we all are
② reminds us of the relative value of time
③ describes a hard life with a happy ending
④ emphasizes the importance of women's roles
⑤ shows how many opportunities there are in Africa

지문 소재별로 자주 출제되는 주요 어휘

moral 도덕적인
timid 소심한
aggressive 공격적인
inherent 내재적인, 고유한, 타고난
describe 기술하다, 묘사하다
celebrated 유명한
charity 자선단체
address 연설
bad temper 성마른 기질
gifted 재능이 있는
earn 얻다
active 활발한, 왕성한
graduate 졸업하다
rural 시골의
found 설립하다
literature 문학
publish 출판하다
edit 편집하다
experiment 실험[하다]
donate 기부하다
reputation 평판, 명성
considerate 사려깊은
committed 헌신적인, 열정적인
illustrate (예를 들어) 설명하다
sympathetic 동정적인, 호의적인
heartbroken 상심한
humorous 유머가 넘치는
childhood 어린 시절
diploma 졸업장
dirt 흙, 먼지
institute (교육) 기관, 대학
urban 도시의
notable 유명한, 저명한
account (있었던 일에 대한) 설명[이야기]
commentary (라디오, 텔레비전 등의) 실황 방송
recognize 알아보다, 인정하다
select 선택하다

Exercise

01 밑줄 친 부분이 가리키는 대상이 나머지 넷과 다른 것은?

Archibald Rutledge, American poet and educator, wrote that one day he met a man whose dog had just been killed in a forest fire. Heartbroken, the man explained to Rutledge how it happened. Because he worked out-of-doors, he often took his dog with him. That morning, he left ① him in a clearing and gave him a command to stay and watch his lunch box while ② he went into the forest. His faithful friend understood, for that's exactly what he did. Then a fire started in the woods, and soon the blaze spread to the spot where the dog had been left. But ③ he didn't move. He stayed right where ④ he was, in perfect obedience to his master's word. With tearful eyes, the dog's owner said, "I always had to be careful what I told ⑤ him to do, because I knew he would do it."

02 다음 글에 드러난 Adam Maguire의 심경으로 가장 적절한 것은?

When a school of dolphins began to go berserk in the waters just south of Brisbane, Australia, Adam Maguire and his friends who were enjoying surfing didn't know what to make of it. Why were the dolphins suddenly diving under their surfboards and poking at them with their noses? When 17-year-old Adam Maguire saw a dolphin charging toward him, he lost his balance and fell into the water. He punched it in the head and jumped on his board. But the dolphin came after him, taking a bite out of his board and his hip and knocking Adam into the water as his friends watched in horror. Suddenly, the dolphins went into a frenzy, beating the water with their tails. During the distraction Adam tried to crawl back on his boards and float back to shore on the next wave.

① calm and lonely
② happy and secure
③ excited and cheerful
④ regretful and relaxed
⑤ embarrassed and frightened

03 주어진 글 다음에 이어질 글의 순서로 가장 적절한 것은?

There once was a little boy who had a bad temper. His father gave him a bag of nails and told him that every time he lost his temper, he must hammer a nail into the fence.

(A) Finally the day came when the boy didn't lose his temper at all. He told his father about it and the father suggested that the boy now pull out one nail for each day that he was able to hold his temper. Finally all the nails were gone.

(B) The father took his son to the fence. He said "you have done well, my son, but look at the holes in the fence. The fence will never be the same. When you say things in anger, they leave a scar just like this one."

(C) The first day the boy had driven 37 nails into the fence. Over the next few weeks as he learned to control his anger, the number of nails hammered daily, ____________ gradually reduced. He discovered it was easier to hold his temper than to drive those nails into the fence.

① (A) – (C) – (B)
② (B) – (A) – (C)
③ (B) – (C) – (A)
④ (C) – (A) – (B)
⑤ (C) – (B) – (A)

Plus Q

윗글의 빈칸에 들어갈 be동사의 알맞은 형태를 쓰시오.

➡

01 heartbroken 상심한 out-of-doors(= outdoors) 야외에서 clearing (숲 속의) 빈터 command 명령 blaze 불길, (대형) 화재 spread(-spread-spread) 퍼지다[확산되다] obedience 순종; 복종
02 school (물고기 · 해양 동물의) 떼, 무리 berserk 광포한, 미친 듯이 날뛰는 poke 찌르다 charge 돌진하다, 공격하다 punch 주먹으로 치다 frenzy 광포함, 광분 distraction 혼란함 crawl 기다, 기어가다
03 temper 기질, 성질 nail 못 lose one's temper 화를 내다 hammer 망치로 두드리다 hold one's temper 화를 참다 be gone 사라지다 scar 상처 drive (못을) 박다 gradually 점차로

소재

교육, 학교

교육, 학교를 다루는 소재는 학습에 영향을 주는 요인, 아동 교육에 있어서의 부모의 역할 등을 다루며, 학생들에게 친숙한 소재로 난이도는 어렵지 않게 출제되는 편이다. 매년 많은 비중의 문항이 출제되고 있다.

대표 예제

다음 글의 주제로 가장 적절한 것은? 수능

도입》 Many disciplines are better learned by entering into the doing than by mere abstract study. This is often the case with the most abstract as well as the seemingly more practical disciplines. 전개1》 For example, within the philosophical disciplines, logic must be learned through the use of examples and actual problem solving. Only after some time and struggle does the student begin to develop the insights and intuitions that enable him to see the centrality and relevance of this mode of thinking. 전개2》 This learning by doing is essential in many of the sciences. For instance, only after a good deal of observation do the sparks in the bubble chamber become recognizable as the specific movements of identifiable particles.

① history of science education
② limitations of learning strategies
③ importance of learning by doing
④ effects of intuition on scientific discoveries
⑤ difference between philosophy and science

한눈에 보는 구조

도입》 **주제 제시**
많은 교과가 추상적인 공부에 의해서보다 실제 행함을 통해 더 잘 학습된다.

전개1》 **주제에 대한 예시 1**
철학 교과에서 논리는 실례의 사용과 실제 문제 해결을 통해 학습되어야 한다.

전개2》 **주제에 대한 예시 2**
행함으로써 배우는 학습은 많은 과학 교과에서 필수적이며, 그 예로서 상당한 양의 관찰이 있은 뒤에야 거품 상자의 불꽃을 인식할 수 있게 된다.

주제를 명시적으로 제시한 후에, 그에 대한 예시로 주제를 부연 설명하고 있는 글이다.

유제 다음 빈칸에 들어갈 말로 가장 적절한 것은? 고2 교육청

When children are very young, you first say no to protect them from danger. You say it because you love your child and because you must teach him to protect himself. Just as saying no is a tool to help ensure your child's physical safety, it also contributes to his emotional security. When you set limits on your child's behavior, whether it's telling a five-year-old he can't hit the baby or telling a teenager he can't stay out past midnight, you're letting him know that his actions don't happen in a vacuum. He is connected to someone(you) who watches and cares what he does. All children need a safe space in which to grow and develop. While it's a child's nature to test the limits of that space, by climbing higher, venturing farther, or asking for more of what he wants, it's also comforting for him ______________________.

① to let his mind drift away
② to know he is not out there alone
③ to realize his venture will succeed
④ to stop thinking about responsibility
⑤ to think he would never be punished

지문 소재별로 자주 출제되는 주요 어휘

perform 수행하다
foster 조성하다
relationship 관계
pupil 학생
improve 개선시키다
behavior 행동
assumption 추정
capability 능력, 역량
curriculum 교육과정
adolescent 청소년
instruction 가르침
consistent 일관된
process 과정
opportunity 기회
incorporate 포함하다
knowledge 지식
preschooler 취학 전 아동
discipline 교과
psychologist 심리학자
influence 영향을 주다
concentrate 집중하다
integrate 통합하다
academic 학문의
conscious 의식적인
perception 인식
individual 개인
interaction 상호작용
immerse 몰두하다
application 적용
development 발달

Exercise

01 다음 글의 주제로 가장 적절한 것은?

The flipped classroom is a pedagogical model in which short video lectures are viewed by students at home before the class session, while in-class time is devoted to exercises, projects, or discussions. In this model, the traditional practice of spending class time for direct instruction and completing content related activities for homework is "flipped." The concept of flipped classroom is gaining popularity, perhaps due to the ubiquitous presence of technology tools that teachers use to accomplish the flip such as YouTube, iPads, and many Learning Management Systems(LMS). The application of these tools, particularly multimedia, exerts a significant influence on flipped learning. Additionally, the current generation of students is accustomed to interacting with audio and video on electronic devices, so it is more likely that technological devices will help students digest educational content in this learning model.

① effects of technology tools on flipped learning
② features of a traditional classroom lecture model
③ limitations of teachers' roles in flipped classroom
④ reasons for teachers to better interact with students
⑤ necessity of technological development in multimedia

02 다음 글의 요지로 가장 적절한 것은?

Parents sometimes fall into the habit of putting all their children's needs before their own, under the pretense that children always come first. Clearly there are times when this is the case, as when a baby gets sick in the middle of the night; then it is appropriate to place all the attention on the baby's wellness. And when a special event comes up, everyone naturally focuses on the special child for the day. But under normal circumstances, it is practical for parents to pay quality attention to their own lives first, knowing that a small amount of daily self-care is oxygen for the spirit. This translates into a calmer adult who reacts less often and responds with more perspective and grace. In short, the first and most crucial way to be better parents for children lies in the healthy, consistent care of you.

① 부모보다 아이들의 요구가 우선되어야 한다.
② 아이들의 관심이 부모의 행복에 영향을 준다.
③ 부모가 자기 자신을 돌보려는 태도가 중요하다.
④ 가족이 모일 특별한 행사를 마련할 필요가 있다.
⑤ 훌륭한 부모가 되기 위해 넓은 관점을 가져야 한다.

03 주어진 글 다음에 이어질 글의 순서로 가장 적절한 것은?

Howard Gardner disputed the belief that "intelligence is a single faculty and that one is either 'smart' or 'stupid' across the board."

(A) So while the conventional method of lecture and note-taking works for some students, it bypasses the needs of many others. Students conclude that they're not good at certain subjects, when [**a / all / approach / different / is / learning / them / they need / to**].

(B) But schools aren't set up to accommodate personal differences. They are supposed to be fair, to make sure that everybody has equal access and no one has special advantages. As Gardner argues, however, "We obviously look different from one another, and have different personalities and temperaments.

(C) Instead, he observed that people rely on a variety of skills that help us resolve problems and difficulties. Furthermore, he discovered that each person uses a different combination of these skills.

① (A)－(C)－(B) ② (B)－(A)－(C) ③ (B)－(C)－(A)
④ (C)－(A)－(B) ⑤ (C)－(B)－(A)

Plus Q

윗글의 괄호 안에 있는 어구들을 어법과 문맥에 맞게 배열하시오.

➡

01 **flip** 뒤집다 **pedagogical** 교육학의 **instruction** 강의 **gain** 얻다 **ubiquitous** 어디에나 있는 **exert influence on** ~에 영향을 미치다 **be accustomed to** ~에 익숙하다 **interact** 상호작용하다
02 **fall into the habit of** ~의 버릇을 들이다 **under the pretense** ~을 핑계삼아, ~의 미명 아래 **wellness** 건강 **circumstance** 상황 **practical** 알맞은, 타당한 **translate into** ~으로 바뀌다 **crucial** 결정적인
03 **faculty** 능력 **across the board** 전반적으로 **conventional** 기존의, 관습적인 **bypass** 무시하다, 건너뛰다 **accommodate** 수용하다 **temperament** 기질 **resolve** 해결하다 **combination** 조합

소재

03 철학, 종교, 심리

철학, 종교, 심리를 다루는 소재는 빈칸 추론, 글의 순서 배열, 문장 삽입, 요약문 완성 등 주로 난이도가 높은 유형의 글감으로 자주 사용되므로 평소에 인문학 관련 배경 지식을 쌓아두는 것이 도움이 된다. 정확하게 해석하고 이해하는 연습이 많이 필요한 소재이다.

대표 예제

다음 빈칸에 들어갈 말로 가장 적절한 것은? 평가원

도입 One remarkable aspect of aboriginal culture is the concept of "totemism," where the tribal member at birth assumes the soul and identity of a part of nature. 전개 This view of the earth and its riches as an intrinsic part of oneself clearly rules out mistreatment of the environment because this would only constitute a destruction of self. Totems are more than objects. They include spiritual rituals, oral histories, and the organization of ceremonial lodges where records of the past travel routes of the soul can be exchanged with others and converted to mythology. The primary motivation is the preservation of tribal myths and a consolidation and sharing of every individual's origins in nature. 결론 The aborigines see ____________, through a hierarchy of totems that connect to their ancestral origins, a cosmology that places them at one with the earth, and behavior patterns that respect ecological balance.

*aboriginal: 원주민의 **consolidation: 병합, 강화

① themselves as incompatible with nature and her riches
② their mythology as a primary motive toward individualism
③ their identity as being self-contained from surrounding nature
④ their relationship to the environment as a single harmonious continuum
⑤ their communal rituals as a gateway to distancing themselves from their origins

한눈에 보는 구조

도입 **주제 제시**
원주민 문화의 두드러진 특징 중 하나는 토테미즘이다.

전개 **주제에 대한 부연 설명**
부족의 신화를 보존하고 모든 개인의 기원을 자연 속에서 병합하고 공유하기 위해 원주민들은 토테미즘을 믿는다.

결론 **주제의 재진술**
원주민들은 토테미즘에 바탕을 둔 사고방식을 통해 환경과 자신과의 관계를 조화로운 연속체로 간주한다.

글의 초반에 토테미즘의 정의에 대해 소개한 후, 그것이 원주민의 사고방식에 어떻게 영향을 주었는지 글의 중반에서 설명하고 있으며, 그런 사고방식을 통해 자신과 세계의 관계에 대해서는 어떻게 생각하는지 글의 결론에서 보여준다.

유제 다음 빈칸에 들어갈 말로 가장 적절한 것은? 고2 교육청

Imagine this scene. There are six people in an elevator with an actor hired by researchers. The actor drops a bunch of coins and pencils. They fall to the floor with a clatter. And then, as the elevator goes down floor by floor, not one person moves a muscle to help. The people in the elevator have to notice the actor picking up the coins and pencils on the floor. Some people may feel uncomfortable and might silently wonder whether to get involved. But each person is surrounded by five others who are doing nothing. If the people knew they were being tested, every one would instantly come to the aid of the stranger. But in the context of everyday life, where people are not thinking deliberately about how others are influencing them, ________________ just feels like the natural thing to do.

*clatter: 땡그랑 소리

① finding fault with others
② maximizing material gains
③ trying to remember faces
④ going along with the group
⑤ declining other people's favor

지문 소재별로 자주 출제되는 주요 어휘

philosophy 철학	**supernatural** 초자연적인	**perspective** 관점
religion 종교	**psychiatrist** 정신과 의사	**ethics** 윤리학
psychology 심리학	**superstition** 미신	**morality** 도덕성
rational 이성적인	**myth** 신화, 통념	**idealism** 이상주의
emotional 감정적인	**skeptical** 회의적인	**realism** 현실주의
sacred 신성한	**critical** 비판적인	**empathy** 공감
enlightenment 계몽	**aesthetics** 미학	**compassion** 연민
counselor 상담사	**origin** 기원	**abnormal** 비정상적인
spiritual 정신적인	**concept** 개념	**recognize** 인식하다
subconscious 잠재의식적인	**follower** 추종자	**perception** 인지
intelligence 지성	**worldview** 세계관	**material** 물리적인

Exercise

01 다음 글의 제목으로 가장 적절한 것은?

One of the greatest benefits of philosophy is that it adds to your quality of life. Parallel to the enjoyment we get from sports, because they help fulfill the physical side of our human nature, intellectual development is also enjoyable because it helps fulfill our spiritual side. Philosophy helps produce a qualitative difference in the thinking person. At one level of education you may read one book a month; at another, four. This, though, is only a quantitative difference. One real value of philosophy is as an aid to understanding how things hang together, which in turn fulfills our intellectual nature and helps make us happy. Do you want to understand yourself and others, political and social movements, the roots of racism, the process of change, and so forth? Then philosophy is for you.

① Why Study Philosophy?
② Careers for Philosophy Majors
③ Philosophy as a Basis for Politics
④ Unsolvable Philosophical Questions
⑤ What Are the Different Types of Intelligence?

02 (A), (B), (C)의 각 네모 안에서 어법에 맞는 표현으로 가장 적절한 것은?

Don't use age or infirmity as justification for your choices. People who use age or limiting physical conditions as an excuse to avoid doing things are headed down a slippery slope (A) [that / where] ultimately can lead to degeneration — even incapacity. If you don't want to do something, be honest about it, both with yourself and with others. If you enjoyed an activity in the past but don't care for it now, (B) [give / giving] yourself permission to eliminate it from your life. If you force yourself to continue, you may well manifest an injury or illness that will give you a reason not to do it anymore. Using advancing age as justification (C) [is / will] likely to cause or worsen signs of age-related degeneration.

	(A)		(B)		(C)
①	that	……	give	……	is
②	that	……	giving	……	will

③ that …… give …… will
④ where …… giving …… will
⑤ where …… give …… is

03 다음 글의 빈칸 (A), (B)에 들어갈 말로 가장 적절한 것은?

If you keep resting your mind on self-criticism, worries, grumbling about others, hurts, and stress, then your brain will be shaped into greater reactivity, vulnerability to anxiety and depressed mood, a narrow focus on threats and losses, and inclinations toward anger, sadness, and guilt. ____(A)____, if you keep resting your mind on good events and conditions(someone was nice to you, there's a roof over your head), pleasant feelings, the things you do get done, physical pleasures, and your good intentions and qualities, then over time your brain will take a different shape, one with strength and resilience hardwired into it, as well as a realistically optimistic outlook, a positive mood, and a sense of worth. ____(B)____, what you pay attention to — what you rest your mind on — is the primary shaper of your brain.

(A) …… (B)
① For example …… However
② For example …… In effect
③ As a result …… Otherwise
④ On the other hand …… In effect
⑤ On the other hand …… Otherwise

Plus Q

윗글의 요지를 본문에 있는 표현을 이용하여 완성하시오.

The brain takes its shape from ____________________.

➡

01 parallel 유사한, 평행한 intellectual 지적인 qualitative 질적인 quantitative 양적인 hang together 잘 들어맞다, 일치하다[일관되다] in turn 결국, 결과적으로
02 infirmity 노환, 허약[병약]함 justification 정당화, 변명 excuse 변명, 구실 slope 경사(면) degeneration 퇴화, 퇴보 incapacity 무능력 eliminate 없애다, 제거하다 manifest 나타내다, 보이다
03 grumbling 불평, 항의 reactivity 반응(성) vulnerability 취약성 inclination 경향, 성향 resilience 회복력 hardwire (행동 양식을) 고정화시키다 outlook 사고방식, 관점

소재

04 문학, 언어, 예술, 문화

수능에서 가장 빈번하게 출제되는 소재 중 하나는 문화에 관련된 것이다. 두 집단 혹은 나라 사이의 다른 문화로 인해 발생하는 다양한 경우의 내용들이 주를 이룬다. 최근에는 문화의 큰 부분을 차지한다고 볼 수 있는 언어, 문학, 예술과 관련된 내용의 지문들의 등장이 빈번해지고 있다. 이러한 지문을 접하기 전에 기본적인 배경지식을 갖추어 놓는다면 지문을 이해하기가 한결 쉬울 것이다.

대표 예제

다음 빈칸에 들어갈 말로 가장 적절한 것은? 평가원

도입 In an increasingly globalized world, literature in translation has an especially important role. Increasingly, writers, readers, and publishers are turning to literature as a bridge between cultures, particularly Western and Arab societies. This growing interest is, in turn, driving a boom in translation. 전개1 However, not surprisingly perhaps, most translations are from English into other languages, not from another language, such as Arabic, into English. Hence, the huge American market is seen as driving the ____________. 전개2 Bookstores in the United States, for example, rarely stock more than Nobel Prize winner Naguib Mahfouz's *Cairo Trilogy*, a masterful, realistic account of life in Cairo and of a merchant family in the mid-20th century. Western readers likely know little of Mahfouz's more experimental work, his political and religious allegories, or his historical dramas. 결론 The result is a kind of one-way mirror between America and the rest of the world.

*allegory: 우화, 풍자

① equality
② diversity
③ interaction
④ imbalance
⑤ uncertainty

한눈에 보는 구조

도입 **소재 소개**
번역 문학이 문화 간의 가교 역할을 하게 되면서 번역이 호황을 누리게 되었다.

전개1 **주제 제시**
대부분의 번역 작품은 영어에서 다른 언어로 된 것으로 미국 시장은 번역 문화의 불균형을 만들어 간다.

전개2 **주제에 대한 예시**
미국의 서점에는 다른 나라의 노벨상을 수상한 작품 이외의 다른 작품의 번역서가 갖추어 있지 않다.

결론 **주제의 재진술**
미국의 번역 시장은 미국과 세계의 다른 나라 사이에서 한쪽 방향만 비추는 거울 같은 것이다.

도입부에서 번역 문학이 두 문화 사이의 가교 역할을 한다는 것이 소개된다. 전개가 시작되는 부분에서 However와 함께 필자가 말하고자 하는 주제가 제시되며 제시된 주제에 대한 예로서 미국의 서점이 다른 나라의 번역 작품을 구비하지 못하고 있음이 설명되어 있다. 이것을 토대로, 미국의 번역 문화는 한쪽 방향만 비추는 거울과 같다고 결론을 내리고 있다.

유제 글의 흐름으로 보아, 주어진 문장이 들어가기에 가장 적절한 곳은? 고2 교육청

This has happened with an Aboriginal language of South Australia called Kaurna.

Even an extinct language can be brought back to life, if conditions are right. There must be people who want the language back. (①) Also, there must be written or audio-recorded material of the language in some form. (②) Its last native speaker died in 1929, but in the 1980s a group of people decided that they wanted their language back. (③) "The language isn't dead," the leader of the group said, "it's only sleeping." (④) Fortunately, material survived from the nineteenth century, so that a linguist was able to make a fresh description and help the Kaurna people start learning the language again. (⑤) It's taught in schools now, and some day, perhaps, some children will start learning it as their mother tongue.

*Aboriginal: 호주 원주민의

지문 소재별로 자주 출제되는 주요 어휘

myth 신화
dialect 방언
verbal 언어[말]의
review 비평, 논평
nonverbal 비언어적인
react 반응하다
enthusiasm 열의, 열정
deliberate 고의의, 계획적인
literary 문학의
interpret (의미를) 해석하다
dominate 지배하다
diversity 다양성
intentional 의도적인
distinction 구별, 차이
translate 번역하다
implicit 내포된, 암시된
interact 상호작용하다
concept 개념
mother tongue 모국어
applicable 적용될 수 있는
colleague 동료
compare 비교하다
non-native 모국어 사용자가 아닌
rationally 온당하게, 합리적으로
distribution 분배, 분포
represent 묘사하다, 기술하다
privilege 특권
prejudice 편견
accumulate 축적하다, 모으다
contemporary 현대의, 당대의
literature 문학
misunderstanding 오해
language 언어

Exercise

01 다음 글에서 전체 흐름과 관계 없는 문장은?

French consumers prefer American television and tune out French programs. American films account for over 70 percent of all box office receipts in France. ① The French government considers this invasion American cultural imperialism and took some steps to minimize its influence. ② France spent $16 billion to produce cultural products in France in 1994, three-quarters of which came from the government. ③ French moviegoers pay an 11 percent tax so the government can provide most of the funding for the French film industry. ④ Now the French entertainment industry is trying to learn how to make programs that can appeal to people in the whole world. ⑤ In addition, the French government demands that French be used on television and radio, in all advertising, and in schools and workplaces.

02 다음 글의 내용을 한 문장으로 요약하고자 한다. 빈칸 (A)와 (B)에 들어갈 말로 가장 적절한 것은?

According to cognitive linguists, the words we use create frames. The idea of frames is similar to the idea of worldview. Frames often imply an ideology, or a set of ideas we have about the way things should be. When we talk about the *Founding Fathers* of our country, for example, we are building and reinforcing a metaphorical frame through which we view our country as a family. The idea of country as family is reinforced by other phrases that we use, such as *sending our sons to war*. Frames help us to talk about things. It is easier to talk about something that your language already has a frame for. If you have a frame for something, you probably have lots of words and phrases that fit comfortably into that frame.

→ The language we use creates the ______(A)______ on things, which, in turn, makes it more ______(B)______ to talk about them.

	(A)		(B)
①	prediction vision	……	convenient
②	prediction vision	……	competitive
③	preference	……	competitive

④ perspective …… emotional
⑤ perspective …… convenient

03 주어진 글 다음에 이어질 글의 순서로 가장 적절한 것은?

When I am speaking English, I say that 9:15 is a quarter past nine and 9:30 is half past nine. When I began learning Czech, I found that 9:15 is a phrase that translates to 'a quarter of ten' and 9:30 is 'half of ten.'

(A) I'm not sure if this way of thinking indicates that Czechs are more future oriented than Americans, but it certainly does suggest a difference, and people who are not careful could miss appointments.

(B) In English, I think about the hour that has just sounded on the clock (a quarter past nine, half past nine) and in Czech I think about the hour that is coming up next (one quarter of the way to ten, half of the way to ten).

(C) This puzzled me for a while, and I had to double-check every appointment I made. Once I figured out the underlying difference between the two systems, however, I found myself thinking about time differently depending on whether I was using English or Czech.

① (A) – (C) – (B)
② (B) – (A) – (C)
③ (B) – (C) – (A)
④ (C) – (A) – (B)
⑤ (C) – (B) – (A)

Plus Q

다음 문장의 빈칸에 들어갈 단어를 윗글에서 찾아 어법에 맞게 쓰시오.

If something __________ you, you do not understand it and feel confused.

➡

01 **consumer** 소비자 **tune out** ~을 무시하다, ~을 듣지 않다 **account for** ~을 차지하다 **box office** 매표소 **receipt** 영수증 **invasion** 침략, 침입 **imperialism** 제국주의 **minimize** 최소화하다 **appeal** 호소하다
02 **cognitive** 인지의 **linguist** 언어학자 **frame** 틀 **imply** 의미하다, 암시하다 **reinforce** 강화하다 **metaphorical** 은유의 **phrase** 어구 **comfortably** 수월하게, 편안[편리]하게
03 **Czech** 체코슬로바키아(= Czechoslovakia) **translate** 해석하다, 번역하다 **indicate** 가리키다 **oriented** ~지향의 **miss** 놓치다 **figure out** 파악하다 **underlying** 기저에 있는, 근본적인

소재

05 역사, 지리

역사, 지리 관련 소재는 고대부터 현대에 이르는 흥미로운 역사적 사건 및 특정 장소를 중심으로 지문이 구성되며, 내용 일치 유형에서 자주 출제된다. 글의 순서 배열, 문장 삽입 유형에서도 출제되는 경향이 있는데, 유형에 따라 난이도가 많이 달라질 수 있다. 2013학년도 9월 모평에서 43번으로 출제된 진시황을 예로 제시한 지문은 글의 순서 배열 문항 중 최고 난이도로 손꼽힐 만큼 어렵게 출제되었다.

대표 예제

주어진 글 다음에 이어질 글의 순서로 가장 적절한 것은?

평가원

도입 Studying history is not about memorizing what we have been told — it requires us to investigate the past. Like a detective, we start with the easy, known pieces of information.

(A) 결론 You have to go further to ask questions such as, "Why was he cruel?" and "What were the results of his rule?" Hence, studying history trains us not to accept everything we read or hear as the truth. Instead, it trains us to use our critical thinking skills to get the full picture of the past.

(B) 전개2 For example, if someone told you that Chinese Emperor Qin Shihuang was a cruel ruler, would you simply accept this as the truth? Or, would you ask questions about the statement and look for information or evidence to support it?

(C) 전개1 We then shuffle the pieces around to see how they fit together. Once all the pieces fit, we have the full picture. As we put the pieces together, we challenge ourselves to think of other ways to describe what we know.

---

① (A) − (C) − (B)　② (B) − (A) − (C)
③ (B) − (C) − (A)　④ (C) − (A) − (B)
⑤ (C) − (B) − (A)

한눈에 보는 구조

도입 **소재 제시**
역사 공부는 암기가 아니라, 우리가 알고 있던 정보에 근거해서 의문을 제기해야 하는 것이다.

전개1 **소재에 대한 부연 설명**
정보의 여러 조각을 짜 맞추며 큰 그림을 그리면서, 우리가 알고 있는 것을 다른 방식으로 생각해 본다.

전개2 **예시 제시**
'진시황제가 잔인했다'는 말을 들었을 때, 이것을 사실로 받아들이겠는가 아니면 이것을 뒷받침할 정보나 증거를 찾겠는가?

결론 **주제 진술**
역사 공부는 과거를 전체적으로 이해할 수 있는 비판적인 사고를 할 수 있도록 우리를 훈련시킨다.

비유적인 표현으로 소재에 대해 쉽게 설명한 후에, 예시로 역사적 인물에 대한 진술을 구체적으로 제시하면서, 올바른 역사 공부 방법이 어떤 것인지 결론을 내리고 있다.

• SUB NOTE p. 72

유제 글의 흐름으로 보아, 주어진 문장이 들어가기에 가장 적절한 곳은? 고2 교육청

> They were constructed that way to minimize property taxes, which were based on the width of a house.

Throughout history, people have changed their behavior to avoid taxes. Centuries ago, the Duke of Tuscany imposed a tax on salt. (①) Tuscan bakers responded by eliminating salt in their recipes and giving us the delicious Tuscan bread we enjoy today. (②) If you visit Amsterdam, you will notice that almost all the old houses are narrow and tall. (③) Consider another architectural example, the invention of the mansard roof in France. (④) Property taxes were often imposed on the number of rooms in a house and, therefore, rooms on the second or third floor were considered just as ratable as those on the ground floor. (⑤) But if a mansard roof was constructed on the third floor, those rooms were considered to be part of an attic and not taxed.

*mansard roof: (2단으로 경사진) 망사르드 지붕

**ratable: 과세할 수 있는

지문 소재별로 자주 출제되는 주요 어휘

ancient 고대의	**traditional** 전통의	**summit** (산의) 정상
native 고유의, 원산의	**range** 산맥; 범위	**folk** 민속의, 전통적인
mild (날씨가) 온화한	**custom** 관습	**equator** 적도
ceremony 의식	**cliff** 절벽	**tropical** 열대의
primitive 원시의, 초기의	**region** 지역	**heritage** 전통, 유산
pasture 목초지	**diverse** 다양한	**glacier** 빙하
civilization 문명	**coast** 해안	**valley** 계곡, 골짜기
ruin 유적, 폐허	**stream** 개울, 시내	**monument** 유물, 기념물
plain 평원, 평지	**era** 시대, 시기	**humid** 습한
contemporary 현대의; 동시대의	**continent** 대륙	**winding** 구불구불한

Exercise

01 주어진 글 다음에 이어질 글의 순서로 가장 적절한 것은?

For more than two centuries, conventional wisdom held that women were incapable of climbing mountains. As he prepared an expedition to climb Mount Everest, for example, Sir Edmund Hillary refused a request to include women.

(A) Fortunately, some women were bold enough to challenge conventional wisdom. Arlene Blum began experimenting with mountain climbs, and she found that she had the leadership, strength, and temperament to make it.

(B) Soon she organized a team of ten American women to prepare a quest in which no American male had ever succeeded: scaling Annapurna, at 26,545 feet the world's tenth highest mountain. In 1978, they succeeded and Blum eventually wrote a book titled *Annapurna: A Woman's Place*.

(C) He allegedly gave three reasons: women didn't have the qualities of leadership, they weren't strong enough to carry the packs, and they would become hysterical at high altitudes.

① (A)－(C)－(B)　② (B)－(A)－(C)
③ (B)－(C)－(A)　④ (C)－(A)－(B)
⑤ (C)－(B)－(A)

02 다음 글의 제목으로 가장 적절한 것은?

Deep in a jungle in Mexico, in 1912, two explorers found a 1,200-year-old temple built by the ancient Indians. The temple was in good condition. They took photographs and tried to plot maps showing where the temple was. Later, other explorers attempted to follow the maps, but they could never find the temple. In 1973, more than 60 years later, some people were making a television film about these ancient Indians. In the jungle, they accidentally found the lost temple, almost completely hidden by jungle plants. It was still in good condition. After so many years, this great discovery had been found again.

① Difficulties Facing Explorers
② Maps Found in a Deep Jungle
③ Rediscovering an Ancient Temple
④ Examples of Accidental Discovery
⑤ Attempted Failures to Find Temples

03 다음 글에서 전체 흐름과 관계 없는 문장은?

On Christmas Eve, millions of American children leave out cookies and milk for Santa Claus to enjoy after his trip down their chimneys with his bag of gifts. ① Some add a few carrots for his trusty reindeer. ② It was during the Great Depression that leaving cookies and milk for Santa took off as an American holiday tradition. ③ In that time of great economic hardship, many parents tried to teach their children that it was important to give to others and to show gratitude for [**receive / were / they / to / the gifts / enough / lucky**] on Christmas. ④ Those parents must remember that many material gifts are soon forgotten. ⑤ Some 80 years later, many children still set out cookies and milk for Santa, whether out of the goodness of their hearts or as a bribe to receive more gifts from the bearded man in the red suit.

Plus Q

윗글의 괄호 안에 있는 어구들을 어법과 문맥에 맞게 배열하시오.

➡

01 conventional wisdom 일반적 통념　incapable 할 수 없는　expedition 원정, 탐험　temperament 기질　make it 해내다　quest 원정　scale (아주 높고 가파른 곳을) 오르다　allegedly 전해진 바에 의하면　hysterical 신경질적인　altitude 고도
02 explorer 탐험가　ancient 고대의　temple 절, 사원　in good condition 상태가 좋은　plot maps 지도를 구상하다　attempt 시도하다　accidentally 우연히　completely 완전히
03 chimney 굴뚝　trusty 믿음직한　reindeer 순록, 사슴　tradition 전통　hardship 어려움　gratitude 감사　material 물질적인　goodness 선량함, 선의　bribe 뇌물

정치, 경제, 사회, 법

정치, 경제, 사회, 법은 난이도가 어려운 유형에 속하는 빈칸 추론, 글의 순서 배열, 문장 삽입, 요약문 완성, 일반 장문 등에 자주 사용되는 소재로 거의 빠짐없이 매년 출제되는 내용이므로 평소 이런 주제와 관련한 글을 많이 읽어둘 필요가 있다.

대표 예제

다음 글에서 전체 흐름과 관계 없는 문장은? 평가원

도입 Roles are like a fence. They allow us a certain amount of freedom, but for most of us that freedom doesn't go very far. 전개 Suppose that a woman decides that she is not going to wear dresses — or a man that he will not wear suits and ties — regardless of what anyone says. ① In most situations, they'll stick to their decision. ② When a formal occasion comes along, however, such as a family wedding or a funeral, they are likely to cave in to norms that they find overwhelming. ③ The increasing social pressure discourages us from fulfilling the social norms and committing ourselves to shared social conventions of behaviour. 결론 ④ Almost all of us follow the guidelines for what is "appropriate" for our roles. ⑤ Few of us are bothered by such restrictions, for our socialization is so thorough that we usually *want* to do what our roles indicate is appropriate.

한눈에 보는 구조

도입 **소재 제시**
(사회적) 역할은 우리에게 일정량의 자유를 허용하지만, 그 범위는 넓지 않다.

전개 **예시 제시**
어떤 경우에도 드레스나 정장을 입지 않겠다고 결심하는 경우라도 결혼식이나 장례식과 같은 격식을 차려야 하는 때가 오면 결국 사회적 역할과 관습에 순응한다.

결론 **주제 진술**
사회적 역할에 따른 제한을 귀찮아하는 사람들은 거의 없는데, 이는 사회적 역할을 그저 따르는 정도가 아니라 적극적으로 그 역할을 하고 싶어 하기 때문이다.

도입에서 사회적 역할에 따른 자유의 범위에 대해 언급하고 있고, 전개 부분에서 사회적 역할로 인해 자유가 제한되는 경우를 예로 들어 제시하고 있으며, 글의 마지막에서는 행동 지침으로서의 사회적 역할을 오히려 우리가 원하고 있다고 결론내리고 있다.

• SUB NOTE p. 74

유제 다음 글의 빈칸 (A), (B)에 들어갈 말로 가장 적절한 것은? 고2 교육청

One of the underlying principles of investing is based upon the relationship between risk and return. The *risk* associated with an investment can be defined as the probability of earning an expected profit. ____(A)____, if you deposit $1,000 into a savings account at your local bank, you would expect this to be a low-risk investment. Banks are generally conservative, and savings accounts are guaranteed by the federal government up to a certain dollar amount. If the bank promises to pay you a 2 percent annual interest rate, the chances are great that at the end of one year you will have $1,020. ____(B)____, there is a high probability that you will earn a 2 percent annual profit, and this would be considered a low-risk investment.

	(A)		(B)
①	For example	……	Thus
②	For example	……	However
③	In addition	……	As a result
④	Nevertheless	……	Similarly
⑤	Nevertheless	……	In contrast

지문 소재별로 자주 출제되는 주요 어휘

politics 정치
economy 경제
sociology 사회학
legal 합법적인
government 정부
interest rate 이자율
democracy 민주주의
representative 대표
election 선거
vote 투표하다

revolution 혁명
autonomy 자율성, 자치권
duty 의무
consumer 소비자
productivity 생산성
industrial 산업의
agricultural 농업의
commercial 상업적인
management 관리, 경영
risk 위험

conflict 갈등
lawyer 변호사
accuse 고소하다
socialization 사회화
judge 판사
capital 자본
cost 비용
depression 불경기, 불황
inflation 인플레이션
investment 투자

Exercise

01 다음 빈칸에 들어갈 말로 가장 적절한 것은?

There was a time when corporations in the US could get away with ignoring diversity issues and hire employees who all looked and thought alike, catering only to one type of consumer. Those days are gone. Also gone is the myth that ________________________. Providing opportunities for people of all backgrounds is the right thing to do from an ethical standpoint. But it is also great for business. Why? Because companies can benefit from a multicultural workforce's expertise. For instance, if your company does business in Asia, having Asian Americans on your negotiating team will greatly improve your chances of success. Even if your organization has no interest in conducting international business, you still need diversity on your staff.

① competition enhances performance
② diversity has little to do with business
③ productivity means cutting costs and jobs
④ managers who use democratic styles are good
⑤ innovation is solely the job of the research team

02 다음 글에서 전체 흐름과 관계 없는 문장은?

Studies have shown over and over again that, on the whole, people in bigger cities move faster than their counterparts from smaller places. ① In one of the earliest studies of this type, Herbert Wright, as part of his classic "City-Town" project, observed the behavior of children in typical city supermarkets and in small-town grocery stores. ② One of the strongest differences between the two environments turned out to be walking speed. ③ The average city child walked nearly twice as fast through the supermarket as the town child did through the smaller grocery. ④ The city supermarkets usually allowed the shoppers to taste, smell, and touch the product before purchasing. ⑤ The town children spent three times as much time interacting with clerks and other shoppers.

03 다음 글의 밑줄 친 부분 중, 문맥상 낱말의 쓰임이 적절하지 않은 것은?

An impact of rural tourism is the conflict that can ① occur between local residents, local councils and National Parks. Although there is a clear need to ② conserve the environment, this can cause conflict with local residents' applications for planning permission, particularly in areas with conservation-area status. Some residents find this even prevents them from diversifying into tourism. In other areas such policy is totally at odds with environmental best practice, ③ reducing the use of solar panels and any other structures that could impact upon the appearance of the area. It can also prove to be expensive to ④ maintain a property in these areas as building materials and style must be in keeping with the heritage and structures already in place. It is often a requirement to replace like for like, which can ⑤ prevent bad feeling and perceived inconvenience for those living in the area.

Plus Q

윗글의 주제를 본문에 있는 단어를 이용하여 완성하시오.

the ____________ of rural tourism on the life of local residents

➡

01 **corporation** 회사 **get away with** (나쁜 짓을 하고도) 처벌을 모면하다[그냥 넘어가다]
cater to ~의 구미에 맞추다 **myth** (근거가 희박한) 통념 **ethical** 윤리적인 **standpoint** 관점, 견지
workforce 노동자, 노동력 **expertise** 전문지식 **negotiating team** 협상 팀

02 **counterpart** (다른 장소나 상황에서 어떤 사람 · 사물과 동일한 지위나 기능을 갖는) 상대, 대응 관계에 있는 사람
observe 관찰하다 **typical** 전형적인 **turn out** ~임이 밝혀지다 **interact with** ~와 서로 교감하다, 상호작용하다

03 **impact** 영향 **rural tourism** 농촌[체험] 관광 **conflict** 갈등 **resident** 주민 **council** 의회
conserve 보존하다 **application for** ~을 위한 신청 **planning permission** (신축 · 증개축의) 건축 허가
conservation-area status 보존 지역으로 지정된 상태 **diversify** 다각화하다 **policy** 정책
at odds with ~와 불화하는, ~와 상충하는 **property** 건물, 재산, 소유지 **heritage** (문화적) 전통[유산]
requirement 필수 조건 **replace** 교체하다 **perceived** 인식[인지]된 **inconvenience** 불편함

소재

07 환경, 자원, 생태계

환경, 자원, 생태계 소재는 근래에 들어 중요한 이슈이므로, 다양한 유형에서 광범위하게 출제되고 있다. 환경오염 문제, 에너지 고갈, 친환경적인 개발, 대체 에너지, 재활용과 같은 시사성이 높은 지문들이 주로 소개되며, 매년 빠지지 않고 출제되는 소재이다. 지문 속에서 답을 추론할 수 있는 명백한 근거가 함께 제시되므로, 소재가 생소해도 차분하게 접근할 필요가 있다.

대표 예제

(A), (B), (C)의 각 네모 안에서 문맥에 맞는 낱말로 가장 적절한 것은? 평가원

도입》 The desert locust lives in two remarkably different styles depending on the availability of food sources and the density of the local locust population. 전개1》 When food is scarce, as it usually is in their native desert habitat, locusts are born with coloring designed for camouflage and lead (A) [solitary / social] lives. 전개2》 But when rare periods of significant rain produce major vegetation growth, everything changes. At first, the locusts continue to be loners, just feasting off the (B) [insufficient / abundant] food supply. 전개3》 But as the extra vegetation starts to die off, the locusts find themselves crowded together. Suddenly, baby locusts are born with bright colors and a preference for company. Instead of avoiding one another and hiding from predators through camouflage and inactivity, these locusts gather in vast groups, feed together, and (C) [overwhelm / overestimate] their predators simply through numbers.

*camouflage: 위장

	(A)		(B)		(C)
①	solitary	……	insufficient	……	overwhelm
②	solitary	……	abundant	……	overwhelm
③	solitary	……	insufficient	……	overestimate
④	social	……	abundant	……	overwhelm
⑤	social	……	insufficient	……	overestimate

한눈에 보는 구조

도입》 **주제 제시**
먹잇감의 입수 가능성과 메뚜기 개체의 밀도에 따라 desert locust(이집트 땅메뚜기)의 살아가는 방식이 다르다.

전개1》 **주제에 대한 부연 설명 1**
먹잇감이 부족할 때에는 혼자서 살아간다.

전개2》 **주제에 대한 부연 설명 2**
많은 비로 먹잇감이 풍부해져도 처음에는 계속 혼자 살아간다.

전개3》 **주제에 대한 부연 설명 3**
초목이 죽어 없어지고 개체수가 엄청나게 많아지면, 떼를 지어 살며 포식자를 압도한다.

먹잇감의 입수 가능성과 메뚜기 개체의 밀도를 세 가지 시기로 나누어 설명하고 있고, 각 시기마다 어휘 추론이 하나씩 들어가 있다.

유제 주어진 글 다음에 이어질 글의 순서로 가장 적절한 것은? 고2 교육청

In a crowded world, an unmanaged commons cannot possibly work. That is an important qualification. If the world is not crowded, a commons may in fact be the best method of distribution.

(A) A plainsman could kill an American bison, cut out only the tongue for his dinner, and discard the rest of the animal. He was not being wasteful in any important sense. Nor did it much matter how a lonely American frontiersman disposed of his waste.

(B) For example, when the pioneers spread out across the United States, the most efficient way was to treat all the game in the wild as an unmanaged commons because for a long time humans couldn't do any real damage.

(C) Today, with only a few thousand bison left, we would be outraged by such careless behavior. As the population in the United States became denser, the land's natural chemical and biological recycling processes were overloaded. Careful management of these resources became necessary, from bison to oil and water.

*commons: 공동 자원, 공유지 **game: 야생의 사냥감

① (A) – (C) – (B)
② (B) – (A) – (C)
③ (B) – (C) – (A)
④ (C) – (A) – (B)
⑤ (C) – (B) – (A)

지문 소재별로 자주 출제되는 주요 어휘

adapt 적응하다	**environment** 환경	**species** (생물의) 종
dispose 처리하다	**resource** 자원	**deplete** 고갈시키다
organism 유기체, 생물	**contaminate** 오염시키다	**generate** 발생시키다
biodiversity 생물 다양성	**exhaust** 고갈시키다	**stability** 안정(성)
ecosystem 생태계	**shortage** 부족	**destruction** 파괴
pollute 오염시키다	**cope** 대처하다	**interaction** 상호작용
chemical 화학 물질	**extinct** 멸종된	**toxic** 유독한
endanger 위험에 빠뜨리다	**source** 원천, 공급원	**discard** 버리다
preserve 보존하다	**damage** 피해(를 주다)	**isolation** 고립
conserve 보존하다	**food chain** 먹이 사슬	**rain forest** 열대 우림

Exercise

01 다음 글에서 전체 흐름과 관계 없는 문장은?

One major advantage with the use of renewable energy is that as it is renewable it is therefore sustainable and so will never run out. ①Renewable energy facilities generally require less maintenance than traditional generators. ②Even more importantly, renewable energy produces little or no waste products such as carbon dioxide or other chemical pollutants, so has minimal impact on the environment. ③Renewable energy often relies on the weather, which is unpredictable and inconsistent. ④Renewable energy projects can also bring economic benefits to many regional areas, which come from the use of local services as well as tourism. ⑤These economic benefits are possible because most projects are located away from large urban centers.

02 주어진 글 다음에 이어질 글의 순서로 가장 적절한 것은?

We lost all of our lifelines immediately after the earthquake. We were unable to use our mobile phones or watch TV. We were so scared that we just could not stay inside our home that night.

(A) We had not been able to drink much liquid for the past two days, so the coffee we were having that day was especially tasty. It's now ten days after the earthquake, and we still do not have running water in our house.

(B) However, I think how lucky we feel to still have this house, especially since there are so many people here who still have not been able to reach their families.

(C) We chose to stay in our car. Not until two days later did the electricity come back on. The gas came on soon after. I can't describe how happy we were to eat warm food under the bright light.

① (A) – (C) – (B)
② (B) – (A) – (C)
③ (B) – (C) – (A)
④ (C) – (A) – (B)
⑤ (C) – (B) – (A)

03 글의 흐름으로 보아, 주어진 문장이 들어가기에 가장 적절한 곳은?

> Finally, the calf stands for the first time on its wobbly legs.

At birth a baby giraffe falls 10 feet from its mother's womb and usually lands on its back. The mother giraffe lowers her head long enough to take a quick look that everything is alright. (①) Then a few minutes later she starts the most incredible process to ensure that her little offspring adapts to the challenges of life. (②) She positions herself directly over her calf, and then she swings her long leg outward and kicks her baby, so that it is sent sprawling, head over heels. (③) When it doesn't get up, the violent process is repeated over and over again to stimulate its efforts. (④) Then the mother giraffe does the most remarkable thing; she kicks it off its feet again. (⑤) The mother giraffe wants its offspring to remember ________________.

Plus Q

윗글의 빈칸에 들어갈 말을 의문사를 포함한 네 단어로 쓰시오.

➡

01 **renewable** 재생 가능한 **sustainable** 지속 가능한 **run out** 다 떨어지다, 바닥나다 **require** 필요로 하다 **maintenance** (건물 · 기계 등을 정기적으로 점검 · 보수하는) 유지 **generator** 발전기 **waste product** 폐기물 **carbon dioxide** 이산화탄소 **pollutant** 오염 물질 **minimal** 최소한의 **inconsistent** 일관성이 없는 **benefit** 혜택, 이득 **regional** 지방[지역]의

02 **lifeline** (사람이 의지하는) 생명선 **immediately** 즉시 **earthquake** 지진 **scared** 무서워하는, 겁먹은 **liquid** 액체 **tasty** 맛있는 **running water** 수돗물 **reach** 연락하다 **electricity** 전기

03 **wobbly** 불안정한 **giraffe** 기린 **womb** 자궁 **incredible** 놀라운 **offspring** 새끼 **position** (특정한 위치에) 두다, ~의 자리를 잡다 **sprawl** 큰 대자로 눕다 **head over heels** 곤두박이가 되어, 거꾸로 **over and over again** 반복적으로 **stimulate** 자극하다 **off one's feet** 발판을 잃어

소재 08 의학, 건강, 식품, 영양

현대인의 가장 큰 관심사 중 하나는 잘 먹고 건강하게 사는 법일 것이다. 수능에서도 이러한 추세와 관련해서 건강과 식품에 대한 지문이 많이 이용되고 있다. 수능 초기에는 다이어트 방법이나 열량과 관련된 내용이 주를 이루었고, 최근에는 의사와 환자와의 관계 혹은 구체적인 영양소의 역할 등을 다룬 소재가 자주 등장하는 편이다.

대표 예제

다음 글의 목적으로 가장 적절한 것은? 평가원

도입 If you're one of the countless people whose mind and body have been overworked, you need a program that will give you a more positive and energetic life: the Health Management Program offered by the ABC Well-Being Institute. 전개 This program lasts for six weeks and consists of three different components: Daily Targets, Walking Plans, and Eating Plans. Each week, you'll be advised by our health experts and introduced to new physical activity targets. 결론 Are you serious about improving your life immediately? Then, you can start by enrolling in our fantastic program today.

① 스포츠 센터 강사를 모집하려고
② 건강관리 프로그램을 홍보하려고
③ 걷기 운동의 효과를 강조하려고
④ 스트레스의 위험성을 경고하려고
⑤ 약물 남용의 부작용을 설명하려고

한눈에 보는 구조

도입 **소재 제시**
몸과 마음이 혹사당해 온 사람에게는 ABC 웰빙 협회에서 제공하는 건강관리 프로그램이 필요하다.

전개 **소재에 대한 세부 설명**
협회에서 제공하는 프로그램은 6주 동안 지속되고, 일일 목표, 걷기 플랜 그리고 식사 플랜으로 구성되어 있으며 건강 전문가들의 조언을 받게 된다.

결론 **글의 목적 제시**
생활을 개선하는 것을 진심으로 원한다면 프로그램에 등록하십시오.

건강관리 프로그램을 홍보하고 있는 안내문으로 프로그램에 대한 내용에 대해 설명한 후, 결론에서 등록을 권유하며 글의 목적을 분명히 드러내고 있다.

유제 다음 글의 빈칸 (A), (B)에 들어갈 말로 가장 적절한 것은?

When it comes to salt and sweets, there's little a parent can do to change a child's inborn desire for them, which begins early in infancy. ____(A)____, there is some evidence that early diet can at least change the circumstances in which children will seek out sweet and salty flavors. As early as six months of age, babies who have been exposed more often to salted food show a stronger preference for salted cereal than babies with less salt experience. ____(B)____, six-month-old babies who have been fed sugar water tend to drink more of it than babies not previously exposed to it. This effect lasts a surprisingly long time, because even if the parents stop giving their baby sugar water by six months of age, she will continue to show a greater preference for it at age two.

*infancy: 유아기

	(A)		(B)
①	However	……	Similarly
②	Moreover	……	Similarly
③	However	……	Therefore
④	Moreover	……	In contrast
⑤	For example	……	Therefore

지문 소재별로 자주 출제되는 주요 어휘

- **diagnose** 진단하다
- **supplement** 보충(제)
- **compound** 화합물
- **refrigeration** 냉장, 냉동
- **flavor** 맛, 향
- **refined** 정제된
- **advance** 발전, 진보
- **ingredient** 재료, 성분
- **serve** (음식을) 차려내다
- **standardized** 표준화된
- **industrialized** 산업화된
- **flour** 밀가루
- **theory** 이론
- **surgery** 수술
- **organ** 장기
- **therapy** 치료, 요법
- **chemical** 화학물질
- **digestion** 소화
- **emergency** 응급, 비상사태
- **prescription** 처방전, 처방
- **abnormal** 비정상적인
- **genetics** 유전적 특징, 유전학
- **identify** 밝히다, 확인하다
- **tissue** 조직
- **organism** 유기체
- **infect** 감염시키다
- **protein** 단백질
- **procedure** 과정
- **physician** 의사
- **muscle** 근육
- **cough** 기침[하다]
- **nutrition** 영양
- **symptom** 증상

Exercise

01 다음 글의 주제로 가장 적절한 것은?

By and large, people who get admitted to medical schools have common attributes: a desire to help people and an aptitude for science. However, over the course of four years of medical school, the time in which aspiring doctors are expected to become acquainted with and understand all the diseases and biologic functions of the human body, they get used to seeing symptoms and signs of illness and injury separate from actual patients. Furthermore, their knowledge of specifics is tested far more than their ability to assess overall patient well-being. Doctors often take these habits with them into medical practice, emphasizing specifics over wholeness, body over mind, leaving many patients not feeling cared by their compassion or interest.

① influence of doctors' character on the patients
② need of changing the curriculum of medical school
③ meanings of giving medical students financial support
④ importance of encouraging studies on medical devices
⑤ reasons doctors in practice do not make patients feel cared for

02 다음 빈칸에 들어갈 말로 가장 적절한 것은?

Slow Food is an association founded in 1986 by Italian Carlo Perini. Forming Slow Food was Mr. Petrini's way of voicing his displeasure over the opening of a McDonald's Restaurant in Rome. The main goal of Slow Food is to promote ____________ in food and wine culture. Since 1986 the association has grown into a worldwide movement existing in over 50 countries. This movement is committed to protecting cultural traditions related to food, food preparation and the use of wild animal and vegetable species. The 83,000 Slow Food members are also opposed to the way foods are quickly becoming similar in taste, or "standardized," around the world. Much of this is caused by restaurant chains that serve the same foods prepared the same way across the globe.

① diversity ② harmony ③ consistency
④ advancement ⑤ advertisement

03 (A), (B), (C)의 각 네모 안에서 어법에 맞는 표현으로 가장 적절한 것은?

Every day, you make hundreds of decisions that are pointing you toward a longer life or a shorter one. Nowhere (A) [are / is] those decisions more clear than at the dinner table. For example, when researchers in Loma Linda University Medical Center tracked the lifestyle habits of 34,000 people in a religious group, (B) [which / whose] members were famous for their longevity, they discovered that those who ate nuts five days a week earned an extra 2.9 years on the planet. Similarly, Italian researchers found that eating as little as one cup of raw vegetables daily can (C) [add / be added] two years to your life. Why are raw vegetables so good for you? Cooking can remove up to 30 percent of the antioxidants in vegetables.

*antioxidant: 산화방지제

	(A)		(B)		(C)
①	are	……	which	……	add
②	are	……	whose	……	be added
③	are	……	whose	……	add
④	is	……	whose	……	be added
⑤	is	……	which	……	add

Plus Q

채소를 조리하지 않고 먹는 것이 좋은 이유를 우리말로 쓰시오.

➡

01 **by and large** 대체적으로 **admit** (단체 · 학교 등에서) 받아들이다, 입학을 허락하다 **attribute** 속성, 특징 **aptitude** 적성 **over the course of~** ~동안 **aspiring** 장차 ~가 되려는 **be acquainted with** ~를 알다[알게 되다] **symptom** 증상 **separate** 분리되다 **specifics** (어떤 주제에 대한 논의 등을 위해 필요한) 세부 사항[내용] **assess** 평가하다 **well-being** 행복, 복지
02 **association** 협회 **found** 설립하다 **voice** (말로) 표현하다, 나타내다 **displeasure** 불만 **promote** 조장하다, 홍보하다 **existing** 존재하는 **committed to** ~에 전념하는 **species** 종 **opposed** (~에) 반대하는 **standardized** 표준화된 **serve** (음식을) 차려내다, 내놓다
03 **point** ~에 이르게 하다 **clear** 명확한, 분명한 **track** 추적하다 **longevity** 장수 **nuts** 견과 **earn** 얻다 **extra** 추가적인 **raw** 조리하지 않은, 날것의 **remove** 제거하다

소재

09 스포츠, 취미, 여행, 여가

여가 시간 및 야외 활동 증가에 따라 다양한 스포츠 활동과 여행지, 여가를 보내는 여러 가지 방법, 많은 취미들이 지문에서 소개되고 있으며, 다양한 유형으로 출제되는 편이다. 소재의 특성상 우리 생활과 밀접하고 친숙하게 느껴지기 때문에 비교적 체감 난이도가 낮은 편이므로, 편안하게 읽으면서 유형에 맞추어 문제를 풀면 된다.

대표 예제

다음 글의 주제로 가장 적절한 것은? 평가원

도입》 Tourism is important for more than just vacationing. 전개1》 Tourism allows people from different places and cultures to come together, and then tourists and host communities learn about each other's differences and similarities. They also learn new tastes and ways of thinking, which may lead to a better understanding between hosts and tourists. 전개2》 Another positive effect of tourism is the aid it provides for the survival of a society's culture, especially the culture's art forms. The opportunity to sell native artworks to tourists or perform folk dances for them may encourage local artists to preserve traditional art forms. 전개3》 For example, Fijians have developed their palm mat and shell jewelry crafts into profitable tourist businesses. They also earn additional income by performing folk dances and fire walking.

① misunderstandings between hosts and tourists
② various ways of creating tourism products
③ negative effects of cultural exchanges
④ disappearance of traditional cultures
⑤ cultural benefits of tourism

한눈에 보는 구조

도입》 **주제 제시**
관광은 휴가를 보내는 것 이상으로 중요하다.

전개1》 **주제에 대한 근거 1**
다른 장소와 문화에서 온 사람들이 함께 모일 수 있도록 해 주고, 관광객과 관광지의 지역사회가 서로에 대해 더 잘 이해할 수 있다.

전개2》 **주제에 대한 근거 2**
지역 예술가들이 전통 예술 형태를 보존하는 데 도움을 준다.

전개3》 **근거 2에 대한 예시**
피지 제도에 사는 사람들은 전통 예술을 응용하여 소득을 얻고 있다.

두괄식으로 주제를 제시한 후, 그 근거를 예시를 통해 구체적으로 설명하고 있는 글이다.

유제 주어진 글 다음에 이어질 글의 순서로 가장 적절한 것은? 고2 교육청

Composition is not just about framing the picture, it is also pressing the camera shutter at exactly the right moment. Get the timing wrong, and the picture may well lose some of its energy.

(A) But with other, less predictable, events there can be magical moments — when constantly changing conditions and people suddenly come together to create a strong, beautiful, energetic composition. Such moments might be when two or more elements combine in a certain way.

(B) For some subjects, the key times at which to take pictures are obvious, such as the moment when a winner crosses the finishing line. On such occasions, preparation and practice count as much as good luck.

(C) On a stormy day, for example, a beautiful building might suddenly be illuminated by a shaft of light, creating a moody scene that might never be recaptured. To make the most of these decisive moments requires patience and the vision to see what might happen, even before it presents itself in the viewfinder.

*composition: 구도

① (A) – (C) – (B)
② (B) – (A) – (C)
③ (B) – (C) – (A)
④ (C) – (A) – (B)
⑤ (C) – (B) – (A)

지문 소재별로 자주 출제되는 주요 어휘

advantage 유리; 장점	**comfortable** 편안한	**divert** 기분전환을 시키다
aboard ~을 타고	**souvenir** 기념품	**opponent** 상대, 적수
reservation 예약; 보류	**crowd** 군중, 관중	**expense** 비용, 경비
athlete 운동선수	**delay** 지연(시키다)	**leisure** 여가; 한가함
accommodation 숙박시설	**spectacular** 볼 만한, 구경거리	**strength** 힘; 강점
scenery 경치; 무대장치	**defeat** 패배(시키다)	**fee** 보수, 수수료
cheer 환호(하다)	**departure** 출발	**pastime** 오락; 기분전환
cancelation 취소	**vessel** 선박	**train** 훈련하다
sightseeing 관광, 유람	**fair** 정정당당한	**passenger** 승객
competition 경쟁; 시합	**destination** 목적지	**relax** (긴장을) 늦추다

Exercise

01 다음 글의 밑줄 친 부분 중, 어법상 틀린 것은?

I went to a football game last week, and it opened my eyes to a whole new way of seeing people. The game was fun, but it was the whole experience, especially the crowd, ① that appeared in a new light. ② Sitting high in the stadium, I could see thousands of people. They all jumped to their feet together, cheered or booed at the same time, did the wave, and ③ encouraged the team. The spectacle made me realize that the crowd was real. It existed, like a huge, dim-witted animal, with joys, angers, fears, and desires of ④ their own. It was more than just a collection of people. It was just as real as the individuals, but different from them. I could see the thing move and change moods with my own eyes, as ⑤ clearly as I could see my friends sitting beside me.

02 다음 글에서 전체 흐름과 관계 없는 문장은?

When you don't know how to spend your free time during summer holidays, gardening is the best option for you. ① With the help of such a primitive but very interesting hobby, you can get some very important benefits. ② Gardening helps you to save money in a grocery shop, because you will soon find all the vegetables that you need right in your backyard. ③ The range of them varies from primitive ones such as onions, paprika or tomatoes to very rare — for example, broccoli and even asparagus. ④ That's why people prefer organically grown vegetables to non-organically cultivated ones. ⑤ Having your own vegetable garden is also very useful, because it brings you positive emotions even on a cloudy day.

• SUB NOTE p. 83

03 글의 흐름으로 보아, 주어진 문장이 들어가기에 가장 적절한 곳은?

> Later in the season when he was able to suit up again, he showed his appreciation by putting the numbers of each of his teammates on his ball cap.

소재 09

Chad Kreuter, a reserve catcher for the Chicago White Sox, severely dislocated and fractured his left shoulder on a play at home. He underwent surgery, and the Sox placed him on the sixty-day disabled list. (①) That's the kind of thing that makes a backup player feel even less like a part of the team. (②) But quite **the opposite** happened. (③) Apparently, Chad's teammates had a strong liking for him; each player put Chad's number 12 on his ball cap to show support. (④) Chad was a member of the team whether he played or not, and that meant a lot to Chad. (⑤) All devoted to one and one devoted to all, and that's what makes a team.

Plus Q

밑줄 친 the opposite을 보여주는 구체적인 예를 본문에서 찾아 쓰시오.

01 crowd 군중, 관중　in a new light 새로운 견해로　jump to one's feet 벌떡 일어서다, 뛰어 일어나다　cheer 환호하다　boo 야유하다　encourage 격려하다　spectacle 광경, 구경거리　exist 존재하다　huge 거대한　dim-witted 우둔한, 멍청한

02 option 선택권　primitive 원시적인　save 절약하다　backyard 뒤뜰, 뒷마당　range 범위　rare 드문　organically 유기농으로　cultivated 재배된

03 suit up 유니폼을 입다　appreciation 감사　reserve catcher 후보 포수　dislocate 탈구시키다　fracture 골절이 되다[되게 하다]　undergo surgery 수술을 받다　apparently 분명히　have a liking for ~을 좋아하다　support 지지

소재

10 컴퓨터, 정보, 미디어, 교통

컴퓨터, 정보, 미디어, 교통 소재는 언론 매체의 특성, 인터넷 사용, 교통 문제 대응과 관련한 내용의 지문이 주로 제시된다. 매년 빠지지 않고 출제되는 소재로서, 특히 빠르게 변화하는 정보, 통신 기술의 발전 동향과 이와 관련하여 주요 이슈로 떠오르는 사회, 문화 현상에 지속적으로 관심을 기울이며 배경지식을 쌓아 두는 것이 중요하다.

대표 예제

다음 글의 빈칸 (A), (B)에 들어갈 말로 가장 적절한 것은? 수능

도입 New media can be defined by four characteristics simultaneously: they are media at the turn of the 20th and 21st centuries which are both integrated and interactive and use digital code and hypertext as technical means. It follows that their most common alternative names are multimedia, interactive media and digital media. By using this definition, it is easy to identify media as old or new. 전개1 ______(A)______, traditional television is integrated as it contains images, sound and text, but it is not interactive or based on digital code. The plain old telephone was interactive, but not integrated as it only transmitted speech and sounds and it did not work with digital code. 전개2 In contrast, the new medium of interactive television adds interactivity and digital code. ______(B)______, the new generations of mobile or fixed telephony are fully digitalized and integrated as they add text, pictures or video and they are connected to the Internet.

	(A)		(B)
①	For example	……	Additionally
②	Nevertheless	……	In other words
③	Therefore	……	Additionally
④	For example	……	In other words
⑤	Nevertheless	……	Consequently

한눈에 보는 구조

도입 주제 제시
새로운 매체는 통합적이고 쌍방향이며 디지털 코드와 하이퍼텍스트를 사용하는 매체로, 이러한 정의를 사용하면 매체가 구식인지 신식인지를 구별하기 쉽다.

전개1 구식 매체의 예시
전통적 텔레비전은 통합적이지만 쌍방향이 아니며 디지털 코드에 기반을 두고 있지 않다. 구식 전화는 쌍방향이었지만 통합적이지 않았고, 디지털 코드로 작동하지 않았다.

전개2 새로운 매체의 예시
쌍방향 텔레비전은 쌍방향성과 디지털 코드가 더해졌고, 새로운 세대의 이동식, 고정식 전화 통신은 완전히 디지털화되고 통합적이다.

글의 도입에서 새로운 매체의 정의를 내린 뒤에 구식 매체와 새로운 매체의 예시를 들고 있는데, 구식 매체와 새로운 매체를 대조하는 방식으로 글이 전개되고 있다.

유제 다음 글의 주제로 가장 적절한 것은? 고2 교육청

Advertising experts have learned that the commercials that we remember will hook us into a story. Think about some of the most memorable and effective advertisements of all time, whether in the form of a printed page or 30-second spot on television. They involved an impressive storyline. Apple Computer's classic "Think Different" campaign is widely considered the best ad of all time because it so dramatically told a powerful story. Coca Cola's "Mean Joe Green" commercial is another example of a story, in which a little boy meets his hero. The goal in all these scenarios is to *move* people, emotionally and personally, creating a close association with the product that is positive and familiar.

*spot: 방송 프로그램 사이에 끼워 넣는 광고

① various lengths of commercials
② roles of ads in increasing sales
③ differences between ads and campaigns
④ uses of personal storytelling in education
⑤ powerful effects of storytelling in advertising

지문 소재별로 자주 출제되는 주요 어휘

access 접근, 접속
distract 산만하게 하다
congestion 혼잡
technical 기술적인
connect 연결하다
process 처리하다
establish 설정하다
scarcity 부족, 결핍
contain 포함하다
involve 수반하다
available 이용 가능한
contemporary 동시대의
promote 촉진하다
excess 초과
eliminate 제거하다
arise 발생하다
rate 비율, 속도
tackle 다루다
advertise 광고하다
transmit 전송하다
exchange 교환하다
multiple 다수의
suggest 시사하다
define 정의하다
solution 해결책
alternative 대안
allocate 할당하다
attribute 속성
reduce 감소시키다
interpret 해석하다

Exercise

01 다음 글의 빈칸 (A), (B)에 들어갈 말로 가장 적절한 것은?

At its core, big data is about predictions. Though it is described as part of the branch of computer science called artificial intelligence, and more specifically, an area called machine learning, this characterization is misleading. Big data is not about trying to "teach" a computer to "think" like humans. ___(A)___, it's about applying math to huge quantities of data in order to infer probabilities; the likelihood that an email message is spam; that the typed letters "teh" are supposed to be "the." The key is that these systems perform well because they are fed with lots of data on which to base their predictions. ___(B)___, the systems are built to improve themselves over time, by keeping a tab on what are the best signals and patterns to look for as more data is fed in.

	(A)		(B)
①	In other words	……	Moreover
②	However	……	Nevertheless
③	Instead	……	Moreover
④	In other words	……	In short
⑤	Instead	……	Nevertheless

02 다음 글에서 전체 흐름과 관계 없는 문장은?

Self-driving vehicles have the potential to radically change the way we think about cars, and the potential is almost limitless. Autonomous taxis could be parked on every street, in every city, so you could summon one using your mobile phone and it would be parked outside your house by the time you walked out of your front door. ① Once it has taken you to your destination, it drives off for its next customer. ② Furthermore, self-driving vehicles could be used to collect children from school, take elderly people to shops and carry out all the usual, everyday journeys. ③ Self-driving cars, if shared, could even solve many of the problems of congestion. ④ In many cities, the number of car sharing providers has increased sharply in the last few years. ⑤ They can communicate with each other to avoid congestion, always taking the shortest and quickest route to your destination.

03 다음 빈칸에 들어갈 말로 가장 적절한 것은?

To be sure, distinctions between analogue and digital media are just ____________. It is important to keep in mind that, **however much our media technologies have changed** in recent decades, the human eyes, ears, and voices have not — that is, we as embodied beings still generate and receive information in resolutely analogue form. The digital codes, for example, that pass between two computers or smartphones, whether in the form of a Skype call, Facebook update, or phone call, begin and end for their human users as analogue information. The emergence of "the digital," in short, does not mean the quick and complete end of "the analogue."

*embodied: 체화된

① one side of the coin
② conventional wisdom
③ technological study results
④ legitimate criteria for media
⑤ proper grounds for development

Plus Q

밑줄 친 however much our media technologies have changed를 우리말로 해석하시오.

➡

01 **core** 핵심 **prediction** 예측 **describe** 기술하다 **artificial intelligence** 인공지능 **characterization** 정의, 묘사 **misleading** 오해의 소지가 있는, 호도[오도]하는 **quantity** 양 **infer** 추론하다 **probability** 확률 **be supposed to** ~하기로 되어 있다 **keep a tab on** ~을 계산[확인]하다

02 **self-driving** 자율주행의 **potential** 잠재력 **radically** 근본적으로 **autonomous** 자율의 **summon** 부르다 **destination** 목적지 **carry out** 수행하다 **congestion** 혼잡 **avoid** 피하다

03 **distinction** 구분 **keep in mind** 명심하다 **generate** 생성하다 **receive** 수용하다 **resolutely** 단호히 **emergence** 출현 **complete** 완전한 **conventional** 관습적인 **legitimate** 타당한 **criteria** 기준 **proper** 적절한 **ground** 이유

There's wall
between you and what you want
and you got to leap it.

- Bob Dylan

PART Ⅲ

Mini Test

Mini Test **01~08**

숨마쿰라우데®

[독해 매뉴얼]

Mini Test 1회

제한 시간	소요 시간	맞은 개수
15분	분	/9문항

01 다음 글에 드러난 'I'의 심경으로 가장 적절한 것은?

It didn't take long for me to realize what had happened. My trapped leg was numb, and the pain seemed to increase with each passing moment. Then I heard a bee buzzing inside my car. It kept flying around my head. The tickling gave me a powerful impulse to shake my head, but I knew that panic would only cause a sting in that most sensitive spot. So I steeled myself not to move. After a few minutes, the bee crawled out of my car and buzzed away. Before I could breathe a sigh of relief, however, I heard a swarm of bees buzzing from my back. I made no movement, trying to hold my breath. I already knew what difference a drop of a pin could make.

① relieved
② envious
③ frightened
④ indifferent
⑤ disappointed

02 다음 글의 요지로 가장 적절한 것은?

Every teen needs to be accepted for who they are, even if they occasionally make choices that you don't agree with. If a teen feels like your love, commitment and emotional support are based on whether or not he can live up to your standards, then he will never feel worthy enough to gain your acceptance or emotionally safe enough to let down his guard. You don't want to devastate them with destructive criticism, do you? Try not to lose faith in a teen when she makes a bad decision. Instead of pointing out how disappointed you are in her as a person, focus your disapproval on her behavior. You can do that by saying something like: *I find it very impolite that* ... Or, *right now I'm annoyed with you because* ... This kind of remark enables a teen to take in what you are saying and understand the main point of your comments.

① 십 대들의 감정 표현에 민감하게 반응하지 마라.
② 십 대들에게 일관성 있는 꾸준한 모습을 보여주어라.
③ 십 대들에게 지시를 내릴 때 명확하게 전달되도록 하라.
④ 십 대들을 다룰 때, 그들이 아닌 그들의 행동을 지적하라.
⑤ 십 대들이 합리적인 의사 결정을 내릴 수 있도록 도움을 주어라.

03 다음 글의 주제로 가장 적절한 것은?

Frequent flying and regularly crossing time zones disrupts your circadian rhythm, or internal clock and causes jet leg. You're knocked out of sync with your environment, making you tired. Symptoms include headaches, irritability, brain fog and low energy. Then how can you be free from such symptoms caused by jet leg? In the days before your flight, stick to a consistent sleep schedule to set a pattern for your body. While on board, drink at least two glasses of water every hour to combat dehydration caused by the plane's dry air. Move around the cabin every so often to improve circulation and prevent swelling. Doing seated stretches by straightening your legs and pointing and flexing your toes will help lessen muscle stiffness. Exposure to sunlight in the morning helps move your circadian rhythm forward.

*circadian rhythm: 24시간 주기 리듬

**brain fog: 머리가 혼란스럽고 안개같이 뿌예서 분명하게 생각하거나 표현하지 못하는 상태

① symptoms of jet leg
② ways of preventing jet leg
③ definition of internal clock
④ how to relax during a flight
⑤ importance of a consistent sleep

04 다음 빈칸에 들어갈 말로 가장 적절한 것은?

For women leaders, the affirmation and support of a larger community are still uncommon. Women leaders can feel alone in the most crowded of rooms. Whether in the ranks of middle management, in the high ranks of the executive, at the helm of entrepreneurial ventures, or in a political arena, they are constantly reminded—subtly and not so subtly—that they are not truly welcome as they attempt to advocate a point of view. This type of __________________ has a profound effect. They doubt their own ideas, intuition, and knowledge. They lose their self-esteem, confidence, and desire to contribute. They do not feel valued or accepted. Although every woman leader knows the personal cost of such marginalization, it is hard to imagine the losses they have caused in organizations as a result.

① mutual interest
② repeated rejection
③ gradual promotion
④ shared information
⑤ overly high expectation

05 다음 빈칸에 들어갈 말로 가장 적절한 것은?

Until recently, medical errors were seldom discussed. The public preferred to believe that errors in medical practice were rare. Health professionals, fearing loss of trust and impaired reputation, sought to ______________________. The adversary climate produced by the threat of legal action against medical errors fueled this "see nothing, do nothing" approach. All this has changed in the past two decades. A new "movement" for patient safety began in 1995, when a series of apparently outrageous errors resulting in death or inappropriate surgery were widely publicized. Hospitals began to recognize that they could do more to prevent patient injuries. The result has been substantial increases in both research on the causes of medical error and implementation of preventive mechanisms.

① recover their prestige
② share medical records
③ depend on legal advice
④ perpetuate that misconception
⑤ contribute more to the society

Mini Test 1회

06 Michael Romanoff에 관한 다음 글의 내용과 일치하지 않는 것은?

Michael Romanoff was a Hollywood restaurateur and actor born in the name of Hershel Geguzin in Lithuania. He was perhaps best known as the owner of the now-vanished Romanoff's, a Beverly Hills restaurant popular with Hollywood stars in the 1940s and 1950s. Geguzin immigrated to New York City at age ten, and changed his name to Michael Romanoff sometime after 1900. In 1931, he pretended to be a famous illustrator, Rockwell Kent, which made the artist happy. Romanoff was so attractive as Kent that he sold more of Kent's art books than the real artist did. He had been expelled to France in May, 1932 to serve time for fraud. According to *U.S.A. Confidential*, Romanoff pretended to be a Russian prince, which made his restaurant popular. He died of a heart attack in Los Angeles, California at the age of 81 in 1971.

① 리투아니아에서 Hershel Geguzin라는 이름으로 태어났다.
② 할리우드 스타들에게 인기 있는 레스토랑의 소유주였다.
③ 유명 삽화가의 행세를 하여 그 삽화가를 불쾌하게 만들었다.
④ 사기죄로 복역하기 위해 1932년에 프랑스로 추방되었다.
⑤ U.S.A. Confidential에 따르면, 러시아의 왕자 행세를 하였다.

07 (A), (B), (C)의 각 네모 안에서 문맥에 맞는 낱말로 가장 적절한 것은?

Distorting reality is not always bad. Sometimes it is (A) [necessary / unnecessary] because of feeling overwhelmed, trauma, or abuse. In such instances, denial helps a person cope with what would otherwise be a highly (B) [carefree / stressful] situation. Other times, denial can be a way to take a mental vacation. From the perspective of mental health, however, the key is knowing when you are "on a fancy trip" from when you are not and not letting some defensive ways of thought become habitual and (C) [block / encourage] pursuit of a healthy and meaningful life. You can do this by learning to observe how your mind works. Such self-knowledge is a goal of meditation, yoga, modern psychotherapies, and other practices that help to focus on awareness and engage one's consciousness.

	(A)		(B)		(C)
①	necessary	……	carefree	……	block
②	necessary	……	stressful	……	block
③	necessary	……	stressful	……	encourage
④	unnecessary	……	carefree	……	encourage
⑤	unnecessary	……	stressful	……	block

08 다음 글의 밑줄 친 부분 중, 어법상 틀린 것은?

When I was a little girl, I accidentally broke a fruit jar. I don't know why, but although several brothers and a sister were nearby ① who could have done it, my father turned to me and asked, "Did you break the jar, Alice?" ② Looking into his large, brown eyes, I knew he wanted me to tell the truth. I also knew he might punish me if I did. But the truth inside of me wanted badly to ③ be expressed. "I broke the jar," I said. The love in his eyes rewarded and embraced me. Suddenly I felt an inner peace ④ where I still recall with gratitude to this day. In the same way, we find that confessing our sins to someone we feel close to ⑤ brings us closer to him.

09 주어진 글 다음에 이어질 글의 순서로 가장 적절한 것은?

The Alcott family finances were very low, but they placed great hopes on Bronson Alcott's latest lecture tour. When he arrived home one night in February, the family gathered around him.

(A) There was a stunned hush in the group around him. Then Mrs. Alcott flung her arms around his neck and said strongly, "I call that doing very well."

(B) They welcomed him, offered him food and drink, and rejoiced in his homecoming. Then a little silence fell, and it was daughter May who asked the question in all their minds: "Did they pay you?"

(C) Slowly Bronson Alcott drew out his pocketbook and displayed its contents. All it had was a single dollar. "Another year I shall do better," he said.

① (A) – (C) – (B)
② (B) – (A) – (C)
③ (B) – (C) – (A)
④ (C) – (A) – (B)
⑤ (C) – (B) – (A)

Mini Test 2회

제한 시간	소요 시간	맞은 개수
15분	분	/9문항

01 다음 글의 목적으로 가장 적절한 것은?

Dear Mr. Tarpley,

According to our computer system, you left your tabby cat "Mitch" with us on February 4, 2016, for leg surgery but failed to pick him up on the 7th as agreed. We have phoned repeatedly in the weeks following to remind you to collect your pet, but we have received no response. If you are unable to do so due to illness or a change in circumstances, we will happily bring him to you, or even see that he is adopted to a loving home. If you fail to contact us within 7 working days, we will have to assume that you have abandoned your cat and will proceed with the adoption process. Please contact us immediately at 601-555-0189.

Sincerely,
M. Baxter

① 입양을 기다리는 애완동물을 소개하려고
② 애완동물의 건강 검진 결과를 통보하려고
③ 희귀한 애완동물을 키워볼 것을 권하려고
④ 잃어버린 애완동물을 찾아준 것을 감사하려고
⑤ 애완동물 처리에 대해 연락할 것을 촉구하려고

02 다음 글의 제목으로 가장 적절한 것은?

Making a significant impact is not common because there are many forces that lead to stagnancy and mediocrity. For example, some people, whether co-workers, managers, or even friends, may not want you to fully engage in the pursuit of great work because it places a responsibility on them to do the same. If you begin to rise above the pack, they will quickly try to bring you back to earth. Also, organizations often make it easy to settle in, providing you with a good salary, a nice title, or a sense of stability — the proverbial "golden handcuffs." It's easy to fall in love with these comfortable perks, but the love of comfort is often the enemy of greatness. There's nothing wrong with experiencing comfort as a by-product of your labor, but you can't make it your chief goal.

*stagnancy: 정체됨

**mediocrity: 평범함

① Try to Be a Better Co-Worker
② Avoid Comfort: It's Dangerous!
③ Good Working Conditions for Workers
④ Is Competition Appropriate in a Cooperative Situation?
⑤ Management Styles: Task-Oriented vs. People-Oriented

03 (A), (B), (C)의 각 네모 안에서 어법에 맞는 표현으로 가장 적절한 것은?

Music is very much a part of the daily lives of Africans. For example, it is called on to cure illnesses, appease gods, and (A) [celebrate / celebrating] the births of babies. There are songs for praising cattle, telling about animal hunts, and paddling a canoe. There is also some music that is simply for entertainment, and a small amount that is played for ceremonies involving a king or chief. Because most African music is functional, it does not take place in a performer / audience situation. Musical performances are truly participatory events (B) [which / in which] there is little distinction between performer and audience. Because African music is functional, its musicians want their work to have an impact. They do not care whether it is considered (C) [beautiful / beautifully] in the sense that Western musicians often think about music.

	(A)		(B)		(C)
①	celebrate	……	which	……	beautiful
②	celebrate	……	in which	……	beautiful
③	celebrate	……	in which	……	beautifully
④	celebrating	……	which	……	beautifully
⑤	celebrating	……	in which	……	beautifully

04 다음 빈칸에 들어갈 말로 가장 적절한 것은?

When I read K. Anders Ericsson's landmark studies of elite performance, I noticed that many people overlooked a factor that significantly influenced performance. While many concentrated on his findings relevant to 10,000 hours of deliberate practice, the other factor that differentiated top performance was sleep. The best performers in these studies slept for 8 hours and 36 minutes per night on average. The average American, in contrast, gets just 6 hours and 51 minutes of sleep on weeknights. Ericsson's studies of elite performers — which included musicians, athletes, actors, and chess players — also suggest that ______________________ boosts achievement. Ericsson found that they take frequent breaks to avoid exhaustion and to ensure that they fully recharge. This allows them to keep improving and perfecting their craft.

① resting more frequently
② taking advanced courses
③ guaranteeing fair treatment
④ exercising on a regular basis
⑤ asking for more information

05 밑줄 친 she[her]가 가리키는 대상이 나머지 넷과 다른 것은?

Cindy Silverman went to a local medical laboratory for a routine blood test. In the next room was a young girl, about five years old, screaming at the top of her lungs. She was supposed to get a blood test, too, but ① she wouldn't let the nurse stick her arm with the needle. It was a nightmare of a scene. Cindy went to the girl's room and asked her mother's permission to talk with ② her, which she received. "Look at me," she empathetically said to the girl. The girl looked at ③ her. "Do you think your mommy loves you?" Cindy asked, kindly. "Yes," ④ she said. "Do you think your mommy would do anything to hurt you?" Cindy asked. "No," the girl said. When the girl had calmed down a bit, she said, "The doctor and Mommy can't make you better unless they do this test." Within two minutes, ⑤ she calmed down and was ready for the needle.

06 다음 글의 내용을 한 문장으로 요약하고자 한다. 빈칸(A)와 (B)에 들어갈 말로 가장 적절한 것은?

At first, hardcore scientists ridiculed Rachel Carson after she published *Silent Spring*, but her evidence and predictions about the horrible effects of pesticides and environmental toxins unfortunately proved to be true; since then, we've made major changes in our lives to help protect our environment. Likewise, many researchers criticized Jane Goodall when she first named the chimpanzees she studied; they didn't believe she'd seen David Graybeard use a blade of grass as a tool for fishing out termites until she showed them a video of this groundbreaking discovery. In the early 1960s, the ideas that an animal had an individual personality (warranting a name) and could make and use a tool (which only humans were thought capable of) were heretical, crazy. Both are now commonplace, self-evident.

*termite: 흰개미

→ At first both Rachel Carson and Jane Goodall were ____(A)____ by some researchers, but the two scientists ____(B)____ their arguments.

	(A)		(B)
①	respected	……	revised
②	respected	……	dismissed
③	influenced	……	proved
④	resisted	……	revised
⑤	resisted	……	proved

Mini Test 2회

07 글의 흐름으로 보아, 주어진 문장이 들어가기에 가장 적절한 곳은?

Neighboring Malawi is very different.

Stephen Buggie, a professor of psychology at Presbyterian College in South Carolina, spent three years teaching in Zambia and nine years in Malawi. (①) "In Zambia," he recalls, "the tempo of life is generally slow, with casual regard toward punctuality and time. (②) Meetings there start more promptly than in Zambia. (③) Malawi's Life President, Kamuzu Banda, practiced medicine in Scotland for 30 years before entering politics back home. (④) He rules the country absolutely and is a stickler for punctuality. (⑤) Back in the 1970s he made it illegal for public clocks to display inaccurate time.

*stickler: 꽤 까다로운 사람

[08~09] 다음 글을 읽고, 물음에 답하시오.

Historians chronicle change over time. While there is continuity between past eras and our own, there has also been significant change. For example, the United States changed considerably between 1776 and 1900: the meaning of the Constitution was defined more clearly by a bloody civil war; the demographic makeup of the country changed immensely with the arrival of new immigrants; and access to democratic practices, such as voting, was gradually applied to nonlandholders, African Americans, and women. Historians trace these changes. Their task is to take their audiences on a journey by shedding light on the ways in which life in past eras was different from the world in which we now live. I am writing this paragraph on July 27, 2012. Earlier this evening I watched, with billions of other people around the world, the opening ceremonies of the London Summer Olympic Games. Many of you will remember these ceremonies for the scene, crafted by film director Danny Boyle, in which James Bond and "Queen Elizabeth" parachuted into the Olympic stadium from a helicopter to the roaring applause of the British faithful. I was struck by the way Boyle's ceremony was based on the historical concept of change over time. The ceremony traced the movement of Great Britain from an agricultural society to an industrial society to a technological society. In essence, Boyle was delivering the world a very expensive and very elaborate history lesson. The historical task is inherently ____________ because the historian is ever aware that things do not stay the same.

08 윗글의 제목으로 가장 적절한 것은?

① History: The Record of Change
② The Present: A Mirror of the Past
③ Historical Narratives: Fact or Fiction?
④ Can the Past Be Changed by the Future?
⑤ History as a Fountain of Imaginative Ideas

09 윗글의 빈칸에 들어갈 말로 가장 적절한 것은?

① subjective
② ambiguous
③ progressive
④ conservative
⑤ contradictory

Mini Test 3회

제한 시간	소요 시간	맞은 개수
15분	분	/9문항

01 다음 글에서 필자가 주장하는 바로 가장 적절한 것은?

One of the mistakes rookie leaders often make is that they try to lead everyone the same way. But let's face it. Everyone doesn't respond to the same kind of leadership. You should try to be consistent with everyone. You should treat everyone with kindness and respect. But don't expect to use the same strategies and methods with everyone. You have to figure out what leadership buttons to push with each individual person on your team. One person will respond well to being challenged; another will want to be nurtured. One will need the game plan drawn up for him; another will be more passionate if she can create the game plan herself. One will require consistent, frequent follow-up; another will want breathing room. If you desire to be an effective leader, you need to take responsibility for conforming your leadership style to what your people need, not expecting them to adapt to you.

① 부하 직원들의 발언권과 재량권을 늘리라.
② 직원의 건의사항에 대해 신속하게 응답하라.
③ 실수의 책임을 부하 직원에게 떠넘기지 말라.
④ 차별 대우 없이 항상 공정하게 사람을 대하라.
⑤ 개인마다 각자에게 적합한 방식으로 지도하라.

02 다음 글에서 전체 흐름과 관계 없는 문장은?

The worship of animals was widespread. The Egyptian deities took animal forms, and many were depicted as people with the heads of nonhumans. ①The relationship was not simple, however, and more than one deity might take the form of a particular animal and certain deities had more than one animal form. ②For instance, Hathor, who was the goddess of love and fertility, often appeared as a cow or with the head of a cow—as did Isis, the goddess of nature. ③Horus, the son of Isis and Osiris, was the ancient Egyptians' national patron god. ④Bastet, the goddess of the home, usually had the head of a cat, but sometimes of a lion. ⑤Mut, mother of the Moon god, bore the head of a vulture or appeared as a lioness.

*deity: 신(神)

03 주어진 글 다음에 이어질 글의 순서로 가장 적절한 것은?

On one flight I happened to be sitting next to a woman who worked for a major software company. I was writing and spell-checking a manuscript, and she asked what program I used.

(A) She recognized that the language we use affects our attitudes. Perhaps the next generation of spell-checking software will reverse its presumptions, prompting writers to refer to animals as "he" or "she," not "it."

(B) I told her and said I was working on a book on animal emotions and that I wished that word-processing software would stop asking me to change the words "who" and "whom" to "that" or "which" when I refer to animals—because animals aren't objects but subjects.

(C) At first she didn't get it, but eventually she did, and she said she'd talk to the people at her company about changing their software. Whether she followed through or not, I was glad that she was open to seeing animals differently.

① (A) – (C) – (B)　　② (B) – (A) – (C)
③ (B) – (C) – (A)　　④ (C) – (A) – (B)
⑤ (C) – (B) – (A)

04 다음 빈칸에 들어갈 말로 가장 적절한 것은?

An innovation does not have a single performance characteristic, but instead there are many, based on ______________________. For example, two cars could be compared based on gas mileage, noise, style, power, and reliability, while the automobile itself can be compared with light rail for efficiency with respect to traffic volume, trip duration, and environmental impact. The performance characteristics of a technology partly determine which alternative will "win" and be widely accepted. However, there is nothing to tell us which characteristics are most important: is it style, mileage, color, or power for a car? The relative importance of various characteristics is socially decided and culturally grounded. For example, environmentalists think that pollution is the main criterion by which a car should be chosen (if choosing a car at all), while most teenagers think that power and style matter more.

*light rail: 경전철

① the production cost of goods
② different potential users' needs
③ the theory of risk management
④ influential experts in financial services
⑤ the level of complexity of the technologies

05 다음 빈칸에 들어갈 말로 가장 적절한 것은?

By *positive* and *good*, I mean what leads to happiness and benefit for oneself and others. *Negative* and *bad* mean what leads to suffering and harm. Positive experiences usually feel good. But some experiences that feel bad have good results, so I'll refer to them as positive. For example, the pain of a hand on a hot stove, the anxiety at not finding your child at a park, and the remorse that helps us take the high road make us feel bad now to help us feel better later. Similarly, negative experiences usually feel bad. But some experiences that feel good have bad results, and I'll call these negative. The buzz from three beers or the vengeance in gossiping about someone who wronged you may feel momentarily pleasurable, but ____________________.

① the costs outweigh the benefits
② honesty is more important than relationships
③ presence of mind is more valuable than wealth
④ positive memories last longer than negative ones
⑤ long-term consistency is better than short-term intensity

06 다음 글의 빈칸 (A), (B)에 들어갈 말로 가장 적절한 것은?

People often make a mistake in their personal development when they focus too much on their weaknesses. As a result, they spend all their time trying to shore up those weaknesses instead of maximizing the strengths they possess. ____(A)____, it's a mistake to focus on the weaknesses of others. The self-proclaimed "experts" who spend their time telling others what's wrong with them never win with people. Most people simply avoid them. ____(B)____, we need to focus on finding people's strengths and pointing them out. Most people have strengths that they rarely get to use. Those strengths may be job skills, knowledge, general abilities, personality characteristics, or other attributes. Every person can do at least one thing better than ten thousand other people. Think about that!

(A)		(B)
① For example	……	Likewise
② For example	……	In other words
③ By contrast	……	Instead
④ Similarly	……	In other words
⑤ Similarly	……	Instead

[07~09] 다음 글을 읽고, 물음에 답하시오.

(A)

One day, Doniece Sandoval happened to pass a young woman sitting on the street. (a) She was crying and saying over and over to herself that she'd never be clean. Doniece lived in San Francisco, where it was impossible to be unaware of the homeless. For years, she had wanted to do more than volunteer or donate to an organization. But it wasn't until that day that she took action, inspired by the words of the young woman.

(B)

Doniece persuaded the city to give her four decommissioned buses that (b) she then had remodeled with $75,000 she'd raised on a crowdfunding website. Each bus connects to a fire hydrant for water, which is heated by large batteries on board. Wastewater is drained into city sewers. The first bus hit the road in July 2014; a second one rolled out in early 2015. Doniece plans to put the other two buses elsewhere in the Bay Area and imagines expanding the program internationally.

(C)

Doniece knew her challenges were deeper than she could imagine, but a light bulb went on in her head as she thought about how (c) she might be able to help the young woman get clean. That night Doniece began to research shower resources for San Francisco's homeless and was shocked by what (d) she learned: there are approximately 16 shower stalls for the more than 3,000 men, women, and children that make the streets of this city home. She thought, if you can put food on wheels, why not showers?

(D)

She did some research and found she wasn't the first person to think about this. There are about half a dozen mostly small communities around the country—all led by faith-based groups—using converted mobile homes and horse trailers. She talked to all of them and they told her stories of transformation; that the homeless using their mobile showers "felt human for the first time in a long time" or "were recovering their sense of dignity." (e) She thought, if they could do it, so could we. So the project, Lava Mae ("Wash Me"), was born.

07 주어진 글 (A)에 이어질 내용을 순서에 맞게 배열한 것으로 가장 적절한 것은?

① (B) – (D) – (C)
② (C) – (B) – (D)
③ (C) – (D) – (B)
④ (D) – (B) – (C)
⑤ (D) – (C) – (B)

08 밑줄 친 (a)~(e) 중에서 가리키는 대상이 나머지 넷과 다른 것은?

① (a)
② (b)
③ (c)
④ (d)
⑤ (e)

09 윗글의 Doniece Sandoval에 관한 내용과 일치하지 않는 것은?

① 자원봉사나 기부하는 것 이상의 남을 돕는 일을 하고 싶었다.
② 모금한 7만 5천 달러로 버스를 리모델링했다.
③ 자신이 만든 프로그램을 세계적으로 확장하는 것을 생각하고 있다.
④ 샌프란시스코의 노숙자를 위한 샤워 시설을 조사했다.
⑤ 이동식 샤워 시설을 제공하는 단체를 최초로 만들었다.

Mini Test 4회

제한 시간	소요 시간	맞은 개수
15분	분	/9문항

01 다음 글의 요지로 가장 적절한 것은?

Conflict can lead to productive growth if it is properly managed and resolved. The process of recognizing and working through a conflict can only happen in an environment of open communication. The old saying, *What doesn't kill us makes us stronger*, is appropriate for conflict. Conflict left under the surface festers and can be fatal. When it is recognized and brought out into the open, its resolution can bring people closer together as they grow in their understanding of each other. Communication is the key element affecting conflict: both its cause and remedy. Open communication is the means by which disagreement can be prevented, managed, or resolved. The lack of open communication can drive conflict underground and worsen misunderstanding and hostility.

*fester: (상처가) 곪다

① 갈등의 원인이 될 수 있는 것은 미리 제거해 두는 것이 좋다.
② 솔직한 의사소통을 할 수 있는 환경 조성이 절실히 필요하다.
③ 갈등이 있다는 것은 서로에 대한 관심이 높다는 것을 의미한다.
④ 솔직한 의사소통을 통해 갈등이 해결되면 상호 이해가 높아진다.
⑤ 서로 간의 불만 표출이 갈등으로 이어지지 않도록 주의해야 한다.

02 다음 글의 제목으로 가장 적절한 것은?

Chris was in charge of international sales for a technology company. He flew all over the world to meet with customers. His interpersonal skills were his greatest strength, a talent that came naturally. He knew instinctively how to build relationships and satisfy customers' needs. Customers were loyal to him beyond the norm. Furthermore, he was often treated as an extended member of the family. Before long, the corporate president made Chris a great offer. However, it was an offer Chris had to refuse. The new position had power and prestige, but it had no customer contact. Recognizing that it would distance him from the unique ability that made him most successful, Chris wisely turned down the opportunity.

① Talent: What You Can Develop
② Make Your Customers Your Family
③ Stick to Where Your Real Talent Lies
④ Only Efforts Lead You to a Higher Position
⑤ Opportunity: Something from the Unexpected

03 다음 빈칸에 들어갈 말로 가장 적절한 것은?

Even the most sophisticated technological advances have little value until they can be demonstrated to ____________________. For instance, the first electronic transistors developed at Bell Labs were considered to have negligible market value, and so the patents were sold for a few thousand dollars to Sony, which had the idea of putting them into portable radios. Sony correctly reasoned that people generally feel better when they are listening to music than when they are not; hence, they would be likely to believe that if they were able to carry their music with them they would be more satisfied than normal. In this manner an entirely new market for the advanced electronic technology, based on the desire for happiness, was created.

① have multiple uses
② enlarge potential value
③ lead general innovation
④ contribute to happiness
⑤ bring benefits to developers

04 다음 빈칸에 들어갈 말로 가장 적절한 것은?

In 1919, eight members of the Chicago White Sox baseball club were accused of taking bribes from gamblers in exchange for intentionally losing the World Series. Although they were never convicted in a court of law, all eight were banned from baseball for life. But one of those players, Buck Weaver, claimed that he had played to win despite knowing about the conspiracy. Though Weaver's performance on the field supported his contention, baseball commissioner Kenesaw Mountain Landis ruled that any player who had knowledge of the scandal, yet chose not to stop it, would still be banned. Weaver was not punished for doing wrong, but for ____________.

① failing to do right
② not keeping his values
③ betraying his colleagues
④ not playing in a fair way
⑤ being involved in the conspiracy

05 글의 흐름으로 보아, 주어진 문장이 들어가기에 가장 적절한 곳은?

> Although there is little question that visual cues are necessary for the successful performance of most technical skills, there are times when vision can prevent athletes from detecting other important sources of sensory information.

Research on perception clearly indicates that vision dominates the other sensory systems. (①) For example, when practicing the golf swing, a player would notice the feel of the swing less if she practiced it with her eyes open than if she did so with her eyes closed. (②) Thus, athletes can often benefit from keeping their eyes closed during technical skill practice. (③) This is particularly true when athletes need to devote more attention to the feel of the action. (④) Closed-eyes practice might also help athletes detect errors in their movements that they would otherwise not notice. (⑤) Finally, more advanced athletes might benefit from closed-eyes practice when they want to reconnect with the feeling associated with their movements.

Harvey University Essay Competition에 관한 다음 안내문의 내용과 일치하지 않는 것은?

Harvey University Essay Competition
Open to all Law Students

Essay topics:
a. The right function of law in society
b. The right application of law in society

* **Deadline**: August 20
The essay should be a maximum of 5,000 words, excluding the footnotes.

* **Prizes**:
1st: $3,000
2nd: $1,000 (The second prize will be awarded to up to 3 persons.)

Certificates of participation will be awarded to all participating students. The winning entries and a few other selected essays will be published in the school magazine.

Submissions to be emailed to: huessaycompetition@gmailcom

① 에세이 주제로 두 가지가 제시되어 있다.
② 에세이는 주석을 제외하고 최대 5천 단어까지이다.
③ 2등상은 3명까지 주어질 수 있다.
④ 모든 참가자는 참가 증명서를 받을 수 있다.
⑤ 수상 작품만 학교 잡지에 실릴 예정이다.

07 다음 글의 밑줄 친 부분 중, 문맥상 낱말의 쓰임이 적절하지 않은 것은?

Many teachers shy away from using contemporary art in their teaching because they do not feel comfortable with their own level of knowledge and are ① reluctant to introduce their students to anything they may not have mastered themselves. This response is not ② unique to educators. As art critic and historian Lucy Lippard has pointed out, the field of contemporary art "has become ③ mystified to the point where many people doubt and are even embarrassed by their responses." To make matters worse, teaching resources are scarce. The ④ absence of curriculum materials about contemporary art reflects the attitude that the only valuable art is that which has "withstood the test of time." This attitude, in turn, reflects the belief that it is ⑤ impossible to establish universal cultural standards that remain fixed and permanent.

08 (A), (B), (C)의 각 네모 안에서 어법에 맞는 표현으로 가장 적절한 것은?

A group of Jews in the Auschwitz concentration camp decide, one afternoon, to put God on trial. God is brought up on charges of cruelty and betrayal and the arguments for and against God (A) [begin / to begin]. Despite believing that God is supposed to counter evil and serve as a comfort to humans, this immediate death camp court finds no evidence of divine intervention in their horrific world nor any forgiving atmosphere (B) [that / what] relieves God of responsibility. The rabbi announces the verdict: God is guilty and, presumably, worthy of death. But then the rabbi glances up at (C) [those / them] assembled and says that the trial has concluded. It is, he tells them, time for the evening prayer.

*Auschwitz concentration camp: 2차 대전 중 독일군에 의해 만들어졌던 수용소

	(A)		(B)		(C)
①	begin	……	that	……	those
②	begin	……	that	……	them
③	begin	……	what	……	those
④	to begin	……	what	……	them
⑤	to begin	……	that	……	those

09 다음 글의 내용을 한 문장으로 요약하고자 한다. 빈칸 (A)와 (B)에 들어갈 말로 가장 적절한 것은?

The researchers extracted some white blood cells from a volunteer and they carefully placed them in a test tube. They then put a probe from a lie detector machine down in that test tube, to measure the person's emotional response. Next, they instructed the same volunteer to go a couple of doors down and watch some violent scenes from an old war movie on television. When this man watched the scenes, even though the blood that was being tested was in another room, when he got all uptight and tense, that lie detector machine went wild. It was detecting his emotional response even though the blood was no longer in his body. The experimenters did this with person after person with the same results.

*probe: 탐침

→ It seems that the blood cells ___(A)___ whom they are ___(B)___ by.

	(A)		(B)
①	remember	……	owned
②	remember	……	found
③	predict	……	abandoned
④	forget	……	owned
⑤	forget	……	abandoned

Mini Test 4회

Mini Test 5

제한 시간	소요 시간	맞은 개수
15분	분	/9문항

01 다음 글의 제목으로 가장 적절한 것은?

I remember one summer day when my ten-year-old son and a friend were getting a pitcher of lemonade from the refrigerator. I'd spent hours that morning scrubbing, waxing, and polishing the kitchen floor, so I wanted the boys not to spill anything. They tried hard to be careful but they accidentally bumped a tray of eggs on the door shelf. It fell, splattering eggs all over my clean floor. The boys' eyes widened with alarm as I exploded angrily. "Get out of here—now!" I shouted, while they headed for the door. By the time I'd finished cleaning up the mess, I had calmed down. To make amends, I set a tray of cookies on the table, along with the pitcher of lemonade and some glasses. But when I called the boys, there was no answer—they'd gone somewhere else to play, somewhere where my angry voice wouldn't reach them. Anger separates us from those we want to be near.

① Anger Shatters Intimacy
② Let Kids Have Time to Play
③ Show Your Emotion The Way It Is
④ Anger: A Basic Emotion of Humans
⑤ Kids Know How to Play by Themselves

02 다음 글의 밑줄 친 부분 중, 어법상 틀린 것은?

"You don't understand! You are going to make me ①die an old maid! You don't even know what romance is!" With that, my 14-year-old daughter raced out of the laundry room. I had just told her that she was too young ②to go on a date on her own. I don't know romance? How does she think she ③brought into the world? But then again, at that moment, I realized that I ④must have looked like a woman who knew only endless cooking, cleaning, and laundry. Physical workouts were done with a broom, a mop and a duster. "Going out" meant a trip to the market. I could see ⑤how someone might believe I had never known romance.

03 주어진 글 다음에 이어질 글의 순서로 가장 적절한 것은?

Almost always, when a person realizes he has been deeply heard, his eyes moisten. I think he is weeping for joy. It is as though he were saying, "Thank goodness! Somebody heard me."

(A) And finally one day he hears some faint tappings which spell out "Yes." By that one simple response he is released from his loneliness; he has become a human being again.

(B) There are many people living in private dungeons today. They give no evidence of it whatsoever on the outside, so you have to listen very sharply to hear the faint messages from the dungeon.

(C) In such moments I have had the fantasy of a prisoner in a dungeon, tapping out day after day a Morse code message, "Does anybody hear me? Is anybody there?"

*dungeon: 지하 감옥

① (A) – (C) – (B)
② (B) – (A) – (C)
③ (B) – (C) – (A)
④ (C) – (A) – (B)
⑤ (C) – (B) – (A)

04 다음 빈칸에 들어갈 말로 가장 적절한 것은?

There is an expression that goes, "The more you know, the more you grow." And the more you grow, the more you owe. What this means is ______________________. Many people often feel like they have nothing to contribute, but this is not true. You can contribute to humanity. Don't underestimate your ability to effect change. Even if you were on the wrong track in the past, you can still help others by educating them about the dangers of engaging in destructive behavior. Think about the people you respect the most. They can be people you know personally or people you've never met whom you greatly admire. How do they pass their knowledge on? I'll bet that they do by letting others know and have their knowledge. And when they do, they become a tremendous source of wisdom and inspiration for others.

① debt is what makes you live productively
② you have to be humble and ready to study
③ you shouldn't be ashamed of asking for help
④ you need to share your knowledge with others
⑤ many good expressions have one thing in common

05 글의 흐름으로 보아, 주어진 문장이 들어가기에 가장 적절한 곳은?

The problem is that different political leaders have different ideas about what is right.

When a political leader puts forth a policy or suggests how we should act, the implied assumption is that the policy or action is right, not wrong. (①) No political leader says, "Here's what you should do. Do it because it is wrong." (②) No political leader puts forth policies on the grounds that the policies don't matter. (③) Political prescriptions are assumed to be right. (④) Moreover, much of moral belief is unconscious. (⑤) We are often not even aware of our own most deeply held moral views.

06 다음 도표의 내용과 일치하지 않는 것은?

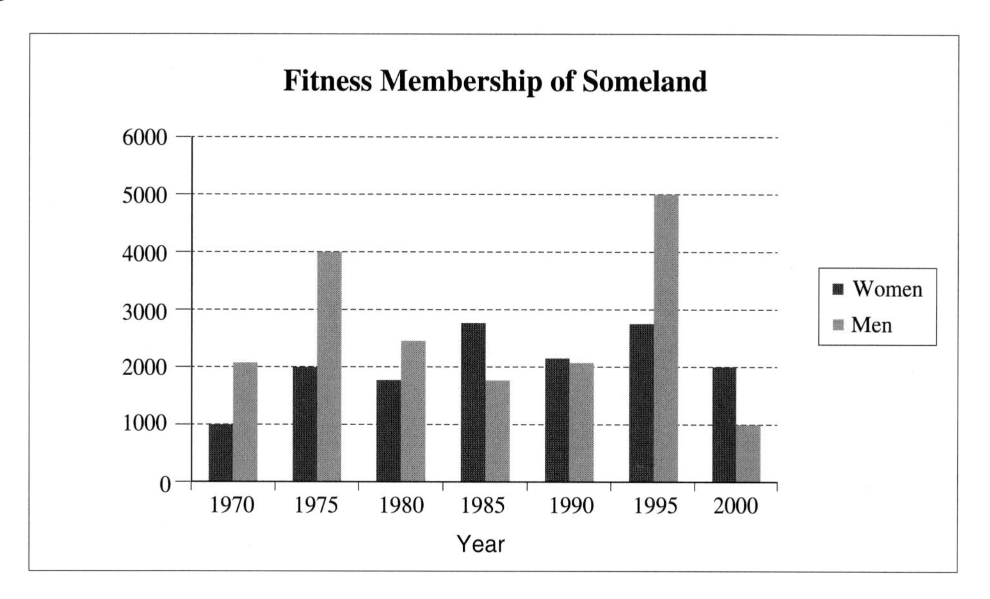

The above graph shows data on the number of male and female fitness members of Someland from 1970 to 2000. ① In 1970, there were more than 2000 male fitness members, while there were only 1000 female fitness members. ② After 5 years, the number of male fitness members increased to 4000, which was almost double compared to the 1970's total male number. ③ Interestingly enough, the number of female fitness members took turns rising and falling every five years. ④ After 1985, the number of female fitness members never fell below that of male fitness members. ⑤ In 2000, the number of female fitness members doubled that of male fitness members.

07 다음 글에서 전체 흐름과 관계 없는 문장은?

Green roofs have been popular in Europe for years, and they have every reason to have been so. First, the vegetation protects the roof's surface from cycles of freezing and thawing that can tear it, as well as from ultraviolet light that can wear it out. ① This doubles the life of a green roof over a conventional one. ② Also, a green roof provides insulation that makes the building envelope more efficient. ③ The vegetation protects the roof from the wind in winter, and when covered in snow, the rooftop can be particularly effective at retaining the building's heat. ④ There are also other ways to reduce its energy bills and protect the environment. ⑤ In summer, the vegetation can cut rooftop temperatures in half, so the rooftop can show off its cooling effects.

[08~09] 다음 글을 읽고, 물음에 답하시오.

Once upon a time there was a bunch of tiny frogs who arranged a running competition. The goal was to reach the top of a very high tower. A big crowd had gathered around the tower to see the race and cheer on the contestants. The race began, and no one in the crowd really believed that any of the tiny frogs would reach the top of the tower. There were statements like: "Oh, way too difficult!" "They will never make it to the top." "Not a chance that they will succeed. The tower is too high!" The tiny frogs began collapsing—one by one. That is, except for those frogs who, in a fresh tempo, were climbing higher and higher. The crowd continued to yell, "It is too difficult! No one will make it!" More tiny frogs got tired and gave up. However, one frog continued higher and higher and higher. This one wouldn't give up! At the end, every frog except for this one had given up climbing the tower, but this frog, after his big effort, reached the top! All of the other tiny frogs naturally wanted to know how this one had managed to do it. A contestant asked the tiny frog how he had found the strength to reach the goal. It turned out that the winner was deaf! The wisdom this frog teaches us is not to listen to people who have the tendency to be __________, as they squash your most wonderful dreams. Be deaf to those who scorn or pessimistically incite you or your goals. And then go out and do it!

08 윗글의 제목으로 가장 적절한 것은?

① Set Your Goals Suitable for You
② Cheer and You Will Get What You Want
③ Believe That Competition Makes You Stronger
④ Don't Care About What Others Say and Just Go
⑤ Willingness Comes From Spirit, Not From Strength

09 윗글의 빈칸에 들어갈 말로 가장 적절한 것은?

① timid ② greedy
③ generous ④ negative
⑤ ambitious

Mini Test 6회

제한 시간	소요 시간	맞은 개수
15분	분	/9문항

01 다음 글의 요지로 가장 적절한 것은?

Ever since its discovery, Mars has always been a source of inspiration and imagination. By early observations through telescopes, some people assumed that water once flowed on its surface. Since then, many people came to believe that Mars was even a habitable planet capable of supporting life. That's why you can find thousands of novels and stories about Mars and "Martians." *The War of the Worlds*(1898), a science fiction novel by English writer H. G. Wells, is about Martians who attempt to invade and conquer Earth. The irresistible fascination about Mars is still going on in the Internet Age. A former programmer, Andy Weir, posted stories about an astronaut trapped on Mars on his blog. They became popular, and he published the novel *The Martian*, which was adapted into a movie that was released in 2015.

① 화성에 생명체가 있을 가능성은 사실상 거의 없다.
② 인터넷의 영향으로 화성에 대한 관심이 증폭되었다.
③ 이야기 속에서 화성인은 주로 인간에 적대적으로 묘사된다.
④ 화성과 화성인을 배경으로 하는 영화를 많이 찾아볼 수 있다.
⑤ 화성에 대한 매료로 많은 사람들은 그에 대한 이야기를 쓰게 되었다.

02 다음 글의 주제로 가장 적절한 것은?

Our society is rapidly moving toward an aged society with the elderly population rising sharply. To meet the demand, new markets are likely to emerge, with a variety of new products targeting old people. One noticeable tendency is that senior customers tend to choose more higher-priced goods than younger ones. For instance, the demand for high-quality furniture and jewelry among senior people is increasing at a rapid pace. Even in foods, consumers of organic products are on the rise despite their high prices. It is an obvious fact that senior people are major customers in these more expensive markets.

① the trend of high prices in most products
② a variety of new products aimed at rich people
③ problems the elderly face with their consumption
④ the impact of an aging population on the economy
⑤ the increasing number of old people in high-priced markets

03 다음 글에 드러난 'I'의 심경 변화로 가장 적절한 것은?

While I was in my second year in law school, my exams caused me to be in a panic. I had prepared well, I believed, but the exams unnerved me and they went very badly. I was convinced that I had failed them. I mentally prepared to receive failing or near-failing grades and began to make plans to find an alternative path in life. I didn't think I could finish my third and final year at law school after such a disaster. I took deep breaths and waited for the bad news about my exam results. When the envelope came, I opened it with calm resignation. But the grades were an A and an A^-. I looked again and blinked. 'How this could be?' Maybe some guardian angels were looking out for me yet again.

① irritated → ashamed
② excited → worried
③ annoyed → regretful
④ frustrated → surprised
⑤ comfortable → delighted

04 다음 빈칸에 들어갈 말로 가장 적절한 것은?

Making mistakes is central to the education of budding scientists and artists of all kinds, who must have the freedom to experiment, try this idea, flop, try another idea, take a risk, and be willing to get the wrong answer. One classic example is Thomas Edison's reply to a reporter who was lamenting Edison's ten thousand experimental failures in his effort to create the first incandescent light bulb. "I have not failed," he told the reporter. "I successfully discovered 10,000 elements that don't work." Most children, however, are denied the freedom to noodle around, experiment, and be wrong in ten ways, let alone ten thousand. The burden of constant testing to measure and standardize children's accomplishments has intensified their deep anxiety about going wrong. It is certainly important for children to learn to succeed; but it is just as important for them to ______________________.

*incandescent light bulb: 백열등

① learn not to fear failure
② fail at least 10,000 times
③ improve their originality
④ concentrate on continuous testing
⑤ discover what they really want to be

05 다음 빈칸에 들어갈 말로 가장 적절한 것은?

Does a bachelor's or master's degree guarantee a bright future? College is not a sure way to a good life and it's no longer true that having a college degree guarantees you a good job. According to one report, however, it seems that there are still ______________________. The Organization for Economic Development and Cooperation, or OECD, reports that the amount and quality of education is intensifying the gap between so-called "haves" and "have-nots." People with poor education levels were paid less than those with higher degrees. Also, they were influenced by the growing number of unemployment more than others. In 34 developed countries in the OECD, the unemployed rate of people with a university degree aged 25 to 34 is just 5% while the rate of those without one is almost 20%. Developing countries are no exception.

① chances to succeed without higher education
② growing gaps between "haves" and "have-nots."
③ many people who want to get a university degree
④ some relationships between level of education and income
⑤ a great number of unemployment rates in developing countries

06 tarantula에 관한 다음 글의 내용과 일치하지 않는 것은?

The whole body of a tarantula, especially its legs, is densely covered with hair. Some of it is short and curly, some long and stiff. Touching this body hair produces one of two distinct reactions. When the spider is hungry, it responds with an immediate and swift attack. At the touch of a cricket's antennae the tarantula seizes the insect so swiftly that a motion picture taken at the rate of 64 frames per second shows only the result and not the process of capture. But when the spider is not hungry, the stimulation of its hairs merely causes it to shake the touched limb. An insect can walk under its hairy belly unharmed. The trichobothria, very fine hairs growing from the legs, were once thought to be the spider's hearing organs, but we now know that they have nothing to do with sound. They are sensitive only to air movement. A light breeze makes them vibrate slowly without disturbing the other hair.

*trichobothria: 감각모

① 몸 부위 중 특히 다리 부위에 털이 빽빽이 나있다.
② 먹이 포획 과정은 초당 64 프레임으로 촬영해야 관찰할 수 있다.
③ 배가 고플 때와 고프지 않을 때에 털의 자극 반응이 다르다.
④ 감각모는 한때 거미의 청각 기관으로 생각되었다.
⑤ 감각모는 오직 공기의 움직임에만 민감하다.

07 밑줄 친 he[his]가 가리키는 대상이 나머지 넷과 다른 것은?

A slave named Androcles once run away from his master and hid in the forest. As he wandered through the woods, ① he heard an animal moaning and groaning and came upon a lion lying down. As he came near, the lion put out his paw, which was all swollen and bleeding, and Androcles found that a huge thorn had got into it, and made him too painful to do anything. ② He pulled out the thorn and bound up the paw of the lion. Before long, both Androcles and the lion were captured, and ③ he was sentenced to be thrown to the lion. Androcles was led out into the middle of the arena. Soon the lion was let loose from ④ his den and rushed towards his victim. But as soon as he came near to Androcles, he recognized his friend and licked ⑤ his hands like a friendly dog.

08 글의 흐름으로 보아, 주어진 문장이 들어가기에 가장 적절한 곳은?

> On the other hand, there is also a case to be made that setting boundaries to divide spheres encourages you to remain detached from different parts of your life so that you can focus better.

To concentrate wisely is to manage the changeable, overlapping boundaries between spheres. (①) The introduction of new media makes the boundaries vague, but also provides tools that we can use to make life more convenient. (②) Sometimes tearing the boundaries apart to merge spheres will allow you to better focus on the thing that is valuable. (③) You can confirm this using an experiment that combines spheres and putting activities together from different parts of your life. (④) You can combine your self, home, and work spheres not only exercising with your spouse but inviting coworkers to your home for a dinner. (⑤) For example, you may decide not to get phone calls from work when you're at home, or not answer personal calls at the office.

09 다음 글의 내용을 한 문장으로 요약하고자 한다. 빈칸 (A)와 (B)에 들어갈 말로 가장 적절한 것은?

Being related to other people seems to be significant to happiness. People who are married, who have good friends, and who are close to their families are happier than those who are not. Similarly, people who get involved in religious communities are happier than those who do not. However, the fact that social ties lead to less freedom is also particularly important. For instance, being someone's friend is to take on heavy responsibilities that may limit your own liberty. The same is true of joining religious institutions. Most religious institutions demand that their members live their lives in a certain way to help enhance the well-being of the other members. So, contrary to how it may appear, what seems to contribute the most to happiness binds us rather than frees us.

→ ____(A)____ in a community seems to make one happier than those who are not involved but to a large extent it may ____(B)____ your liberty.

	(A)		(B)
①	Withdrawal	……	eradicate
②	Withdrawal	……	restrict
③	Participation	……	restrict
④	Connection	……	support
⑤	Participation	……	support

Mini Test 6회

Mini Test 7회

제한 시간	소요 시간	맞은 개수
15분	분	/9문항

01 다음 글의 목적으로 가장 적절한 것은?

Dear Mayor Smith:

As a long-time resident of Obion County, I am deeply concerned about the disaster that hit our town 5 days ago. As you know, some worn-out electrical wiring caused a fire to break out and eventually destroyed an entire block of houses in our town. From the very beginning, the fire was fanned by strong winds, but it would not have spread so rapidly, if the firefighters had been able to arrive at the scene earlier. Our town has only one fire station. As this latest disaster has shown, that is simply not enough. In order to prevent another similar tragedy from happening again, Obion County needs more fire stations. I look forward to your prompt reply regarding this issue.

Best regards,
Kurt Jackson

① 소방서 신설을 요청하려고
② 소방 시설의 노후화를 고발하려고
③ 결함이 있는 전선의 수리를 요구하려고
④ 강풍으로 인한 재산 피해를 보고하려고
⑤ 소방관의 도착시간 연착으로 인한 피해를 알리려고

02 다음 글의 제목으로 가장 적절한 것은?

Melatonin is a naturally occurring hormone controlled by light exposure that helps regulate your sleep-wake cycle. When it's dark, your brain sends out more melatonin to make you sleepy and sends out less during the day when it's light, because you want to stay awake and alert. However, many aspects of modern life can disrupt your body's natural production of melatonin and throw off your sleep-wake cycle. For example, spending long days in an office away from natural light can impact your daytime wakefulness and make your brain sleepy. Then bright lights at night—especially from hours spent in front of the TV or computer screen — can suppress your body's production of melatonin and make it harder to sleep.

① The Importance of Natural Bright Lights
② Ways to Control the Release of Melatonin
③ A Few Tips to Help You Sleep Better Tonight
④ Melatonin: The Most Essential Hormone in Your Body
⑤ Daily Habits Can Unbalance Melatonin Secretion Levels

03 다음 글의 빈칸 (A), (B)에 들어갈 말로 가장 적절한 것은?

People often make the mistake of assuming that because vitamins, minerals, or other supplements are sold over the counter, they are completely safe to take, even in high doses. In the 1990s there was even a trend of "megadosing" antioxidants like vitamin C, beta carotene, and vitamin E. Even though no scientific studies have ever proven that large doses of vitamin C can prevent or cure colds, many people still think this is true. ___(A)___, large doses of some vitamins have been shown to be dangerous and even toxic, causing a bad impact on overall health. For example, too much vitamin C can interfere with the body's ability to absorb copper, a metal that's needed by the body. ___(B)___, too much iron can cause digestive upset, organ failure and even death in extreme cases. Because our bodies cannot get rid of large doses of these supplements quickly, they end up causing more harm than good.

	(A)		(B)
①	Therefore	……	In addition
②	However	……	In short
③	Furthermore	……	In short
④	However	……	In addition
⑤	Therefore	……	For example

04 다음 빈칸에 들어갈 말로 가장 적절한 것은?

Needless to say, stillbirths are catastrophic and painful for families. The causes of many stillbirths are unknown, but the research by Queensland University of Technology (QUT) suggested there's a relationship between temperature and the possibility of stillbirths. The researchers recorded temperature, humidity and air conditions on a weekly basis for 101,870 pregnancies over four years. They found out the risks were at the lowest level in the coolest weeks and warm temperatures around 23℃ could be as dangerous as the hottest weeks. This could be because most pregnant women would likely be trying to remain cool on the hottest days and would generally seek air conditioning. They estimated at 15℃ there would be 3.53 stillbirths per 1000 pregnancies while 6.1 stillbirths per 1000 pregnancies at 23℃. So, they advised pregnant women should ________________________ to reduce the risk of stillbirths.

*stillbirth: 사산

① be aware of their body temperature
② avoid long baths that are too hot or too cold
③ be especially careful when traveling in winter
④ avoid excessive sweating during their workouts
⑤ protect themselves from overheating and stay cool

05 다음 빈칸에 들어갈 말로 가장 적절한 것은?

If you've ever made room for dessert even though you're already full or dove into a pint of ice cream when you're feeling down, you've experienced emotional eating. Emotional eating is using food to make yourself feel better—eating to fill emotional needs, rather than to fill your stomach. We cannot say that using food to cheer you up or to reward yourself is always wrong. But whenever you're upset, angry, lonely, stressed, exhausted, or bored, if eating is your primary emotional coping mechanism, you get stuck in an unhealthy cycle. ________________________ Eating may feel good in the moment, but the feelings that triggered the eating are never addressed and are still there. And you often feel worse than you did before because of the unnecessary calories you consumed. This may make the problem worse, as you may have a harder time controlling your weight rather than learning healthier ways to deal with your emotions, and also feel increasingly powerless over both food and your feelings.

① Emotional emptiness may be temporary.
② Emotional hunger can't be filled with food.
③ Controlling your body weight can be dangerous.
④ Appropriate food intakes are not always a good option.
⑤ Teens who have an eating disorder are increasing every year.

06 다음 글의 내용을 한 문장으로 요약하고자 한다. 빈칸 (A)와 (B)에 들어갈 말로 가장 적절한 것은?

You may know that genes determine a big part of how you look and act. What you might not know is that not only your genes but also your environment has an effect on your appearance and behavior. However, you should know that your environment isn't just the air you breathe and the food you eat. In fact, a big part of your environment is culture. Culture is composed of the common things members of a community learn from family, friends, school, and even strangers from outside. These are the things that influence how they look, act, and communicate. But, you don't even know you're learning these things because they become second nature to you, for example, the way you shake hands with someone, the kind of things you find funny, or how you identify with others around you.

→ Unlike the belief that only ____(A)____ make what you are, the culture surrounding you also ____(B)____ how you behave.

	(A)		(B)
①	inherited traits	……	affects
②	inherited traits	……	evaluates
③	certain habitations	……	affects
④	certain habitations	……	decides
⑤	unique habits	……	evaluates

07 다음 글에서 전체 흐름과 관계 없는 문장은?

The victory of antibiotics over deadly bacteria is one of modern medicine's greatest achievements of mankind. Since these medicines first became widely used in the early 1940s, they have saved many people's lives and prevented serious diseases and infections. ① However, after the extensive use for over 60 years, a lot of antibiotics don't have the same effect that they first had. ② Sideeffects range from mild to very serious depending on the antibiotics used. ③ Over time, some bacteria have developed ways to resist the power of antibiotics. ④ Extensive use of antibiotics makes evolutionary changes in bacteria that allow them to survive these medicines. ⑤ Resistance to antibiotics gives mankind two big troubles: it makes it harder to eliminate infections from our bodies and it increases the risk of hospital-acquired infection.

08 글의 흐름으로 보아, 주어진 문장이 들어가기에 가장 적절한 곳은?

> She says that within a few months you will be surrounded by many close and loyal friends.

Imagine that you are feeling a bit down because you have just moved to a new neighborhood and are finding it difficult to meet people. Just for fun, you decide to go along to the local fortuneteller to find out what the future holds for you. (①) The fortuneteller gazes into her crystal ball, smiles and says that the future looks bright. (②) You are reassured by her comments and walk away feeling much happier than when you arrived. (③) Because you now feel happy and confident about the future, you smile more, go out more and chat to more people. (④) After a few weeks you find that you are indeed surrounded by a close circle of friends. (⑤) In fact, it is quite possible that the fortuneteller did not actually see into the future but instead actually helped to create it.

09 주어진 글 다음에 이어질 글의 순서로 가장 적절한 것은?

An unmanned aerial vehicle (UAV), commonly known as a drone and also referred by several other names, is an aircraft without a human pilot aboard.

(A) The trend for these uses of UAV technology in commercial aerial surveillance is expanding rapidly with increased development of automated object detection approaches.

(B) This unmanned aerial vehicle has mostly found military and special operation applications, but it is increasingly finding uses in civil applications, such as policing, surveillance and firefighting, and nonmilitary security work.

(C) For example, aerial surveillance of large areas is made possible with low-cost UAV systems. Surveillance applications include livestock monitoring, wildfire mapping, pipeline security, and home security.

① (A) – (C) – (B)
② (B) – (A) – (C)
③ (B) – (C) – (A)
④ (C) – (A) – (B)
⑤ (C) – (B) – (A)

Mini Test 8회

제한 시간	소요 시간	맞은 개수
15분	분	/9문항

01 다음 글의 요지로 가장 적절한 것은?

Some interviewers explain the way you act sends important messages about you and how much you care about the job that you want. Your interviewer will read your character and form his or her impressions about you from your posture, facial expressions, eye contact, use of space, tone of voice, wariness and so on. Avoiding eye contact with interviewers may show you are trying to hide something you don't want to expose. And yet too much eye contact like direct staring can seem intimidating. When you are rehearsing your answers to potential questions, make sure to get feedback on your body language, and then use the right body language during the job search process.

*wariness: 신중함

① 면접에서는 숨기는 것이 없어야 한다.
② 면접에서는 언어 구사력이 가장 중요하다.
③ 면접관과 가급적 눈을 자주 마주쳐야 한다.
④ 면접을 보기 전에 사전 연습을 충분히 해야 한다.
⑤ 면접에서는 비언어적인 요소들을 중요하게 여긴다.

02 다음 글의 주제로 가장 적절한 것은?

You may have avoided a situation where you could encounter some people on social occasions because their conversations struck you as boring. On the other hand, you may know those who can enliven any discussion. How can you improve your conversational skills to become a welcome sight at every party and social event you attend? Most people prefer to talk about themselves rather than hear about you, so asking questions is a great way to start a good conversation. Also, praising someone whenever you can is a good way to improve your ability to communicate with others. For example, if someone has lost lots of weight or has a stylish new haircut, then show that you have noticed it by giving a genuine compliment.

① what makes your words boring
② the importance of social gatherings
③ how to be a good conversationalist
④ impressing others with false compliments
⑤ the reason why you shy away from awkward situations

03 narwhal에 관한 다음 글의 내용과 일치하지 <u>않는</u> 것은?

The narwhal is a medium-sized whale that lives in the icy waters of the Arctic seas. They have two teeth in their upper jaw and one of the teeth grows outward, spirally. It is often thought to be the unicorn of the sea because of the long and impressive tusk. The female's tusk doesn't grow as long and prominent as the male's. The function of the tusk is uncertain, but some believe it is important in mating rituals. This mysterious creature can grow to be about 13 to 20 feet excluding the tusk, and it weighs about 1600 kg. Narwhals swim in groups and are normally observed in pods of two to ten. They feed on fish, shrimp, squid, and other marine animals. They are preyed upon by man (Inuit hunters), polar bears, or walruses.

*walruse: 바다코끼리

① 북극해의 얼음물에 사는 고래이다.
② 한 개의 엄니가 나선형으로 길게 자란다.
③ 수컷보다 암컷의 엄니가 더 두드러진다.
④ 엄니의 길이를 제외하고 약 20피트까지 자란다.
⑤ 사람이나 북극곰, 바다코끼리에 의해 잡아먹힌다.

04 다음 빈칸에 들어갈 말로 가장 적절한 것은?

"________________________," said Oliver Cromwell to the artist Lely. "If you leave out the scars and wrinkles, I will not pay you a shilling." Even in such a trifle, Cromwell showed good sense. He did not wish all that was characteristic in his facial expression to be lost, in a vain attempt to give him regular features and smooth cheeks. He was content that his face should show all the signs put on it by time, by war, by sleepless nights, by anxiety, perhaps by regret but with valor, policy, authority, and public care written on it as well. If great men knew what was in their best interests, it is thus that they would wish their minds to be portrayed.

① Paint me as I am
② Paint me as a perfect person
③ Paint me as if I've been tired for long
④ Paint me as a totally different person
⑤ Paint me like a person who doesn't exist

05 다음 빈칸에 들어갈 말로 가장 적절한 것은?

In a 2009 article in the *Philosophical Transactions of the Royal Society*, the French psychologists Sylvie Droit-Volet and Sandrine Gil described what they call the paradox of time: "although humans are able to accurately estimate time as if they possess a specific mechanism that allows them to measure time," they wrote, "their representations of time ________________________." They describe how our sense of time changes with our emotional state. When we're agitated or anxious, for example, time seems to crawl; we lose patience. Our social environment, too, influences the way we experience time. Studies suggest, write Droit-Volet and Gill, that "individuals match their time with that of others." The "activity rhythm" of those around us alters our own perception of the passing of time.

① are abstract and subtle
② are all down to inaccuracy
③ depend on their physical condition
④ are easily distorted by the context
⑤ essentially emphasize the passing of time

Mini Test 8회

06 주어진 글 다음에 이어질 글의 순서로 가장 적절한 것은?

> Gender pricing is the act of charging men and women differently for the same products or services. Commonly, women have to pay more than men for almost the same things.

(A) Car insurance is another: Men pay an estimated $15,000 more over their lifetime for car insurance than women do. Therefore, women are not always victims of gender pricing.

(B) However, for certain kinds of services, men typically pay more — like manicures and waxing for instance — because they supposedly require more work.

(C) For example, women usually pay more for dry cleaning than men. In terms of products, women usually pay more for clothing like jeans, personal care products like razors, and toys like scooters.

① (A) – (B) – (C)
② (A) – (C) – (B)
③ (B) – (C) – (A)
④ (C) – (A) – (B)
⑤ (C) – (B) – (A)

07 밑줄 친 부분이 가리키는 대상이 나머지 넷과 다른 것은?

When the fire broke out last night, people ran out of the house, shouting and crying in confusion. And the next day, there was no one still in the house except Henry, the last son of the Smiths. Nobody thought of ① him. Because Mr. and Mrs. Smith had both died in the fire, people thought Henry was also dead. But ② his friend Thomas believed Henry was alive and looked for him. Walking down the blackened hall, he kept calling "Henry! It's me, Thomas!" From the panic room where he had hid, Henry finally heard his friend's voice. With ③ his help, he was able to get out of the house safely. When he woke up the next day in Thomas's room, his parents told him ④ he could live together with them. He was relieved that ⑤ he wouldn't be alone in the world.

08 글의 흐름으로 보아, 주어진 문장이 들어가기에 가장 적절한 곳은?

> Factors such as insufficient rest, bad posture, and physical stress may cause this tension to become more severe and frequent.

Among all headaches diagnosed, "tension headaches" are most common and account for approximately 90% of all. (①) There's no single cause known, and tension headaches aren't hereditary. (②) People sometimes have tightened muscles in their necks and scalps and the tightness may cause a tension headache. (③) Environmental or mental stress can also cause tension headaches. (④) Among the most common sources of mental stress are social relationships, family, friends, school, and work. (⑤) Doctors suggest rest, stress reduction and pain relievers such as aspirin as effective treatments for tension headaches.

다음 글의 내용을 한 문장으로 요약하고자 한다. 빈칸 (A)와 (B)에 들어갈 말로 가장 적절한 것은?

고 난도

In the U.S., about 30% to 40% of all food is wasted, or about $161 billion worth of food, according to Agriculture Department estimates. While it is unclear how much of that is due to consumers misreading 'date labels,' a recent survey of over 1,000 grocery shoppers by the Food Marketing Institute showed that nearly half of consumers said they threw out food either "fairly often" or "every time" after the sell-by or best-by date. Yet, terms such as sell-by, use-by and best-before don't indicate the safety of food, as many people believe. The dates are typically set by the manufacturer to indicate when food is at its peak quality. Still, many consumers believe that not sticking to those dates could make them sick. Most products are still safe to eat after the dates listed on the packaging. The sell-by date is just meant for retailers to control stock.

→ Even though the expired best-by date doesn't mean that the food is ____(A)____, people naturally think that it should be ____(B)____.

	(A)		(B)
①	inedible	……	heated up
②	insufficient	……	heated up
③	inactive	……	thrown away
④	inedible	……	thrown away
⑤	insufficient	……	packed up

M.E.M.O

M.E.M.O

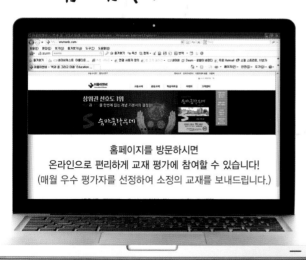

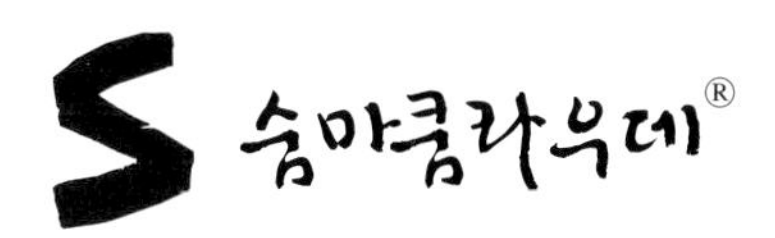

독해

ENGLISH READING COMPREHENSION

MANUAL

秘 서브노트 SUB NOTE

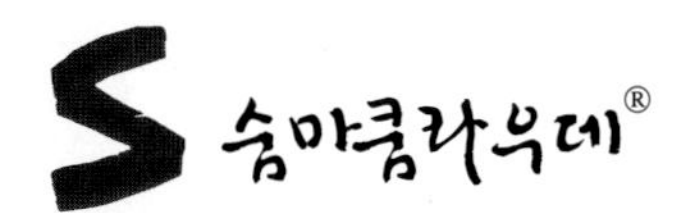

독해

ENGLISH READING COMPREHENSION

MANUAL

秘 서브노트 SUB NOTE

Part Ⅰ 유형편

유형 01 요지, 주장

p. 10

대표 예제

정답 ⑤

소재 내적 동기 부여에 기초를 둔 학습법의 효과

전문 해석

성적과 같은 외적인 동기 부여 요인의 부정적인 영향은 다양한 문화권 출신의 학생들에게서 서류로 입증되어 왔다. 비록 이 문제가 단지 모든 외적인 보상을 학습을 통제하거나 감소시키는 것으로 여기는 것보다 더 복잡하지만, 우리는 다양한 문화에 걸쳐 있는 사람들은 그들의 주된 목표가 외적이기보다는 내적일 때 그들의 삶에 더 만족감을 표현할 가능성이 있다는 Richard Ryan과 그의 동료들에게 동의한다. 또 다른 일관된 연구 결과는 어떤 외적인 보상을 얻기 위해 명시적으로 어떤 학습 활동을 할 때 사람들은 그 보상을 보장해 주는 가장 덜 힘든 방식을 추구함으로써 반응한다는 것이다. 외적인 보상을 통제하는 체제를 가진 지배적인 가르침이 질 낮은 학습의 원인이 될 수도 있다는 30년간의 증거가 있기 때문에, 내적인 동기 부여 이론에 기초를 둔 교수법을 사용하는 것이 문화적으로 다양한 학생들 사이에서 학습을 증진시키는 데 더 합리적이고 효과적인 접근법인 것 같다.

문제 해설

다양한 문화권 출신의 학생들을 대상으로 한 연구 결과를 보면 외적인 동기 부여보다는 학습을 위한 내적인 동기 부여의 접근법이 더 효과적이라는 내용이므로, 글의 요지로 가장 적절한 것은 ⑤이다.

구문 분석

[13행] Since there are three decades of evidence [**that** dominating instruction with a system of controlling external rewards may contribute to inferior learning], using a pedagogy [**based** on theories of intrinsic motivation] appears to be a more reasonable and effective approach to enhancing learning among culturally diverse students.

▶ [that ~]는 three decades of evidence의 동격어구이며, [based ~]는 분사구로 a pedagogy를 수식한다.

어휘

extrinsic 외적인 **motivator** 동기를 부여하는 것
document 서류로 입증하다, 뒷받침하다
diminish 감소시키다 **consistent** 일관된, 지속적인
explicitly 명시적으로 **dominating** 지배적인
contribute to ~의 원인이 되다, ~에 기여하다
motivation 동기 부여 **enhance** 증진시키다

Exercise

01 ② 02 ④ 03 ② 04 ② 05 ③ 06 ④

Plus Q

03 결코 반대하지 않고, 항상 동의하며, 늘 모든 것이 멋있기를 원하고, 그리고 다른 사람들이 그들이 하기를 바라는 것만 하는 것

06 what the puzzle will look like

01

정답 ②

소재 풍부한 상상력이 주는 혜택

전문 해석

어린 시절을 회상해 보라. 어떻게 놀았는가? 상상력을 사용하는 것이 어떻게 느껴졌는가? 상상력이 풍부하다는 것은 우리에게 행복감을 주고 삶에 흥분을 더한다. 이제 그런 감정들로 돌아갈 때이다. 놀이를 통해서 가졌던 기쁜 감정들로 돌아갈 수 있다면 스스로에 대해 더 행복하다고 느끼는 것을 알게 될 것이다. 여러분은 책을 쓰거나 뭔가를 발명하기 위해 상상력을 활용할 수 있다. 여러분이 상상 속으로 들어갈 때 얼마나 창의적일 수 있는지는 끝이 없다. 또한, 상상력은 일상적인 과업을 더욱 흥미롭게 만들어서 당면한 과업을 완수하는 데 집중할 수 있게 해 줄 것이다.

문제 해설

어린 시절에 풍부한 상상력을 통해 행복감과 흥분을 가졌던 것처럼 현재 일을 할 때도 상상력을 통해서 창의적이 될 수 있으며 과업을 흥미롭게 느끼고 그것을 완수할 수 있을 거라는 내용의 글이다. 따라서 필자가 주장하는 바로 가장 적절한 것은 ②이다.

구문 분석

[7행] It will also keep(V) you(O) focused(O.C) on completing the tasks at hand because imagination makes(V′) everyday tasks(O′) more interesting(O.C′).

▶ 「keep+목적어+목적보어」 구문이 사용되었으며, 의미는 '~가 …하도록 유지시키다'이다. 또한 「make+목적어+목적보어」 구문도 함께 사용되었는데, 목적보어로 형용사인 interesting이 쓰였다.

02 정답 ④

소재 인간다움과 문명의 초석인 인간의 호기심

전문 해석

호기심은 생명체의 핵심적 특성이다. 인간을 포함한 동물들은 어디서 먹을 것을 찾아야 하는지, 어떻게 포식자를 피해야 하는지, 어디서 짝을 찾아야 하는지와 같은, 그들에게 유용한 것과 그들의 생존을 위해서 필요한 것을 모르고서는 살아갈 수 없다. 그러나 우리가 개인적인 욕구를 훨씬 넘어서는 지식을 갈망하기 때문에 인류는 다른 동물들과는 다르다. 우리는 주변을 둘러보고 궁금해한다. 우리는 우리 주변에 대해서 그리고 가까운 곳과 먼 곳에서 관찰한 것에 대해서 궁금해하고 그것을 모두 이해하고 싶어 한다. 실로, 우리는 미지의 것을 두려워한다. 이러한 궁금증과 이해하고 싶은 욕망은 우리를 인간답게 할 뿐만 아니라 문명의 초석을 이루는 것 중 하나이다.

문제 해설

인류는 개인적인 욕구를 넘어서는 지식에 대한 호기심을 가지고 있는 존재이며, 이러한 특성이 인간을 인간답게 하며 문명의 초석이 되었다는 내용의 글이다. 따라서 글의 요지로 가장 적절한 것은 ④이다.

구문 분석

[8행] This sense of wonder and desire for understanding(S) **not only** makes(V₁) us human, **but** is(V₂) **also** one of the foundation stones of civilization.

▶ 'This ~ understanding'이 문장의 주어이며 동사는 「not only A but also B」를 통해 병렬을 이루고 있는 makes와 is이다.

03 정답 ②

소재 상담사의 바람직한 모습

전문 해석

자기주장은 일부 사람들에게는 상담사답지 않은 것처럼 보일 수도 있다. 만약 상담사에 대한 여러분의 마음속 그림이 결코 반대하지 않고, 항상 '동의하며,' 늘 모든 것이 멋있기를 원하고, 그리고 다른 사람들이 그들이 하기를 바라는 것만 하는 그런 누군가라면, 이것은 확신에 찬 상담사에 대한 모습이 아니다. 확신에 차 있다는 것이 무례하다는 것을 의미해야만 하는 것은 아니다. 상담사가 된다는 것은 누군가가 인종차별적인 농담을 할 때 그저 침묵한다는 것을 의미하지 않는다. 확신에 찬 상담사는 어떻게 그것이 듣는 사람의 기분을 상하게 했는지 설명하고, 그리고 유사한 농담을 피할 수 있는 방법을 제안하면서 그 농담이 인종차별적인 것이라는 사실에 그 사람의 주의를 환기시키는 방법을 찾을 것이다. 확신에 차 있는 것은 매우 잘 개발된 기술이다. 즉 그것은 상담사의 기법 목록에 잘 어울리는 것이다.

문제 해설

자기주장은 상담사에게 잘 어울리지 않는 특성처럼 보이지만, 상담사가 된다는 것은 늘 동의하고 남들이 하기를 기대하는 것만 하는 것이 아니라 자신의 생각을 분명히 드러낼 줄도 알아야 한다는 내용이다. 따라서 필자의 주장으로 가장 적절한 것은 ②이다.

오답 풀이

첫 문장이 주제문일 수 있다는 원칙을 섣불리 적용해서 첫 문장을 필자가 말하고자 하는 주된 내용으로 오인하여 상담사가 상대방의 감정을 해치는 농담을 하지 말아야 한다거나 상담사는 항상 친절한 태도로 상담을 진행해야 한다는 것을 필자의 주장으로 여기지 않도록 주의한다.

구문 분석

[7행] An assertive counselor would find a way to **call that person's attention to the fact that** the joke is racist, [explaining how it offended the hearer], and [suggesting ways similar jokes could be avoided].

▶ 「call one's attention to the fact that ~」 구문이 사용되었으며 의미는 '~라는 사실에 …의 주의를 환기시키다'이다. 두 개의 [ ]로 표시된 부분은 분사구문으로 and에 의해 병렬을 이루고 있다.

Plus Q

지시대명사가 가리키는 것은 보통 같은 문장의 앞부분이나 앞 문장 속에 있으므로, 지시대명사의 앞부분을 유심히 살펴야 한다.

04 정답 ②

소재 현재에 충실한 삶

전문 해석

내가 알고 있는 어떤 사람은 늘 미래 속으로 부리나케 달려 들어가는 경향이 있었다. 우리가 퇴근 후 한 잔을 하기 위해 만나면, 그가 맨 처음 하는 것은 대부분의 사람들이 그러한 것처럼 음료를 주문하는 것이 아니라 저녁 먹으러 어디로 갈 것인가에 대해 말하는 것이다. 저녁을 먹다가는 디저트를 급하게 먹고 영화 보러 갈 준비를 한다. 영화관에서는 마지막 화면이 사라지기도 전에 자리에서 일어난다. 그는 내일, 내주, 내년에 대한 계획을 수립하고 있었다. 결코 지금 이 순간 속에 머물러 있은 적이 없었다. 결과적으로 그는 인생을 온전히 즐길 수가 없었다. 인생은 시간표가 있다. 아기가 되는 데에는 9개월이 걸리고, 성인이 되는 데에는 21년이 걸린다. 현재에 집중하고, 모든 에너지를 그 안에 쏟아 부어라. 그것이 바로 인생이다.

문제 해설

필자는 늘 미래만을 생각하느라 현재를 충분히 즐기지 못하는 친구의 사례를 들며 현재에 충실하면서 살 것을 권유하고 있다. 따라서 글의 요지로 가장 적절한 것은 ②이다.

구문 분석

[1행] If we met for a drink after work, the first thing [he did] was (to) talk about where we'd go for dinner, not about ordering drinks like most people typically do.

▶ was와 talk 사이에 to가 생략되어 있다. 주어에 동사 do가 있으면(ex. all you have to do) be동사의 보어 역할을 하는 to부정사에서 to를 생략하고 쓸 수 있다.

[6행] **Never did he live** in the here and now.

▶ 부정의 부사(여기서는 never)가 주어보다 앞에 나오면 도치가 되어 「조동사+주어+동사 ~」의 어순이 된다.

05 정답 ③

소재 자아의 가치를 판단하는 시각

전문 해석

어느 날 총명하고 호감이 가는 학생이 한 번은 내게 자신이 창의적인 작문 과제 때문에 아주 괴롭다고 말을 한 적이 있다. A보다 못한 어떤 점수를 받는다는 예상이 그가 깊이 낙담을 느끼도록 만들었다. 결국 그는 왜곡된 사실, 즉 "우리 문화에서는 목표에 도달하지 못하면 살 가치가 없습니다."라는 사실을 말했다. 나는 그에게 "완전하지 않은 사람이 가치가 없다는 것이 어디에 쓰여 있지?"라고 물었다. 그는 잠시 생각하고 나서, "그것(그렇게 묻는 것)이 내가 훌륭하게 되기 위해서 완전할 필요가 없다고 누군가 내게 처음으로 말해준 거예요."라고 말했다. 여러분이 특정한 봉급을 벌지 못하고, 논쟁에서 지거나 실수를 한다면 여러분은 자신의 가치에 대해 의구심을 품을지 모른다. 그것은 여러분이 기필코 피해야 할 일이다. 여러분이 여러분 자신을 판단해야 한다면 (여러분의) 핵심적인 자아가 아니라 성과만 판단하려고 해야 한다.

문제 해설

필자는 A보다 못한 점수를 받고서 낙담해하는 학생에게 완전하지 않은 사람도 가치가 있다고 위로하면서 특정 분야에서 잘 하지 못한다 하더라도 자신의 핵심적인 자아에 대해 의구심을 품지 말고 그 분야의 성과만 판단하라고 설명하고 있다. 따라서 필자가 주장하는 바로 가장 적절한 것은 ③이다.

구문 분석

[8행] You might question your worth [**should** you **fail** to earn a certain salary, **lose** an argument, or **make** a mistake].

▶ [should ~]는 원래 if you should fail ~의 형태였는데 if가 생략되면서 should와 you가 도치된 형태이다. fail, lose, make가 should에 이어지며 병렬구조를 이룬다.

06 정답 ④

소재 조직의 전체적인 비전을 제시하는 지도자의 임무

전문 해석

어떠한 조직에서든지, 사람들은 조직이라는 퍼즐의 서로 다른 조각을 가지고 있다. 구성원들은 자신들의 역할과 책임에 대한 세부적인 묘사를 가지고 있을 지도 모르지만, 아주 종종 그들은 '큰 그림', 즉 조직의 전체적인 비전에 대한 정보가 부족하다. 사람들은 자신들이 가지고 있는 조각들이 맞도록 만들려고 시도하면서 여기저기에 되는대로 그것을 집어넣으며, 어쨌든 그 퍼즐에 대해 작업을 할 수 있을지 모르지만 그들은 자신들이 전체에 기여하는 것을 가능케 할 필수적인 정보가 부족하다. 임의적인 많은 시도 후에 끈질긴 몇몇 사람들은 그 퍼즐을 결국 맞출 것이다. 많은 다른 참가자들이 좌절하게 되고 흥미를 잃고 그래서 그만두게 되는 일이 더 많이 발생할 수 있다. 지도자의 일은 큰 그림을 그리고, 비전을 전달하고 사람들에게 모든 사람이 조각들을 제자리에 두었을 때 그 퍼즐이 어떠한 모습일지에 대한 분명한 느낌을 주는 것이다.

문제 해설
조직 내에서 구성원들이 맡은 일을 할 때 조직의 전체적인 정보가 부족하면 사람들이 일을 하다가 좌절하고 그만두게 되므로, 지도자는 큰 그림을 그리고 조직의 전체적인 비전에 대한 분명한 의식을 제시해야 한다는 내용의 글이다. 따라서 글의 요지로 가장 적절한 것은 ④이다.

오답 풀이
이 글은 조직의 발전에 필수적인 정보에 대한 언급을 하고 있는 것이 아니라 '지도자의 역할은 조직의 전체적인 비전을 제시하는 것이다' 라는 것이 이 글의 초점이므로, ②번의 '조직의 발전에 필수적인 정보는 조직 내에서 충분히 공유되어야 한다.'는 글의 요지라고 볼 수 없다.

구문 분석
[4행] While people may be able to work on the puzzle anyway, [**randomly sticking** their pieces here and there in an attempt to make them fit], they lack the essential information [**that** will enable them to contribute to the whole].

▶ [randomly sticking ~]는 분사구문으로서 and randomly stick ~으로 이해할 수 있다. [that ~]는 관계절로 the essential information을 수식한다.

Plus Q
의문사절의 주어는 the puzzle이며, 동사구는 will look이다. like는 전치사로서 의문대명사인 what을 목적어로 받는다. what the puzzle will look like는 '그 퍼즐이 어떠한 모습일지'로 해석한다.

유형 02 주제, 제목

p. 16

대표 예제

정답 ①

소재 생활 연령과 생물학적 연령

전문 해석
우리가 어떤 사람이 그의 생활 연령에 비해 '젊어 보인다' 고 놀라면서 말할 때 우리는 우리 모두가 생물학적으로 서로 다른 속도로 나이가 든다는 것을 말하고 있는 것이다. 과학자들은 이 겉으로 보이는 차이가 진짜라는 타당한 증거를 갖고 있다. 나이 변화는 서로 다른 시기에 신체의 서로 다른 부위에서 시작되고 매년의 변화 속도는 사람마다 다른 것은 물론 다양한 세포, 조직 그리고 기관마다 다를 가능성이 있다. 시간의 경과와 달리 생물학적 노화는 쉬운 측정을 방해한다. 우리가 갖고 싶은 것은 예를 들어, 생활 연령으로 80세인 어떤 사람이 생물학적으로 60세라고 말할 수 있도록 시간의 경과와는 관계없이 모든 다른 생물학적 나이 변화를 반영하는 하나 또는 몇 개의 측정 가능한 생물학적 변화이다. 이런 종류의 측정은 80세인 한 사람이 생물학적으로 80 또는 심지어 90세인 또 다른 80세인 사람보다 그렇게 훨씬 더 많은 젊음의 특징을 가진 이유를 설명하는 데 도움을 줄 것이다.

문제 해설
우리가 갖고 싶은 것은 생활 연령으로 80세인 어떤 사람이 생물학적으로 60세라고 말할 수 있도록 시간의 경과와는 관계없이 모든 다른 생물학적 나이 변화를 반영하는 하나 또는 몇 개의 측정 가능한 생물학적 변화라고 했으므로, 글의 제목으로 가장 적절한 것은 ① '생물학적 노화를 반영하는 거울을 찾아서'이다.

② 현대 시대에서 느린 노화의 이유들
③ 생활 연령을 짐작할 수 있는 몇 가지 비결
④ 밝혀진 생물학적 노화의 비밀들
⑤ 청춘의 샘 찾기

구문 분석
[4행] Scientists have good evidence [**that** this apparent difference is real].

▶ [that ~]는 good evidence와 동격 관계에 있고, that은 동격절을 이끄는 접속사이다.

[10행] [**What** we would like to have] **is** one or a few measurable biological changes [**that** mirror all other biological age changes without reference to the passage of time], **so that** we could say, for example, that someone [**who** is chronologically eighty years old] is biologically sixty years old.

▶ [what ~]는 문장의 주어로서 단수 취급하고, what은 선행사를 포함하고 있는 관계대명사이다. [that ~]는 관계대명사절로서 선행사 changes를 수식한다. 「so that+주어+조동사 ~」는 목적을 나타내며 '~하기 위해, ~할 수 있도록'으로 해석한다. [who ~]는 관계대명사절로서 선행사 someone을 수

식한다.

어휘

chronological age 역연령(曆年齡), 생활 연령
biologically 생물학적으로 **rate** 속도, 비율
apparent 외관상의, 겉보기의 **annual** 매년의, 연례의
tissue 조직 **organ** 기관, 장기 **mirror** 반영하다
without reference to ~에 관계없이
quality 특징, 특성 **Fountain of Youth** 청춘의 샘

Exercise

01 ③ 02 ⑤ 03 ② 04 ② 05 ② 06 ①

Plus Q
03 human penance, the curse of the poor, a privilege of the free
06 Each sound

01 정답 ③

소재 감정의 의미

전문 해석

감정은 보통 평판이 나쁘다. 감정은 종종 조절되거나 관리되어야 할 것으로 여겨진다. 심지어 사람들은 감정이 통제되지 않으면 해롭다고 생각한다. 하지만 모든 감정은 나름의 의미가 있다. 감정은 우리의 진화 역사에서 중요한 역할을 했으며 우리가 생존하는 데 도움을 주었다. 예를 들면, 곰팡이가 낀 음식을 제공 받은 사람의 얼굴에 드러난 혐오감을 봄으로써 우리는 위험한 것을 먹지 않고 피할 수가 있었다. 우리는 행복감을 전달함으로써 유익한 사회적 상호작용을 발전시킬 수 있었다. 심지어 분노도 우리의 조상들에게 중요한 감정이었는데, 배고플 때 음식을 찾고 포식자를 물리치고 부족한 자원을 위해 경쟁하도록 자극했다.

문제 해설

인간의 진화 역사에서 감정이 생존에 도움을 주고 중요한 역할을 수행했다는 내용이므로, ③ '인간의 생존에 대한 감정의 기여'가 글의 주제로 가장 적절하다.

① 우리가 감정을 숨겨야 하는 이유
② 다른 사람의 감정을 파악하는 것의 어려움
④ 다양한 문화에서 감정을 표현하는 방법
⑤ 감정적 반응과 신체적 반응의 차이

구문 분석

[7행] Even anger was an important emotion to our ancestors, [**motivating** us **to seek** food when we were hungry, **to fight** off predators and **to compete** for scarce resources].

▶ [ ]로 표시된 부분은 motivating이 이끄는 분사구문이다. to seek, to fight, to compete는 병렬구조로 연결되는데 「motivate+사람+to+동사원형」 구문의 'to+동사원형'에 해당하는 부분이다.

02 정답 ⑤

소재 아이들의 음식 선택권

전문 해석

아이들에게 선택권을 주고 그들이 얼마나 많이 먹기를 원할지, 그들이 먹고 싶어 할지 또는 아닐지, 그리고 그들이 무엇을 먹기를 원할지에 대해 자신이 결정하게 허락하라. 예를 들어, "Lisa, 파스타와 미트볼을 먹고 싶니 아니면 닭고기와 구운 감자를 먹고 싶니?"라고 여러분이 저녁 식사를 위해 만들려고 생각하고 있는 것에 대한 의사결정 과정에 그들을 포함하라. 그들이 저녁 식사 동안 얼마나 먹어야 하는지를 의논할 때, 그들에게 적당량의 음식을 차려줘라. 만약 그들이 (식사를) 끝낸 후에도 여전히 '배고프다'고 주장하면, 그들에게 5분에서 10분 동안 기다리라고 요청하고, 만약 그들이 계속 허기를 느끼면, 그때 그들은 또 한 접시의 음식을 먹을 수 있다. 제대로 배우면, 이것들은 훌륭한 자신감과 자기통제를 가르쳐 주는 멋진 행동이다.

문제 해설

뭘 먹고 싶은지, 얼마나 먹고 싶은지, 진짜로 배고픈 것인지 여부를 아이들이 결정할 수 있도록 해주면, 음식을 통해 자신감과 자기통제를 가르칠 수 있다는 내용이므로, ⑤ '아이들에게 음식에 대한 자립심을 가르쳐라'가 글의 제목으로 가장 적절하다.

① 자녀들에게 역할 모델이 되라
② 허기: 아이들에게 최고의 반찬
③ 식사 예절: 그것이 중요한가?
④ 충분한 영양 섭취: 아이들의 지적 능력

구문 분석

[1행] Give children options and allow them to make their own decisions — **on** [how much they would like to eat], [whether they want to eat or not], and [what they would like to have].

▶ 세 개의 간접의문문이 병렬구조를 이루며 전치사 on의 목적어로 사용되고 있다.

03 정답 ②

소재 노동에 대한 인식

전문 해석

노동은 한때 에덴동산에서의 악의 시초에 대한 인간의 속죄로 여겨졌다. 여러 해를 거치면서 사회경제적 계층이 중세 시대 사회에서 생겨남에 따라, 노동은 가난한 사람들에 대한 저주로 여겨지기 시작했다. 사회의 부유한 사람들은, 아마도 숭고한 것으로 여겨졌던 전쟁을 제외하고는, 노동을 피하기 위해 할 수 있는 모든 것을 했다. 마침내 St. Thomas Aquinas와 그의 동시대인들과 같은 계몽된 철학자들은, 특히 우리가 다른 사람들을 돕기 위해 우리의 잉여를 사용한다면, 노동이 중요하다고 가르쳤다. 그들의 가르침은 Martin Luther와 같은 개혁가들에게 영향을 주었는데, 그는 만약 같은 인간과의 관계에서 우리가 진실성을 지니고 정직하다면 노동은 고결하다고 설명했다. 이후에 미국과 캐나다가 새로운 영토로 확장해가면서, 당대 사회에서의 노동은 자유인의 특권으로 묘사되었다. 그러고 나서, 우리가 1900년대에 들어서면서, Henry Ford와 다른 기업가들은 노동이 우리 사회와 가정의 발전으로 이어진다는 것을 우리에게 확신시켰다.

문제 해설

시대의 흐름에 따라 노동에 대한 인식이 변했다는 내용의 글이므로, ② '시간에 따른 노동에 대한 인식의 변화'가 글의 주제로 가장 적절하다.

① 근로 여건을 향상시키는 다양한 방법들
③ 노동자의 권리에 대한 인식을 높이려는 노력
④ 노동 계층이 현대 사회에 미치는 영향
⑤ 근로 시간과 생산성의 관계

구문 분석

[7행] Their teachings influenced reformers such as Martin Luther, [**who** explained {that work was virtuous *if* we *had* integrity and *were* honest in our dealings with our fellow men}].

▶ [who ~]는 관계절로 Martin Luther를 부가적으로 설명한다. [who ~] 안의 동사 explained의 목적어에 해당되는 { }에 부사절이 포함되어 있으며, 부사절의 동사 had와 were가 병렬구조를 이루고 있다.

Plus Q

에덴동산에서의 악의 시초에 대한 인간의 속죄가 노동이라는 인식, 중세 시대에는 가난한 사람들에 대한 저주가 노동이라는 인식, 현대 사회에서는 자유인의 특권이 노동이라는 인식이 있다.

04 정답 ②

소재 주식 소유주들의 판단 기준

전문 해석

회사를 대중이 소유하는 것은 자본주의의 관대함을 널리 퍼뜨리기 위해 의도되었다. 그러나 주식 소유주와 그들이 투자하는 회사와의 관계는 비인간적인 경향이 있다. 그들은 회사가 무엇을 만드는가, 즉 그것이 값싼 무기인지, 독성이 있는 살충제인지 혹은 우스꽝스러운 오락물인지에 대해 거의 신경 쓰지 않는다. 그들은 그것(회사)이 제품에 대해 어떻게 마케팅을 하는지 혹은 그것이 고객을 어떻게 다루는지 혹은 그것이 영업을 하는 지역사회에 어떻게 영향을 주는지에 대해 거의 신경을 쓰지 않는다. 회사가 이득을 낸다면 그들은 회사의 경영진을 지지한다. 하지만 한 분기에 최고 경영자의 실적이 하락하도록 두게 되면 그들은 서둘러 자신들의 자금 밑천을 다른 곳으로 가지고 간다. 당연히 관리자들은 분기 보고가 절대적인 힘을 가지고 있다는 것을 빠르게 알게 되며 그 뒤로 그것의 되풀이되어 발생하는 그늘을 무서워하며 산다.

문제 해설

주식 소유주들은 회사가 하는 일에 대해서는 신경을 쓰지 않고, 오직 회사가 이득을 내는가에만 관심을 가지고 있으며 이에 따라 행동한다는 내용의 글이다. 따라서 글의 제목으로 가장 적절한 것은 ② '이익: 주식 소유주들의 판단 기준'이다.

① 투자는 모험 그 자체이다
③ 더 많이 가지면 가질수록 우리는 덜 만족하게 된다
④ 투자자들: 다른 어느 누구보다도 더 영리한
⑤ 회사: 자본에 의해 운영되는 유기체

오답 풀이

이 글은 이득에 따라서 움직이는 투자자들에 대한 내용이며, 회사 자체가 자본에 따라 운영된다는 내용이 아니므로 ⑤ '회사: 자본에 의해 운영되는 유기체'를 고르지 않도록 주의한다.

구문 분석

[5행] They pay little attention **to** [how it markets its products], or [how it treats its customers], or [how it affects the community where it operates].

▶ 세 개의 [ ]로 표시된 의문사절은 전치사 to의 목적어이며 or에 의해 병렬을 이루고 있다.

05 정답 ②

소재 낮잠의 생산성

전문 해석

여러분은 아마도 느꼈을 것이다. 소화가 된 후, 눈꺼풀이 무거워지기 시작하면서 졸음에 정신은 오락가락하게 되는 오후의 그러한 이른 몇 시간을 말이다. 낮잠을 자고 정신이 말짱하게 깨어난 후 다시 일을 할 채비를 하는 것이 훨씬 더 낫다. 그리고 일하는 중에 자고 있는 것을 상사에게 들키면 이는 모두 생산성을 향상시키기 위한 것이라고 상사에게 말하라. 하버드 대학의 한 연구에서 30명의 사람들이 얼마나 신속하게 정보를 처리할 수 있는지에 관한 테스트를 하루에 네 차례 받았다. 스크린에 번쩍하고 나타났다 사라지는 선의 이미지를 보여주고 그 선이 어느 방향으로 기울었는지를 확인해 달라고 요청하였다. 내내 잠을 자지 않은 열 사람들의 실적이 마지막 테스트에서 50퍼센트까지 떨어진 반면 정오를 막 지나서 한 시간 정도 낮잠을 잔 사람들은 처음 테스트와 마지막 테스트의 결과가 거의 같았다. 30분 정도 낮잠을 잔 사람들도 잠을 자지 않은 사람들보다 나았다.

문제 해설

낮잠을 조금이라도 잔 사람들이 테스트에서 좋은 결과를 낸 실험 결과를 바탕으로 낮잠이 생산성에 영향을 미친다는 것을 보여주고 있으므로, ② '낮잠이 생산성에 미치는 영향'이 글의 주제로 가장 적절하다.

① 생산성을 향상시키는 방법
③ 유용한 정보를 고르는 방법
④ 적절한 낮잠 시간
⑤ 직장에서 어울리는 것의 중요성

구문 분석

[7행] They *were shown* flashing images of lines on a screen and *asked* to identify [**which direction** they were slanted].

▶ shown과 asked는 병렬구조로 were에 이어진다. [which direction ~]는 의문사절로 identify의 목적어로 사용되었다.

06 정답 ①

소재 감정을 가지고 음악 듣기

전문 해석

음악 작품에서 각각의 소리는 알아차려지기만 하면 일정한 반응을 불러일으킨다. 변화된 리듬, 화음의 음표, 혹은 멜로디를 연주하는 악기가 듣는 사람의 반응에 영향을 끼친다. 음악에서 들리는 것에 대한 자극 감응은 그것을 기억하는 것만큼이나 중요하다. 감정 없이 음악을 듣는 것은 득점이 없는 축구 경기를 보는 것과 마찬가지일 것이다. 마찬가지로, 감정 없이 음악을 듣는 것은 의미가 없다. 심리적으로 관여가 안 되고, 오로지 빈약한 지적 경험만 남게 된다. 음악 소리에 어떻게 하면 더 반응하게 될 수 있을까? 간단한 것처럼 보이지만 듣는 것에 그저 좀 더 민감해지려고 하는 것이 좋은 첫 걸음이다. 음악의 속성에 눈을 떠라. 곡의 어떤 짧은 구간을, 가령 5초 정도의 구간을 연주해도 좋다. 그런 다음 그 음악의 그 부분에 내가 어떤 반응을 보였지? 라고 자문해라.

문제 해설

음악을 감정 이입 없이 듣는 것을 득점 없는 축구 경기에 비유하며 감정을 가지고 음악을 듣는 방법에 대해 알려 주고 있으므로, ① '음악에 감정적으로 반응하라'가 글의 제목으로 가장 적절하다.

② 음악 소리: 우리를 치유하는가, 그렇지 않은가
③ 여성이 남성보다 감수성이 뛰어난가?
④ 심리학이 지적 호기심으로 이어진다
⑤ 음악과 축구 사이에 공통점이 무엇인가?

구문 분석

[4행] Listening to music with no feeling must be something like watching a soccer game [**in which** the goals have been removed].

▶ which는 a soccer game을 선행사로 하는 관계대명사이며, 앞의 전치사 in과 함께 where로 대체될 수 있다. 여기서 must는 추측을 나타내는 조동사로 쓰였다.

Plus Q

it은 앞에 나온 명사를 가리키는데, '각각의 소리는 (그것이) 알아차려지기만 하면 일정한 반응을 불러일으킨다'는 내용이므로, it은 주절의 주어인 Each sound를 가리킨다는 것을 알 수 있다.

유형 03 글의 목적

p. 22

대표 예제 정답 ②

소재 체조 캠프 프로그램 참가

전문 해석

Johnson 코치님께
제 이름은 Christina Markle이고, Bradley Markle의 엄마입니다. Bradley와 저는 올해 또 다시 귀하의 하계 체조 캠프가 열린다는 것을 알고 몹시 기뻤습니다. 그래서 저는 주저하지 않고 등록을 했고 7월 13일부터 17일까지 열리는 두 번째 주 프로그램에 환불이 안 되는 보증금을 지불했습니다. 그러나 오늘 저는 우리 가족이 7월 13일에 여행에서 돌아올 예정이라는 것을 기억해 냈고, 그래서 Bradley가 프로그램의 바로 첫날에 참가할 수가 없을 것 같습니다. 그가 그날을 거르게 하기보다는 세 번째 주 프로그램으로 바꿀 수 있는지 알기 위해 확인을 하고 싶습니다. 그게 가능하다면 저희에게 알려 주시기 바랍니다. 감사합니다.
Christina Markle 드림

문제 해설
하계 체조 캠프의 두 번째 주 프로그램에 아이를 등록시켰는데, 프로그램이 시작되는 첫날 아이의 출석이 어려워 세 번째 주 프로그램으로 바꿀 수 있는지를 문의하고 있는 내용이므로, 글의 목적으로는 ②가 가장 적절하다.

구문 분석
[5행] So I didn't hesitate **to sign up** and (to) **pay** the non-refundable deposit for the second week program, **which** is from July 13 to 17.

▶ to sign up과 pay는 and에 의해 병렬구조로 연결되어 있으며 pay 앞에 to가 생략된 구문이다. 콤마(,)와 함께 쓰인 which는 the second week program을 부연 설명하는 계속적 용법의 관계대명사이다.

어휘
learn 알다 **hold** 개최하다 **gymnastics** 체조
hesitate 망설이다 **sign up** 등록하다
non-refundable 환불되지 않는 **deposit** 보증금
make it 참석하다
very (장소 · 시간을 강조하여) 맨[가장], 바로
skip 거르다 **switch** 바꾸다

Exercise

01 ⑤ 02 ⑤ 03 ⑤ 04 ④ 05 ④ 06 ③

Plus Q
03 20 containers, 2,000 clear trash bags
06 Expressing

01 정답 ⑤

소재 학교 다목적실 사용 협조 요청

전문 해석
학생회 귀중,
우리는 11학년 밴드부 구성원들입니다. 현재, 우리만의 연습실이 없어 다목적실에서 일주일에 두 번 연습해야 합니다. 지난 2주 동안, 다른 그룹들이 다목적실을 사용할 필요가 있어 밴드 연습이 취소되었습니다. 밴드 경연 대회가 한 달밖에 남지 않았기에, 이번 달 내내 방과 후에 다목적실을 사용하는 유일한 그룹이 되길 요청합니다. Cooper 교장 선생님께서는 우리의 제안에 대해 학생회 전체가 투표를 해야 한다고 말씀하셨습니다. 우리의 상황을 이해하고 우리를 지지하여 투표해 주길 소망합니다.
11학년 밴드부 드림

문제 해설
밴드부 구성원들이 연습을 위해 필요한 다목적실의 단독 사용을 원하여 학생회를 대상으로 지지를 요청하는 내용의 글이므로, 글의 목적으로 가장 적절한 것은 ⑤이다.

구문 분석
[5행] Since the band tournament is only one month away, we are asking to be the only group **to use** the multipurpose room after school for this entire month.

▶ to부정사의 형용사적 용법이 쓰였으며 '다목적실을 사용할[하는] 유일한 그룹'으로 해석한다.

02 정답 ⑤

소재 직원 정보 요청에 대한 대응

전문 해석
Jayden Corporation에서는 이전과 현재의 모든 직원들의 사생활을 보호하기 위해 노력하고 있습니다. 만약 이전 직원에 관련된 정보를 얻기 위해 전화, 이메일, 또는 서면 요청을 받으면, 근무 사항과 관련된 어떠한 세부 내용도 제공하지 마세요. 그러한 문의 사항을 인사부로 전달하세요. 어떠한 문의 사항이든 합당한 사유 때문인지는 인사부에서 결정할 것입니다. 특정 상황 시 인사부에서 이전 직원에게 외부 기관이나 기업, 또는 개인에게 정보를 제공하는 것에 대한 동의를 요청하기 위해 연락을 취할 수도 있습니다. 이러한 정책에 대해 질문이 있다면 인사부로 연락주세요.

문제 해설
이전 직원에 대한 정보 요청을 받은 경우 어떠한 내용도 전

달하지 말고 인사부에 문의하여 처리하라는 내용의 글이므로, 글의 목적으로 가장 적절한 것은 ⑤이다.

오답 풀이

④번은 '개인 정보 수집' 이라는 지문과 관련된 내용을 포함하지만, '동의를 요청'한다는 내용은 제시되지 않으므로 이 글의 목적으로 볼 수 없는 선택지이다.

구문 분석

[6행] In certain situations, the HR Department may contact a former employee **to request** permission **to provide** information **to** an outside agency, business, or individual.

▶ 문장 속에서 다양하게 쓰인 to의 용법과 해석에 유의해야 한다. to request는 to부정사의 부사적 용법 중 목적의 의미로 '~하기 위해'로 해석한다. to provide는 to부정사의 형용사적 용법으로 '~할, 하는'으로 해석한다. 마지막에 쓰인 to는 전치사로 '~에게'로 해석한다.

03 정답 ⑤

소재 종이 재활용 프로그램

전문 해석

C&G Waste Services 귀중

Westwood 고등학교는 현재 종이 재활용 프로그램을 마련 중에 있습니다. 저희는 학생과 교직원의 도움을 받아, 종이를 재활용함으로써 쓰레기로 나가는 종이의 양을 크게 줄이는 것을 목표로 하고 있습니다. 저희에게는 현재 종이 재활용을 수용할 대형 쓰레기 수거함은 있지만, 저희의 목표를 달성할 수 있도록 각 교실의 수거함이 필요합니다. 저희는 20개의 수거함을 요청하고자 합니다. 저희는 또한 학생과 교직원이 종이를 대형 재활용 수거함으로 가져갈 수 있도록 2,000개의 투명 쓰레기 봉투도 필요합니다. 그래서 저희가 우리의 천연자원을 보존하는 데 기여할 수 있도록 귀사에서 이러한 물품들을 기증해 주실 수 있는지 문의드리는 바입니다. 질문이 있으시면 저에게 연락해 주십시오. 저희는 C&G Waste Services와 협력 관계를 구축하기를 기대합니다. 저희는 이러한 협력 관계가 저희가 지역사회에 기여하고 우리 학생들이 환경을 돕기 위해 취할 수 있는 행동들을 강화시키는 데 도움을 준다는 것을 알고 있습니다.

Anna Wilson 드림

문제 해설

학교에서 실시하고자 하는 재활용 프로그램에 필요한 교실용 수거함과 투명 쓰레기 봉투와 같은 물품을 기증해 줄 것을 문의하는 내용의 글이므로, 글의 목적으로 가장 적절한 것은 ⑤이다.

구문 분석

[11행] We know that these types of partnerships **help** us **give** back to the community and enhance actions [(which / that) our students can take towards helping the environment].

▶ 「help+목적어+목적보어」는 '~가 …하는 것을 돕다'의 의미로, 목적보어로 동사원형인 give가 쓰였다. [ ]로 표시된 부분은 목적격 관계대명사 which나 that이 생략된 관계대명사절로 선행사인 actions를 수식한다.

Plus Q

these items가 본문에서 가리키는 것은 Westwood 고등학교가 C&G Waste Services로부터 기증받기를 희망하는 20 containers와 2,000 clear trash bags이다. 둘 중 한 가지 품목만 적지 않도록 유의해야 한다.

04 정답 ④

소재 추천서 제공에 대한 안내

전문 해석

저는 당신이 곧 우리 회사를 떠날 것이라는 사실을 알게 되었습니다. 우리는 당신의 업무가 항상 최고로 만족스러웠고 앞으로도 여러 해 동안 당신이 J&E에 남아주기를 바라고 있었기 때문에 당신을 잃는다는 것이 매우 유감입니다. 당신이 이 회사와는 아무런 관계가 없는 개인적 이유로 떠난다는 점을 이해합니다. 당신이 요청한다면 저는 기꺼이 추천서를 작성해 드리겠습니다. 제 추천서는 당신이 새로운 지역에서 다른 회사의 일자리를 얻는 데 도움이 될 것입니다. 당신이 떠나기 전에 추천서를 준비해 둘 수 있도록 이 문제에 대한 당신의 생각을 제 비서에게 알려주시기 바랍니다. J&E의 모두를 대표하여 당신의 앞날에 행운이 있기를 바랍니다.

문제 해설

회사를 떠나려는 직원을 대상으로 쓴 글로 원할 경우 추천서를 작성해 제공하겠다는 내용이므로, 글의 목적으로 가장 적절한 것은 ④이다.

구문 분석

[6행] You may **find** this **helpful** *in securing* a position with another firm in your new locale.

▶ 「find+목적어+목적보어」는 '~가 …하다고 여기다'의 의

미로, 목적보어로 형용사인 helpful이 쓰였다. 「in+동사-ing」는 '~하는 데 있어서'의 의미이다.

[7행] Please **advise** my secretary **of** your intent in this matter, so that we can **have** it **prepared** for you before your departure.

▶ 「advise A of B」는 'A에게 B를 알리다'의 의미이다. 사역동사 have 다음의 목적어 it과 목적보어의 관계가 수동이므로 과거분사 prepared가 쓰였다.

05 정답 ④

소재 물품 배송 결함에 대한 사과

전문 해석

최근 귀하의 물품 배송에 결함이 있었던 점에 대해 유감입니다. 저희는 귀하의 실망을 이해하며, 이것이 귀사에 가져왔을 모든 불편에 대해 사과드립니다. 저희 제품의 전체적인 품질과 그것들이 배송되는 방식을 향상시키려는 노력으로 저희는 새로운 배송 회사와 포장으로 바꾸었습니다. 이 노력으로 저희 제품에 대한 피해를 예방하고 주문을 더 신속히 처리할 수 있을 것입니다. 저희는 귀하의 전체 주문을 교체하고 이번 주 안으로 그것을 배송할 것입니다. 이번 일이 우리 측의 실수 때문이므로 귀하께서는 아무런 비용도 들지 않습니다. 저희는 계속하여 귀사를 모실 수 있기를 고대하며 귀하께서 저희로부터 제품 주문을 지속해 줄 것을 바랍니다. 귀하의 불편을 줄이기 위해 저희가 할 수 있는 또 다른 일이 있다면 편히 저희에게 연락해 주시기 바랍니다.

문제 해설

물품 배송에 결함이 발생하여 이에 대해 사과하는 내용의 글이므로 글의 목적으로 가장 적절한 것은 ④이다.

구문 분석

[8행] We **look forward to continuing** serving your business and hope that you will continue ordering products from us.

▶ 「look forward to ~」는 '~를 기대하다' 라는 뜻으로 to가 전치사이므로 뒤에 동명사인 continuing이 쓰였다.

06 정답 ③

소재 업무 처리 관련 시스템 개선

전문 해석

고객님을 더욱 정성껏 모시고 업무 처리를 개선하기 위해, 저희는 전사적 자원관리 시스템에 대한 중요한 업그레이드를 실시하고 있습니다. 곧 있을 변화를 계획함에 있어 저희는 사업 파트너들에게 미칠 혼란을 최소화하기 위해 모든 노력을 기울이고 있습니다. 그러나 고객님들께서 아시길 바라는 몇 가지 사항이 있습니다. 그것은 주문과 선적의 일시적 중단, 개설된 거래 조회번호의 변경 그리고 거래 서류 형식의 수정입니다. 저희는 고객께서 이러한 변화를 예상하고, 선적이 중단되는 동안 업무에 어떤 피해도 입지 않기 위해 충분한 재고 보유량을 확실히 확보하시도록 이 정보를 인지하시기를 바랍니다. BD Biosciences의 제품을 지원해 주시는 고객님께 감사드리며, 앞으로도 저희는 이번의 중요한 변화에 대해 고객들과 계속 소통해 나갈 것입니다. 문의사항이 있으시면, 고객서비스 무료전화 855-236-2772로 연락주시기 바랍니다.

문제 해설

시스템 업그레이드 실시에 따른 주문 및 선적의 일시 중단, 서류 형식 수정 등의 변경 사항들을 알리고 있으므로, 글의 목적으로 가장 적절한 것은 ③이다.

구문 분석

[4행] There are, however, <u>a few things</u> (S) [(which / that) we **want** you **to know** about]:

▶ [ ]로 표시된 부분은 목적격 관계대명사 which나 that이 생략된 관계대명사절로 선행사 a few things를 수식한다. 「want+목적어+to부정사」는 '목적어가 ~하길 바라다'의 의미이다.

[7행] We want you to be aware of this information so you **could anticipate** these changes and (could) **ensure** that you have sufficient inventory on-hand ~.

▶ could anticipate와 ensure는 병렬구조로 연결되어 있으며 ensure 앞에 could가 생략된 구문이다.

Plus Q

'표시하면서'의 의미가 되어야 하므로 능동인 현재분사 Expressing으로 고쳐 써야 한다. 이 부분은 분사구문으로 접속사와 주어가 생략된 형태이며 As we express로 바꿀 수 있다.

유형 04 심경, 분위기

p. 28

대표 예제

정답 ①

소재 아마존 탐험에 대한 흥분과 기대

전문 해석

나는 마침내 내일 아침 일찍 떠날 것이다! 나는 항상 미지의 신비스러운 세계인 아마존을 탐험하고 싶었다. 이 시각이면, 멋진 Emerald Amazon Explorer가 나의 승선을 기다리면서 항구에 와 있을 것이다. 민물돌고래가 즐거운 강에서 나를 호위할 것이며, 500종의 새들, 6종의 원숭이들, 그리고 수많은 화려한 나비들이 나를 맞이해 그들의 왕국으로 데려갈 것이다. 야생에서 야영을 하면서 모기, 뱀, 그리고 거미들과 함께 즐길 수 있다면 좋겠다. 나는 세계에서 가장 큰 열대우림을 집으로 만들고 싶다. 내 가슴은 나의 불룩한 가방만큼 많이 부풀어 오르지만, 길고 힘든 여행을 앞두고 있으니 잠을 좀 자는 편이 낫겠다.

문제 해설

내일 아침 Emerald Amazon Explorer에 승선해 아마존을 탐험하게 될 필자는 탐험 여행에 대한 기대로 한껏 부풀어 있으므로, 글에 드러난 필자의 심경으로 가장 적절한 것은 ① '흥분된'이다.

② 지친 ③ 실망한 ④ 무관심한 ⑤ 안심한

구문 분석

[8행] **I wish I could** *camp* in the wild and *enjoy* the company of mosquitos, snakes, and spiders.

▶ 「wish+동사의 과거형(could)」의 가정법 현재 구문이 사용되었다. 의미는 '(현재) ~할 수 있다면 좋을 텐데[~하고 싶다]'이며 could에 camp와 enjoy가 병렬관계로 연결되어 있다.

어휘

explore 탐험하다 **mysterious** 신비한
get on board (배에) 승선하다 **freshwater** 민물
escort 호위하다 **species** 종 **numerous** 수많은
camp 야영하다 **mosquito** 모기 **swell** 부풀다
chubby 불룩한, 통통한 **tough** 힘든

Exercise

01 ② 02 ① 03 ⑤ 04 ③ 05 ④ 06 ②

Plus Q

03 While[After] she[Gabby] recalled this 또는 While[After] she[Gabby] was recalling this

06 pale

01 정답 ②

소재 응급 센터에 걸려온 전화에 대한 대처 상황

전문 해석

응급 센터에서의 첫날 내가 막 커피를 마시려고 하는데 첫 번째 전화가 왔다. 나는 재빨리 "9-1-1" 전화를 집어 들었다. 내 목소리는 떨리고 있었고 내 심장은 아주 빨리 고동치고 있었다. "내 남편이 숨을 쉬고 있지 않아요!"라고 한 여자가 절규했다. 나는 그녀에게 심폐소생술을 시작하라고 지시했다. 가능한 한 침착해지려 애를 쓰고 있었지만 나는 떨고 있었다. 상황은 절대적으로 위급했다. 그 여자가 심폐소생술을 실시하고 있는 동안 나는 즉시 가까운 병원에 알렸다. 긴장된 순간이 지난 후 그 여자가 다시 전화로 돌아와서 "앰뷸런스는 어디에 있나요?"라고 외쳤다. "앰뷸런스는 가능한 한 빨리 그곳으로 가고 있습니다." 라고 나는 대답했다.

문제 해설

필자가 응급 센터에서 근무하는 첫날 한 여자가 전화를 걸어 그녀의 남편이 숨을 쉬고 있지 않다고 말하자 필자가 떨면서 이에 대응하는 상황이므로, 글에 나타난 분위기로 가장 적절한 것은 ② '긴급한'이다.

① 축제의 ③ 낭만적인 ④ 신비로운 ⑤ 단조로운

구문 분석

[7행] I replied, "It's getting there as quickly as it can."

▶ 문장의 마지막에 나오는 can 뒤에 문맥상 get there quickly가 생략된 것으로 이해할 수 있다.

02 정답 ①

소재 집시 여인에게 친절을 베푼 젊은 여성

전문 해석

어느 날 오후, 내가 호텔 근처의 가게 주위를 돌아다니고 있을 때, 나는 한 불쌍한 집시 여자가 지하철 역 밖에 있는

보도에 앉아 있는 것을 보았다. 그녀는 지치고 외로워 보였으며 그녀의 눈은 땅에 단단히 고정되어 있었다. 어린 아이가 엄마의 슬픔을 모르고 즐겁게 그녀의 발치에서 놀고 있었다. 그때 근처 여행객을 위한 가게에서 일하던 한 젊은 여성이 약간의 음식을 들고 가게 밖으로 나왔다. 그녀는 그 집시 여자에게 다가가서 아이를 향해 미소를 지으며 그 음식을 건네주었다. 나는 그 가게 점원이 그 아기가 장난스럽게 만지는 손길을 즐겁게 받아주고 있는 동안 그 집시 여자의 얼굴에 미소가 스쳐 지나가는 것을 보았다. 마음이 따뜻해지는 순간이었다. 그날 나는 인간의 친절함에 대해 한 가지 교훈을 배웠다.

문제 해설

지치고 외로워 보이는 한 집시 여인에게 젊은 여성이 음식을 가지고 와서 건네주는 것을 보면서 인간의 친절함에 대한 교훈을 얻었다는 내용의 글이다. 따라서 글에 드러난 필자의 심경으로 가장 적절한 것은 ① '감동한'이다.

② 지루한 ③ 불안한 ④ 무관심한 ⑤ 우울한

구문 분석

[4행] Then, a young woman (S) [**who** worked at a nearby tourist shop] came (V) out of the shop, [**holding** some food].

▶ [who ~]는 관계대명사절로 주어인 a young woman을 수식하고 있으며, [holding ~]는 분사구문으로 and held의 의미로 이해할 수 있다.

03 정답 ⑤

소재 연설을 하게 된 Gabby의 걱정과 이를 극복하게 되는 과정

전문 해석

마이크로 다가가면서, Gabby는 땀이 자신의 얼굴과 목에 흘러내리기 시작하고 있는 것을 느낄 수 있었다. 그녀는 심호흡을 하려고 애를 썼지만, 그렇게 할 수가 없었다. 자신의 이름이 불렸을 때, Gabby는 많은 청중 앞에서 연설한다는 것이 더 두려워졌다. 그러고 나서 그녀는 똑같은 두려움을 서서히 극복해 낸 여자가 "두려움, 빠른 심장 박동, 가쁜 호흡 그리고 땀이 나는 것은 단지 우리가 싸울 준비가 되어 있다는 것을 신체가 선언하는 것입니다."라고 한 말이 갑자기 생각났다. 이것을 상기하면서, Gabby는 진정했고, 자신이 해야 할 말을 또렷하게 생각해 냈다. 자신감이 생긴 Gabby는 미소를 지으며 연설하기 시작했다. 말은 물처럼 흘러나왔고, 그녀의 고동치는 심장으로 인해 그녀는 정신력이 더욱더 강해졌다. 과업 수행(연설)은 성공적이었다. 그녀는 자신의 두려움을 극복해냈다.

문제 해설

많은 청중 앞에서 연설을 해야 하는 Gabby가 두려움에 땀을 흘리고 심호흡도 제대로 못하는 상황이었다가 똑같은 두려움을 극복해 낸 여자가 한 말을 생각하면서 진정되고 자신감이 생겨 연설을 성공적으로 해냈다는 내용의 글이다. 따라서 Gabby의 심경 변화로 가장 적절한 것은 ⑤ '걱정하는 → 자신감 있는'이다.

① 기대에 부푼 → 무서워하는
② 무관심한 → 상쾌한
③ 질투하는 → 기뻐하는
④ 불안해하는 → 당황한

오답 풀이

Gabby가 많은 청중 앞에서 연설한다는 것이 두려워졌다는 것을 보고 Gabby의 불안해하는 심경을 파악한 다음에 지문의 뒷부분을 보지 않고 정답을 ④번으로 고르지 않도록 주의한다.

구문 분석

[8행] **Assured**, Gabby smiled and started to deliver her speech.

▶ Assured는 Being이 생략된 분사구문으로 원래 문장은 Gabby was assured and의 의미로 이해할 수 있다.

Plus Q

원래의 문장에서 접속사와 주어가 생략되고 동사의 원형을 -ing 형태로 바꾸어 분사구문을 만든 것으로 보거나, 원래 문장에서 동사 부분을 was recalling의 형태로 보고 was가 being이 되고 being이 생략되면서 recalling이 남은 것으로 볼 수도 있다.

04 정답 ③

소재 학생들의 깜짝 선물

전문 해석

수업 마지막 날에 학교 건물에 들어서자 교장이 날 맞이했다. "나와 함께 가실까요? 선생님 방에 문제가 좀 있어요."라고 그는 준엄하게 말했다. 그는 나를 복도 아래로 이끌면서 곧장 앞만 일직선으로 응시했다. 지금 뭘 어쩌라는 거야? 나는 의아해했다. 내가 교실에 도착했을 때 난 내가 본 것을 믿을 수가 없었다. 놀라웠다! 각 구석마다 꽃다발이, 학생들의 책상과 파일용 캐비닛 위에 부케가, 그리고 내 책상 위에 거대한 꽃바구니가 놓여 있었다. 아이들이 이런 일을 어떻게 해냈을까 궁금했다. 그들 대부분은 극빈 가정 출신이어서 옷과 음식도 학교 지원 프로그램에 의존

하고 있었다. 나는 울음을 터뜨렸고 아이들도 같이 울었다. 하지만 그것이 그들이 내게 표한 유일한 경의가 아니었다. 2년 후, 14명의 모든 학생이 졸업을 했고, 6명은 대학교 장학금을 받았다.

문제 해설

필자의 마지막 수업 날에 가난한 집안 출신의 학생들이 교실을 꽃으로 장식하고 필자에게 경의를 표해 주었다는 내용의 글이므로 글에 드러난 필자의 심경으로 가장 적절한 것은 ③ '아주 기뻐하는'이다.

① 부러워하는
② 유감스러운
④ 동정어린
⑤ 실망한

구문 분석

[7행] Most of them came from families **so** poor **that** they relied on the school assistance program for clothing and meals.

▶ 「so+형용사/부사+that(너무 ~해서 …하다)」 구문이 쓰였으며, 여기서 so poor는 앞의 families를 수식하고 있다. families who were so poor에서 who were가 생략된 구조이다.

05 정답 ④

소재 양식장에 빠진 Chris Jenkins

전문 해석

Chris Jenkins는 호주에 있는 그의 송어 양식장에서 밀렸던 마당일을 하기로 마음먹었다. 그의 개인 Ziggy가 그와 함께 있었는데, 그의 친구인 Stella는 약 60야드 떨어진 곳에서 낮잠을 자고 있었다. Chris는 기지개를 켜려고 일어섰을 때, 양식장 주위에 있는 난간에 머리를 부딪친 다음, 중심을 잃고 미끄러져 차가운 물속으로 빠졌다. 불행하게도, Chris는 수영을 할 줄 몰랐으며 설상가상으로, 그의 무거운 옷이 그의 무게를 늘려 가라앉도록 만들었다. 아마도 Ziggy는 자신이 너무나 가벼워서 그를 밖으로 끌어낼 수 없다는 것을 알았던지 Stella를 깨우기 위해 미친 듯이 짖었다. 몇 초안에 Stella는 호수 안으로 돌진해 들어갔고, 그곳에서 Chris는 그녀의 다리를 잡고 버틸 수 있었다.

문제 해설

물에 빠진 Chris Jenkins를 살리기 위해 그의 개가 옆에서 자고 있던 Chris Jenkins의 친구인 Stella를 깨우고 Stella가 Chris를 구하고 있는 상황이므로, 글에 나타난 분위기로 가장 적절한 것은 ④ '절박하고 긴급한'이다.

① 엄숙하고 진지한
② 재미있고 즐거운
③ 적막하고 침울한
⑤ 편안하고 한가로운

구문 분석

[3행] ~, he **banged** his head on the railing around the fishing area, **lost** his balance, and **slipped** into the icy water.

▶ banged, lost, slipped가 he를 수어로 공유하며 병렬을 이루고 있다.

[6행] Perhaps Ziggy knew that she was **too light to pull** him out, **barking** frantically to wake up Stella.

▶ 「too+형용사/부사+to부정사」는 '너무 …해서 ~할 수 없다' 라는 뜻이다. barking은 동시동작을 나타내는 분사구문을 이끈다.

06 정답 ②

소재 사진으로만 보았던 Mr. Johnson을 만나게 되는 Hana

전문 해석

이른 아침의 안개가 가벼운 빗줄기가 되었으며 부두에는 검은 우산들이 여기저기 눈에 띄어서, Johnson 씨를 알아보는 것을 더욱 어렵게 만들었다. Hana는 자신이 아주 오래 그리고 열심히 살펴보았던 사진과 닮은 얼굴을 절실하게 찾았다. 그가 오지 않았다면 어쩌지? 혼자서 어떻게 그의 집에 갈 수 있을까? Hana는 깊이 숨을 들이마시고는 머리를 들었다. 그때 그녀는 검은 코트를 입고 우산을 든 한 남자가 자신 쪽으로 빠르게 걸어오는 것을 보았다. 그는 홀쭉한 체격이었고 그녀보다 크지 않았으며 얼굴은 창백했다. 어색하게 고개를 숙이며 그는 중얼거렸다. "긴 여행을 하셨군요, Omiya 양." Hana는 숨을 멈췄다. "당신이 Johnson 씨인가요? 오 이런! 당신이 나타나지 않으면 어떻게 할지 걱정하고 있었어요."

문제 해설

Hana는 사진으로만 보았던 Mr. Johnson을 만나고자 한다. 그가 나오지 않으면 그의 집에 혼자서 어떻게 찾아갈지를 걱정하고 있다가 Mr. Johnson을 만나게 되어 Hana의 마음은 안도하는 심정이 되었을 것이다. 따라서 Hana의 심경 변화로 가장 적절한 것은 ② '걱정하는 → 안도해 하는'이다.

① 외로운 → 기쁜

③ 흥분된 → 당황한
④ 무서워하는 → 놀라는
⑤ 동정하는 → 무관심한

오답 풀이
우산들 때문에 Johnson 씨를 알아보는 것이 더욱 어렵게 된 상황을 Hana가 외로워하는 것으로 오해하지 않도록 주의한다.

구문 분석
[1행] ~, and on the pier black umbrellas were seen here and there, [**making** recognizing Mr. Johnson even harder].

▶ [making ~]는 분사구문으로, 분사 making의 의미상의 주어는 black umbrellas이다. recognizing Mr. Johnson은 making의 목적어이다.

[5행] At that moment, she **saw a man** [in a black coat], [carrying an umbrella], **come** quickly to her side.

▶ 「지각동사+목적어+목적보어」 구문이며 목적보어로 동사원형인 come이 쓰였다. [ ]로 표시된 전치사구와 분사구가 목적어인 a man을 모두 수식하고 있다.

Plus Q
pale은 '창백한, (색깔이) 옅은'이라는 뜻을 가진다.
어떤 것이 창백하다면, 그것은 색이 아주 연하거나 거의 하얗다.

유형 05 내용 일치 p. 34

대표 예제 정답 ④

소재 고대 그리스 화가 Protogenes

전문 해석
자신의 그림들 각각에 대한 헌신 때문에 알려진 Protogenes는 고대 그리스의 화가이자 Apelles의 라이벌이었다. 그는 Caria의 해안에 있는 Caunus에서 태어났지만 삶의 대부분을 Rhodes에서 살았다. 그에 대해 그 밖에 다른 것은 거의 알려지지 않는다. 그러나 그의 그림에 대한 몇 가지 기술은 있다. 'Ialysus'와 'Satyr'는 그의 작품 중에서 가장 잘 알려진 작품이었다. Protogenes는 Rhodes의 한 마을의 지역 영웅의 묘사인 'Ialysus'를 그리는 데 대략 7년을 보냈다. 적어도 200년 동안 Rhodes에 남아 있은 다음에 그것은 로마로 옮겨졌다. 그곳에서 나중에 그것은 화재로 파괴되었다. Protogenes는 Demetrius Poliorcetes가 기원전 305년에서 304년 동안에 Rhodes를 공격할 때 'Satyr'를 작업했다. 흥미롭게도, 그가 'Satyr'를 그린 정원은 적의 막사 한가운데에 있었다. Protogenes는 'Satyr'가 완성되었을 때 약 70세였다고 한다.

문제 해설
'Satyr'를 그린 정원은 적진의 한가운데에 있었다(the garden in which he painted the *Satyr* was in the middle of the enemy's camp)고 했으므로 글의 내용과 일치하지 않는 것은 ④이다.

구문 분석
[7행] Protogenes **spent** approximately seven years **painting** [the *Ialysus*], [a depiction of a local hero of a town in Rhodes].

▶ 「spend+시간+-ing」는 '~하는 데 시간이 걸리다'라는 의미이다. 콤마(,)로 연결된 두 개의 [ ]는 동격 관계에 있다.

[15행] Protogenes is said **to have been** about seventy years of age when the *Satyr* was completed.

▶ 완료부정사(to have been)가 사용된 것은 이 어구가 기술하는 상황(그림을 완성했을 때 70세였다)이 주절이 기술하는 상황(현재 전해진다)보다 앞서 일어났기 때문이다.

어휘
devotion 헌신, 몰두 **account** 설명, 기술
depiction 묘사, 서술 **camp** (군인들의) 막사
complete 완성하다

Exercise

01 ⑤ 02 ⑤ 03 ⑤ 04 ④ 05 ③ 06 ③

Plus Q
03 차량의 바깥쪽 바퀴를 더 잘 볼 수 있도록 하기 위해, 통행을 보다 안전하도록 하기 위해
06 식습관을 조절하지 못해서

01 정답 ⑤

소재 addax의 특징

전문 해석

addax는 사하라 사막의 일부 지역에서 발견되는 영양의 일종이다. 그것은 나선형 뿔과 짧고 두꺼운 다리를 갖고 있다. 그것은 멸종 위기에 처한 포유동물이며 야생에 대략 500마리만 남아 있다. addax의 머리와 몸의 길이는 150~170센티미터이다. 수컷은 암컷보다 약간 더 크다. addax의 털은 계절에 따라서 색이 변한다. 겨울에 addax는 회갈색이며 다리는 흰색이다. 여름 동안에 그것들의 털은 더 밝아져서, 거의 완전히 흰색이다. addax는 모래가 많은 사막 지역과 돌이 많은 사막을 선호한다. addax는 사막의 더위 때문에 주로 밤에 활동적이다.

문제 해설

사막의 더위 때문에 주로 밤에 활동적(The addax is mostly active at night due to the heat of the desert)이라고 했으므로 글의 내용과 일치하지 않는 것은 ⑤이다.

구문 분석

[4행] The coat of the addax changes in color **depending on** the season.

▶ depending on은 '~에 따라서, ~에 달려 있는'의 의미를 나타낸다.

02 정답 ⑤

소재 tarsier의 특징

전문 해석

Tarsier는 쥐보다 크지 않은 크기의 작은 영장류이다. 전체 몸통보다 훨씬 더 긴 가는 꼬리 때문에 쥐와의 유사성이 더욱 부각된다. 모든 tarsier는 완전히 야행성이고, 이러한 생활 방식을 위하여 많은 뛰어난 신체적 적응 장치들이 있다. 그들은 뛰어난 청력을 갖고 있다. Tarsier는 또한 몸 크기에 비해 굉장히 큰 눈을 갖고 있는데, 눈이 얼굴 크기의 약 4분의 1을 차지한다. Tarsier의 서식지는 대개 열대우림 지역이며, 빽빽한 대나무 숲에서 발견된다. 낮 동안에는, 나무 둥치의 구멍이나, 어둡고 두꺼운 엉킨 초목에서 누워 있다. 밤에는 벌레, 거미, 그리고 작은 도마뱀을 사냥한다. Tarsier는 그들의 머리를 최소 180도 돌릴 수 있는데, 이는 먹이를 찾기 위한 넓은 시야를 확보해 준다.

문제 해설

Tarsier는 벌레, 거미, 그리고 작은 도마뱀을 사냥한다(they hunt for insects, spiders, and small lizards)고 했으므로 글의 내용과 일치하지 않는 것은 ⑤이다.

구문 분석

[1행] Tarsiers are little primates [**not much bigger than rats**].

▶ 형용사구(not much ~ rats)가 앞에 나온 명사구(little primates)를 수식하고 있다. little primates 뒤에는 「주격 관계대명사+be동사」인 'that/which/who are'가 생략되어 있다. much는 비교급을 강조하며 '훨씬'의 의미이다.

03 정답 ⑤

소재 'Death Road'로 알려져 있는 North Yungas Road

전문 해석

'Death Road'로 알려져 있는 North Yungas Road는 북부 볼리비아의 Yungas 지역과 수도인 La Paz를 이어준다. 그 도로는 1930년대 Chaco 전쟁 중에 파라과이인 전쟁 포로들에 의해 만들어졌다. La Paz에서 시작되어, 이 도로는 처음에는 4,650미터까지 올라가고, 그런 다음 Coroico 마을이 있는 1,200미터까지 점차 내려간다. 이 내리막은 세계에서 가장 길게 뻗어 지속되는 내리막길 중 하나이다. 그것은 대부분이 가드레일이 없는 일차선 도로이고, 600미터에 이르는 절벽을 가지고 있다. 위험 요인에는 산사태와 굴러 떨어지는 바위들, 지속적인 안개, 열대성 폭우와 제한된 시야가 포함된다. 볼리비아의 다른 지역과는 달리, 그 지역 도로 규칙 중 하나는 운전자에게 차량의 바깥쪽 바퀴에 대한 더 나은 시야를 주고 통행을 더 안전하게 하기 위해 차량을 도로의 왼편에서 운행해야 할 것을 명시하고 있다.

문제 해설

North Yungas Road에서 차량은 도로의 왼편에서 운행해야 한다(specifies that vehicles are required to drive on the left side of the road)고 언급되어 있으므로 글의 내용과 일치하지 않는 것은 ⑤이다.

구문 분석

[8행] Unlike the rest of Bolivia, **one** (S) [of the local road rules] **specifies** (V) that vehicles are required to drive on the left side of the road *to give* the driver a better view of the vehicle's outside wheel and (*to*) *make* passing safer.

▶ 「one of+복수명사」의 주어는 one이므로 단수동사가 와야 한다. give와 make는 to에 병렬구조로 연결되어 있으며 여기서의 to부정사는 '~하기 위해'의 목적 용법으로 쓰였다.

Plus Q

마지막 문장에서 to부정사를 활용하여 그 목적을 밝히고 있다. (to give the driver a better view of the vehicle's outside wheel, (to) make passing safer)

04 정답 ④

소재 Dorothy Hodgkin의 삶

전문 해석

Dorothy Hodgkin은 1910년 이집트의 카이로에서 태어났으며, 그녀의 아버지 John Crowfoot는 영국의 고고학자였다. 제1차 세계 대전 동안에 Dorothy와 그녀의 여동생들은 안전상의 이유로 영국으로 보내졌다. 그녀는 Sir John Leman School에서 학교 교육을 받았다. 그 학교를 졸업한 후에 Dorothy는 옥스퍼드 대학에 있는 Somerville 여자 단과 대학에 들어갔다. 다행스럽게도, 그녀는 등록금을 낼 때 그녀의 친척 중 한 명으로부터 재정적으로 지원을 받을 수 있었다. 그녀는 1932년에 옥스퍼드 대학에서 자신의 학사 학위를 받았다. 그런 다음 그녀는 캠브리지 대학의 유명한 결정학자인 John Desmond Bernal의 조수로 일했다. 1934년에 Hodgkin은 자신의 가르치는 일을 위해서 뿐만 아니라 자신의 박사 학위를 마치기 위해서 옥스퍼드로 돌아왔다. 제2차 세계 대전 후에 Hodgkin은 복잡한 화학물질의 분자 구조를 분석하기 위해 영국에서 컴퓨터를 사용한 최초의 과학자가 되었으며, 이런 일로 인해 그녀는 3차원 모델을 만들어낼 수 있었다.

문제 해설

Hodgkin은 옥스퍼드 대학에서 학사 학위를 받았으며, 캠브리지 대학에서는 John Desmond Bernal의 조수로 일을 했다고 했으므로, 글의 내용과 일치하지 않는 것은 ④이다.

구문 분석

[10행] After World War II, Hodgkin became the first scientist in Britain [**to use** a computer] [**to analyze** the molecular structure of complex chemicals] ~.

▶ [to use ~]는 the first scientist in Britain을 수식하는 to부정사의 형용사적 용법이며, [to analyze ~]는 '~하기 위해'로 해석되는 to부정사의 부사적 용법이다.

05 정답 ③

소재 장애를 극복한 불굴의 육상 선수

전문 해석

Wilma Rudolph는 22명의 자식 중 20번째였다. 그녀는 조산으로 태어났고 의사들은 그녀가 살 것으로 예상하지 않았다. 그녀는 살았지만 4살 때, 양측 폐렴과 성홍열에 걸렸으며, 그로 인해 왼쪽 다리가 마비되었다. 9살에 그녀는 과거 5년간 의지했던 금속 의족을 제거했고 그것 없이 걷기 시작했다. 13살에 그녀는 규칙적으로 걷게 되었는데, 의사들은 그것을 기적이라고 말했다. 같은 해에, 그녀는 달리기를 시작하고 싶어 했다. 그녀는 첫 달리기 대회에 참가해서 꼴찌로 들어왔다. 그 후 3년 동안, 그녀는 참가할 수 있는 모든 대회에 참가했다. 그녀는 자신이 경주에서 이기는 날이 올 때까지 계속 달렸다. 결국, 살지 못할 것으로 예상되었던 그리고 그때 다시 걷지 못할 것으로 예상되었던 어린 소녀가 세 개의 올림픽 금메달을 획득하였다.

문제 해설

첫 번째 달리기 대회에서 꼴찌로 들어왔으므로 중도에 포기하지는 않았다. 따라서 글의 내용과 일치하지 않는 것은 ③이다.

구문 분석

[5행] By thirteen, she had developed a rhythmic walk, **which** (doctors said) was a miracle.

▶ which는 was a miracle의 주어 역할을 하고 있으며 앞 절의 내용을 받는 관계사이다. doctors said가 삽입된 구조이다.

06 정답 ③

소재 체중 증가에 민감했던 여성

전문 해석

Ellen West는 신경성 식욕부진과 아마도 다른 정신질환을 겪은 걱정스러운 환자였다. Ellen은 체중의 등락이 심했고 체중이 증가하는 것에 대한 극단적인 두려움을 가지고 있었다. 그것이 결국 우울증의 발병으로 이어졌다. 날씬함을 유지하기 위해서 그녀는 약을 복용하기 시작했다. 그녀는 28살의 나이에 사촌과 결혼하도록 허락을 받았다. 그녀는 아이를 갖는 것에 집착하게 되었지만 그녀는 식습관을 조절하지 못했고, 그것이 유산으로 이어졌다. 그녀는 임신하기 위해서 약을 끊기로 결심하였으나 체중 증가에 대한 두려움이 그녀를 압도해서 그녀는 다시 약을 사용하기 시작했다. 그녀는 30살이 되었을 때 날씬한 모습을 유지하기 위한 바람에서 채식주의자가 되기로 결심했다. 그녀가 남편에게 자신의 심한 식이 장애와 우울증에 관해 알린 것은 결혼한 지 3년이 지난 후에서였다.

문제 해설

Ellen West는 아이를 갖는 것에 집착했다(She became obsessed with wanting a child)고 했으므로 글의 내용과 일치하지 않는 것은 ③이다.

구문 분석

[10행] **It wasn't until** after three years of marriage **that** she informed her husband of her severe eating disorder and depression.

▶ 「It is not until A that ~」은 '~한 것은 A하고 나서이다.'라는 의미이다. It is ~ that으로 'not until A'를 강조하고 있다.

Plus Q

아이를 낳고 싶었지만 식습관을 조절하지 못해서 유산으로 이어졌다고 6행에 기술되어 있다.

유형 06 실용문의 이해

p. 40

대표 예제

정답 ④

소재 십 대 프로그래머 연례회의

전문 해석

2015 십 대 프로그래머 연례 회의
11월 21과 22일, 오전 10시부터 오후 5시까지

십 대 프로그래머 협회에 의해 주최됨

컴퓨터 화면이 여러분의 우주입니까? 그렇다면 West 주립 대학의 Brilliance Hall에서 개최되는 저희 회의에 참여하여 스스로에게 도전해 보십시오! 여기서 여러분은 현대 컴퓨터 과학의 선도자들을 만나게 될 것입니다.

회의에 포함된 내용:

- Warwick Meade를 포함한, 유명한 업계 인물들의 강연
- 하드웨어와 소프트웨어, 프로그래밍, 그리고 새로운 응용 프로그램에 관한 10개의 개별 세미나
- 12개 주요 회사들의 최신 제품 전시회

입장권 가격:

- Total Pass(전체 행사 입장권): 25달러 (점심 뷔페를 포함)
- 강연과 세미나만: 15달러
- 전시회만: 10달러

예약은 필수입니다. www.tiinprogrammers.org에서 입장권을 예약하십시오.

문제 해설

전체 행사 입장권(Total Pass)에 점심 뷔페가 포함된다(Total Pass: $25 (includes buffet lunch))고 언급되어 있으므로 ④가 안내문의 내용과 일치한다.

구문 분석

[4행] Then join our conference [(which/that is) held at West State University's Brilliance Hall], ~.

▶ [ ]는 주격 관계대명사 which나 that과 동사 is가 생략된 관계대명사절로 선행사 our conference를 수식한다.

어휘

annual 연례의 **conference** 회의
association 협회 **renowned** 유명한
industry figure 업계 인물 **separate** 별개의
application 응용 프로그램
exhibition 전시회 **latest** 최신의
reserve 예약하다

Exercise

01 ④ 02 ③ 03 ④ 04 ③

Plus Q

02 to become
04 (금요일이나 토요일의 1박 예약은) 일주일 전에 이뤄져야 한다.

01

정답 ④

소재 동물원 사육사 체험

전문 해석

Dudley 동물원 사육사 체험

동물원 사육사 체험을 하는 동안, 여러분은 동물을 돌보는 직업에 종사하는 데 무엇이 필요한지를 다음과 같은 활동에 참여하면서 알게 될 것입니다.

- 동물 먹이 준비하기
- 동물의 무게를 재고 돌보는 일 돕기

• 동물 훈련에 참여하기

대상: 9세에서 18세까지의 동물 애호가
시간: 오전 9시 30분 ~ 오전 11시 30분
– 우리 동물원은 하루에 한 번 동물원 사육사 체험 활동을 운영합니다.
가격: 50달러
– 동물원 입장료가 포함되어 있습니다.
준비물: 물병과 본인 카메라
– 사진을 찍을 수 있는 기회가 제공됩니다.
예약을 위해 우리 홈페이지 www.dudleyzoo.com을 방문해 주십시오.

문제 해설
가격(COST)에 동물원 입장료가 포함된다(Zoo admission is included)고 언급되어 있으므로 ④가 안내문의 내용과 일치하지 않는다.

구문 분석
[2행] ~, you will learn [**what** it takes to work in an animal care career], **participating** in the following activities:

▶ [what ~]는 learn의 목적어 역할을 하는 명사절로 쓰였으며 participating 이하는 부대상황을 나타내는 분사구문으로, 'as you participate ~'로 바꿔 쓸 수 있다.

02 정답 ③

소재 전국 에세이 대회

전문 해석

2015 전국 에세이 대회

Evergreen 재단은 2015 전국 에세이 대회를 위한 작품 제출을 부탁드리게 되어 매우 기쁩니다! 이 대회는 고등학교 학생들이 우리의 환경에 대한 중요성을 더 의식하도록 권장하기 위해 계획되었습니다.

대회 주제
• 어떻게 우리는 우리의 숲을 보존할 수 있는가?

필수 조건 및 제출 지침
• 고등학생만 가능
• 학생 1인당 1편의 에세이만 가능
• 에세이는 1,500에서 2,000단어 사이여야만 함.
• 2015년 7월 15일까지 마감

올해의 대회 수상자는 2015년 8월 15일에 발표할 예정입니다.

에세이는 이메일로 제출된 것만 접수됩니다.
(이메일: 2015essay@evergreeners.org)

더 많은 정보를 원하시면 www.evergreeners.org를 방문해 주시기 바랍니다.

문제 해설
필수 조건 및 제출 지침에서 학생 1인당 1편의 에세이만 가능(Only one essay per student)하다고 했으므로 ③이 안내문의 내용과 일치한다.

오답 풀이
① 대회 주제는 '어떻게 우리는 우리의 숲을 보존할 수 있는가?'이다.
② 고등학생만 가능하다고 되어 있다.
④ 수상자는 2015년 8월 15일에 발표할 예정이다.
⑤ 에세이 접수는 이메일로만 받는다.

구문 분석
[13행] Only essays [(which / that are) submitted by email] will be accepted.

▶ [ ]는 주격 관계대명사 which나 that과 동사 are가 생략된 관계대명사절로 선행사 essays를 수식한다.

Plus Q
5형식 동사 encourage의 목적격 보어이므로 to부정사 형태인 to become으로 고쳐 써야 한다.

03 정답 ④

소재 하계 캠프 청소년 자원봉사 프로그램

전문 해석

하계 캠프 청소년 자원봉사 프로그램

2016년 여름 신청은 이제 마감되었습니다. 2016년 하계 캠프에 지원했다면 여기 다음 단계가 있습니다.
• 4월 8일: 모든 봉사자들이 선정되며 일정이 배정됩니다.
• 6월 4, 5, 혹은 15일: 모든 봉사자들은 한 번의 예비교육에 참석해야 합니다.

청소년 봉사자들은 비공식적인 과학 교육을 지원하면서 우리 하계 캠프에서 함께 일하게 됩니다. 그들은 교육자와 보조원의 교실 준비와 관리를 돕고, 아이들과 함께 실험 및 활동에 참여합니다. 봉사자들은 6월 13일부터 8월 26일까지 Durham의 박물관에서 열리는 캠프 기간 동안 참가자들의 과학 탐험을 지원하며, 즐겁고 안전한 환경을 제공하는 데 도움을 줍니다. 봉사자들은 오전 8시 30분부터 오후 3시 30분까지 일해야 합니다.

자격 조건

- 어린 아이들을 대하고 책임지는 자리에서 근무한 경험이 있어야 합니다.
- 봉사자들은 2주간 캠프에서 근무할 수 있어야 합니다. 2주가 연속될 필요는 없습니다.

문의 사항은 봉사 프로그램 진행자에게 이메일(emman@ncmls.org)을 보내주시기 바랍니다.

문제 해설

책임이 필요한 자리에서 일한 경험이 있어야 한다(have experience working in positions of responsibility)고 했으므로 ④가 안내문의 내용과 일치한다.

오답 풀이

① 모든 봉사자들은 한 번의 예비교육에 참석해야 한다.
② 봉사자들을 위한 별도의 과학 교육에 대한 언급은 없다.
③ 하계 캠프는 6월 13일부터 8월 26일까지 진행되므로 3개월이 채 되지 않는다.
⑤ 봉사자들은 2주간 캠프에서 근무할 수 있어야 하지만 2주가 연속될 필요는 없다.

구문 분석

[9행] Volunteers help provide a fun and safe environment [**while assisting** campers **in** their exploration of science] ~.

▶ [while ~]는 분사구문으로 의미를 명확하게 하기 위하여 접속사 while을 생략하지 않은 형태이다. 「assist+사람+in 명사(구)」는 '~가 …하는 것을 돕다'는 의미이다.

04 정답 ③

소재 Breitenbush 온천

전문 해석

Breitenbush 온천

워크숍, 개인 휴양, 혹은 당일 방문을 위해 찾아주세요!
(모든 방문에 예약이 필수입니다.)

예약 시간: 월요일~토요일 오전 9시~오후 4시
2016년 9월까지 예약을 받고 있습니다.

숙박비 포함 내역:

- 매일 3번의 풍성한 유기농 채식류 식사
- 24시간 온천 이용

중요한 정보

주말 저녁 예약은 최소 이틀을 예약하셔야 합니다. 금요일이나 토요일 1박은 1주일 전에 예약하셔야 합니다.

할인

7일 이상을 머무시는 고객께는 숙박비를 10퍼센트 할인해 드립니다. 중복 할인은 제공하지 않습니다.

추가적인 정보를 원하시면, office@breitenbush.com으로 이메일을 보내주시기 바랍니다.

문제 해설

24시간 온천 이용(Round-the-clock access to the hot springs)이 가능하다고 했으므로, 정해진 시간에 온천 이용이 가능하다는 ③은 안내문의 내용과 일치하지 않는다.

구문 분석

[14행] **Guests** (S.) [**who** stay 7 days or more] **receive** (V) a 10% lodging discount.

▶ [who ~]는 주격 관계대명사 who가 쓰인 관계대명사절로 앞의 Guests를 선행사로 수식하며, 이 문장의 동사는 receive이다.

Plus Q

「시간+in advance」는 '~의 시간 전에'라는 뜻으로서 must be made one week in advance라고 했으므로 '(금요일이나 토요일의 1박 예약은) 일주일 전에 이뤄져야 한다'는 조건을 지켜야 한다.

유형 07 도표의 이해

p. 46

대표 예제 정답 ③

소재 부모와 다른 성인들이 도서관에서 하는 활동

전문 해석

위의 도표는 2012년에 시행된 한 조사의 결과를 보여준다. 그것은 미성년 자녀의 부모(이후부터는 부모라고 한다)의 비율과 다른 성인의 비율을 그들의 6개의 도서관 활동 참여의 관점에서 비교한다. 아주 현저하게도, 부모의 비율은 모든 활동 유형에서 다른 성인의 비율보다 더 높았다. 서가를 둘러본 부모의 비율은 인쇄된 책을 빌린 부모의 비율과 같다. 부모와 다른 성인의 비율의 차이는 수업이나 행사에 참가하는 활동에서 가장 크고 컴퓨터나 인터넷을 사용하는 활동에서 가장 작다. 서가를 둘러본 다른 성인의 비율은 DVD, CD 또는 비디오테이프를 빌린 다른 성인의 비율보다 두 배 더 높다. 마지막으로, 전자 도서를

빌린 부모의 비율은 10퍼센트보다 더 적지만 똑같은 활동을 한 다른 성인의 비율보다 더 높다.

문제 해설
부모와 다른 성인의 참여율 차이가 가장 큰 것은 수업이나 행사 참가 활동(33% point)이 맞지만, 부모와 다른 성인의 참여율 차이가 가장 작은 것은 컴퓨터나 인터넷을 사용하는 활동(13% point)이 아니라 전자 도서를 빌리는 것(4% point)이므로 ③이 도표의 내용과 일치하지 않는다.

구문 분석
[12행] The percentage of other adults [who browsed shelves] is **twice as high as** that of other adults [who borrowed DVDs, CDs, or videotapes].
▶ 첫 번째 [ ]는 who가 이끄는 관계사절로 other adults를 수식하고 있으며, 두 번째 [ ] 역시 other adults를 수식하고 있다. '두 배 더 높다'는 twice as high as 또는 twice higher than으로 표현할 수 있다.

어휘
survey 조사 **conduct** 시행하다
minor 미성년의 **hereafter** 이후로
in terms of ~의 관점에서
involvement 참여 **notably** 현저히
browse (가게 안의 물건들을) 둘러보다
e-book 전자 도서

Exercise

01 ③ 02 ④ 03 ③ 04 ②

Plus Q
02 to
04 the size of urban female population of each age group

01 정답 ③

소재 11세 호주 학생들의 고민 상담 대상

전문 해석
위 그래프는 11세 호주 여자아이들과 남자아이들이 문제가 생겼을 경우 누구에게 조언을 구하는지를 보여준다. 여자아이들과 남자아이들은 문제가 생겼을 경우 어머니에게 가장 많이 조언을 구했다. 남자아이들의 경우, 아버지에게 두 번째로 많이 조언을 구했고, 친구가 그 뒤를 이었다. 선생님에게 조언을 구한 여자아이들의 비율은 아버지에게 조언을 구한 여자아이들의 비율보다 20퍼센트 포인트 더 높았다. 선생님에게 조언을 구한 남자아이들의 비율은 여자아이들의 비율보다 4퍼센트 포인트 더 높았다. 자신에게 문제가 생겼을 경우, 친구에게 간 여자아이들이 남자 형제나 여자 형제에게 간 여자아이들보다 더 많았다.

문제 해설
선생님에게 조언을 구한 여자아이들의 비율(40%)은 아버지에게 조언을 구한 여자아이들의 비율(60%)보다 20퍼센트 포인트 낮으므로 ③이 도표의 내용과 일치하지 않는다.

구문 분석
[6행] The percentage of boys who consulted teachers was higher than **that** of girls who consulted teachers **by** 4 percentage points.
▶ 같은 명사의 반복을 피하기 위해 the percentage 대신 that이 사용되었다. by는 정도를 나타내는 전치사이다.

02 정답 ④

소재 미국 이주민 출신지의 비율

전문 해석
위 두 개의 원 그래프는 1960년과 2013년 사이의 다섯 개의 미국 이주민 출신지의 비율 변화를 보여준다. 1960년에는 유럽/캐나다가 미국 이주민들의 가장 큰 출신지였지만, 2013년에는 4위로 떨어졌다. 2013년에 미국 이주민들에게 있어서 가장 큰 출신지는 멕시코였다. 1960년에는 멕시코와 그 외 라틴 아메리카의 비율이 합쳐서 10퍼센트만을 차지하였으나, 2013년에는 그것이 증가하여 50퍼센트를 초과하였다. 남/동아시아에서 태어난 이주민들의 비율은 2013년에 26퍼센트로 증가했고, 이것은 1960년의 비율의 일곱 배보다 많았다. 1960년에는 유럽/캐나다가 미국 이주민들의 80퍼센트를 넘게 차지하며 지배적인 출신지였으나, 2013년에는 어떤 단일 출신지도 30퍼센트를 넘게 차지하지 못했다.

문제 해설
2013년에 남/동아시아에서 태어난 이주민 비율(26%)은 1960년의 비율(4%)의 일곱 배보다 적으므로 ④는 도표의 내용과 일치하지 않는다.

구문 분석
[7행] The percentage of immigrant population born

in South/East Asia increased to 26% in 2013, **which** was more than **seven times that** of 1960.

▶ '~의 몇 배, ~의 반'이라고 할 때 전치사 of를 쓰지 않는 경우가 일반적이다. 여기서 that은 the percentage를 받고 있으며, which는 계속적 용법으로 쓰여 앞문장 전체를 받는다.

Plus Q

도표에서 전치사의 쓰임을 잘 아는 것이 중요한데, by+수치는 '정도'를, to+수치는 '증감을 통해 그 수치에 이르렀다'는 의미이므로 여기서는 to가 들어가야 한다.

03 정답 ③

소재 자녀 보육에 대한 Tompkins 카운티 부모들의 주당 지출 규모

전문 해석

위의 그래프는 미국의 Tompkins 카운티의 부모들이 주당 자녀 보육에 얼마나 많은 비용을 지불하는지를 보여준다. 3백 5명의 부모들이 이러한 조사에 응답했다. 부모들 중에서 가장 많은 수가 아이 보육에 한 주당 100달러에서 200달러의 돈을 지불한다고 답했는데, 이러한 부모들은 27.2 퍼센트를 차지한다. 두 번째로 많은 수이며 16.7 퍼센트를 차지하는 부모들은 자녀 보육에 한 주당 200달러에서 300달러의 돈을 지불한다고 말했다. 무료 자녀 보육 프로그램을 이용하는 부모들의 수는 14.1 퍼센트를 자치하는데, 이것은 순위가 세 번째이다. 자녀 보육에 한 주당 200에서 300달러를 지불하는 부모들의 수는 한 주당 300에서 400달러를 지불하는 부모들의 수보다 두 배 이상이 많다. 가장 적은 수의 부모들이 자녀 보육에 대해 한 주당 400에서 500달러를 지불한다고 응답했으며, 이것은 전체에서 2.6 퍼센트를 차지한다.

문제 해설

무료 자녀 보육 프로그램을 이용하는 부모들은 14.1 퍼센트가 맞지만 전체에서 네 번째에 해당하므로 ③은 도표의 내용과 일치하지 않는다.

구문 분석

[7행] **The number** (S) of parents [who pay 200 to 300 dollars per week] for child care **is** (V) more than twice as many as **that** of parents [who pay 300 to 400 dollars per week].

▶ 문장의 주어는 The number이고, 단수 취급하므로 단수 동사 is가 쓰였다. The number의 반복을 피하기 위해 that이 사용되었다.

04 정답 ②

소재 20~49세 사이의 도시 여성 인구

전문 해석

위 그래프는 세 개의 연령집단(20~29세, 30~39세, 40~49세)의 1991년과 2011년의 도시 여성 인구 구성을 보여준다. 2011년에 각 연령 집단의 도시 여성 인구 규모가 1991년의 그것보다 두 배 이상 올랐다. 2011년에, 직장을 다니고 있는 20~29세 집단의 도시 여성 인구는 같은 집단의 일자리를 찾는 도시 여성 인구와 거의 같았지만 직장을 다니고 있는 30~39세 집단의 도시 여성 인구는 같은 집단의 일자리를 찾는 도시 여성 인구보다 적었다. 두 해 모두에서, 직장을 다니고 있는 40~49세의 도시 여성 인구는 다른 두 연령 집단의 직장을 다니고 있는 도시 여성 인구보다 적었다. 두 해 모두에서, 직장을 가지고 있지 않은 20~29세 집단은 다른 두 집단의 그들보다 더 많았다. 2011년에 일자리를 구하는 모든 연령 집단의 도시 여성 인구의 규모는 1991년의 그들의 그것(인구 규모)보다 더 많았다.

문제 해설

2011년에 직장을 다니고 있는 30~39세 집단의 도시 여성 인구는 같은 집단의 일자리를 찾는 도시 여성 인구보다 많았으므로 ②가 도표의 내용과 일치하지 않는다.

구문 분석

[4행] ~, the urban female population of the 20-29 group in workforce was almost the same as **that** of the same group seeking work, ~.

▶ that은 'the urban female population'을 받는 대명사이다. 전치사구의 수식을 받으며 앞에 나온 명사를 받는 대명사는 단수의 경우 that으로, 복수의 경우 those로 받는다.

Plus Q

대명사 that은 앞에 나온 단수 명사(구)를 받는데, 주로 뒤에 수식어구가 동반되는 명사 대신 사용된다. 여기서는 of 1991이 수식어구의 역할을 하고 있다.

유형 08 어휘 추론

p. 52

대표 예제 정답 ③

소재 Atitlán 호수에 Atitlán Giant Grebe의 수가 적어지게 된 이유

전문 해석

Atitlán Giant Grebe는 훨씬 더 널리 퍼져 있던 더 작은 Pied-billed Grebe(얼룩부리논병아리)에서 진화한 날지 못하는 큰 새였다. 1965년 무렵에는 Atitlán 호수에 약 80 마리만이 남아 있었다. 한 가지 직접적인 원인은 알아내기 매우 쉬웠는데, 현지의 인간들이 맹렬한 속도로 갈대밭을 베어 넘어뜨리는 것이었다. 이런 파괴는 빠르게 성장하는 매트 제조 산업의 필요에 의해 추진되었다. 그러나 다른 문제들이 있었다. 한 미국 항공사가 그 호수를 낚시꾼들의 관광지로 개발하는 데 강한 관심을 보였다. 하지만 이 생각에 큰 문제가 있었는데, 그 호수에는 적절한 스포츠용[낚시용] 물고기가 없었다! 이런 다소 분명한 문제점을 해결하기 위해 Large-mouthed Bass(큰입농어)라 불리는 특별히 선택된 물고기 종이 도입되었다. 그 도입된 개체는 즉각 그 호수에 사는 게와 작은 물고기에게 관심을 돌렸고, 이리하여 몇 마리 안 남은 논병아리와 먹이를 놓고 경쟁하였다. 또한, 가끔 그들[큰입농어들]이 얼룩말 줄무늬가 있는 Atitlán Giant Grebe 새끼들을 게걸스럽게 먹어치웠다는 데 의심의 여지가 거의 없다.

문제 해설

(A) 인간들이 맹렬한 속도로 갈대밭을 베어 넘어뜨리는 행위를 대신하는 표현이 와야 하므로 '파괴'의 의미인 destruction이 적절하다. accommodation은 '적응, 조화, 화해'의 의미이다.

(B) 관광지로서 호수가 가지고 있는 문제점을 해결하기 위해 Large-mouthed Bass를 도입했다고 언급하고 있으므로 그 호수에는 스포츠용[낚시용] 물고기가 없었다는 것을 알 수 있다. 따라서 '없었다'의 의미인 lacked가 적절하다. support는 '지지[지원]하다'의 의미이다.

(C) Atitlán Giant Grebe가 Atitlán 호수에서 생존에 어려움을 겪게 된 원인을 설명하고 있는 글이므로, 새로 도입된 Large-mouthed Bass가 먹이를 두고 Atitlán Giant Grebe와 경쟁하게 되었다는 것을 알 수 있다. 따라서 '경쟁하였다'의 의미인 competing이 적절하다. cooperate는 '협력하다'의 의미이다.

구문 분석

[16행] The introduced individuals immediately turned their attentions to the crabs and small fish [**that** lived in the lake], [**thus competing** with the few remaining grebes for food].

▶ [that ~]는 관계대명사절로 the crabs and small fish를 수식하고 있으며, [thus competing ~]는 분사구문으로 'and thus competed ~'로 이해할 수 있다.

어휘

flightless 날지 못하는 **evolve** 진화하다
spot 알아내다, 발견하다 **reed bed** 갈대밭
furious 맹렬한, 몹시 화가 난
intent 강한 관심을 보이는
tourist destination 관광지
compensate for ~을 보충[보상]하다
obvious 분명한 **defect** 결함
chick 새끼 새, 병아리

Exercise

01 ④ 02 ② 03 ④ 04 ② 05 ⑤ 06 ①

Plus Q
03 had gone
06 상상력은 좌절의 원천일 수 있다는 것

01 정답 ④

소재 최저임금법의 기능

전문 해석

역사적인 증거들에서 적절한 법의 부재 시 고용주들에 의해 착취당하는 노동자들을 볼 수 있다. 이것은, 노동자들이 경제 이론이 제시하는 것처럼, 그들의 증가된 생산성에 대해, 즉, 그들의 기여분에 대해 항상 보상받는 것은 아니라는 것을 의미한다. 만약 고용주들이 법적으로 제약을 받지 않는다면 노동자들을 착취할 수 있을 것이다. 따라서 최저임금법은 어쩌면 많은 노동자들이 빈곤선 위(→ 아래)의 월급으로 노동하는 것을 못하게 막는 유일한 방법일 수 있다. 이러한 관점은 최저임금법이 효율적인 결과를 창출해내는 시장의 힘을 강화시키면서 현존하는 시장의 실패를 수정하는 원천이라는 것을 의미한다.

문제 해설

최저임금법을 통해 고용주들이 노동자들을 착취하는 것을 법적으로 막을 수 있다는 내용의 글이므로 ④의 above를 below로 바꿔야 한다.

구문 분석

[7행] This point of view means that minimum wage laws are a source of correcting for existing market failure, [**enhancing** the power of markets **to create** efficient results].

▶ [enhancing ~]는 분사구문으로서 'while they (= minimum wage laws) are enhancing~'으로 이해할 수 있다. to create는 to부정사의 형용사적 용법으로 the power of markets를 수식한다.

02 정답 ②

소재 가족 간의 갈등에 대처하는 방법

전문 해석

가족 간의 갈등에 대처하는 데 가장 좋은 처방 중 하나를 아는가? 'I'm sorry.' 라는 두 단어이다. 몇몇 사람들이 그 말을 하는 것을 얼마나 어려워하는지는 놀랍다. 그들은 그것이 약함이나 패배를 의미한다고 생각한다. 전혀 그렇지 않다. 사실, 정확하게 반대이다. 갈등을 덜어 주는 또 다른 좋은 방법은 말다툼이다. 바다는 폭풍 후에 훨씬 더 잔잔해진다. 말다툼은 또 다른 이점을 갖고 있다. 화가 날 때, 입 밖에 내지 않은 진실이 일반적으로 나오게 된다. 그것들은 특히 그 순간에 약간 감정을 상하게 할 수도 있다. 그러나 끝에 가서는 서로를 조금 더 잘 알게 된다. 마지막으로, 아이들 간의 갈등과 싸움의 대부분은 자연스러운 것이다. 그것들이 지속적인 것처럼 보일 때조차, 현명한 부모는 지나치게 걱정하지 않는다.

문제 해설

(A) 일부 사람들은 미안하다고 하는 말이 약함이나 패배를 의미한다고 생각하지만 필자는 그것이 가족 간의 갈등에 대처하는 데 가장 좋은 처방 중 하나라고 보고 있으므로, 일부 사람들이 생각하는 것과는 '반대'라는 문맥이 되어야 한다. 따라서 opposite이 적절하다. same은 '같은'이라는 뜻이다.

(B) 말다툼이 갈등을 덜어 주는 좋은 방법이라고 했으므로 말다툼은 '이점'을 갖는다는 문맥이 되어야 한다. 따라서 advantage가 적절하다. disadvantage는 '불리한 점'이라는 뜻이다.

(C) 현명한 부모들은 아이들 간의 갈등과 싸움에 대해 지나치게 걱정하지 않는다고 했으므로 아이들 간의 갈등과 싸움은 '자연스러운' 것이라는 맥락이 되어야 한다, 따라서 natural이 적절하다. risky는 '위험한'이라는 뜻이다.

구문 분석

[8행] Lastly, **most of** the tensions and quarrels (S) between children **are** (V) natural.

▶ 「most of+명사」의 수는 명사가 단수이면 단수동사가, 명사가 복수이면 복수동사가 온다. most of 뒤에 복수명사인 the tensions and quarrels가 와서 복수동사인 are가 사용되었다.

03 정답 ④

소재 협상에서 변호사를 입회시키는 것에 대한 캐나다인과 이집트인의 관점 차이

전문 해석

캐나다인 손님을 접대한 후에, 한 이집트인 중역이 그에게 새로운 벤처 사업에서의 합작 제휴를 제의했다. 그 제의에 기뻐서, 캐나다인은 세부 사항을 마무리하기 위해 다음 날 아침에 각자의 변호사와 함께 다시 만날 것을 제안했다. 이집트인은 결코 나타나지 않았다. 놀라고 실망한 캐나다인은 무엇이 잘못된 것인지 이해하려고 했다. 이집트인은 시간 엄수 관념이 없었는가? 그 이집트인이 수정 제안을 기대하고 있었는가? 카이로에서는 변호사를 구할 수 없었는가? 이들 설명 중 어떤 것도 올바른 것으로 판명되지 않았다. 오히려, 문제는 캐나다인과 이집트인이 변호사를 불러들이는 것에 두는 서로 다른 의미에 의해 야기되었다. 그 캐나다인은 변호사의 부재(→ 입회)를 협상의 성공적인 마무리를 용이하게 하는 것으로 여겼고, 그 이집트인은 그것을 캐나다인이 그의 구두 약속을 불신하는 것을 암시하는 것이라고 해석했다. 캐나다인은 흔히 합의를 끝내기 위해 변호사의 도움을 받는, 사사로움에 치우치지 않는 형식상의 절차를 이용한다. 이와 대조적으로 이집트인은 같은 목적을 완수하기 위해 거래 상대자 간의 개인적인 관계에 더 자주 의존한다.

문제 해설

변호사와 함께 다시 만날 것을 제안한 캐나다인은 변호사가 입회한 상태에서 협상을 마무리하는 것이 협상을 성공적으로 끝내는 데 도움이 된다고 생각했을 것이므로, ④의 absence를 presence로 바꿔야 한다.

오답 풀이

이 글은 캐나다인과 이집트인들이 협상을 벌일 때 변호사의 입회에 대한 관점이 다르다는 것을 설명한다. 따라서 이 두 국민들 간의 차이를 마무리 짓는다고 섣불리 추론하면서 ⑤번의 agreements가 differences와 같은 단어로 바뀌어야 한다고 결론내리지 않도록 주의한다.

구문 분석

[2행] The Canadian, [**delighted** with the offer], **suggested** that they **meet** again the next morning with their respective lawyers to finalize the details.

▶ [delighted ~]는 분사구문으로 'as he(=the Canadian) was delighted with the offer'로 이해할 수 있다. 주절에 '주장, 제안, 요구, 명령, 충고' 등의 동사가 오고 문맥상 '당위'의 의미가 성립될 때 that이 이끄는 목적절의 동사는 「(should)+동사원형」의 형태가 된다. 이때 should는 보통 생략된다.

Plus Q

놀라고 실망한 캐나다인이 이해하려고 했던 것은 시제상 과거보다 그 이전에 일어난 일이므로 대과거 형태인 had gone이 어법상 옳다.

04 정답 ②

소재 시각을 통해 습득해가는 아기의 인지 능력

전문 해석

그것은 거의 본능적이다. 여러분은 사랑스런 아기를 보면 반응을 유도하기 위해 미소를 짓거나 얼굴 표정을 짓기 시작한다. 그러나 여러분이 멍하니 바라보는 눈길을 받는다고 할지라도, 아기가 아무것도 안 하고 있다고 생각하지는 마라. 사실, 아기는 여러분 입과 얼굴의 형태와 리듬의 모든 변화를 처리하고 있다. 아기들은 태어나면서부터 어떤 언어와 얼굴 표정도 받아들인다. 시간이 흘러가면서 아기들은 자신들이 노출되어 있는 언어의 소리, 언어를 쓸 때의 근육 움직임과 얼굴의 리듬에 집중하는 법을 배운다. 그것은 모두 아기가 배워가는 과정의 일부이다. 심지어 언어조차도 시각적 자극에 달려있는 것 같다. 따라서 당신이 만나는 다음 아기에게 다가가 미소를 지어라. 단지 표현으로 두드러지게 하라.

문제 해설

(A) 아기가 아무것도 안 하고 있다고 생각하게 만들어야 하므로 '멍한'의 의미인 blank가 적절하다. meaningful은 '의미 있는' 이라는 의미이다.
(B) 아기들은 태어나면서부터 언어와 얼굴 표정을 받아들일 준비가 되어 있고 시간이 흘러가면서 좀 더 세심한 것들을 받아들인다는 문맥이므로 receptive가 적절하다. blind는 '눈 먼, 모르는' 이라는 의미이다.
(C) 다음에 아기를 만나게 되면 미소를 짓고, 표현적이 되라는 내용이 뒤이어 이어지므로, visual이 적절하다. audible은 '들을 수 있는' 의 의미이다.

구문 분석

[6행] With time, they learn to focus on the sounds, muscle movements and facial rhythms of the language **to which** they are exposed.

▶ which는 전치사의 목적어인 the language를 선행사로 받는 관계대명사이며 which 앞의 to는 be exposed to에 걸리는 to로 자신의 목적어인 it(= the language)을 찾아 그 앞에 위치한 것이다. 전치사의 목적어가 선행사로 사용되는 관계대명사절에서 전치사는 관계대명사 앞에 위치할 수도 있고, 문장 끝에 남아 있을 수도 있다.

05 정답 ⑤

소재 아이들의 성장 과정에서 나타나는 자율성과 순응

전문 해석

일 년여 동안 열심히 의존을 한 후에 유아들은 자신들의 자율성을 주장할 필요성을 느끼기 시작한다. 어떠한 수준에서 자신들의 행동에 대해 책임을 지기 시작하지 않는다면 그들이 온전하게 기능을 하는 사람들로 성장하지 못할 것이라는 것을 느낀다. 결과적으로 그들은 자신의 방식대로 일을 하겠다고 우기고, 그들이 그렇게 하는 것을 방해받는다면 그들은 짜증을 낼 준비가 되어 있는데, 그때가 전형적인 '끔찍한 두 살'의 나이이다. 집 밖에 있는 세상의 광대함을 인식하게 되면서 대부분의 아이들은 결국 그들 자신의 하찮음에 의해 겁을 먹게 된다. 그때에, 그들은 자신들의 또래와 어울리는 것과 가족보다 더 큰 공동체에 의해 받아들여지고 인정을 받는 일에 대해 걱정한다. 이것이 반항(→ 순응)의 단계이며, 아주 많은 사람들에게 있어, 그때가 개인적인 발전으로 가는 길의 시작이다.

문제 해설

세상의 광대함에 비해 자신들의 하찮음으로 겁을 먹고 또래와 어울리는 것과 가족보다 더 큰 공동체에 의해 받아들여지고 인정을 받는 것에 대해 걱정하게 되므로 이때는 자신이 속한 공동체에 순응을 하는 시기라고 볼 수 있다. 따라서 ⑤의 disobedience는 conformity(순응)와 같은 단어로 바꿔야 한다.

오답 풀이

아이들이 자율성을 주장하게 되는(assert) 것은 일을 자신의 마음대로 하는 것을 우기는(insist) 것과 통하며, 세상의 광대함에 비해 자신들의 하찮음(insignificance)으로 겁을 먹는 것과 또래들과 어울리고 가족보다 더 큰 공동체에 의해 받아들여지고 인정을 받는 것을 걱정하는(concerned) 것이 일맥상통한다.

구문 분석

[8행] At that point, they become concerned [with fitting in with their peers] and [with being accepted and recognized by a community larger than the family].

▶ [ ]로 표시된 부분이 and에 의해 병렬을 이루며 concerned에 이어지고 있다.

06 정답 ①

소재 상상력에 의존할 때 입을 수 있는 폐해

전문 해석

풍부한 상상력이 새로운 지식을 추구하는 데 있어 영감의 원천이긴 하지만 그것은 또한 강한 비판에 의해 균형이 잡히지 않는다면 위험할 수 있다. 물론 이것은 그것(풍부한 상상력)이 억눌리거나 짓밟아져야 한다고 말하는 것과는 아주 다르다. 이러한 상상력은 우리가 지니는 희미한 지식의 빛에 의해 재미있는 것처럼 보이는 어떤 것을 힐끗 볼 수도 있는 미지의 어두움 속으로 단지 돌아다니는 것을 가능케 한다. 그러나 그것을 밖으로 가지고 와서 그것을 더 면밀히 검토할 때, 그것의 반짝거림이 우리의 관심을 끌었던 쓰레기에 지나지 않은 것으로 드러날 수 있을 것이다. 분명하게 보이지 않는 것들은 종종 기괴한 형태를 띤다. 상상력은 좌절의 원천일 수도 있다. 이러한 사실을 잊는 것은 절망을 자초하는 것이다. 사실 상상력에서 나온 많은 가설들은 그들의 기원이 무엇이든지 간에 틀린 것으로 드러난다.

문제 해설

(A) 상상력이 영감을 얻는 데 있어 중요하긴 하지만 균형이 잡히지 않으면 위험할 수 있고, 이것이 상상력을 억압해야 한다고 말하는 것은 아니라고 언급하고 있으므로 문맥상 criticism이 적절하다. support는 '지지'라는 의미이다.
(B) 흥미로워 보이는 것을 꺼내서 조사한다는 내용이 뒤에 나오므로 그것을 힐끗 본다는 문맥이 자연스럽다. 따라서 glimpse가 적절하다. overlook은 '간과하다'의 의미이다.
(C) 상상력이 좌절의 원천이며, 이것을 잊는 것은 절망을 자초하는 것이라는 앞의 내용을 통해 상상력에서 나온 가설들이 틀린 것으로 드러난다는 문맥이 되어야 자연스럽다. 따라서 wrong이 적절하다. right은 '옳은'이라는 의미이다.

구문 분석

[4행] This imagination merely enables us to wander into the darkness of the unknown [**where**, by the dim light of the knowledge {**that** we carry}, we may glimpse something that seems interesting].

▶ [where ~]는 관계부사절로서 the darkness of the unknown을 수식한다. {that ~}는 관계대명사절로서 the dim light of the knowledge를 수식한다.

Plus Q

지시대명사가 가리키는 것은 대개 같은 문장의 앞부분이나 앞 문장 속에 있다. 이 경우는 앞 문장의 내용을 가리킨다.

유형 09 어법성 판단

p. 58

대표 예제 정답 ②

소재 활성 산소의 이중적 역할

전문 해석

중요한 것은 바로 산소이다. 역설적이게도, 우리에게 생명을 주는 것이 결국 그것(생명)을 죽인다. 궁극적인 생명력은 우리가 들이쉬는 거의 모든 산소를 태우는, 미토콘드리아라고 불리는 아주 작은 에너지 세포 공장에 있다. 그러나 호흡에는 대가가 있다. 우리를 살아있게 하고 활동적이게 유지하는 산소 연소는 활성 산소라고 불리는 부산물을 내보낸다. 그것들(활성 산소)은 지킬박사와 하이드 씨의 특징을 가지고 있다(서로 다른 이중적인 특징을 가지고 있다). 한편으로, 그것들은 우리의 생존 보장을 돕는다. 예를 들어, 감염원과 싸워 물리치기 위해 신체가 동원될 때, 그것(신체)은 침입자들을 매우 효율적으로 파괴하기 위해 한바탕 활성 산소를 생산한다. 다른 한편으로, 활성 산소는 통제할 수 없을 정도로 신체를 돌아다니면서 세포를 공격하고, 세포의 단백질을 부식시키고, 세포막을 뚫고 세포의 유전 암호를 변질시켜 마침내 그 세포는 제대로 기능을 하지 못하게 되고 때로는 포기하여 죽어버린다. 보호자인 동시에 보복자로 생명체의 일부가 되어 있는 이런 사나운 활성 산소는 노화의 강력한 동인이다.

문제 해설

② 이 문장에는 문장의 필수 성분인 동사가 현재 없다. 따라서 sending을 문장의 주어인 The combustion of oxygen에 이어질 수 있는 동사 형태인 sends로 고쳐야 한다.

오답 풀이

① that은 tiny cellular factories of energy를 선행사로 취하는 주격 관계대명사이다.
③ to fight는 목적을 나타내는 to부정사로 부사적 용법으로 쓰였다.
④ 부사인 uncontrollably를 사용하여 동사 move를 수식

하고 있다.
⑤ 의미상 주어인 These fierce radicals가 분사가 나타내는 동작의 대상이므로 과거분사 built를 사용하고 있다.

구문 분석

[5행] The combustion of oxygen [**that** keeps us alive and active] sends out by-products {(which / that are) called oxygen free radicals}.

▶ 문장의 주어인 The combustion of oxygen을 주격 관계대명사 that을 이용하여 수식하고 있다. 「keep+목적어+목적보어(형용사)」는 '~을 …하게 유지하다'라는 의미이며 { }는 선행사인 by-products를 수식하는 관계사절로 주격 관계대명사 which 혹은 that과 동사 are가 생략되어 있다.

어휘

combustion 연소 **mobilize** 동원되다
infectious agent 감염원(전염병의 병원체)
burst 한바탕 터뜨림 **uncontrollably** 통제할 수 없게
rust 녹슬다; 부식시키다 **pierce** 뚫다
corrupt 오염[변질]시키다 **genetic code** 유전 암호
dysfunctional 제대로 기능을 하지 않는
avenger 보복자 **agent** 동인(動因), 요인

Exercise

01 ③ 02 ⑤ 03 ③ 04 ④ 05 ⑤ 06 ③

Plus Q
03 has been shown by the increase in websites
06 with

01 정답 ③

소재 언어의 기능과 역할

전문 해석

언어는 인간을 다른 동물과 구분하는 주요한 특징 중 하나이다. 돌고래, 고래, 그리고 새를 포함한 많은 동물들이 소리, 냄새, 그리고 다른 화학물질의 패턴이 있는 체계, 또는 움직임을 통해 실제로 서로 의사소통을 한다. 게다가, 인간이 아닌 어떤 영장류는 인간과 의사소통을 하기 위해 손짓을 사용하도록 가르침을 받아왔다. 하지만 인간 언어의 복잡성, 미묘한 차이가 있는 감정과 생각을 전달하는 그것의 능력, 그리고 사회적 동물로서 우리의 존재에 있어서의 그것의 중요성은 그것을 다른 동물들이 사용하는 의사소통 체계와 구분짓는다. 여러 가지 면에서 언어는 문화의 본질이다. 그것은 다른 문화 집단들이 구별되게 하는 단 하나의 가장 보편적인 변인을 제공한다. 언어는 혁신의 문화적 확산을 촉진할 뿐 아니라, 그것은 또한 우리가 환경에 대하여 생각하고, 인지하고, 이름을 붙이는 방식을 형성하도록 돕는다.

문제 해설

③ 문장을 구성하기 위해 필요한 동사가 빠져 있으므로 setting을 복수 주어에 맞게 set으로 고쳐야 한다.

오답 풀이

① 동사 communicate를 강조하기 위해 조동사 do가 쓰였다.
② 주어 some nonhuman primates(어떤 영장류)가 '가르침을 받아온' 것이므로 현재완료의 수동태를 써야 한다.
④ the single most common variable를 선행사로 하는 「전치사+관계대명사」 구문이다.
⑤ think, perceive, name의 동사가 병렬구조를 이루고 있다.

구문 분석

[11행] Language **not only** facilitates the cultural diffusion of innovations, (**but**) it **also** helps to shape the way ~.

▶ 상관접속사 「not only A but also B」가 쓰였으며 but은 생략되어 있다. 「help+(to) 동사원형」 구문은 '~하는 것을 돕다' 라는 의미로 to를 생략할 수 있다.

02 정답 ⑤

소재 과제 수행 메커니즘

전문 해석

우리가 정해진 절차를 만들어 두면, 매일 모든 일에 우선순위를 정하는 데 소중한 에너지를 쏟을 필요가 없다. 우리는 정해진 절차를 만들어 내기 위해 단지 적은 양의 초기 에너지만 쓰면 되고, 그러고 나서 해야 할 남은 일이라고는 그것을 따르는 것이다. 그 메커니즘을 설명하는 방대한 양의 과학적 연구가 있는데, 그 메커니즘에 의해서 정해진 절차가 어려운 일들이 쉬워지는 것을 가능하게 한다. 간단히 설명하자면 우리가 반복적으로 어떤 과제를 수행할 때 신경세포인 뉴런이 '시냅스' 라고 부르는 전달 관문을 통해 새로운 연결을 만들어 낸다. 반복을 통해, 그 연결이 강력해지고 뇌가 그 연결을 활성화시키는 것이 좀 더 쉬워진다. 예를 들어, 당신이 새로운 단어 하나를 배울 때 그 단어가 숙달되기 위해서는 다양한 간격으로 여러 번 반

복하는 것이 필요하다. 나중에 그 단어를 기억해내기 위해서 당신은 그 단어에 대해 의식적으로 생각하지 않고도 결국 그 단어를 알게 될 때까지 똑같은 시냅스를 활성화시킬 필요가 있을 것이다.

문제 해설

(A) 뒤의 문장이 완전한 문장이 오므로 「전치사+관계대명사」의 형태가 와야 한다. 따라서 which가 아닌 by which가 적절하다.

(B) 주어 the neurons에 이어질 수 있는 동사 make를 쓰는 것이 적절하다.

(C) the word를 지칭하는 대명사 it이 적절하다.

구문 분석

[8행] ~ and **it** becomes easier **for** the brain [**to** activate them].

▶ it은 가주어이고 to 이하가 진주어이며 the brain이 의미상의 주어로 쓰였다.

03 정답 ③

소재 청소년들에게서의 인터넷과 과학기술의 역할 증대

전문 해석

인터넷과 통신 기술은 선진 사회에 있는 젊은이들의 사회생활에서 점점 더 큰 역할을 수행한다. 청소년들은 대부분 소통하기 위해 인터넷을 사용하면서 빠르게 과학기술에 몰두해 왔다. 젊은이들은 휴대전화를 생활에 꼭 필요한 필수품으로 다루고 친구들과 소통하기 위해 문자 메시지를 사용하기를 보통 선호한다. 젊은이들은 소셜 네트워킹 웹사이트에도 점점 더 많이 접속한다. 과학기술과 인터넷이 젊은이들에게 친숙한 수단이기에, 그들이 이 정보원에서 도움을 구할 것이라는 것은 논리적이다. 이것은 젊은이들을 위한 치료법 정보를 제공하는 웹사이트의 증가에서 증명되었다. 많은 수의 '젊은이 친화적인' 정신 건강 웹사이트들이 개발되어 왔다. 제공되는 정보는 '자주 묻는 질문', 자료표, 추천 링크의 형태를 자주 띤다. 그러므로 젊은이들에게 온라인 상담을 제공해주는 것은 논리적으로 보일 것이다.

문제 해설

③ 뒤에 주요 구성 요소를 모두 갖춘 절이 왔으므로 what을 쓸 수 없으며, 형식상의 주어 it이 대신하는 내용상의 주어를 이끌 수 있는 접속사 that이 필요하다. 따라서 what을 that으로 고쳐야 한다.

오답 풀이

① with를 이용한 분사구문으로 대부분의 청소년들(most)이 '사용하는' 것이므로 능동의 의미로 현재분사 using이 쓰였다.

② increasingly는 부사로서 동사 access를 수식한다.

④ 「a number of+복수 명사」는 복수 취급하므로 동사 have가 쓰였다.

⑤ 정보가 '제공되는' 것이므로 과거분사인 presented의 형태가 쓰였다.

구문 분석

[2행] Adolescents **have been quick to** immerse themselves in technology ~.

▶ 과거부터 현재까지 이어지는 상황이므로 현재완료 시제가 쓰였으며, 「be quick to 동사원형」 구문은 '재빠르게 ~하다'라는 뜻이다.

[13행] **It** would seem, therefore, logical [**to** provide online counselling for young people].

▶ It은 가주어이며 to 이하의 [ ]부분이 진주어이다.

Plus Q

'증명이 되어 온' 것이므로 현재완료의 수동태 구문 has been shown을 쓴다. 이어서 수단을 나타내는 전치사 by 뒤에 '~의 수 증가'를 뜻하는 「increase in+명사」 구문을 이용하여 the increase in websites를 배열한다.

04 정답 ④

소재 생각의 힘과 신경언어프로그래밍(NLP)

전문 해석

지구상의 다른 모든 생물을 뛰어 넘는 인간의 능력은 사고력이다. 모든 성공적인 사람들은 그들의 삶을 향상시키고 운명을 통제하기 위해 그것을 사용한다. 당신만이 당신의 생각 속에 있는 힘을 촉발시키는 첫발을 내딛을 수 있다. 그 힘은 엄청나며 때로는 무섭기까지 하다. 그러나 인간에게는 많은 사람들이 믿을 수 없는 혹은 믿지 않을 생각의 힘이 있다. Anthony Robbins는 최근 신경언어프로그래밍(NLP)의 이론, 생각의 힘, 생각의 통제 및 사용법을 설명하는 '무한한 힘'이라는 제목의 책을 저술했다. 신경언어프로그래밍은 본래 John Grinder에 의해 중추신경계를 사용하는 의사소통체계로서 개발되었다. 이 체계를 통해 Robbins는 당신이 아마도 불가능하다고 느꼈을 목표를 이루는 방법에 관한 완벽한 틀을 제시해냈다.

문제 해설

④ a communication system을 수식하는 분사로, 의사소통체계가 중추신경계를 '사용하는' 것이므로 used를 현재분사 using으로 고쳐야 한다.

오답 풀이

① 그 힘이 '무섭게 만드는' 것이므로 능동인 frightening이 적절하다.

② 선행사인 power of the mind를 수식하는 목적격 관계대명사 that이 쓰였다.

③ a book을 수식하는 분사로, 책의 제목이 '붙여진' 것이므로 과거분사 entitled가 적절하다.

⑤ goals를 선행사로 하는 관계사절의 동사이므로 복수동사 were가 쓰였다.

구문 분석

[11행] ~ how to achieve goals [**that** {you probably felt} were impossible].

▶ 주격 관계대명사 that과 동사 were 사이에 you probably felt가 삽입되었다. 관계대명사가 이끄는 문장에서의 삽입절은 관계대명사 바로 뒤에 위치한다.

05 정답 ⑤

소재 유기농 식품

전문 해석

우리는 제철이 아닌 외국의 과일과 채소를 먹는 데 너무 익숙해서 제철 유기농 과일과 채소를 구할 수 있다는 사실을 처음에는 받아들이기가 어렵다. 물론 많은 유기농 식품이 외국에서 생산되어 우리가 다니는 슈퍼마켓으로 운반됨으로써 쉽게 구입할 수 있지만, 식품이 먼 거리를 이동하게 되면 비타민과 미네랄 성분이 손실된다. 따라서 지역에서 생산된 식품을 구입하는 것이 훨씬 더 좋다. 많은 슈퍼마켓들은 유기농이 큰 사업을 의미한다는 사실을 인식하고 있다. 하지만 특히 가공된 경우에, 단지 통에 유기농 식품이라고 쓰여 있다고 해서 당신에게 더 좋다는 것을 의미하지는 않는다는 것을 기억하라. 예를 들어, 일단 유기농 식품이 케이크나 비스킷이 되면, (유기농이 아닌) 기존 형태의 이러한 식품에 수반되는 걱정을 똑같이 하게 될 것이다. 그것은 바로 많은 당분과 지방이다.

문제 해설

(A) 문맥상 '~에 익숙하다'라는 의미가 되어야 하므로 「be used to+동명사」가 적절하다.

(B) 5형식 동사 make의 목적격 보어 자리이므로 형용사인 available이 적절하다.

(C) 주어 it(유기농 식품)이 '가공되는' 것이므로 현재완료 수동태인 has been processed가 적절하다.

구문 분석

[1행] We're **so** used to having exotic fruits and vegetables out of season **that** at first it's difficult to accept **that** we can get organic fruits and vegetables [**that** are in season].

▶ 「so ~ that ...」은 '매우 ~해서 …하다'는 뜻이다. accept의 목적어로 쓰인 명사절을 이끄는 접속사 that이 쓰였으며 [ ]는 주격 관계대명사 that이 이끄는 관계절로 선행사인 organic fruits and vegetables를 수식한다.

[6행] It's therefore **much** better to buy locally produced products.

▶ 비교급 better를 강조하는 부사로 much가 쓰였으며, far, even, still, a lot 등으로 바꿔 쓸 수 있다.

06 정답 ③

소재 문화에 따른 식습관의 이해

전문 해석

수많은 인종, 종교, 지역의 집단이 생겨나면서 미국의 인구는 점점 다인종으로 이루어져 가고 있다. 이 집단의 각각에는 소위 전형적인 미국인의 대다수 식습관과 약간 혹은 상당히 다른 전통적 식습관들이 있다. 효과적인 영양 상담, 교육, 외식 산업을 위해서 이러한 차이점들을 문화적 맥락 안에서 인정하고 이해할 필요가 있다. 자민족 중심적인 추정을 피하기 위해 필요한 폭넓은 분석과 (앞에서) 언급한 각 집단을 연구하는 데 도움이 되는 영양 정보를 영양사, 영양학자, 외식산업 전문가들에게 제공하는 것이 우리의 목표이다. 우리는 다른 건강 전문가들에게도 도움이 되는 방식으로 개념적 측면과 기술적 측면을 결합하려고 시도해 왔다.

문제 해설

③ 「'주장, 요구, 제안, 명령' 동사+that+주어+(should)+동사원형」 구문이다. 요구의 의미를 갖는 동사인 require가 쓰였으므로 are를 동사원형인 be로 고쳐야 한다.

오답 풀이

① moving 이하는 부대상황을 나타내는 분사구문으로, 'as it(=the population) moves~'로 바꿔 쓸 수 있다.

② 「Each of+복수명사」는 단수 취급을 하므로 단수동사의 형태인 has가 적절하다.

④ the broad overview에 '필요한'의 의미로 과거분사 needed가 쓰였다.

⑤ 「attempt to+동사원형」은 '~하려고 시도하다'는 의미이다.

구문 분석

[6행] **It** is our goal [**to provide** dietitians, nutritionists, and food service professionals with the broad overview {(which / that is) needed to avoid ethnocentric assumptions} and the nutrition specifics {(which / that are) helpful in working~}].

▶ It은 가주어이며 to provide 이하의 [ ]가 진주어이다. { }는 주격 관계대명사 which나 that과 동사가 생략된 관계대명사절로 각각 선행사 the broad overview, the nutrition specifics를 수식한다.

Plus Q

문맥상 「provide A with B」, 「combine A with B」 구문이 쓰여야 적절하므로 공통으로 들어갈 전치사는 with이다.

유형 10 지칭 추론

p. 64

대표 예제

정답 ④

소재 힙합 춤 대결

전문 해석

댄서들은 두 계단 위에 있는 무대에 서 있어서 춤을 추러 온 사람들과 보러 온 사람들 간에 자연스러운 간격이 있었다. 진행자가 모자에서 무작위로 Linx라는 잘 알려진 댄서의 이름을 뽑았다. 사람들은 환호했다. 구성 방식에 따라, Linx는 무대에서 대결할 또 다른 댄서를 '호명'해야 했다. 하지만 찬찬히 고르는 대신에 그는 자신을 인간 회전판으로 만들어 자신의 상대를 무작위로 선택하기로 했다. 그는 백스핀(등을 바닥에 두고 빙글빙글 도는 춤 동작)으로 자신을 돌아가게 했고, 자신의 눈을 가렸고, 자신의 머리 위로 팔을 뻗었다. 그의 몸이 마침내 도는 것을 멈췄을 때, 그의 팔은 무대 위의 댄서들을 벗어나, 관중 속에 서있는 Dan Tres를 똑바로 가리켰다. 사람들은 "오!"라는 (놀라움의) 탄성을 터뜨렸는데, 왜냐하면 그가 여러 해 동안 힙합을 추지 않은 더 나이 든 가정이 있는 남자인 반면, 훨씬 더 어린 Linx는 동작이 날렵한 비보이이기 때문이었다. Linx는 당황한 것처럼 보였지만, 그럼에도 불구하고 그는 대결하기 위해 그 존경받는 연장자를 호명했다.

문제 해설

①, ②, ③, ⑤는 모두 Linx를 가리키지만, ④는 Dan Tres를 가리킨다.

구문 분석

[1행] The dancers stood on a two-step elevated stage, **so that** there was a natural gap between **those** [**who** came to dance] and **those** [**who** came to watch].

▶ 「so that+주어+동사 ~」는 '그래서 ~가 …하다'라고 해석할 수 있다. 「those who ~」는 '~하는 사람들'이라는 의미이다.

[15행] The crowd **erupted** in "Ohhhhs!" because he was an older family man [who **had not danced** hip-hop in many years], ~.

▶ [ ]로 표시된 관계대명사절에서 과거완료가 사용된 것은 주절보다 이 절이 기술하는 상황(힙합 춤을 추지 않았던 것)이 앞서 일어났기 때문이다.

어휘

host 진행자 **randomly** 무작위로
deliberately 찬찬히, 신중하게 **opponent** 상대, 적수
extend 뻗다, 늘리다, 연장하다 **spectator** 관중
erupt (강한 감정을, 특히 고함과 함께) 터뜨리다, 분출하다

Exercise

01 ③ 02 ③ 03 ③ 04 ③ 05 ④ 06 ④

Plus Q

03 got better
06 매우 소중한 사람(것)

01 정답 ③

소재 아버지의 용서

전문 해석

간디는 열다섯 살 때, 형의 팔찌에서 금 한 조각을 훔쳤다. 간디는 죄책감으로 너무 괴로워 어느 날 그는 아버지께 자신이 한 일을 말씀드리기로 했다. 그는 아버지께 자신을 벌해 달라고 요청하는 편지를 썼다. 그런 다음 간디는 병석에 누워 계신 아버지께 그 편지를 건네 드렸다. 그의 아버지는 조용히 일어나 앉아 편지를 읽고는 그 편지를 자신의 눈물로 흠뻑 적셨다. 잠시 후 그의 아버지는 그 편지를 찢었다. 편지를 찢는 아버지의 행동을 통해서, 간디는 자신이 용서받았음을 알았다. 그날 이후 그는 항상 아버지의 눈물과 사랑을 마음속에 간직했으며 계속 나아가 위대한

지도자가 되었다.

문제 해설

①, ②, ④, ⑤는 모두 간디를 가리키지만 ③은 간디의 아버지를 가리킨다.

구문 분석

[2행] Gandhi was **so troubled** by his guilt **that** one day he decided to tell his father what he had done.

▶ 「so+형용사/부사+that ~」을 활용한 구문으로 '너무나 ~ 해서 …하다'의 의미를 나타낸다.

02 정답 ③

소재 한 소년의 비행에 대한 꿈

전문 해석

Jake 자신의 비행하는 꿈은 어떤 마을 축제에서 시작됐다. 그는 4살이었다. 그의 삼촌은 키 크고 과묵한 비행기 조종사로, 자선 가판대에서 빨간 파티 풍선을 그에게 사 주고 그것을 Jake의 셔츠 맨 위 단추에 묶었다. 풍선은 그것 스스로의 의지를 가진 것처럼 보였다. Jake는 그 당시 이것을 이해하지 못했지만, 그것은 공기보다 네 배 가벼운 헬륨으로 채워져 있었다. 신기하게 그것은 그의 단추를 잡아당겼다. "아마 너는 날게 될 거야." Jake의 삼촌이 말했다. 그는 그들이 축제 전체를 살펴볼 수 있도록 그(삼촌)의 조카를 풀이 무성한 강둑으로 데리고 갔다. Jake 아래에 작은 텐트들과 가판대들이 펼쳐져 있었다. 그의 머리 위로 반짝이고 아름다운 큰 빨간 풍선이 까닥까닥 움직였다. 그것은 계속 하늘 쪽으로 그를 잡아당겼고, 그는 자기 발이 불안정하다고 느끼기 시작했다. 그때 그의 삼촌은 그의 손을 놓았고, Jake의 꿈이 시작되었다.

문제 해설

①, ②, ④, ⑤는 모두 Jake를 가리키지만, ③은 Jake의 삼촌을 가리킨다.

구문 분석

[6행] He led his nephew up a grassy bank **so they could** look over the whole festival.

▶ 「so that+주어+조동사」나 「so+주어+조동사」 또는 「that+주어+조동사」는 모두 '~할 수 있도록'이라는 의미의 목적을 나타낸다.

03 정답 ③

소재 오랜 친구에게 준 도움

전문 해석

Carlos Sanchez의 오랜 친구인 Frank Sandoval은 재정적으로 힘든 시기를 겪으면서 막 자기 집을 잃을 참이었다. Frank의 아내는 병이 들었고 그들의 어린 두 아이들은 일시적으로 Frank의 어머니와 지내고 있었다. Carlos는 몇 달 동안 Frank와 직접 접촉이 없었는데 어느 날 그에게 전화를 걸어 그가 어떻게 지내고 있는가를 알아보기로 했다. Frank가 자신의 상황에 관해 Carlos에게 털어놓자, Carlos는 곧장 Frank의 집으로 갔다. 집에 들어갔을 때 그는 매우 여위고 허약한 자기 친구를 보고는 충격을 받았다. 그는 Frank와 함께 앉아서 그가 얼마나 많은 돈이 필요한지를 물었다. Frank는 절망적인 상황이며, 갚기에는 너무 많은 금액이라고 그에게 말했다. Carlos는 자신의 수표책을 꺼내서 그에게 5만 달러짜리 수표를 써주었다. 그는 Frank에게 상황이 좋아질 것이라고 말했고, 상황은 좋아졌다. 3년 뒤, Frank는 이자를 붙여 Carlos에게 돈을 갚았다.

문제 해설

①, ②, ④, ⑤는 모두 Frank를 가리키지만, ③은 Carlos를 가리킨다.

구문 분석

[8행] Frank told him [it was hopeless], [**that** it was too much to pay back].

▶ 콤마(,)가 접속사 and의 역할을 하고 있다. 두 개의 [ ]는 told의 목적어이다. 두 개의 that절이 목적어로 사용되고 있는데, 목적절을 이끄는 that은 생략할 수 있으나, 이처럼 두 개의 목적어인 경우, 앞의 that은 생략하고 뒤의 that은 남겨두는 것이 일반적이다.

Plus Q

did는 대동사로 'get better'를 받고 있는데, 과거의 일이므로 동사의 시제를 과거로 써야 한다.

04 정답 ③

소재 무게를 속여 왔던 제빵사를 다루는 농부의 재치

전문 해석

제빵사에게 1파운드의 버터를 판 농부가 있었다. 어느 날 제빵사는 자신이 1파운드를 받고 있는지를 알아보기 위해서 버터의 무게를 재기로 했고, 그는 자신이 그러지 못하고 있다(1파운드를 받지 않고 있다)는 것을 알게 되었다. 이것은 그를 화나게 해서 그는 농부를 법정으로 데리고 갔다. 판사는 농부에게 그가 어떠한 도량 단위를 사용하고 있는지를 물었다. 그 농부는, "존경하는 재판장님, 저는 미개한 사람입니다. 저는 적절한 도량 단위가 없지만 저울은 하나 가지고 있습니다." 라고 대답했다. 그 판사는, "그렇다면 당신은 어떻게 버터의 무게를 잽니까?" 라고 물었다. 그 농부는, "존경하는 재판장님, 제빵사가 저에게서 버터를 사가기 시작하기 오래 전에 저는 그에게서 1파운드가 되는 덩어리의 빵을 구매해 왔습니다. 매일 그 제빵사가 빵을 가져올 때마다 저는 그것을 저울에 올려놓고 그에게 같은 무게의 버터를 줍니다. 어느 누구라도 비난받아야 한다면 그것은 제빵사입니다."

문제 해설

③은 농부를 가리키지만 나머지는 모두 제빵사를 가리킨다.

구문 분석

[1행] One day the baker decided to weigh the butter to see if he was getting a pound, and he found that **he was not**.

▶ not 뒤에 생략된 내용은 문맥상 getting a pound이다.

05 정답 ④

소재 터무니없는 기사를 쓰는 기자

전문 해석

Louis Stone은 1890년대에 창의력이 풍부한 신문 기자였다. 그는 Connecticut 주 Winstead 시에 소재한 Evening Citizen에서 일했다. 전형적인 따분한 뉴스 기사에서 탈피한 그는 대신에 터무니없는 허풍 기사를 썼다. 그러나 독자들은 그의 기사가 사실이 아님을 알고 있을 때조차도 그의 기사를 좋아했다. Evening Citizen의 독선적인 편집장은 그를 해고하지 않았다. 대신에, 그는 발행 부수의 갑작스런 증가에 의기양양했다. 그에게 계속 터무니없는 허풍 기사를 쓰게 해서 그는 Stone이 Winstead Liar로 유명해지도록 도왔다. 편집장의 전폭적인 지지로 그는 또한 "Yankee Doodle"을 휘파람으로 불 수 있었던 고양이, 잎이 없는 사과를 재배한 나무, 7월 4일(미국 독립기념일)에 빨간, 하얀, 파란 달걀을 낳은 암탉, 그리고 파리를 쫓기 위해 자신의 대머리에 거미줄을 그린 남자의 이야기를 썼다.

문제 해설

④는 편집장을 가리키지만, 나머지는 모두 Louis Stone을 가리킨다.

구문 분석

[8행] With the full support of the editor, he also wrote accounts **of** a cat [**that** could whistle "Yankee Doodle,"] a tree [**that** grew baked apples], a hen [**that** laid red, white, and blue eggs on the Fourth of July], and a man [**who** painted a spider web on his bald head to keep flies away].

▶ 전치사 of 뒤에 4개의 목적어가 각각 관계사절을 수식어로 취하며 병렬구조를 이루고 있다.

06 정답 ④

소재 사랑하는 아들을 사고로 잃었지만 여전히 아내를 챙기는 남편

전문 해석

한 사내아이가 11년간의 결혼 생활을 한 부부에게서 태어났다. 그들은 서로를 사랑하는 부부였으며 그 아이는 그들에게 매우 소중한 존재였다. 아이가 두 살 무렵이었던 어느 날 아침, 나가는 길에 남편은 약병의 뚜껑이 열려있는 것을 보았다. 그는 출근이 늦어서 아내에게 병의 마개를 닫고 찬장에 그것을 다시 두라고 부탁했다. 아내는 부엌일에 바쁜 나머지 남편이 그녀에게 하라고 부탁한 것을 완전히 잊고 있었다. 사내아이는 약병이 있는 곳으로 가서 그것을 전부 먹었다. 그것은 하필이면 어른들이 소량으로 복용하도록 되어 있었던 독성이 있는 약이었다. 그가 구토하기 시작하자 아내는 그를 병원으로 데려갔는데, 그곳에서 아이는 죽고 말았다. 아내는 망연자실했다. 넋이 나간 남편은 병원에 와서 죽은 아이를 보았다. 그러고 나서 그는 아내를 보고는 단 네 단어를 입 밖에 냈다. "여보 사랑해."

문제 해설

④는 아들을 가리키는 반면, 나머지는 모두 남편을 가리킨다.

구문 분석

[4행] He was late for work, so he **asked his wife to cap** the bottle and **put** it back in the cupboard.

▶ 「ask+사람+to부정사(~에게 …해달라고 부탁하다, 요청하다)」 구문을 활용한 문장이다. cap과 put이 to에 걸리는 병렬구조이며 it는 the bottle을 받는다.

Plus Q

the apple of one's eye는 '눈동자', '매우 소중한 사람(것)'의 의미이며, 여기서는 '매우 소중한 사람(것)'이라는 의미로 쓰였다.

유형 11 빈칸 추론

p. 70

대표 예제

정답 ②

소재 문화 교류

전문 해석

두 문화가 접촉할 때, 그 두 문화가 모든 문화 항목을 교환하는 것은 아니다. 만약 그렇다면, 오늘날 세계에는 전혀 문화적 차이가 없을 것이다. 대신에 단지 적은 수의 문화적 요소들만 늘 한 문화에서 다른 문화로 퍼진다. 어떤 문화 항목이 받아들여지는가는 그 항목의 용도 및 이미 존재하는 문화적 특성과의 양립 가능성에 대체로 달려있다. 예를 들어, '흰머리를 피하려고' 고안된 남성용 머리 염색약은 나이가 들어감에 따라 사람의 지위가 올라가는 아프리카의 시골 지역으로 퍼질 것 같지는 않다. 어떤 혁신적인 것이 한 사회의 필요와 일치할 때조차도, 여전히 그것이 받아들여질 것이라는 보장은 없다. 예를 들어, 미국의 관습적 단위(예컨대, 인치, 피트, 야드, 마일 등)를 사용하는 미국의 대부분의 사람들은, 그러한 변화를 이루는 것이 미국인들로 하여금 세계의 다른 나라들과 더 효율적으로 접촉할 수 있게 할 터임에도 불구하고, 미터법 채택에 저항해 왔다.

문제 해설

예시는 앞의 내용을 구체화시키는 역할을 하므로, 빈칸이 속한 문장이 뒤에 나오는 예시 문장에서 어떻게 다른 방식으로 표현되었는지 비교해보면 답을 찾기 쉽다. 문맥상 예시에서 빈칸의 내용에 해당하는 것이 making such a change(자신들의 관습적 단위를 버리고 미터법을 채택하는 것)이므로 빈칸에 가장 적절한 것은 ② '혁신적인 것'이다.

① 범주화 ③ 조사 ④ 관찰 ⑤ 설명서

구문 분석

[8행] ~, **it** is not likely {**that** men's hair dyes [**designed** to "get out the gray"] will spread into parts of rural Africa [**where** a person's status is elevated with advancing years]}.

▶ it은 가주어이고 { }로 표시된 that절이 진주어이다. 염색약은 사람에 의해 만들어진 것이기 때문에 수동을 뜻하는 과거분사 designed를 써서 hair dyes를 수식한다. [where ~]는 관계부사절로 parts of rural Africa를 수식한다.

[14행] For example, **most people** (S) in the United States [**using** US customary units (e.g., inch, foot, yard, mile, etc.)] **have resisted** (V) adopting the metric system~.

▶ 미국인들이 관습적 단위를 능동적으로 사용하는 것이기 때문에 현재분사(using)를 써서 주어(most people)를 수식한다. 이 문장의 동사는 have resisted이다.

어휘

come into contact 접촉하다 **trait** 특성
dye 염색약; 염색하다 **elevate** 올리다, 높이다
with advancing years 나이가 들어감에 따라
consistent 일치하는, 일관된
guarantee 보장, 확약, 보증서
resist 저항하다
interface with ~와 접촉[접속]하다
efficiently 효율적으로

Exercise

01 ② 02 ④ 03 ① 04 ④ 05 ① 06 ④
07 ③ 08 ② 09 ②

Plus Q

03 Furthermore, In addition, Moreover, Besides 또는 On top of that 등 첨가, 부연의 의미를 가지는 연결어라면 모두 가능하다.
09 accidentally

01 정답 ②

소재 이웃에게 베푼 호의가 발명으로 이어진 경우

전문 해석

여러분이 자신의 파이 한 조각을 간절히 얻고 싶을 때, 다른 사람들이 그들의 파이 한 조각을 얻을 수 있도록 그들에게 도움을 주는 데 여러분이 왜 관심을 기울이겠는가? Ernest Hamwi가 1904년 세계 박람회에서 페르시아의 아주 얇은 와플 zalabia를 팔고 있었을 때, 그런 마음가짐을 가지고 있었더라면, 그는 거리의 상인으로 생을 마감했을지도 모른다. Hamwi는 인근의 아이스크림 상인이 고객에게 줄 아이스크림을 담을 그릇이 동난 것을 보게 되었다. 대부분의 사람들은 "내 문제가 아니야" 라고 콧방귀를 뀌며 말했을 것이며, 아마도 심지어 그 아이스크림 상인의 불행이 자신들에게 더 많은 고객을 의미하기를 바랐을 것이다. 대신에 Hamwi는 와플을 말아 올려 꼭대기에 한 숟가락의 아이스크림을 놓아서, 세계 최초의 아이스크림콘

중의 하나를 만들었다. 그는 자신의 이웃을 도왔으며, 그 과정에서 많은 돈을 벌었다.

문제 해설

이웃 상인을 돕기 위해서 한 행동이 최초의 아이스크림콘의 발명으로 이어져 엄청나게 많은 돈을 벌었다는 내용이므로, 빈칸에 가장 적절한 것은 ② '자신의 이웃을 도왔으며'이다.

① 새로운 상점을 열었으며
③ 그 큰 행사에 참여했으며
④ 자신의 조리법을 비밀로 했으며
⑤ 자신의 실패로부터 배웠으며

구문 분석

[2행] **If** Ernest Hamwi **had taken** that attitude when he was selling zalabia, a very thin Persian waffle, at the 1904 World's Fair, he **might have ended** his days as a street vendor.

▶ 가정법 과거완료의 대표적 예이다. 가정법 과거완료는 과거 사실에 대한 반대를 가정할 때 사용하며, 「If+주어+had+과거분사, 주어+과거형 조동사(would, could, might, should)+have+과거분사」의 형태를 취한다.

02 정답 ④

소재 환자의 치료에 대한 전문의의 의견

전문 해석

여러 질환에서 누가 치료를 받아야 하는지에 대해 전문의들 사이에서 다른 의견이 있을 수 있다는 것을 환자들이 알고 있어야 한다. 예를 들어, 유럽과 미국의 전문가 위원회는 고혈압을 언제 치료할지에 대해 서로 다른 지침을 마련했다. 미국 전문가 집단은 가벼운 혈압 상승의 경우 치료로 얻는 이득이 위험을 넘어선다고 믿었다. 그들은 가벼운 혈압 상승 증상이 있는 환자들이 약을 복용할 것을 제안하는 지침을 작성했다. 하지만 유럽에서 같은 과학적 데이터를 접한 전문가 위원회는 가벼운 혈압 상승의 경우 치료를 권하지 않는 다른 지침을 마련했다. 유럽에서는 동일한 증상이 있는 사람들에게 약을 복용하라고 권하지 않을 것이다. 서로 다른 전문가 집단은 무엇이 '최선의 (의료) 행위'인가에 대해 의견이 상당히 다를 수 있다.

문제 해설

환자가 치료를 받아야 할지에 대해 전문가 집단 사이에서 지침이 다르다는 내용의 글이므로 빈칸에 가장 적절한 것은 ④ '전문의들 사이에서 다른 의견이 있을 수 있다'이다.

① 보편적 지침이 있다
② 도덕적 고려 사항이 있을 수 있다
③ 가족이 의사 결정에 책임이 있다
⑤ 주치의의 충고를 따르는 데에서 이득을 얻는다

구문 분석

[5행] They wrote guidelines [**suggesting** that patients with mild blood pressure elevation **take** medicine].

▶ suggesting은 분사로 guidelines를 수식한다. suggest는 '~해야 할 것을 제안'하는 동사이므로 that절의 동사는 「(should)+동사원형」의 형태가 된다.

03 정답 ①

소재 정상급 선수들의 팀 승리에 대한 기여도

전문 해석

Emmitt Smith와 같이 매우 뛰어난 선수가 득점 기록판에 점수를 올려 팀의 승리 가능성을 높이는 것은 부정할 수 없지만, 새로운 연구는 정상급 기량의 선수들이 팀에 가져오는 이점에는 한계가 있다는 것을 보여준다. 연구자들은 팀의 개인적 기량의 양과 팀의 승리를 비교해서, 더 많은 수의 정상급 선수가 팀에 해를 입힌다는 것의 주목할 만한 예를 찾아냈다. 연구자들은 세 가지의 운동, 즉 농구, 축구, 그리고 야구를 조사해 보았다. 각각의 운동에서 각 팀의 정상급 기량의 선수의 비율과 팀의 승리를 몇 년 동안 계산해 냈다. 농구와 축구 둘 다의 경우, 그들은 정상급 기량의 선수가 실제로 팀의 성공을 예견했지만, 단지 어떠한 시점까지만임을 알아냈다. 더욱이, 정상급 기량의 선수와 관련해서 수확 체감의 시점이 있을 뿐만 아니라, 실제로 손실도 있었다. 뛰어난 운동선수가 비율적으로 가장 많은 농구와 축구팀은 최고 수준의 선수 비율이 그다지 많지 않은 팀들보다 더 안 좋은 성과를 냈다.

문제 해설

정상급의 선수들로 구성된 팀이 오히려 더 안 좋은 성적을 냈다는 내용이 이어지고 있으므로 빈칸에 가장 적절한 것은 ① '더 많은 수의 정상급 선수가 팀에 해를 입힌다'이다.

② 연습이 완벽을 이끈다
③ 정상급 선수들이 더 협력적이다
④ 감독이 팀 관리의 핵심이다
⑤ 팬들이 게임의 흐름을 방해한다

구문 분석

[1행] While **there is no denying** that exceptional players like Emmitt Smith can put points on the board and enhance team success, new research suggests there is a limit to the benefit [top talents bring to a team].

▶ 「there is no+-ing」는 '~하는 것은 불가능하다'의 의미이다. [ ]는 목적격 관계대명사가 생략된 관계절로 앞에 있는 the benefit을 수식한다.

Plus Q

문맥상 첨가, 부연을 나타내는 연결어가 들어가는 것이 적절하므로 Furthermore, In addition, Moreover, Besides, On top of that 등이 들어 갈 수 있다.

04 정답 ④

소재 남을 비판하고 싶을 때 고려 사항

전문 해석

아무도 완벽하지는 않다. 찾고자하면 누구에 대해서라도 비판할 점을 항상 찾을 수 있을 것이다. 그러나 여러분 역시 완벽하지 않다는 것을 기억하라. 사람들을 계속적으로 비판하고 기를 꺾는 것보다는 그들을 있는 그대로 받아들이고 어떤 관계든지 최대한 이용하는 것을 배우는 것이 훨씬 낫다. 지구상의 가장 위대한 지도자들조차 많은 결점을 갖고 있었지만 그들은 자신들의 실수로부터 배웠고 이 교훈들을 자신들의 발전을 위해 이용했다. 간디, 만델라, 그리고 테레사 수녀는 모두 어떤 때는 거부를 당했었고 젊었을 때 모두 실수를 저질렀다. 하지만 그들은 자신만의 방법으로 불멸적인 인물이 되었다. 남들을 비난하는 것에 대해 생각할 때 이것을 염두에 두는 것이 좋을 것이다.

문제 해설

자신을 포함해서 아무도 완벽한 사람은 없고 위인들 역시 결점이 있었고 실수하기도 했으나 그것으로부터 배워서 발전할 수 있었다는 내용으로 남을 비난할 마음이 들 때 이런 점을 염두에 두라는 맥락이다. 따라서 빈칸에 가장 적절한 것은 ④ '비난하는 것'이다.

① 돕는 것
② 교육하는 것
③ 보호하는 것
⑤ 격려하는 것

구문 분석

[3행] **It** is much better [**to accept** people as they are, and **(to) learn** to make the best of any relationship, than to continuously criticize them and beat them down].

▶ It은 형식상의 주어(가주어)이고 [to accept ~]가 내용상의 주어(진주어)이다. accept와 learn은 둘 다 to부정사에 이어지는 동사로 병렬구조를 이룬다.

05 정답 ①

소재 자기 인식의 필요성

전문 해석

우리는 항상 자신과 함께 있지만 우리 중 많은 이가 사실은 자신에 관해 많이 모르고 있다는 것이 놀랍다. 왜 그럴까? 그것은 우리가 내면의 원천과 연결하는 데 시간을 들이지 않기 때문이다. 우리의 양육과 교육을 통해 우리는 흔히 우리의 핵심적인 자아와의 접촉을 잃는다. 그리고 시간 투자와 결합된 깊은 사색, 자기 평가, 그리고 진심에서 우러난 노력을 통해서만 우리는 이 접촉을 회복할 수 있다. 하지만 인간인 우리는 역동적인 존재이기 때문에 우리는 또한 항상 변한다. 이것은 우리 자신을 알게 되는 것이 끝이 없는 과정이라는 것을 의미한다. 그리고 그것이 그 과정을 수고를 아끼지 않는 노력으로 만든다. 그러나 그것은 해볼 만한 가치가 있는데, 그 이유는 우리가 자신을 더 잘 알게 되기만 하면 훨씬 더 많은 것을 할 수 있기 때문이다. 우리는 자신이 좋아하는 것과 싫어하는 것, 우리가 선호하는 목적, 그리고 스스로 행복하고 만족하는 것을 유지하는 방법을 알 수 있을 것이다.

문제 해설

자신을 알아가는 것은 중요한 과정인데 사람은 항상 변하기 때문에 그 과정은 끝이 없는 것이라는 맥락이므로 빈칸에 가장 적절한 것은 ① '끝이 없는 과정'이다.

② 아주 혼란스러운 상황
③ 거의 일어나지 않는 것
④ 사회화를 위한 주요 필수 조건
⑤ 세상을 이해하는 것과 다른

구문 분석

[4행] And **it is** [only through deep contemplation, self-evaluation, and genuine efforts, combined with an investment of time], **that** we can restore this contact.

▶ [ ]로 표시된 부분이 「it is~that 강조 구문」에 의해 강조되고 있다.

06 정답 ④

소재 결과를 염두에 두고 선택하기

전문 해석

우리가 쉬운 해결책을 먼저 선택한 다음 불편한 감정으로 그것에 대한 대가를 치를 때, 예를 들어 아이스크림을 먹는다면 한동안은 기분이 좋겠지만 나중에 체중 증가로 그에 대한 대가를 치를 때 쾌락 욕구 원칙이 우리를 통제한다. 우리가 가게에 들어가 지불할 돈이 부족한 어떤 것을 볼 때 우리는 신용 카드를 사용한다. 지금 그것을 갖지 못할 이유가 뭔가? 어떤 구매를 연기하는 것의 가치를 알기는 어렵다. 우리는 신용 카드로 구매될 수 있는 멋진 저녁 식사, 새로운 휴대전화, 또는 예쁜 옷을 볼 수 있을 따름이다. 청구서 지불 날짜가 될 때까지는 아무런 고통도 희생도 없다. 어떤 사람들은 신용 카드 빚에 족쇄로 묶인다. 우리가 선택을 할 때 그런 순간들을 의식하고 일정하게 더 어려운 단기적인 출구를 택하려고 노력해라, 예를 들면 TV를 보는 대신 운동을 하고 초콜릿 바 대신에 사과를 사라.

문제 해설

아이스크림을 먹는 것이 당장은 맛있지만 체중 증가라는 결과로 대가를 치르게 되고 신용 카드로 구매를 하는 것이 당장은 좋지만 지불 날짜가 오면 부담스럽고 빚에 묶이게 되듯이 어떤 행동을 할 때 결과를 염두에 두고 선택하라는 내용의 글이다. 따라서 빈칸에 가장 적절한 것은 ④ '더 어려운 단기적인 출구를 택하려고'이다.

① 착하고 이기심 없는 행동을 하려고
② 최신 연구 결과와 접하려고
③ 여러분이 즐기는 것을 할 시간을 내려고
⑤ 공동체를 위한 프로젝트가 진행되고 있게 하려고

구문 분석

[6행] {All [one can see]} **is** an evening of elegant dining, a new mobile phone or the beautiful clothes that can be purchased with credit cards.

▶ { }가 주어이고 동사는 is이다. [ ]는 All을 수식하는 관계절로 목적격 관계대명사가 생략되어 있다.

07 정답 ③

소재 실제로 해보는 경험을 통해 재능을 발견한 Gardner

전문 해석

종종, 우리는 우리의 재능이 어떤 것인지에 대한 적절한 생각을 가지고 있지 못한데, 왜냐하면 우리는 그것을 시도해 볼 기회를 가져본 적이 없었기 때문이다. 예를 들면, John Gardner는 그가 제2차 세계 대전 동안에 군대에 징집되기 전까지는 보통의 대학 교수였다. 복무 중에 그는 어쩔 수 없이 관리를 하는 책임을 맡게 되었는데, 그 일이 가르치는 일보다 그의 재능과 훨씬 더 잘 맞는다는 것을 알게 되었다. 그가 민간인의 생활로 돌아왔을 때 그가 카네기 재단의 의장으로 임명된 다음, Lyndon B. Johnson 대통령에 의해 건강, 교육과 복지를 담당하는 최초의 장관으로 근무해 줄 것을 부탁받을 때까지 그는 점점 더 까다로운 행정 일을 부여받았다. 이러한 종류의 경험은 우리 대부분이 단지 우리의 선천적인 능력의 작은 부분만을 사용하며 아마도 우리가 정말로 할 수 있는 일을 발견하지 못하고 있다고 Gardner를 확신시켰다.

문제 해설

Gardner는 보통의 대학 교수였지만 전쟁 중에 맡게 된 관리직을 통해 자신이 그 일에 재능이 있다는 것을 발견하게 되고 나아가서는 장관직까지 맡게 된다는 내용의 글이다. 따라서 빈칸에 가장 적절한 것은 ③ '그것을 시도해 볼 기회를 가져본 적이 없었기'이다.

① 우리의 재능이 과장되도록 했기
② 불공정한 기준에 의해 판단되었기
④ 우리가 과거에 만났던 장애물을 극복하지 못했기
⑤ 의무와 책임을 파악하지 못했기

구문 분석

[3행] In the service he was forced to take on managerial responsibilities, which **(he discovered)** fit his talents even better than teaching **did**.

▶ he discovered는 삽입어구이다. which가 이끄는 관계절의 선행사인 managerial responsibilities는 관계절 내의 동사인 fit의 주어 역할을 한다. did는 fit를 받는 대동사로 쓰였다.

08 정답 ②

소재 사람을 판단할 수 있는 능력

전문 해석

운명적인 사람을 만날 때 어떤 일이 벌어지는가? 이내, 심장이 마구 요동질치고, 혀가 사포처럼 느껴지고, 손바닥이 분수로 변한다. 갑자기 'Hello'가 영어에서 가장 어려운 단어가 된다. 왜 이런 특정 인물이 이동 주택 캠프장을 휩쓸고 간 토네이도처럼 당신을 휩쓸고 가는가? 그것은 당신 뇌 깊숙이 사람을 즉시 가늠하는 능력이 묻혀 있기 때문이다. 이 기술은 "싸워야 하나 혹은 도망쳐야 하나"의 순간의 결정이 삶과 죽음의 문제였던 시절로 거슬러 올라가는 강한 진화적 뿌리를 가지고 있다. 여러분은 누군가가 함께 있으면 즐거울지, 누가 당신의 필요할 부분을 실현시켜 줄 것인가를 알아차릴 놀라운 잠재적 능력을 개발해왔다.

문제 해설

운명적인 사람을 만났을 때, 생물학적인 반응이 곧장 나타나는 것은 순간의 결정이 중요한 문제가 되었던 시절에서 그 진화적 뿌리를 갖는다는 내용이므로, 빈칸에 가장 적절한 것은 ② '사람을 즉시 가늠하는'이다.

① 옳고 그름을 구별하는
③ 과거 경험으로부터 배우는
④ 새로운 환경에 쉽게 적응하는
⑤ 생물학적 징후를 즉시 감지하는

구문 분석

[1행] **In no time**, your heart pounds **as strongly as it can**, your tongue feels like sandpaper, and your palms turn into a waterfall.

▶ 'In no time'은 '이내, 곧'의 의미이다. as strongly as it can은 as strongly as possible로 대체하여 사용할 수 있다.

09 정답 ②

소재 생각 없이 한 행동의 가치 결정

전문 해석

생각 없이 한 행동의 가치는 우연에 달려 있다. 우리의 행동은 우리가 생각해보고 더 나아가 탐험해 볼 어떤 것으로 우리를 인도할 수도 있고, 혹은 아무것도 안 될 수도 있다. 아기가 언어를 배우는 방식이 좋은 예이다. 아기가 듣거나 만들어내는 많은 소리는 언어에 관한 한 아무것도 아니다. 아기가 큰 소리를 내거나, 차가 지나쳐 가거나, 숟가락이 마루에 떨어지거나, 혹은 아기가 유아용 침대에 부딪히기도 한다. 이런 것들은 모두 언어에서 의미가 없는 소리들이다. 그러나 다른 소리들은 단순히 다른 누군가가 우연히 듣게 됨으로써 대단한 의미를 가질 수 있다. 예를 들어, 아기가 우연히 'mama'와 비슷한 어떤 것을 말하는데, 그것이 우연히 그것을 들은 엄마를 행복하게 한다. 그러면 그 언어 소리는 거듭해서 반복되고, 그것들이 의미를 갖게 된다. 소위 말하는 통계적 학습이 시작된다.

문제 해설

아기가 의미 있는 단어와 관련된 비슷한 것을 말하는데, 엄마가 그것을 우연히 듣고, 행복해하는 모습을 보이자, 아기가 그 비슷한 것을 반복해서 말하면서 학습이 이루어진다는 예를 통해서, 아무 생각 없이 한 행동이 '우연'에 의해서 가치를 갖기도 하고 못 갖기도 한다는 것을 알 수 있다. 따라서 빈칸에 가장 적절한 것은 ② '우연'이다.

① 호기심 ③ 수용 ④ 의지 ⑤ 기여

구문 분석

[8행] ~, a baby accidentally says **something close** to "mama," which **makes** the mother [**who** happens to hear it] **happy**.

▶ '-thing'으로 끝나는 명사는 형용사가 뒤에서 수식한다. 「makes+목적어+목적보어(형용사)」 구문이 쓰였으며 목적어에 [who ~]는 관계절로 the mother를 수식한다.

Plus Q

by chance, by accident, accidentally는 모두 '우연히'라는 의미이며, intentionally, deliberately 등이 반의어이다.

유형 12 연결어 추론

p. 78

대표 예제 정답 ①

소재 피드백을 주는 시기

전문 해석

피드백은 특별히 여러분의 목적이 누군가에게 어떤 기술을 가르치는 것이라면 가급적 빨리 줄 때 일반적으로 가장 효과적이다. 예를 들어, 여러분이 친구에게 자신의 훌륭한 에그롤을 만드는 방법을 가르치고 있다면, 여러분은 자신의 제자(친구)를 지켜보면서 단계적인 설명을 제공한다. 그가 실수를 하면, 여러분은 에그롤이 끝날 때까지 기다리지 않고 그에게 양배추를 빠뜨렸다고 말한다. 나머지 연속 과정을 성공적으로 마치기 위해서 그에게는 즉각적인 피드백이 필요하다. 하지만, 때때로 어떤 사람이 어떤 일에 관해 이미 예민하고 당황해하고 있다면, 피드백을 미루는 것이 현명할 수 있다. 피드백이 언제 가장 이로울 것인지를 분석하기 위해 여러분의 비판적 사고 기능을 활용하라. 기계적으로 즉각적인 수정을 제공하기보다는, 적기의 접근법(필요할 때 피드백을 제공하는 접근법)을 사용하고 그 사람이 또 다른 실수를 하기 바로 전에 피드백을 제공하라.

문제 해설

(A) 빈칸 앞에서 피드백을 가급적 빨리 줄 때 효과가 가장 크다는 내용을 언급하고, 그 예로 친구에게 에그롤을 만드는 방법을 가르치는 경우를 빈칸 뒤에서 설명하고 있으므로, For example이 적절하다.

(B) 빈칸 앞에서 피드백을 가급적 빨리 줄 때 효과가 가장 큰 것이 일반적이라는 내용을 다루고 있지만, 빈칸 뒤에서는 이와는 대조적으로 피드백을 미루고 필요할 때 피드백을 제공하는 접근법을 사용해야 하는 경우도 있다는 내용을 다루고 있으므로, however가 적절하다.

② 예를 들어 – 결과적으로
③ 더욱이 – 사실
④ 마찬가지로 – 게다가
⑤ 마찬가지로 – 따라서

구문 분석

[13행] **Rather than** automatically offering immediate correction, *use* the just-in-time approach and *provide* feedback just before the person might make another mistake.

▶ 「rather than~」은 '~보다는[~대신에]'라는 뜻이고, 주절의 동사인 use와 provide가 명령문의 형태를 띠며 병렬을 이루고 있다.

어휘

at the earliest opportunity 가급적 빨리
objective 목적 **commentary** 설명
pupil 학생; 제자 **leave out** ~을 빼다, ~을 제외하다
immediate 즉각적인 **sequence** 연속 과정
sensitive 예민한 **upset** 당황한 **analyze** 분석하다
do good 이롭다, 이익을 주다 **correction** 수정
just-in-time 적기의, 적시의

Exercise

01 ① 02 ④ 03 ① 04 ⑤ 05 ② 06 ②

Plus Q
03 acquire
06 that

01 정답 ①

소재 스포츠를 정의하는 것의 어려움

전문 해석
누군가에게 스포츠 이름 세 가지를 말하라고 요청하면, 그 사람은 필시 쉽게 대답할 수 있을 것이다. 어쨌든, 거의 모든 사람이 어떤 유형의 활동이 스포츠로 여겨지고 어떤 것이 그렇지 않은지에 대한 생각을 가지고 있다. 우리 대부분은 무엇이 스포츠인지 안다고 생각한다. 하지만, 스포츠, 여가 활동, 놀이의 사례들 사이에 그어지는 선이 항상 분명한 것은 아니다. 사실, 어떤 유형의 활동이 포함되어야 하고 제외되어야 하는지를 둘러싼 규정 요소들을 분명하고 깔끔하게 규명하는 정의를 궁리하는 것은 비교적 어렵다. 오늘날 놀이로 여겨지는 활동이 미래에 스포츠의 지위를 얻을 수도 있다. 예를 들어, 많은 사람이 예전에 자기 뒤뜰에서 배드민턴을 쳤지만 이 활동은 거의 스포츠로 여겨지지 않았다. 하지만 1992년 이래 배드민턴은 올림픽 스포츠가 되었다!

문제 해설
(A) 빈칸의 앞에는 우리 대부분이 무엇이 스포츠인지 안다고 생각한다는 내용이 나오고, 뒤에는 스포츠를 규정하는 요소들을 깔끔하게 규명하는 것이 비교적 어렵다는 내용이 나오므로 역접의 연결어인 However가 적절하다.
(B) 빈칸의 앞에는 오늘날 놀이로 여겨지는 활동이 미래에 스포츠의 지위를 얻을 수도 있다는 내용이 나오고, 뒤에는 그에 대한 예로 배드민턴이 나오므로 For example이 적절하다.

② 하지만 – 결론적으로
③ 게다가 – 결론적으로
④ 마찬가지로 – 예를 들어
⑤ 마찬가지로 – 다시 말해서

구문 분석

[5행] In fact, [devising a definition {**that** establishes clear and clean parameters around what types of activities should be included and excluded}] **is** (V) relatively difficult to do.

▶ [ ]로 표시된 부분이 문장의 주어이고 동사는 is이다. {that ~}는 a definition을 수식하는 관계절이다.

02 정답 ④

소재 점점 더 늘어나는 수산물에 대한 수요

전문 해석
어업은 가장 명백한, 바다에 기초를 둔 경제 활동이다. 많은 해안 지역에 사는 사람들은 어업으로 먹고 살고 물고기와 조개류는 그들의 주식을 구성한다. 사실, 전 세계적으로 약 십억의 사람들이 그들의 동물성 단백질의 주요 공급원으로 물고기에 의존한다. 어업을 경제 활동으로 볼 때, 세계 어업의 가장 큰 부분은 상업적인 어업이다. 상업적인 어부들에 의해 잡히는 물고기는 연어, 참치, 조개 그리고 오징어와 같이 다른 먹을 수 있는 종을 포함한다. 소비자

들은 이러한 해산물을 전 세계의 식료품점, 식당, 그리고 마을 시장에서 사는 데 익숙하다. 하지만, 공급은 무한하지 않다. 세계 인구가 증가하면서, 수산물에 대한 수요가 물고기 개체에 강한 압력을 주고 있다. 전 세계 바다에서의 어획량이 2003년 8천백만 톤에서 2010년 1억 4천 8백만 톤으로 늘어났다.

문제 해설

(A) 빈칸의 앞에는 많은 해안 지역에 사는 사람들이 물고기와 조개류를 주식으로 삼고 있다는 내용이 나오고, 빈칸의 뒤에는 이에 대한 내용에 대해 부연 설명을 하고 있으므로 In fact가 적절하다.
(B) 빈칸의 앞에는 소비자들이 해산물을 식료품점, 식당과 마을 시장에서 사는 것에 익숙하다는 내용이 나오고, 빈칸의 뒤에는 그럼에도 공급이 무한하지 않다는 내용이 나오므로 However가 적절하다.

① 대신에 – 마찬가지로
② 대신에 – 그러나
③ 사실 – 마찬가지로
⑤ 예를 들어 – 더욱이

구문 분석

[6행] Fish [**caught** by commercial fishermen] include salmon, tuna, shellfish and other edible species such as squid.

▶ [caught ~]는 분사구로 주어인 Fish를 수식한다.

03 정답 ①

소재 합리적인 문제와 비합리적인 문제를 다루는 방법

전문 해석

문제는 그것들이 합리적인지 혹은 비합리적인지에 따라 구분될 수 있다. 합리적인 문제는 단계적인 방식으로 해결될 수 있는 종류이다. 크로스워드 퍼즐(십자말해설)이 이런 성격이다. 충분한 어휘가 주어지면 빈 공간을 하나씩 채울 수 있다. 그에 반해, 비합리적인 문제는 누군가가 해결책에 도달할 수 있기 전에 반드시 알아야 하는 어떤 '속임수'나 '함정'을 과업에 포함하고 있기 때문에 이런 방식으로 다룰 수 없다. 이런 특성은 '상황이 겉보기와는 다르다' 라는 인식이 없이 진행되는 단계적인 과정이 어느 것이든 방해한다. 그러므로, 이런 경우에 있어서의 성공적인 문제 해결은 속임수의 성격에 대한 통찰을 그 사람이 습득해야 함을 요구한다. 수수께끼가 그런 통찰 문제의 아주 흔한 사례를 제공하는데, 스핑크스가 오이디푸스에게 제기했던 고전적인 수수께끼 같은 것이다.

문제 해설

(A) 빈칸의 앞에는 합리적인 문제에 대한 예로서 크로스워드 퍼즐이 제시되어 있으며, 빈칸의 뒤에는 비합리적인 문제에 대해 언급하고 있으므로 역접의 연결어인 in contrast가 적절하다.
(B) 빈칸의 앞에는 비합리적인 문제를 다룰 때 '상황이 겉보기와는 다르다' 라는 인식을 갖지 못하는 단계적 과정은 좌절하게 된다는 내용이 나오고, 빈칸의 뒤에는 그래서 이런 경우에 취해야 할 자세를 설명하고 있으므로 Hence가 적절하다.

② 그에 반해 – 그럼에도 불구하고
③ 예를 들어 – 그러므로
④ 예를 들어 – 게다가
⑤ 더욱이 – 그럼에도 불구하고

오답 풀이

빈칸 (B)의 앞에는 비합리적인 문제를 풀 때는 '상황이 겉보기와는 다르다' 라는 인식이 없으면 안 된다는 내용이 나오고, 뒤에는 따라서 속임수의 성격에 대한 통찰이 필요하다는 인과 관계의 내용이 나오므로 '그러므로'가 적절하다. 이것을 단순히 하나의 정보를 추가하는 것으로 오인하지 않도록 주의한다.

구문 분석

[7행] This feature frustrates any step-by-step process [**that** proceeds without the realization {**that** "things aren't what they seem."}]

▶ [ ]로 표시된 부분은 관계사절로 any step-by-step process를 수식하며, { }로 표시된 부분은 동격절로 the realization을 부연 설명한다.

Plus Q

'주장(insist), 요구(ask, require), 명령(order), 제안(suggest, move), 조언(advise)' 등의 동사가 주절에 오고, that절이 '당위성'을 나타내도록 해석되는 맥락일 경우 that 절의 동사 형태는 「(should)+동사원형」이 되며, 이때 should는 대개 생략된다.

04 정답 ⑤

소재 고통과 불편함을 다루는 방법

전문 해석

우리가 고통 혹은 불편함을 경험할 때 자연스런 성향은 고통을 피하려고 하거나 고통의 원천을 없애기 위해 어떤 일을 하려고 하는 것이다. 예를 들어, 이웃의 시끄러운 라디오에 의해 유발되는 외부에서 오는 불편함의 경우에 소음으로부터 탈출하기 위해서 드라이브를 갈 수도 있고 혹은

그 이웃에게 소리를 줄여달라고 요청할 수도 있을 것이다. 그러나 내부의 고통에 대해 보자면, 이러한 종류의 접근법은 대개는 역효과를 낳는다. 예를 들어 극심한 공포의 공격을 두려워하는 사람은 긴장하다가 그것과 싸우려고 한다. 이것은 극심한 공포의 공격을 더 강렬하고 더 오래 지속되도록 만든다. 더 나은 접근법은 편히 쉬고 그 공격이 오게 하고 지나가도록 하는 방법일 것이다. 마찬가지로, 대단히 충격적인 사건을 경험한 사람들은 헛되게 그 기억들을 없애려고 할지 모른다. 그 기억을 받아들이고 처리하는 것이 더 나을 것이다. 어떤 사람이 만성적인 고통을 경험하면 할 수 있는 최악의 일들 중 하나는 긴장하다가 그것과 싸우는 것이다.

문제 해설

(A) 빈칸의 앞에는 우리가 고통을 경험할 때 고통을 피하려 하거나 그 원천을 없애려 한다는 내용이 나와 있으며, 뒤에는 라디오 소음과 관련된 예가 나오므로 (A)에는 for example이 적절하다.

(B) 빈칸의 앞에는 극심한 공포의 공격에 대한 더 나은 접근법은 그것이 온 다음에 지나가도록 하는 것이라는 내용이 오고, 뒤에는 충격적인 사건을 경험한 사람들도 그 기억을 없애려 하지 말고 받아들이고 처리하는 것이 더 나은 방법이라는 비슷한 맥락의 내용이 나오므로 (B)에는 Similarly가 적절하다.

① 결과적으로 – 마찬가지로
② 결과적으로 – 게다가
③ 사실 – 게다가
④ 예를 들어 – 따라서

오답 풀이

(B)의 경우, 빈칸의 앞뒤에 내적인 고통을 대하는 유사한 방법들이 제시되어 있는데, 이것을 또 다른 접근법이 추가되어 있는 것처럼 잘못 생각해서 Besides를 선택하지 않도록 주의한다.

구문 분석

[1행] When we experience pain or discomfort, the natural inclination **is to** [try to avoid the pain] or [do something to get rid of the source of the pain].

▶ 두 개의 [ ]로 표시된 부분은 to를 공유하며 병렬을 이루고 있으며, to와 함께 동사 is의 주격보어 역할을 하고 있다.

05 정답 ②

소재 총체적인 체험을 하게끔 재설계되고 있는 쇼핑몰들

전문 해석

전자 유통 체계의 성장은 마케팅의 성질에서의 근본적인 변화를 만들어내고 있다. 고객들은 이전에 고정된 장소에 위치해 있으면서 고정된 시간에 영업을 하는 공급자와 얼굴을 맞대고 하는 접촉으로부터 '어디서든지, 언제든지' 영업을 하는 원거리 접촉으로 이동하고 있다. 더욱 더 많은 서비스들이 이제는 얼굴을 맞대고 하는 상호작용보다는 오히려 팔을 뻗으면 닿는 거리(컴퓨터를 이용해서 쇼핑을 하는 경우를 말함)의 관계의 범주에 속한다. 그러나, 고객들은 여전히 시장을 없애는 것이 어렵다는 것을 알고 있는데, 왜냐하면 그들을 이끄는 것은 사람들이 특별히 찾는 리조트의 경우처럼 물리적인 환경이기 때문이다. 더욱이, 그 물리적인 환경은 발전하고 있다. 이전에는 소매 상점만 있었던 쇼핑몰들은 이제 '총체적인 체험'을 할 수 있도록 재설계되고 있다. 다른 말로 하자면, 재설계된 몰들은 음식 서비스, 헬스클럽, 오락, 전시회와 무엇보다도 사교활동을 할 수 있는 기회를 제공하는 것을 추구한다.

문제 해설

(A) 빈칸의 앞에는 더욱 더 많은 서비스들이 팔을 뻗으면 닿는 거리, 즉 컴퓨터를 이용해서 쇼핑을 하는 범주에 속한다는 내용이 나왔으며, 빈칸의 뒤에서는 그래도 시장을 없애는 것이 어렵다는 내용이 나오므로 역접의 연결어인 However가 적절하다.

(B) 빈칸의 앞에서는 '총체적인 체험'을 할 수 있도록 쇼핑몰들이 재설계되고 있다는 내용이 나와 있고, 빈칸의 뒤에서는 총체적인 체험에 대해 설명하고 있으므로 In other words가 적절하다.

① 그러나 – 그럼에도 불구하고
③ 마찬가지로 – 그럼에도 불구하고
④ 마찬가지로 – 다른 말로 하자면
⑤ 게다가 – 결과적으로

구문 분석

[2행] The customers are moving **from** [face-to-face contacts with the suppliers {who were earlier located in fixed locations} {that operate during fixed hours}], **to** [remote contacts that operate "anywhere, anytime"].

▶ 「from A to B」 구문이 사용되었다. 첫 번째 [ ]로 표시된 부분이 A에 해당되며, 두 번째 [ ]로 표시된 부분이 B에 해당한다. 첫 번째 [ ]로 표시된 부분 안에 두 개의 { }로 표시된 관계대명사절이 the suppliers를 수식하고 있다.

06 정답 ②

소재 생리(현상)을 통제하는 것의 효과

전문 해석

수 년 동안 나는 사람들이 그들의 정신을 통제하는 것을 돕기 위해 노력해왔다. 내가 알게 된 가장 중요한 것들 중 하나는 여러분이 여러분 자신의 느낌과 행동을 바꾸길 원한다면 여러분이 생리(현상)을 이용하는 방식을 바꾸라는 것이다. 예를 들어, 여러분이 우울함을 느끼고 있지만 똑바로 서서 가슴을 내밀고 얼굴에 미소를 띤다면 여러분은 더 이상 우울함을 느끼지 않을 것이다. 과학자들은 이 점을 확인해왔다. 그들은 사람들이 진실을 말하고 있을 때와 유사한 생리적인 (신체) 상태, 자세 그리고 호흡 패턴 속에 자신들을 놓음으로써 거짓말 탐지기를 이겨왔다는 것을 밝혀냈다. 따라서, 여러분이 여러분의 신체와 사고 과정을 이용하는 방식을 바꿈으로써 여러분 자신의 프로그램을 다시 만들어볼 수 있다.

문제 해설

(A) 빈칸의 앞에는 생리 현상을 이용하는 방식을 바꾸라는 내용이 나오고, 뒤에는 그에 대한 구체적인 예가 제시되고 있으므로 For example이 적절하다.
(B) 빈칸 앞에 나오는 내용들에 대한 결론을 맺고 있는 문장이 나오고 있으므로, Therefore가 적절하다.

① 예를 들어 – 게다가
③ 마찬가지로 – 게다가
④ 그러나 – 따라서
⑤ 그러나 – 다른 말로 하자면

구문 분석

[6행] ~ people have beaten lie detectors by putting themselves in a physiological state, posture, and breathing pattern [**similar** to that of when they are telling the truth].

▶ a physiological state, posture와 breathing pattern은 전치사 in의 목적어로 and에 의해 병렬을 이루고 있다. [ ]로 표시된 부분은 similar가 이끄는 형용사구로 a physiological state, posture, and breathing pattern을 수식한다.

Plus Q

문맥상 '진실을 말하고 있을 때의 그것과 비슷한 생리적인 (신체) 상태, 자세, 그리고 호흡 패턴'의 의미가 되어야 하므로 빈칸에는 a physiological state, posture, and breathing pattern을 가리키는 대명사이어야 한다. 이러한 대명사로 적절한 것은 that이다. 이때의 대명사는 가리키는 명사의 수에 따라 결정되는데, 가리키는 명사가 단수이면 that, 복수이면 those가 사용된다. 여기서는 a physiological state, posture, and breathing pattern을 하나의 이어지는 의미로 보고 단수 취급한다.

유형 13 무관한 문장 찾기

p. 84

대표 예제 정답 ③

소재 음식 섭취를 위한 감각의 사용

전문 해석

음식 섭취는 모든 생물의 생존을 위해 필수적이다. 상했거나 독이 있는 음식을 감지하지 못하면 치명적인 결과가 생길 수 있다. 따라서 인간이 음식의 질을 분석하기 위해 자신의 모든 오감을 사용하는 것은 놀랍지 않다. 음식 재료의 가치에 대한 최초의 판단은 그것의 외관과 냄새를 바탕으로 이뤄진다. 매력적으로 보이고 냄새도 매혹적인 음식은 입속으로 들어가게 된다. (특정한 음식의 가치는 비타민, 미네랄, 칼로리의 수준에 근거하여 그것이 얼마나 좋으냐에 대한 평가이다.) 여기에서 단지 미각에만 국한되지 않고, 후각, 촉각, 그리고 청각도 포함하는 복합적인 감각 분석을 토대로, 음식의 섭취나 거부에 대한 최종 결정이 이뤄진다. 빈번히, 이러한 서로 다른 감각 간의 복합적 상호작용은 여러 가지 감각을 사용하기 때문에 향미 지각으로 불리는 편이 더 낫겠지만, 부적절하게도 '맛'이라고 불린다.

문제 해설

음식을 섭취하기 전에 인간은 자신의 모든 감각을 사용하여 음식을 섭취할지 여부를 결정한다는 내용의 글이므로, 특정한 음식의 가치는 비타민, 미네랄, 칼로리의 수준에 근거하여 그것이 얼마나 좋으냐에 대한 평가라는 내용의 ③은 글의 흐름과 관계가 없다.

구문 분석

[3행] Therefore, **it** is not surprising [**that** humans use all their five senses to analyze food quality].

▶ it은 가주어이고, [that ~]가 진주어이다.

[10행] Here, based on a complex sensory analysis [**that** is not only restricted to the sense of taste but also includes smell, touch, and hearing], ~.

▶ [that ~]는 주격 관계대명사 that이 쓰인 관계대명사절로 선행사인 a complex sensory analysis를 수식한다. 「not only A but also B」는 'A뿐만 아니라 B도'의 뜻이다.

어휘

intake 섭취 **organism** 생물 **toxic** 유독성의
deadly 치명적인 **consequence** 결과
analyze 분석하다 **attractive** 매력적인
estimation 평가, 판단 **sensory** 감각의
restrict 제한하다 **include** 포함하다 **swallow** 섭취하다
interaction 상호작용 **inappropriately** 부적절하게
refer to 부르다 **perception** 지각

Exercise

01 ④ 02 ③ 03 ③ 04 ③ 05 ③ 06 ⑤

Plus Q

03 그 직사각형 격자무늬 체계는 이로운 만큼이나[도움이 된 만큼이나] 많은 해로움도 초래했다

06 the personal and professional aspects (of an individual's life)

01 정답 ④

소재 소리에 관한 조류와 포유류의 차이

전문 해석

포유류와 조류 둘 다 시끄러운 동물이다. 일반적으로 그것들은 소리로 자신들의 존재가 느껴지도록 만들고 소통을 하지만, 조류가 그것에 훨씬 더 능숙하다. 많은 포유류가 각기 다른 물체에 대해 각기 다른 소리를 내지만, 조류가 낼 수 있는 유의미한 소리의 범위에 필적할 수 있는 포유류는 거의 없다. 인간을 제외하고는 포유류는 대체로 노래하지 못하며, 그것들이 그렇게 하려 한다는 증거도 거의 없다. 몇몇 포유류가 큰 소리로 울부짖기는 하지만, 인간과 아마도 고래를 제외하고는 노래하는 포유류는 거의 없다. (몇몇 포유류는 사는 장소, 돌아다니는 방식, 먹는 것에 있어서 서로 다르다.) 하지만 많은 조류는 노래로 유명하며, 가장 멋진 명금(고운 소리로 우는 새) 중의 일부는 우리가 가장 흔하게 마주치는 것들이다.

문제 해설

소리를 내는 것에 있어 조류가 포유류보다 훨씬 능숙하다는 내용의 글이므로, 포유류가 사는 장소와 먹는 것 등을 언급한 ④는 글의 흐름과 관계가 없다.

구문 분석

[9행] ~ **some** of the most glorious songsters **are** the ones [(which / that) we encounter most often].

▶ 「some+of+the+복수명사」 구문으로 동사 are가 쓰였다. some, most, all과 같은 부정대명사의 경우 뒤에 오는 명사의 수에 따라 동사를 일치시킨다. [ ]는 관계대명사 which 혹은 that이 생략된 목적격 관계대명사절로 the ones를 수식한다.

02 정답 ③

소재 블랙 아이스의 위험성

전문 해석

블랙 아이스는 표면의 반짝이는 얇은 얼음막을 지칭한다. 실제로 검은색은 아니고, 사실상 투명하며, 아래에 있는 검은색 아스팔트 도로나 표면이 그것을 통해 보여지기에 '블랙 아이스'라고 불린다. 블랙 아이스는 사실상 자주 운전자나 그 위를 걷는 사람에게 보이지 않는다. 따라서 갑작스러운 미끄러짐과 뒤따르는 사고의 위험이 있다. (안전한 운전을 위해서 출발하기 전에 당신의 차를 점검하는 것이 최선이다.) 2013년 12월 1일에 추수감사절 후 주말에 Massachusetts 주 Worcester에 있는 서쪽행 I-290 고속도로에서 교통 체증이 블랙 아이스를 만났다. 세 대의 견인 트레일러와 60대가 넘는 다른 차량의 연쇄 충돌 사건이 생겼던 것이다.

문제 해설

블랙 아이스에 관해 이야기하고 있는 글이므로, 안전한 운전을 위해 차량을 점검해야 한다는 ③은 글의 흐름과 관계가 없다.

구문 분석

[1행] [**While** (**it is**) not truly black], it is virtually transparent, [**allowing** black asphalt roadways or the surface below **to** be seen through it ~].

▶ 부사절의 주어가 주절의 주어와 일치할 때 「부사절의 주어+be동사」를 생략할 수 있다. allowing은 분사구문으로 쓰였으며 「allow+목적어+to부정사」는 '목적어가 ~하도록 허용하다'의 의미이다.

03 정답 ③

소재 해로움을 초래한 자연 체계에 대한 인식

전문 해석

20세기 초에 생태학이 부상한 이후에야 사람들은 땅을 서로 연결된 부분을 가진 하나의 자연 체계로 진지하게 생각하기 시작했다. 한 세기 전에, Thomas Jefferson은 Northwest Territory에서 시작하여 미국 땅을 질서 정연하게 나누는 것을 활발히 추진했었다. 측량사들이 그 땅에 직사각형의 격자무늬를 그리도록 파견되어, 지형이나 다른 자연적 특징에 대한 고려는 거의 하지 않고 야생의 자연을 자치주, 군구, 그리고 궁극적으로는 정부 공여 농지로 나누었다. (그들은 그 안에서 이득을 예상하지는 않았지만 그래도 환경 친화적인 체계를 택했다.) 그 체계는 그 나름의 장점을 가지고 있었지만, 머지않아 생태는 그 선들이 인위적으로 보이게 만들었다. 몇몇 관찰자들이 그것에 대해 알게 되었을 바와 같이, 그 직사각형 격자무늬 체계는 이로운 만큼이나 많은 해로움도 초래했다.

문제 해설
자연적 특징을 고려하지 않고 땅에 격자무늬를 그려 분할하는 체계가 해로움을 초래했다는 내용이므로, 환경 친화적인 체계를 택했다는 ③은 글의 흐름과 관계가 없다.

구문 분석
[1행] **Not** until the rise of ecology at the beginning of the twentieth century **did** people **begin** to think seriously of land as a natural system ~.

▶ 부정어인 Not이 문두에 왔으므로 「부정어+조동사+주어+동사」의 어순이 쓰였다. 일반동사는 조동사 do[does / did]를 이용해서 도치한다. 「think of A as B」는 'A를 B로 여기다'라는 뜻이다.

[9행] ~ ecology **made** the lines **appear** artificial.

▶ made가 사역동사이므로 목적격 보어로 동사원형인 appear가 쓰였다. 또한 불완전 자동사인 appear의 보어로 형용사가 쓰였다.

Plus Q
「as+much+명사+as」는 '~만큼 많은 …'의 뜻이며 do good은 '이롭다, 도움이 되다'의 의미이다.

04 정답 ③

소재 난민 문제의 원인, 결과 및 대응

전문 해석
난민이란 인권 남용과 분쟁을 피해 달아나기 위해 국경을 넘는 사람들을 말한다. 그러나 난민은 단지 인권 문제 이상이다. 난민 이동 또한 국제 정치에 내재해 있는 일부이다. 난민의 원인 및 결과와 그에 대한 대응 모두는 세계 정치와 밀접하게 연관되어 있다. 예를 들어, 난민 이동의 원인은 분쟁, 국가 실패, 국제 정치 경제의 불평등에 바탕을 둔다. (세계 경제는 정치 환경의 변화뿐만 아니라 사람들의 결정에 근거가 되는 추정에 의해서도 영향을 받는다.) 이러한 이동의 결과는 안보를 비롯하여 분쟁, 테러, 다국적주의의 확산과 연관성을 지녀왔다. 따라서 난민 문제에 대응한다는 것은 세계 질서와 정의, 그리고 국제 협력의 활성화에 대한 도전에 해당한다.

문제 해설
난민 문제의 원인, 결과, 그에 대한 대응이 세계 정치와 밀접하게 연관되어 있다는 내용이므로, 정치 환경의 변화와 사람들의 추정이 세계 경제에 영향을 준다고 언급한 ③은 글의 흐름과 관계가 없다.

구문 분석
[7행] The world's economy is influenced **not only** *by changes* in political circumstances **but also** *by assumptions* [on which people base their decisions].

▶ 「not only A but also B」 구문이 쓰였으며 A와 B는 문법상 대등한 병렬구조를 취해야 하므로 「전치사 by+명사」 구조가 이어지고 있다. assumptions를 선행사로 하는 「전치사+관계대명사」 구문으로 on which가 쓰였다. 「base A on B」는 'A의 근거를 B에 두다'라는 뜻이다.

05 정답 ③

소재 정보 과부하

전문 해석
정보화 시대에서 우리는 정보가 더 이상 희소하지 않고, 오히려 엄청나게 많은 지점에 도달했다. 정보의 양은 일부 사람들을 불안하고 긴장하도록 만들며 정보 과부하로 이어진다. 이것은 정보 공급량이 제한된 인간의 정보 처리 용량을 초과할 때 발생한다. 그러한 사람들은 읽고 이해할 것이 여전히 너무 많기 때문에 집중력의 큰 감소, 높은 스트레스, 죄책감을 느낀다. (그러나 중요한 것은 정보가 사람에게 무엇을 하느냐가 아니라 사람이 정보를 가지고 무엇을 하느냐이다.) 결과적으로, 그들은 압도당하고 정보의 흐름에 대처할 수 없다고 느낀다. 지난 20년 동안에 엄청나게 증가한 정보의 흐름은 기술에 있어서는 아무런 문제도 제기하지 않지만, 우리의 뇌는 그것에 대한 올바른 해답을 찾아내지 못했다.

문제 해설
정보의 양이 너무 많아져서 사람들이 정보 과부하를 경험한다는 내용의 글이므로, 사람이 정보를 가지고 무엇을 하느냐가 중요하다는 ③은 글의 흐름과 관계가 없다.

구문 분석

[1행] ~, we have arrived at a point [**where** information is no longer scarce; instead, it's overwhelming].

▶ where가 이끄는 관계부사절인 [ ]는 선행사인 a point를 수식한다.

[7행] ~, **it** is *not* what information does to people **that counts**, *but* what people do with information.

▶ it은 가주어이고, that counts가 진주어이다. 「not A but B」 구문은 'A가 아니라 B'의 뜻이다.

06 정답 ⑤

소재 일과 삶의 균형

전문 해석

오늘날의 기업 세계에서 인간의 잠재력을 괴롭히는 주요 문제 중의 하나는 '일과 삶의 균형'이다. 최근 기업의 풍경을 지배해 온 일과 삶의 균형에 대한 대화에서 일과 삶은 분리된 것으로 여겨진다. 이렇게 보면 우리는 일과 삶을 서로 대치시키게 되며, 이어서 드는 생각은 당신이 일만 너무 많고 삶이 매우 적거나 혹은 그 반대라는 것이다. 일이 한 인간의 삶에 있어 매우 보람 있는 일부가 될 수 있고, 많은 경우에 개인적이어야 한다는 점을 입증할 우리의 능력을 깎아내리고 있어서, 일과 삶의 균형이라는 용어 자체에 치명적인 결함이 있다. 당신은 한 사람의 삶이 갖는 개인적 부분과 직업적인 부분을 분리할 수 없다. 당신은 통찰력을 얻기 위해 그들을 분리하여 생각할 수는 있지만, 이 둘의 실질적 분리는 불가능하다. (따라서, 그것들이 서로 연관이 거의 없다는 것을 당신이 이해할 때만 일과 삶의 균형이 얻어질 수 있다.)

문제 해설

삶에서 개인적인 부분과 직업적인 부분을 분리할 수 없다는 내용의 글이므로, 이 두 가지가 서로 연관이 거의 없다는 점을 이해할 때만 일과 삶의 균형을 얻을 수 있다는 ⑤는 전체 글의 흐름에서 벗어난다.

구문 분석

[6행] ~ is fatally flawed **for** it diminishes our ability to prove [**that** work can be a richly rewarding part of a person's life and should {in many ways} be personal].

▶ for는 접속사로 '~ 때문에'라는 뜻이다. [that ~]에서 that은 prove의 목적어 역할을 하는 명사절 접속사로 쓰였으며 동사 can be와 should be의 주어는 work이다. 조동사 should와 동사 be 사이에 in many ways가 삽입되었다.

Plus Q

실질적인 분리가 불가능한 대상이므로 바로 앞 문장에서 제시된 '(한 사람의 삶이 갖는) 개인적인 부분과 직업적인 부분'이다.

유형 14 글의 순서 배열

p. 90

대표 예제 정답 ②

소재 의도적인 변화에 대한 태도의 차이

전문 해석

살면서 의도적인 변화를 거의 하지 않는 사람들이 있다. 물론, 시간이 지나면서 그들은 더 뚱뚱해지고, 주름살이 늘어나고, 그리고 머리가 희끗희끗해질 것이다. (B) 그러나 그들은 편안하고 예측 가능한 삶이 쉽다는 이유만으로 똑같은 방식의 머리를 하고, 똑같은 상표의 신발을 사고, 똑같은 아침을 먹으며 판에 박힌 일상을 고수한다. 하지만 연구와 실제 삶이 모두 보여 주듯이, 다른 많은 사람들은 실제로 중요한 변화를 한다. (A) 그들은 마라톤을 위해 훈련을 하고, 담배를 끊고, 분야를 바꾸고, 희곡을 쓰고, 기타를 배우고, 또는 살면서 전에 한 번도 춤을 춰 본 적이 없다고 해도 탱고를 배운다. 이 두 집단의 사람들 사이에 있는 차이는 무엇인가? (C) 그것은 그들의 시각이다. 변화하는 사람들은 변화가 가능한지를 묻지 않으며 변화할 수 없는 이유를 찾지 않는다. 그들은 그저 자신이 원하는 변화를 결정하고 그것을 성취하는 데 필요한 것을 한다. 항상 확고한 결심에서 생겨나는 변화는 최우선이 된다.

문제 해설

주어진 글은 의도적인 변화를 원치 않아 시간이 지나면서 더 뚱뚱해지고, 주름살이 늘어나며, 머리가 희끗희끗해지는 사람들이 있다고 언급한다. 이 뒤에는, 그러나 그들은 이를 바꾸려 시도하지 않고 판에 박힌 일상을 고수한다는 (B)의 첫 문장이 이어져야 한다. 그리고 (B)의 두 번째 문장인 다른 많은 사람들은 실제로 중요한 변화를 한다는 내용에 이어 그 변화의 예시를 보여주는 (A)가 와야 하며, (A)의 마지막 문장인 "이 두 집단의 사람들 사이에 있는 차이는 무엇인가?"라는 질문에 대한 대답인 (C)가 이어져야 하므로 글의 순서로 가장 적절한 것은 ② (B)-(A)-(C)이다.

구문 분석

[13행] People [**who** change] **do not** *question* [whether change is possible] or *look for* reasons they cannot change.

▶ [who ~]는 People를 수식하는 관계절이다. question과 look for는 둘 다 do not에 이어지는 동사이다. [whether ~]는 question의 목적어 역할을 하는 명사절이다.

어휘

intentional 의도적인 **switch** 바꾸다
take up ~을 배우다, 시작하다 **stick to** ~을 고수하다
routine 판에 박힌 일상
for no reason other than ~라는 이유만으로
predictable 예측 가능한 **accomplish** 성취하다
stem from ~에서 생기다 **firm** 확고한
job number one 최우선, 가장 중요한 것

Exercise

01 ④ 02 ② 03 ④ 04 ② 05 ③ 06 ⑤

Plus Q

03 vicious cycle
06 Rice stalks lower their heads when they are mature and corn kernels remain on the shoots even when they are ripe.

01 정답 ④

소재 성공과 성취의 차이

전문 해석

몇몇 사람에게는 성공에 역설적인 점이 있다. 대단한 성공을 이뤄낸 많은 사람이 그 성공을 항상 느끼는 것은 아니다. (C) 예를 들면, 명성을 얻은 사람은 그 명성에 자주 수반되는 고독에 대해 이야기한다. 그것은 성공과 성취가 같은 것이 아니기 때문인데, 그래도 우리는 너무 자주 한쪽을 다른 쪽으로 오인한다. (A) 성취는 목표처럼 여러분이 도달하거나 달성하는 어떤 것이다. 그것은 실체가 있고 분명히 정의되며 측정할 수 있는 어떤 것이다. 그것은 여러분이 원하는 것을 추구하고 얻을 때 온다. (B) 그에 반해서, 성공은 느낌, 곧 어떠한 상태이다. 우리는 이런 '어떠한' 상태를 넌지시 나타내기 위하여 'be' 동사를 사용하여 "그녀는 성공적이라고 느낀다. 그녀는 성공적'이다'." 라고 말한다.

문제 해설

성공을 얻은 사람이라도 항상 그것을 느끼는 것은 아니라는 주어진 글 다음에 그것의 사례로 명성을 얻은 사람이 그에 수반되는 외로움에 대해 언급한다는 (C)가 이어지고 성공과 성취가 같은 것이 아니라는 말 다음에 성취를 정의하는 (A)가 오며 그 다음에 '그에 반해서(in contrast)' 라는 연결사를 갖고 있는 (B)가 이어지는 것이 글의 흐름상 자연스럽다. 따라서 글의 순서로 가장 적절한 것은 ④ (C)-(A)-(B)이다.

구문 분석

[8행] For example, some [**who** achieve fame] talk about the loneliness [**that** often goes with it].

▶ [who ~]는 some을 수식하는 관계절이고 [that ~]는 the loneliness를 수식하는 관계절이다.

02 정답 ②

소재 수업 시간에 '공식 질문자'를 선정하는 것의 효과

전문 해석

매일, 수업 시간마다 나는 무작위로 '공식 질문자'의 칭호를 부여받는 두 명의 학생을 정한다. 이 학생들에게는 그 수업 시간 동안 최소한 하나의 질문을 해야 하는 책임이 부여된다. (B) 나의 학생 중 한 명인 Carrie는 그 날의 공식 질문자가 된 후 사무실로 나를 찾아왔다. 나는 그냥 서먹서먹한 분위기를 깨려고 쾌활하게 "이번 학기 첫 번째 '공식 질문자' 중 한 명으로 지명되어 영광이었니?"라고 물었다. (A) 그녀는 진지한 어조로, 수업이 시작될 때 내가 자기를 (공식 질문자로) 지명했을 때 매우 긴장했다고 말했다. 하지만 그 후 그 수업 동안에 그녀는 다른 강의에서 느꼈던 것과는 아주 다른 느낌이 들었다. (C) 그 강의는 다른 강의들과 비슷했지만, 그녀는 이번에 더욱 높은 의식 수준을 가져야 했고, 강의와 토론의 내용을 더 잘 알게 되었다고 말했다. 또한 결과적으로 자기가 그 수업으로부터 더 많은 것을 얻게 되었다고 인정했다.

문제 해설

수업 시간에 '공식 질문자'를 선정한다는 주어진 글 다음에 그것에 선정된 한 학생인 Carrie가 등장하는 (B)가 이어지고 '공식 질문자'로 뽑힌 것이 어떠냐는 질문에 대해 그녀가 대답하기 시작하는 (A)가 그 다음에 이어지며 똑같은 수업이라도 그런 역할이 주어지니 수업에 임하는 자신의 태도가 달라졌다는 (C)가 마지막에 이어지는 것이 글의 흐름상 자연스럽다. 따라서 글의 순서로 가장 적절한 것은 ② (B)-(A)-(C)이다.

구문 분석

[2행] These students **are assigned the responsibility** to ask at least one question during that class.

▶ are assigned라는 수동형 다음에 명사인 the responsibility가 이어지는 것은 assign이 능동형에서 「assign A B」구문으로 쓰이기 때문이며, 그것은 'A에게 B를 할당[부여]하다'라는 의미이다.

03 정답 ④

소재 회피 훈련

전문 해석

때때로 처벌이 몇 번 가해진 후에는 그것(처벌)이 계속될 필요가 없는데, 그 이유는 처벌하겠다고 단순히 위협만 해도 바라는 행동을 끌어내기에 충분하기 때문이다. (C) 당사자가 처벌 결과의 가능성을 피하는 법을 배우고 있으므로 심리학자들은 이것을 회피 훈련이라고 부른다. 일상의 많은 행동이 회피 훈련에 기인한다. 그것(회피 훈련) 때문에 여러분은 비가 올 것 같으면 젖게 되는 처벌을 피하고자 우산을 가져가고, 화상의 처벌을 피하고자 뜨거운 다리미에서 손을 멀리하는 법을 배웠다. (A) 그러나 회피 훈련이 항상 우리에게 유리하게 작용하는 것은 아니다. 예를 들어, 수학에서의 부진한 (학업) 성취로 반복해서 꾸지람을 들은 아이는 더 이상의 처벌을 면하기 위해 어려운 수학 문제를 요리조리 피하는 방법을 배우게 될 것이다. (B) 불행하게도 이러한 회피 때문에 그 아이는 자신의 수학 기술을 발전시키지 못하고, 따라서 자신이 갖춘 능력을 개선하지 못하게 되며, 그래서 악순환이 시작된 것이다. 이 (악순환의) 고리를 끊기 위해서는 회피는 수학에서의 몇 가지 긍정적인 경험을 통해 (그것을) 배우지 않았던 상태로 되돌려져야 한다.

문제 해설

처벌이 몇 번 반복되면 처벌하겠다는 위협만으로도 바라는 행동을 끌어낼 수 있다는 주어진 글 다음에는 이런 행동에 대한 최초의 정의를 내리는 (C)가 와야 하며, 이런 행동이 우리에게 유익한 점이 있다는 (C)의 두 번째 문장 다음에는 이와 대조를 이루는 (A)가 이어져야 한다. 그리고 처벌을 면하기 위해 어려운 수학 문제를 피하는 법을 배우게 되는 한 아이(a child)에 대한 (A)의 두 번째 문장 다음에 그 아이(the child)가 이로 인해 겪게 되는 수학 공부의 악순환과 그 악순환의 해결 방법이 제시된 (B)가 와야 한다. 따라서 글의 순서로 가장 적절한 것은 ④ (C)-(A)-(B)이다.

구문 분석

[4행] For instance, a child [**who** has been repeatedly criticized for poor performance on math] may learn to dodge difficult math problems **in order to** avoid further punishment.

▶ [who ~]는 a child를 수식하는 관계절이다. in order to는 '~하기 위해서'라는 의미이다.

Plus Q

더 많은 살충제를 쓸수록 벌레들이 더 저항력을 갖게 되고 그래서 심지어 더 많은 살충제를 써야 한다. 그것이 악순환이다.

04 정답 ②

소재 회사에 대한 정보 수집

전문 해석

어느 최고 금융 분석가가 인터넷을 이용해서 자기가 추적하고 있던 회사인 Waste Management Incorporated (WMI)에 관한 어떤 새로운 소식을 알아냈다. (B) 여러 투자 채팅방을 방문함으로써, 그 분석가는 Waste Management의 직원들이 연이은 혼란 상태에 관해 드러내고 있다는 것을 알게 되었는데, 많은 것이 그 회사의 서로 다른 단위에서 서로 호환되지 않는 컴퓨터 시스템 탓이었다. (A) 일부 고객들은 여러 장의 청구서를 받고 있었고 다른 고객들은 전혀 청구서를 받고 있지 않았다. 너무 자주 쓰레기가 정시에 수거되고 있지 않았다. 그 분석가는 채팅방 게시물을 출발점으로 이용했다. 그는 직원 다수와 이메일 접촉을 전개했고 자신의 정보 수집에 추가했다. (C) 다른 문제뿐만 아니라 회사 전체의 부적절한 시스템을 보여주는 분명한 증거로 무장한 채 그 분석가는 자기 고객들에게 WMI에 뭔가 썩은 냄새가 난다고 충고했다. 그 회사를 멀리 했던 투자자들은 몇 개월 후에 WMI의 주가가 폭락했을 때 안도의 한숨을 쉬었다.

문제 해설

어느 금융 분석가가 인터넷을 통해 WMI라는 회사에 관한 정보를 캐냈다는 주어진 글 다음에 그 회사 직원들이 회사의 혼란에 대해 채팅방에 드러내고 있는데 그 이유가 서로 호환되지 않는 컴퓨터 때문이라는 (B)가 이어지고 그 결과로 고객들에게 청구서가 잘못 가거나 쓰레기 수거가 정시에 이루어지지 않는다는 내용이 있는 (A)가 그 다음에 이어지며 마지막으로 그가 자기 고객들에게 그 회사를 멀리 하라고 권고했고 실제로 그 회사의 주가가 폭락했다는 (C)가 이어지는 것이 글의 흐름상 자연스럽다. 따라서 글의 순서로 가장 적절한 것은 ② (B)-(A)-(C)이다.

구문 분석

[12행] [**Armed** with clear evidence suggesting

inadequate firmwide systems, as well as other problems], **the analyst** advised his clients that something smelled rotten at WMI.

▶ [Armed ~]는 Being이 생략된 분사구문이며 의미상의 주어는 주절의 주어인 the analyst이다.

05 정답 ③

소재 토테미즘

전문 해석

'totem'이라는 단어는 캐나다의 Algonquin 사람인 Ojibwa에게서 나온 것이다. (B) 'totem'이라는 단어가 유래한 'ototeman'이라는 표현은 대략 '그는 나의 친척이다'라는 의미이고 종족 외 결혼으로 맺어진 집단의 구성원임을 나타낸다. Ojibwa 부족은 동물 종의 이름을 따서 사람들은 'makwa nth-totem'('나의 부족은 곰이다')라고 말할 수 있었다. (C) 그 후의 연구자들은 다른 곳에서의 비슷한 현상에 대해 문자 그대로 'totemism'이라는 용어를 적용했고 그것은 사회 집단과 물질적 대상의 하나 또는 더 많은 집단, 구체적으로 동물과 식물 사이에 특별한 관계가 존재한다고 여겨지는 어떤 상황을 가리키면서 일반적인 개념으로 사용하게 되었다. (A) 흔히 그 관계는 의식(儀式)적인 것이고 그 동물은 신성하게 여겨지고 그것과 관련된 구체적인 금기사항이 있으며 그 집단의 구성원들은 스스로 그 토템인 생물 종의 후손이라고 믿을 정도이기도 하다.

문제 해설

토템의 어원적인 의미를 소개하는 (B)가 그 단어가 Ojibwa 부족에게서 나온 말이라는 주어진 글 다음에 오고 그런 현상에 대해 연구자들이 토테미즘이라는 용어를 적용했다는 (C)가 그 다음에 이어지며, 토템으로 여겨지는 동물과 식물에 대해 특별한 관계가 있었다는 (C)의 내용 다음에 그것을 신성시하고 그 토템의 후손이라고까지 생각했다는 (A)가 마지막에 이어지는 것이 글의 흐름상 자연스럽다. 따라서 글의 순서로 가장 적절한 것은 ③ (B)-(C)-(A)이다.

구문 분석

[3행] Frequently [the relationship is a ritual one], [the animal is considered sacred, and there are specific taboos associated with it], and [the members of the group may even believe themselves to be descended from the totemic species].

▶ 각각의 문장인 세 개의 [ ]가 and로 이어지면서 서로 병렬구조를 이루고 있다.

06 정답 ⑤

소재 돌연변이종인 벼와 옥수수

전문 해석

벼는 익었을 때 자기의 머리를 낮추고 옥수수 알은 익었을 때조차 햇가지에 매달려 있다. (C) 이것은 이상하게 보이지 않을지도 모르지만 사실은 이런 유형의 쌀과 옥수수는 아마 자연에서 살아남지 못할 것이다. 보통의 경우에는 그것이 익었을 때 씨는 발아하기 위해 땅으로 떨어져야 한다. (B) 그러나 쌀과 옥수수는 돌연변이이고 편리하고 효율적인 수확을 위해 씨가 붙어 있도록 변화되었다. 인간들은 계속적으로 품종 개량 기술을 통해 이런 현상이 발생하도록 그런 변종을 선택하고 키웠다. (A) 이런 변종 씨앗은 의도적으로 확산되었고 그것은 그 식물이 자연에서 발견되지 않는, 씨앗을 원래 상태대로 유지하도록 품종 개량된 인위적인 종이 되었다는 것을 의미한다. 이런 재배 변종 식물을 키움으로써 가장 선호되는 씨앗이 생산된다.

문제 해설

다 익었는데도 벼와 옥수수의 낟알이 떨어지지 않고 있는 것을 묘사한 주어진 글 다음에 사실 그것이 일반적인 자연 현상이 아니라고 언급한 (C)가 이어지고, 그렇게 된 것은 수확이 편하라고 인간이 그런 변종을 선택하고 키워왔기 때문이라고 설명한 (B)가 그 다음에 이어지며 마지막으로 이런 변종 씨앗(These mutant seeds)이라고 언급하면서 그것이 만들어진 과정을 상술하는 (A)가 이어지는 것이 글의 흐름상 자연스럽다. 따라서 글의 순서로 가장 적절한 것은 ⑤ (C)-(B)-(A)이다.

구문 분석

[3행] These mutant seeds have been spread intentionally, **which** means that the plants have become artificial species [**not found** in nature], having been bred to keep their seeds intact.

▶ which는 앞 문장 내용을 선행사로 하는 계속적 용법의 관계대명사로 쓰였다. [not found ~]는 artificial species를 수식한다.

Plus Q

This는 주어진 글의 '벼는 익었을 때 자기의 머리를 낮추고 옥수수 알은 익었을 때조차 햇가지에 매달려 있다'는 내용을 가리킨다. 이 글은 벼와 옥수수가 그렇게 되는 이유가 인간이 수확을 위해 인위적으로 만든 품종이어서 그렇다는 것을 설명하는 내용이다.

유형 15 문장 삽입

p. 96

대표 예제

정답 ⑤

소재 개들이 감각을 사용하는 방식

전문 해석

여러분이 어렸고 어른들은 무한한 힘을 가졌다고 상상하던 때를 기억하는가? 분명 자동차를 운전하고, 주스 용기를 열고, 개수대에 손이 닿을 수 있는 사람은 비를 그치게 할 수 있을 것이었다. 개와 냄새를 맡는 그들의 능력에 관해서도 우리는 똑같은 기대를 갖고 있다고 나는 생각한다. 그들이 코를 사용하는 능력이 아주 뛰어나서 우리는 그들이 어느 때건 뭐든지 냄새를 맡을 수 있다고 추정한다. 그렇지만 개들은 다른 감각도 사용하고, 인간과 개 양쪽 모두의 뇌는 한 번에 한 가지 감각을 증강하는 경향이 있다. 많은 주인들은 머리 모양을 새로 하거나 새 코트를 입고 집에 돌아왔을 때, 개가 달려든 적이 있다. 낯선 검은 윤곽이 집으로 밀고 들어오는 것을 보고 깜짝 놀라, 이 개들은 코 대신 눈을 사용하고 있었다. 그들의 코가 뛰어날 수 있지만, 늘 켜져 있는[작동되는] 것은 아니다.

문제 해설

주어진 문장은 개가 주인에게 달려든 이유를 설명하는 내용이므로, 주인이 새로운 머리 모양이나 새로운 코트를 입고 나타났다가 개가 달려든 적이 있다는 내용 다음에 이어져야 자연스럽다. 따라서 주어진 문장이 들어가기에 가장 적절한 곳은 ⑤이다.

구문 분석

[5행] Surely someone [**who** could *drive* the car, *open* the juice container, and *reach* the sink] could make it stop raining.

▶ [who ~]는 관계사절로 주어인 someone을 수식하고 있으며, 관계절 내의 동사인 drive, open, reach는 could에 이어지며 병렬을 이루고 있다.

어휘

silhouette 검은 윤곽, 실루엣 **infinite** 무한한
expectation 기대 **with respect to** ~에 관하여
assume 추정하다 **intensify** 증강하다
snap at ~에 달려들다, ~을 덥석 물려하다
hairdo 머리 모양 **remarkable** 뛰어난, 놀라운
switch on (스위치를) 켜다

Exercise

01 ⑤ 02 ④ 03 ④ 04 ③ 05 ③ 06 ③

Plus Q

03 exhausted
06 survive

01

정답 ⑤

소재 한 집단 내의 다른 종류의 은어들

전문 해석

언어학자들에게 있어서 은어를 파악하는 것은 실제로 상당히 어려운 일이다. 학교나 마을에서 사용하는 지역 은어가 있을 것이고, 그것이 무엇인지를 나에게 말해 주지 않으면 그것에 대해 알아낼 방법이 없다. 사실상, 여러분이 사는 지역에는 몇 가지 다른 종류의 은어가 아마 있을 것이다. 초등학교에서 아이들이 사용하는 은어는 중등학교에서 사용되는 것과 다를 가능성이 있다. 만약 마을에 여러 학교가 있다면, 각각의 학교에서 들리는 은어의 종류가 흔히 다르다. 그리고 심지어 한 학교 내에서 서로 다르게 사용되는 어휘들도 있을 수 있다. 나는 이전에 고등학교 졸업반 학생의 한 집단과 일했는데, 그 학생들은 자신들의 학교에서 사용되는 은어를 주의 깊게 들었다. 그들은 1학년 학생들이 사용하는 은어가 자신들의 것과 매우 다르다는 것을 발견했다.

문제 해설

주어진 문장은 필자가 일한 고등학교 졸업반 학생들이 자신들의 학교에서 사용되는 은어를 주의 깊게 들었다는 내용이다. 이 문장 뒤에는 주의 깊게 들은 내용의 결과가 나와야 하므로 주어진 문장이 들어가기에 가장 적절한 곳은 ⑤이다.

구문 분석

[6행] The slang (S) [**that** kids use in primary school] is (V) likely to be different from what is used in secondary school.

▶ [that ~]는 관계절로 문장의 주어인 The slang을 수식하고 있으며 동사는 is이다.

[10행] They found {that the slang (S′) [**used** by first-year students] was (V′) very different from their own}.

▶ [used ~]는 분사구로 that절의 주어인 the slang을 수식하고 있으며 that절의 동사는 was이다.

02 정답 ④

소재 남성들이 몸단장하는 이유

전문 해석

남성 몸단장 제품의 인기가 크게 상승해왔다. 전 세계의 남성들은 화장품에서 성형 수술에 이르는 모든 것에 수십억 달러의 돈을 쓰고 있다. 남성들이 몸단장하는 이유에 관해 전문가들은 남성들이 그들의 외모를 사회적 성공의 중요한 요소로 간주한다고 이야기한다. 나아가 전문가들은 다양한 나라의 그런 사례를 남성들의 몸단장 역사에서 찾아보았다. 예를 들면, 금발로 염색을 하는 것은 고대 로마 남성들 사이에서는 흔한 관행이었는데, 이는 그들이 금발이 더 젊어 보이게 한다고 믿었기 때문이었다. 마찬가지로, 고대 이집트 남성들은 정기적으로 몸의 털을 깎았고 피부에 다양한 화장품을 발랐다. 외모가 과거에 남성들에게 중요했으며 현재의 남성들에게도 확실히 그렇다고 말할 수 있다.

문제 해설

주어진 문장은 고대 로마 남성들이 금발로 염색을 하는 것이 흔한 관행이었다는 내용을 예로 들고 있으므로 남성들의 몸단장 사례를 역사 속에서 찾아볼 수 있다는 내용 다음에 이어져야 자연스럽다. 따라서 주어진 문장이 들어가기에 가장 적절한 곳은 ④이다.

구문 분석

[5행] Men all over the world are **spending** billions of dollars **on** everything [from cosmetics to plastic surgery].

▶ 「spend+돈/시간+on」 구문이 사용되었으며, '~에 돈/시간을 쓰다'의 의미이다. [ ]로 표시된 부분은 everything을 수식하고 있다.

03 정답 ④

소재 지구의 환경 수용력에 대한 다양한 관점

전문 해석

우리는 똑같은 생태 공간 속에서 그 공간의 자원을 소비하며 우리의 생활 수준을 유지할 수 있을까? 이 질문은 우리가 유가는 치솟고 인간의 탄소 발자국은 끊임없이 커지는 시대에 살고 있기 때문에 특히 적절하다. 어떤 이들은 우리가 지구의 유한한 환경 수용력을 거의 다 써버렸기 때문에 우리가 이미 한계점에 이르러 있다고 주장한다. 그러나 혁신과 문화적인 변화가 지구의 수용력을 확장할 수도 있다는 것이 가능하다. 세계 경제가 점점 더 태양 에너지와 수소 에너지 같은 '녹색'의 재생 가능한 산업을 바라보고 있으므로 우리는 이미 이것을 목격하고 있다. 하지만, 많은 이들이 우리가 결국 자원의 유한한 특성과의 갈등이 불가피한 지점에 도달하게 될 것이라 믿는다. 그것은 생존이 궁극적으로 인구를 환경 수용력 아래로 낮추는 것에 의해 결정될 수 있다는 것을 의미한다. 그렇지 않으면 인구 통제 없이 자원에 대한 수요가 결국 그것을 제공할 생태계의 능력을 초과할 것이다.

문제 해설

주어진 문장은 재생 가능한 에너지를 통해 지구의 수용력을 늘릴 수 있다는 ④의 앞에 나온 내용과 반대되는 내용이다. 그리고 ④의 다음에 나오는 That means의 That이 가리키는 것이 바로 주어진 문장의 내용이다. 따라서 주어진 문장이 들어가기에 가장 적절한 곳은 ④이다.

오답 풀이

주어진 문장이 ③에 들어갈 수 없는 이유는 ③의 뒤의 문장 속에 있는 this가 문맥상 innovations and cultural changes can expand Earth's capacity를 가리켜야 하므로 주어진 문장은 ③에 들어갈 수 없다.

구문 분석

[9행] We are already seeing this **as** the world economies are increasingly looking at "green," renewable industries like solar and hydrogen energy.

▶ as는 '이유'를 나타내는 접속사로 부사절을 이끌고 있다.

Plus Q

- 그녀는 잠깐만 걸어도 기진맥진했다.
- 3년 안에 그들은 자신들의 자원을 다 써버렸다.

exhaust는 '기진맥진하게 하다, ~을 다 써버리다'의 의미를 가지고 있다.

04 정답 ③

소재 직장 동료의 실수

전문 해석

다른 경우라면 유능했을 동료가 중요한 잠재적 거래를 망쳐 놓았다고 가정해보자. 여러분의 첫 경향은 화나고, 실망하고, 좌절이 드러나는 메모나 이메일을 급히 보내는 것일지도 모른다. 다시 잘 생각해 보고서 여러분은 수석 부사장이 어쩌다 복사본을 보면 여러분 동료의 업무 수행이 심각하게 문제가 되거나 그것보다 안 좋은 상황에 처하게 될 것이라고 걱정하게 된다. 여러분은 그것을 원하지는 않을 것이므로 글을 쓰는 대신에 개인적인 논의가 여러분에게 오히려 적합할 것이라고 결정을 내린다. 그 불쌍한 영혼은 여전히 여러분의 말투와 얼굴 표정을 통해 여러분이 느끼는 바를 인지할 수 있을 것이다. 게다가, 여러분이 느끼는 강한 실망은 표현이 될 것이지만 일이 가끔씩 잘못되기도 한다는 것을 여러분이 이해한다는 점도 또한 표현이 될 것이다. 개인적인 감정은 없고 단지 여러분의 요점을 전달하도록 해주지만 듣는 사람으로 하여금 여러분이 그 사람을 싫어하지 않는다는 것을 알게 해주는 친근한 간단한 대화일 뿐이라고 여러분은 말할 수 있을 것이다.

문제 해설

주어진 문장의 that은 ③의 바로 앞 문장인 수석 부사장이 동료가 잘못한 것을 알게 되어 동료가 심각한 곤경에 처하는 내용을 가리키므로 주어진 문장이 들어가기에 가장 적절한 곳은 ③이다.

구문 분석

[9행] Moreover, the strong disappointment [**you feel**] will be expressed, but **so** too **will your understanding** {**that** occasionally things go wrong}.

▶ [you feel]이 the strong disappointment를 수식하고 있다. 「so+will+주어 ~」는 '~도 역시 마찬가지이다'라는 의미이다. {that ~}는 동격을 나타낸다.

05 정답 ③

소재 근대 시대에 강조되어진 품성

전문 해석

내세에 있을 곳을 확보하는 데 개인적인 관심이 더 집중되었던 중세 시대에는, 선행은 모든 훌륭한 기독교인이 열망하던 것이었다. 덕이 높은 삶을 살고 아주 선하게 되는 것이 영원한 구원을 보장해 주었던 것이다. 사회가 점차로 생산 지향적이 되어가면서 근대 시대에는, 선행은 가장자리로 표류해가기 시작했다. 결국 그것은 유산계급에 의해 품성으로 대체되었다. 19세기경에 '품성'은 영어 어휘에서 가장 중요한 묘사적인 단어들 중 하나가 되었다. '품성'이라는 말은 근면, 부지런함, 검소, 청렴 등과 관련을 가지게 되었다. 좋은 품성을 가진 사람이라는 것은 유산계급의 남녀에게 표할 수 있는 최고의 칭찬이었다.

문제 해설

주어진 문장은 결국 선행이 유산계급에 의해 품성으로 대체되었다는 내용이다. 이 문장의 it은 virtue를 가리키며, 이 문장 속에 있는 Eventually와 어울리기 위해서는 앞에 선행의 지위가 흔들리기 시작했다는 내용이 와야 한다. 따라서 주어진 문장이 들어가기에 가장 적절한 곳은 ③이다.

구문 분석

[4행] To lead a virtuous life and to **be of good virtue** assured eternal salvation.

▶ 「of+추상명사」는 형용사의 역할을 한다. 따라서 of good virtue는 '아주 선한'의 의미가 된다.

06 정답 ③

소재 조림지가 숲의 생태계에 미치는 영향

전문 해석

숲의 손실 속도는 아프리카, 라틴 아메리카, 캐리비언 지역과 많은 아시아 지역에서 특히 높다. 보고에 따르면, 예외 지역은 중국과 인도인데, 이곳에서는 숲 조림지에 대한 많은 투자가 자료를 왜곡해 현재 진행 중인 천연 숲의 손실 속도를 숨긴다. 그러나, 산업 목재 조림지는 실제 숲과는 아주 다르다. 조림지들의 목표는 실제 숲이 제공하는 많은 다른 서비스, 자원과 서식지에 대한 고려를 거의 혹은 전혀 하지 않으면서 나무 제품을 생산하는 것이다. 이러한 목적을 위해 그것들(조림지들)은 대개 열심히 관리되고, 고르게 공간이 띄워지며, 가장 높은 나무 수확량을 내는 수입종으로 이루어진 단일 작물이 재배되는 들판이다. 그러한 조림지는 생물학적 다양성, 병에 대한 저항 혹은 사람들과 동물들이 생존을 위해 의존하는 목재가 아닌 많은 다른 숲의 생산물의 제공에 도움이 되지 못한다. 나무 조림지는 일반적으로 숲에 사는 종들 중 겨우 10퍼센트만을 부양할 수가 있어서 '녹색 사막'으로 가장 잘 묘사된다!

문제 해설

주어진 문장은 조림지들의 목표를 기술하고 있다. 그러므로 이 문장의 뒤에는 이 목표를 이루기 위해 행해지는 내용들이 나오는 것이 글의 흐름상 자연스러우므로 주어진 문장이 들어가기에 가장 적절한 곳은 ③이다.

오답 풀이

주어진 문장이 들어갈 위치를 파악할 때 단순히 어휘가 중복되는 것을 힌트로 삼아서 들어갈 위치를 정해서는 안 된다. 예를 들면, 주어진 문장의 서두에 나오는 plantations라는 단어와 ④의 바로 뒤 문장의 앞부분에 나오는 Such plantations를 기계적으로 연결하려고 해서는 안 된다.

구문 분석

[1행] The goal of plantations is to produce wood products, with little or no regard **to** *the many other services, resources,* and *habitat* [**that** real forests provide].

▶ the many other services, resources, habitat가 전

치사 to를 공유하여 and에 의해 병렬을 이루고 있으며, [that ~] 관계절의 수식을 받고 있다.

Plus Q

산업 목재를 생산하는 조림지는 그 숲에 사는 종들이 생존하는 데 필요한 충분한 자원을 제공하지 못한다.

나무 조림지는 일반적으로 숲에 사는 종들의 10퍼센트만 부양할 수 있다고 했으므로 숲에 사는 종들이 생존하는 데 충분한 자원을 제공하지 못한다고 볼 수 있다. 본문에는 명사인 survival이 나와 있으므로 동사형인 survive를 빈칸에 넣는 것이 적절하다.

유형 16 요약문 완성

p. 102

대표 예제

정답 ②

소재 실적 평가에서 고려해야 할 요인들

전문 해석

실적은 개인의 통제 범위를 벗어난 실적에 미친 영향보다는 평가를 받는 개인의 통제 하에 있는 것의 측면에서 판단되어야 한다. 판단을 받고 있는 모든 사람의 실적을 억제하는, 때로는 경제적 성격을 띠는, 광범위한, 영향을 미치는 요인이 있을 수 있다. 한 가지 예가 매출액에 관한 것이다. 일반적인 경제적 경기 침체가 있어서 상품이나 서비스가 이전 해와 동일한 빈도로 구매되지 않고 있다면, 매출액이 예를 들어 평균 15%만큼 감소될 수 있다. 그렇다면 이 15%(사실은 −15%) 수치는 '평균' 실적을 나타낼 것이다. 아마도 그 해의 가장 우수한 영업사원은 이전 해에 비해서 매출액이 3%만 감소했을 것이다. 따라서 이러한 상황에서 '훌륭한' 실적이란 어떤 평균 혹은 기준 집단과 비교했을 때 더 적은 양의 감소를 말한다.

→ 실적 평가에 있어서 우리는 수치에만 의존하기보다는 개인의 실적에 영향을 미치는 상황적 요인들을 고려해야 한다.

문제 해설

개인의 실적을 평가할 때에 단순히 그 수치만을 보기보다는 업무를 수행한 당시의 상황을 고려하여 평가해야 한다는 내용의 글이므로 요약문의 빈칸 (A), (B)에는 각각 contextual(상황적인)과 rely on(의존하다)이 들어가는 것이 가장 적절하다.

① 상황적인 – 제쳐놓다
③ 통제할 수 있는 – 제쳐놓다
④ 긍정적인 – 무시하다
⑤ 긍정적인 – 의존하다

구문 분석

[4행] There can be broad, influential factors, [sometimes of an economic nature], [that hold down the performance of everyone being judged].

▶ 첫 번째 [ ]로 표시된 부분은 전치사구로 broad, influential factors를 수식하며, 두 번째 [ ]로 표시된 부분은 관계대명사절로 역시 broad, influential factors를 수식한다.

어휘

performance 실적, 업무 수행 **in terms of** ~의 면에서
evaluate 평가하다 **influential** 영향을 미치는
factor 요인 **hold down** ~을 억제하다
downturn (경기) 침체 **purchase** 구매하다
frequency 빈도 **previous** 이전의
drop 감소, 하락 **norm group** 기준 집단, 준거 집단

Exercise

01 ① 02 ① 03 ② 04 ①

Plus Q

02 If the fig trees should disappear
04 their colleagues

01

정답 ①

소재 학습 내용을 효과적으로 외우는 방법

전문 해석

내가 8학년이었을 때, 우리는 지리 시간에 경도와 위도를 공부하고 있었다. 일주일 동안 매일 우리는 쪽지시험을 보았는데, 나는 계속해서 경도와 위도를 혼동했다. 나는 집에 가서 거의 울 뻔했는데, 왜냐하면 너무도 좌절하고 창피해서 그 말들을 제대로 기억할 수 없었기 때문이었다. 나는 그 단어들을 바라보고 바라보다가, 마침내 무엇을 해야 할지를 갑자기 알게 되었다. longitude(경도)에서 'n'을 보면, 그것은 'north(북쪽)'라는 어휘를 떠올리게 할 것이

라고 나는 중얼거렸다. 그래서 경도선은 북에서 남으로 간다고 기억하는 것이 쉬워질 거야. 그것은 효과가 있었고, 나는 다음 쪽지시험에서, 그리고 다음 번에서, 그리고 시험에서도 그것들을 전부 맞히었다.

→ 위 이야기는 여러분이 배우는 것을 이미 알고 있는 것과 관련지어 생각하는 것이 학습 내용을 외우는 데 도움이 된다는 것을 시사한다.

문제 해설

필자가 8학년이었을 때의 한 지리 시간에 longitude(경도)에서 'n'을 보고, 'north(북쪽)'라는 어휘를 떠오르게 하는 방법을 통해 그것을 기억했다는 일화이므로 빈칸 (A), (B)에는 각각 associating(관련지어 생각하는 것)과 memorize(외우다)가 들어가는 것이 가장 적절하다.

② 관련지어 생각하는 것 – 출판하다
③ 제시하는 것 – 출판하다
④ 대체하는 것 – 평가하다
⑤ 대체하는 것 – 외우다

구문 분석

[3행] I went home and almost cried because I was **so** frustrated and embarrassed **that** I couldn't keep them straight in my mind.

▶ 「so+형용사/부사+that...」 구문이 사용되었으며, '너무 ~해서 …하다'라는 의미이다.

02 정답 ①

소재 생태계를 보존해주는 기능을 하는 무화과나무

전문 해석

특정 종들은 다른 종들보다 자신들의 생태계 유지에 더 결정적이다. 그러한 종들은 핵심종이라 불리며 전체 생태계의 특성과 구조를 결정하는 데에 매우 중요하다. 다른 종들이 핵심종에 의존하거나 크게 영향을 받는다는 사실은 핵심종이 제거되었을 때 드러난다. 바로 이런 관점에서 우리는 무화과나무에 주의를 기울여야 한다. 서로 다른 종의 무화과나무들이 열대우림에서는 핵심종일 수 있다. 무화과가 집단으로 지속적인 과실의 수확을 창출하지만, 열대우림의 과실을 먹는 원숭이, 새, 박쥐, 그리고 다른 척추동물들은 일반적으로 자신들의 먹이에서 많은 양의 무화과를 먹지 않는다. 그러나 한 해 중 다른 과실들이 덜 풍부한 시기 동안에 무화과나무는 과실을 먹는 척추동물을 먹여 살리는 데 중요해진다. 무화과나무가 사라지면 과실을 먹는 척추동물들이 대부분 없어질 것이다. 그러한 열대우림 생태계에서 무화과나무를 보호하는 것은 원숭이, 새, 박쥐, 그리고 다른 척추동물들의 생존 가능성을 높여 주기 때문에 중요한 보존 목표이다.

→ 열대우림의 핵심종으로서 무화과나무는 다른 과실들이 불충분할 때 과실을 먹는 동물들의 생존을 유지해 주며, 그리하여 그들의 생태계를 보존해 준다.

문제 해설

무화과나무가 다른 과실이 덜 풍부할 때 과실을 먹는 척추동물의 생존에 중요한 역할을 하여 생태계 보존에 이바지한다는 내용의 글이다. 따라서 요약문의 빈칸 (A), (B)에는 각각 insufficient(불충분한)와 preserve(보존하다)가 들어가는 것이 가장 적절하다.

② 불충분한 – 창조하다
③ 독이 있는 – 정화하다
④ 독이 있는 – 모양을 새로 만들다
⑤ 풍부한 – 깨끗하게 하다

오답 풀이

무화과나무가 지속적인 과실의 수확을 창출한다는 내용을 보고 기계적으로 (A)에 들어갈 단어를 abundant(풍부한)로 고르지 않도록 주의한다. 또한 무화과나무가 생태계를 위해 하는 일은 새, 박쥐, 그리고 다른 척추동물들의 생존 가능성을 높여주는 일이므로 생태계를 깨끗하게 해주는 일과는 관련이 없음에 유의한다.

구문 분석

[3행] The fact [**that** other species *depend* on or *are* greatly *affected* by the keystone species] is revealed when the keystone species is removed.

▶ [that ~]는 The fact를 설명해 주는 동격절이며, 동격절 안에서 depend와 are affected가 주어인 other species를 공유하며 병렬을 이루고 있다.

Plus Q

「If+주어+should+동사원형 ~」의 가정법 구문에서 If가 생략될 경우 「Should+주어+동사원형」의 어순을 취한다.

03 정답 ②

소재 남성다움에 대한 인식

전문 해석

요즈음 남성다움이라는 단어를 언급하면 사람들은 아마도 여러분을 킥킥대는 웃음으로 맞이할 것이다. 오늘날 많은 사람들은 남성다움을 소파에 앉아서 맥주를 마시며 중요한 경기를 관람하는 남성의 만화와 같은 이미지와 연관시킨다. 혹은 그들은 남성다움을 전혀 중요하게 생각하지 않을 확률 또한 못지않게 높다. 여러분이 '남성다움'에 대해서 언급할 때 그들이 무슨 이미지를 염두에 두고 있든지 간에, 그것은 그저 웃음거리일 뿐이고 아마도 미덕과는 아무 관계가 없을 것이다. 그러나 여러분이 서구식 사고에 관한 기록을 살펴보면 남성다움에 관한 이러한 천박한 개념이 비교적 새로운 것임을 발견하게 될 것이다. 2,000년 동안 세계의 위대한 사상가들 중 상당수가 남성다움이라는 주제를 조사했으며 그것을 어리석은 것으로 그려내지 않았다. 대신 그들은 남성다움을 남성의 일생에서 표현되는 것처럼 미덕의 정점으로 간주했다. 남성다움은 그 자체로 미덕으로 간주되었으며 그것의 달성을 적극적으로 추구해야 했다.

→ 요즘에는 비록 남성다움이 일반적으로 부정적인 것으로 묘사되긴 하지만, (예전에는) 추구할 가치가 있는 것으로 여겨졌었다.

문제 해설

남성다움을 언급하면 킥킥거리고, 웃음거리 정도로 생각하는 요즘과는 달리 예전에는 미덕의 정점으로 사람들이 남성다움을 추구하려고 했다는 내용이므로 빈칸 (A), (B)에는 각각 negative(부정적인)와 pursuing(추구할)이 들어가는 것이 가장 적절하다.

① 부정적인 – 탈출할
③ 용인되는 – 추구할
④ 용인되는 – 보고할
⑤ 비교적인 – 탈출할

구문 분석

[10행] Instead, they **considered** it **as** the culmination of the virtues **as** expressed in the life of a man.

▶ 「consider A as B(A를 B라고 여기다, 간주하다)」 표현을 활용한 구문이다. 뒤에 나오는 as 뒤에는 it was가 생략되었으며, 이때 as는 접속사로서 '~한 것처럼'의 의미이다.

04 정답 ①

소재 언어를 통한 공유에 의해 얻게 되는 과학적 지식

전문 해석

과학이 물질적인 것들과 물리적인 관계에 관한 것이고, 기술과 인공물로 대표된다고 할지라도 그것은 말과 공식들을 통해 공유된다. 예를 들어, 어떠한 생물학자가 진화 이론에 대해 알고 있는 거의 모든 것은 물질적인 증거를 관찰함으로써 온 것이 아니고 언어를 통해서 다른 생물학자들과 의사소통을 함으로써 온 것이다. 화학자들에게 주기율표에 대해 설명해달라고 요청하면, 그들은 다른 화학자들로부터 받은 원소들의 이름을 이용할 것이다. 천문학자들과 물리학자들은 '초신성'에 대해 알고 있다. 그러나 그들이 알고 있는 것은 자신들의 망원경을 통해서 본 것의 결과일 뿐만 아니라 그들의 동료들이 그들의 마음대로 그 데이터를 어떻게 설명하려고 했는지를 읽고 들은 것에서 나온 결과이다.

→ 과학적 지식의 대부분은 과학자의 개별적인 과학적 경험에 의한 것이 아니라 자신이 알고 있는 것을 언어를 통해 공유함으로써 얻어진 것이다.

문제 해설

과학에 대한 지식의 대부분은 과학자 자신이 개별적으로 관찰함으로써가 아니라 언어를 통해 다른 동료들과 공유함으로써 얻어진다는 내용의 글이다. 따라서 빈칸 (A), (B)에는 각각 individual(개별적인)과 sharing(공유함)이 들어가는 것이 가장 적절하다.

② 개별적인 – 주장함으로써
③ 필수적인 – 공유함으로써
④ 예기치 않은 – 주장함으로써
⑤ 예기치 않은 – 명시함으로써

오답 풀이

글의 핵심적인 내용은 과학적 지식의 대부분은 과학자의 개별적인 경험에 의해서가 아니라, 언어를 통해 다른 과학자들의 업적을 공유하는 과정을 통해 이루어진다는 것이다. 따라서 이러한 핵심적인 내용과 관련이 없는 unexpected나 essential과 같은 선택지를 고르지 않도록 주의한다.

구문 분석

[8행] ~ however, what they know is **not just** the result [of looking through their telescopes] **but** [of reading and hearing how their colleagues have tried to explain the data at their disposal].

▶ 「not just A but (also) B」 구문으로 의미는 'A뿐만 아니라 B도'이다. 두 개의 [ ]로 표시된 부분은 result를 공유하며 병렬을 이루고 있다.

Plus Q

지시대명사가 가리키는 것은 같은 문장의 바로 앞부분이나 앞 문장 속에 있기 마련이다. 여기서 their가 가리키는 것은 how가 이끄는 절 속에 있는 their colleagues이다.

유형 17 장문 독해(1) 일반 장문

p. 108

대표 예제

정답 01 ① 02 ②

소재 기초과학의 가치

전문 해석

우리는 아무런 알려진 실용적 가치를 지니지 않은 과학을 기초과학 혹은 기초연구로 기술할 수 있다. 목성과 같은 세계에 대한 우리의 탐사는 기초과학으로 불릴 것이며, 기초과학은 아무런 알려진 실용적 용도를 지니지 않으므로 노력과 비용을 들일만한 가치가 없다고 주장하기 쉽다. 물론, 문제는 우리가 어떤 지식을 얻을 때까지는 그 지식이 쓸모가 있을 것인지를 알아낼 방법이 우리에게 없다는 것이다. 19세기 중반에, Victoria 여왕이 물리학자인 Michael Faraday에게 전기와 자성에 관한 그의 실험이 무슨 도움이 되느냐고 물었다고 한다. 그는 대답하기를, "여왕님, 아기는 무슨 도움이 됩니까?"라고 했다. 물론, Faraday의 실험은 전자 시대의 시작이 되었다. 우리의 세상을 채우고 있는 많은 과학적 지식의 실용적 사용, 이를 테면 트랜지스터, 백신, 플라스틱은 기초연구로 시작되었다. 기초과학 연구는 기술과 공학에서 문제점을 해결하기 위해서 사용하는 원료를 제공한다.
기초과학 연구는 또 다른 한 가지 중요한 용도를 지니고 있는데, 그것은 매우 중요한 것이어서 그것을 단순히 기능적인 것으로 언급하는 것은 모욕적인 말처럼 들린다. 과학은 자연을 연구하는 학문이며, 우리가 자연이 어떻게 작용하는지에 대해 더 많이 학습함에 따라 우리는 이 우주 안에서의 우리의 존재가 우리에게 무엇을 의미하는지에 대해 더 많은 것을 알게 된다. 외부 세계에 대한 우주탐사기로부터 우리가 얻는 비실용적인 지식으로 보이는 것이 우리의 행성에 대해 우리에게 알려주고 자연의 체계 안에서의 우리 자신의 역할에 대해 알려준다. 과학은 우리가 어디에 있으며 우리가 무엇인지 우리에게 말해주며, 그러한 지식은 가치를 넘어서는 것이다.

문제 해설

01

기초과학과 기초연구가 우리에게 왜 필요한지 그리고 그것이 우리에게 어떤 도움이 되는지에 대해 설명한 글이다. 따라서 글의 제목으로 가장 적절한 것은 ① '기초과학이 우리에게 무엇을 가져다 주는가?'이다.

② 기초과학 연구자들의 위기
③ 과학과 기술의 공동 목표
④ 기술: 기초과학의 궁극적인 목표
⑤ Michael Faraday, 전자 시대의 개척자!

02

외부 세계에 대한 우주탐사기로부터의 지식이 '비실용적인' 것으로 보일 수 있지만 그것이 우주 안에서의 인간 존재의 의미와 자연 체계 내에서의 인간의 역할 등에 대해 말해준다고 하는 것이 문맥상 자연스럽다. 따라서 빈칸에 들어갈 말로 가장 적절한 것은 ② '비실용적인'이다.

① 적용되는
③ 부정확한
④ 값을 매길 수 없는
⑤ 지략이 풍부한

구문 분석

[6행] Of course, the problem is [**that** we have no way of knowing {**what** knowledge will **be of use**} until we acquire that knowledge].

▶ [that ~]는 보어 역할을 하는 명사절이다. {what ~}는 knowing의 목적어 역할을 한다. be of use는 be useful이라는 의미이다.

어휘

practical 실용적인 **exploration** 탐사
acquire 습득하다 **physicist** 물리학자
magnetism 자성, 자력 **raw material** 원자재, 원료
engineering 공학 **insult** 모욕적인 말
seemingly 겉보기에는 **scheme** 체계, 계획

Exercise

01 ⑤ 02 ① 03 ① 04 ① 05 ③ 06 ②
07 ⑤ 08 ①

Plus Q

01~02 This growing emphasis on ethical consumption
05~06 Periodic

01 정답 ⑤ **02** 정답 ①

소재 윤리적 소비

전문 해석

오늘날의 소비자들은 적정한 가격의 괜찮은 제품을 찾고 있는 것만이 아니다. 그들은 제품이나 서비스를 넘어서 그것을 제공하는 기업의 윤리까지 살펴보고 있다. 소비자들에 의한 주안점의 전환은 그들이 물건을 구매하는 기업에 대한 관심에서 분명히 드러난다. 예를 들면, 노동 관행, 환경 정책, 그리고 사회적 책임에 대한 관심이 커져 가고 있다. 또한, 금전적인 결과만이 아니라 사회적 그리고 환경적 결과와 영향을 기업이 제시하도록 하는 압력이 있다. 기업은 그 압력에 대응할 필요가 있는데, 고객들이 그들의 관심사를 상점에 대한 불매 동맹하기에서부터 기업에 대한 고소에 이르기까지 모든 방법으로 목소리를 내고 있기 때문이다. 몇몇 다국적 기업은 최근 윤리적 소비자의 분노를 겪었으며, 평판과 기업으로서의 존재를 보호하기 위해 재빨리 반응하도록 강요받아 왔다.
윤리적 소비에 대한 이런 커지는 중요성은 무시될 수 없는 추세이다. 그것은 사라지지 않을 것이다. 윤리적 소비자가 다음 몇 십 년간 성장하는 세력으로 계속 존재할 것임을 알려주는 몇몇 중요한 세계적인 변화가 있다. 기업들은 이 추세를 잘 이해하고 대처하려 노력하는 것이 현명할 것이다.

문제 해설

01

금전적인 이득만 추구하는 소비자가 아니라 기업의 사회적, 환경적 영향에 대해 주목하는 윤리적 소비자들이 많아지고 있으므로 기업들도 이들의 태도에 주의를 기울여야 한다는 내용이므로 글의 제목으로는 ⑤ '계속 증가하는 윤리적 소비주의 경향'이 적절하다.

① 실업률에 대한 커지는 우려
② 다양한 마케팅 전략의 중요성
③ 다국적 기업: 국가에는 부담
④ 공정 무역 대 자유 무역: 경쟁 개념

02

기업의 사회적, 환경적 영향에 대해 주목하면서 소비자들이 불매 운동과 기업 고소에 이르기까지 자신의 목소리를 내고 있다는 내용 다음에 일부 다국적 기업들이 이런 소비자들의 '분노'를 겪었다는 맥락이므로 빈칸에는 ① '분노'가 적절하다.

② 감소
③ 정직하지 못함
④ 비효율
⑤ 무력함

구문 분석

[13행] There are some important changes in the world [**indicating** {**that** ethical consumers will continue to be a growing force in the next few decades}].

▶ [indicating ~]는 앞에 있는 changes를 수식한다. {that ~}는 indicating의 목적어 역할을 하는 명사절이다.

Plus Q

밑줄 친 '이 추세'는 두 번째 문단의 처음에 언급한 '윤리적 소비에 대한 이런 커지는 중요성'을 가리킨다.

03 정답 ①　　04 정답 ①

소재 욕설 없는 블로그를 운영하는 모범 사례

전문 해석

'The Atlantic Monthly'의 선임 편집자인 Ta-Nahesi Coates는 여러 해 동안 개인 블로그를 운영했다. Coates는 영화, 정치, 경제적 불평등, 남북전쟁, TV 프로그램, 좋아하는 시, 또는 프로 미식축구 시합이 너무 위험하지 않은지 등등 광범위한 주제에 대해 매일 글을 올린다. 아프리카계 미국인인 Coates는 또한 인종 문제에 대해 설득력 있는 글을 쓰는 사람으로 잘 알려져 있고 그는 그것에 관해 자주 글을 올린다. 그러나 그의 블로그는 놀라울 정도로 욕설이 없는데, 댓글이 정도를 벗어나지 않으면서 수백 개가 쏟아져 나온다. "이것은 미국에서 가장 뜨거운 이슈이고, 사람들은 상당한 분별력을 유지해 왔습니다."라고 그는 말한다.

그 비결은 Coates가 자기의 토론 게시판에 투입하는 작업이다. 블로거가 되기 전에 그는 자기가 좋아하는 정치 블로그들에서 끔찍한 댓글들을 봤다. Coates는 부정적인 댓글들이 하나의 순환 고리를 만든다는 사실을 깨달았는데, 그것들이 건설적인 게시물을 올리는 사람들을 쫓아내면서 분위기를 망치는 것이다. 그래서 그는 자기 개인 블로그를 시작했을 때 그 고리를 끊기로 작정했다. 모욕적인 것을 보는 즉시 그것을 삭제하곤 하면서 반복적으로 남의 감정을 해치는 사람들을 막았다. 한편 재치 있는 사람들을 격려하는 데 특별히 공을 들여 그들에게는 개인적으로도 공개적으로도 반응을 보여서 그들이 블로그에 머물면서 발언하도록 유도하였다. 그리고 Coates 자신도 변함없이 예의 바르고 공손하여, 커뮤니티의 기준을 세우는 데 도움이 되었다. 곧 수십 명의 고정적으로 댓글을 다는 사람들이 나타났고 그들은 서로를 알게 되었고 Coates에게 말을 거는 만큼이나 자기들끼리도 대화를 나누었다. 그들의 결속은 예의바름의 문화를 훨씬 더 견고하게 하는 데 도움이 되었는데, 오늘 그 블로그를 보는 누구라도 금방 이 커뮤니티는 불쾌함을 용인하지 않을 것이라는 사실을 알 수 있다.

문제 해설

03

Ta-Nahesi Coates가 자기 블로그를 운영하면서 욕설을 삭제하고 무례한 사람들은 차단하며 긍정적인 댓글을 다는 사람들을 격려하는 등의 방법으로 자신의 블로그를 욕설과 비방이 없는 곳으로 관리하고 있다는 내용이므로 글의 제목으로는 ① '한 성공적인 블로거가 댓글을 관리하는 방법을 안다'가 적절하다.

② 블로깅은 사업을 홍보하는 좋은 방법이다
③ 블로그: 다른 외국 문화를 보는 창
④ 블로그를 통해서 사람들과 취미를 나누세요
⑤ 블로그를 통해 개인 정보가 새나간다

04

욕설과 비방이 없는 블로그로 관리하면서 불쾌함을 용인하지 않는다는 것을 금방 알 수 있다는 맥락이므로 빈칸에는 ① '예의바름'이 적절하다.

② 경쟁 ③ 독립 ④ 불신 ⑤ 사생활

구문 분석

[13행] **The instant** he saw something abusive, he'd delete it, [**banning** repeat offenders].

▶ The instant는 '~하는 즉시'라는 의미로 부사절을 이끈다. banning은 he를 의미상 주어로 하는 분사구문을 이끈다.

05 정답 ③ 06 정답 ②

소재 인터넷으로 인해 달라진 주식 투자 방식

전문 해석

인터넷은 예전에는 전문 투자자들에게만 이용 가능했던 이점과 혜택을 제공한다. 주요한 것은 언제라도 엄청난 양의 주식시장 자료와 정보에 접속할 수 있는 편리함이다. 불안한 투자자들은 자신들의 주식 중개인으로부터 중요한 정보를 알아내기 위해 정기 근무 시간까지 더 이상 기다릴 필요가 없다. 이 정보는 이제 그들의 집, 사무실, 또는 그들이 인터넷에 접속할 수 있는 어떤 장소에서라도 접속될 수 있다.
인터넷 이용자는 더 이상 신문이나 TV나 라디오의 마감 방송과 같은 간헐적인 소식통을 통한 진부한 뉴스에 제한되지 않는다. 뉴스가 발표되거나 인터넷에 뜨자마자 인터넷 이용자들은 실시간으로 그 정보에 접속할 수 있다. 그런 신속한 정보의 확산은 개인 투자자들을 이롭게 한다. 적시의 정보는 그들이 더 정보에 밝은 결정을 할 수 있게 한다. 게다가 온라인 주식 중개 서비스를 이용하는 많은 투자자들은 자신들의 거래가 주식 중개인에게 매입/매각 전화를 할 때보다 훨씬 더 효율적이고 신속하게 실행된다는 것을 알고 있다. 인터넷은 또한 진지한 투자자들에게 광범위하게 다양한 분석 도구를 제공한다. 이런 도구들은 간단한 그래프와 역사적 자료의 도표에서 주가의 동향을 예측하는 복잡한 기술적 분석에 이른다. 이 모든 도구들은 투자자의 투자 결정에 영향을 미치는 더 나은 정보를 제공함으로써 투자자를 돕는다.

문제 해설

05

인터넷을 통해 이제 주식 중개인을 통하지 않고서도 개인 투자자가 실시간으로 주식 거래에 관한 정보를 얻을 수 있게 되었고 주식 거래를 직접 할 수 있게 되었으며 자료 분석 도구도 얻을 수 있게 되었다는 내용이므로 글의 제목으로는 ③ '인터넷이 개인 투자자에게 미치는 영향'이 적절하다.

① 성공적인 주식 중개인이 되는 방법
② 인터넷 마케팅에 대한 투자 부족
④ 조심해라, 인터넷에서 틀린 정보를 피해라
⑤ 거래에 중독된: 온라인 투자자가 도박사가 된다

06

주식 중개인을 통하거나 신문이나 TV나 라디오의 마감 뉴스를 보고서야 정보를 알 수 있었던 것이 인터넷 덕분에 실시간으로 정보를 얻을 수 있게 되었다는 맥락이므로 빈칸에는 ② '적시의'가 적절하다.

① 가공하지 않은
③ 개인적인
④ 역사적인
⑤ 양적인

구문 분석

[15행] These tools **range from** simple graphs and charts of historical data **to** a complex technical analysis [**that** predicts the movement of stock prices].

▶ 「range from A to B」는 '범위가 A에서 B까지 이른다'라는 의미이다. [that ~]는 a complex technical analysis를 수식한다.

Plus Q

주기적인 사건이나 상황은 아주 규칙적인 간격을 두고 이따금 일어난다.

'periodic은 '주기적인, 간헐적인'의 의미를 갖는 형용사이다.

07 정답 ⑤ 08 정답 ①

소재 매운 맛에 중독되는 이유

전문 해석

왜 한국인들이 다른 어떤 나라보다 더 많이 매운 고추를 좋아하는지 이해하기 어렵다. 그들의 고추 소비는 1998년에 1인당 하루 5.2그램에서 2005년에 7.2그램으로 40% 늘어났다. 1인당 연간 소비는 2.6킬로그램으로 세계 최고 기록이다. 왜 그들은 매운 고추가 그토록 매운 데도 그것을 좋아할까? 1997년에 San Francisco에 있는 California 대학의 David Julius 교수팀이 이 비밀을 풀었다. 우리 몸의 여러 열 감지센서 중의 하나인 TRPV1은 화상을 막기 위해 섭씨 43도가 넘는 높은 온도를 감지한다. 우리가 매운 고추를 먹을 때 고추 속에 든 캅사이신이 TRPV1과 결합하여 대뇌로 열과 통증 신호를 보낸다. TRPV1은 또한 와사비와 서양고추냉이의 매운 맛의 화학 성분인 즉, allyl isothiocyanates(이소티오시안염)를 감지한다. 이 화학 물질로부터 실제 온도 상승은 없지만 TRPV1은 열 감지 신호를 보내 버린다. 뇌는 우리가 높은 온도에 노출되었다고 생각하고 열을 낮추기 위해 반응하고 몸이 땀을 흘리게 만든다. 뇌의 관점에서는 그게 완전히 속은 것이지만, 우리는 고추를 먹은 후에 정말 열을 느끼고 spicy(매운)라는 말의 유의어로 hot이라는 기술(記述)적인 단어를 쓴다. 이 열과 통증을 인지한 뒤에는 Endorphin이 배출된다. 이것은 우리 몸이 통증을 느낄 때 뇌에서 자연스럽게 분비되는 화학 물질로, 마약보다 100배 더 강력한 진통 효과를 갖고 있다. 이것이 사람들이 매운 음식에 중독되는 이유이다. 더 많은 캅사이신이 섭취될수록 TRPV1에 대한 더 많은 자극이 발생하고 뇌는 더 많은 endorphin을 배출하고 전반적으로 매운 것에 대해 쾌락을 느끼는 정도가 늘어난다.

문제 해설

07

매운 음식을 좋아하고 그것에 중독되는 이유를 과학적으로 설명하는 내용으로 매운 맛을 열과 통증으로 인지하여 땀을 배출하고 진통 효과가 있는 endorphin이 배출되는 과정을 보여주고 있으므로 글의 제목으로는 ⑤ '우리가 매운 음식을 좋아하는 이유를 과학이 설명하다'가 적절하다.

① 양념의 의학적 이용
② 서로 다른 지역, 서로 다른 양념
③ 고추를 주재료로 하는 몸에 좋은 요리법
④ 양념 속에 담긴 영양가

08

매운 음식을 먹으면 실제로 온도 상승은 없는데도 뇌는 열이라고 감지하여 땀을 배출해서 식히려고 한다는 맥락으로 뇌의 입장에서는 속는다고 볼 수 있으므로 빈칸에는 ① '속은'이 적절하다.

② 변한 ③ 손상된 ④ 검토된 ⑤ 보호된

구문 분석

[15행] This is a chemical substance [**released** naturally from the brain when our body feels pain], **which** has a pain-relieving effect 100 times stronger than narcotics.

▶ [released ~]는 앞에 있는 a chemical substance를 수식한다. which는 a chemical substance를 설명하는 관계절을 이끈다.

유형 18 장문 독해(2) 순서 장문

p. 118

대표 예제

정답 01 ⑤ 02 ② 03 ⑤

소재 졸업식날 고등학교 생활 회상

전문 해석

(A) 한낮의 태양은 빛났다. 고등학교 운동장은 화려한 드레스와 정장을 입고 쾌활한 사진사들을 위해 포즈를 취하는, 옷을 잘 차려입은 사람들로 가득 찼다. 축하, 포옹, 그리고 웃음이 전파되었다. Hannah는 지난 몇 년 동안 자신의 삶의 일부였던 모든 친숙한 얼굴들을 바라보았다. 곧 그녀의 어머니가 그들과 합류할 것이었다. 그녀는 불안해하는 많은 신입생들의 한가운데에서 자신이 똑같은 곳에 서 있었던 학교에서의 첫날을 기억해냈는데, 그들 중 몇 명은 그녀의 가장 친한 친구들이 되었다.

(D) 그날은 마치 불가사의한 뭔가가 앞에 있는 것처럼 평소와 달리 안개가 자욱했다. Hannah는 긴장하고 떨고 있었다. 교장 선생님은 고등학교 생활의 도전과 스릴에 대해 이야기하면서 그들에게 힘차게 말씀하고 있었지만, 그녀는 집중할 수가 없었다. 후에 키가 크고 엄격해 보이는 남자가 자기 자신을 그녀의 담임선생님으로 소개했다. 교실은 낡았지만, 정돈되어 있었고 마음을 끌어 당겼다. Hannah는 창가 자리를 원했지만 복도 쪽 다섯 번째 줄에 앉았다. 고등학교 생활은 교장 선생님이 예측했던 대로 도전적이라는 것이 곧 드러났다.

(C) Hannah는 그 많은 수업 시간, 끝없는 과제, 그리고 시험과 씨름했다. 하지만, 운동회 날과 학교 축제처럼 신

나는 행사도 있었다. 그녀가 어떻게 자신의 두 번째 해를 잊을 수 있겠는가! 선풍적인 공연의 일환으로 그녀는 축제에서 친구들과 함께 노래를 부르고 춤을 추었다. 그 후에 그녀는 자신감이 더 생기고 활동적이 되었다. 그녀의 생각이 떠도는 사이에 Hannah는 어렴풋이 자신의 어머니의 목소리를 들었다. "자 여기 있어!" 그녀의 어머니가 서둘러 다가와 그녀에게 백합과 장미 한 다발을 주고 강한 포옹을 해 주었다.

(B) "Hannah, 너 아주 심각해 보여. 뭘 생각하고 있니?" "아, 엄마, 그저, 아시잖아요." 그녀의 어머니는 미소를 지었다. "넌 이곳을 그리워할 거야, 그렇지 않니?" Hannah는 고개를 끄덕였다. "빨리, 저쪽으로 서서… 그리고 미소를 지으렴, Hannah. 넌 아주 예쁘게 미소를 짓잖아."라고 그녀의 어머니가 말했다. 그녀는 자신의 휴대전화를 서둘러 꺼내, 줌 렌즈로 자신의 딸을 서서히 확대하고서, 자신이 한 어린 숙녀를 바라보고 있다는 것을 갑자기 깨달았다. "넌 다 컸구나." 라고 그녀는 속삭였다. Hannah는 학교 정원에서 선생님들과 사진을 더 찍었다. 그녀는 모든 추억이 자신의 마음속에 영원히 남아 있기를 바랐다.

문제 해설

01

(A)의 마지막 문장 the first day of school과 (D)의 첫 문장 That day, (D)의 마지막 문장 challenging과 (C)의 첫 문장 struggled, (C)의 마지막 문장 Her mother와 (B)의 두 번째 문장 Mom이 연결 고리를 형성한다. 따라서 주어진 글 (A)에 이어질 적절한 글의 순서는 ⑤ (D)-(C)-(B)이다.

02

(b)는 Hannah의 어머니를 가리키고, 나머지는 모두 Hannah를 가리킨다.

03

Hannah는 창가 자리를 원했지만 복도 쪽에 앉았다(Hannah was seated in the fifth row, hallway side, even though she had wanted a window seat.)는 내용으로 보아 ⑤가 글의 내용과 일치하지 않는다.

구문 분석

[C 7행] {Her thoughts wandering}, Hannah vaguely heard her mother's voice.

▶ {　　}로 표시된 부분은 분사구문인데, 주절의 주어와 부사절의 주어가 달라서 부사절의 주어(Her thoughts)를 생략하지 못했다.

[D 3행] The principal was energetically addressing them, **talking of** the challenges and thrills of high school life, but she could not concentrate.

▶ talking of는 동시동작을 나타내는 분사구문으로 '~에 대해 이야기하면서'라고 해석한다.

어휘

glorious 빛나는　**fancy** 화려한
contagious 전파하는　**recall** 기억해내다
anxious 불안한
zoom in on (줌 렌즈로) ~을 서서히 확대하다
sensational 선풍적인　**performance** 공연
confident 자신감 있는　**wander** (정처 없이) 떠돌다
vaguely 어렴풋이　**bundle** 다발, 묶음　**tremble** 떨다
energetically 힘차게　**neat** 정돈된　**hallway** 복도
predict 예측하다

Exercise

01 ④	02 ③	03 ③	04 ⑤	05 ④	06 ④
07 ②	08 ③	09 ⑤	10 ④	11 ④	12 ④

Plus Q

01~03 late-night reading
07~09 최악의 상황 또는 최악의 상태

01 정답 ④　02 정답 ③　03 정답 ③

소재 William Miller의 야간 책 읽기 습관

전문 해석

(A) William Miller는 가족이 잠자리에 든 후 잠자지 않고 아침까지 책을 읽었다. 양초가 비쌌지만 관솔이 많이 있어 그는 숲에서 관솔을 모으기만 하면 되었다. 그래서 William은 밤에 책을 읽는 데 필요한 불빛을 위해 벽난로에 관솔을 태우는 습관을 갖게 되었다.

(D) 하지만 그의 아버지는 그 습관을 좋아하지 않았고 그 습관을 그만두게 하려 애썼다. 그의 아버지는 아들의 늦은 밤 독서가 그 다음 날의 일에 필요한 그의 힘을 줄일 것이라고 느꼈다. 그리고 농장은 자기 아들로부터 그가 얻어낼 수 있는 모든 노동이 필요했다. 그는 나머지 가족들이 잠자리에 들 때 William이 잠자리에 들어야 한다고 강하게 주장했다. 그리고 그의 아버지는 커가는 소년이 밤 내내 푹 자야 한다고 생각했다.

(B) 하지만 William의 '비밀 생활'은 한동안 지속되었다. 밤마다 그는 할 수 있는 한 오랫동안 책을 읽은 후 위층으

로 (그가) 다시 올라가 아침에 하는 집안일을 할 시간이 될 때까지 잠을 잤다. 그러던 어느 날 밤 그가 예상치 못했던 일이 생겼다. 그의 아버지가 잠에서 깨어 아래층의 불빛을 보게 되었던 것이다. 집에 불이 난 것으로 생각하여 자신의 집과 가족이 불길에 휩싸이는 것으로부터 구하려고 그(아버지)는 계단을 급히 달려 내려왔다.
(C) 그러나 그는 집에 난 불 대신 자기 아들 William이 벽난로 앞에 태평하게 누워 이웃으로부터 빌린 책을 읽고 있는 모습을 보았다. 그의 아버지는 빗자루를 움켜잡고는 방에서 아들을 쫓아다니며 "이놈, 지금 당장 잠자리에 들지 않으면 집에서 내쫓을 거야!" 라고 소리 질렀다. William은 적어도 이날 밤만은 자러 갔다. 그는 그저 그 마을에 있는 선생님들로부터 얻을 수 없었던 교육을 얻으려 애쓰고 있었을 뿐이었다.

문제 해설

01

관솔을 태워서 그 불빛으로 책을 읽는 William의 습관에 관한 내용 뒤에는 아버지가 그 습관을 싫어했다는 내용과 그 이유를 설명한 (D)가 나오고, 그러한 아버지의 반대에도 불구하고 그 습관(비밀 생활)을 한동안 지속했다는 내용의 (B)가 나온 다음, 그 비밀 습관 때문에 발생한 해프닝을 설명한 (C)가 마지막에 나와야 한다.

02

(c)는 William의 아버지를 가리키지만, 나머지는 모두 William을 가리킨다.

03

아버지는 벽난로 앞에서 누워 책을 읽고 있는 William의 모습을 보았다고 했으므로, ③이 글의 내용과 일치하지 않는다.

구문 분석

[D 3행] He **insisted** that William **retire** for the night when the rest of the family **did**.

▶ 주절의 동사가 '주장, 제안, 요구, 동의, 명령' 등을 나타내고 의미가 당위성을 내포할 때 that절의 동사는 「(should)+동사원형」이 되어야 한다. did는 대동사로 앞에 나온 동사 retire의 과거형을 대신하고 있다.

Plus Q

늦은 밤 독서가 농장에서 노동 일을 하는 데 필요한 힘을 줄이며, 커가는 소년은 밤에 잠을 푹 자야 한다는 이유로 아버지가 반대하고 있는데, 이를 어기고 몰래 하는 비밀 생활을 가리키므로 William의 비밀 생활은 '늦은 밤 독서'이다.

04 정답 ⑤ 05 정답 ④ 06 정답 ④

소재 아버지로부터 배운 낚시

전문 해석

(A) 매달 마지막 토요일은 Adrian의 삶에서 항상 가장 빛나는 순간이었다. 그와 그의 아버지에게는 정기적으로 낚시를 가는 날이 있었다. Adrian은 이 여행에서 낚시와 인생에 관해서 많은 것을 배웠다. 그의 아버지는 바다가 잔잔해 보일 때에도 올라가기에 너무 위험한 바위가 몇 군데 있다고 지적했다. 그곳이 낚시에 완벽한 장소처럼 보일지라도, 물가에 너무 가까이 있는 바위는 보기와는 달리 위험할 수 있는 것이다.
(D) 조심성 없는 많은 낚시꾼들이 이 바위에서 목숨을 잃었다. 이 사람들이 바다에 휩쓸려 들어간 곳에는 콘크리트로 만든 십자가가 표시되어 있었다. Adrian은 무모하게 물가에 너무 가까이 갔다가 가까스로 벗어난 적이 몇 번 있었다. 그는 대양의 강력한 파도를 존중하는 법을 빨리 배웠다. Adrian의 아버지는 또한 그에게 다양한 종류의 물고기를 잡는 데 어떤 미끼가 적합한지를 가르쳤고, 그는 또한 어느 낚시 추가 서로 다른 낚시 장소에 맞는지를 배웠다.
(C) 그뿐만 아니라, 그는 곧 정확히 두 밧줄의 양끝을 잇는 매듭(피셔맨스 노트)을 만드는 방법과 까다롭게 꼬인 낚싯줄의 매듭을 푸는 법을 알았다. 그러나 Adrian이 항상 아버지의 충고를 열심히 받아들인 것은 아니었다. 그의 아버지가 그에게 낚싯바늘을 미끼에 거는 방법을 그에게 보여줬을 때, 그는 낚싯바늘이 약간 항상 밖으로 튀어나와야 한다고 말했지만, Adrian은 다르게 생각했다. 그는 미끼가 낚싯바늘을 감추는 것이 합당하다고 생각해서 아버지를 무시했지만, 꽤 여러 날 동안 아무것도 잡지 못하고 나서는 아버지의 조언을 따르기로 했다.
(B) 그렇게 하자 그는 정말로 큰 물고기를 잡기 시작했고, 그의 어머니는 저녁 식사로 요리할 수 있는 신선한 물고기에 기뻐했다. Adrian은 위험한 장소에 대한 경험과 지식을 가진 사람들의 말을 듣는 것이 이득이 된다는 것을 차츰 깨달았다. 그는 또한 자신에게 공짜로 귀중한 조언을 해 준 아버지의 조언을 듣지 않은 것이 참으로 어리석은 일임을 깨달았다!

문제 해설

04

물가에 너무 가까이 있는 바위는 보기와는 달리 위험할 수 있다는 것을 아버지에게 배웠다는 (A)의 내용 뒤에는 실제 이 바위에서 많은 낚시꾼들이 목숨을 잃었으며 Adrian도 무모하게 물가에 너무 가까이 갔다가 가까스로 위기에서 벗어난 경험이 있었다고 언급하는 내용의 (D)가 이어지는 것이 자연스럽다. (C)에는 그 외에도 또 아버지에게 배운 것들을 설명하고 있으므로 (D)의 뒤에 (C)가 나와야 하고, (C)의 말미에 낚싯바늘에 대한 아버지의 조언을 무시하고 자기 생각대로 하다가 여러 날을 아무것도 잡지 못하고 나서 비로소 아버지의 조언을 따르기로 했다는 내용이 나오므로, 그 결과 큰 물고기를 잡게 되었고 아버지의 조언을 듣지 않은 것이 어리석은 것이었음을 깨달았다는 내용의 (B)가 마지막에 오는 것이 글의 흐름상 적절하다.

05

나머지는 모두 Adrian을 가리키고, (d)는 그의 아버지를 가리킨다.

06

아버지의 조언을 따르기 시작하고부터는 물고기를 잡기 시작했다고 되어 있으므로 ④는 글의 내용과 일치하지 않는다.

구문 분석

[C 5행] He **thought it logical for the bait to hide** the hook, so he ignored his dad ~.

▶ 「think+목적어+목적보어(형용사)」는 '목적어가 ~하다고 (주어가) 생각하다'의 의미인데, it은 가목적어이고 to hide가 진목적어이다. 「for+목적어」는 to부정사의 의미상의 주어이다.

[D 1행] Concrete crosses marked the spots [**where** these people had been swept into the sea].

▶ [where ~]는 the spots를 수식하는 관계부사절이다.

07 정답 ② 08 정답 ③ 09 정답 ⑤

소재 이웃 간의 갈등

전문 해석

(A) Palmer 씨가 자신의 새 집으로 이사왔을 때, 그와 그의 새 이웃은 잘 지냈다. 그들은 진입로에서 마주치면 활짝 웃으며 인사하고 손을 흔들곤 했다. 그들의 마당 사이에는 담장도 없었고, 그들은 담장이 필요할 것처럼 보이지 않았다.

(C) 문제는 Palmer의 아이들이 그들의 마당에서 개똥을 밟기 시작하면서 시작되었다. 이웃집에는 푸들이 두 마리가 있었는데 그는 그들이 범인이라고 확신하고 있었기에 어느 날 그 민감한 문제를 이웃에게 제기했다. 그러나 그는 푸들이 문제라는 것을 인정하지 않았고 얼마 후 두 이웃은 적대감의 지저분한 소용돌이 속으로 들어갔다.

(B) Palmer의 마음속에서 다른 문제가 표면화되었을 때 갈등이 최악에 상태에 도달했다. 어느 날 그는 그의 적대적인 이웃으로부터 두 집 사이에 있는 토지 경계선에 굳세게 서 있는 죽은 느릅나무를 벨 것을 암시하는 내용의 쪽지를 받았다. Palmer는 관련된 비용을 나누어 내자는 생각이 마음에 들지 않아서 그 편지를 무시했다.

(D) 몇 달이 지난 후, 그는 밖에서 갑자기 동력 사슬톱 소리를 들었다. 그는 창밖을 내다보았고 이웃이 토지 경계선에 있는 죽은 느릅나무의 중앙을 수직으로 톱질하여, 나머지 반을 그의 땅에 서 있게 한 것을 보았다. 그는 그것을 몇 년 동안 대화거리로 방치해 두었다가 마침내 잘라냈다. 적대감에 대한 대가치고는 얼마나 컸던가!

문제 해설

07

잘 지내던 이웃과의 관계에 대해 언급한 (A)의 내용 뒤에는 문제가 생기기 시작했다는 내용의 (C)가 이어지고, 또 다른 문제(죽은 느릅나무의 처리 문제)로 인해 갈등이 최악의 상태에 도달했다는 내용의 (B)가 나와야 하며, 마지막으로 갈등이 두 가족에게 얼마나 큰 피해를 주었는가를 지적한 (D)가 와야 한다.

08

나머지는 모두 Palmer를 가리키지만, (c)는 그의 이웃을 가리킨다.

09

죽은 느릅나무의 반을 벤 것은 몇 년이 지난 후였으므로 ⑤는 글의 내용과 일치하지 않는다.

구문 분석

[A 3행] There was no fence between their yards, and it appeared they would never need **one**.

▶ one은 정해지지 않은 가산 명사를 대신하며 여기서는 a fence를 의미한다.

[B 2행] One day he received a note from his hostile neighbor [**suggesting** that the dead elm tree {**that** stood squarely on the lot line between them} should be cut down].

▶ [suggesting ~]는 a note를 수식하고 있으며, {that ~}는 관계절로 the dead elm tree를 수식하고 있다.

[D 2행] ~ watched the dead elm tree on the lot line **as** it was sawn vertically down the middle, leaving half standing on his property.

▶ as 이하는 벌어지는 상황에 대해 설명하고 있다. it은 the dead elm tree를 받으며, 누가 했는지를 굳이 드러내지 않아도 되어서 수동태로 처리하였으나 해석을 능동으로 하는 것

이 자연스럽다.

Plus Q

low point는 '최악의 상태 혹은 최악의 상황'이라는 의미이며, 여기서는 이웃집 개의 똥 문제로 갈등이 생긴 가운데, 또 하나의 문제(두 집 사이에 걸쳐 있는 느릅나무 처리)가 생겼다는 내용이 나오므로 문맥상 그 의미를 유추할 수 있다.

10 정답 ④ 11 정답 ④ 12 정답 ④

소재 삶과 죽음을 결정하는 삶의 의의

전문 해석

(A) 1942년 9월에 비엔나에서 저명한 유대인 정신과 의사이자 신경과 전문의인 Viktor Frankl이 체포되어 아내와 부모님과 함께 나치 수용소로 이송되었다. 3년 후, 수용소가 해방되었을 때 임신한 아내를 포함하여 그의 가족 대부분이 죽었지만 죄수 번호 119104였던 그는 살았다. 1946년에 쓴 자신의 베스트셀러 책 'Man's Search for Meaning'에서 그는 수용소에서의 자신의 경험에 대해서 썼다.

(D) 그 책에서 Frankl은 살아남은 사람들과 죽은 사람들 사이의 차이는 한 가지로 귀결된다고 결론지었다. 바로 그 한 가지는 (삶의) 의의였는데, 그것은 그가 어린 시기에 다가간 통찰력이었다. 그가 고등학생이었을 때 그의 과학 선생님 중 한 분이 반 학생들에게 "인생은 연소 과정, 산화 과정에 불과하다." 라고 단호히 말했다. Frankl은 의자에서 벌떡 일어나서, "선생님, 그렇다면 인생의 의미는 무엇이 될 수 있을까요?" 라고 응답했다.

(B) 그로부터 구체적인 답변은 없었지만 그것은 Frankl이 인생의 의미에 대해 곰곰이 생각해 볼 좋은 기회로 작용했다. 그가 수용소에서 목격한 것처럼, 심지어 가장 끔찍한 상황에서도 (삶의) 의의를 찾은 사람들은 그렇지 못한 사람들보다 고통을 덜 받았다. "사람에게서 한 가지를 제외하고는 뭐든지 가져갈 수 있어요. 인간 자유의 마지막 항목, 즉 주어진 상황에서의 인간의 태도를 선택하는 자유, 자기 방식대로 선택할 수 있는 자유를 제외하고 말이죠,"라고 Frankl은 'Man's Search for Meaning'에 적고 있다.

(C) 수용소에서 (심리)치료사로 일을 한 Frankl은 그의 책에서 그러한 한 사례를 소개했는데, 그는 그가 그곳에서 만난 자살을 시도한 한 수감자였다. 수용소의 많은 다른 사람들처럼, 그는 희망이 없었고 인생에서 더 기대할 만한 것도, 살아야 할 이유도 없다고 생각했다. "그의 경우에는, 인생이 여전히 그에게 뭔가를 기대하고 있다는 것, 미래의 뭔가가 그에게 기대된다는 것을 깨닫게 만들 수 있느냐의 문제였어요." 라고 Frankl은 (책에) 적고 있다. 그 남자에게는 그것은 당시 외국에 살고 있었던 그의 어린 아이였다. 그리고 그는 살아남았다.

문제 해설

10

수용소에서의 경험을 적은 책을 언급하면서 끝난 (A)의 뒤에는, 그 책 내용을 설명하는 (D)가 와야 하며, 삶의 의의가 있는지의 여부가 삶과 죽음을 결정한다는 내용의 (D) 다음에는 이를 좀 더 구체적으로 설명한(삶의 의의가 있는 사람은 그렇지 않은 사람보다 고통을 잘 이겨냄) 내용의 (B)가 오고, 마지막으로 그 한 사례를 설명한 (C)가 와야 글의 연결이 자연스럽다.

11

나머지는 모두 Frankl을 가리키지만, (d)는 Frankl이 수용소에서 만난 수감자를 가리킨다.

12

자신의 어린 아이 때문에 살기로 마음먹고 결국 살아남은 수감자에 관한 내용을 책에 적었으므로 ④가 글의 내용과 일치하지 않는다.

구문 분석

[B 2행] As he saw in the camps, **those who** found meaning even in the most terrible circumstances **were less likely to** suffer than **those who** did not.

▶ 「those who ~」는 '~한 사람들'의 의미이며, 「be less likely to」는 '~할 가능성이 더 적다' 라는 의미이다.

[C 6행] For the man, it was his young child, [**who** was then living in a foreign country].

▶ 「who ~」는 선행사인 his young child를 부연 설명하고 있다.

Part Ⅱ 소재편

소재 01 인물, 일화

p. 132

대표 예제

정답 ③

소재 Georg Dionysius Ehret의 삶

전문 해석

18세기는 식물화의 황금기라고 불리고, Georg Dionysius Ehret는 흔히 당대의 가장 위대한 식물 화가로 칭송된다. 독일의 Heidelberg에서 태어난 그는 미술과 자연에 대해서 그에게 많은 것을 가르쳐 준 정원사의 아들이었다. 젊은 시절, Ehret은 식물들을 관찰하고 자신의 미술 기법을 발전시키면서 주로 도보로 유럽을 여행했다. 네덜란드에서, 그는 스웨덴의 박물학자인 Carl Linnaeus를 알게 되었다. Linnaeus를 비롯한 다른 이들과의 공동 작업을 통해서, Ehret은 많은 중요한 원예 출판물의 삽화를 제공했다. 과학적 정확성에 대한 그의 명성은 그가 부유한 후원자, 특히 영국에 있는 후원자로부터 많은 일을 위탁받게 했고, 그는 결국 그곳에 정착했다.

문제 해설

젊은 시절 주로 도보로 유럽을 여행했다고 했으므로 ③은 글의 내용과 일치하지 않는다.

구문 분석

[13행] ~ gained him many commissions from wealthy patrons, particularly in England, [**where** he eventually settled].

▶ [where ~]는 계속적 용법의 관계부사절로서 and there (= in England)로 바꾸어 쓸 수 있다.

어휘

botanical 식물의
be acquainted with ~와 알게 되다, ~의 낯을 익히다
naturalist 박물학자 **collaboration** 공동 작업
illustration 삽화 **publication** 출판(물)
reputation 명성
commission (그림 제작 등의) 의뢰[주문]
patron 후원자

유제

정답 ①

소재 스웨터를 통해 발견한 우리 모두의 연결된 삶

전문 해석

Acumen Fund의 설립자인 Jacqueline Novogratz는 우리 모두가 어떻게 연결되어 있는지를 보여주는 이야기를 해준다. 그녀의 이야기는 파란 스웨터 하나를 중심으로 전개된다. 그것은 그녀가 열두 살 때 삼촌 Ed로부터 받은 것이었다. "저는 줄무늬 소매와 얼룩말 두 마리가 앞에 있는 그 부드러운 모직 스웨터를 좋아했어요."라고 그녀는 말한다. 그녀는 심지어 꼬리표에 자신의 이름을 썼다. 그러나 그녀가 자라면서 그 스웨터는 그녀에게 너무 작아졌다. 그래서 고등학교 1학년 때 그녀는 그것을 자선단체에 기증했다. 11년 후, 그녀는 빈곤 여성을 위한 지원 프로그램을 시작하기 위하여 일하던 Rwanda의 Kigali에서 조깅을 하고 있었다. 갑자기 그녀는 비슷한 스웨터를 입고 있는 한 어린 소년을 발견했다. 그것일까? 그녀는 그에게 달려가서 꼬리표를 확인했다. 그래, 거기에 그녀의 이름이 있었다. 그것은 Jacqueline뿐만 아니라 나머지 우리들에게도 서로에 대한 우리의 인연이 실처럼 연결되어 있음을 상기시켜 주기에 충분했다.

문제 해설

Jacqueline Novogratz가 자선단체에 기증한 자신의 스웨터를 입고 있는 한 소년을 발견하면서 우리의 인연이 실처럼 연결되어 있음을 상기하게 된다는 내용이므로 빈칸에 들어갈 가장 적절한 것은 ① '우리 모두가 어떻게 연결되어 있는지를 보여주는'이다.

② 시간의 상대적 가치를 우리에게 상기시켜 주는
③ 행복한 결말이 있는 힘든 생애를 묘사하는
④ 여성의 역할의 중요성을 강조하는
⑤ 아프리카에 얼마나 많은 기회가 있는지 보여주는

구문 분석

[5행] But the sweater got too tight for her **as** she grew older.

▶ as는 부사절을 이끄는 접속사로서 '~하면서'의 의미이다.

어휘

founder 설립자 **striped** 줄무늬의

sleeve 소매　zebra 얼룩말
tag 꼬리표　donate 기부하다
charity 자선단체　set up 시작하다, 설립하다
spot 발견하다　remind 생각나게 하다
thread 실　demonstrate 보여주다
relative 상대적인　emphasize 강조하다

Exercise

01 ②　02 ⑤　03 ④

Plus Q
03　was

01 정답 ②

소재　주인의 말에 끝까지 순종했던 충실한 개

전문 해석

미국의 시인이자 교육자인 Archibald Rutledge는 어느 날 산불로 자신의 개가 막 죽음을 당한 한 남자를 만난 일에 대해 썼다. 상심한 그 남자는 Rutledge에게 그 일이 어떻게 일어났는지를 설명했다. 그는 야외에서 일을 했기 때문에 종종 자신의 개를 데리고 갔다. 그날 아침, 그는 그를(자신의 개를) 숲 속의 빈터에 남겨두고 자신이 숲으로 가 있는 동안에 그에게 머물면서 자신의 점심 도시락을 지켜보라는 명령을 내렸다. 그의 충직한 친구는 알아들었는데, 왜냐하면 그 일이 바로 그가 했던 일이었기 때문이다. 그런 다음 숲에서 화재가 시작되었고, 곧 불길이 개가 남겨져 있던 장소로 퍼졌다. 그러나 그는(그 개는) 움직이지 않았다. 그는 자신이 있던 바로 그곳에 그의 주인의 말에 완벽하게 순종하면서 머물러 있었다. 눈에 눈물을 머금으면서 그 개의 주인은 "내가 그에게 하라고 말했던 것에 대해 항상 주의를 기울여야 했어요. 왜냐하면 나는 그가 그 일을 하리라는 것을 알고 있었기 때문입니다." 라고 말했다.

문제 해설

②는 개의 주인을 가리키지만 나머지는 모두 개를 가리킨다.

구문 분석

[6행] Then a fire started in the woods, and soon the blaze spread to the spot [**where** the dog had been left].

▶ [where ~]는 관계부사절로서 the spot을 수식한다.

02 정답 ⑤

소재　광포해진 돌고래들이 있는 호주 Brisbane에서의 서핑

전문 해석

한 떼의 돌고래들이 호주 Brisbane의 바로 남쪽 바다에서 광포해지기 시작했을 때, 서핑을 즐기고 있었던 Adam Maguire와 그의 친구들은 그 상황에서 어떻게 해야 할지 몰랐다. 왜 돌고래들이 갑자기 서핑보드 밑으로 들어가서 코로 보드를 찌르고 있는 것일까? 17세의 Adam Maguire는 돌고래 한 마리가 그를 향해 돌진해오고 있는 것을 보았을 때 그는 균형을 잃고 물 속으로 빠졌다. 그는 그 돌고래의 머리를 주먹으로 친 후에 보드에 뛰어 올랐다. 하지만 그의 친구들이 두려움에 떨며 (그 광경을) 보고 있었을 때 그 돌고래는 그의 뒤를 쫓아 와서 보드와 그의 엉덩이를 물고는 Adam을 쳐서 물 속에 빠뜨렸다. 갑자기 돌고래들이 광포한 상태가 되어 꼬리로 물을 쳤다. 혼란스러운 상황 동안에 Adam은 보드로 다시 기어 올라와서 다음 번 파도를 타고 해안가로 돌아오려고 시도했다.

문제 해설

Adam Maguire는 돌고래들이 처음에 갑자기 서핑보드를 찌르는 것에 당혹해 하다가 돌고래의 공격에 의해 몸을 다치게 되자 무서운 감정이 들었을 것이다. 따라서 글에 드러난 Adam Maguire의 심경으로 가장 적절한 것은 ⑤ '당혹스럽고 무서운'이다.

① 침착하고 외로운
② 행복하고 안심하는
③ 신나고 활기찬
④ 유감스럽고 안도해하는

구문 분석

[6행] He **punched it in the head** and jumped on his board.

▶ 「동작[접촉]동사+동작의 대상+in[on or by] the 신체의 일부」를 나타내는 구문이다.
cf. kiss him on the cheek (그의 뺨에 뽀뽀를 하다)
　grab me by the arm (내 팔을 잡다)

03 정답 ④

소재　화를 잘 내는 아들에게 주는 아버지의 교훈

전문 해석

이전에 성마른 기질이 있는 한 어린 소년이 있었다. 그의 아버지는 그에게 못 한주머니를 주면서 그가 화가 날 때마다 못 하나를 담장에 망치로 박으라고 말을 했다. (C) 첫날에 그 소년은 담장에 37개의 못을 박아 넣었다. 이후 몇

주 동안 자신의 화를 조절하는 법을 배우면서 매일 망치로 박아 넣은 못의 수가 점차로 감소되었다. 그는 담장에 그 못을 박는 것보다 화를 참는 것이 더 쉽다는 것을 알게 되었다. (A) 마침내 그 소년이 화를 전혀 내지 않는 날이 왔다. 그는 자신의 아버지에게 그 사실에 대해 말을 했고, 아버지는 그 소년이 이제 화를 참을 수 있는 날마다 못 하나를 빼라고 제안했다. 마침내 모든 못들이 (담장에서) 없어졌다. (B) 아버지는 아들을 담장으로 데리고 갔다. 그는 "아들아, 아주 잘했다. 하지만 담장에 있는 구멍을 보거라. 담장은 결코 같은 상태가 되지 않을 것이다. 네가 화가 나서 어떠한 말을 할 때는 그 말들이 이것처럼 상처를 남긴단다."라고 말했다.

문제 해설

주어진 글은 화를 잘 내는 아들에게 아버지가 화가 날 때마다 담장에 못을 박으라고 말하는 내용이다. 아들이 아버지 말대로 하다가 화를 참는 것이 못을 박는 것보다 더 쉽다는 것을 느끼는 (C)가 온 다음, 아버지가 이제 담장에 박은 못을 빼라고 말하는 내용의 (A)가 오고, 담장에 생긴 못이 만든 구멍을 보며 아버지가 교훈을 말하는 내용의 (B)가 와야 글의 흐름이 가장 적절하다.

오답 풀이

이야기를 소재로 하는 글의 순서 배열 문제는 이야기의 발단부터 결말까지를 고려해야 한다. (C)에서 소년이 화를 참는 것이 더 쉽다는 것을 발견하자마자 아버지가 담장으로 데리고 가서 칭찬하는 (B)로 이어진다고 오인하지 않도록 주의한다. (B)는 이야기의 결말이 담겨있는 부분이기 때문이다.

구문 분석

[11행] Over the next few weeks **as** he learned to control his anger, the number of nails [**hammered** daily], was gradually reduced.

▶ as는 '~하면서'로 해석되는 부사절 접속사이며, [hammered ~]는 nails를 수식한다.

Plus Q

글의 전체 시제는 과거이며, 문장의 주어는 the number이므로 어법상 올바른 be동사의 형태는 was이다.

소재 02 교육, 학교

p. 136

대표 예제

정답 ③

소재 행함으로써 배우는 학습

전문 해석

많은 교과가 단순한 추상적인 공부에 의해서보다 실제로 행함으로써 더 잘 학습된다. 이것은 표면적으로 더 실용적인 교과뿐만 아니라 가장 추상적인 교과에서도 흔히 그러하다. 예를 들어, 철학 교과 내에서 논리는 실례의 사용과 실제적 문제 해결을 통해서 학습되어야 한다. 어느 정도의 시간과 노력이 있은 뒤에야 학습자는 이런 사고방식의 중요성과 타당성을 알 수 있게 해주는 통찰력과 직관력을 발달시키기 시작한다. 행함으로써 배우는 이런 학습은 많은 과학 교과에서 필수적이다. 예를 들어, 상당한 양의 관찰이 있은 뒤에야 거품 상자의 불꽃은 확인 가능한 미립자의 구체적 운동으로서 인식될 수 있게 된다.

문제 해설

실용적인 교과뿐만 아니라 철학, 과학과 같은 추상적인 교과에서도 실제로 행함으로써 배우는 학습이 중요하다는 내용의 글이므로, 글의 주제로는 ③ '행함으로써 배우는 학습의 중요성'이 가장 적절하다.

① 과학 교육의 역사
② 학습 전략의 한계
④ 직관력이 과학적 발견에 미치는 영향
⑤ 철학과 과학 사이의 차이점

구문 분석

[6행] [**Only** after some time and struggle] **does** the student begin to develop the insights and intuitions that *enable* him *to* see ~.

▶ Only로 시작하는 부사구 [ ]가 문두로 나오면서 도치되었다. 일반동사 begin이 쓰여 조동사 does가 사용된 형태이다. enable은 목적격 보어로 to부정사를 취한다.

어휘

discipline 교과, (학문의) 분야 **abstract** 추상적인
seemingly 표면적으로, 외관상 **logic** 논리, 논리학
insight 통찰력 **intuition** 직관(력)
centrality 중요성, 중심임 **relevance** 타당성, 관련성
essential 필수적인, 본질적인, 매우 중요한
a good deal of 상당한 양의
bubble chamber [물리학] 거품(기포) 상자(방사선의 궤적(軌

跡)을 측정하기 위한 원자핵 실험 장치)
identifiable 확인 가능한 **particle** 미립자

유제 정답 ②

소재 아이들의 안전 보장과 정서적 안정

전문 해석

아이들이 아주 어릴 때, 당신은 그들을 위험에서 보호하기 위해 먼저 안 된다고 말한다. 당신이 그렇게 말하는 것은 당신의 아이를 사랑하기 때문이고 아이에게 스스로를 보호하도록 가르쳐야 하기 때문이다. 안 된다고 말하는 것이 당신 아이의 신체적 안전을 보장하도록 돕는 수단인 것처럼, 그것은 또한 그의 정서적 안정에도 기여한다. 당신이 아이의 행동을 제한할 때, 5살짜리 아이에게 아기를 때리면 안 된다고 말하든 또는 10대에게 자정이 지나 밖에 머물면 안 된다고 말하든, 당신은 그에게 그의 행동이 외부와 고립되어 생겨나는 것은 아님을 알려주고 있는 것이다. 그는 자신이 하는 일을 지켜보고 관심을 가지는 사람(당신)과 연결되어 있다. 모든 아이들은 자라나고 성장할 안전한 공간을 필요로 한다. 더 높이 기어오르고, 위험을 무릅쓰고 더 멀리 가보고, 또는 자신이 원하는 것 그 이상을 요구함으로써, 그 공간의 한계를 시험해 보는 것은 아이의 본성인 반면, 그에게 있어 자신이 저 바깥에 홀로 있지 않음을 아는 것은 위로가 되기도 한다.

문제 해설

부모가 아이에게 안 된다고 말하는 것은 그들이 아이를 사랑으로 지켜보고 있다는 것을 의미하면서 아이에게 혼자가 아니라는 정서적 안정감을 제공한다는 내용이므로 빈칸에 들어갈 말로 가장 적절한 것은 ② '자신이 저 바깥에 홀로 있지 않음을 아는 것'이다.

① 자신의 마음이 표류하도록 내버려 두는 것
③ 자신의 모험이 성공할 것이라고 인지하는 것
④ 책임감에 대해 생각하는 것을 그만두는 것
⑤ 자신이 전혀 벌을 받지 않을 거라고 생각하는 것

구문 분석

[8행] All children need a safe space **in which** to grow and develop.

▶ a safe space를 선행사로 하는 「전치사+관계대명사」 구문으로, 이때 in which는 관계부사 where로 바꿔 쓸 수 있다. in which 뒤에는 문장이 to부정사구로 축약된 형태이다.

어휘

ensure 보장하다 **contribute to** ~에 기여하다
security 안정 **in a vacuum** 외부와 단절된 상태에서
nature 본성 **venture** 위험을 무릅쓰고 가다
comforting 위로가 되는

Exercise

01 ① 02 ③ 03 ⑤

Plus Q

03 all they need is a different approach to learning them

01 정답 ①

소재 기술을 활용한 거꾸로 교실

전문 해석

거꾸로 교실은 수업 시간 전에 학생들이 집에서 짧은 영상 강의를 보는 반면에, 수업 도중의 시간은 실습, 연구과제, 혹은 토론에 전념하는 교육 모형이다. 이 모형에서는 직접적인 강의를 하는 데 수업 시간을 보내고 숙제로 내용 관련 활동을 완성하는 전통적 관행이 '뒤집히게' 된다. 거꾸로 교실의 개념은 인기를 얻고 있는데, 이것은 아마도 YouTube, iPads, 그리고 많은 학습관리체계(LMS)와 같이 교사들이 거꾸로 교육을 이루기 위해 사용하는 기술 도구들이 어디에서나 흔히 존재하기 때문인 듯하다. 특히 멀티미디어와 같은 이러한 도구들의 적용은 거꾸로 학습에 중대한 영향을 미친다. 게다가, 현 세대의 학생들은 전자장치의 시청각 자료로 상호작용하는 데 익숙해져 있으므로, 이 학습 모형에서 학생들이 교육 내용을 이해하는 데 이러한 기술적 장치들이 도움을 줄 가능성이 더 많다.

문제 해설

다양한 기술 도구들이 거꾸로 교실 방식에 큰 영향을 미치며, 이런 방식이 학생들의 교육자료 이해에도 도움을 줄 것이라는 내용의 글이므로, 글의 주제로는 ① '거꾸로 학습에 대한 기술 도구들의 영향'이 가장 적절하다.

② 전통적인 교실 강의 형식의 특징
③ 거꾸로 교실에서 교사 역할의 한계
④ 교사가 학생들과 더 잘 상호작용해야 할 이유
⑤ 멀티미디어의 기술적 발전의 필요성

구문 분석

[10행] ~, the current generation of students **is accustomed to** interacting with audio and video on electronic devices, so **it** is more likely [**that** technological devices ~].

▶ 「be accustomed to + 동명사」는 '~에 익숙하다'는 뜻으로 이때 to는 전치사이다. 「be used to + 동명사」로 바꿔 쓸 수 있다. it은 가주어이고 that 이하의 [ ]로 표시된 부분이 진주어이다.

02 정답 ③

소재 부모의 자기 관리의 필요성

전문 해석

아이들이 항상 우선이라는 구실로 부모들은 때때로 자신들의 것보다 그들의 아이들의 모든 욕구를 더 우선시하는 버릇을 들인다. 아기가 한밤중에 아플 때와 마찬가지로 분명히 이것이 사실일 때가 있고 그러면 모든 관심을 아기의 건강에 기울이는 것이 적절하다. 그리고 특별한 행사가 있을 때, 모두가 자연스럽게 그날의 특별한 아이에게 집중한다. 하지만 일반적인 상황에서, 적은 양의 매일의 자기 관리가 정신을 위한 산소라는 점을 인지하면서, 부모들은 그들 자신의 삶에 우선 양질의 관심을 기울이는 것이 바람직하다. 이로써 덜 자주 (본능적인) 반응을 보이고 더 많은 관점과 위엄을 갖고 (합리적으로) 대응하는 더욱 차분한 성인으로 바뀌게 된다. 요약하면, 아이들에게 더 나은 부모가 되는 최우선이자 가장 결정적인 방법은 당신에 대한 건강하고 일관적인 관리에 있다.

문제 해설

좋은 부모가 되기 위해 부모의 자기 관리가 중요하다는 것이 글의 요지이므로 정답은 ③이다.

구문 분석

[6행] ~, **it** is practical **for parents** [**to pay** quality attention to their own lives first], knowing {**that** a small amount of daily self-care is oxygen for the spirit}.

▶ it은 가주어, for parents는 의미상 주어, to pay 이하의 [ ]로 표시된 부분이 진주어이다. 접속사 that 이하의 { } 로 표시된 부분은 현재분사인 knowing의 목적절이다.

03 정답 ⑤

소재 다중지능 이론과 학교 교육

전문 해석

Howard Gardner는 '지능은 독립된 능력이며 그 능력은 전반적으로 '똑똑한' 것이거나 '어리석은' 것'이라는 믿음에 이의를 제기했다. (C) 대신에, 그는 우리가 문제와 어려움을 해결하는 데 도움을 주는 다양한 능력에 사람들이 의존한다는 것을 알아냈다. 게다가, 그는 각각의 사람이 이러한 능력들의 다른 조합을 사용한다는 것을 발견했다. (B) 하지만 학교는 개인적인 차이들을 수용하도록 만들어지지 않는다. 학교는 반드시 모두가 동등한 접근을 갖고 아무도 특별한 이점을 갖지 않기 위해 공정해야 한다. 하지만 Gardner가 주장하듯, "우리는 명백히 서로 외모가 다르며, 다른 성격과 기질을 갖고 있다." (A) 그래서 기존의 강의와 필기 방식이 일부 학생들에게는 효과가 있지만, 그것은 다른 많은 학생들의 요구들을 채우지 못한다. 학생들은 그들이 특정 과목에 능력이 없다고 결론을 내리며, 그때 그들이 필요한 전부는 그 과목들을 배우는 데 대한 다양한 접근법이다.

문제 해설

Howard Gardner가 지능이 독립된 능력이라는 믿음에 이의를 제기했다는 주어진 글 다음에, 사람들은 다양한 능력을 서로 다르게 조합하여 사용한다는 점을 알아냈다는 내용의 (C)가 오고, 그러나 학교들은 이러한 개인의 차이를 수용하도록 만들어지지 않지만 Gardner는 우리의 외모, 성격, 기질이 다르다고 주장했다고 언급한 (B)가 온 다음, 기존의 강의, 필기 방식이 많은 다른 학생들의 요구를 충족하지 못해서 서로 다른 학습법이 필요한 학생들이 특정 과목에 대해 능력이 없다고 결론을 내린다는 내용의 (A)가 마지막에 오는 것이 가장 적절하다.

구문 분석

[12행] ~ people rely on a variety of skills [**that** help us resolve problems and difficulties].

▶ 주격 관계대명사 that 이하의 [ ]는 선행사인 a variety of skills를 수식하는 관계대명사절이다. 「help + 목적어 + (to) 동사원형」은 '~가 …하는 것을 돕다'의 의미로, 목적보어로 동사원형인 resolve가 쓰였다.

Plus Q

주어인 '그들이 필요한 전부'는 목적격 관계대명사 that이 생략된 all (that) they need로 표현하며, '~하는 데 대한 접근법'은 전치사 to가 쓰여 approach to learning으로 표현한다.

소재 03 철학, 종교, 심리

p. 140

대표 예제 정답 ④

소재 토테미즘의 의미와 사고방식에 미치는 효과

전문 해석

원주민 문화의 한 가지 두드러진 측면은 부족의 구성원이 태어날 때 자연의 일부의 영혼과 정체성을 취한다는 '토테미즘'의 개념이다. 지구와 지구의 풍요를 자신의 고유한 일부로 보는 이 견해는 환경을 학대하는 것을 분명히 배제하는데, 이것은 자신을 파괴하는 것이 될 뿐이기 때문이다. 토템은 물체 그 이상의 것이다. 그것들은 영적 제사, 구전 역사, 그리고 영혼의 과거 여행길 기록들이 다른 사람들과 교환될 수 있고 신화로 전환될 수 있는 의식용 신당의 조직을 포함한다. 그 주된 동기는 부족의 신화를 보존하고 모든 개인의 기원을 자연 속에서 병합하고 공유하는 것이다. 원주민들은 자신들의 조상대대의 기원과 연결된 토템들의 위계, 자신들을 지구와 하나가 되게 놓아주는 우주론, 그리고 생태적 균형을 존중하는 행동 패턴을 통해 환경과 자신과의 관계를 하나의 조화로운 연속체로 간주한다.

문제 해설

토테미즘을 통해 원주민들은 지구와 지구의 풍요를 자신의 고유한 일부로 간주한다고 했으므로 빈칸에 들어갈 말로 가장 적절한 것은 ④ '환경과 자신과의 관계를 하나의 조화로운 연속체로'이다.

① 자신들이 자연과 자연의 풍요와 양립하지 않는다고
② 자신들의 신화를 개인주의를 향한 주요한 동기로
③ 자신들의 정체성을 주변의 자연과 독립된 것으로
⑤ 자신들의 공동 의식을 기원으로부터 자신들을 멀리 떨어뜨리는 관문으로

구문 분석

[1행] One remarkable aspect of aboriginal culture is the concept of "totemism," [**where** the tribal member at birth assumes the soul and identity of a part of nature].

▶ [where ~]는 the concept of "totemism"을 설명하는 관계절이고 where는 관계부사이다.

어휘

remarkable 두드러진 **aspect** 측면, 양상
tribal 부족의 **at birth** 태어날 때 **assume** 취하다, 띠다
soul 영혼 **identity** 정체성, 신원
intrinsic 고유한 **rule out** ~을 배제하다
mistreatment 학대 **constitute** ~이 되다, ~을 구성하다
destruction 파괴 **object** 물체, 물건 **ritual** 의식, 제사
ceremonial 의식(용)의 **lodge** 오두막, 신당
convert 전환하다, 바꾸다 **mythology** 신화 **myth** 신화
hierarchy 위계, 계급 제도 **ancestral** 조상(대대)의
cosmology 우주론 **ecological** 생태적인
incompatible 양립하지 않는
self-contained 자족적인, 독립된 **harmonious** 조화로운
continuum 연속체

유제 정답 ④

소재 심리 실험

전문 해석

이 장면을 상상해 보라. 여섯 명의 사람이 연구원들에 의해 고용된 연기자와 함께 한 엘리베이터에 있다. 배우가 한 움큼의 동전과 연필을 떨어뜨린다. 그것들은 땡그랑 소리와 함께 바닥에 떨어진다. 그 후, 엘리베이터가 한 층 한 층 내려가는 동안 도와주기 위해 한 사람도 조금도 움직이지 않는다. 엘리베이터의 그 사람들은 이 연기자가 바닥에서 동전과 연필을 줍는 것을 알아차려야 한다. 몇몇 사람들은 불편하게 느꼈을 것이고, 관여해야 할 것인지 어떤지에 대해 조용히 고민했을지도 모른다. 그러나 사람들은 각각 아무것도 하지 않는 다섯 명의 사람들에게 둘러싸여 있다. 만약 사람들이 자신이 실험 대상이라는 것을 안다면 모두 즉시 그 낯선 사람을 도와줄 것이다. 그러나 타인이 자기에게 어떻게 영향을 미치는지에 대해 일부러 생각하지 않는 일상의 상황 속에서 사람들은 집단을 따르는 것이 그냥 자연스러운 것이라고 느낀다.

문제 해설

상대를 도와줄 수도 있는 상황에서 만약 주변에 있는 다른 사람들이 아무도 그 사람을 도와주지 않으면 자신도 무리의 행동을 따라하는 것이 자연스럽다고 생각한다는 내용이므로 빈칸에는 ④ '집단을 따르는 것'이 적절하다.

① 다른 사람을 비난하는 것
② 물질적 이득을 극대화하는 것
③ 얼굴을 기억하려고 애쓰는 것
⑤ 다른 사람의 호의를 거절하는 것

구문 분석

[9행] But in the context of everyday life, [**where** people are not thinking deliberately about how others are influencing them], {going along with the group}(S) just **feels**(V) like the natural thing to do.

▶ where는 the context of everyday life를 설명하는

관계절을 이끌고 있다. 이 문장의 주어는 {　　}이고 동사는 feels이다.

어휘

scene 장면　**hire** 고용하다　**floor** (건물의) 층
notice 알아차리다　**involve** 관여하게 하다
surround 둘러싸다　**instantly** 즉시　**aid** 도움
stranger 낯선 사람　**context** 상황　**deliberately** 일부러
influence 영향을 미치다　**maximize** 극대화하다
go along with ~을 따르다　**decline** 거절하다
favor 호의

Exercise

01 ①　**02** ①　**03** ④

Plus Q

03 what you rest your mind on 또는 what you pay attention to

01 정답 ①

소재　철학을 배우는 것의 이점

전문 해석

철학의 가장 큰 이점들 중의 하나는 그것이 여러분의 삶의 질에 보탬이 된다는 것이다. 스포츠가 우리의 인간 본성의 신체적인 측면을 완성하는 데 도움이 되기 때문에 그것으로부터 우리가 얻는 즐거움과 유사하게, 지적인 발전은 우리의 정신적인 측면을 완성하는 데 도움이 되기 때문에 그것 또한 즐겁다. 철학은 생각하는 사람에게서 질적인 차이를 만들어내는 데 도움이 된다. 교육의 한 단계에서 여러분은 한 달에 책 한 권을 읽을지도 모르고 다른 단계에서 네 권을 읽을지도 모른다. 하지만 이것은 그저 양적인 차이이다. 철학의 진정한 한 가지 가치는 상황이 어떻게 맞물리는지 이해하는 데 도움이 되는 것으로 그것이 결국 우리의 지적인 본성을 완성하고 우리가 행복해지도록 만드는 데 도움이 된다. 자신과 다른 사람들, 정치적, 사회적 운동, 인종차별주의의 뿌리, 변화의 과정, 기타 등등을 이해하고 싶은가? 그렇다면 철학은 여러분을 위한 것이다.

문제 해설

철학을 배움으로써 우리의 정신적인 측면을 완성할 수 있고 질적인 변화를 얻을 수 있으며 상황이 어떻게 맞물리는지 이해할 수 있다는 내용이므로 글의 제목으로는 ① '왜 철학을 공부하는가?'가 적절하다.
② 철학 전공자를 위한 직업
③ 정치학의 기본으로서의 철학
④ 해결할 수 없는 철학적 문제들
⑤ 서로 다른 지능의 유형들은 무엇인가

구문 분석

[7행] One real value of philosophy is as an aid to understanding [**how** things hang together], **which** in turn *fulfills* our intellectual nature and *helps* make us happy.

▶ [how ~]는 understanding의 목적어 역할을 한다. which가 이끄는 관계절 안에서 fulfills와 helps는 병렬구조를 이룬다.

02 정답 ①

소재　노화를 부추기는 태도

전문 해석

나이나 병약함을 여러분의 선택에 대한 정당화로 이용하지 마라. 나이나 제한하는 신체 조건을 어떤 것을 하는 것을 피하기 위한 변명으로 이용하는 사람은 궁극적으로 퇴보, 심지어 무능력을 가져올 수 있는 미끄러운 경사면 아래로 향한다. 어떤 일을 하고 싶지 않다면 그것에 대해 자신과 남들에게 솔직해라. 과거에 어떤 활동을 즐겼으나 이제는 그것을 좋아하지 않는다면 여러분의 생활에서 그것을 없애도록 스스로에게 허락해라. 계속하도록 자신을 강요하면 더 이상 그것을 하지 않을 이유를 줄 부상이나 질병을 나타낼 가능성이 크다. 나이 들어가는 것을 정당화로 이용하는 것은 나이와 관련된 퇴보의 징후를 유발하거나 악화시킬 가능성이 클 것이다.

문제 해설

(A) 뒤에 있는 can lead의 주어 역할을 하면서 앞에 있는 a slippery slope를 수식하는 관계절을 이끌어야 하므로 주격 관계대명사로 쓸 수 있는 that이 어법에 맞다.
(B) 뒤에 다른 동사가 없으므로 give를 써서 명령문이 되는 것이 어법에 맞다.
(C) 뒤에 to cause가 이어지므로 is가 어법에 맞다. 조동사인 will을 쓰면 그 다음에 이어지는 동사가 없어서 적절하지 않다.

구문 분석

[7행] If you force yourself to continue, you **may well** manifest an injury or illness [**that** will give you a reason not to do it anymore].

▶ may well은 '~할 가능성이 크다, ~하는 것도 무리가 아니다'라는 의미이다. [that ~]는 an injury or illness를 수식하는 관계절이다.

03 정답 ④

소재 뇌 형성에 영향을 주는 마음가짐

전문 해석

마음을 계속 자기비판, 근심, 남들에 대한 불평, 상처, 그리고 스트레스에 둔다면 여러분의 뇌는 걱정과 우울한 기분에 대한 더 큰 반응성과 취약함, 위협과 상실에 대한 좁은 집중, 그리고 분노, 슬픔, 죄책감을 향한 성향으로 형성될 것이다. 반면에, 마음을 계속 좋은 일과 조건(누군가 여러분에게 친절했다, 거처할 곳이 있다), 즐거운 감정, 여러분이 완수한 일, 육체적 기쁨, 그리고 여러분의 좋은 의도와 자질에 둔다면 시간이 흐름에 따라 여러분의 뇌는 다른 형태를 갖게 될 것인데, 현실적으로 낙관적인 관점, 긍정적인 기분, 그리고 자존감뿐만 아니라 그 안에 힘과 회복력이 내장된 형태가 될 것이다. 사실상 여러분이 무엇에 주목하는가, 즉 마음을 무엇에 두는가가 기본적으로 여러분의 뇌를 형성하는 것이다.

문제 해설

(A) 앞에서 부정적인 마음가짐이 뇌 형성에 영향을 준다는 내용 다음에 긍정적인 마음가짐이 뇌 형성에 영향을 준다는 내용이 이어지므로 상반됨을 나타내는 On the other hand가 적절하다.

(B) 앞에서 언급한 내용들을 재확인하는 문장이 이어지므로 In effect가 적절하다.

① 예를 들어 - 그러나
② 예를 들어 - 사실상
③ 그 결과 - 그렇지 않으면
⑤ 반면에 - 그렇지 않으면

구문 분석

[7행] ~, then over time your brain will take a different shape, **one** with strength and resilience hardwired into it, **as well as** a realistically optimistic outlook, a positive mood, and a sense of worth.

▶ 「A as well as B」는 'B뿐만 아니라 A도'라는 뜻이다. 여기서 one은 a shape을 의미한다.

Plus Q

뇌는 여러분이 마음을 두는 것으로부터 자신의 형태를 취한다.

부정적인 마음가짐을 지니면 뇌가 그에 따라 형성되고 긍정적인 마음가짐을 가지면 뇌는 또 그에 따라 그것의 형태를 취한다는 내용이므로 빈칸에는 '여러분이 마음을 두는 것'이 적절하다.

소재 04 문학, 언어, 예술, 문화

p. 144

대표 예제 정답 ④

소재 다른 나라의 작품 번역에 소극적인 미국의 번역 시장

전문 해석

점점 더 세계화되는 세상에서, 번역 문학은 특히 중요한 역할을 한다. 점점 더 작가, 독자, 출판업자들은 특히 서양 사회와 아랍 사회 문화 간의 가교로서 문학에 관심을 기울이고 있다. 그 결과 이처럼 커지는 관심은 번역의 호황을 일으키고 있다. 하지만 아마 놀라운 일도 아닐 것인데, 대부분의 번역 작품은 영어에서 다른 언어로 된 것이고 아랍어와 같은 다른 언어에서 영어로 된 것이 아니다. 그리하여 거대한 미국 시장은 그런 불균형을 만들어 간다고 생각된다. 예를 들어, 미국의 서점은 20세기 중엽의 카이로의 삶과 상인 가족에 대해 대가답고 사실적으로 그린 노벨상 수상 작가 Naguib Mahfouz가 쓴 '카이로 3부작' 이외의 작품을 좀처럼 갖추어 놓지 않는다. 서양 독자들은 Mahfouz가 쓴 더 실험적인 작품이나 그의 정치적 · 종교적 우화나 그의 사극에 대해 거의 알지 못할 가능성이 있다. 그 결과는 미국과 세계의 다른 나라 사이에서 한쪽 방향만 비추는 거울 같은 것이다.

문제 해설

번역 작품 대부분이 영어에서 다른 언어로 된 것이고 아랍어와 같은 다른 언어에서 영어로 번역된 것이 아니라고 했으므로, 빈칸에 들어갈 말로 가장 적절한 것은 ④ '불균형'이다.

① 평등 ② 다양성 ③ 상호작용 ⑤ 불확실성

구문 분석

[11행] ~ rarely stock more than Nobel Prize winner **Naguib Mahfouz's *Cairo Trilogy***, [a masterful, realistic account of life in Cairo and of a merchant family in the mid-20th century].

▶ [ ]로 표시된 부분은 Naguib Mahfouz's *Cairo Trilogy*를 부연 설명해주는 동격어구이다.

어휘

literature 문학　translation 번역
publisher 출판업자
turn to ~에 관심을 기울이다, ~에 의지하다
boom 호황, 붐　huge 거대한　stock 갖추다, 채우다
trilogy 3부작　masterful 대가다운, 능란한
account 기술, 이야기, 말　merchant 상인
historical drama 사극　imbalance 불균형

유제

정답 ②

소재　사멸된 언어가 다시 살아나기 위한 조건

전문 해석

만약 조건이 적합하다면, 사멸된 언어조차도 다시 살아날 수 있다. 그 언어를 다시 원하는 사람들이 있어야 한다. 또한, 문자로 쓰여 있거나 녹음된 그 언어의 자료가 어떤 형태로 있어야 한다. Kaurna라고 불리는 호주 남부 원주민의 한 언어에서 이런 일이 일어났다. 그 언어의 마지막 원어민은 1929년에 죽었지만, 1980년대에 한 집단의 사람들이 그들의 언어를 되살리고 싶다는 결정을 내렸다. "그 언어는 죽지 않았습니다. 단지 자고 있을 뿐입니다." 라고 그 집단의 지도자가 말했다. 다행히도, 19세기 자료가 남아있어서 한 언어학자가 그 언어를 생생하게 기술할 수 있었고 Kaurna인들이 그 언어를 다시 배우기 시작하도록 도울 수 있었다. 오늘날, 그 언어는 학교에서 가르쳐지고 있으며, 아마도 언젠가 일부의 아이들이 자신의 모국어로 배우기 시작할 것이다.

문제 해설

주어진 문장은 Kaurna라고 불리는 호주 남부 원주민의 한 언어에서 이런 일이 일어났다는 내용이다. 따라서 이 문장의 뒤부터는 '이런 일'에 대한 설명이 시작되어야 하므로 주어진 문장이 들어가기에 가장 적절한 곳은 ②이다.

구문 분석

[8행] ~, material survived from the nineteenth century, **so that** a linguist was able to make a fresh description and [help the Kaurna people start] learning the language again.

▶ so that은 결과를 나타내는 접속사로서 '그래서 ~이다'의 의미이다. [　]로 표시된 부분은 「help+목적어+(to) 동사원형」 구문이다.

어휘

extinct 사멸된, 멸종한　condition 조건
fortunately 다행히도　linguist 언어학자
description 기술, 묘사　mother tongue 모국어

Exercise

01 ④　02 ⑤　03 ⑤

Plus Q

03 puzzles

01

정답 ④

소재　자국의 연예 산업과 언어를 지키려는 프랑스 정부의 노력

전문 해석

프랑스 소비자들은 미국 텔레비전을 선호하고 프랑스의 프로그램을 무시한다. 미국의 영화들은 프랑스의 모든 (극장의) 매표소 영수증의 70퍼센트 이상을 차지한다. 프랑스 정부는 이러한 침입을 미국의 문화적 제국주의라고 여기며, 그것의 영향력을 최소화하기 위해 몇 가지 조치를 취했다. 프랑스는 1994년에 프랑스의 문화적 제품을 생산하기 위해 160억을 썼는데, 이 액수의 4분의 3은 정부에서 나온 것이었다. 프랑스의 영화 관람객들은 11퍼센트의 세금을 지불하므로 정부는 프랑스의 영화 산업을 위한 자금의 대부분을 공급할 수 있다. (이제 프랑스의 연예 산업은 전 세계의 사람들에게 매력을 줄 수 있는 프로그램을 만드는 법을 배우려고 노력하고 있다.) 게다가, 프랑스 정부는 텔레비전과 라디오, 모든 광고와 학교와 직장에서 프랑스어가 사용되어질 것을 요구한다.

문제 해설

프랑스 소비자들은 미국의 프로그램을 선호하는데, 프랑스 정부는 이것을 문화적 제국주의라 생각하면서 이것을 막기 위한 조치를 취한다는 내용의 글이다. ④는 프랑스 연예 산업이 전 세계인들의 흥미를 끌 수 있는 프로그램을 만드는 법을 배우려고 한다는 내용이므로 글의 흐름과 관계 없는 문장이다.

구문 분석

[5행] France spent $16 billion to produce cultural products in France in 1994, **three-quarters of which** came from the government.

▶ three-quarters of which는 and three-quarters of $16 billion과 같은 의미이다.

02 정답 ⑤

소재 언어의 사용을 통해 만들어지는 상황을 보는 틀

전문 해석

인지 언어학자들에 따르면 우리가 사용하는 말은 틀을 만들어낸다. 틀에 대한 개념은 세계관에 대한 개념과 비슷하다. 틀은 종종 이데올로기, 다른 말로 하자면 상황이 어떤 식으로 존재해야 하는가에 대해 우리가 갖는 개념들의 집합을 의미한다. 예를 들어, 우리가 우리나라의 'Founding Fathers(건국의 아버지들)'에 대해 말할 때 우리는 그것을 통해서 우리나라를 가족으로 보는 은유적인 틀을 만들고 강화시키고 있는 것이다. 나라를 가족으로서 보는 개념은 'sending our sons to war(우리의 아들들을 전쟁에 보내는 것)'처럼 우리가 사용하는 다른 어구들에 의해 강화된다. 틀은 우리가 상황에 대해 말하는 것을 돕는다. 여러분의 언어가 이미 틀을 가지고 있는 어떤 것에 대해 말하는 것은 더 쉽다. 여러분이 어떤 것에 대한 틀을 가지고 있다면 여러분은 아마도 그러한 틀에 잘 맞는 많은 단어와 어구들을 가지고 있을 지도 모른다.

→ 우리가 사용하는 언어는 상황에 대한 관점을 만들어내는데, 이것은 결국 우리가 상황에 대해 말하는 것을 더 편리하게 만든다.

문제 해설

우리가 사용하는 언어는 틀을 만들어내고 그 틀은 상황이 어떤 식으로 존재해야 하는가에 대한 개념들의 집합인 이데올로기를 의미하는데, 이것은 상황에 대한 관점이라고 볼 수 있다. 또한 우리의 언어가 어떠한 것에 대해 틀[관점]을 가지고 있을 때 우리가 상황에 대해 말하는 것이 더 쉽다고 했으므로, 요약문의 빈칸 (A)와 (B)에는 각각 perspective(관점)와 convenient(편리한)가 적절하다.

① 예지력 – 편리한
② 예지력 – 경쟁적인
③ 선호(도) – 경쟁적인
④ 관점 – 감정적인

구문 분석

[2행] Frames often imply an ideology, or [a set of ideas we have about the way things should be].

▶ [ ]로 표시된 부분은 an ideology를 부연 설명하는 동격어구이다. or는 '다른 말로 하자면'의 의미로 사용되었다.

03 정답 ⑤

소재 시간 기술에 대한 미국과 체코 방식의 차이

전문 해석

내가 영어를 말할 때 나는 9시 15분이 9시를 지난 15분이라고 말하고 9시 30분을 9시를 지난 30분이라고 말한다. 내가 체코어를 배우기 시작했을 때 9시 15분이 '10시의 15분', 9시 30분이 '10의 반'으로 해석되는 어구임을 알게 되었다. (C) 이것은 잠시 동안 나를 이해할 수 없게 만들어서 나는 내가 한 모든 약속을 다시 한 번 확인해야 했다. 그러나 내가 그 두 가지 체계의 기저에 있는 차이점을 파악한 후에 나는 내 자신이 영어를 사용하느냐 혹은 체코어를 사용하느냐에 따라 시간을 다르게 생각하고 있음을 발견했다. (B) 영어에서는, 나는 시계에서 소리 나는 대로의 시간(9시 15분, 9시 30분)에 대해 생각하고, 체코어에서는 다음에 오는 시간(10시로 가는 방향의 15분, 10시로 가는 방향의 30분)에 대해 생각한다. (A) 이러한 사고방식이 체코인들이 미국인들보다 더 미래 지향적이라는 것을 가리킨다고 확신하진 않지만 그것은 확실히 차이점을 의미해서, 신경을 쓰지 않는 사람들은 약속을 놓칠 수도 있다.

문제 해설

주어진 글은 필자가 영어와 체코어의 시간을 기술하는 방식에 차이가 있음을 발견했다는 내용이다. 이러한 것이 필자를 당혹하게 만들었고, 그 두 가지 체계의 차이점에 대해 파악했다는 내용의 (C)가 온 다음, 자신이 영어와 체코어를 사용할 때 생각하는 방식에 대해 설명하는 (B)가 오고, 이러한 사고방식이 체코인들이 더 미래 지향적이라는 것을 의미하진 않지만 분명히 차이가 있음을 의미한다는 내용의 (A)가 와야 가장 자연스러운 글의 흐름이 된다.

오답 풀이

글의 흐름을 파악할 때 내용적인 흐름을 파악하는 것이 가장 중요하지만 대명사를 이용하는 것도 방법이 될 수 있다. 예를 들어 (C)의 This는 주어진 글을 가리키고, (A)의 this way of thinking은 (B)에서 제시된 필자가 영어와 체코어를 사용할 때 생각하는 방식을 가리킨다. 이렇게 대명사를 이용하면 오답으로 가는 길을 확실히 예방할 수 있다.

구문 분석

[12행] ~, however, I **found myself thinking** about time differently depending on [**whether** I was using English or Czech].

▶ 「find+목적어+-ing」 형식이 사용되었으며 '~가 …하고 있는 것을 발견하다'의 의미이다. [whether ~]는 전치사 on의 목적어이다.

Plus Q

어떤 것이 당신을 어리둥절하게 한다면, 당신은 그것을 이해하지 못해서 혼란스러움을 느끼게 된다.

puzzle은 동사의 의미로 '어리둥절하게[이해할 수 없게] 만들다' 이다.

소재 05 역사, 지리

p. 148

대표 예제

정답 ⑤

소재 올바른 역사 공부 방법

전문 해석

역사 공부는 우리가 들어왔던 것을 기억해내는 것이 아니라 그것은 우리에게 과거를 조사할 것을 요구한다. 탐정처럼, 우리는 쉽고 알려진 정보로부터 시작한다. (C) 그러고 나서 그 정보들이 어떻게 서로 들어맞는지를 알아보기 위해 조각들을 이리저리 맞춰본다. 모든 조각들이 들어맞기만 하면, 우리는 큰 그림을 가질 수 있다. 우리가 모든 정보를 짜 맞출 때, 우리는 우리 자신에게 우리가 알고 있는 것을 설명할 수 있는 다른 방식에 대해 생각해 볼 것을 요구한다. (B) 예를 들어, 어떤 사람이 당신에게 중국 진시황제가 잔인한 통치자였다고 말한다면, 당신은 이것을 사실로 단순히 받아들이겠는가? 아니면 그 말에 대해서 질문을 하고 그것을 뒷받침할 정보나 증거를 찾겠는가? (A) 당신은 더 나아가 "왜 그는 잔인했을까?" 그리고 "그의 통치의 결과는 무엇인가?"와 같은 질문을 해야 한다. 그러므로, 역사를 공부하는 것은 우리가 진실이라고 읽거나 들은 모든 것을 사실로 받아들이지 않도록 우리를 훈련시킨다. 대신에, 그것은 과거를 전체적으로 이해할 수 있는 비판적인 사고의 기술을 사용하도록 우리를 훈련시킨다.

문제 해설

역사 공부는 암기가 아니라 기존에 사실이라고 알려진 것에 대해 의문을 제기하며 비판적인 사고를 해야 하는 것이라는 내용의 글이다. 쉽고 알려진 정보에서 시작한다는 내용의 주어진 글 다음에, (C) 정보의 여러 조각을 짜 맞추며, 우리가 알고 있는 것을 다른 방식으로 생각해봐야 한다는 내용이 이어지고 (B) 진시황을 통한 예를 제시하는 내용이 나온 후 (A) 글에 대한 결론을 지으며 비판적인 사고를 하는 훈련을 해야 한다는 내용이 나와야 한다.

구문 분석

[9행] Instead, it **trains** us **to use** our critical thinking skills [**to get** the full picture of the past].

▶ train은 목적격보어로 to부정사를 취하므로 to use로 쓰였다. [ ]에서 to get은 동사 train을 수식하는 부사적 용법(~하기 위해서)으로 해석해도 되고, 명사 skills를 수식하는 형용사적 용법(~하는)이라고 해석해도 된다.

[16행] We then shuffle the pieces around [**to see** how they fit together].

▶ [ ]에서 to see는 목적의 의미(~하기 위해서)로 해석되며, 타동사로 쓰인 see의 목적어절로 간접의문문이 왔다.

어휘

investigate 조사하다 **detective** 탐정
go further 더 나아가다 **cruel** 잔인한 **rule** 통치, 통치하다
hence 그러므로 **train** 훈련하다, 훈련시키다
get the picture 이해하다 **emperor** 황제
ruler 통치자 **shuffle** 이리저리 바꾸다, 정리하다
put ~ together 조립하다, 짜 맞추다
challenge (상대방에게 도전이 될 일을) 요구하다

유제

정답 ③

소재 세금을 피하기 위한 사람들의 행동 방식의 변화

전문 해석

전 역사에 걸쳐 사람들은 세금을 피하기 위해 그들의 행동을 바꾸어왔다. 몇 세기 전에, 토스카나의 공작은 소금에 세금을 부과했다. 토스카나의 제빵업자들은 그들의 조리법에서 소금을 없애고 우리가 오늘날 즐겨 먹는 토스카나의 맛있는 빵을 우리에게 선사하는 것으로 응수했다. 여러분이 암스테르담을 방문한다면, 여러분은 오래된 집들이 모두 거의 다 좁고 높다는 것을 알아챌 것이다. 그것들은 재산세를 최소화하기 위해서 그런 식으로 건축되었는데, 이(재산세)는 집의 폭을 근거로 한 것이었다. 또 다른 건축 사례인, 프랑스의 망사르드 지붕의 발명을 생각해보자. 재산세는 흔히 집에 있는 방의 개수에 부과되었고, 따라서 2층이나 3층에 있는 방들도 1층에 있는 방들처럼 과세할 수 있는 것으로 여겨졌다. 그러나 3층에 망사르드 지붕이 만들어지면, 그 방들은 다락방의 일부로 간주되었고 과세되지 않았다.

문제 해설

역사적으로 사람들이 세금을 피하기 위해 어떻게 행동을 바꾸어왔는지 토스카나, 암스테르담, 프랑스의 사례를 통해 설명하고 있는 글이다. 주어진 문장은 집의 폭을 근거로 하는 재산세를 최소화하기 위해 그에 맞게 건축했다는 내용이다. ③의 앞 문장에 쓰인 'narrow and tall'이라는 개념이 주어진 문장의 핵심어 'width'와 연결되므로 주어진 문장은 ③에

들어가는 것이 가장 적절하다.

오답 풀이
②에 주어진 문장을 넣으면, 주어진 문장 속의 They가 가리키는 대상이 ②의 앞 문장에 없으므로 글이 연결되지 않는다.

구문 분석
[4행] Tuscan bakers **responded by** *eliminating* salt in their recipes and *giving* us the delicious Tuscan bread [we enjoy today].

▶ respond는 자동사이므로 목적어를 필요로 하지 않는다. 「by -ing」는 '~함으로써'라고 해석하는데 eliminating과 giving이 병렬구조로 쓰였다. Tuscan bread를 수식하는 [ ]에서 목적격 관계대명사 which[that]이 생략되었다.

[10행] ~, therefore, rooms(S) on the second or third floor were considered(V) just as **ratable** as **those** on the ground floor.

▶ 이 문장의 주어는 rooms이므로 복수형 동사 were가 쓰였다. 이 문장을 능동태로 고치면 'people considered rooms on the second or third floor just as ratable as those ~'가 된다. consider는 목적격보어로 형용사를 취하므로, 부사가 아니라 ratable이 와야 한다. 또한 같은 명사의 반복(rooms)을 피하기 위해 those를 사용하였다.

어휘
minimize 최소화하다 **property tax** 재산세 **width** 폭
throughout ~내내, 도처에 **impose** (세금을) 부과하다
eliminate 없애다, 제거하다 **recipe** 조리법
architectural 건축학의 **attic** 다락(방)

Exercise

01 ④ 02 ③ 03 ④

Plus Q
03 the gifts they were lucky enough to receive

01 정답 ④

소재 통념을 깨뜨린 여성 등반가

전문 해석
두 세기 이상 동안에, 여성들은 등반을 할 수 없다는 것이 일반적인 통념이었다. 예를 들어, Sir Edmund Hillary는 에베레스트 산을 등반하기 위한 여행을 준비하고 있었을 때, 여성을 포함시키자는 요구를 거절했다. (C) 전해진 바에 의하면 그는 세 가지 이유를 들었다. 여성은 지도력의 자질이 없고, 짐을 운반할 만큼 체력이 강하지 않으며 고도가 높은 곳에서 과민성 반응을 보인다는 것이었다. (A) 다행스럽게도, 몇몇 여성들은 일반적인 통념에 도전할 만큼 대담했다. Arlene Blum은 등반을 시험해보기 시작했으며 자신이 (등반을) 성공하기 위한 지도력, 체력, 기질이 있음을 발견했다. (B) 이내 그녀는 어떤 미국 남성도 성공해본 적이 없었던 원정인 세계에서 10번째로 높은 26,545피트에 있는 Annapurna 등반을 준비하기 위해 10명의 미국 여성들로 이루어진 팀을 조직했다. 1978년에 그들은 성공했으며 Blum은 결국 'Annapurna: A Woman's Place'라는 제목의 책을 썼다.

문제 해설
사회적 통념에 따라 에베레스트 산 등반에 여성을 포함시키자는 요구를 거절했다는 주어진 글 뒤에는 거절의 이유를 설명한 (C)가 와야 한다. 그 뒤에는 사회적 통념에 도전하는 대담함을 보인 여성에 대해 설명하고 있는 내용의 (A)가 나오고, 그녀가 여성들로만 조직한 등반 팀이 남자들보다 앞서서 Annapurna 등반에 성공했다는 내용의 (B)가 마지막에 나와야 한다.

구문 분석
[8행] Soon she organized a team of ten American women to prepare a quest **in which** no American male had ever succeeded: ~.

▶ in which에서 which는 a quest를 받는 관계대명사이고 in은 동사 succeeded에 걸리는 전치사이다.

02 정답 ③

소재 고대 사원의 발견

전문 해석
1912년에 멕시코의 깊은 정글에서 두 명의 탐험가가 고대 인도인들이 지은 1,200년 된 사원을 발견하였다. 그 사원은 좋은 상태를 유지하고 있었다. 그들은 사진을 찍고 사원의 위치를 나타내는 지도를 그려보려고 시도했다. 훗날, 다른 탐험가들이 그 지도를 따라가려고 시도했으나, 사원을 발견할 수가 없었다. 60년 이상이 지난 1973년, 일부 사람들이 이 고대 인도인들에 관한 TV 영화를 만들고 있었다. 정글에서 그들은 우연히 사라진 사원을 발견하였는데, 그 사원은 정글에 있는 나무들로 거의 완전히 덮여있었다. 사원은 여전히 좋은 상태를 유지하고 있었다. 수십

년이 지난 후, 그 위대한 발견물(사원)이 다시 발견된 순간이었다.

문제 해설
두 차례에 걸쳐서 발견된 고대 인도인들이 지은 사원에 관한 내용이므로 ③ '고대 사원의 재발견'이 제목으로 가장 적절하다.

① 탐험가들이 직면한 어려움
② 깊은 정글에서 발견된 지도
④ 우연한 발견의 예들
⑤ 절을 찾기 위해 시도된 실패들

구문 분석
[6행] In the jungle, they accidentally found the lost temple, **almost completely hidden** by jungle plants.
▶ 'almost completely hidden'은 분사구이며, which was 혹은 and it was가 생략되었다고 볼 수도 있다.

03 정답 ④

소재 산타클로스와 관련된 관습의 유래

전문 해석
크리스마스이브에 수백 만 명의 미국 어린이들이 산타클로스가 선물 가방을 가지고 굴뚝 아래로 내려오고 난 후에 먹을 수 있도록 쿠키와 우유를 놓아둔다. 어떤 아이들은 그의 믿음직한 순록을 위해 당근을 조금 더하기도 한다. 산타클로스를 위해 쿠키와 우유를 내놓는 것이 미국 명절의 전통으로 시작된 것은 대공황의 와중에서였다. 엄청난 경제적 고난의 그 시기에 많은 부모들은 자식들에게 다른 사람에게 주는 것이 중요하며 크리스마스에 운이 좋아서 받게 된 선물에 대해서 감사를 표하는 것이 중요하다고 가르치려고 했다. (그런 부모들은 많은 물질적 선물들이 이내 잊혀진다는 것을 기억해야 한다.) 80여년이 지난 지금, 많은 아이들이 선의의 마음에서 혹은 빨간 옷을 입고 수염을 기른 남자로부터 더 많은 선물을 받아 내기 위한 뇌물로 여전히 쿠키와 우유를 산타를 위해 내놓고 있다.

문제 해설
산타클로스를 위해 쿠키와 우유를 내놓는 것이 미국 명절의 전통이 된 유래에 대해 설명하는 글이므로 물질적 선물에 대한 망각을 지적한 내용의 ④는 글의 흐름과 관계 없는 문장이다.

구문 분석
[3행] **It was** during the Great Depression **that** leaving cookies and milk for Santa took off as an American holiday tradition.
▶ 「it is ~ that」 강조 용법을 활용하여 during the Great Depression을 강조한 구문이다.

Plus Q
문맥상 '크리스마스에 운이 좋아서 받게 된 선물'의 의미이며 목적격 관계절이 선행사(the gifts)를 수식하는 구조가 되어야 한다. enough는 to부정사를 동반하여 부사나 형용사를 뒤에서 수식함에 유의한다.

소재 06 정치, 경제, 사회, 법

p. 152

대표 예제 정답 ③

소재 행동 지침으로서의 사회적 역할

전문 해석
역할은 담장과 같다. 역할은 우리에게 일정량의 자유를 허용하지만, 우리 대부분에게 있어 그 자유는 매우 멀리까지 가지는 않는다. 누가 무슨 말을 하든지 관계없이 한 여성이 드레스를 입지 않기로 하거나, 한 남성이 양복과 넥타이를 착용하지 않기로 한다고 가정해 보라. 대부분의 상황에서 그들은 자신들의 결정을 고수할 것이다. 하지만 가족 결혼이나 장례식 같은 공식적인 행사가 생길 때 그들은 저항하기 힘들다고 느껴지는 규범에 어쩔 수 없이 따르기 쉽다. (증가하는 사회적 압력은 우리가 사회적 규범을 이행하고 행동에 대한 공유된 사회적 관례에 충실하지 못하게 한다.) 우리 중 거의 모두는 우리의 역할에 '적절한' 것에 대한 지침을 따른다. 우리 중 그러한 제한을 귀찮아하는 사람들은 거의 없는데, 그 이유는 우리의 사회화가 매우 철저해서 우리는 대개 우리의 역할이 적절하다고 말해 주는 것을 하기 '원하기' 때문이다.

문제 해설
글의 주요 내용은 사람은 각자 자신이 맡은 역할을 수행하리라 기대하는 사회적 규범을 벗어나 행동하기는 어렵다는 것인데 ③은 오히려 그 반대되는 내용으로 사회적 압력의 증가로 인해 사회적 규범을 이행하지 못한다고 언급하고 있다. 따라서 ③이 글의 전체 흐름과 관계가 없다.

구문 분석
[9행] The increasing social pressure **discourages** us **from** [fulfilling the social norms] and [committing ourselves to shared social conventions of behaviour].

▶ 두 개의 [ ]는 모두 from에 이어지며 병렬구조를 이루고 있다. 「discourage A from -ing」는 'A가 ~하지 못하게 하다[막다]'라는 의미이다.

어휘
fence 담장, 울타리 **regardless of** ~에 관계없이
stick to ~을 고수하다 **occasion** 행사, 일
come along 생기다 **funeral** 장례식
cave in to (어쩔 수 없이) ~에 따르다, ~에 굴복하다
norms 규범 **overwhelming** 저항하기 힘든, 압도적인
fulfill 이행하다 **commit** 충실하다, 전념하다, 헌신하다
convention 관례, 관습 **bother** 귀찮게 하다
restriction 제한, 제약 **thorough** 철저한

유제

정답 ①

소재 위험률이 낮은 투자

전문 해석
투자의 근본 원리 중 하나는 위험과 수익 간의 관계를 토대로 한다. 투자와 관련된 '위험'은 기대 수익을 얻을 가능성으로 규정될 수 있다. 예를 들어, 여러분이 지역 은행에 있는 예금 계좌에 1,000달러를 예금한다면, 여러분은 이것을 위험이 낮은 투자라고 예상할 것이다. 은행은 일반적으로 보수적이고, 예금 계좌는 특정한 달러 액수까지 연방 정부에 의해 보장받는다. 그 은행이 여러분에게 2퍼센트의 연이율을 지급한다고 약속한다면, 여러분은 연말에 1,020달러를 받을 가능성이 크다. 따라서, 여러분은 2퍼센트의 연간 수익을 얻을 가능성이 크고, 이것은 위험이 낮은 투자로 여겨질 것이다.

문제 해설
(A) 투자와 관련된 '위험'에 대한 정의를 언급한 다음에 투자금을 안정적으로 되돌려 받을 수 있는 은행에 예금하는 예를 언급하고 있으므로 For example이 적절하다.
(B) 앞서 언급한 예를 가지고 위험과 기대 수익금을 받을 수 있는 가능성의 관계에 대해 마무리하고 있으므로 Thus가 적절하다.

② 예를 들어 - 그러나
③ 게다가 - 결과적으로
④ 그럼에도 불구하고 - 마찬가지로
⑤ 그럼에도 불구하고 - 그에 반해서

구문 분석
[9행] ~, there is a high probability [**that** you will earn a 2 percent annual profit], and this would be considered a low-risk investment.

▶ a high probability와 [that ~]는 동격 관계이고, that은 동격 명사절을 이끄는 접속사이다.

어휘
underlying 근본적인 **principle** 원리, 원칙 **return** 수익
associated 관련된 **probability** 확률, 가능성
deposit 예금하다 **savings account** 예금 계좌
conservative 보수적인 **guarantee** 보장하다
annual interest rate 연이율

Exercise

01 ② 02 ④ 03 ⑤

Plus Q
03 impact

01

정답 ②

소재 직원 구성의 다양성

전문 해석
미국에서 기업들이 다양성 문제를 무시하고도 별탈이 없고 한 유형의 소비자의 구미에만 맞추면서 모두 비슷해 보이고 비슷하게 생각하는 직원을 고용할 수 있었던 때가 있었다. 그런 시절은 사라졌다. 또한 다양성이 사업과 거의 관련이 없다는 통념도 사라졌다. 갖가지 출신 배경의 사람들에게 기회를 주는 것은 윤리적인 관점에서 옳게 행동하는 것이다. 그런데 그것은 또한 사업에도 유익하다. 왜 그럴까? 회사가 다문화적인 인력의 전문지식으로부터 이익을 볼 수 있기 때문이다. 예를 들어, 아시아에서 사업을 하는 회사라면 아시아계 미국인이 협상 팀에 있는 것이 성공할 가능성을 크게 늘려줄 것이다. 세계적인 사업을 하는 데 관심이 없는 조직이라도 여전히 직원 구성에 다양성이 필요하다.

문제 해설
기업이 다양한 문화적 배경을 가진 직원들로 구성되어 있어야 그들의 전문지식을 이용할 수 있고 사업에 유익하다는 내용이므로 빈칸에는 ② '다양성이 사업과 거의 관련이 없다'가 적절하다.

① 경쟁이 업무 수행을 향상시킨다
③ 생산성은 비용과 일자리를 줄이는 것을 의미한다
④ 민주적인 방식을 이용하는 관리자가 좋다

⑤ 혁신은 오로지 연구팀이 할 일이다

구문 분석

[1행] There was a time [**when** corporations in the US could {get away with ignoring diversity issues} and {hire employees who all looked and thought alike, catering only to one type of consumer}].

▶ [when ~]는 a time을 수식하는 관계절이고 when은 관계부사이다. 두 개의 { }는 모두 could에 이어지며 병렬구조를 이룬다.

02 정답 ④

소재 도시와 읍내의 생활 속도의 차이

전문 해석

전반적으로 더 큰 도시에 사는 사람들이 더 작은 곳에 사는 사람들보다 더 빨리 움직인다는 것을 연구들이 반복적으로 보여주었다. 이런 유형의 가장 초기의 연구 중 하나에서 Herbert Wright는 자기의 고전적인 '도시와 읍내' 프로젝트의 일환으로 전형적인 도시의 슈퍼마켓과 작은 읍내 식료품 가게에서 아이들의 행동을 관찰했다. 그 두 환경 사이에 가장 강력한 차이점 중의 하나는 걷는 속도라는 것이 드러났다. 평균적인 도시 아이는 읍내 아이가 더 작은 식료품 가게를 가로질러 걷는 것보다 슈퍼마켓을 거의 두 배는 빨리 가로질러 걸었다. (도시의 슈퍼마켓은 보통 쇼핑객들이 구매하기 전에 식품을 맛보고, 냄새 맡아보며 만져볼 수 있게 허용했다.) 읍내 아이들은 점원과 다른 쇼핑객들과 어울리면서 세 배나 많은 시간을 보냈다.

문제 해설

도시의 슈퍼마켓과 읍내의 식료품 가게에서 도시의 아이들과 읍내의 아이들이 걷는 속도의 차이를 보였다는 내용의 글이다. ④는 구매 전에 식품을 맛보고 냄새 맡고 만져볼 수 있게 한다는 내용이므로, 글의 흐름과 관계 없는 문장이다.

구문 분석

[6행] The average city child walked nearly **twice as fast** through the supermarket **as** the town child **did** through the smaller grocery.

▶ twice as fast as는 '~보다 두 배나 빨리'라는 의미이다. did는 앞에 있는 walked를 대신한다.

03 정답 ⑤

소재 관광 자원 보존이 지역 주민에게 미치는 불편함

전문 해석

농촌 관광의 한 가지 영향은 지역 주민, 지역 의회와 국립공원 사이에 일어날 수 있는 갈등이다. 환경을 보존할 분명한 필요가 있지만 이것은, 특히 보존 지역으로 지정된 상태의 지역에서, 지역 주민의 건축 허가 신청과의 갈등을 초래할 수 있다. 일부 주민들은 이것이 자신들이 관광업으로 다각화하는 것을 막기까지 한다는 것을 알게 된다. 다른 지역들에서 그런 정책은 지역의 외양에 영향을 줄 수 있는 태양열 전지판과 여타 구조물의 사용을 줄이면서 최적의 환경 관리 방안과도 완전히 불화한다. 건축 자재와 스타일이 이미 자리를 잡고 있는 유산과 구조물과 맞아야 하기 때문에 이런 지역에서 건물을 유지하는 것은 비용이 많이 든다는 것도 입증될 수 있다. 흔히 비슷한 것으로 대체하는 것이 필수조건이고 그것이 그 지역에 사는 사람들에게 나쁜 감정과 인지된 불편함을 예방할(→ 초래할) 수 있다.

문제 해설

건축 자재와 스타일을 이미 자리를 잡고 있는 유산과 구조물에 맞춰서 유지하는 것이 돈이 많이 들고, 관광 자원이 되도록 지역의 외양을 보존하는 것이 지역 주민에게 불편함을 초래한다는 맥락이므로 ⑤prevent를 cause로 고쳐야 한다.

구문 분석

[8행] **It** can also prove to be expensive [**to maintain** a property in these areas] **as** building materials and style must be in keeping with the heritage and structures already in place.

▶ It이 가주어, [ ]로 표시된 부분이 진주어로 쓰였다. as는 '~이기 때문에'라는 의미의 접속사로 이유의 부사절을 이끈다.

Plus Q

외지인들이 농촌 관광을 오도록 지역에 있는 유산과 구조물, 환경을 보존해야 하므로 신축 건물 허가 신청에서부터 태양열 전지판 설치까지 제한을 받게 되고 기존 건물의 재료와 스타일에 맞춰 자기 건물을 유지하는 데 돈이 많이 들어 불편을 초래할 수 있다는 내용이므로 글의 주제로는 '농촌 관광이 지역 주민의 생활에 미치는 영향'이 적절하고 빈칸에는 impact를 찾아 써야 한다.

소재 07 환경, 자원, 생태계

p. 156

대표 예제

정답 ②

소재 먹잇감의 입수 가능성과 메뚜기 개체의 밀도

전문 해석

desert locust(이집트 땅메뚜기)는 먹잇감의 입수 가능성과 지역 메뚜기 개체의 밀도에 따라 현저하게 다른 두 가지 방식으로 살아간다. 그들이 원래 사는 사막 서식지에서 보통 그렇듯 먹잇감이 부족할 때는 메뚜기들이 위장을 위해 고안된 색깔을 갖고 태어나며 홀로 살아간다. 그러나 드물긴 하지만 상당량의 비가 내리는 기간이 와서 초목이 크게 성장하게 되면, 모든 것이 변한다. 처음에는, 그 메뚜기들이 그저 풍부한 먹잇감을 마음껏 먹어 치우면서 계속 홀로 살아간다. 그러나 그 여분의 초목이 죽어 없어지기 시작하면, 메뚜기들은 자신들의 수가 많아져서 혼잡하다는 것을 알게 된다. 갑자기, 밝은 색을 띠고 함께 있기를 선호하는 새끼 메뚜기들이 태어난다. 서로를 피하고 위장과 활동하지 않음을 통해 포식자들로부터 몸을 숨기는 대신, 이 메뚜기들은 거대한 떼를 지어 함께 먹으며, 순전히 숫자를 통해 자신의 포식자들을 압도한다.

문제 해설

(A) 많은 비로 먹이가 풍부해져도 처음에는 계속 혼자 살아간다는 내용이 뒤에 나오므로 '(다른 사람 없이) 혼자 하는'이라는 뜻의 solitary가 적절하다. social은 '사회적인'이라는 의미이다.

(B) 많은 비로 인해 초목이 크게 성장하게 된다는 내용이 앞에 나오는 것으로 보아 풍부한 먹잇감을 먹어 치운다는 내용이 되어야 하므로 abundant가 적절하다. insufficient는 '불충분한'이라는 의미이다.

(C) 메뚜기들이 거대한 떼를 지어서 포식자들을 압도한다는 내용이 되어야 하므로 overwhelm이 적절하다. overestimate는 '과대평가하다'라는 의미이다.

구문 분석

[5행] ~ locusts *are* born with coloring **designed** for camouflage and *lead* solitary lives.

▶ 이 문장의 주어 locusts의 복수형 동사 are와 lead가 병렬구조를 이루고 있다. coloring(색깔)은 수동적으로 만들어지는 대상이므로 과거분사 designed에 의해 수식을 받는다.

어휘

locust 메뚜기 **remarkably** 두드러지게, 현저하게
availability 유효성; (입수) 가능성
density 밀도 **scarce** 부족한 **habitat** 서식지
significant 중요한, 상당한 **vegetation** 초목
feast 마음껏 먹다[포식하다] **preference** 선호
predator 포식자 **inactivity** 활동하지 않음

유제

정답 ②

소재 공동 자원의 분배와 관리

전문 해석

혼잡한 세상에서는 관리되지 않은 공동 자원이 아마도 제대로 기능하지 못할 것이다. 그것은 중요한 조건이다. 만약 세상이 혼잡하지 않다면, 공동 자원은 아마도 사실상 최선의 분배 방식일지도 모른다. (B) 예를 들어, 개척자들이 미국 전역에 흩어져 있었을 때, 가장 효율적인 방법은 모든 야생의 사냥감을 관리되지 않은 공동 자원으로 다루는 것이었는데, 왜냐하면 오랫동안 인간이 어떤 실질적인 피해를 입힐 수 없었기 때문이다. (A) 평원의 주민은 아메리카 들소를 죽여서 저녁 식사로 오로지 혀만을 잘라내고 그 동물의 나머지 부분은 버릴 수 있었다. 그는 그 어떤 중요한 의미에서도 낭비하고 있던 것이 아니었다. 외로운 미국 변경 개척자가 어떻게 자신의 쓰레기를 처리하는가도 그다지 중요하지 않았다. (C) 오늘날, 오직 몇 천 마리의 들소만이 남은 상태에서, 우리는 그러한 부주의한 행동에 격분할 것이다. 미국의 인구 밀도가 높아지면서 땅의 자연적인 화학적, 생물학적 재활용 과정에 과부하가 걸렸다. 들소에서부터 석유와 물에 이르는, 이런 자원에 대한 주의 깊은 관리가 필요해졌다.

문제 해설

'세상이 혼잡하지 않다면, 공동 자원은 최선의 분배 방식일 것이다'라는 내용의 주어진 글 다음에, 이에 대한 예시로 미국 개척자들은 사냥감을 관리되지 않은 공동 자원으로 다루었다는 내용의 (B)가 온 다음, 평원의 주민은 공동 자원을 필요한 부분만 사용하고 나머지 부분을 버려도 낭비하는게 아니었다고 앞의 내용을 구체적으로 상술하고 있는 (A)가 오고, 그러나 오늘날에는 자원에 대한 주의 깊은 관리가 필요해졌다 라는 결론적 내용의 (C)가 와야 글의 흐름이 적절하다.

구문 분석

[6행] **Nor did it** much **matter** [how a lonely American frontiersman disposed of his waste].

▶ 부정어(Nor)가 문장 앞에 쓰이면서 도치되었다. 본동사가 일반동사일 경우, 「부정어+do(es)/did+주어+동사원형~」의 어순으로 써야 한다. it은 가주어이고, [ ]로 표시한 부분이 진주어이다.

[11행] Today, **with** only a few thousand bison **left**, we would be outraged by such careless behavior.

▶ 「with+목적어+분사~」 구문으로 「목적어가 ~한 채 / 목적어가 ~하기 때문에」 등으로 해석한다. 목적어와 분사의 관계가 수동(들소가 남겨진 상황)이므로 과거분사인 left를 써야 한다.

어휘

qualification 자격, 조건 **distribution** 분배
plainsman 북미 대평원의 주민 **bison** 들소
discard 버리다 **matter** 중요하다, 문제되다
frontiersman 개척자
dispose of ~을 처리하다, ~를 없애다
pioneer 개척자, 선구자 **do damage** 손해를 입히다
outrage 격노하게 만들다 **dense** 빽빽한, 밀도가 높은
overloaded 과적된, 과부하가 걸린

Exercise

01 ③ 02 ④ 03 ④

Plus Q
03 how it got up 또는 how to get up

01 정답 ③

소재 재생 가능한 에너지의 장점

전문 해석

재생 가능한 에너지 사용의 한 가지 주요 장점은 재생 가능하기 때문에 지속 가능하다는 것이고 따라서 결코 고갈되지 않을 것이라는 점이다. 재생 가능한 에너지 시설은 일반적으로 전통적인 발전기보다 유지 보수를 덜 필요로 한다. 재생 가능한 에너지가 이산화탄소 혹은 기타 화학 오염 물질과 같은 폐기물을 거의 혹은 전혀 만들어내지 않으므로 환경에 미치는 영향이 미미하다는 것이 훨씬 더 중요하다. (재생 가능한 에너지는 날씨에 의존하는데, 날씨는 예측 불가능하고 일관적이지 않다.) 재생 가능한 에너지 사업은 또한 많은 지방에 관광 산업뿐만 아니라 지역 서비스 사용에서 나오는 경제적 이득을 가져다 줄 수 있다. 이러한 경제적 이득은 대부분의 사업이 대도시 중심지에서 떨어져 있기 때문에 가능하다.

문제 해설

재생 에너지 사용의 장점에 관한 내용이므로, 재생 가능한 에너지의 단점에 대해 언급하고 있는 ③은 전체 글의 흐름에서 벗어난다.

구문 분석

[4행] Even more importantly, renewable energy produces little or no waste products such as carbon dioxide or other chemical pollutants, so has minimal impact on the environment.

▶ Even more importantly는 문두 부사로, 문장 앞에 나오고 뒤에 쉼표가 나오는 형태의 부사를 지칭한다. 이런 경우 'It is even more important that ~'의 의미이다.

02 정답 ④

소재 지진으로 인한 피해

전문 해석

우리는 지진 직후에 모든 생명선을 잃었다. 우리는 휴대전화를 사용할 수도 TV를 볼 수도 없었다. 우린 너무 무서운 나머지 그날 밤 그저 집안에 머물러 있을 수가 없었다. (C) 우리는 차에 머무르는 것을 선택했다. 이틀이 지나서야 전기가 들어왔다. 이내 가스가 작동됐다. 밝은 불빛 아래에서 따뜻한 음식을 먹게 되어 얼마나 행복했는지 설명할 수가 없다. (A) 우리는 지난 이틀 동안 마실 것이 많지 않아서 그날 마시고 있었던 커피는 특히 맛이 있었다. 지금 지진이 난 후 10일이 지났는데, 우린 아직도 집에 수돗물이 안 나온다. (B) 그러나, 나는 특히, 가족과 아직도 연락이 되지 않는 사람이 이곳에 매우 많이 있기 때문에 여전히 이 집을 소유하게 되어 매우 운이 좋다고 생각한다.

문제 해설

지진으로 인한 두려움 때문에 집안에 머물러 있을 수 없었다는 주어진 글 뒤에는 차 안에서 머물 것을 선택했다는 내용의 (C)가 와야 한다. 지진이 난 지 10일이 지났는데도 여전히 수돗물이 나오지 않는다는 내용의 (A)가 이어지고, 아직 수돗물이 나오지 않아 불편하지만 가족과 연락이 닿지 않고 있는 사람들과 비교하면 그래도 행복하다는 내용의 (B)가 마지막에 나와야 한다.

구문 분석

[10행] Not until two days later **did the electricity come** back on.

▶ 부정어(not)가 포함된 부사구가 주어보다 앞에 위치하면서 도치가 일어나서 「조동사(did)+주어(the electricity)+동사원형」의 어순이 되었다.

03 정답 ④

소재 기린의 새끼 적응 교육

전문 해석

태어날 때 새끼 기린은 엄마의 자궁에서 10피트를 떨어지는데 대체로 등부터 떨어진다. 엄마 기린은 모든 것이 괜찮은지를 빨리 살펴보기에 충분한 시간만큼 자신의 머리를 낮춘다. 그런 다음 몇 분 후에 그녀는 자신의 어린 새끼가 인생의 난관에 적응하도록 확실히 해두기 위해 가장 놀라운 과정을 시작한다. 그녀는 자신의 새끼 바로 위에 자리를 잡고는 자신의 긴 다리를 바깥쪽으로 휘둘러서 새끼를 차고, 그래서 새끼는 큰 대자로 뻗으면서 곤두박이가 된다. 새끼가 일어나지 않으면, 새끼의 노력을 자극시키기 위해 그 폭력적인 과정은 반복적으로 되풀이된다. 마침내, 새끼가 불안정한 다리를 딛고 처음으로 일어선다. 그때 엄마 기린이 가장 놀랄만한 일을 하는데 그녀는 새끼를 다시 차서 서 있지 못하게 한다. 엄마 기린은 새끼가 자신이 어떻게 일어났는지를 기억하기를 원하는 것이다.

문제 해설

엄마 기린이 새끼 기린을 강하게 단련시키는 과정을 설명한 글로, 엄마 기린의 폭력적인 과정을 딛고 마침내 불안정한 다리로 일어섰다는 주어진 문장은, 그 폭력적인 과정이 진행된 부분과 일어나고 나서 다시 쓰러뜨리는 엄마 기린의 행동을 설명한 문장 사이에 와야 하므로 ④에 들어가는 것이 적절하다.

구문 분석

[3행] The mother giraffe lowers her head **long enough to take** a quick look that everything is alright.

▶ enough는 to부정사를 동반하여 부사 혹은 형용사를 뒤에서 수식한다.

Plus Q

'When it doesn't get up, the violent process is repeated over and over again to stimulate its efforts.' 에서 알 수 있듯이 엄마 기린은 새끼 기린이 일어나는 방법을 터득할 수 있도록 혹독하게 훈련시키고 있으므로, how it got up 또는 how to get up이 빈칸에 들어갈 말로 적절하다.

소재 08 의학, 건강, 식품, 영양

p. 160

대표 예제 정답 ②

소재 건강관리 프로그램 홍보

전문 해석

만약 여러분이 마음과 몸이 혹사당해온 무수한 사람 중의 한 명이라면, 여러분에게는 더 긍정적이고 활기에 찬 생활을 제공해 줄 프로그램인 ABC 웰빙 협회에서 제공하는 건강관리 프로그램이 필요합니다. 이 프로그램은 6주 동안 지속되고, 3개의 상이한 요소인 일일 목표, 걷기 플랜 그리고 식사 플랜으로 구성됩니다. 매주 저희 건강 전문가들이 여러분에게 조언을 해드릴 것이고, 여러분은 새로운 신체 활동 목표를 접하게 될 것입니다. 여러분의 생활을 즉시 개선하는 것에 대해 진지하십니까? 그러시다면, 저희의 환상적인 프로그램에 오늘 등록함으로써 시작하실 수 있습니다.

문제 해설

마음과 몸이 혹사당하는 사람들을 위해 제공하는 건강관리 프로그램을 홍보하는 내용의 글이므로, 글의 목적으로는 ②가 가장 적절하다.

구문 분석

[1행] If you're one of the countless people [**whose** mind and body have been overworked], you need a program [**that** will give you a more positive and energetic life]: [the Health Management Program offered by the ABC Well-Being Institute].

▶ 첫 번째 [ ]로 표시된 부분은 the countless people을 수식하는 관계대명사절이며, 두 번째 [ ]로 표시된 부분은 a program을 수식하는 관계대명사절이다. 세 번째 [ ]로 표시된 부분은 a program을 부연 설명하는 동격어구이다.

어휘

countless 무수한, 셀 수 없이 많은
overworked 혹사당하는, 과로한 **positive** 긍정적인
energetic 정력적인, 활기에 찬
institute 협회, 학회, 연구소
consist of ~로 구성되다
component 요소
expert 전문가 **immediately** 즉시, 즉각
enroll in ~에 등록하다

유제 정답 ①

소재 아이의 소금과 단 것에 관한 욕구를 조절하는 법

전문 해석

소금과 단 것에 관해서 아이의 선천적인 욕구를 바꾸기 위하여 부모가 할 수 있는 것은 거의 없는데, 그 욕구는 유아기 초기에 시작된다. 하지만, 어릴 때 먹는 것으로 아이가 단 맛과 짠 맛을 찾게 될 상황을 적어도 바꾸어줄 수 있다는 몇몇 증거가 있다. 불과 생후 6개월일 때에도, 소금 간을 한 음식에 더 자주 노출된 아기들은 소금을 덜 맛본 아기들보다 소금을 가미한 시리얼에 대해 더 강한 선호를 보인다. 마찬가지로, 설탕물을 먹어본 적이 있는 6개월 된 아기들은 전에 그것에 노출되지 않은 아기들보다 그것을 더 많이 마시는 경향이 있다. 이러한 효과는 놀라울 정도로 오랜 기간 지속되는데, 그 이유는 심지어 생후 6개월이 되어 부모가 아기에게 설탕물을 주는 것을 멈추더라도 그 아기는 두 살에도 그것에 대한 더 큰 선호를 지속적으로 보일 것이기 때문이다.

문제 해설

(A) 앞에서 아이의 소금과 단 것에 대한 선천적인 욕구를 바꾸기 위해 부모가 할 수 있는 것이 거의 없다는 내용이 나오고, 뒤에서는 아이가 단 맛과 짠 맛을 찾게 될 상황을 적어도 바꾸어줄 수 있는 몇몇 증거가 있다는 내용이 나오므로 역접의 연결어인 However가 적절하다.

(B) 앞 문장에서 소금 간을 한 음식에 더 자주 노출된 아기들이 소금을 가미한 시리얼에 대해 더 강한 선호를 보인다는 내용이 나와 있으며, 뒤에서도 같은 맥락의 내용을 설탕물을 들어 설명하고 있으므로 Similarly가 적절하다.

② 게다가 – 마찬가지로
③ 하지만 – 그러므로
④ 게다가 – 그와는 반대로
⑤ 예를 들어 – 그러므로

구문 분석

[7행] ~, six-month-old babies [**who** have been fed sugar water] tend to drink more of it than babies [not previously exposed to it].

▶ 첫 번째 [ ]로 표시된 부분은 관계대명사절로 주어인 six-month-old babies를 수식하며, 두 번째 [ ]로 표시된 부분은 분사구로서 babies를 수식한다.

어휘

when it comes to ~에 관해서 **inborn** 선천적인, 타고난
evidence 증거 **at least** 적어도, 최소한
circumstance 상황, 환경 **seek out** ~을 찾다
flavor 맛 **expose** 노출시키다 **preference** 선호
cereal 시리얼, 곡물 식품 **tend to** ~하는 경향이 있다
previously 전에, 이전에 **surprisingly** 놀라울 정도로

Exercise

01 ⑤ 02 ① 03 ③

Plus Q

03 조리를 하게 되면 채소에 있는 산화방지제가 30퍼센트까지 없어질 수 있기 때문이다.

01 정답 ⑤

소재 환자에 대한 의사들의 태도 변화

전문 해석

대체적으로, 의과대학에 입학하는 사람들은 공통적인 속성을 가지고 있다. 즉 사람들을 돕고자 하는 바람과 과학에 대한 적성을 가지고 있다. 그러나, 장차 의사가 되려는 사람들이 인체의 모든 병과 생물학적 기능을 알고 이해하리라고 기대되는 시기인 4년간의 의과대학 기간 동안 그들은 병과 부상의 증상과 징후를 실제 환자들과 분리된 것으로 보는 것에 익숙해진다. 더욱이, 구체적인 사실에 대한 그들이 갖고 있는 지식은 전반적인 환자의 행복을 평가하는 그들의 능력보다 훨씬 더 많이 시험을 받는다. 의사들은 이러한 습관을 종종 (개업을 해서) 의료 행위를 하는 데까지 가지고 가게 되고, 전체보다는 (병에 대한) 구체적인 사실을, 정신보다는 신체를 강조하게 되어, 많은 환자들이 연민이나 관심으로 배려를 받지 않는다고 느끼도록 만든다.

문제 해설

의사들은 의과대학 과정을 거치고 의료 행위를 하게 되면서 처음에 가졌던 마음인, 환자들을 돕겠다는 태도가 변하게 된다는 내용의 글이다. 따라서 글의 주제로 가장 적절한 것은 ⑤ '의료 행위를 하는 의사들이 환자들이 배려를 받고 있다고 느끼도록 만들지 못하는 이유'이다.

① 의사들의 성격이 환자에게 미치는 영향
② 의과대학의 교육과정을 바꾸어야 할 필요성
③ 의대생들에게 재정적인 지원을 하는 것의 의미
④ 의료 장비에 대한 연구를 조장하는 것의 중요성

오답 풀이

의대생들이 4년간의 교육을 받으면서 병과 부상의 증상과 징

후를 실제 환자들과 분리된 것으로 보는 것에 익숙해진다는 도입부의 내용을 통해 의과대학의 교육과정을 바꾸어야 한다는 것이 주제라고 섣불리 판단하지 않도록 주의한다.

구문 분석

[8행] Doctors often take these habits with them into medical practice, [**emphasizing** specifics over wholeness, body over mind], [**leaving** many patients not feeling cared by their compassion or interest].

▶ [ ]로 표시된 부분은 병렬을 이루고 있는 분사구문으로 'emphasize ~, and leave ~'로 이해할 수 있다. 「leave+목적어+목적보어」 형태가 사용되었으며 목적보어로 현재분사가 사용되었다. 의미는 '~가 …한 상태로 있게 하다'이다.

02 정답 ①

소재 Slow Food의 설립 배경

전문 해석

Slow Food는 1986년 이탈리아 사람인 Carlo Perini에 의해 설립된 협회이다. Slow Food를 만든 것은 Petrini 씨가 로마에 맥도날드 음식점이 개장되는 것에 대한 자신의 불만을 표하는 방식이었다. Slow Food의 주된 목표는 음식과 포도주 문화에 있어 다양성을 조장하는 것이다. 1986년부터 그 협회는 50개국 이상에서 존재하는 전 세계적인 운동으로 성장해왔다. 이 운동은 음식, 음식 준비와 야생 동물과 채소의 종을 사용하는 것과 관련된 문화적 전통을 보호하는 데 전념하고 있다. 8만 3천 개의 Slow Food 회원들은 또한 음식이 재빠르게 맛 측면에서 비슷하게 되는 것, 다시 말하면 전 세계적으로 '표준화되는' 방식에 반대한다. 이러한 일의 많은 부분이 전 세계적으로 같은 방식으로 준비되는 같은 음식을 내놓은 식당 체인에 의해 유발된다.

문제 해설

Slow Food는 음식과 음식 준비 등과 관련된 문화적 전통을 보호하고, 음식이 표준화되는 것에 반대하고자 설립되었다는 내용의 글이다. 따라서 빈칸에 들어갈 말로 가장 적절한 것은 ① '다양성'이다.

② 조화 ③ 일관성 ④ 발전 ⑤ 광고

구문 분석

[10행] Much of this is caused by restaurant chains [**that** serve the same foods {**prepared** the same way across the globe}].

▶ [that ~]는 restaurant chains를 수식하는 관계대명사절이며, {prepared ~}는 분사구로 the same foods를 수식한다.

03 정답 ③

소재 장수를 위해 해야 할 노력들

전문 해석

매일, 여러분은 더 오래 살거나 혹은 더 짧게 사는 쪽으로 가도록 하는 수백 가지의 결정을 내린다. 그러한 결정은 그 어느 곳에서도 저녁 식탁에서보다 더 명확하지 않다. 예를 들어, Loma Linda 대학 의료 센터의 연구자들이 구성원들이 장수로 유명한 한 종교 집단의 3만 4천명의 사람들의 생활 방식 습관을 추적했을 때, 그들은 일주일에 5일을 견과를 먹은 사람들이 지구상에서 2.9년을 추가적으로 얻었다는 것을 발견했다. 마찬가지로, 이탈리아의 연구자들은 매일 한 컵 정도 생채소를 먹는 것이 여러분의 삶에 2년을 더할 수 있다는 것을 알아냈다. 왜 생채소는 여러분에게 매우 좋은가? 조리하는 것은 채소에 있는 산화방지제를 30퍼센트까지 제거할 수 있다.

문제 해설

(A) 문장의 주어는 those decisions이므로 동사는 이와 어울리는 are가 되어야 적절하다. 부정의 부사어(구)가 문두로 나갈 때 주어와 동사는 도치된다.
(B) 선행사인 a religious group이 관계대명사절 내에서 자리를 차지하려면 소유격 형태가 되어야 하므로 whose가 적절하다.
(C) 문장의 주어는 eating이며 '먹는 것이 2년을 더할 수 있다'는 문맥이 되어야 하므로 동사는 능동의 의미인 add가 되어야 적절하다.

구문 분석

[2행] **Nowhere** are those decisions more clear than at the dinner table.

▶ 부정의 부사어구(no, not only, never, little, few 등)가 문두로 나가게 되면 동사가 일반동사일 경우는 「do[does / did]+주어+동사원형」의 형태가 된다. 동사가 be동사일 경우는 「be동사+주어」 형태가 된다.

Plus Q

'Cooking can remove up to 30 percent of the antioxidants in vegetables.'를 통해 채소를 조리하지 않고 먹는 것이 좋은 이유를 알 수 있다.

소재 09 스포츠, 취미, 여행, 여가

p. 164

대표 예제

정답 ⑤

소재　관광의 문화적인 이점

전문 해석

관광은 단지 휴가를 보내는 것 이상을 위해서 중요하다. 관광은 다른 장소와 문화에서 온 사람들이 함께 모일 수 있도록 해 주고, 관광객과 관광지의 지역사회가 서로의 차이점과 유사점에 대해 배운다. 그들은 또한 새로운 취향과 사고방식을 배우는데, 그것이 관광지에 사는 사람들과 관광객들 사이의 보다 나은 이해로 이어질 수 있다. 관광의 또 다른 긍정적인 효과는 그것이 한 사회의 문화, 특히 그 문화의 예술 형태의 생존을 위해 제공하는 도움이다. 관광객들에게 고유의 미술품을 팔거나 그들을 위해 민속춤을 공연할 기회는 지역 예술가들에게 전통적인 예술 형태를 보존하도록 용기를 북돋아 줄 수 있다. 예를 들면, 피지 제도에 사는 사람들은 야자수 깔개와 조개껍질로 만든 장신구를 돈벌이가 되는 관광 사업으로 발전시켰다. 그들은 또한 민속춤과 불 속 걷기 공연을 함으로써 추가적인 소득을 얻고 있다.

문제 해설

관광을 통해 서로 다른 문화를 가진 사람이 함께 모여 서로의 차이점과 유사점을 더 잘 이해할 수 있으며 지역 예술가들이 전통 예술 형태를 보존하는 데 도움을 준다는 내용의 글이다. 따라서 글의 주제로 가장 적절한 것은 '⑤ 관광의 문화적인 이점'이다.

① 현지인과 관광객 사이의 오해
② 관광 상품을 만드는 다양한 방법
③ 문화적 교류의 부정적인 영향
④ 전통 문화의 소실

구문 분석

[5행] They also learn new tastes and ways of thinking, **which** may lead to a better understanding between hosts and tourists.

▶ 관계대명사 which가 계속적 용법으로 쓰일 경우, 선행사에 대해 추가적인 설명을 하는 것이다. 이때 선행사는 앞 문장 전체나 두 단어 이상의 어구도 가능하다. 여기에서는 which가 앞 문장 전체를 가리킨다.

[10행] The opportunity {**to sell** native artworks to tourists or **perform** folk dances for them} may **encourage** local artists **to preserve** traditional art forms.

▶ {　}로 표시한 부분에서 to sell과 (to) perform이 병렬 구조를 이루며 opportunity를 수식한다. encourage는 목적격보어로 반드시 to부정사를 써야 한다.

어휘

tourism 관광　**host** 주인, 주최국, 진행자
community 지역사회, 공동체　**similarity** 유사성
aid 도움　**folk** 민속의　**local** 지역의, 현지의
preserve 보존하다　**palm mat** 야자수로 만든 깔개
craft (수)공예　**profitable** 수익이 되는
additional 추가적인　**income** 소득, 수입

유제

정답 ②

소재　사진 촬영 시 타이밍의 중요성

전문 해석

구도는 사진을 구성하는 것일 뿐만 아니라, 또한 정확하게 적절한 순간에 카메라 셔터를 누르는 것이다. 타이밍을 잘못 잡으면 사진은 그것의 활력의 일부를 잃게 되는 것이 당연하다. (B) 어떤 피사체들에 있어서, 사진을 찍을 중요한 순간들은 한 우승자가 결승선을 통과하는 순간과 같이 분명하다. 그런 경우들에서, 준비와 연습은 행운만큼이나 중요하다. (A) 그러나 덜 예측 가능한 다른 사건들의 경우에는 끊임없이 변화하는 상황들과 사람들이 갑자기 합쳐져서 어떤 강력하고, 아름다우며, 활기 넘치는 구도를 만들어내는 마법적인 순간들이 있을 수 있다. 이러한 순간들은 두 개 또는 그 이상의 요소들이 어떤 한 방식으로 결합되는 때일 것이다. (C) 예를 들어, 어느 폭풍우 치는 날 한 아름다운 건물이 갑자기 한 줄기 빛에 의해 빛나게 되면서, 결코 다시는 포착될 수 없을 분위기 있는 장면을 만들어 낼 수 있다. 이러한 결정적인 순간들을 최대한 활용하는 것은 인내심과 통찰력을 요구하는데, 이 통찰력은 심지어 그것이 뷰파인더에 그 모습을 드러내기도 전에 무엇이 일어날지를 알아볼 수 있는 것이다.

문제 해설

'주어진 글은 사진을 찍을 때 정확하게 적절한 순간을 잡는 것이 중요하다는 글의 주제를 제시하고 있다. 사진을 찍을 때 그러한 적절한 순간이 분명하여 준비와 연습을 하는 것이 중요하다는 내용의 (B)가 온 다음, 앞의 내용에 대한 반대의 내용, 즉 여러 요소들이 결합하여 예측이 어려운 순간도 있다는 내용의 (A)가 오고, 이에 대한 구체적인 예를 제시하는 (C)가 와야 글의 흐름이 가장 적절하다.

구문 분석

[8행] For some subjects, the key times [**at which** to take pictures] are obvious, such as the moment {**when** a winner crosses the finishing line}.

▶ [at which ~]는 the key times를 수식하며 {when ~}는 관계부사절로 the moment를 수식한다.

[13행] To make the most of these decisive moments requires patience and the vision [to see what **might** happen, even before it presents itself in the viewfinder].

▶ to부정사가 주어로 쓰이면 단수 취급한다. [ ]로 표시된 부분은 the vision을 뒤에서 수식하며, 이 문장에서 might는 과거 시제를 나타내는 것이 아니라 미래에 대한 추측을 완곡하게 표현하기 위해 사용된 것이다.

어휘

frame 틀에 넣다, 표현하다
may well (~하는 것도) 당연하다, 아마 ~일 것이다
predictable 예측할 수 있는 **constantly** 끊임없이
combine 결합하다 **subject** 소재, 주제, 피사체
count 중요하다 **illuminate** (~에 불을) 비추다, 밝히다
shaft (빛 · 햇살 등의) 줄기[가닥]
moody 기분 변화가 심한, 감수성을 자극하는
make the most of ~을 최대한 활용하다
decisive 결정적인

Exercise

01 ④ 02 ④ 03 ⑤

Plus Q

03 each player put Chad's number 12 on his ball cap

01 정답 ④

소재 풋볼 경기에서 본 관중

전문 해석

나는 지난주에 풋볼 게임에 갔고, 그것은 사람들을 보는 완전히 새로운 방식에 내 눈을 뜨게 했다. 경기가 재미있었지만, 새로운 관점으로 보게 된 것은 그 완전한 경험, 특히 관중이었다. 경기장 높은 곳에 앉아서 나는 수천 명의 사람들을 볼 수 있었다. 그들 모두가 함께 벌떡 일어서고, 동시에 환호하거나 야유를 보냈고, 파도타기를 했으며, 팀을 응원했다. 그 광경은 내가 관중이 실제로 존재한다는 것을 깨닫게 했다. 관중은 자신만의 기쁨, 분노, 두려움, 욕망을 가지고 있는, 거대하고 우둔한 동물처럼 존재했다. 그것은 단지 사람들의 집합체 이상이었다. 그것은 개인들 못지않은 존재감을 뽐냈지만, 개인들과는 달랐다. 내 옆에 앉아 있는 친구들을 볼 수 있는 것만큼 분명하게 나는 그 실체가 움직이고 분위기를 바꾸는 것을 내 눈으로 볼 수 있었다.

문제 해설

④ 주어가 It이므로 their가 아니라 its를 써야 한다.

오답 풀이

① 「it was ~ that」 구문으로 주어를 강조하고 있다.
② 주절과 주어가 같은 부사절을 생략하여 분사구로 처리한 것이므로 적절하다.
③ jumped, cheered or booed, did, encouraged가 병렬구조로 사용되었다
⑤ 동사 see를 수식하므로 부사 clearly를 사용한 것은 적절하다.

구문 분석

[2행] ~, but **it was** the whole experience, especially the crowd, **that** appeared in a new light.

▶ 「it is (was) ~ that」 구문으로 주어인 the whole experience를 강조한 구문이다.

02 정답 ④

소재 정원 가꾸기의 이점

전문 해석

여름 휴가 동안 여가 시간을 보내는 방법을 모르고 있을 때, 정원 가꾸기가 여러분에게 가장 좋은 선택권이다. 그런 원시적이지만 굉장히 흥미로운 취미의 도움으로 여러분은 몇 가지 매우 중요한 이득을 얻을 수 있다. 정원 가꾸기는 여러분이 필요로 하는 모든 채소를 바로 뒤뜰에서 곧 발견할 것이기 때문에 식료품점에서 돈을 절약하도록 도움을 준다. 채소의 범위는 양파, 파프리카 혹은 토마토와 같은 원시적인 것에서부터 매우 드문 가령 브로콜리와 심지어 아스파라거스와 같은 채소에 이르기까지 다양하다. (그것이 바로 사람들이 유기농으로 재배하지 않은 채소보다 유기농으로 재배된 채소를 선호하는 이유이다.) 자신의 채소 정원을 가지는 것은 흐린 날에도 긍정적인 감정을 가져다주기 때문에 또한 매우 유용하다.

문제 해설

채소 정원 가꾸기를 하면서 갖게 되는 이점에 대해 설명한

글이므로, 사람들이 유기농 채소를 선호한다는 내용의 ④는 전체 글의 흐름과 무관하다.

구문 분석

[6행] The range of them **varies from** primitive ones such as onions, paprika or tomatoes **to** very rare — for example, broccoli and even asparagus.

▶ 「vary from A to B」는 'A에서 B에 이르기까지 다양하다'의 의미이다. very rare 뒤에는 ones(= vegetables)가 생략되어 있다.

03 정답 ⑤

소재 후보 선수의 부상

전문 해석

Chad Kreuter는 Chicago White Sox의 예비 포수였는데, 홈구장에서 경기를 하다가 왼쪽 어깨가 심하게 골절 탈구되었다. 그는 수술을 받았으며 그 Sox팀은 그를 60일자 부상자 명단에 올려 놓았다. 그것은 후보 선수를 팀의 일원으로 덜 느끼게끔 만드는 그런 종류의 조치였다. 하지만 정확히 반대의 일이 벌어졌다. 분명히, Chad의 팀 동료들은 그를 매우 좋아했으며 각각의 선수는 지지를 보여주기 위해 야구 모자에 Chad의 번호 12번을 새겨 넣었다. Chad가 경기를 뛰든 안 뛰든지 간에 그는 팀의 일원이었으며 그것은 Chad에게 많은 것을 의미했다. 시즌 후반에 그가 다시 유니폼을 입을 수 있게 되었을 때, 그는 모든 팀 동료들의 번호를 그의 야구 모자에 새겨 넣는 것으로 감사를 나타냈다. 모두가 하나가 되었고 하나가 모두가 되었는데, 그것이 바로 팀을 만드는 것이다.

문제 해설

주어진 문장은 Chad가 다시 유니폼을 입게 되었을 때, 모든 동료 선수들의 번호를 자신의 모자에 새기는 것으로 감사를 나타냈다는 내용이므로, 선수들이 Chad를 배려한 행동이 나타난 이후에 들어가야 한다. 따라서 주어진 문장은 ⑤에 들어가는 것이 가장 적절하다.

구문 분석

[6행] That's the kind of thing [**that** makes a backup player feel even less like a part of the team].

▶ [that ~]는 관계절로 the kind of thing을 수식한다. 「make+목적어+목적보어(동사원형)」 구문은 '~로 하여금 …하게 하다'라는 의미이다.

Plus Q

후보 선수를 대하는 구단의 홀대와 반대되는 것을 나타내는 것이어야 하므로 '모든 팀 동료 선수가 Chad의 번호 12를 야구 모자에 새겨 넣었다'가 이에 해당한다.

소재 10 컴퓨터, 정보, 미디어, 교통

p. 168

대표 예제 정답 ①

소재 새로운 매체

전문 해석

새로운 매체란 네 가지 특징에 의해 동시에 정의될 수 있는데, 그것들은 모두 통합적이고 쌍방향이며 기술적 수단으로 디지털 코드와 하이퍼텍스트를 사용하는, 20세기와 21세기의 전환기의 매체이다. 그렇기에 그것들의 가장 일반적인 다른 이름이 다중 매체, 쌍방향 매체, 디지털 매체라는 이야기가 된다. 이 정의를 사용하면 매체가 구식인지 신식인지를 구별하는 것이 쉽다. 예를 들어, 전통적인 텔레비전은 그것이 이미지, 소리, 글을 포함하고 있기 때문에 통합적이지만, 쌍방향이 아니며 디지털 코드에 기반을 두고 있지도 않다. 평범한 구식 전화는 쌍방향이었지만, 그것은 오로지 말과 소리만 전송하기 때문에 통합적이지 않았으며, 디지털 코드로 작동하지 않았다. 대조적으로, 쌍방향의 텔레비전이라는 새로운 매체는 쌍방향성과 디지털 코드를 더한다. 게다가, 새로운 세대의 이동식 또는 고정식 전화 통신은 글, 그림 또는 영상을 추가하고 인터넷과 연결되기 때문에 완전히 디지털화되고 통합적이다.

문제 해설

(A) 앞에서 새로운 매체의 정의를 이용하여 어떤 매체가 구식인지 신식인지를 구별하기 쉽다는 내용이 나온 후 이에 대한 구체적인 예를 들고 있으므로 For example이 적절하다.
(B) 새로운 매체의 예를 추가적으로 제시하고 있으므로 Additionally가 적절하다.

② 그럼에도 불구하고 - 다시 말해서
③ 따라서 - 게다가
④ 예를 들어 - 다시 말해서
⑤ 그럼에도 불구하고 - 결과적으로

구문 분석

[2행] ~ they are media at the turn of the 20th and 21st centuries [**which** are both integrated and interactive and use digital code and hypertext as technical means].

▶ 주격 관계대명사 which 이하의 [ ]는 선행사인 media를 수식하는 관계대명사절이다. 상관접속사 「both A and B」 구문은 'A와 B 둘 다'라는 뜻으로 형용사 integrated와 interactive가 병렬구조를 이루고 있다.

어휘

simultaneously 동시에 **integrated** 통합적인, 통합된
interactive 쌍방향의, 상호작용하는 **hypertext** 하이퍼텍스트(문장 중의 어구나 그것에 붙은 표제, 표제를 모은 목차 등이 서로 연결된 문자 데이터 파일)
alternative 대안의 **identify** 확인하다, 식별하다
transmit 전송하다, 송신하다

유제 정답 ⑤

소재 광고 속 이야기의 효과

전문 해석

광고 전문가들은 우리가 기억하는 광고 방송들이 우리를 이야기 속으로 끌어들이는 경향이 있다는 것을 알게 되었다. 인쇄된 종이 형태든 방송 프로그램 사이에 끼워 넣는 30초짜리 텔레비전 광고의 형태든, 역대 가장 기억에 남고 효과적인 몇몇 광고들을 생각해 보자. 그것들은 인상적인 줄거리를 포함한다. Apple 컴퓨터의 걸작인 'Think Different' 캠페인은 매우 극적으로 강력한 이야기를 들려주었기 때문에 역대 최고의 광고로 널리 여겨진다. Coca Cola의 'Mean Joe Green' 광고 방송은 이야기를 담은 또 하나의 사례인데, 그 이야기에서 어린 소년은 자신의 영웅을 만난다. 이런 모든 시나리오에서의 목적은 상품과 긍정적이고 친숙한 연상을 밀접하게 만들면서 사람들을 정서적으로 그리고 개인적으로 '감동시키는' 것이다.

문제 해설

역대 가장 기억에 남고 효과적인 몇몇 광고들이 인상적인 줄거리를 포함하며, 이야기를 담은 광고 사례를 제시하는 내용의 글이므로, 글의 주제로는 ⑤ '광고에서 이야기를 하는 것의 강력한 효과'가 가장 적절하다.

① 광고 방송의 다양한 길이
② 매출 증대에 있어서의 광고의 역할
③ 광고와 캠페인의 차이점
④ 교육에서 개인적인 이야기를 하는 것의 효용

구문 분석

[5행] ~ "Think Different" campaign **is** widely **considered the best ad** of all time ~.

▶ consider가 쓰인 5형식 문장이 수동태로 전환된 문장으로, 명사 the best ad가 주격 보어로 사용되었다.

어휘

expert 전문가 **commercial** 광고 방송, 상업 광고
hook ~ into ... ~을 …로 끌어들이다
of all time 역대 **involve** 포함하다
scenario 시나리오, 각본 **emotionally** 정서적으로
personally 개인적으로 **association** 연상; 연관

Exercise

01 ③ 02 ④ 03 ①

Plus Q

03 우리의 미디어 기술들이 아무리 많이 변하였더라도

01 정답 ③

소재 빅데이터의 핵심

전문 해석

본질적으로 빅데이터는 예측에 관한 것이다. 비록 그것이 인공지능이라 불리는 컴퓨터 과학 분야의 일부분, 더욱 구체적으로는 기계 학습이라 불리는 영역이라고 기술되지만, 이러한 정의는 오해의 소지가 있다. 빅데이터는 컴퓨터를 인간처럼 '생각'하도록 '가르치려는' 시도에 관한 것이 아니다. 대신에, 그것은 확률을 추론하기 위해 막대한 양의 데이터에 대한 수학의 적용에 관한 것이다. 이메일 메시지가 스팸이거나 'teh'라고 입력된 철자가 'the'일 가능성이 그 예이다. 핵심은 그들의 예측의 기반이 될 많은 데이터를 공급받기 때문에 이러한 체계들이 역할을 능숙히 수행한다는 것이다. 게다가, 이 체계들은 더 많은 데이터를 공급받으면서 어떤 것이 최상의 신호와 패턴일지를 계산함으로써, 시간이 지남에 따라 스스로를 개선하도록 만들어져 있다.

문제 해설

(A) 빈칸 앞에서는 빅데이터의 정의에 대해 컴퓨터를 인간처럼 생각하도록 가르치려는 시도에 관한 것이 아니라는 내용이 나오지만, 빈칸 이후에는 수학의 적용에 관한 것이라고 언급하고 있으므로, Instead가 적절하다.
(B) 이 체계들이 많은 데이터를 공급받기 때문에 역할을 잘 수행한다는 내용에 이어서 시간이 지남에 따라 스스로를 개선하도록 만들어져 있다고 언급하고 있으므로, 첨가의 뜻을 가진 연결사 Moreover가 적절하다.

① 다시 말해서 – 게다가
② 그러나 – 그럼에도 불구하고
④ 다시 말해서 – 요약하면
⑤ 대신에 – 그럼에도 불구하고

오답 풀이
In other words는 '다시 말해서' 라는 뜻으로 같은 개념이나 문장을 다르게 바꾸어 표현할 때 쓰인다. 주어진 지문에서 빈칸 (A)의 앞뒤 내용이 서로 다르므로 답이 될 수 없다.

구문 분석
[5행] Instead, it's about applying math to huge quantities of data **in order to** infer probabilities; ~.
▶ 「in order to+동사원형」은 '~하기 위해서'의 뜻으로 쓰인 부사적 용법의 to부정사구이다.

02 정답 ④

소재 자율주행 자동차의 잠재력

전문 해석
자율주행 자동차는 차에 대한 우리의 생각을 근본적으로 바꿀 잠재력이 있으며, 그 잠재력은 거의 무한하다. 자율주행 택시는 모든 거리와 도시에 주차할 수 있어서, 당신은 휴대전화를 이용하여 자율주행 택시를 호출할 수 있고, 그것은 당신이 집 문앞을 나섰을 때쯤 당신의 집 밖에 주차되어 있을 것이다. 일단 그 택시가 당신을 목적지에 데려다 주고 나면, 그것은 다음 승객을 태우러 떠난다. 더욱이, 자율주행 자동차는 하교하는 아이들을 태우고, 노인을 가게로 데려다주며, 모든 흔한 일상의 여정을 수행하는 데 사용될 수 있다. 자율주행 자동차는 그들이 만약 공유된다면 혼잡의 많은 문제들을 해결할 수도 있다. (많은 도시에서 자동차 공유 제공업자들의 수가 지난 몇 년간 급격히 증가했다.) 그들은 당신의 목적지에 대해 항상 최단거리의 가장 빠른 경로를 택하며 혼잡을 피하기 위해 서로 소통할 수 있다.

문제 해설
자율주행 자동차의 다양한 잠재력에 대해 설명하고 있는 글이므로, 자동차 공유 제공업자들의 증가를 언급한 ④는 글의 전체 흐름과 관계가 없다.

구문 분석
[4행] ~ **it would be** parked outside your house **by the time you walked** out of your front door.
▶ 「by the time+주어+과거동사」는 '~가 ~했을 때쯤' 이라는 의미이다.

03 정답 ①

소재 아날로그와 디지털 미디어의 관계

전문 해석
확실히, 아날로그 미디어와 디지털 미디어의 구분은 단지 동전의 한 면일 뿐이다. 최근 수십 년 간 우리의 미디어 기술들이 아무리 많이 변하였더라도 인간의 눈, 귀, 목소리는 변하지 않았으며, 다시 말해, 체화된 존재로서 우리는 아직도 변함없이 아날로그 형태로 정보를 생성하고 수용한다는 것을 명심하는 것이 중요하다. 예를 들어, 두 대의 컴퓨터나 스마트폰 사이의 디지털 코드는 그 형태가 스카이프 전화든, 페이스북 업데이트든, 혹은 전화통화든, 그들의 인간 사용자들에게 아날로그 정보로써 시작되고 끝난다. 요약하면, '디지털'의 출현은 '아날로그'의 빠르고 완전한 종말을 의미하지는 않는다.

문제 해설
디지털 미디어가 아무리 발전해왔더라도 인간은 정보를 아날로그 형태로 생성, 수용하기 때문에 두 미디어를 명확히 구분 지을 수 없고 디지털의 출현이 아날로그의 종말을 의미하지 않는다는 내용의 글이므로, 빈칸에는 ① '동전의 한 면'이 가장 적절하다.

② 사회적 통념
③ 기술적 연구 결과
④ 미디어를 위한 타당한 기준들
⑤ 발전을 위한 적절한 이유

구문 분석
[2행] **It** is important [**to keep** in mind that, however much our media technologies have changed in recent decades, the human eyes, ears, and voices have not (changed) ~].
▶ It은 가주어이며 to keep 이하의 [ ]가 진주어이다. have not 다음에 changed가 생략되었다.

Plus Q
「however+부사+주어+동사」 구문은 '아무리 ~하더라도'의 뜻으로, 이때 복합관계부사 however는 no matter how로 바꿔 쓸 수 있다.

Part Ⅲ Mini Test

Mini Test 1

p. 174~179

01 ③ 02 ④ 03 ② 04 ② 05 ④ 06 ③
07 ② 08 ④ 09 ③

01 정답 ③

소재 무방비 상태에서 마주하게 된 벌 떼

전문 해석
내가 무슨 일이 벌어졌는지를 파악하는 데에는 오래 걸리지 않았다. 나의 갇힌 다리는 마비 상태였고 고통은 시간이 지나가면서 더해지는 것 같았다. 그때 나는 벌 한 마리가 차 안에서 윙윙거리는 소리를 들었다. 그것은 내 머리 주변에 계속 날았다. 간지러움 때문에 머리를 흔들고자 하는 강한 충동을 느꼈지만 (그렇게 할 경우) 벌이 놀라서 그 가장 민감한 부위(머리)에 침을 쏠 것이라는 것을 나는 알고 있었다. 그래서 나는 움직이지 않으려고 마음을 단단히 먹었다. 잠시 후, 벌이 차 밖으로 나갔고, 윙윙거리는 소리도 멀어졌다. 그러나 안도의 한숨을 채 내쉬기도 전에, 나는 벌 떼들이 등 뒤에서 윙윙대는 소리를 들었다. 나는 꼼짝도 하지 않았고, 숨도 쉬지 않으려고 했다. 핀 하나만 떨어져도 어떤 결과가 발생할지 나는 이미 알고 있었다.

문제 해설
차 안에 발이 갇혀져 있는 상태에서 벌 떼들의 등장으로 필자는 숨을 죽인 채 꼼짝도 안 하고 있으며, 약간의 움직임이 있으면 벌 떼들의 공격을 받을 것이라고 생각하고 있는 상황이므로 ③ '무서운'이 필자 'I'의 심경으로 가장 적절하다.

① 안도한 ② 부러워하는 ④ 무관심한 ⑤ 실망한

구문 분석
[8행] I already knew what difference **a drop of a pin could** make.

▶ could는 가정법 과거를 나타내는 조동사이다. '핀 하나라도 떨어지면'의 가정의 의미를 주어 a drop of a pin이 담고 있다.

어휘
numb 감각이 없는 **buzz** 윙윙거리다
tickling 간지러움 **impulse** 충동 **sting** (곤충 따위의) 침
sensitive 민감한 **steel oneself** 단단히 마음먹다
crawl (곤충이) 기어가다 **a sigh of relief** 안도의 한숨
a swarm of 한 떼의 **hold one's breath** 숨을 죽이다

02 정답 ④

소재 십 대 다루기

전문 해석
모든 십 대들은 설령 그들이 여러분이 동의하지 않는 선택을 가끔씩 한다고 할지라도 그들의 있는 그대로의 모습을 위해 받아들여질 필요가 있다. 십 대는 여러분의 사랑, 헌신 그리고 정서적 지지가 자신이 여러분의 기준에 부응할 수 있느냐의 여부에 바탕을 두고 있다고 느낀다면 그러면 그는 여러분의 수락을 얻을 만큼의 값어치가 없다고 느끼거나 자신이 방심해도 될 만큼 충분히 정서적으로 안전하다고 느끼지 않을 것이다. 여러분은 그들을 파괴적 비난으로 망연자실하게 만들고 싶지는 않을 것 아닌가? 그들이 형편없는 결정을 내릴 때 십 대를 신뢰하는 마음을 잃지 않도록 해라. 인간으로서 그녀에게 얼마나 실망하고 있는지를 지적하지 말고 여러분의 비난을 그녀의 행동에 집중시켜라. '나는 … 하는 것이 매우 무례하다고 생각한다', 혹은 '지금 너에게 화가 나 있는데 그 이유는 … 때문이다'와 같이 말해서 그렇게 할 수 있다. 이런 식의 말은 십 대에게 여러분이 말하고 있는 것을 받아들이게 해 줄 것이고 여러분이 말한 것의 요지를 이해할 수 있게 해 준다.

문제 해설
십 대들이 잘못된 결정이나 행동을 할 때 그들이 아닌 그들의 행동에 대해 지적을 하면 십 대들이 더 잘 이해할 것이라는 내용이므로 ④가 요지로 가장 적절하다.

구문 분석
[2행] If a teen feels like your love, commitment and emotional support are based **on** [whether or not he can live up to your standards], then he will never feel worthy **enough to gain** your acceptance or emotionally safe **enough to let** down his guard.

▶ [whether ~]는 명사절로 전치사 on의 목적어로 사용되었다. 「enough to+동사원형」은 부사나 형용사를 뒤에서 수

식한다.

어휘
occasionally 이따금씩 **commitment** 헌신
live up to (다른 사람의 기대에) 부응하다
worthy 가치가 있는 **let down one's guard** 방심하다
devastate 망연자실하게 하다 **criticism** 비난
disapproval 반감, 반대 **take in** 받아들이다

03 정답 ②

소재 시차 예방

전문 해석
빈번한 비행과 일정하게 표준 시간대를 넘나드는 것이 당신의 24시간 주기 리듬 혹은 체내 시계에 지장을 주고 시차를 유발한다. 환경과의 조화가 깨진 것이고, 그것이 당신을 피곤하게 만든다. 증상은 두통, 과민성, 머리가 안개같이 뿌예진 상태, 그리고 낮은 에너지를 포함한다. 그렇다면 시차에 의해 야기된 이러한 증상으로부터 어떻게 자유로울 수 있을까? 비행을 앞둔 며칠 간, 당신의 몸에 맞는 패턴을 설정하기 위해 일관된 수면 일정을 고수하라. 비행기에서는 비행기의 건조한 공기에 의해 유발되는 탈수증을 막기 위해 매시간 적어도 물 두 잔을 마셔라. 순환을 원활하게 하고 붓는 것을 막기 위해 가끔 기내를 돌아다녀라. 다리를 뻗고 발가락을 특정 방향으로 향하게 하고 구부리고 하면서 앉은 자세로 스트레치를 하는 것이 근육이 덜 당기게 하는 데 도움이 될 것이다. 아침에 햇볕을 쬐는 것이 당신의 24시간 주기 리듬을 앞당기는 데 도움이 된다.

문제 해설
잦은 비행으로 발생하는 시차를 예방하는 방법에 관해 설명하고 있는 내용의 글이므로 ② '시차를 예방하는 방법'이 글의 주제로 가장 적절하다.

① 시차의 증상
③ 체내 시계의 정의
④ 비행 동안 휴식을 취하는 방법
⑤ 일관되게 잠을 자는 것의 중요성

구문 분석
[6행] While on board, drink at least two glasses of water every hour to combat dehydration [**caused** by the plane's dry air].

▶ [caused ~] 앞에 which is가 생략된 관계절로 dehydration을 수식한다. to combat은 '목적'을 나타내는 부정사이다.

어휘
time zone 표준 시간대 **internal clock** 체내 시계
jet leg 시차 **out of sync with** 협조 관계가 아닌
irritability 과민성, 화를 잘 냄 **stick to** ~을 고수하다
combat 방지하다, 싸우다 **dehydration** 탈수증
every so often 가끔[종종] **circulation** 순환
swelling 붓기 **flex** 구부리다 **lessen** 줄다[줄이다]
stiffness 당김, 뻣뻣함

04 정답 ②

소재 여성 지도자들에 대한 지지의 부재

전문 해석
여성 지도자들에게 더 큰 집단의 긍정과 지지는 여전히 흔한 일이 아니다. 여성 지도자들은 가장 붐비는 방에서 외로움을 느낄 수 있다. 중간 관리자 계급에 있든, 임원이라는 높은 계급에 있든, 실업가의 모험적 사업을 책임지고 있든, 혹은 정치계에 몸담고 있든, 그들은 관점을 주장하려고 시도할 때 그들이 진정으로 환영받는 것은 아니라는 것을 알게 모르게 항상 깨닫게 된다. 이런 방식의 반복되는 거절은 심오한 영향을 미친다. 그들은 자신의 구상, 직관 그리고 지식을 의심한다. 그들은 자부심, 자신감, 그리고 기여하고자 하는 열망을 잃는다. 그들은 가치를 인정받고 있다거나, 받아들여지고 있다고 느끼지 않는다. 모든 여성 지도자가 그러한 주변적인 존재로 만드는 것으로 인한 개인적인 손실을 알고 있지만 그 결과로 그들이 조직에 초래한 손실을 상상하는 것은 어렵다.

문제 해설
여성 지도자들이 뭔가를 주장하려고 할 때마다 탐탁지 않게 여기는 분위기를 계속 깨닫게 되고, 그런 것이 스스로가 낸 아이디어, 직관, 지식에 대한 불신으로 이어진다는 내용이므로 빈칸에는 ② '반복되는 거절'이 가장 적절하다.

① 상호간의 이익
③ 점진적인 승진
④ 공유된 정보
⑤ 지나치게 높은 기대

구문 분석
[9행] Although every woman leader knows the personal cost of such marginalization, **it** is hard [**to imagine** the losses {**they have caused in organizations as a result**}].

▶ 주절의 it이 형식상의 주어(가주어), [ ]로 표시된 부분이 내용상의 주어(진주어)인 구문으로, 진주어 속 { }로 표시된 부분은 관계절로 the losses를 수식한다.

어휘

affirmation 긍정, 단언
at the helm ~을 책임지고 있는
entrepreneurial 실업가의 **venture** 모험적 사업
arena 활동 장소 **advocate** 주장하다, (공개적으로) 지지하다
profound 심오한 **intuition** 직관
self-esteem 자부심

05 정답 ④

소재 의료 과실에 대한 인식 변화

전문 해석

최근까지, 의료 과실은 거의 논의되지 않았다. 대중은 의료 행위에서의 과실은 드물다고 믿는 것을 선호했다. 신뢰의 상실과 손상된 명예를 우려한 건강 전문가들은 그 그릇된 생각을 영속화하려고 했다. 의료 과실에 대한 법적 소송이라는 위협에 의해서 만들어진 반대 분위기가 이 '아무것도 보지 말고, 아무것도 하지 말라'는 접근 방식에 부채질을 했다. 이 모든 것이 지난 20년간에 바뀌었다. 환자 안전을 위한 새로운 '운동'이 1995년에 시작되었는데, 그 해에 죽음 혹은 부적절한 수술로 이어진 일련의 명백하게 터무니없는 과실이 널리 알려지게 되었다. 병원들은 환자 부상을 예방하기 위해 더 많은 것들을 할 수 있다는 것을 인정하기 시작했다. 결과는 의료 과실의 원인들에 대한 연구와 예방을 위한 장치의 이행에서의 상당한 증가였다.

문제 해설

최근까지 의료 과실이 거의 논의되지 않았던 것은 의료 과실은 드문 현상이라는 사람들의 믿음 때문이었고, 의료 과실로 인한 손실과 이미지 실추를 두려워한 건강 전문가들 입장에서는 그러한 믿음이 계속되는 것을 원했을 것이라는 내용이 되어야 하므로 빈칸에는 ④ '그 그릇된 생각을 영속화하다'가 가장 적절하다.

① 그들의 명성을 회복하다
② 의료 기록을 공유하다
③ 법적 자문에 의존하다
⑤ 사회에 더욱 기여하다

구문 분석

[6행] A new "movement" for patient safety began in 1995, **when** a series of apparently outrageous errors [**resulting** in death or inappropriate surgery] were widely publicized.

▶ when은 관계부사로 그 이하에서는 1995년에 벌어진 내용을 설명하고 있다. [resulting ~]는 a series of apparently outrageous errors를 수식한다.

어휘

medical practice 의료 행위 **rare** 드문
impaired 망가진, 손상된 **reputation** 명성
apparently 명백히 **outrageous** 터무니없는
inappropriate 부적절한 **publicize** 공표하다, 선전하다
recognize 인정하다 **substantial** 상당한, 실질적인
implementation 이행 **preventive** 예방을 위한
mechanism 장치 **prestige** 명성
perpetuate 영속화하다
misconception 그릇된 생각, 오해

06 정답 ③

소재 Michael Romanoff의 생애

전문 해석

Michael Romanoff는 리투아니아에서 Hershel Geguzin이라는 이름으로 태어난 할리우드의 레스토랑 경영자이자 배우였다. 그는 아마도 지금은 없어진, 1940년대와 1950년대에 할리우드 스타들에게 인기가 있던 Beverly Hills 레스토랑인 Romanoff's의 소유주로 가장 잘 알려져 있을 것이다. Geguzin은 10살의 나이에 뉴욕으로 이민을 왔으며 1900년 이후 이름을 Michael Romanoff로 바꾸었다. 1931년에 그는 유명한 삽화가 Rockwell Kent의 행세를 했는데, 그것이 그 예술가를 행복하게 해 주었다. Romanoff는 Kent 못지않게 매력적이어서 그는 Kent의 미술책을 그 실제 예술가가 판매한 것보다 더 많이 팔았다. 그는 1932년 5월에 사기죄로 복역하기 위해 프랑스로 추방되었다. 'U.S.A. Confidential'에 따르면 Romanoff는 러시아 왕자 행세를 했는데, 그것이 레스토랑을 인기가 있게 만들었다. 그는 1971년 81세의 나이로 캘리포니아 주 LA에서 심장마비로 사망했다.

문제 해설

Michael Romanoff가 삽화가의 행세를 한 것이 그 삽화가를 행복하게 해 주었다고 했으므로 ③은 글의 내용과 일치하지 않는다.

구문 분석

[7행] Romanoff was **so attractive as** Kent **that** he sold **more** of Kent's art books **than** the real artist did.

▶ 원급 비교(so ~ as)와 「so ~ that(너무나 ~해서 …하다)」구문이 결합되어 있고 that절 속에는 비교 구문과 대동사 did(= sold)가 활용되어 문장을 형성하고 있다.

어휘

restaurateur 레스토랑 경영자
now-vanished 지금은 사라진
popular with ~에게 인기가 있는
pretend ~인 체하다, 가장하다 **illustrator** 삽화가
expel 추방하다
serve time for fraud 사기죄로 복역하다
heart attack 심장마비

07 정답 ②

소재 왜곡의 장점

전문 해석

현실을 왜곡하는 것이 항상 나쁜 것은 아니다. 압도당하고 있다는 느낌, 정신적 외상, 혹은 학대 때문에 가끔씩 현실 왜곡이 필요하다. 그러한 경우에, 부정은 사람으로 하여금 다른 경우라면 매우 스트레스가 많은 상황을 다루는 데에 도움을 준다. 다른 때에는 부정이 정신적 휴가를 얻는 방법이 될 수 있다. 하지만 정신 건강의 관점에서 보면 중요한 것은 '멋진 여행을 하고 있는' 시점과 그렇지 않은 시점을 구별해내서, 몇몇 방어적인 사고방식이 습관화가 되어서 건강하고 의미 있는 삶의 추구를 차단하도록 허락하지 않는 것이다. 마음이 어떻게 작동하는지를 지켜보는 것을 배워서 이것을 해 낼 수 있다. 그러한 자기 이해는 명상, 요가, 현대식 심리치료, 그리고 의식에 집중하고 자각을 끌어들이는 데 도움을 주는 기타 관행들의 목적이다.

문제 해설

(A) 바로 앞 문장에서 현실 왜곡이 나쁜 것만은 아니라고 했으므로 현실 왜곡이 필요할 상황도 있다는 내용이 이어져야 자연스럽다. 따라서 necessary가 적절하다. unnecessary는 '불필요한'이라는 뜻이다.
(B) 왜곡하지 않으면 스트레스가 될 수밖에 없는 상황을 다루는 데 도움을 준다는 내용이 되어야 하므로 stressful이 적절하다. carefree는 '근심 없는'이라는 뜻이다.
(C) 방어적인 사고가 습관화가 되어서 건강하고 의미 있는 삶의 추구를 '차단'하는 것을 못하게 한다는 내용이 되어야 하므로 block이 적절하다. encourage는 '장려하다'의 뜻이다.

구문 분석

[2행] In such instances, denial helps a person cope with what would **otherwise** be a highly stressful situation.

▶ otherwise는 가정법 대용어구로 사용되는 부사로 '다른 경우라면, 그게 아니라면'의 의미로 현재 사실의 반대를 가정할 때 사용한다.

어휘

distort 왜곡하다 **overwhelmed** 압도되는
trauma 정신적 외상, 마음의 쇼크 **denial** 부인, 부정
from the perspective of ~의 관점으로
know 구별하다 **pursuit** 추구 **meditation** 명상
psychotherapy 심리치료, 심리 요법
awareness 의식, 자각
engage (주의 · 관심을) 사로잡다[끌다]
consciousness 의식, 자각

08 정답 ④

소재 진실을 통한 아버지의 사랑 확인

전문 해석

내가 어린 소녀였을 때, 나는 우연히 과일 단지를 깨뜨렸다. 이유는 모르겠지만 과일 단지를 깨뜨렸을 수도 있었던 오빠들 여럿과 언니가 근처에 있었지만, 아빠는 내 쪽으로 방향을 돌리고는 "Alice, 네가 단지를 깨뜨렸니?" 하고 물으셨다. 아빠의 큰 갈색 눈을 들여다 본 나는 아빠가 내게 진실을 말해주기를 원하고 있음을 알았다. 나는 또한 내가 진실을 말하면 아빠가 나를 꾸짖을지도 모른다는 것을 알고 있었다. 하지만 나의 내면 속 진실은 표현되어지기를 간절히 원했다. "제가 단지를 깨뜨렸어요,"라고 내가 말했다. 아빠의 사랑의 눈길이 내게 상이었고 안아줌이었다. 갑자기 나는 내가 지금까지 아직도 감사하게 기억하고 있는 내적 평화를 느꼈다. 똑같은 방식으로, 우리는 친근하게 느끼는 사람에게 죄를 고백하는 것이 우리를 그와 더 가까운 곳으로 데려다준다는 것을 알게 된다.

문제 해설

④ 선행사인 an inner peace 뒤에 이어지는 문장에서 recall의 목적어가 없으므로, '관계사와 목적어'의 역할을 동시에 수행할 수 있는 관계대명사 that 혹은 which로 고쳐야 한다.

오답 풀이

① several brothers and a sister를 선행사로 하는 주격 관계대명사이다.
② 주어(I)가 같아서 부사절을 분사구로 대체한 것이므로 Looking은 적절하다.
③ the truth와 express와의 관계는 수동이므로 be expressed는 적절하다.
⑤ that절에서 confessing이 주어이고 동사가 필요한 자리

이므로 brings는 적절하다.

구문 분석

[8행] In the same way, we find [**that** confessing our sins to someone {**we feel close to**}] brings us closer to him.

▶ that절의 주어는 동명사인 confessing이다. {we feel ~}는 목적격 관계대명사가 생략된 관계사절로 someone을 수식하고 있다.

어휘

accidentally 우연히 **jar** 단지
want badly 간절히 원하다 **reward** 상을 주다
embrace 안다, 포옹하다 **gratitude** 감사
confess 고백하다 **feel close to** ~와 가깝다고 느끼다

09 정답 ③

소재 아내의 따뜻한 격려

전문 해석

Alcott 집안의 경제 사정은 매우 안 좋았으나, 그들은 Bronson Alcott의 최근 강의 투어에 큰 희망을 걸었다. 2월의 어느 날 밤에 그가 집에 돌아왔을 때, 가족들이 그의 주변에 모였다. (B) 그들은 그를 환영했고, 그에게 음식과 음료를 제공했으며 그의 귀환을 기뻐했다. 그런 다음 약간의 침묵이 엄습했고, "그들이 돈을 주었나요?" 라는 가족들 모두의 마음속에 있던 그 질문을 한 것은 다름 아닌 딸 May였다. (C) Bronson Alcott은 천천히 지갑을 끄집어내고는 그 안의 내용물을 보여주었다. 지갑에 있는 것이라고는 1달러가 다였다. "내년에는 내가 더 잘 할 거야," 라고 그가 말했다. (A) 그를 둘러싼 집단에서 아찔한 침묵이 흘렀다. 그러고 나서 Alcott 부인이 팔로 그의 목을 껴안고는 단호하게 말했다. "나는 그것을 매우 잘 하고 있다고 여겨요."

문제 해설

집안의 경제 사정이 안 좋은 가운데, 모든 가족들이 가장이 강의 투어에서 벌어 올 수입을 기대하고 있었고, 가장이 돌아왔으며 그런 가장의 주변에 가족이 모였다는 주어진 글 뒤에는 그를 환영하는 모습을 담은 (B)가 와야 하고, (B)의 말미에서 얼마나 벌었는지를 묻고 있으므로 1달러가 그가 번 전부라고 설명하는 (C)가 온 다음, 기대하다가 실망한 가족 가운데 아내가 나서서 애쓰고 온 남편을 자랑스럽게 표현한 (A)가 마지막에 나와야 한다.

구문 분석

[8행] ~, and **it was** daughter May **who** asked the question in all their minds: "Did they pay you?"

▶ 「it is~that」강조 구문이다. 강조하는 내용이 사람이므로 그에 맞게 that을 who로 바꾸어 사용하였다.

어휘

finance 재정, 경제
place great hopes on ~에 큰 희망을 걸다
stunned (놀람 등으로) 어리벙벙하게 하는 **hush** 침묵, 고요
fling(-flung-flung) (몸이나 신체 일부를 갑자기 힘껏) 던지다
rejoice 크게[대단히] 기뻐하다
fall (어둠 · 침묵 등이 갑자기) 닥치다[찾아오다]
pocketbook 지갑 **display** 보여주다
content (*pl.*) 내용물

Mini Test 2

p. 180~185

01 ⑤ 02 ② 03 ② 04 ① 05 ③ 06 ⑤
07 ② 08 ① 09 ③

01 정답 ⑤

소재 애완동물 처리에 관한 연락

전문 해석

Tarpley 씨에게,
저희 컴퓨터시스템에 따르면 귀하께서 귀하의 얼룩 고양이 'Mitch'를 2016년 2월 4일에 다리 수술을 위해 저희에게 맡기셨는데 합의된 대로 7일에 고양이를 데려가지 않으셨습니다. 저희가 고양이를 데려가라고 귀하께 상기시켜 드리려고 그 후 몇 주간 반복적으로 전화를 드렸습니다만 응답하지 않으셨습니다. 편찮으시거나 환경이 달라져서 데려갈 수 없으시면 저희가 기꺼이 고양이를 귀하에게 데려다주거나 애완동물을 사랑하는 가정에 그 고양이가 입양되도록 할 수도 있습니다. 7일 간의 근무일 안에 저희에게 연락하지 않으시면 귀하가 고양이를 버린 것이라고 생각할 수밖에 없고 입양 과정을 진행하겠습니다. 601-555-0189로 저희에게 즉시 연락해 주십시오.
M. Baxter 드림

문제 해설

다리 수술을 위해 맡긴 고양이를 찾아가지 않는 주인에게 고양이를 어떻게 할지 연락하지 않으면 버린 것으로 간주하고 입양 과정을 진행하겠다는 내용이므로 글의 목적으로 가장 적절한 것은 ⑤이다.

구문 분석

[4행] If you are unable to do so **due to illness or a change in circumstances**, we will happily [bring him to you], or [even see that he is adopted to a loving home].

▶ illness와 a change in circumstances는 둘 다 due to에 이어진다. 두 개의 [ ]는 we will에 이어지며 병렬구조를 이룬다.

어휘

tabby cat 얼룩 고양이 surgery 수술
adopt 입양시키다 assume 추측하다
abandon 버리다
proceed (일을) 진행하다

02 정답 ②

소재 편안함에 안주하는 것

전문 해석

정체됨과 평범함으로 이끄는 많은 힘들이 있어서 중요한 영향을 주는 것은 흔하지 않다. 예를 들어 동료이든, 관리자이든, 또는 심지어 친구이든 어떤 사람들은 여러분이 위대한 일을 온전히 추구하는 것을 원치 않을지도 모르는데 그것이 그들에게 똑같이 하라는 책임을 부과하기 때문이다. 여러분이 무리의 수준을 넘어서 돋보이기 시작하면 그들은 재빨리 여러분을 다시 끌어내리려고 애쓸 것이다. 또한, 조직들은 흔히 여러분에게 좋은 임금과 멋진 직함이나 안정감을 제공하면서 적응하는 것을 쉽게 만드는데 속담에도 나오듯이 '황금 수갑'인 것이다. 이런 편안한 특전과 사랑에 빠지는 것은 쉽지만 편안함을 좋아하는 것은 흔히 위대함의 적이다. 노고의 부산물로 편안함을 누리는 것은 잘못된 것이 아니지만 그것을 주요한 목적으로 삼을 수는 없다.

문제 해설

주변에서 여러분이 편안함에 안주하도록 유도할지라도 그것에 안주하는 것은 위대함의 적이고, 노력의 부산물로 편안함을 누리는 것은 상관없지만 애초에 그것을 목적으로 삼아서는 안 된다는 내용이므로 글의 제목으로는 ② '편안함을 피하라: 그것은 위험하다!'가 적절하다.

① 더 나은 동료가 되도록 노력하라
③ 근로자를 위한 좋은 근로 조건
④ 협동하는 상황에서 경쟁은 적절한가?
⑤ 경영 방식: 과제 지향적인 방식 대 사람 지향적인 방식

구문 분석

[6행] Also, organizations often make **it** easy **to settle in**, [**providing** you with a good salary, a nice title, or a sense of stability]—the proverbial "golden handcuffs."

▶ it은 형식상의 목적어이고 to settle in이 내용상의 목적어이다. [providing ~]는 organizations를 의미상 주어로 하는 분사구문이다.

어휘

in the pursuit of ~을 추구하는 **pack** 무리, 떼
bring ~ back to earth ~를 (흥분에서 깨어) 현실로 되돌리다
settle in (자리를 잡고) 적응하다 **stability** 안정성
proverbial 속담의
golden handcuffs 황금 수갑(직원의 전직을 막기 위한 고액의 돈이나 다른 혜택)
perk (급료 이외의) 특전 **by-product** 부산물

03 정답 ②

소재 아프리카 음악의 특징

전문 해석

음악은 아프리카 사람들의 일상생활에서 상당한 일부이다. 예를 들어, 질병을 치료하고 신을 달래며 아기의 탄생을 축하하기 위해 음악이 요청된다. 소를 찬양하고 사냥에 관해 말하고 카누의 노를 젓기 위한 노래가 있다. 그저 오락을 위한 일부 노래도 있고 왕이나 추장과 관련된 행사를 위해 연주되는 소량의 곡이 있다. 대부분의 아프리카 음악은 기능적이기 때문에 연주자/청중이라는 상황에서 일어나지 않는다. 음악 연주는 연주자와 청중 사이의 구별이 거의 없는 진짜 참여적인 행사이다. 아프리카 음악은 기능적이기 때문에 그 음악가들은 자기들의 작품이 효력이 있기를 원한다. 그들은 서양의 음악가들이 흔히 음악에 관해 생각하는 의미에서 그것이 아름답게 여겨지는지에 관해 신경 쓰지 않는다.

문제 해설

(A) 앞에 있는 cure, appease와 병렬구조를 이루므로 celebrate가 적절하다.
(B) 뒤에 이어지는 절이 문장의 요소를 모두 갖추고 있으므로 in which가 적절하다.
(C) is considered 다음에 이어지는 보어이므로 형용사인 beautiful이 적절하다.

구문 분석

[3행] There are songs for [praising cattle], [telling

about animal hunts], and [paddling a canoe].

▶ 세 개의 [ ]는 모두 for에 이어지며 서로 병렬구조를 이루고 있다.

어휘

call on ~을 요청하다 **appease** 달래다, 진정시키다
paddle 노를 젓다 **take place** 발생하다, 일어나다
participatory 참여적인 **distinction** 구별

04 정답 ①

소재 휴식의 필요성

전문 해석

내가 엘리트의 과제 수행에 관한 K. Anders Ericsson의 획기적인 연구를 읽었을 때 나는 많은 사람들이 과제 수행에 중요하게 영향을 미친 한 요소를 간과했다는 것을 알게 되었다. 많은 사람들이 1만 시간의 계획적인 연습과 관련된 그의 연구 결과에 집중한 반면에 최고 기량을 보인 사람들을 구별했던 또 다른 요소는 잠이었다. 이 연구들에서 최고 기량을 보인 사람들은 평균 매일 밤 8시간 36분을 잤다. 이와 대조적으로 평균적인 미국인은 고작 평일 밤에 6시간 51분의 잠을 잔다. 음악가, 운동선수, 배우, 그리고 체스 선수를 포함하는 Ericsson의 엘리트 과제 수행자에 관한 연구는 또한 더 자주 쉬는 것이 성취를 높인다는 것을 보여준다. Ericsson은 그들이 기진맥진해지는 것을 피하고 자신들이 완전히 재충전되는 것을 확실하게 하기 위해 자주 휴식 시간을 가진다는 것을 알게 되었다. 이것이 그들이 자신들의 솜씨를 계속 향상시키고 완벽하게 만들 수 있게 한다.

문제 해설

최고 기량을 보이는 사람들은 평균적인 미국인보다 잠을 더 많이 잤고 자신들의 에너지가 고갈되지 않도록 자주 휴식 시간을 가진다고 했으므로, 빈칸에는 ① '더 자주 쉬는 것'이 적절하다.

② 고급 과정을 수강하는 것
③ 공정한 대접을 보장하는 것
④ 규칙적으로 운동하는 것
⑤ 더 많은 정보를 요구하는 것

구문 분석

[3행] **While** many concentrated on his findings relevant to 10,000 hours of deliberate practice, the other factor [**that** differentiated top performance] was sleep.

▶ While은 '~인 반면에'라는 의미의 접속사로 부사절을 이끈다. [that ~]는 the other factor를 수식하는 관계절이다.

어휘

landmark 획기적인 **overlook** 간과하다
finding 연구 결과 **relevant to** ~에 관련된
deliberate 계획[의도]적인, 신중한
differentiate 구별하다, 구분 짓다 **weeknight** 평일의 밤
boost 향상시키다 **exhaustion** 고갈, 소모
recharge 재충전하다 **craft** 솜씨, 기술

05 정답 ③

소재 아이 달래기

전문 해석

Cindy Silverman은 일상적인 혈액 검사를 받으러 지역 의료실에 갔다. 옆방에 대략 다섯 살 정도인 어린 여자아이가 큰 소리로 소리치고 있었다. 그녀 역시 혈액 검사를 받기로 되어 있었지만 그녀는 간호사가 자기 팔에 바늘을 찌르도록 허락하려고 하지 않았다. 그것은 악몽 같은 장면이었다. Cindy는 그 소녀가 있는 방으로 가서 그녀와 이야기를 해도 되는지 그녀의 엄마의 허락을 구했고 그녀는 허락을 받았다. "나를 봐라." 라고 그녀는 그 소녀에게 공감어린 목소리로 말했다. 그 소녀는 그녀를 봤다. "네 엄마가 너를 사랑한다고 생각하니?" 라고 Cindy는 친절하게 물었다. "네." 라고 그녀는 말했다. "네 엄마가 너를 아프게 할 어떤 것을 할 거라고 생각하니?" 라고 Cindy는 물었다. "아니요." 라고 그 소녀는 말했다. 그 소녀가 약간 진정했을 때 "그들이 이 검사를 하지 않으면 의사 선생님과 엄마는 너를 더 낫게 만들 수가 없단다." 라고 그녀는 말했다. 2분 안에 그녀는 진정했고 바늘을 찌를 준비가 되었다.

문제 해설

③은 Cindy Silverman을 가리키고, 나머지는 어린 소녀를 가리킨다.

구문 분석

[4행] Cindy went to the girl's room and asked her mother's permission to talk with her, [**which** she received].

▶ [which ~]의 선행사는 her mother's permission to talk with her이고 which는 목적격 관계대명사이다.

어휘

local medical laboratory 지역 의료실
routine 일상적인 **scream** 소리치다
at the top of one's lungs (목청이 터지도록) 큰 소리로

stick 찌르다　permission 허락
empathetically 공감하면서

06 정답 ⑤

소재 무시되었으나 자기의 주장을 입증한 과학자들

전문 해석

처음에 강경한 과학자들은 Rachel Carson이 '침묵의 봄'을 출간한 후에 그녀를 비웃었지만 살충제와 환경적 독소의 끔찍한 영향에 관한 그녀의 증거와 예언이 불행하게도 사실임이 입증되었고 그때 이래로 우리는 환경을 보호하는 데 도움이 되고자 우리의 생활에 주요한 변화를 이루었다. 이와 유사하게, 많은 연구자들이 Jane Goodall이 처음에 자기가 연구했던 침팬지에게 이름을 붙였을 때 그녀를 비판했는데, 그들은 그녀가 David Graybeard가 흰개미를 꺼내기 위해 풀잎을 도구로 사용하는 것을 보았다는 것을 그녀가 그들에게 이 획기적인 발견의 동영상을 보여줄 때까지 믿지 않았다. 1960년대 초반에 동물이 (이름을 정당화하는) 개별적인 개성을 가졌고 (인간만이 할 수 있다고 여겨졌던) 도구를 만들고 이용할 수 있다는 생각은 이단이었고 미친 생각이었다. 둘 다 이제는 평범하고 자명하다.

→ 처음에 Rachel Carson과 Jane Goodall 둘 다 일부 과학자들에 의해 저항을 받았으나, 그 두 과학자들은 자신들의 주장을 입증했다.

문제 해설

Rachel Carson과 Jane Goodall은 둘 다 처음에는 과학자들에 의해 조롱당하고 비판을 받았으나 자신들의 주장을 증명했다는 내용이므로 요약문의 빈칸 (A)에는 resisted가, (B)에는 proved가 적절하다.

① 존경했다 – 변경했다
② 존경했다 – 묵살했다
③ 영향을 미쳤다 – 입증했다
④ 저항했다 – 변경했다

구문 분석

[8행] In the early 1960s, the ideas(S) [**that** an animal had an individual personality (warranting a name) and could make and use a tool (which only humans were thought capable of)] were(V) heretical, crazy.

▶ [that ~]는 the ideas와 동격 관계이다. 주어가 the ideas이고 동사가 were이다.

어휘

hardcore 강경한　ridicule 비웃다, 조롱하다
prediction 예언　pesticide 살충제
toxin 독소　blade of grass 풀잎
fish out ~을 꺼내다[빼내다]　groundbreaking 획기적인
personality 개성　warrant 보장하다, 정당화하다
heretical 이단의, 이설의　commonplace 평범한
self-evident 자명한

07 정답 ②

소재 Zambia와 Malawi 사이의 시간관념의 차이

전문 해석

South Carolina 주의 Presbyterian 대학의 심리학 교수인 Stephen Buggie는 Zambia에서 가르치면서 3년을 보냈고 Malawi에서 9년을 보냈다. "Zambia에서는 시간 엄수와 시간에 대해 격식을 차리지 않는 태도로 생활 속도는 일반적으로 느리다." 라고 그는 기억한다. 이웃에 있는 Malawi는 아주 다르다. 그곳에서 만남은 Zambia에서보다 더 신속하게 시작한다. Malawi의 종신 대통령인 Kamuzu Banda는 고향으로 돌아와 정치에 입문하기 전에 30년 동안 스코틀랜드에서 의사로 개업했다. 그는 절대적으로 그 나라를 장악하고 시간 엄수에 대해 꽤 까다로운 사람이다. 1970년대 당시 그는 공공 시계가 정확하지 않은 시간을 보이는 것을 불법으로 만들었다.

문제 해설

②의 앞부분에서는 Zambia에서 생활 속도가 느리다고 언급했고 ②의 다음 문장에서는 그곳에서의 만남이 Zambia에서보다 신속하다고 했으므로 주어진 문장에 있는 Malawi가 아주 다르다는 언급은 ②에 들어가야 한다.

구문 분석

[8행] Back in the 1970s he made **it** illegal [for public clocks to display inaccurate time].

▶ it은 형식상의 목적어이고 [ ]가 내용상의 목적어이다. 형용사인 illegal이 목적보어이다.

어휘

recall 기억하다, 상기하다　casual 격식을 차리지 않는
regard 주목, 주의　punctuality 시간 엄수
promptly 신속히, 재빨리
practice medicine 의사로 개업하다　illegal 불법적인
display 보이다　inaccurate 부정확한

08 정답 ①　09 정답 ③

소재 역사가 보여주는 것

전문 해석

역사가들은 시간의 흐름에 따른 변화를 연대순으로 기록한다. 과거의 시대와 우리가 사는 시대 사이에 지속성이 있는 한편, 중요한 변화 또한 있었다. 예를 들어, 미국은 1776년과 1900년 사이에 상당히 변했다. 즉, 헌법의 의미는 유혈 내전에 의해 더 분명하게 정의되었고, 나라의 인구 구성은 새로운 이민자들이 도착하면서 엄청나게 달라졌으며 투표와 같은 민주주의적인 관습에 대한 접근은 점진적으로 지주가 아닌 사람, 흑인, 그리고 여성에게 적용되었다. 역사가들은 이런 변화를 추적한다. 그들의 과제는 과거 시대의 삶이 지금 우리가 사는 세계와 다른 방식을 조명함으로써 자신들의 청중을 여행으로 안내하는 것이다. 나는 이 문단을 2012년 7월 27일에 쓰고 있다. 오늘 저녁 일찍 나는 전 세계 수십억 명의 다른 사람들과 함께 하계 런던 올림픽 게임의 개막식을 봤다. 여러분 가운데 많은 사람들이, James Bond와 'Elizabeth 여왕'이 헬리콥터에서 열광하는 영국 지지자들의 환호 속으로 올림픽 경기장을 향해 낙하산을 타고 내려오는, 영화감독 Danny Boyle이 만든 그 장면으로 이 행사를 기억할 것이다. 나는 Boyle이 연출한 개막식이 시간의 흐름에 따른 변화라는 역사적 개념에 바탕을 둔 방식이라는 생각이 들었다. 그 개막식은 농업 사회에서 산업 사회로, 기술 사회로 대영제국의 변화를 추적했다. 기본적으로 Boyle은 세상 사람들에게 아주 비싸고 아주 공들인 역사 수업을 하고 있었다. 역사가는 상황이 똑같은 상태로 머물지 않는다는 것을 항상 자각하고 있기 때문에 역사적 과제는 본질적으로 꾸준히 진행된다.

문제 해설

08

역사는 과거의 시대와 우리가 사는 시대 사이에 달라진 점을 파악하고 기록하는 작업이라는 내용의 글이므로, 글의 제목으로는 ① '역사: 변화의 기록'이 가장 적절하다.

② 현재: 과거의 거울
③ 역사 서술: 사실인가 허구인가?
④ 과거는 미래에 의해 바뀔 수 있는가?
⑤ 상상력이 풍부한 아이디어의 원천인 역사

09

헌법에 의한 통치를 이루어내고, 이민을 받아들이며, 선거권이 확대되는 등의 변화가 일어나고 농업 사회에서 산업 사회를 거쳐 기술 사회로 발전한다는 내용을 볼 때 빈칸에는 ③ '꾸준히 진행된다'가 가장 적절하다.

① 주관적인
② 애매모호한
④ 보수적인
⑤ 모순적인

구문 분석

[8행] Their task is to take their audiences on a journey by shedding light on the ways [**in which** life in past eras was different from the world {**in which** we now live}].

▶ [in which ~]는 the ways를 수식하는 관계절이고 {in which ~}는 the world를 수식하는 관계절이다.

[19행] The historical task is inherently progressive [**because** the historian **is** ever **aware that** things do not stay the same].

▶ [because ~]는 이유를 나타내는 부사절이고 「be aware+that절」은 '~을 알다' 라는 의미이다.

어휘

chronicle 연대순으로 기록하다 **continuity** 지속성
era 시대 **constitution** 헌법 **demographic** 인구(학)의
makeup 구성 **immensely** 엄청나게 **access** 접근
nonlandholder 지주가 아닌 사람 **trace** 추적하다
shed light on ~을 비추다, 밝히다, 해명하다 **craft** 만들다
parachute 낙하산으로 강하하다 **roaring** 환호하는
applause 박수 **faithful** 충실한 지지자
struck by ~라는 생각이 들다 **elaborate** 공들인
inherently 본질적으로

Mini Test 3

p. 186~191

01 ⑤ 02 ③ 03 ③ 04 ② 05 ① 06 ⑤
07 ③ 08 ① 09 ⑤

01 정답 ⑤

소재 각자에게 맞는 지도 방식

전문 해석

초보 지도자가 흔히 저지르는 실수 중의 하나는 똑같은 방식으로 모든 사람을 지도하려고 애쓰는 것이다. 그러나 그 점을 직시하자. 모든 사람이 똑같은 종류의 리더십에 반응을 보이지는 않는다. 모든 사람에게 일관된 태도를 보이도록 노력해야 한다. 모든 사람을 친절함과 존중하는 마음으로 대해야 한다. 하지만 모든 사람에게 똑같은 전략과 방법을 이용하려고 기대하지마라. 여러분의 팀에 있는 각 개인에게 어떤 리더십의 단추를 누를 것인지 생각해내야 한

다. 어떤 사람은 도전을 받는 것에 잘 반응할 것이고 다른 사람은 보살핌을 받기를 원할 것이다. 어떤 사람은 그 사람을 위한 전략을 작성해주어야 할 필요가 있을 것이고 다른 사람은 스스로 전략을 만들 수 있다면 더 열정적이게 될 것이다. 어떤 사람에게는 지속적이고 빈번한 후속 조치가 필요할 것이고 다른 사람은 숨 쉴 여지를 원할 것이다. 실력 있는 지도자가 되고 싶다면 여러분이 맡은 사람들이 여러분에게 적응하기를 기대하지 말고 그들이 무엇을 필요로 하는가에 여러분의 리더십 방식을 맞추는 책임을 질 필요가 있다.

문제 해설

일관된 태도로 부하 직원에게 친절하고 그들을 존중하는 것이 마땅하지만 각자에게 서로 다른, 각자에게 적합한 방식으로 그들을 지도할 필요가 있다는 내용이므로 필자가 주장하는 바로 가장 적절한 것은 ⑤이다.

구문 분석

[10행] If you desire to be an effective leader, you need to take responsibility for conforming your leadership style to [**what** your people need], not expecting them to adapt to you.

▶ [what ~]는 전치사인 to의 목적어 역할을 하고 what은 선행사를 포함한 관계사이다.

어휘

rookie 초보자 **face** 직면[직시]하다
consistent 일관된 **strategy** 전략
challenge 도전하다 **nurture** 보살피다, 육성[양성]하다
draw~up (세심한 생각 · 계획이 필요한 것을) 만들다[작성하다]
follow-up 후속 조치 **conform** 순응하다, 따르게 하다

02 정답 ③

소재 동물 형상을 띤 신(神)

전문 해석

동물 숭배는 널리 퍼져 있었다. 이집트의 신들은 동물 형상을 갖고 있었고 많은 신들이 인간이 아닌 것의 머리를 가진 사람으로 그려졌다. 그러나 그 관계는 단순하지 않았고 여러 신들이 특정한 하나의 동물의 형태를 가질 수 있었고 어떤 신들은 여러 동물 형상을 가졌다. 예를 들어, 사랑과 풍요의 여신인 Hathor는, 자연의 여신인 Isis가 그랬던 것처럼, 흔히 소로 나타나거나 소의 머리를 갖고 있다. (Isis와 Osiris의 아들인 Horus는 고대 이집트 국가의 수호신이었다.) 가정의 여신인 Bastet는 보통 고양이의 머리를 가졌지만 때로는 사자의 머리를 갖고 있기도 했다. 달의 신의 어머니인 Mut는 독수리의 머리를 지녔거나 암사자로 나타났다.

문제 해설

동물 숭배 사고방식의 영향으로 이집트의 여러 신들이 동물의 형상을 지녔다는 내용의 글이므로, Horus는 고대 이집트 국가의 수호신이라고 언급한 ③은 글의 전체 흐름과 관계가 없다.

구문 분석

[5행] For instance, Hathor, [**who** was the goddess of love and fertility], often appeared **as a cow or with the head of a cow**—as did Isis, the goddess of nature.

▶ [who ~]는 앞에 있는 Hathor를 설명하는 관계절이다. as a cow와 with the head of a cow는 둘 다 appeared에 이어지는 표현이다.

어휘

worship 숭배 **widespread** 널리 퍼진
depict 묘사하다 **nonhuman** 인간이 아닌 것
fertility 풍요, 다산성 **patron god** 수호신
vulture 독수리

03 정답 ③

소재 동물을 지칭하는 표현

전문 해석

한 비행에서 나는 주요한 소프트웨어 회사에서 일하는 한 여성 옆 자리에 우연히 앉아 있게 되었다. 나는 원고를 쓰고 철자 검사를 하고 있었고 그녀는 내가 무슨 프로그램을 이용하는지 물었다. (B) 나는 그녀에게 말해주었고 내가 동물의 감정에 관한 책을 쓰고 있고 워드 프로세싱 소프트웨어가 내가 동물을 가리킬 때 나에게 'who'와 'whom'이라는 단어를 'that'이나 'which'로 바꾸라고 요청하지 말았으면 좋겠다고 말했다. 왜냐하면 동물은 사물이 아니라 주체니까. (C) 처음에 그녀는 그 말을 이해하지 못했지만 마침내 이해하게 되었고 자기가 자기 회사 사람들에게 그 회사의 소프트웨어를 바꾸라고 얘기하겠다고 말했다. 그녀가 그 일을 이행하든 아니든 나는 그녀가 동물을 다르게 보는 것에 대해 열려 있어서 기뻤다. (A) 그녀는 우리가 이용하는 언어가 우리의 태도에 영향을 미친다는 것을 인식했다. 아마 차세대 철자 검증 소프트웨어는, 동물을 'it'이 아니라 'he'나 'she'로 지칭하라고 글을 쓰는 사람에게 촉구하면서 그것이 가진 가정(假定)을 번복할 것이다.

문제 해설

비행기에서 옆 자리에 앉은 여성이 무슨 철자 검증 프로그램을 이용하는지 물었다는 내용의 주어진 글 다음에 그 질문에 답하면서 동물을 지칭할 때 사물을 가리키는 대명사로 바꾸라는 지시가 거슬린다고 말한 (B)가 이어지고, 그녀가 처음에는 말뜻을 이해하지 못하다가 이해한 다음에는 자기 회사 사람들에게 소프트웨어를 바꾸라는 말을 하겠다고 말하는 (C)가 이어진 다음, 마지막으로 차세대 철자 검증 소프트웨어는 지금과는 반대로 동물을 사람처럼 지칭하라고 지적할지도 모른다는 내용의 (A)가 오는 것이 자연스럽다.

구문 분석

[12행] [**Whether** she followed through or not], I was glad that she was open **to seeing** animals differently.

▶ [Whether ~]는 양보의 부사절이고 whether는 '~이든 아니든'이라는 의미이다. to가 전치사이므로 뒤에 동명사인 seeing이 이어진다.

어휘

happen to ~ 우연히 ~하다
spell-check 철자를 검사하다 **manuscript** 원고
affect 영향을 주다 **reverse** 뒤엎다, 번복하다
presumption 추정, 추론 **prompt** 촉구하다
object 사물 **subject** 주체
follow through (시작한 일을) 다 끝내다

04 정답 ②

소재 선택의 기준

전문 해석

혁신은 단 하나의 성능 특성을 가진 것이 아니라 오히려 여러 다른 잠재적 이용자들의 필요에 기초한 많은 성능 특성들이 있다. 예를 들어, 두 대의 자동차는 연비, 소음, 스타일, 힘, 그리고 신뢰도에 바탕을 두고 비교될 수 있으나, 한편 자동차 그 자체는 교통량, 주행 기간, 그리고 환경적 영향에 관련된 효율성의 면에서 경전철과 비교될 수 있다. 기술의 성능 특성은 부분적으로 어떤 대안이 '우세할' 것이고 널리 수용될 것인지를 결정한다. 그러나 어느 특성이 가장 중요한지, 즉 자동차의 스타일인지, 연비인지, 색깔인지, 아니면 힘인지를 우리에게 말해주는 것은 없다. 다양한 특성의 상대적인 중요성은 사회적으로 결정되고 문화적으로 기반을 둔다. 예를 들어, 환경보호론자들은 (만약 어쨌든 자동차를 골라야 한다면) 오염도가 자동차를 선택하는 주요 기준이라고 생각하는 반면, 대부분의 십 대들은 힘과 스타일이 더 중요하다고 생각한다.

문제 해설

혁신의 성능 특성 중에 어느 것이 우세할지는 사회적으로 결정되고 문화적인 기반을 둔다고 했으며 환경보호론자와 십 대는 서로 중시하는 성능 특성이 다르다는 내용이므로 빈칸에는 ② '여러 다른 잠재적 이용자들의 필요'가 가장 적절하다.

① 상품의 생산비
③ 위기관리 이론
④ 금융 서비스에서의 영향력 있는 전문가
⑤ 테크놀로지의 복잡성 정도

구문 분석

[7행] However, there is nothing [**to tell** us {**which** characteristics are most important}]: is it style, mileage, color, or power for a car?

▶ [to tell ~]는 nothing을 수식하는 to부정사구이다. {which ~}는 tell의 목적어 역할을 하는 명사절이다.

[10행] For example, environmentalists think that pollution is the main criterion by which a car should be chosen (if choosing a car at all), **while** most teenagers think [**that** power and style(S′) matter(V′) more].

▶ while은 '반면에'라는 의미의 접속사이다. [that ~]는 think의 목적어 역할을 하는 명사절이고 명사절 내 주어는 power and style이고 동사는 matter이다.

어휘

innovation 혁신
gas mileage 연비(휘발유 1갤런 당 주행 마일 수)
reliability 신뢰도 **with respect to** ~에 관해서
duration 지속 기간 **determine** 결정하다
alternative 대안 **ground** 기반을 두다
environmentalist 환경보호론자
criterion 기준 **matter** 중요하다

05 정답 ①

소재 긍정적인 경험과 부정적인 경험

전문 해석

'긍정적인'과 '좋은'이라는 말로 나는 자신과 남들을 위해 행복과 이익을 가져오는 것을 의미한다. '부정적인'과 '나쁜'이라는 말은 고통과 해악을 가져오는 것을 의미한다. 긍정적인 경험은 흔히 기분을 좋게 한다. 그러나 기분이 나쁜 일부 경험은 좋은 결과를 가져서 나는 그 경험들을 긍정적이라고 부른다. 예를 들어, 뜨거운 난로에 손이 데

인 아픔과 공원에서 아이를 찾지 못해서 걱정하는 것, 그리고 우리가 가장 확실한 길을 찾아가도록 도움이 되는 후회는 당장은 우리를 기분 나쁘게 만들지만 나중에 우리가 더 기분이 좋게 느끼도록 돕는다. 이와 유사하게, 부정적인 경험은 흔히 기분을 나쁘게 한다. 그러나 기분이 좋은 일부 경험은 나쁜 결과를 가지고 나는 이 경험들을 부정적이라고 부른다. 세 잔의 맥주로 얼큰히 취하거나 여러분을 부당하게 다루었던 누군가에 대해 험담하는 복수는 일시적으로 즐거울 수 있지만 그 대가가 이익보다 더 크다.

문제 해설

당장은 기분이 나쁘더라도 나중에 유익한 결과를 가져오는 경험은 긍정적인 것인 반면, 당장은 기분이 좋더라도 후에 나쁜 결과를 가져오는 경험은 부정적인 것이라는 내용의 글이다. 빈칸이 있는 문장은 당장에는 기분이 좋지만 후에 나쁜 결과를 가져오는 것에 대한 사례에 해당하므로 빈칸에는 ① '그 대가가 이익보다 더 크다'가 적절하다.

② 솔직함이 관계보다 더 중요하다
③ 마음의 평온함이 부보다 더 가치가 있다
④ 긍정적인 기억은 부정적인 기억보다 더 오래 지속된다
⑤ 장기적인 지속성이 단기적인 강렬함보다 더 낫다

구문 분석

[4행] For example, [the pain of a hand on a hot stove], [the anxiety at not finding your child at a park], and [the remorse that helps us take the high road] **make** **us** **feel** bad now to help us feel better later.
(make: V, us: O, feel: O.C)

▶ 세 개의 [ ]는 서로 병렬구조를 이루면서 주어 역할을 하고 동사는 make이다. make 다음에 목적어인 us, 목적보어로 동사원형인 feel이 이어진다.

어휘

stove 난로 **remorse** 후회, 양심의 가책
take the high road 가장 확실한 길을 택하다
buzz 얼큰히 취함 **vengeance** 복수, 앙갚음
gossip 험담하다 **wrong** 나쁜 짓을 하다, 부당하게 취급하다
momentarily 일시적으로 **outweigh** ~보다 더 크다

06 정답 ⑤

소재 약점보다 강점에 집중할 필요성

전문 해석

사람들이 자신들의 약점에 지나치게 초점을 둘 때 그들의 개인적인 발달에서 흔히 실수를 저지른다. 그 결과, 그들은 자신들이 소유한 강점을 최대화하는 대신 그 약점들을 강화하느라 애쓰면서 자신들의 모든 시간을 보낸다. 이와 비슷하게, 다른 사람들의 약점에 초점을 두는 것은 잘못이다. 남들에게 뭐가 잘못되었다고 말하면서 자신의 시간을 보내는 자칭 '전문가'들은 결코 사람을 얻지 못한다. 대부분의 사람들은 그저 그들을 피한다. 그 대신, 사람들의 강점을 찾고 그것을 가리키는 데 초점을 둘 필요가 있다. 대부분의 사람들은 거의 사용하지 않는 강점을 지니고 있다. 그 강점들은 일하는 능력, 지식, 전반적인 능력, 성격의 특성, 또는 여타 속성들일 수 있다. 모든 사람은 다른 만 명보다 적어도 한 가지는 더 잘 할 수 있다. 그 점을 생각해라!

문제 해설

(A) 자신의 강점보다 약점에 초점을 두는 실수에 대한 언급 다음에 남의 강점보다 약점에 초점을 두는 실수가 이어지므로 그 사이에는 Similarly가 적절하다.
(B) 남의 약점을 지적하는 데 초점을 두는 사람들을 피한다는 언급 다음에 남의 강점을 찾는 데 초점을 두라는 내용이 이어지므로 Instead가 적절하다.

① 예를 들어 – 마찬가지로
② 예를 들어 – 다시 말하면
③ 그에 반해서 – 그 대신
④ 이와 비슷하게 – 그 대신

구문 분석

[4행] The self-proclaimed "experts" [**who** *spend their time telling* others what's wrong with them] never win with people.
(The self-proclaimed "experts": S)

▶ [who ~]는 The self-proclaimed "experts"를 수식하는 관계절이다. 「spend+시간+-ing」는 '~하는 데 시간을 보내다'라는 의미이다.

어휘

shore up (약한 것을) 지원[강화]하다
maximize 최대화하다 **possess** 소유하다
self-proclaimed (다른 사람들의 동의 · 허락 없이) 자기 혼자 주장하는, 자칭의
attribute 속성

07 정답 ③ 08 정답 ① 09 정답 ⑤

소재 노숙자에게 샤워 시설을 제공하는 버스

전문 해석

(A) 어느 날, Doniece Sandoval은 길가에 앉아 있는 젊은 여자를 우연히 지나쳤다. 그녀는 울면서 자기는 결코 깨끗해질 수 없을 거라고 계속해서 혼잣말하고 있었다.

Doniece는 샌프란시스코에 살았고 그곳에서 노숙자를 의식하지 않기란 불가능했다. 수년 간 그녀는 단체에 자원봉사나 기부하는 것 이상의 일을 하고 싶었다. 그러나 그 젊은 여자의 말에 영감을 받은 그날에서야 비로소 그녀는 행동에 나섰다.

(C) Doniece는 자신의 도전이 자기가 상상할 수 있는 것보다 더 깊다는 것을 알았지만 자기가 그 젊은 여자가 깨끗해지는 것을 어떻게 도울 수 있을지도 모른다는 것에 대해 생각할 때 자기의 머릿속에서 아이디어가 번쩍 떠올랐다. 그날 밤 Doniece는 샌프란시스코의 노숙자를 위한 샤워 시설을 조사하기 시작했고, 이 도시의 거리를 집으로 삼는 3천 명이 넘는 남자와 여자, 그리고 아이들을 위해 대략 16개의 샤워 스톨이 있다는 자기가 알게 된 것에 의해 충격을 받았다. 그녀는 음식을 차에 실을 수 있다면 샤워기는 왜 안 되겠는가라고 생각했다.

(D) 그녀는 약간의 조사를 했고 자기가 이 문제에 대해 생각한 최초의 인물이 아니라는 것을 알게 되었다. 전국적으로 대략 여섯 개의 대부분은 작은 공동체가 있는데, 모두 신앙을 바탕으로 한 집단이 이끌며 개조된 이동식 주택과 말이 끄는 트레일러를 이용하고 있었다. 그녀는 그 공동체 모두와 이야기를 했고 그들은 그녀에게 변화의 이야기를 전했는데, 그들의 이동식 샤워 시설을 이용하는 노숙자들은 "오랜만에 처음으로 인간임을 느꼈다"거나 "자신의 존엄에 관한 의식을 회복하고 있었다." 그녀는 그들이 그 일을 할 수 있다면 우리 역시 할 수 있다고 생각했다. 그래서 Lava Mae('나를 씻자')라는 프로젝트가 탄생했다.

(B) Doniece는 자기에게 4대의 사용이 중지된 버스를 주도록 시 당국을 설득한 다음 그녀는 그 버스들을 시민 기금 웹사이트에서 자기가 모금한 7만 5천 달러로 리모델링했다. 각 버스는 소화전에 연결하여 물을 얻고 그 물은 버스에 설치된 큰 배터리로 데운다. 하수는 시의 하수도로 배수된다. 첫 번째 버스는 2014년 7월에 길에 나왔고 두 번째 버스는 2015년 초에 나왔다. Doniece는 Bay Area의 다른 곳에 나머지 두 대를 둘 계획이고 그 프로그램을 세계적으로 확장하려고 생각하고 있다.

문제 해설

07

Doniece가 길에서 울고 있는 여자를 보고 노숙자가 씻지 못하는 처지에 대해 알게 되었다는 내용 다음에 샌프란시스코의 노숙자를 위한 샤워 시설의 실태를 조사했다는 내용의 (C)가 이어지고, 자기와 같은 문제 의식을 가지고 노숙자에게 이동식 샤워 시설을 제공하는 단체들을 만나봤다는 (D)가 그 다음에 이어지며, 마지막으로 모금한 돈으로 버스를 리모델링하여 샤워 시설을 제공하는 버스를 운영하기 시작했다는 (B)가 이어지는 것이 적절하다.

08

(a)는 길에 앉아 울고 있는 젊은 여자를 가리키고 나머지는 Doniece Sandoval을 가리킨다.

09

노숙자에게 샤워 시설을 제공하는 문제에 대해 생각한 최초의 인물이 아니라는 것을 알게 되었다고 했고 이미 6개의 공동체가 이동식 샤워 시설을 제공하고 있었으므로 ⑤는 글의 내용과 일치하지 않는다.

구문 분석

[A 5행] But **it was**n't until that day **that** she took action, inspired by the words of the young woman.

▶ it was ~ that은 not until that day를 강조하는 구문이고, not until that day는 '그날이 되어서야 비로소'라는 의미이다.

어휘

donate 기부하다 **take action** 조치[행동]을 취하다
inspire 영감을 주다 **persuade** 설득하다
decommission (사용을) 중지하다, 퇴역하다
crowdfunding 시민 기금(웹사이트나 다른 온라인 도구를 통해 여러 사람으로부터 기금을 모아서 프로젝트의 자금을 대는 것)
fire hydrant 소화전 **on board** 승차[탑승]한
drain 배수하다 **sewer** 하수도 **roll out** 공개[출시]하다
a light bulb goes on (아이디어 등이) 번득이다, 번쩍 떠오르다
approximately 대략
shower stall 샤워 스톨(샤워할 때 주위를 막기 위해 이용되는 칸막이)
faith-based 신앙[종교]을 바탕으로 한 **converted** 개조된
trailer 트레일러, 이동 주택 **dignity** 존엄

Mini Test 4

p. 192~197

01 ④ 02 ③ 03 ④ 04 ① 05 ① 06 ⑤
07 ⑤ 08 ① 09 ①

01 정답 ④

소재 솔직한 의사소통과 갈등의 관계

전문 해석

갈등은 적절히 관리되고 해결되면 생산적인 성장으로 이어질 수 있다. 갈등을 인식하고 그것을 통해 일하는 과정

은 솔직한 의사소통의 환경에서만 일어날 수 있다. 옛 속담인, '우리를 죽이지 못하는 것은 우리를 더욱 강하게 만든다.' 는 갈등에 적합한 것이다. 표면 밑에 남겨진 갈등은 곪아서 치명적일 수 있다. 그것을 인식하고 열린 곳으로 가지고 나왔을 때 그것의 해결은 사람들을 더 가깝게 모이도록 하는데 왜냐하면 사람들이 서로에 대한 이해 속에서 성장하기 때문이다. 의사소통은 갈등에 영향을 주는 핵심적인 요소인, 그것의 원인과 치료책이다. 솔직한 의사소통은 의견 충돌이 예방되고, 관리되고 혹은 해결될 수 있는 수단이다. 솔직한 의사소통의 부족은 갈등을 안보이는 곳으로 몰아가서 오해와 적대감을 악화시킬 수 있다.

문제 해설

갈등이 해결되기 위해서 솔직한 의사소통이 필요하고 이것을 통해 사람들은 서로를 더 이해하게 된다는 내용의 글이므로 글의 요지로 가장 적절한 것은 ④이다.

구문 분석

[5행] When it is recognized and brought out into the open, its resolution can bring people closer together [**as** they grow in their understanding of each other].

▶ [ ]로 표시된 부분은 부사절 접속사 as가 이끄는 절이며, as는 '이유'를 나타내는 접속사로 사용되었다.

어휘

conflict 갈등 **properly** 적절하게 **resolve** 해결하다
process 과정 **recognize** 인식하다
appropriate 적절한 **surface** 표면 **fatal** 치명적인
resolution 해결 **element** 요소 **affect** 영향을 미치다
remedy 치료책 **means** 수단
disagreement 의견 충돌 **underground** 지하의
worsen 악화시키다 **misunderstanding** 오해
hostility 적대(감)

02 정답 ③

소재 적성에 맞는 일자리의 중요성

전문 해석

Chris는 한 기술 회사에서 국제 판매를 책임지고 있었다. 그는 전 세계를 다니며 고객들과 만났다. 그의 개인 간의 관계를 잘 처리하는 기술은 가장 강한 강점이며 선천적으로 갖게 된 재능이었다. 그는 관계를 맺고 고객들의 요구를 충족시키는 방법을 본능적으로 알았다. 고객들은 그에게 보통을 넘어서는 충실함으로 그를 대했다. 더욱이, 그는 종종 확대된 가족의 구성원으로서 대우를 받았다. 얼마 후에, 회사의 사장은 Chris에게 큰 제안을 했다. 그러나 그 제안은 Chris가 거절해야 했던 것이었다. 새로운 자리는 권력과 위엄이 있는 자리였지만 그 자리는 고객과의 접촉이 없었다. 그 자리가 자신에게 큰 성공을 주었던 자신만의 독특한 능력으로부터 멀어지게 할 것이라는 것을 인식하며, Chris는 그 기회를 현명하게 거절했다.

문제 해설

Chris는 고객들을 만나는 일을 아주 잘함으로 인해 사장으로부터 더 좋은 자리를 제안받지만 그것이 자신의 강점을 살릴 수 없는 자리임을 알고 거절했다는 내용이므로 글의 제목으로 가장 적절한 것은 ③ '여러분의 실제적인 재능이 있는 곳에 머물러 있어라'이다.

① 재능: 여러분이 개발할 수 있는 것
② 여러분의 고객을 여러분의 가족으로 만들라
④ 노력만이 여러분을 더 높은 직위로 이끈다
⑤ 기회: 예기치 않은 일로부터 오는 것

구문 분석

[8행] [Recognizing that it would distance him from the unique ability {**that** made him most successful}], Chris wisely turned down the opportunity.

▶ [Recognizing ~]는 분사구문으로 'As he(=Chris) recognized ~'로 이해할 수 있다. {that ~}는 the unique ability를 수식하는 관계대명사절이다.

어휘

in charge of ~을 맡고 있는 **meet with** ~을 만나다
naturally 선천적으로 **instinctively** 본능적으로
loyal 충실한, 충성스러운 **norm** 보통, 표준
extended 확장된 **before long** 곧, 머지않아
corporate 회사의 **prestige** 위엄, 위신
distance 멀어지게 하다 **turn down** 거절하다

03 정답 ④

소재 사람들의 행복을 통해 보는 기술의 가치

전문 해석

가장 정교한 기술적인 진보조차도 그것들이 행복에 기여한다고 증명될 수 있을 때까지 가치를 거의 가지고 있지 못하다. 예를 들어, Bell의 실험실에서 개발된 최초의 전기 트랜지스터라디오는 하찮은 시장 가치를 가지고 있는 것으로 생각되어서 특허권은 Sony에게 몇 천 달러에 팔렸는데, Sony는 그것을 휴대용 라디오에 넣는다는 생각을 가지고 있었다. Sony는 정확하게 사람들이 음악을 듣지 않고 있을 때보다 음악을 듣고 있을 때 일반적으로 더 기

분 좋게 느낀다고 판단을 내렸다. 그러므로 사람들은 자신들이 음악을 가지고 다닐 수 있다면 보통 때보다 더 만족스러워 할 것임을 믿기 쉬울 것이다. 이런 식으로 발전된 전기 기술에 대한 완전히 새로운 시장이 행복에 대한 소망을 기반으로 만들어졌다.

문제 해설

빈칸의 뒤에서 제시된 예는 Sony가 사람들은 음악을 듣고 있을 때 더 기분 좋게 느낀다고 판단하고 트랜지스터를 휴대용 라디오에 넣게 되었다는 것이다. Sony는 전기 트랜지스터 기술이 행복에 기여한다고 판단을 내렸던 것이다. 따라서 빈칸에 들어갈 말로 가장 적절한 것은 ④ '행복에 기여한다고'이다.

① 다양한 용도를 가지고 있다고
② 잠재적 가치를 확대한다고
③ 전반적인 혁신을 이끈다고
⑤ 개발자들에게 혜택을 가지고 온다고

오답 풀이

Sony의 트랜지스터라디오가 많이 팔리게 되면 개발자인 Sony도 많은 혜택을 받게 될 것이다. 하지만 이런 내용은 언급되지 않았으며 글의 핵심 내용이 아니므로 정답으로 ⑤ '개발자들에게 혜택을 가지고 온다고'를 고르지 않도록 주의한다.

구문 분석

[2행] For instance, the first electronic transistors [**developed** at Bell Labs] were considered to have negligible market value, and so the patents were sold for a few thousand dollars to Sony, [**which** had the idea of putting them into portable radios].

▶ [developed ~]는 분사구로 the first electronic transistors를 수식하며, [which ~]는 계속적 용법의 관계대명사절로 Sony를 부연 설명하고 있다.

어휘

sophisticated 정교한 **technological** 기술적인
advance 진보, 발전 **demonstrate** 증명하다, 보여주다
negligible 하찮은, 무시할 수 있는 **patent** 특허
portable 휴대용의 **reason** 판단을 내리다, 추론하다
normal 보통의, 정상의 **entirely** 완전히, 전체적으로
advanced 발전된

04 정답 ①

소재 비리를 알면서도 막지 못한 Buck Weaver

전문 해석

1919년에, 시카고 화이트 삭스 야구팀의 여덟 명의 선수가 미국 프로야구 월드시리즈에서 고의로 게임에 져 준다는 조건으로 도박꾼들로부터 뇌물을 받았다는 혐의로 고소되었다. 그 여덟 명의 야구 선수들은 법정에서는 어떤 유죄 판결도 받지 않았지만, 그들 모두 다 평생 동안 프로야구 선수생활을 하는 것이 금지되었다. 그러나 그 선수들 중 한 명인 Buck Weaver는 그 음모를 알고 있었음에도 불구하고 이기기 위해 경기를 했다고 주장했다. 경기장에서 보여주었던 Weaver의 모습이 그의 주장을 뒷받침해주었지만 프로야구협회 회장 Kenesaw Mountain Landis는 스캔들을 알고 있으면서도 그것을 막지 않기로 결정한 선수도 마찬가지로 선수 생활을 금지시키기로 결정을 내렸다. Weaver는 잘못한 일 때문에 처벌받은 것이 아니라 옳은 일을 하지 못했기 때문에 처벌받은 것이다.

문제 해설

Buck Weaver는 자신은 그 음모에 가담하지 않았으며 그 경기를 이기도록 하기 위해 노력했다고 주장했지만 결국 그 음모를 알고 있으면서도 막지 않았음으로 인해 선수생활 금지 처분을 받는다. 막지 않았던 것은 옳은 일을 하지 못한 것으로 해석될 수 있으므로 빈칸에 들어갈 말로 가장 적절한 것은 ① '옳은 일을 하지 못했기'이다.

② 자신의 가치관을 지키지 못했기
③ 자신의 동료들을 배신했기
④ 공정한 방식으로 경기하지 못했기
⑤ 음모에 가담했기

오답 풀이

Buck Weaver 또한 결국에는 같은 잘못을 한 것이라고 섣불리 판단해서 ⑤ '음모에 가담했기'를 고르지 않도록 주의한다.

구문 분석

[4행] But one of those players, Buck Weaver, **claimed** that he **had played** to win despite knowing about the conspiracy.

▶ 주절에 '주장'의 의미를 가진 동사가 나왔지만 문맥상 '당위성'의 의미로 종속절이 해석되지 않으므로 「should+동사원형」이 쓰이지 않았으며, 시제와 문맥을 고려해 had played가 사용되었다.

어휘

accuse A of B A를 B로 고소[고발]하다 **bribe** 뇌물
in exchange for ~대신의, 교환으로
intentionally 고의적으로 **convict** 유죄를 선고하다
ban 금지하다 **claim** 주장하다 **contention** 주장
commissioner 야구협회의 최고 책임자 **rule** 판결을 내리다

scandal 추문

05 정답 ①

소재 운동선수들이 눈을 감고 연습할 때 얻는 이점

전문 해석

인식에 대한 연구는 시각이 다른 감각 체계를 지배한다는 것을 나타낸다. 시각적 단서가 대부분의 전문적인 기술을 성공적으로 수행하는 데 필요하다는 데 의문은 거의 없지만 시각은 운동선수들이 다른 중요한 감각 정보의 출처를 찾아내는 것을 막을 수 있는 때들이 있다. 예를 들어, 골프 스윙을 연습할 때 선수는 눈을 감은 채로 연습할 때보다 눈을 뜬 채로 연습한다면 스윙의 느낌을 덜 의식할 것이다. 그러므로 운동선수들은 기교적인 기술 연습을 하는 동안에 눈을 감고 있는 것으로부터 종종 이득을 볼 수 있다. 특히나 운동선수들이 동작에 대한 느낌에 더 많은 주의를 기울일 필요가 있을 때 그러하다. 눈을 감고 하는 연습은 또한 운동선수들이 그렇지 않으면(눈을 감지 않으면) 의식하지 못할 동작 실수를 찾아내는 것을 도와줄 수도 있다. 마지막으로, 더 상급의 선수들은 그들이 자신들의 동작과 결부된 느낌을 다시 연결하고 싶을 때 눈을 감고 하는 연습으로부터 이득을 얻을 수도 있다.

문제 해설

주어진 문장은 시각이 운동선수들이 다른 중요한 감각 정보의 출처를 찾아내는 것을 막을 수 있는 때들이 있다는 내용이다. 이 문장의 뒤에는 구체적인 예가 이어지는 것이 자연스러우므로 주어진 문장이 들어가기에 가장 적절한 곳은 ①이다.

구문 분석

[6행] For example, when practicing the golf swing, a player would notice the feel of the swing **less** [if she practiced it with her eyes open] **than** [if she did so with her eyes closed].

▶ 「less A than B」 비교 구문이 사용되었다. A에 해당하는 것이 첫 번째 [ ]로 표시된 부분이며, B에 해당하는 것은 두 번째 [ ]로 표시된 부분이다.

[11행] Closed-eyes practice might also help athletes detect errors in their movements that they would **otherwise** not notice.

▶ otherwise는 문맥상 if they practiced with their eyes not closed로 이해할 수 있다.

어휘

visual 시각의 **cue** 단서, 실마리
technical 기교적인, 기술적인 **vision** 시각
athlete 운동선수 **detect** 찾아내다
sensory 감각의 **perception** 인식
indicate 나타내다 **dominate** 지배하다
notice 의식하다, 알아차리다 **benefit** 이득을 얻다
particularly 특히 **advanced** 상급의, 고급의
reconnect 다시 연결하다, 재결합하다
associate 연상 짓다, 결부하다

06 정답 ⑤

소재 Harvey University 에세이 대회

전문 해석

Harvey University 에세이 대회
모든 법과 대학 학생들에게 개방됨.

에세이 주제:
a. 사회에서의 법의 올바른 기능
b. 사회에서의 법의 올바른 적용

* 마감일: 8월 20일
에세이는 주석을 제외하고 최대 5천 단어이어야 합니다.

* 상
1등: 3천 달러
2등: 1천 달러(2등상은 3명까지 수여될 것입니다.)

참가 증명서는 모든 참가 학생들에게 수여될 것입니다.
수상 작품과 몇몇 다른 선발된 에세이들이 학교 잡지에 게재될 것입니다.

제출물은 huessaycompetition@gmailcom으로 이메일을 보내주십시오.

문제 해설

수상 작품과 몇 개의 선발된 에세이들이 학교 잡지에 실릴 것이라고 했으므로 ⑤는 안내문의 내용과 일치하지 않는다.

구문 분석

[12행] [The winning entries and a few other selected essays] will be published in the school magazine.

▶ [ ]로 표시된 부분은 문장의 주어이다.

어휘

competition 대회, 경쟁 **function** 기능
application 적용 **maximum** 최대한의
excluding ~을 제외하고
footnote 각주(각 페이지 하단에 붙이는 주석)
award 수여하다 **entry** 출품[참가] 작
publish 게재하다, 출판하다

07 정답 ⑤

소재 교사들의 현대 미술에 대한 관점

전문 해석

많은 교사들은 가르칠 때 현대 미술을 사용하는 것을 피하는데, 왜냐하면 그들은 자신들의 지식 수준에 대해 편안해하지 않아서 그들이 직접 정통하지 않을 수도 있는 어떤 것이든지 학생들에게 소개하는 것을 꺼려하기 때문이다. 이러한 반응은 교육자들에게만 독특한 것이 아니다. 예술 비평가이자 역사가인 Lucy Lippard가 지적한 것처럼, 현대 미술 분야는 '많은 이들이 의문을 갖고 그들의 반응에 의해 당혹하게 되기조차 한 정도까지 혼란스럽게 되었다.' 설상가상으로, 교수 자료는 드물다. 현대 미술 교육과정 자료의 부재는 가치있는 미술만이 '시대의 시험을 견뎌낸' 미술이라는 태도를 반영한다. 결과적으로 이러한 태도는 고정되고 영구적인 상태를 유지하는 보편적인 문화적 표준을 확립하는 것이 불가능하다는(→ 가능하다는) 믿음을 반영한다.

문제 해설

현대 미술의 교육과정 자료의 부재는 '시대의 시험을 견뎌낸' 미술만이 가치 있는 미술이라는 것을 반영한다는 내용이 나오는데, 시대의 흐름을 견뎌왔다는 것은 고정되고 영구적인 상태를 유지하는 보편적인 문화적 표준이 될 수 있다는 것을 의미하므로, 이러한 표준을 확립하는 것이 가능하다는 것을 추론할 수 있다. 그러므로 ⑤의 impossible은 possible로 고쳐야 한다.

오답 풀이

교육자들이 현대 미술을 학생들에게 소개하는 것을 꺼려하는 것에 대해 많은 이들이 의문을 품고 당혹해한다는 내용으로 보아 많은 이들이 혼란스러워한다는 것은 문맥상 적절하다. 그러므로 ③ mystified(혼란스러운)는 적절하게 사용된 어휘이다.

구문 분석

[1행] Many teachers shy away from using contemporary art in their teaching **because** they *do not feel* comfortable with their own level of knowledge and *are* reluctant to introduce their students to anything [they may not have mastered themselves].

▶ 부사절 접속사 because가 이끄는 절에서 do not feel과 are가 주어인 they를 공유하며 병렬을 이루고 있다. [ ]로 표시된 부분은 anything을 수식하는 관계사절로 관계대명사 that이 생략되어 있다.

어휘

shy away 피하다 **contemporary** 현대의, 동시대의
master 정통하다 **unique** 독특한
point out ~을 지적하다 **mystify** 혼란스럽게 하다
scarce 드문, 희귀한, 부족한 **curriculum** 교육과정
reflect 반영하다 **attitude** 태도
withstand 견뎌[이겨]내다 **in turn** 결과적으로
establish 확립하다 **universal** 보편적인
standard 표준 **permanent** 영구적인

08 정답 ①

소재 재판에 회부된 신

전문 해석

아우슈비츠 수용소 캠프에 있었던 유대인 무리들은 어느 오후 신을 재판에 회부하기로 결정한다. 신은 잔인함과 배신이라는 죄목으로 회부되어지고 신을 옹호하고 반대하는 논쟁들이 시작된다. 신은 악을 막아야 되고 인간들에게 위안을 주는 역할을 해야 된다는 것을 믿음에도 불구하고 죽음의 수용소에서 이루어진 즉석에서 벌어진 재판은 그들이 처한 끔찍한 세상에서 신이 간섭을 했다는 증거를 찾지 못하고 신에게서 책임감을 덜어주고자 하는 용서하는 분위기도 찾아내질 못한다. 랍비는 신은 유죄이며, 아마도 죽을 가치가 있다는 판결을 발표한다. 그러나 그때 랍비는 모인 사람들을 힐끗 쳐다보고는 그 재판은 끝났다고 말한다. 그는 저녁 기도를 위한 시간이라고 그들에게 말한다.

문제 해설

(A) 문장의 주어는 arguments이며 동사가 필요하므로 begin을 쓰는 것이 적절하다.
(B) 관계대명사 뒤의 문장에서 주어가 빠져 있으므로 선행사인 atmosphere를 주어 자리에 넣어 해석하는 것이 자연스럽다. what은 그 자체에 선행사를 포함하고 있으므로 what이 될 경우 자체 선행사(thing)와 atmosphere가 주어로 겹치게 되므로 적절치 않다. 따라서 주격 관계대명사 역할을 하는 that이 적절하다.
(C) them, him, her와 같은 목적격 대명사는 분사나 형용사의 수식을 받을 수 없으므로 those가 적절하다.

구문 분석

[3행] Despite believing that God is supposed to counter evil and serve as a comfort to humans, this immediate death camp court **finds** [no evidence of divine intervention in their horrific world] **nor** [any forgiving atmosphere {**that** relieves God of responsibility}].

▶ 두 개의 [ ]로 표시된 부분은 동사 finds의 목적어로 nor에 의해 병렬을 이루고 있다. { }로 표시된 부분은 관계대명사절로 any forgiving atmosphere를 수식한다.

어휘

concentration 수용소
put ~ on trial ~을 재판에 회부하다
on charge of ~의 죄목으로 **cruelty** 잔인함
betrayal 배신 **argument** 논쟁, 논의
counter ~에 반대하다, 거스르다
serve as ~의 역할을 하다 **evidence** 증거
intervention 간섭 **horrific** 끔찍한
atmosphere 분위기
relieve A of B A에게서 B를 덜어주다
verdict 판결 **presumably** 아마도
glance up 힐끗 쳐다보다 **assemble** 모으다

09 정답 ①

소재 자신들이 온 곳을 기억하는 혈액 세포

전문 해석

연구자들은 한 자원자로부터 백혈구 세포를 조금 빼내 시험관에다 그것들을 조심스럽게 집어넣었다. 그들은 그런 다음 거짓말 탐지기에 연결된 탐침을 그 시험관에 집어넣어 그 사람의 감정적인 반응을 측정하였다. 다음으로 그들은 같은 지원자에게 몇 개의 문을 지나가서 TV를 통해 오래된 전쟁 영화에서 나오는 폭력적인 장면들을 보도록 지시를 내렸다. 이 사람이 그 장면들을 보고 있었을 때, 비록 검사를 받고 있는 피는 다른 방에 있었지만, 자원자가 완전히 초조해하며 긴장되어 있었을 때, 그 거짓말 탐지기는 격렬한 반응을 보였다. 피가 그의 몸속에 더 이상 있지 않았지만 그것은 그의 감정적인 반응을 탐지하고 있었던 것이다. 실험자들은 여러 사람에 대해 이러한 실험을 해보았지만 같은 결과를 얻었다.
→ 혈액 세포들은 자신들이 누구에게 소유되어 있는지를 기억하고 있는 것처럼 보인다.

문제 해설

글의 내용은 실험자들에게서 뽑아낸 백혈구 세포들이 실험관에 담겨진 후, 멀리 떨어져 있어도 실험자의 기분의 변화에 따라 같이 반응한다는 것, 즉 세포들이 자신이 속해있던 곳을 기억한다는 내용이다. 따라서 빈칸 (A)와 (B)에 들어갈 말로 가장 적절한 것은 각각 remember와 owned이다.

② 기억하다 – 발견하다
③ 예측하다 – 버리다
④ 잊어버리다 – 소유하다
⑤ 잊어버리다 – 버리다

구문 분석

[4행] Next, they **instructed** the same volunteer **to go** a couple of doors down and (to) **watch** some violent scenes from an old war movie on television.
▶ 「instruct+목적어+to 부정사」 형태가 사용되었으며, to 부정사 to go와 (to) watch가 병렬을 이루고 있다.

어휘

extract 추출하다 **volunteer** 자원자 **test tube** 시험관
lie detector machine 거짓말 탐지기
measure 측정하다 **emotional** 감정적인
violent 폭력적인 **uptight** 초조해하는, 불안해하는
tense 긴장된 **experimenter** 실험자

Mini Test 5

p. 198 ~ 203

01 ① 02 ③ 03 ④ 04 ④ 05 ④ 06 ④
07 ④ 08 ④ 09 ④

01 정답 ①

소재 화로 인해 깨진 친밀감

전문 해석

나는 어느 여름날이 기억나는데 그날 세 살짜리 아들과 친구가 냉장고에서 레모네이드가 든 주전자를 꺼내고 있었다. 나는 그날 오전 몇 시간을 들여서 마룻바닥을 문지르고, 왁스칠하고 광을 냈기에 아이들이 아무것도 쏟지 않기를 원했다. 그들은 조심하려고 애를 썼지만 우연히 냉장고 선반에 있는 계란 접시와 부딪혔다. 계란 접시는 떨어졌고 깨끗한 마루 위에 계란을 사방으로 튀겼다. 내가 화가 폭발했을 때 아이들의 눈은 불안한 마음으로 휘둥그레졌다. "당장 여기서 나가!" 그들이 문을 향해 가는 동안 나는 소리를 질러댔다. 어질러진 것의 청소가 끝날 무렵에 나는 진정이 되었다. 보상을 하려고 나는 레모네이드 주전자와 잔 몇 개와 함께 쿠키 접시를 테이블 위에 차려 놓았다. 그러나 내가 아이들을 불렀을 때, 대답이 없었다. 그들은 나의 화난 목소리가 미치지 않는 다른 어딘가로 놀러 가버렸다. 분노는 우리가 근처에 있기를 원하는 사람들을 우리로부터 분리시킨다.

문제 해설

광을 내서 청소한 마룻바닥에 달걀을 떨어뜨려 더럽힌 아들과 그의 친구에게 순간 벌컥 화를 냈다가 나중에 화를 낸 것을 보상하는 차원에서 아들과 친구를 불렀지만 그들은 이미 목소리가 미치지 않는 곳으로 가버렸다는 내용의 글이다. 글의 마지막 부분에서 분노는 우리가 가까이 두고 싶어 하는 사람을 우리에게서 분리시킨다고 했으므로 ① '분노가 친밀감을 산산조각 내다'가 글의 제목으로 가장 적절하다.

② 아이들에게 놀 시간을 허락하다
③ 감정을 있는 그대로 표출하라
④ 분노: 인간의 기본적인 감정
⑤ 아이들은 혼자 노는 법을 안다

구문 분석

[2행] I'd **spent** hours that morning **scrubbing, waxing, and polishing** the kitchen floor, so I wanted the boys **not to spill** anything.

▶ 「spend+시간+-ing」 구문이 쓰였으며 scrubbing, waxing, polishing이 병렬구조로 연결되어 있다. to부정사(to spill)의 부정은 일반적으로 to부정사 앞에 not이나 never를 써서 나타낸다.

어휘

pitcher 주전자 **scrub** 문지르다 **wax** 왁스칠하다
polish 광내다 **spill** 엎지르다 **accidentally** 우연히
bump 부딪히다 **splatter** 튀기다 **explode** 폭발하다
make amends 보상하다

02 정답 ③

소재 딸아이를 통해 돌아 본 나의 모습

전문 해석

"엄마는 이해하지 못 해요! 엄마는 저를 노처녀로 죽게 만들 거예요! 엄마는 로맨스가 뭔지도 몰라요!" 이 말을 하고는 14살짜리 딸이 세탁실을 뛰쳐나갔다. 나는 그저 그녀가 혼자서 데이트를 하러 나가기에는 나이가 너무 어리다고 말을 했을 뿐인데 말이다. 내가 로맨스를 모른다고? 그녀는 도대체 자신이 어떻게 태어났다고 생각하는 것일까? 그런데, 다시 한 번 생각해 보니 그 순간에 난 내가 끝도 없이 요리를 하고, 청소를 하고, 빨래만을 하는 그런 여자처럼 보였을 수도 있겠다는 것을 깨달았다. 신체적 운동은 빗자루, 마대, 청소기를 가지고 하는 것들이었다. '외출'이라는 것은 장보는 것을 의미했다. 나는 어떻게 해서 누군가가 내가 전혀 로맨스를 몰랐던 사람이라고 믿을 수 있을 것인지 알 수 있었다.

문제 해설

③ brought가 타동사인데 뒤에 목적어가 없음을 알 수 있다. bring ~ into the world는 '~를 낳다'라는 의미인데, 목적어가 문장의 주어로 나갔으므로 수동태가 되어야 한다. 따라서 brought를 was brought로 고쳐야 한다.

[오답 풀이]

① 사역동사 make는 목적보어로 동사원형을 취하므로, die는 적절하다.
② 「too+형용사/부사+to부정사」는 '~하기에는 너무 …한'이라는 뜻이고, 이때의 to부정사는 '~하기에는'의 의미이다.
④ 「must have p.p.」는 '했었음이 틀림없다'라는 의미로, 과거 사실에 대한 강한 추측의 표현이다.
⑤ 의문사 how는 「how+주어+동사」의 간접의문문의 형태로, 문장 내에서 목적어 역할을 하고 있다.

구문 분석

[5행] ~ I realized that I **must have looked** like a woman who knew only endless cooking, cleaning, and laundry.

▶ 「must have+p.p.」는 과거에 벌어진 일에 대한 확신이나 강한 추측의 표현이다.

어휘

old maid 노처녀 **laundry** 세탁 **on one's own** 혼자서
bring ~ into the world ~를 낳다
workout 운동

03 정답 ④

소재 경청의 가치

전문 해석

거의 항상, 자신의 말을 누군가가 열심히 들어준다는 것을 깨닫게 될 때, 그 사람의 눈은 촉촉해진다. 나는 그가 기뻐서 눈물을 흘리고 있다고 생각한다. "감사합니다. 누군가가 제 말을 들어주었어요."라고 말하고 있는 것처럼 말이다. (C) 그런 순간에 나는 지하 감옥에서 매일 매일 "누가 내 말을 듣고 있나요? 거기 누구 없어요?"라는 모스 부호 메시지를 치고 있는 죄수에 대한 환상을 가져본다. (A) 그리고 마침내, 어느 날 그는 "있어요."라는 내용의 희미하게 들리는 소리를 듣는다. 그 단 하나의 단순한 반응에 의해서 그는 외로움에서 해방된다. 그는 다시 인간이 된 것이다. (B) 오늘날 사적인 지하 감옥에서 살고 있는 사람들이 많다. 그들은 겉으로 보기에는 그런 증거를 전혀 보이지 않기 때문에, 지하 감옥에서 나오는 희미한 메시지를 들으려면 여러분은 매우 집중해서 들어야 한다.

문제 해설

누군가가 자신의 말을 진정으로 들어주고 있음을 알게 될 때 기쁨의 눈물을 흘린다는 주어진 글 뒤에는 그런 순간에 지하 감옥에 있는 사람을 떠올리게 된다는 (C)가 나오고, 지하 감옥에서 모스 부호 메시지를 보내면 누군가가 들어주기를 간절히 원하는 모습을 묘사한 (C)의 마지막 부분에 이어질 내용으로는 마침내 반응을 듣고 인간으로서의 가치를 느끼게 된다는 내용의 (A)가 이어지며, 오늘날 누군가가 들어주기를 간절히 원하는 사람들이 많지만 그들은 겉으로 그런 내색을 하지 않으므로 그들의 메시지를 들어 주려면 매우 집중해서 들어야 한다는 내용의 (B)가 마지막에 나와야 한다.

구문 분석

[10행] In such moments I have had the fantasy of a prisoner in a dungeon, **tapping out** day after day a Morse code message, "Does anybody hear me? Is anybody there?"

▶ tapping out은 a prisoner가 하는 구체적인 행동을 묘사해주고 있는데, who taps out ~ 로 바꾸어 쓸 수 있다.

어휘

deeply 열심히, 깊이 **moisten** 촉촉해지다
weep 눈물을 흘리다 **faint** 희미한
tapping 가볍게 두드리는 소리
release 풀어 주다, 해방하다 **evidence** 증거
fantasy 환상, 공상
Morse code message 모스 부호 메시지

04 정답 ④

소재 지식 공유를 통한 사회에의 기여

전문 해석

'많이 알면 알수록, 더 많이 성장한다.' 라는 표현이 있다. 그리고 더 많이 성장하면 할수록, 더 많이 빚지고 있다. 이것이 의미하는 것은 당신의 지식을 다른 사람들과 공유할 필요가 있다는 것이다. 많은 사람들은 자신들이 공헌할 것이 없다고 종종 느끼지만 그것은 사실이 아니다. 여러분은 인류에 기여할 수 있다. 변화를 초래하는 여러분의 능력을 과소평가하지 마라. 설령 여러분이 과거에 잘못된 길을 갔다고 할지라도, 여러분은 여전히 파괴적 행동에 관여하는 것의 위험성에 관해서 사람들에게 교육함으로써 다른 사람을 도울 수 있다. 여러분이 가장 존경하는 사람에 대해 생각해 보아라. 그들은 여러분이 개인적으로 아는 사람 일 수도 있고, 여러분이 대단히 존경하지만 만나본 적이 없는 사람일 수도 있다. 그들이 자신의 지식을 어떻게 전달하는가? 확신하건데, 그들은 자신의 지식을 다른 사람들이 알게 하고 가지게 함으로써 그렇게 할 것이다. 그리고 그들이 그렇게 할 때 그들은 다른 사람들에게 지혜와 영감의 엄청난 출처가 된다.

문제 해설

빈칸 뒤에서 사람은 누구나 사회에 기여할 수 있으며, 기여하는 방식은 상대방으로 하여금 자신이 알고 있는 것을 알게 하는 것이라고 말하고 있으므로 지식의 공유를 통해 인류에 기여할 수 있다는 말임을 알 수 있다. 따라서 빈칸에는 ④ '당신의 지식을 다른 사람들과 공유할 필요가 있다'가 가장 적절하다.

① 빚은 사람을 생산적으로 살게 만든다
② 겸손하고 배울 준비가 되어 있어야 한다
③ 도움을 청하는 것을 부끄럽게 생각하지 말아야 한다
⑤ 많은 좋은 표현들은 한 가지 공통점이 있다.

구문 분석

[8행] They can be people [you know personally] or people [you've never met whom you greatly admire].

▶ 첫 번째 [ ]로 표시된 부분은 people을 수식한다. 두 번째 [ ]로 표시된 부분에서 you've never met과 whom you greatly admire의 두 관계절이 people을 수식하고 있다.

어휘

owe 빚지다 **humanity** 인류
underestimate 과소평가하다 **effect** 초래하다
on the wrong track 잘못된 길을 가서
engage in ~에 관여하다 **tremendous** 엄청난
inspiration 영감

05 정답 ④

소재 옳음에 대한 정치 지도자의 다양한 믿음

전문 해석

정치 지도자가 정책을 발의하거나 우리가 어떻게 행동해야 하는지 말할 때, 그 정책이나 행동이 잘못된 것이 아닌 옳은 것이라는 가정을 함축하고 있다. 어떤 정치 지도자도 "여기 여러분이 하셔야 할 일이 있습니다. 그것이 잘못된 것이니까 그것을 하세요."라고 말하지는 않는다. 어떤 정치 지도자도 정책이 중요하지 않다는 것을 이유로 정책을 발의하지는 않는다. 정치적인 처방은 맞는 것으로 여겨진다. 문제는 각기 다른 정치인들은 무엇이 옳은지에 대한 생각이 다르다는 점이다. 게다가, 도덕적 믿음의 상당수가 무의식적이다. 우리는 종종 우리의 가장 깊숙이 자리 잡은

도덕적 견해를 심지어 알지 못하기도 한다.

문제 해설

주어진 문장은 정치 지도자마다 옳다고 생각하는 것이 제각각인 점이 문제라고 지적하고 있다. 따라서 정치 지도자가 하려고 하는 것은 모두 옳은 것에 기반을 두고 있다는 내용의 문장과, 또 다른 문제점을 언급하는 Moreover로 시작하는 문장의 사이인 ④에 주어진 문장이 들어가야 한다.

구문 분석

[3행] When a political leader **puts** forth a policy or **suggests** how we should act, the implied assumption is [**that** the policy or action is right, not wrong].

▶ puts와 suggests가 a political leader에 이어지는 병렬구조이다. [that ~]는 that이 이끄는 명사절로 문장에서 보어 역할을 하고 있다.

어휘

put forth 앞으로 내놓다, 발의하다 **implied** 함축된, 암시적인
assumption 가정 **on the grounds that** ~의 이유로
prescription 처방 **assume** 추정하다
unconscious 모르는, 깨닫지 못하는, 무의식의

06 정답 ④

소재 남녀 피트니스 회원의 수

전문 해석

위 도표는 1970년부터 2000년까지 Someland의 남녀 피트니스 회원의 수에 관한 자료를 보여준다. 1970년에 2,000명이 넘는 남성 피트니스 회원이 있었지만 여성 피트니스 회원은 불과 1,000명이었다. 5년 후에, 남성 피트니스 회원의 수가 4000명으로 늘었는데 이는 1970년의 총 남성 숫자와 비교해볼 때 거의 두 배였다. 흥미롭게도, 여성 피트니스 회원의 수는 5년마다 교대로 등락을 했다. 1985년 이후로, 여성 피트니스 회원의 수는 남성 회원의 수 아래로 떨어진 적이 없었다. 2000년에는 여성 피트니스 회원의 수가 남성 피트니스 회원의 그것보다 두 배가 되었다.

문제 해설

1995년에는 남성 피트니스 회원의 수가 여성 피트니스 회원의 수보다 월등히 많았으므로 ④는 도표의 내용과 일치하지 않는다.

구문 분석

[4행] ~ the number of male fitness members increased to 4000, **which** was almost double **compared to** the 1970's total male number.

▶ which는 관계대명사로 4000 혹은 4000으로 늘어난 내용을 선행사로 받고 있다고 볼 수 있다. compared to는 '~와 비교해 볼 때'라는 의미의 표현으로 도표에서 많이 사용된다.

어휘

double 두 배의, 두 배가 되다 **total** 총
take turns -ing 교대로 ~하다 **rise** 오르다
fall 떨어지다 **below** ~아래에

07 정답 ④

소재 녹색 지붕의 장점

전문 해석

녹색 지붕은 유럽에서는 수년 동안 인기 있는 지붕이었으며 그렇게 되었을 만한 충분한 이유가 있다. 우선, 초목이 지붕을 헐어서 못쓰게 만들 수 있는 자외선뿐만 아니라 지붕을 찢어놓을 수 있는 얼고 녹는 반복적 주기로부터 지붕의 표면을 보호해준다. 이것이 전통적인 지붕보다 녹색 지붕의 수명을 두 배로 늘려준다. 또한 녹색 지붕은 건물 외피를 좀 더 효율적으로 만들어주는 절연체를 공급해준다. 초목은 겨울에는 바람으로부터 지붕을 보호하고 눈에 뒤덮여 있을 때에는 지붕이 건물의 열을 보유하는 데 특히 효율적일 수 있다. (또한 그것의 에너지 비용을 줄이고 환경을 보호할 다른 방법들이 있다.) 여름철에는 초목이 지붕의 온도를 반으로 줄일 수 있기 때문에 지붕은 냉각 효과를 과시할 수 있다.

문제 해설

녹색 지붕(지붕 위에 초목을 설치한 것)의 장점을 설명한 글이다. 따라서 에너지 비용과 환경을 보호할 다른 방법들에 대해 언급한 ④는 전체 글의 흐름과 관계가 없다.

구문 분석

[1행] Green roofs have been popular in Europe for years, and they have every reason **to have been so**.

▶ so는 popular를 받는 대형용사이다. to뒤에 완료부정사 have been을 쓴 이유는 과거부터 줄곧 그래왔으므로 현재의 시점보다 시제가 앞서기 때문이다.

어휘

vegetation 식물, 초목 **thaw** 녹다
ultraviolet light 자외선 **insulation** 절연
retain 보유하다
show off 과시하다, 자랑하다

08 정답 ④ 09 정답 ④

소재 작은 개구리 떼의 경주

전문 해석

옛날에, 달리기 대회를 준비한 작은 개구리 떼가 있었다. 목표는 매우 높은 탑의 정상에 도달하는 것이었다. 많은 군중들이 경주를 보고 참가자들을 응원하기 위해 탑 주변에 모였다. 경주가 시작되었고, 군중들 중 누구도 작은 개구리들 중 어느 한 개구리라도 탑의 꼭대기에 도달하리라고 믿는 이는 없었다. "오, 너무 어려운 일이야!" "그들은 절대 정상에 도달하지 못 할 거야." "그들이 성공할 확률은 없어. 탑이 너무 높아!"와 같은 말들이 나왔다. 작은 개구리들은 하나씩 무너지기 시작했다. 즉, 기운찬 속도로 점점 더 높이 올라가는 그런 개구리들을 제외하고 말이다. "그것은 너무 어려워! 아무도 해내지 못 할 거야," 라고 군중들은 계속 소리를 질렀다. 더 많은 작은 개구리들이 피곤해져서 포기했다. 하지만 한 개구리는 계속해서 더 높이, 더 높이, 더 높이 올라갔다. 그 개구리는 포기하려 들지 않았다! 끝내는 이 개구리를 제외한 모든 개구리가 탑에 올라가는 것을 포기했지만 이 개구리는 대단한 노력 끝에 꼭대기에 도달했다! 다른 작은 개구리들은 모두 자연스럽게 어떻게 이 개구리가 그것을 해낼 수 있었는지를 알고 싶어 했다. 한 참가 개구리가 그 작은 개구리에게 목표 지점에 도달할 힘을 어떻게 찾아냈는지를 물었다. 그 결과 승자는 귀머거리였던 것이 밝혀졌다! 이 개구리가 우리에게 가르치는 지혜는 부정적인 경향이 있는 사람들의 말을 듣지 말라는 것이다. 그런 말들은 여러분의 가장 멋진 꿈을 짓누르기 때문이다. 여러분이나 여러분의 목표를 비웃거나 비관적으로 선동하는 사람들의 말을 듣지 마라. 그러고 나서 나가서 그것을 해라!

문제 해설

08

해낼 수 없다는 많은 부정적인 말들이 있었지만 들을 수 없었기에 묵묵히 올라가서 탑의 정상에 도달할 수 있었다는 내용이므로 ④ '다른 사람이 하는 말을 신경 쓰지 말고 그냥 나아가라'가 제목으로 가장 적절하다.

① 당신에게 맞는 목표를 설정하라
② 기운을 내라, 그러면 당신이 원하는 것을 얻을 것이다
③ 경쟁이 당신을 더 강하게 한다는 것을 믿어라
⑤ 의지는 힘으로부터가 아니라 정신으로부터 나온다

09

'해낼 수 없다'는 많은 부정적인 말들을 듣지 못했기 때문에 정상에 오를 수 있었다는 내용이므로 '부정적인' 경향을 보이는 사람의 말을 귀담아 듣지 말라는 것이 이 내용을 통해서 얻을 수 있는 지혜이다. 따라서 빈칸에 들어갈 말로는 ④ '부정적인'이 가장 적절하다.

① 소심한 ② 탐욕스러운 ③ 관대한 ⑤ 야심 있는

구문 분석

[15행] The wisdom [this frog teaches us] is not to listen to people who have the tendency to be negative, **as** they squash your most wonderful dreams.

▶ [ ]로 표시한 부분은 관계절로 주어인 The wisdom을 수식하고 있고 is가 동사, not to listen~ 이 보어이다. as는 '이유'를 나타내는 접속사이다.

어휘

once upon a time 옛날에 **bunch** 떼, 무리
arrange 준비하다 **competition** 대회
statement 말 **make it to** ~에 도달하다
collapse 무너지다 **in a fresh tempo** 활기찬 속도로
tendency 경향 **squash** 짓누르다, 으깨다
scorn 비웃다, 무시하다 **pessimistically** 비관적으로
incite 선동하다

Mini Test 6

p. 204~209

01 ⑤ 02 ⑤ 03 ④ 04 ① 05 ④ 06 ②
07 ④ 08 ⑤ 09 ③

01 정답 ⑤

소재 영감과 상상력의 원천이 되어 온 화성

전문 해석

발견된 이래로, 화성은 언제나 영감과 상상력의 원천이 되어왔다. 망원경을 통한 초기의 관측으로 인해 일부 사람들은 한때 그것의 표면에 물이 흘렀다고 추정했다. 그 이후로 많은 사람들은 화성이 생명을 유지할 수 있는, 서식도 가능한 행성이었다고 믿게 되었다. 그것이 여러분이 화성과 '화성인'에 대한 수많은 소설과 이야기들을 찾을 수 있는 이유이다. 영국의 작가 H. G. Wells가 지은 공상 과학 소설인 '우주전쟁'(1898)은 지구를 침략해 정복하려는 화성인들에 대한 소설이다. 화성에 대한 거부할 수 없는 매력은 인터넷 시대에도 여전히 계속되고 있다. 전직 프로그래머인 Andy Weir는 화성에 갇힌 한 우주인에 대한 이야

기를 자신의 블로그에 게재했다. 그 이야기는 인기를 얻었고, 그는 소설 '마션'을 출판했는데, 이는 영화로 각색되어 2015년에 개봉되었다.

문제 해설
사람들은 화성에 대해 관심을 가져왔으며, 이러한 화성에 대한 여러 가지 가정을 많은 소설과 이야기들 속에서 찾을 수 있다는 내용의 글이므로, 이 글의 요지로는 ⑤가 가장 적절하다.

구문 분석
[4행] That's [**why** you can find thousands of novels and stories about Mars and "Martians."]

▶ [why ~]는 명사절로 보어 역할을 하고 있다. why는 의문부사로 명사절을 이끌며 절 내에서 부사 역할을 하므로 뒤에는 완전한 절이 온다. That is why는 '그것이 ~이 일어난 이유이다.'라는 의미이다.

어휘
discovery 발견 **inspiration** 영감
imagination 상상력 **observation** 관측, 관찰
telescope 망원경 **assume** 추정하다
habitable 거주 가능한 **attempt** 시도하다
invade 침략하다 **conquer** 정복하다
irresistible 억누를 수 없는, 거부할 수가 없는
fascination 매력, 매혹 **former** 과거[이전]의
astronaut 우주인 **trap** 가두다 **publish** 출간하다
release 개봉하다

02 정답 ⑤

소재 노년층의 고가의 소비 추세

전문 해석
우리 사회는 노인 인구가 급격히 증가함에 따라 고령화 사회로 빠르게 이동하고 있다. 그 요구를 충족시키기 위해, 다양한 새로운 제품들이 노년층을 대상으로 하면서 새로운 시장이 생겨나는 것 같다. 분명한 한 가지 추세는 노인 고객들이 젊은 고객들보다 좀 더 고가의 물건들을 선택하는 경향이 있다는 것이다. 예를 들면, 고급 가구와 보석에 대한 수요는 노인들 사이에서 빠른 속도로 증가하고 있다. 음식에서조차 높은 가격에도 불구하고 유기농 제품의 소비자들이 증가하고 있다. 노인들이 이러한 더 고가의 시장에서 주요 소비자들이라는 것은 분명한 사실이다.

문제 해설
노인 인구가 급격히 증가함에 따라 노년층을 대상으로 한 새로운 시장이 형성되고 있고, 노인들은 젊은 사람들보다 고가의 물건들을 선택하는 경향을 보인다는 내용의 글이므로, 글의 주제로 가장 적절한 것은 ⑤ '고가의 시장에서 증가하는 노인의 수'이다.

① 대부분의 제품에서의 고가의 추세
② 부유한 사람들을 겨냥한 다양한 새로운 제품
③ 노인들이 소비에서 직면하는 문제들
④ 노령화 인구가 경제에 미치는 영향

구문 분석
[3행] One noticeable tendency is that senior customers tend to choose **more** higher-priced goods **than** younger **ones**.

▶ more ~ than의 비교급 구문이 사용되었으며 senior customers와 younger customers를 비교하고 있다. 같은 명사의 반복을 피하기 위해 customers를 ones로 대신 받았다. 대체되는 명사가 단수인지 복수인지에 유의한다.

어휘
society 사회 **demand** 수요 **emerge** 등장하다
noticeable 뚜렷한, 현저한 **tendency** 경향
senior 연장자, 손윗사람 **organic** 유기농의
obvious 확실한[분명한] **aimed at** ~를 목표로 한

03 정답 ④

소재 뜻밖의 시험 결과

전문 해석
로스쿨(법학전문대학원) 2학년 동안 시험으로 인해 나는 공황 상태에 빠지게 되었다. 내 생각에 나는 잘 준비했으나 시험이 나를 불안하게 만들었고 결과는 매우 나빴다. 나는 시험에 실패했다고 확신했다. 나는 낙제점을 받거나 거의 낙제 점수라고 마음속으로 준비하고 인생에서 다른 대안의 길을 찾으려고 계획하기 시작했다. 나는 그런 재난(시험을 망친) 이후에 로스쿨에서 3학년과 마지막 학년을 끝낼 수 있을 거라고는 생각하지 못했다. 나는 깊이 숨을 쉬고 시험 결과에 대한 나쁜 소식을 기다렸다. 그 봉투가 왔을 때 나는 조용히 체념한 채 그것을 열었다. 그러나 점수는 A와 A⁻였다. 나는 다시 보고서 눈을 깜빡였다. '이것이 어떻게 가능했지?' 어쩌면 어떤 수호천사들이 나를 위해 다시 한 번 보살펴주고 있었을지 모른다.

문제 해설
필자는 시험 결과가 매우 좋지 않을 거라고 생각하고 좌절하였으나, 시험 결과가 A와 A⁻로 나쁘지 않게 나오자 눈을 깜빡이며 놀라워하고 있다. 따라서 필자의 심경 변화로 가장 적절한 것은 ④ '좌절감을 느끼는 → 놀라워하는'이다.

① 화난 → 부끄러운
② 흥분한 → 걱정스러운
③ 짜증난 → 후회하는
⑤ 편안한 → 기쁜

구문 분석

[1행] **While** I was in my second year in law school, my exams **caused** me **to** be in a panic.

▶ While은 시간을 나타내는 부사절을 이끌며, '~동안'이라는 의미이다. cause는 목적격보어로 to부정사를 취한다.

어휘

panic 극심한 공포, 공황 **unnerve** 불안하게 만들다
convince 확신시키다 **mentally** 정신적으로
grade 성적, 점수 **alternative** 대안적인, 대체 가능한
path 길, 방향 **disaster** 재앙
take a deep breath 심호흡하다 **envelope** 봉투
blink 눈을 깜빡이다 **guardian angel** 수호천사

04 정답 ①

소재 실패를 두려워하지 않는 것의 중요성

전문 해석

실수를 하는 것은 이제 막 성장하는 모든 종류의 과학자들과 예술가들의 교육에 있어서 중요한데 그들은 실험하며 한 생각을 시도하였다가 완전히 실패하고, 또 다른 생각을 시도하고, 위험을 무릅쓰며 기꺼이 잘못된 답을 얻을 수도 있는 자유를 지녀야 한다. 전형적인 한 예는 첫 번째 백열등을 만들기 위해 1만 번의 실험의 실패를 경험한 Edison을 애석해했던 기자에 대한 Thomas Edison의 대답이다. "나는 실패하지 않았습니다." 그는 기자에게 말했다. "나는 (백열등이) 작동하지 않는 만 가지의 원리를 성공적으로 발견했습니다." 그러나 대부분의 아이들은 시험 삼아 해보고 실험하며, 만 번은 고사하고, 10가지 방법에서도 틀릴 수 있는 자유를 빼앗긴다. 아이들의 성취를 측정하고 표준화하는 끊임없는 시험에 대한 부담은 일이 잘못되는 것에 대한 아이들의 깊은 걱정을 강화시켰다. 아이들이 성공하는 법을 배우는 것은 분명 중요하지만 아이들이 실패를 두려워하지 않는 법을 배우는 것도 똑같이 중요하다.

문제 해설

아이들이 시험 삼아 해보고, 시도하며, 기꺼이 잘못된 답을 얻을 수도 있어야 한다는 내용의 글이므로, 빈칸에는 ① '실패를 두려워하지 않는 법을 배우는'이 들어가는 것이 가장 적절하다.

② 적어도 만 번의 실패를 하는
③ 그들의 독창성을 향상시키는
④ 끊임없는 시험에 집중하는
⑤ 진짜 원하는 것을 발견하는

구문 분석

[11행] **It** is certainly important for children [**to learn** to succeed]; but ~.

▶ It은 가주어, [to learn ~]가 진주어이며, for children은 to부정사의 의미상 주어이다.

어휘

central 가장 중요한 **budding** 신예의, 싹트기 시작한
flop 완전히 실패하다 **lament** 애통해하다, 아쉬워하다
deny 부정하다, 사실이 아니라고 말하다
noodle around 시험 삼아 해보다
let alone ~은 말할 것도 없이 **standardize** 표준화하다
intensify 강화하다

05 정답 ④

소재 교육 수준과 소득 사이의 상관관계

전문 해석

학사나 석사 학위가 밝은 미래를 보장하는가? 대학이 좋은 삶으로 가는 확실한 방법은 아니며, 대학 학위를 갖는 것이 좋은 직장을 보장한다는 것은 더 이상 사실이 아니다. 하지만 어떤 보고에 따르면 교육 수준과 소득 사이에는 어떤 관련성이 여전히 있는 것으로 보인다. 경제협력개발기구(OECD)는 교육의 양과 질이 소위 '가진 자'와 '못 가진 자' 사이의 격차를 심화시키고 있다고 보고한다. 낮은 교육 수준을 가진 사람들은 더 높은 학위를 가진 사람들보다 적은 급여를 받았다. 또한 그들은 다른 이들보다 증가하고 있는 실업률의 영향을 더 받았다. OECD의 34개 선진국 중에서 대학 학위를 가진 25세에서 34세 사이의 사람들의 실업률은 단지 5퍼센트인 반면, 학위가 없는 사람들의 실업률은 거의 20퍼센트이다. 개발도상국도 예외는 아니다.

문제 해설

교육 수준이 낮은 사람들이 더 높은 학위를 가진 사람들보다 적은 급여를 받으며, 실업률의 영향을 더 많이 받는다는 내용의 글이므로 빈칸에는 ④ '교육 수준과 소득 사이에는 어떤 관련성'이 들어가는 것이 가장 적절하다.

① 고등 교육 없이 성공할 가능성
② '가진 자'와 '못 가진 자' 사이의 증가하는 격차
③ 대학 학위를 얻고 싶어하는 많은 사람들
⑤ 개발도상국에서의 많은 실업률

구문 분석

[5행] ~ the amount and quality of education is intensifying **the gap between** so-called "haves" **and** "have-nots."

▶ 「the gap between A and B」는 'A와 B 사이의 격차[차이]'라는 의미이고, 둘 사이의 격차나 간극을 말할 때 사용되는 표현이다.

어휘

bachelor's degree 학사 학위
master's degree 석사 학위 **guarantee** 보장하다
gap 차이 **so-called** 소위, 이른바
haves 가진 자들, 부자들
have-nots 가진 것 없는[돈 없는] 사람들
influence 영향을 미치다
unemployment 실업(률)
developed country 선진국
developing country 개발도상국
be no exception 예외가 아니다

06 정답 ②

소재 타란튤라의 몸의 특징

전문 해석

타란튤라의 전체 몸, 특히 다리는, 털로 빽빽이 덮여 있다. 털 중 일부는 짧고 동그랗게 말려 있고 다른 일부는 길고 뻣뻣하다. 이러한 몸의 털을 만지는 것은 뚜렷이 다른 두 가지 반응 중 하나를 보이게 된다. 이 거미가 배가 고프면, 즉각적이고 재빠른 공격으로 반응한다. 귀뚜라미의 더듬이 접촉만으로, 타란튤라는 그 곤충을 아주 재빠르게 붙잡아서 초당 64 프레임의 속도로 촬영되는 영화도 오로지 포획된 결과만 보여줄 뿐, 포획의 과정은 보여주지 못한다. 그러나 거미가 배고프지 않을 때, 거미 털의 자극은 단지 접촉된 사지를 흔들어대는 데에만 반응한다. 곤충은 다치지 않고 털이 덥수룩한 거미의 배 아래를 지나갈 수 있다. 감각모는 아주 미세한 털로 다리에 나있는데, 한때 거미의 청각 기관으로 생각되어지기도 했으나 현재는 소리와는 관계가 없는 것으로 알고 있다. 그 털들은 오직 공기의 움직임에 (감각이) 예민하다. 가벼운 바람은 다른 털들을 방해하지 않으면서 그것(감각모)들을 천천히 진동시킨다.

문제 해설

타란튤라는 배가 고플 때 먹이를 포획하는 속도가 너무 빨라 초당 64 프레임의 속도로 촬영을 해도 그 과정은 볼 수 없고 오직 결과만 보여줄 수 있다고 했으므로 글의 내용과 일치하지 않는 것은 ②이다.

구문 분석

[5행] ~ the tarantula seizes the insect **so** swiftly **that** a motion picture [**taken** at the rate of 64 frames per second] **shows** only the result and not the process of capture.

(a motion picture: S′, shows: V′)

▶ 「so+형용사/부사+that+주어+동사 ~」는 '너무 ~해서 ~하다' 라는 의미이다. [taken ~]는 a motion picture를 수식한다. that절 안의 주어는 a motion picture이고, 동사는 shows이다.

어휘

densely 질게, 빽빽이 **be covered with**~로 뒤덮이다
curly 곱슬곱슬한, 동그랗게 말린 **stiff** 뻣뻣한
distinct 뚜렷이 다른, 별개의 **cricket** 귀뚜라미
seize 와락 붙잡다, 움켜잡다
frame (영화 · 비디오의) 한 장면[프레임] **capture** 포획
stimulation 자극, 흥분 **limb** (하나의) 팔(다리)
belly 배, 볼록한 부분 **unharmed** 다치지 않은, 손상되지 않은
organ 장기 기관 **sensitive** 예민한 **breeze** 미풍, 연풍
vibrate 진동시키다, 진동하다 **disturb** 방해하다

07 정답 ④

소재 Androcles에게 은혜를 갚는 사자

전문 해석

Androcles라고 불리는 한 노예가 어느 날 그의 주인에게서 도망쳐 숲에 숨었다. 그가 그 숲을 헤매고 있었을 때, 그는 동물의 신음소리를 들었고 우연히 누워있는 한 마리의 사자를 만났다. 그가 가까이 가자, 그 사자는 모두 붓고 피가 나는 그의 발을 꺼내 놓았고 Androcles는 큰 가시가 그 속에 박혀있어서 그 사자가 너무 고통스러워 어떤 것도 할 수 없다는 것을 알게 되었다. 그는 가시를 빼내었고 그 사자의 발을 붕대로 매 주었다. Androcles와 그 사자는 모두 곧 잡혔고 그는 그 사자에게 던져지는 형벌을 받았다. Androcles는 원형투기장의 한가운데 이끌려 나왔다. 곧 그 사자는 그의 동굴에서 풀려났고 그의 희생자에게 돌진했다. 그러나 그가 Androcles에게 가까이 다가가자마자 그는 친구를 알아보았고 마치 다정한 개처럼 그의 양손을 핥았다.

문제 해설

④는 사자를 가리키지만 나머지는 모두 Androcles를 가리킨다.

구문 분석

[2행] As he wandered through the woods, he **heard**

an animal **moaning and groaning** and came upon a lion [lying down].

▶ 지각동사 hear는 목적보어로 동사원형 뿐만 아니라 현재분사 형태도 취하는데, 동작, 상태의 진행을 강조하고 싶을 때 쓰인다. [lying ~]는 a lion을 수식한다.

어휘

forest 숲 **wander through** 돌아다니다, 헤매다
come upon ~을 우연히 만나다[발견하다]
paw (동물의 발톱이 달린) 발 **swollen** 부어 오른
thorn 가시 **lick** 핥다

08 정답 ⑤

소재 영역 사이의 경계 조정

전문 해석

현명하게 집중하려면 잘 변하고, 겹치기도 하는 각 영역 사이의 경계를 잘 조정해야 한다. 새로운 매체들의 도입은 그 경계를 애매하게도 하지만 삶을 더 편리하게 해주기 위해 우리가 이용할 수 있는 도구를 제공하기도 한다. 때때로 영역을 통합하기 위해 경계를 허무는 것은 당신이 귀중한 일에 더 잘 집중할 수 있게 해줄 것이다. 당신은 영역을 결합하는 실험을 하고 삶의 다른 부분들에서 하던 활동들을 한데 모음으로써 이를 확인해 볼 수 있다. 당신은 배우자와 함께 운동을 하는 것을 통해서 뿐만 아니라 저녁식사를 위해 직장동료를 집으로 초대하는 것을 통해서도 자아, 가정 그리고 일의 영역을 결합시킬 수도 있는 것이다. 반면, 영역을 분리하여 경계를 설정하면서 당신을 삶의 여러 가지 부분에서 분리시켜, 당신이 더 잘 집중하게 되는 경우도 있을 것이다. 예를 들어, 집에 있을 때는 직장에서 전화가 와도 받지 않겠다거나 직장에 있을 때는 개인적인 전화는 받지 않겠다고 결심할 수도 있다.

문제 해설

주어진 문장은 영역을 분리하여 경계를 설정해 집중력을 향상시킬 수 있다는 내용을 담고 있으므로 이에 대한 구체적인 부연 설명이 이어지고 있는 문장 앞에 위치해야 한다. 따라서 주어진 문장은 ⑤에 들어가는 것이 가장 적절하다.

오답 풀이

①을 정답으로 오인할 가능성이 있다. 그러나 주어진 문장은 삶의 여러 활동에 있어서 경계를 설정하면 당신이 더 집중할 수 있다는 내용이며 이는 그 예시가 ⑤의 다음 문장에서 이어지고 있기 때문에 ①의 위치에 들어가는 것은 적절하지 않다.

구문 분석

[8행] You can **confirm** this [**using** an experiment that combines spheres] and [**putting** activities together from different parts of your life].

▶ 동사 confirm은 this를 목적어로 삼으며, [using ~]와 [putting ~]는 you를 의미상 주어로 하는 분사구문이다. using과 putting 앞에는 의미상 전치사 by가 생략되어 있으며, by가 없더라도 동시상황 구문으로 해석을 한다면 무리가 없는 문장이다.

어휘

boundary 경계 **sphere** 영역, 분야 **detached** 분리된
overlap 겹치다, 포개다 **tear apart** 떼어내다, 잡아 뜯다
merge 결합하다, 합병하다 **put together** 한데 모으다, 합치다
spouse 배우자

09 정답 ③

소재 참여가 가지는 자유의 제한성

전문 해석

다른 사람들과 관련이 된다는 것은 행복에 있어서 중요한 것 같아 보인다. 결혼한 사람들, 좋은 친구들을 가진 사람들, 가족과 가까운 사람들은 그렇지 않은 사람들보다 더 행복하다. 이와 마찬가지로, 종교적인 단체에 관여하는 사람들은 그렇지 않은 사람들보다 더 행복하다. 그러나 사회적 유대감이 자유를 감소시킨다는 사실 또한 특히 중요하다. 예를 들어, 누군가의 친구가 된다는 것은 당신 자신의 자유에 제한을 둘지도 모르는 무거운 책임을 지는 것이다. 종교 단체에 참여하는 것도 마찬가지이다. 대부분의 종교 단체들은 나머지 구성원들의 복지를 증진시키는 것을 돕기 위해 그들의 구성원들이 어떤 특정한 방식으로 생활해야 한다고 요구한다. 그래서 보이는 것과는 반대로 행복에 가장 기여하는 것처럼 보이는 것이 우리를 해방시키는 것보다 오히려 우리를 속박한다.

→ 공동체에 참여하는 것은 그렇지 않은 사람들보다 사람들을 더 행복하게 만들어 주는 것처럼 보이지만 대체로 그것은 당신의 자유를 제한할 지도 모른다.

문제 해설

사회적으로 연결되어 살아가고 여러 단체에 참여하는 사람들이 그렇지 않은 사람보다 행복할 수 있지만 책임을 강요당할 수 있어서 자유를 감소시키고 속박할 수 있다는 내용의 글이다. 따라서 요약문의 빈칸 (A)에는 Participation이, (B)에는 restrict가 가장 적절하다.

① 탈퇴 – 근절하다
② 탈퇴 – 제한하다
④ 연관 – 지지하다
⑤ 참여 – 지지하다

구문 분석

[9행] So, contrary to how it may appear, [what seems to contribute the most to happiness] **binds** us rather than frees us.

▶ [what ~]는 문장에서 주어 역할을 하고 있으며 선행사를 포함한 관계대명사는 단수 취급하므로 동사로 binds가 쓰였다.

어휘

related to ~와 관련 있는 **significant** 중요한
be married 결혼하다 **be close to** ~와 가깝다
get involved in ~에 관련되다 **social tie** 사회적 유대
freedom 자유 **take on** (책임을) 지다
responsibility 책임 **liberty** 자유
the same is true of ~에서도 마찬가지다
appear 보이기 시작하다, 나타나다
contribute ~의 원인이 되다 **bind** 구속하다, 의무를 지우다
to a large extent 대체로, 대부분

Mini Test 7

p. 210~215

01 ① 02 ⑤ 03 ④ 04 ⑤ 05 ② 06 ①
07 ② 08 ② 09 ③

01 정답 ①

소재 소방서 신설에 대한 요청

전문 해석

Smith 시장님께

저는 Obion County의 오래된 주민으로서, 5일 전에 우리 마을에 닥친 재난에 대해 깊게 걱정하고 있습니다. 시장님도 아시다시피 일부 닳아 해진 전기 배선이 화재를 발생시켰고 결국에는 우리 마을 한 구역의 집들을 모두 파괴했습니다. 초기부터 강한 바람이 일어 화재가 번졌으나 소방관들이 그 장소에 더 빨리 도착할 수 있었다면 아주 빠르게 번지지는 않았을 것입니다. 우리 마을에는 소방서가 하나뿐입니다. 이 최근의 재난이 보여 주듯이 그것은 충분하지 않습니다. 또 다른 비슷한 비극이 다시 발생하지 않기 위해서 Obion County는 더 많은 소방서가 필요합니다. 이 문제와 관련한 당신의 신속한 답변을 기다리겠습니다.

Kurt Jackson 드림

문제 해설

마을에 소방서가 하나밖에 없어서 화재가 더 큰 피해로 이어졌다고 말하며, 더 많은 소방서 신설을 요구하고 있으므로 글의 목적으로 가장 적절한 것은 ①이다.

구문 분석

[6행] ~, but it **would not have spread** so rapidly, **if** the firefighters **had been** able to arrive at the scene earlier.

▶ 「if+주어+had p.p ~, 주어+would(조동사의 과거형)+have p.p ...」는 가정법 과거완료 구문으로 과거 시점에서의 과거의 상태나 사실을 반대로 가정할 때 쓰인다.

어휘

disaster 재해, 재난 **worn-out** 닳은
wiring 배선 (공사) **break out** 발생하다
destroy 파괴하다 **fan** (바람을 일으켜 불길을) 거세게 하다
spread 퍼지다 **tragedy** 비극

02 정답 ⑤

소재 현대 생활로 인한 멜라토닌 분비의 억제

전문 해석

멜라토닌은 자연적으로 발생하는 호르몬으로 빛의 노출에 의해 조절되며 수면 각성 주기를 통제하는 것을 돕는다. 어두워졌을 때, 당신을 졸리게 만들기 위해서 뇌는 멜라토닌을 더 많이 분비하고 빛이 있는 낮에는 멜라토닌을 적게 분비하는데 이는 당신이 깨어있고 긴장하기를 원하기 때문이다. 그러나, 현대 생활의 많은 면들은 신체의 자연스러운 멜라토닌 생산을 방해하고 수면 각성 주기를 벗어나게 할 수 있다. 예를 들어 자연적인 빛이 닿지 않는 사무실에서 긴 하루를 보내는 것은 낮 동안의 각성에 영향을 줄 수 있으며 뇌를 졸리게 만들 수 있다. 그리고 나서 특히 TV나 컴퓨터 모니터 앞에서 몇 시간을 보내는 것으로부터 밤에 밝은 빛을 보는 것은 신체의 멜라토닌 생산을 억제할 수 있고 잠자기를 더 어렵게 만들 수 있다.

문제 해설

현대 생활의 많은 부분들이 멜라토닌의 생성을 방해하고 수면 각성 주기에 혼란을 준다는 내용의 글이므로 이 글의 제목으로 가장 적절한 것은 ⑤ '일상 습관이 멜라토닌 분비 수치의 균형을 깨뜨릴 수 있다'이다.

① 자연적인 밝은 빛의 중요성
② 멜라토닌 분비를 통제하는 방법들
③ 밤에 더 잘 자도록 하는 몇 가지 조언
④ 멜라토닌: 당신의 몸의 가장 필수적인 호르몬

구문 분석

[8행] Then bright lights at night—especially from hours [**spent** in front of the TV or computer screen] —can suppress your body's production of melatonin and **make** *it* **harder to sleep**.

▶ [spent ~]는 분사구로 hours를 수식하고 있다. 동사 make 다음에 오는 it은 가목적어이며 진목적어는 to sleep이다. 목적격보어는 진목적어에 대한 보어이기 때문에 해석할 때 주의하며, 가목적어 it을 빠뜨리지 않고 쓰도록 한다.

어휘

occurring 일어나고 있는 **exposure** 노출
regulate 규제하다, 통제하다
sleep-wake cycle 수면 각성 주기
send out ~을 내보내다 **awake** 깨어 있는, 잠들지 않은
alert 기민한 **aspect** 측면, 양상 **disrupt** 방해하다
throw off 떨쳐 버리다, 벗어 던지다
impact 영향을 주다 **wakefulness** 각성
suppress 억제하다 **secretion** 분비

03 정답 ④

소재 비타민 과다 복용의 위험성

전문 해석

사람들은 종종 비타민, 미네랄, 또는 다른 보충제들을 의사 처방 없이 살 수 있기 때문에, 심지어 매우 높은 복용량을 섭취하더라도 완전히 안전하다고 가정하는 실수를 한다. 1990년대에는 심지어 비타민 C, 베타카로틴, 비타민 E와 같은 산화방지제의 '대량 복용'의 추세가 있었다. 비타민 C가 감기를 예방하거나, 치료할 수 있다고 증명된 어떠한 과학적인 증거가 없음에도, 많은 사람들은 여전히 그것이 사실이라고 생각한다. 그러나, 다량의 일부 비타민은 위험하고 전반적인 건강에 안 좋은 영향을 주면서 심지어 독성일 수 있다고 밝혀졌다. 예를 들어, 너무 많은 비타민 C는 몸에 필수적으로 필요한 금속인 구리를 흡수할 수 있는 능력을 방해할 수 있다. 게다가, 너무 많은 철은 소화불량, 장기기능 부전, 그리고 심할 경우에는 죽음까지도 야기할 수 있다. 우리 몸은 많은 양의 보충제들을 빠르게 제거 할 수 없기 때문에 그것들은 좋기는 커녕 도리어 해로움을 야기시키게 된다.

문제 해설

(A) 사람들은 비타민이 안전하고 건강에 좋을 거라고 생각한다고 언급한 후, 그것과는 달리 비타민이 위험하고 독성일 수 있다는 내용이 이어지므로 역접의 연결사 However가 적절하다.

(B) 앞에서 비타민 C의 과다 복용의 문제점에 대해 언급하고 있으며, 뒤에서도 철의 과다 복용이 문제가 될 수 있다고 첨가하여 말하고 있으므로, In addition이 적절하다.

① 그러므로 - 게다가
② 그러나 - 요약하자면
③ 게다가 - 요약하자면
⑤ 그러므로 - 예를 들면

구문 분석

[6행] However, large doses(S) of some vitamins have been shown(V) to be dangerous and even toxic, **causing** a bad impact on overall health.

▶ 이 문장의 주어는 large doses이며 동사는 have been shown으로 연결사를 추가하지 않는 이상 동사를 또 사용할 수가 없다. 따라서 cause라는 동사는 causing의 분사 형태로 변경하여 의미를 추가할 수 있으며, 이는 분사구문의 '동시 상황'의 의미가 된다.

어휘

assume 추정하다, 생각하다 **supplement** 보충제
over the counter 처방전[특별 허가] 없이 (살 수 있는)
dose 1회 복용량 **megadose** 대량 투여
antioxidant 산화 방지제 **cold** 감기 **toxic** 유독한
overall 전반적인 **interfere with** 방해하다
absorb 흡수하다 **copper** 구리 **digestive** 소화의
organ failure 장기 기관의 기능 부전

04 정답 ⑤

소재 기온과 사산 사이의 연관 관계

전문 해석

말할 것도 없이, 가족들에게 사산은 재앙이며 고통이다. 많은 사산의 원인은 알려져 있지 않지만 퀸스랜드 공과 대학(QUT)의 연구는 기온과 사산의 가능성 사이에 연관이 있음을 제시했다. 연구자들은 4년 동안 101,870명의 임신에 대해 매주 기온, 습도, 공기 상태를 기록했다. 그들은 그 위험은 가장 시원한 주에서 가장 낮았으며 23도 정도의 따뜻한 기온은 가장 더운 주만큼 위험할 수 있음을 발견했다. 이는 대부분의 임신한 여성들이 가장 더운 날씨에서는 시원한 상태를 유지하려고 하고 보통 에어컨을 찾게 될 것이기 때문이다. 그들은 15도에서 1000명의 임신당 3.53명의 사산이 있는 반면 23도에서는 1000명의 임신당 6.1명의 사산이 있을 것임을 추산했다. 따라서 임신부는 사산의 위험을 줄이기 위해 그들이 너무 덥지 않도록 보호하고 서늘하게 유지해야 한다고 그들은 조언했다.

문제 해설

15도의 서늘한 기온일 때 사산의 위험이 가장 적고, 23도 정도만 되도 아주 더운 날씨만큼이나 사산의 위험이 높다는 연구 결과에 비추어 보아, 사산의 위험을 낮추려면 덥지 않고 서늘하게 있어야 함을 알 수 있다. 따라서 빈칸에는 ⑤ '너무 덥지 않도록 보호하고 서늘하게 유지해야'가 가장 적절하다.

① 자신의 체온을 인지해야
② 너무 뜨겁거나 차가운 장시간의 목욕을 피해야
③ 특히 겨울에 이동할 때 조심해야
④ 운동하는 동안 과도한 땀을 흘리는 것을 피해야

오답 풀이

사산의 위험은 기온이 높을 때 더 높아진다고 했으므로 단지 자신의 체온을 인지해야 한다는 내용의 ①은 정답이 될 수 없다.

구문 분석

[10행] They estimated at 15℃ there would be 3.53 stillbirths per 1000 pregnancies **while** 6.1 stillbirths per 1000 pregnancies at 23℃.

▶ while은 '~인 반면에'라는 의미로 앞뒤의 내용 사이의 대조를 나타내는 접속사이다. 여기서는 while 뒤에 there would be가 생략되어 있다.

어휘

catastrophic 큰 재앙의, 비극적인 **painful** 고통스러운
possibility 가능성 **humidity** 습도
on a weekly basis 매주 **pregnancy** 임신
estimate 추정하다 **be aware of** ~을 알다
excessive 과도한 **workout** 운동
protect ~ from -ing …로부터 ~을 지키다
overheat 과열되다

05 정답 ②

소재 정서적 섭식의 문제점

전문 해석

만약 당신이 이미 배가 부른데도 디저트를 먹기 위한 배를 만들었거나 기분이 안 좋을 때 파인트 크기의 아이스크림에 손을 집어넣었다면, 당신은 정서적 섭식을 경험한 것이다. 정서적 섭식이란 음식을 이용해서 당신의 기분을 좋게 만드는 것이다. 즉 배를 채우기 위해서가 아니라, 정서적인 필요를 채우기 위해 먹는 것을 말하는 것이다. 여러분을 기분 좋게 하거나 여러분 자신에게 보상하기 위해 음식을 이용하는 것이 항상 잘못된 것이라고 말할 수는 없다. 그러나 당신이 긴장하고, 화나고, 외롭고, 스트레스를 받고, 지치거나 지루할 때마다 먹는 것이 당신의 주요한 감정 대응기제라면, 당신은 건강하지 않은 순환에 갇힌 것이다. 감정적인 굶주림은 음식으로 채울 수 없다. 먹는 것은 잠시 기분을 좋게 해줄 수 있지만 먹는 것을 유발한 감정은 전혀 다루어지지 않은 채로 그대로 있을 것이다. 그리고 당신은 불필요한 칼로리를 섭취했기 때문에 종종 그전보다 기분이 더 안 좋을 것이다. 이것은 문제를 더 안 좋게 만들 수 있는데 왜냐하면 당신은 감정에 대처하는 좀 더 건강한 방법들을 배운다기보다는 몸무게를 조절하는 데에 더 힘든 시간을 보내게 될 수 있고 또한 음식과 당신의 감정 모두에게서 갈수록 무력함을 느끼게 될 수 있기 때문이다.

문제 해설

정서적인 필요를 채우기 위해 먹은 음식은 잠시 기분을 좋게 해주지만 감정은 그대로 남아 있으며 오히려 문제를 더 악화시킬 수 있다는 내용의 글이므로 빈칸에는 ② '감정적인 굶주림은 음식으로 채울 수 없다'가 가장 적절하다.

① 감정적인 공허함은 일시적일 것이다.
③ 체중을 조절하는 것은 위험할 수 있다.
④ 적절한 식사 섭취가 항상 좋은 선택은 아니다.
⑤ 섭식 장애를 가진 십 대들이 매년 증가하고 있다.

구문 분석

[1행] **If** you've ever made room for dessert **even though** you're already full or dove into a pint of ice cream **when** you're feeling down, you've experienced emotional eating.

▶ 이 문장은 if 조건절, 양보의 even though절, 시간 부사절인 when절이 주절 앞에 연달아 나온 구조이다. 주절과 종속절들을 구별할 필요가 있다.

어휘

make room for ~을 위해 자리를 만들다
dive into (가방 · 호주머니 속에) 손을 쑥 집어[찔러]넣다
stomach 배, 복부 **primary** 주된, 기본적인, 최초의
mechanism 기계 장치, 메커니즘
get stuck 꼼짝 못하게 되다 **trigger** 촉발시키다
address (문제 · 상황 등에 대해) 고심하다[다루다]
consume 섭취하다 **powerless** 무력한

06 정답 ①

소재 문화가 우리 행동 방식에 미치는 영향

전문 해석

당신은 유전자가 당신의 모습과 행동 방식에 큰 부분을 결정한다는 것을 알지도 모른다. 당신이 모를 수도 있는 것은 당신의 유전자뿐만 아니라 당신의 환경 또한 당신의 생

김새와 행동에 영향을 준다는 것이다. 그러나, 당신은 당신의 환경이 단지 당신이 숨을 쉬는 공기 그리고 당신이 먹는 음식뿐이 아니라는 것을 알아야 한다. 사실상, 당신의 환경의 가장 큰 부분은 문화이다. 문화는 한 지역 사회의 일원들이 가족, 친구, 학교 그리고 심지어 외부 이방인들에게서 배우는 흔한 것들로 구성되어 있다. 이것들은 그들의 모습, 행동 방식, 그리고 의사소통 방법에 영향을 미치는 것들이다. 그러나 당신은 심지어 당신이 이것들을 배우고 있다는 것을 모른다. 왜냐하면 그것들은 당신에게 제2의 천성이 되기 때문인데 예를 들면 그것들은 당신이 누군가와 악수하는 방법, 당신이 재미있다고 하는 것들의 종류, 또는 당신을 둘러싼 다른 사람들에게 동질감을 갖는 방식을 말한다.

→ 오직 선천적인 특성만이 당신을 만든다는 믿음과는 달리 당신을 둘러싸고 있는 문화도 당신이 어떻게 행동하는지에 영향을 미친다.

문제 해설

사람들은 보편적으로 유전자만이 당신의 모습과 행동 방식을 결정한다고 생각하지만 후천적인 환경, 특히 가장 큰 부분인 문화 또한 그것들에 영향을 준다는 내용의 글이다. 따라서 요약문의 빈칸 (A)와 (B)에는 각각 inherited traits와 affects가 가장 적절하다.

② 선천적인 특성 – 평가하다
③ 특정 거주지 – 영향을 미치다
④ 특정 거주지 – 결정하다
⑤ 고유한 습관 – 평가하다

구문 분석

[2행] **What** you might not know(S) is(V) that **not only** your genes **but also** your environment has an effect on your appearance and behavior.

▶ what절은 what이 선행사를 포함하고 있기 때문에 불완전한 절을 이끈다. 이 문장에서 know의 목적어를 what이 포함하고 있으며 is의 주어 역할도 동시에 하고 있다. 반면에 that은 수반되는 절이 완전한데 이는 that 자체는 접속사 역할만 하며 선행사를 포함하고 있지 않기 때문이다. 「not only A but also B」에서 A와 B에 해당하는 부분이 서로 대구를 이루고 있다.

어휘

gene 유전자 **determine** 결정하다, 결심하다
environment 환경 **effect** 영향, 효과
appearance 외모 **behavior** 행동 **breathe** 숨을 쉬다
compose ~을 구성하다 **community** 지역 공동체
influence 영향을 미치다
identify with 동일시하다, 동질감을 갖다

07 정답 ②

소재 항생제에 대한 박테리아의 저항력

전문 해석

치명적인 박테리아에 대한 항생제의 승리는 인류에 있어서 현대 의학의 최고의 업적 중 하나이다. 이러한 약물이 처음 1940년대 초기에 널리 사용되기 시작한 이래로, 그것들은 많은 사람들의 생명을 살려왔고 심각한 질병과 감염을 예방해왔다. 그러나, 60년이 넘게 광범위하게 사용된 이후 많은 항생제들은 처음 가져왔던 것과 같은 효과를 가지지 않는다. (부작용은 사용된 항생제에 따라 가벼운 것부터 매우 심각한 것까지 있다.) 일부 박테리아는 항생제의 힘에 저항하는 방법들을 시간에 걸쳐 발달시켜왔다. 항생제의 광범위한 사용이 그것들이 이러한 약물들에서도 살아남을 수 있도록 해주는 진화적인 변화들을 박테리아에 가져다 준 것이다. 항생제에 대한 저항력은 인류에게 두 가지 큰 문제를 주었는데 그것은 우리 몸에서 감염원들을 제거하기 더 어렵게 만들고 병원에서 감염되는 감염의 위험을 증가시킨다.

문제 해설

시간의 흐름에 따른 항생제의 광범위한 사용으로 인해 박테리아가 항생제에 대해 저항력을 갖게 되었다는 내용의 글이므로, 항생제의 부작용을 언급하고 있는 ②는 글의 전체 흐름과 관계가 없다.

구문 분석

[9행] Resistance to antibiotics gives mankind two big troubles: it **makes** *it* harder [**to eliminate** infections from our bodies ~].

▶ 이 문장에서 동사 makes 앞의 it은 앞 문장의 Resistance to antibiotics를 가리키는 주어이며 동사 makes 뒤의 it은 가목적어로 진목적어인 [to eliminate ~]를 대신 받는다.

어휘

antibiotics 항생제, 항생 물질
deadly 생명을 앗아가는, 치명적인
achievement 업적
mankind 인류 **infection** 감염
extensive 광범위한
depending on ~에 따라
evolutionary 진화의 **resistance** 저항(력)
hospital-acquired infection 병원 내 감염

08 정답 ②

소재 점을 통해 얻을 수 있는 긍정적 효과

전문 해석

당신은 막 새로운 지역으로 이사를 했고 사람들을 만나기가 어렵다는 것을 알아가고 있기 때문에 기분이 약간 울적하다고 생각해보자. 그저 재미로, 당신은 어떤 미래가 당신을 기다리고 있을지 알아보기 위해 그 지역의 점쟁이에게 가기로 결정한다. 그 점쟁이는 그녀의 크리스탈 공을 응시하고, 웃음을 지으면서 그 미래는 밝을 것이라고 말한다. 그녀는 몇 달 안에 당신이 많은 가깝고 충실한 친구들로 둘러싸이게 될 것이라고 말한다. 당신은 그녀의 말에 안심을 하고는 도착했을 때보다 훨씬 행복한 기분으로 자리를 떠난다. 당신은 현재 행복감을 느끼고 미래에 대한 확신을 느끼기 때문에, 당신은 더 미소를 짓고, 더 밖으로 나가서 좀 더 많은 사람들과 대화를 한다. 몇 주가 지나고 나서 정말로 당신은 친한 친구들로 둘러싸여 있다는 것을 알게 된다. 사실상, 그 점쟁이가 실제로는 미래를 보지 못했지만 그 대신 미래를 만드는 데 사실상 도움을 주었을 가능성이 아주 크다.

문제 해설

주어진 문장은 앞 문장의 구체적인 내용을 서술하고 있으며 여기서 She는 앞 문장의 The fortuneteller를 지칭하므로 주어진 문장이 들어가기에 가장 적절한 곳은 ②이다.

오답 풀이

⑤를 정답으로 오인할 가능성이 있다. 그러나 대명사 She를 지칭하는 명사를 그 앞 문장에서 찾아볼 수 없으며 주어진 문장은 가까운 친구로 둘러싸이기 전의 예언인데 이미 그러한 일이 행해진 ④ 다음 문장의 뒤에 올 수 없으므로 적절하지 않다.

구문 분석

[4행] Just for fun, you decide to go along to the local fortuneteller to find out [**what** the future holds for you].

▶ find out의 목적절인 what 이하의 문장은 「what+주어+동사 ~」의 어순이다. 이처럼 의문사절이 목적절로 사용이 될 때에는 간접의문문의 어순을 따른다.

어휘

surround 둘러싸다 **feel down** 마음이 울적하다
neighborhood 이웃, 근처 **fortuneteller** 점쟁이
gaze into 응시하다, 지켜보다 **reassure** 안심시키다
comment 논평, 언급 **indeed** 정말, 확실히

09 정답 ③

소재 민간에서의 드론의 이용

전문 해석

흔히 드론으로 알려져 있으며 또한 몇몇 다른 이름들로 불리는 무인 공중 차량(UAV)은 사람 조종사가 타지 않은 항공기이다. (B) 이러한 무인 공중 차량은 주로 군사 교육이나 특수한 작업의 이용에서 발견되지만 점진적으로 방범, 감시, 소방 그리고 비군사적인 안보 작업과 같은 민간의 이용들에서 그 사용이 찾아지고 있다. (C) 예를 들면, 넓은 지역에 있어서의 공중 감시는 적은 비용의 UAV 시스템으로 가능해졌다. 감시 이용은 가축 관찰, 야생 산불 분포 측정, 수송관의 보안, 가옥 보안을 포함한다. (A) 민간의 항공 감시에 있어서 UAV 기술의 이러한 사용 경향은 자동화된 물체 탐지 접근의 증가된 발전과 함께 빠르게 확산하고 있다.

문제 해설

무인 공중 차량인 드론에 대한 정의가 서술되어 있는 주어진 글 다음에, (B) 이러한 무인 공중 차량의 이용에 대해 언급한 (B)가 이어지고, (B)에서는 드론이 군사적인 목적으로 사용될 뿐 아니라 민간의 사용도 증가하고 있다고 했는데 그 예로 (C)에서 가축을 관찰하고, 야생 산불 분포를 측정하는 등에 사용한다고 했으므로 (C)가 그 다음에 이어져야 한다. (A)는 (C)에서 언급된 민간의 사용이 점차 확대되고 있다고 글을 마무리하고 있으므로 마지막에 와야 한다.

구문 분석

[1행] An unmanned aerial vehicle (UAV) (S), commonly **known** as a drone [and] also **referred** by several other names, is (V) an aircraft without a human pilot aboard.

▶ 과거분사 known과 referred가 and로 병렬구조를 이루고 있으며 An unmanned aerial vehicle (UAV)를 수식하고 있다. 문장의 주어는 An unmanned aerial vehicle이며, 동사는 is이다.

어휘

commonly 흔히, 보통 **aboard** 탑승한
commercial 민간의, 민영의 **surveillance** 감시
detection 발견, 탐지 **application** 적용, 이용, 사용
livestock 가축

Mini Test 8

p. 216~221

01 ⑤ 02 ③ 03 ③ 04 ① 05 ④ 06 ⑤
07 ③ 08 ③ 09 ④

01 정답 ⑤

소재 면접에서의 비언어적인 행동의 중요성

전문 해석

일부 면접관은 당신이 행동하는 방식이 당신과 당신이 원하는 그 직업에 대해 일마나 신경을 쓰는지에 대한 중요한 메시지를 보낸다고 설명한다. 당신의 면접관은 당신의 자세, 얼굴 표정, 눈맞춤, 공간 사용, 목소리 톤, 신중함 등으로부터 당신의 성격을 읽고 당신에 대한 인상을 형성할 것이다. 면접관과 눈을 맞추는 것을 피하는 것은 당신이 노출하고 싶지 않은 무언가를 감추는 것처럼 보일 수 있다. 그렇지만 직접적으로 빤히 쳐다보는 것과 같이 너무 많이 눈을 맞추는 것은 위협적으로 보일 수 있다. (면접에 나올) 가능성이 있는 질문에 대한 대답을 연습하고 있다면, 반드시 당신의 몸짓 언어에 대한 피드백을 얻어서 구직 과정에서 올바른 몸짓 언어를 사용하라.

문제 해설

면접관들은 면접에서의 비언어적인 요소들에 대해 중요하게 여기므로, 면접 자리에서 비언어적인 행동을 올바르게 할 필요가 있다는 내용의 글이므로 ⑤가 글의 요지로 가장 적절하다.

구문 분석

[1행] Some interviewers explain (that) the way you act sends important messages about you and how much you care about the job [**that** you want].

▶ explain 뒤에 목적절을 이끄는 that이 생략되어 있는데 목적절을 이끄는 that은 종종 생략이 가능하다. [that ~]는 the job을 수식한다.

어휘

interviewer 면접관; 인터뷰 진행자 **character** 특성, 성격
impression 인상, 감명 **posture** 자세, 태도
facial 얼굴의, 안면의 **avoid** 막다, 피하다
expose 노출하다, 드러내다 **direct** 직접적인
intimidating 겁을 주는[겁나는]
rehearse 리허설[예행연습]을 하다

02 정답 ③

소재 좋은 대화자가 될 수 있는 방법

전문 해석

당신은 사교 모임에서 몇몇 사람들과 마주치는 상황을 피해본 적이 있을 것인데, 그 이유는 그들과의 대화가 당신에게 지루하다는 인상을 주기 때문이었을 것이다. 반면에, 당신은 어떤 토론에도 활기를 불어 넣는 사람을 알고 있을지도 모른다. 어떻게 하면 당신이 참석하는 모든 파티와 사교 모임에서 반가운 사람이 되기 위해 당신의 대화 기술을 향상시킬 수 있을까? 대부분의 사람들은 당신에 대해 듣기보다는 자신에 대해 말하는 것을 더 선호하므로, 질문을 던지는 것은 대화를 잘 시작할 수 있는 멋진 방법이다. 또한 당신이 할 수 있을 때마다 누군가를 칭찬하는 것은 다른 사람들과 의사소통을 하는 당신의 능력을 향상시킬 수 있는 좋은 방법이다. 예를 들어, 누군가 몸무게가 많이 빠졌거나 세련되고 새로운 머리 모양을 하고 있다면, 진심으로 칭찬을 던져 당신이 그것을 알아차렸다는 것을 보여 주어라.

문제 해설

사교 모임에서 환영 받는 사람이 되기 위해서 대화 기술을 향상시킬 수 있는 방법에 대해 알려 주고 있는 내용의 글이므로 글의 주제로 가장 적절한 것은 ③ '좋은 대화자가 되는 방법'이다.

① 당신의 말을 지루하게 만드는 것
② 사교 모임의 중요성
④ 사실이 아닌 칭찬으로 다른 사람에게 감동 주기
⑤ 당신이 어색한 상황에서 벗어나야 하는 이유

구문 분석

[1행] You may have avoided a situation [**where** you could encounter some people on social occasions] because their conversations struck you as boring.

▶ 관계부사 where는 a situation을 수식하고 있으며, [where ~]는 문장 성분이 부족하지 않은 완전한 절의 형태로 구성된다.

어휘

encounter 마주치다 **occasion** 경우, 기회, 이유
strike [생각 등이] (사람의) 머리에 떠오르다, ~이 생각나다
enliven 활기띠게 하다 **praise** 칭찬하다
genuine 진짜의, 진실한 **compliment** 칭찬
awkward 어색한, 불편한

03 정답 ③

소재 narwhal의 특징

전문 해석

narwhal(일각고래)은 북극해의 얼음물에 사는 중간 크기의 고래이다. 그들은 위턱에 두 개의 이빨을 갖고 있는데, 그중 하나가 밖으로 나선형으로 자란다. 그것은 길고 인상적인 엄니 때문에 바다의 유니콘으로 종종 생각된다. 암컷의 엄니는 수컷의 엄니만큼 길고 두드러지게 자라지 않는다. 엄니의 기능은 정확하지 않지만 어떤 사람들은 그것이 짝짓기 의식에 중요하다고 믿는다. 이 기이한 생명체는 엄니를 제외하고 약 13피트에서 20피트까지 자랄 수 있으며 무게는 약 1600kg이다. Narwhal은 무리로 수영하며 주로 2~10마리의 떼로 관찰된다. 그들은 물고기, 새우, 오징어 및 기타 해양 동물을 주식으로 한다. 그들은 인간(이뉴잇족 사냥꾼들), 북극곰, 바다코끼리에게 잡아먹힌다.

문제 해설
암컷의 엄니는 수컷의 엄니만큼 길고 두드러지게 자라지 않는다고 했으므로 ③은 글의 내용과 일치하지 않는다.

구문 분석
[4행] The female's tusk doesn't grow **as** long and prominent **as** the male's.

▶ 주어인 The female's tusk와 뒤의 as 다음에 나오는 male's (tusk)를 「as ~ as ...」로 비교하고 있다. male's 뒤에는 tusk가 반복을 피하기 위해 생략되었다. 원급 자리에는 형용사나 부사가 올 수 있는데 여기서는 형용사 long and prominent가 와서 '~만큼 길고 주목할 만한[두드러지는]'이라는 뜻으로 쓰였다.

어휘
Arctic 북극(의) **upper** 위쪽의 **jaw** 턱
outward 밖으로 향하는 **spirally** 나선형으로
impressive 인상적인 **tusk** 엄니, 상아
prominent 두드러진, 현저한 **mating** 짝짓기
ritual 의식 **excluding** ~을 제외하고
weigh 무게가 ~이다 **observe** 관찰하다
pod (물개 · 고래 등의) 작은 떼
feed on ~을 먹다[먹고 살다]
marine 해양의 **prey upon** ~을 잡아먹다

04 정답 ①

소재 Oliver Cromwell의 초상화에 대한 일화

전문 해석
"나를 있는 그대로 그려주시오"라고 Oliver Cromwell이 화가인 Lely에게 말했다. "만약 상처나 주름을 생략해 버린다면, 나는 한 푼도 당신에게 지불하지 않을 거요." 심지어 아주 사소한 것에 있어서도, Cromwell은 타고난 감각을 드러냈다. 그는 자신을 균형 잡힌 얼굴과 매끈한 볼로 그리려는 헛된 시도로 그의 얼굴 표정에 드러나 있는 특유한 모든 것들이 사라지는 것을 원치 않았다. 그는 그의 얼굴에 시간, 전쟁, 잠을 못잔 밤들, 걱정, 어쩌면 후회가 묻어나지만 용맹함과, 정책과, 지위, 그리고 대중에 대한 관심이 또한 얼굴에 쓰여 있는 그러한 모든 흔적들이 나타난다는 것에 만족해했다. 만약 위대한 사람이 무엇이 그들에게 가장 최상의 이익이 되는지 안다면, 그것은 바로 그들 자신의 마음이 스케치에 (그대로) 그려질 수 있도록 바라는 것이다.

문제 해설
Oliver Cromwell은 자신의 상처나 주름을 빼고 그림을 그리면 돈을 한 푼도 지불하지 않겠다고 했으며, 얼굴 표정에 드러나 있는 특유한 모든 것들이 사라지는 것을 원치 않았다고 했으므로, 빈칸에는 ① '나를 있는 그대로 그려주시오'가 가장 적절하다.

② 나를 완벽한 사람으로 그려주시오
③ 나를 오랫동안 피곤해 왔던 것처럼 그려주시오
④ 나를 완전히 다른 사람처럼 그려주시오
⑤ 나를 존재하지 않는 사람처럼 그려주시오

구문 분석
[3행] He did not wish all [**that** was characteristic in his facial expression] **to be lost**, in a vain attempt to give him regular features and smooth cheeks.

▶ [that ~]는 all을 수식하고 있으며, all과 lose의 관계가 수동이므로, to부정사의 수동 표현인 to be lost가 쓰였다.

어휘
leave out ~을 빼다, 생략하다 **wrinkle** 주름
shilling 실링(영국에서 1971년까지 사용되던 주화)
trifle 하찮은 것 **characteristic** 특유의
vain 헛된, 소용 없는 **feature** (*pl.*) 이목구비; 얼굴
content 만족하는 **sleepless** 잠을 못 자는, 불면의
valor 용기, 용맹 **authority** 지휘권, 권한
portray 그리다, 나타내다

05 정답 ④

소재 문맥에 의해 왜곡되기 쉬운 시간

전문 해석
2009년도 'Philosophical Transactions of the Royal Society'에 실린 한 기사에서, 프랑스의 심리학자인 Sylvie Droit-Volet과 Sandrine Gil은 시간의 역설이라 부르는 것에 대해 설명했는데 "비록 인간이 마치 그들이

시간을 측정하도록 허용한 특정한 작동 방식을 소유하고 있는 것처럼 정확하게 시간을 추정할 수 있더라도, 그들의 시간에 대한 묘사는 문맥에 의해 쉽게 왜곡된다"는 것이다. 그들은 어떻게 우리의 시간 감각이 우리의 감정 상태에 따라 변하는지를 설명한다. 예를 들어, 우리가 동요되어 있거나 긴장할 때는 시간이 느리게 가는 것처럼 보이고 우리는 인내심을 잃어버린다. 우리의 사회적인 환경 또한 우리가 시간을 경험하는 방식에 영향을 미친다. Droit-Volet과 Gill의 연구는 '개인들이 그들의 시간과 타인들의 시간을 맞춘다'는 것을 시사한다. 우리 주변 사람들의 '활동 리듬'은 시간의 경과에 대한 우리의 인식을 바꾸어 놓는다.

문제 해설

인간은 감정 상태에 따라 시간 감각을 다르게 느끼며, 사회적인 환경도 시간을 경험하는 방식에 영향을 미친다는 내용의 글이므로 빈칸에는 '문맥에 의해 쉽게 왜곡된다'가 가장 적절하다.

① 추상적이고 모호하다
② 모두 부정확성으로 귀결된다
③ 그들의 신체 상태에 달려있다
⑤ 본질적으로 시간의 흐름을 강조한다

오답 풀이

②를 정답으로 오인할 가능성이 있는데 '모두 부정확성으로 귀결되다.'라는 것은 상황에 따라 다르다는 것을 모두 부정확하다고 이야기하는 것으로, 지나치게 일반화시키는 주장이다. 따라서 ②는 정답이 될 수 없다.

구문 분석

[3행] ~ "although humans are able to accurately estimate time **as if** they possess a specific mechanism [**that** allows them to measure time]," ~.

▶ as if는 '마치 ~처럼'이라는 의미이며, [that ~]는 a specific mechanism을 수식하고 있다.

어휘

article 기사 **psychologist** 심리학자
paradox 역설 **accurately** 정확하게
estimate 평가하다, 추정하다
representation 묘사, 표현 **agitated** 동요된, 불안해하는
crawl 몹시 느리게 가다 **perception** 인식
abstract 추상적인 **subtle** 미묘한, 모호한
inaccuracy 부정확성 **depend on** ~에 의지하다
physical condition 신체적 상태 **distort** 왜곡하다
emphasize 강조하다

06 정답 ⑤

소재 성별에 따른 가격 책정

전문 해석

성별에 따른 가격 책정은 남성과 여성에게 같은 제품이나 서비스에 대해 다르게 가격을 부여하는 행동이다. 일반적으로 여성이 남성보다 거의 같은 물건에 더 많은 돈을 지불해야 한다. (C) 예를 들어, 여성들은 대부분 남성들보다 드라이클리닝을 하는 데에 돈을 더 많이 지불한다. 제품에 있어서 여성들은 대개 청바지와 같은 의류, 면도기와 같은 개인 관리 제품, 스쿠터(외발 롤러스케이트)와 같은 장난감에서도 더 많은 비용을 지불한다. (B) 그러나, 예를 들어 매니큐어나 제모와 같은 특정한 종류의 서비스에 대해서는 전형적으로 남성들이 더 많이 지불하는데 왜냐하면 아마도 더 많은 작업이 필요하기 때문이다. (A) 차 보험이 또 다른 예인데 남성들은 여성들이 지불하는 것보다 일생 동안 약 15,000달러 이상을 자동차 보험료로 지불한다. 따라서 여성들이 항상 성별에 따른 가격 책정의 피해자는 아니다.

문제 해설

성별에 따른 가격 책정에서 여성이 남성보다 거의 같은 물건에 대해 더 많은 돈을 지불한다는 내용의 주어진 글 다음에, 그것에 대한 예를 제시한 (C)가 온 다음, 반대로 남성이 여성보다 돈을 더 지불하는 사례에 대해 언급하고 있는 (B)가 오고, 차 보험을 남성이 여성보다 돈을 더 지불하는 또 하나의 예로 제시하고 있는 (A)가 마지막에 와야 글의 흐름이 가장 적절하다.

구문 분석

[4행] ~ Men pay an **estimated** $15,000 more over their lifetime for car insurance than women **do**.

▶ estimated는 대략적인 수치 앞에서 사용하는 형용사로, 동사나 과거분사로 착각하지 않도록 주의한다. do는 pay를 대신하여 쓰인 대동사이다.

어휘

charge (지불 · 손해 등을) ~의 부담으로 하다
commonly 일반적으로, 흔하게 **insurance** 보험
estimated 어림잡은, 추측의 **victim** 희생자
waxing 제모 **supposedly** 아마, 추정상
require 필요로 하다 **razor** 면도기

07 정답 ③

소재 화재로 홀로 남겨진 Henry

전문 해석

지난밤 화재가 발생했을 때, 사람들은 혼란스러워 하며 소

리를 지르고, 울며 그 집에서 뛰쳐 나갔다. 그리고 그 다음 날, 그 집에는 Smith 부부의 막내 아들 Henry를 제외하고 여전히 아무도 없었다. 아무도 그를 생각하지 않았다. 왜냐하면 Smith 부부가 모두 화재로 사망해서, 사람들은 Henry 역시 죽었다고 생각했기 때문이다. 그러나 그의 친구 Thomas는 Henry가 살아있다고 생각했고 그를 찾아 나섰다. 검게 그을린 복도를 따라 걸으면서 그는 "Henry! 나야, Thomas!" 라고 계속 불렀다. 패닉룸(안전방)에 숨어 있었던 Henry는 마침내 그의 친구의 목소리를 들었다. 그의 도움으로, 그는 그 집에서 안전하게 빠져 나올 수 있었다. 그가 다음 날 Thomas의 방에서 일어났을 때 Thomas의 부모님께서 그가 그들과 함께 살아도 된다고 말씀해 주셨다. 그는 자신이 세상에서 혼자라는 기분을 느끼지 않아도 되었기에 다행이라고 생각했다.

문제 해설

나머지는 모두 Henry를 가리키고, ③은 그의 친구인 Thomas를 가리킨다.

구문 분석

[8행] When he woke up the next day in Thomas's room, his parents **told** him (I.O) (that) he could live together with them. (D.O)

▶ tell은 4형식 동사로 쓰여 목적어를 두 개 취할 수 있는데 이 문장에서는 직접목적어로 쓰인 that 명사절에서 that이 생략되어 있다.

어휘

run out of ~로부터 도망 나오다 **shout** 소리 지르다
confusion 혼란 **alive** 살아 있는 **look for** ~을 찾다
blacken 검게 하다 **panic room** 안전방

08 정답 ③

소재 긴장성 두통의 원인과 치료법

전문 해석

진단되는 모든 두통 중에서 '긴장성 두통'은 가장 흔하며 전체 중 거의 90퍼센트를 차지한다. 알려진 어떤 한 원인은 없으며 긴장성 두통은 자녀로 전해지지 않는다. 사람들은 때때로 목이나 두피의 근육이 굳어지는데 이 긴장은 긴장성 두통을 유발할 수 있다. 이러한 긴장은 불충분한 휴식, 나쁜 자세, 육체적인 스트레스와 같은 요소들에 의해 더욱 심해지고 빈번해질 수 있다. 환경 또는 정신적인 스트레스 또한 긴장성 두통을 유발할 수 있다. 정신적인 스트레스의 가장 흔한 원인들로는 사회적 관계, 가족, 친구, 학교, 직장이 있다. 긴장성 두통에 대한 효과적인 치료법은 휴식, 스트레스 감소, 아스피린과 같은 진통제라고 의사들은 제안한다.

문제 해설

주어진 문장은 ③의 바로 앞 문장에 대해 추가적인 설명을 하고 있으며, 주어진 문장의 this tension이 the tightness를 가리키므로 주어진 문장은 ③에 들어가는 것이 적절하다.

구문 분석

[3행] Among all headaches **(that / which are)** diagnosed, "tension headaches" are most common and account for approximately 90% of all.

▶ headaches와 diagnosed 사이에는 「주격 관계대명사 that[which]+be동사」, 즉 that[which] are가 생략되어 있다. '진단되는 모든 두통'이라는 의미로, 주격 관계대명사가 생략될 때에는 언제나 뒤의 be동사와 함께 생략된다는 것에 유의한다.

어휘

factor 요소 **insufficient** 불충분한 **posture** 자세
tension 긴장 상태 **severe** 극심한, 심각한
frequent 잦은, 빈번한 **headache** 두통
diagnose 진단하다 **account for** (부분 · 비율을) 차지하다
approximately 거의, 대략
hereditary 유전적인, 부모로부터 물려받은
tighten (몸의 일부가) 굳어지다 **muscle** 근육
scalp 두피 **tightness** 긴장, 견고함
environmental 환경의 **mental** 정신의, 마음의
reduction 감소, 축소 **pain reliever** 진통제
treatment 치료

09 정답 ④

소재 유통 기한의 의미

전문 해석

농무부의 추정에 따르면 미국에서 모든 음식의 약 30퍼센트에서 40퍼센트 즉, 약 천육백십억 달러 가치의 음식이 버려진다고 한다. '날짜 표시'를 잘못 읽은 소비자들 때문에 버려지는 음식이 얼마인지는 불명확하지만, 음식 홍보 기관에 의해 1,000명이 넘는 식료품점에서 쇼핑을 하는 사람들을 대상으로 한 최근 조사에 따르면 거의 소비자들의 절반이 유효 기간 혹은 유통 기한이 지난 후에는 '상당히 자주' 또는 '매번' 음식을 내다 버린다고 말했다고 한다. 그러나 유효 기간, 사용 기한, 그리고 유통 기한과 같은 용어들은 많은 사람들이 믿는 것처럼 음식의 안전성을 나타내지는 않는다. 날짜들은 일반적으로 음식이 언제 최상의

품질을 나타내는지에 대한 것을 표시하기 위해 제조자들이 설정한 것이다. 여전히, 많은 소비자들이 그러한 날짜들을 고수하지 않는 것은 그들을 아프게 할 수 있다고 믿는다. 대부분의 제품들은 포장에 등록되어진 날짜들이 지난 후에 섭취하여도 여전히 안전하다. 그 유효 기한은 단지 소매업자가 재고를 조절하기 위한 것이다.

→ 만기된 유통 기한이 그 음식을 먹을 수 없다는 것을 의미하지 않음에도 불구하고, 사람들은 자연스럽게 그것이 버려져야 한다고 생각한다.

문제 해설

유통 기한이 음식의 안전성을 나타내 주는 것이 아니며, 표기된 날짜가 지나서 음식을 섭취하더라도 여전히 안전한데 사람들은 날짜를 지키지 않는 것은 몸을 아프게 할 수 있다고 믿고 있다는 내용의 글이다. 따라서 요약문의 빈칸 (A)와 (B)에는 각각 inedible과 thrown away가 가장 적절하다.

① 먹을 수 없는 – 데우다
② 불충분한 – 데우다
③ 사용되지 않는 – 버리다
⑤ 불충분한 – 포장하다

구문 분석

[1행] In the U.S., about **30% to 40% of all food** (S) is (V) wasted, or about $161 billion worth of food, according to Agriculture Department estimates.

▶ 주어에 퍼센트나 분수가 나올 때는 퍼센트나 분수 뒤에 나오는 명사의 수에 의해 동사의 형태를 결정한다. 여기서는 퍼센트 뒤에 all food가 단수 취급을 하므로, 동사로 is가 쓰였다.

어휘

waste 낭비하다, 버리다 **worth** 가치, 값어치
consumer 소비자 **misread** 잘못 읽다, 오해하다
typically 전형적으로 **manufacturer** 제조업자
peak 최고의 **stick to** 고수하다 **stock** 재고
expired 만료된, 기한이 지난

M.E.M.O

M.E.M.O

M.E.M.O